E. M. Ackermann

Franklin Grove, Ill. 1912

WORLD'S FAMOUS LITERATURE

PLUTARCH'S

LIVES OF ILLUSTRIOUS MEN

Translated from the Greek by John Dryden
and Others. The Whole Carefully
Revised and Corrected, to
which is Prefixed ·

A LIFE OF PLUTARCH

COMPLETE IN THREE VOLUMES

VOL. II

PHILADELPHIA
DAVID McKAY, Publisher
610 South Washington Square

CONTENTS

VOLUME II.

	PAGE
Pyrrhus	7
Caius Marius	41
Lysander	81
Sylla	107
Comparison of Lysander with Sylla	143
Cimon	147
Lucullus	167
Comparison of Lucullus with Cimon	208
Nicias	211
Crassus	241
Comparison of Crassus with Nicias	272
Sertorius	276
Eumenes	301
Comparison of Sertorius with Eumenes	318
Agesilaus	320
Pompey	355
Comparison of Pompey and Agesilaus	430
Alexander	435
Cæsar	503
Phocion	555

PLUTARCH'S LIVES.

VOLUME II.

PYRRHUS.

OF the Thesprotians and Molossians after the great inundation, the first king, according to some historians, was Phaethon, one of those who came into Epirus with Pelasgus. Others tell us that Deucalion and Pyrrha, having set up the worship of Jupiter at Dodona, settled there among the Molossians. In after time, Neoptolemus, Achilles's son, planting a colony, possessed these parts himself, and left a succession of kings, who, after him, were named Pyrrhidæ; as he in his youth was called Pyrrhus, and of his legitimate children, one was borne of Lanassa, daughter of Cleodæus, Hyllus's son, had also that name. From him Achilles came to have divine honors in Epirus, under the name of Aspetus, in the language of the country. After these first kings, those of the following intervening times becoming barbarous, and insignificant both in their power and their lives, Tharrhypas is said to have been the first who, by introducing Greek manners and learning, and humane laws into his cities, left any fame of himself. Alcetas was the son of Tharrhypas, Arybas of Alcetas, and of Arybas and Troas his queen, Æacides; he married Phthia, the daughter of Menon, the Thessalian, a man of note at the time of the Lamiac war, and of highest command in the confederate army next to Leosthenes. To Æacides were born of Phthia, Deidamia and Troas, daugthters, and Pyrrhus, a son.

The Molossians, afterwards falling into factions and expelling Æacides, brought in the sons of Neoptolemus, and such friends of Æacides as they could take were all cut off; Pyrrhus, yet an infant, and searched for by the enemy, had been stolen away and carried off by Androclides and Angelus; who, however, being obliged to take with them a few servants, and women to nurse the child, were much impeded and retarded in their flight, and when they were now overtaken, they delivered the infant to Androcleon, Hippias, and Neander, faithful and able young fellows, giving them in charge to make for Megara, a town of Macedon, with all their might, while they themselves, partly by entreaty, and partly by force, stopped the course of the pursuers till late in the evening. At last, having hardly forced them back, they joined those who had the care of Pyrrhus; but the sun being already set, at the point of attaining their object they suddenly found themselves cut off from it. For on reaching the river that runs by the city they found it looking formidable and rough, and endeavoring to pass over, they discovered it was not fordable; late rains having heightened the water, and made the current violent. The darkness of the night added to the horror of all, so that they durst not venture of themselves to carry over the child and the women that attended it; but, perceiving some of the country people on the other side, they desired them to assist their passage, and showed them Pyrrhus, calling out aloud, and importuning them. They, however, could not hear for the noise and roaring of the water. Thus time was spent while those called out, and the others did not understand what was said, till one recollecting himself, stripped off a piece of bark from an oak, and wrote on it with the tongue of a buckle, stating the necessities and the fortunes of the child, and then rolling it about a stone, which was made use of to give force to the motion, threw it over to the other side, or, as some say, fastened it to the end of a javelin, and darted it over. When the men on the other shore read what was on the bark, and saw how time pressed, without delay they cut down some trees, and lashing them together, came over to them. And it so fell out, that he who first got ashore, and took Pyrrhus in his arms, was named Achilles, the rest being helped over by others as they came to hand.

Thus being safe, and out of the reach of pursuit, they addressed themselves to Glaucias, then king of the Illyrians, and finding him sitting at home with his wife, they laid down the child before them. The king began to weigh the matter, fearing Cassander, who was a mortal enemy of Æacides, and, being in deep consideration, said nothing for a long time, while Pyrrhus, crawling about on the ground, gradually got near and laid hold with his hand upon the king's robe, and so helping himself upon his feet against the knees of Glaucias, first moved laughter, and then pity, as a little, humble, crying petitioner. Some say he did not throw himself before Glaucias, but catching hold of an altar of the gods, and spreading his hands about it, raised himself up by that; and that Glaucias took the act as an omen. At present, therefore, he gave Pyrrhus into the charge of his wife commanding he should be brought up with his own children and a little after, the enemies sending to demand him, and Cassander himself offering two hundred talents, he would not deliver him up; but when he was twelve years old, bringing him with an army into Epirus, made him king. Pyrrhus in the air of his face had something more of the terrors, than of the augustness of kingly power; he had not a regular set of upper teeth, but in the place of them one continued bone, with small lines marked on it, resembling the divisions of a row of teeth. It was a general belief he could cure the spleen, by sacrificing a white cock and gently pressing with his right foot on the spleen of the persons as they lay down on their backs, nor was any one so poor or inconsiderable as not to be welcome, if he desired it, to the benefit of his touch. He accepted the cock for the sacrifice as a reward, and was always much pleased with the present. The large toe of that foot was said to have a divine virtue; for after his death, the rest of the body being consumed, this was found unhurt and untouched by the fire. But of these things hereafter.

Being now about seventeen years old, and the government in appearance well settled, he took a journey out of the kingdom to attend the marriage of one of Glaucias's sons, with whom he was brought up; upon which opportunity the Molossians again rebelling, turned out all of his party, plundered his property, and gave themselves up to Neoptolemus. Pyrrhus having thus lost the kingdom, and being in want of all things, applied to Demetrius, the son of Antigonus, the husband of his sister Deidamia, who, while she was but a child, had been in name the wife of Alexander, son of Roxana, but their affairs afterwards proving unfortunate, when she came to age, Demetrius married her. At the great battle of Ipsus, where so many kings were engaged, Pyrrhus, taking part with Demetrius, though yet but a youth, routed those that encountered him, and highly signalized himself among all the soldiery; and afterwards, when Demetrius's fortunes were low, he did not forsake him then, but secured for him the cities of

Greece with which he was intrusted; and upon articles of agreement being made between Demetrius and Ptolemy, he went over as an hostage for him into Egypt, where both in hunting and other exercises, he gave Ptolemy an ample proof of his courage and strength. Here observing Berenice in greatest power, and of all Ptolemy's wives highest in esteem for virtue and understanding, he made his court principally to her. He had a particular art of gaining over the great to his own interest, as on the other hand he readily over looked such as were below him; and being also well-behaved and temperate in his life, among all the young princes then at court, he was thought most fit to have Antigone for his wife, one of the daughters of Berenice by Philip, before she married Ptolemy.

After this match, advancing in honor, and Antigone being a very good wife to him, having procured a sum of money, and raised an army, he so ordered matters as to be sent into his kingdom of Epirus, and arrived there to the great satisfaction of many, from their hate to Neoptolemus, who was governing in a violent and arbitrary way. But fearing lest Neoptolemus should enter into alliance with some neighboring princes, he came to terms and friendship with him, agreeing that they should share the government between them. There were people, however, who, as time went on, secretly exasperated them, and fomented jealousies between them. The cause chiefly moving Pyrrhus is said to have had this beginning. It was customary for the kings to offer sacrifice to Mars, at Passaro, a place in the Molossian country, and that done to enter into a solemn covenant with the Epirots; they to govern according to law, these to preserve the government as by law established. This was performed in the presence of both kings, who were there with their immediate friends, giving and receiving many presents; here Gelo, one of the friends of Neoptolemus, taking Pyrrhus by the hand, presented him with two pair of draught oxen. Myrtilus, his cup-bearer, being then by, begged these of Pyrrhus, who not giving them to him, but to another, Myrtilus extremely resented it, which Gelo took notice of, and, inviting him to a banquet (amidst drinking and other excesses, as some relate, Myrtilus being then in the flower of his youth), he entered into discourse, persuading him to adhere to Neoptolemus, and destroy Pyrrhus by poison. Myrtilus received the design, appearing to approve and consent to it, but privately discovered it to Pyrrhus, by whose command he recommended Alexicrates, his chief cup-bearer, to Gelo, as a fit instrument for their design. Pyrrhus being very desirous to have proof of the plot by several evidences. So Gelo being deceived, Neoptolemus, who was no less deceived, imagining the design went prosperously on, could not forbear, but in his joy spoke of it among his friends, and once at an entertainment at his sister Cadmea's, talked openly of it, thinking none heard but themselves. Nor was any one there but Phænarete the wife of Samon; who had the care of Neoptolemus's flocks and herds. She, turning her face towards the wall upon a couch, seemed fast asleep, and having heard all that passed, unsuspected, next day came to Antigone, Pyrrhus's wife, and told her what she had heard Neoptolemus say to his sister. On understanding which Pyrrhus for the present said little, but on a sacrifice day, making an invitation for Neoptolemus, killed him; being satisfied before that the great men of the Epirots were his friends, and that they were eager for him to rid himself of Neoptolemus, and not to content himself with a mere petty share of the government, but to follow his own natural vocation to great designs, and now when a just ground of suspicion appeared, to anticipate Neoptolemus by taking him off first.

In memory of Berenice and Ptolemy, he named his son by Antigone, Ptolemy, and having built a city in the peninsula of Epirus, called it Berenicis. From this time he began to revolve many and vast projects in his thoughts; but his first special hope and design lay near home, and he found means to engage himself in the Macedonian affairs under the following pretext. Of Cassander's sons, Antipater, the eldest, killed Thessalonica, his mother, and expelled his brother Alexander, who sent to Demetrius entreating his assistance, and also called in Pyrrhus; but Demetrius being retarded by multitude of business, Pyrrhus, coming first, demanded in reward of his service the districts called Tymphæa and Parauæa in Macedon itself, and of their new conquests, Ambracia, Acarnania, and Amphilochia. The young prince giving way, he took possession of these countries, and secured them with good garrisons and proceeded to reduce for Alexander himself other parts of the kingdom which he gained from Antipater. Lysimachus, designing to send aid to Antipater, was involved in much other business, but knowing Pyrrhus would not disoblige Ptolemy, or deny him anything, sent pretended letters to him as from Ptolemy, desiring him to give up his expedition, upon the payment of three hundred talents to him by Antipater. Pyrrhus, opening the letter, quickly discovered the fraud of Lysimachus ; for it had not the accustomed style of salutation, "The father to the son, health," but "King Ptolemy to Pyrrhus, the king, health ;" and reproaching Lysimachus, he notwithstanding made a peace, and they all met to confirm it by a solemn oath upon sacrifice. A goat, a bull, and a ram being brought out, the ram on a sudden fell dead. The others laughed, but Theodotus the prophet forbade Pyrrhus to swear, declaring that Heaven by that portended the death of one of the three kings, upon which he refused to ratify the peace.

The affairs of Alexander being now in some kind of settlement, Demetrius arrived, contrary, as soon appeared, to the desire and indeed not without the alarm of Alexander. After they had been a few days together, their mutual jealousy led them to conspire against each other ; and Demetrius taking advantage of the first occasion, was beforehand with the young king, and slew him, and proclaimed himself king of Macedon. There had been formerly no very good understanding between him and Pyrrhus ; for besides the inroads he made into Thessaly, the innate disease of princes, ambition of greater empire, had rendered them formidable and suspected neighbors to each other, especially since Deidamia's death ; and both having seized Macedon, they came into conflict for the same object, and the difference between them had the stronger motives. Demetrius having first attacked the Ætolians and subdued them, left Pantauchus there with a considerable army, and marched direct against Pyrrhus, and Pyrrhus, as he thought, against him ; but by mistake of the ways they passed by one another, and Demetrius falling into Epirus wasted the country, and Pyrrhus, meeting with Pantauchus, prepared for an engagement. The soldiers fell to, and there was a sharp and terrible conflict, especially where the generals were. Pantauchus, in courage, dexterity, and strength of body being confessedly the best of all Demetrius's captains, and having both resolution and high spirit, challenged Pyrrhus to fight hand in hand ; on the other side Pyrrhus, professing not to yield to any king in valor and glory, and esteeming the fame of Achilles more truly to belong to him for his courage than for his blood, advanced against Pantauchus through the front of the army. First they used their lances, then came to a close fight, and managed their swords both with art and force ; Pyrrhus receiving one wound, but returning two for 1, one in the thigh and the other near the neck, repulsed and overthrew Pantauchus, but did not kill him outright, as he was rescued by his friends. But the Epirots exulting in the victory of their king, and admiring his courage, forced through and cut in pieces the phalanx of the Macedonians, and pursuing those that fled, killed many, and took five thousand prisoners.

This fight did not so much exasperate the Macedonians with anger for their loss, or with hatred to Pyrrhus, as it caused esteem, and admiration of his valor, and great discourse of him among those that saw what he did, and were engaged against him in the action. They thought his countenance, his swiftness and his motions expressed those of the great Alexander, and that they beheld here an image and resemblance of his rapidity and strength in fight; other kings merely by their purple and their guards, by the formal bending of their necks, and lofty tone of their speech, Pyrrhus only by arms, and in action, represented Alexander. Of his knowledge of military tactics and the art of a general, and his great ability that way, we have the best information from the commentaries he left behind him. Antigonus, also, we are told, being asked who was the greatest soldier, said, "Pyrrhus, if he lives to be old," referring only to those of his own time; but Hannibal of all great commanders esteemed Pyrrhus for skill and conduct the first, Scipio the second, and himself the third, as is related in the life of Scipio. In a word, he seemed ever to make this all his thought and philosophy, as the most kingly part of learning: other curiosities he held in no account. He is reported, when asked at a feast whether he thought Python or Caphisias the best musician, to have said, Polysperchon was the best soldier, as though it became a king to examine and understand only such things. Towards his familiars he was mild, and not easily incensed; zealous, and even vehement in returning kindnesses. Thus when Aeropus was dead, he could not bear it with moderation, saying, he indeed had suffered what was common to human nature, but condemning and blaming himself, that by puttings off and delays he had not returned his kindness in time. For our debts may be satisfied to the creditor's heirs, but not to have made the acknowledgment of received favors, while they to whom it is due can be sensible of it, afflicts a good and worthy nature. Some thinking it fit that Pyrrhus should banish a certain ill-tongued fellow in Ambracio, who had spoken very indecently of him, "Let him rather," said he, "speak against us here to a few, than rambling about to a great many." And others who in their wine had made reflections upon him, being afterward questioned for it, and asked by him whether they had said such words, on one of the young fellows answering, "Yes, all that, king : and should have said more if we had had more wine ; " he laughed and discharged them. After Antigone's death, he married several wives to enlarge his interest and power. He had the daughter of Autoleon, king of the Pæonians, Bircenno, Bardyllis the Illyrian's daughter, Lanassa, daughter of Agathocles the Syracusan, who brought with her in dower the city of Corcyra, which had been taken by Agathocles. By Antigone he had Ptolemy, Alexander by Lanassa and Helenus, his youngest son, by Bircenna : he brought them up all in arms, hot and eager youths, and by him sharpened and whetted to war from their very infancy. It is said, when one of them, while yet a child, asked him to which he would leave the kingdom, he replied, to him that had the sharpest sword, which indeed was much like that tragical curse of Oedipus to his sons :—

Not by the lot decide,
But with the sword the heritage divide.

So unsocial and wild-beast-like is the nature of ambition and cupidity.

After this battle Pyrrhus, returning gloriously home, enjoyed his fame and reputation, and being called " Eagle " by the Epirots, " By you," said he, " I am an eagle ; for how should I not be such, while I have your arms as wings to sustain me ? "   A little after, having intelligence that Demetrius was dangerously sick, he entered on a sudden into Macedonia, intending only an incursion, and to harass the country ; but was very near seizing upon all, and taking the kingdom without a blow. He marched as far as Edessa unresisted, great numbers deserting, and coming in to him. This danger excited Demetrius beyond his strength, and his friends and commanders in a short time got a considerable army together and with all their forces briskly attacked Pyrrhus, who, coming only to pillage, would not stand a fight, but retreating lost part of his army, as he went off, by the close pursuit of the Macedonians.   Demetrius, however, although he had easily and quickly forced Pyrrhus out of the country, yet did not slight him, but having resolved upon great designs, and to recover his father's kingdom with an army of one hundred thousand men, and a fleet of five hundred ships, would neither embroil himself with Pyrrhus, nor leave the Macedonians so active and troublesome a neighbor; and since he had no leisure to continue the war with him, he was willing to treat and conclude a peace, and to turn his forces upon the other kings. Articles being agreed upon, the designs of Demetrius quickly discovered themselves by the greatness of his preparation. And the other kings, being alarmed, sent to Pyrrhus ambassadors and letters, expressing their wonder that he should choose to let his own opportunity pass by, and wait till Demetrius could use his; and whereas he was now able to chase him out of Macedon, involved in designs and disturbed, he should expect till Demetrius at leisure, and grown great, should bring the war home to his own door, and make him fight for his temples and sepulchres in Molossia; especially having so lately, by his means, lost Corcyra and his wife together. For Lanassa had taken offence at Pyrrhus for too great an inclination to those wives of his that were barbarians, and so withdrew to Corcyra, and desiring to marry some king, invited Demetrius, knowing of all the kings he was most ready to entertain offers of marriage; so he sailed thither, married Lanassa, and placed a garrison in the city. The kings having written thus to Pyrrhus, themselves likewise contrived to find Demetrius work, while he was delaying and making his preparations. Ptolemy, setting out with a great fleet, drew off many of the Greek cities. Lysimachus out of Thrace wasted the upper Macedon; and Pyrrhus, also, taking arms at the same time, marched to Berœa, expecting, as it fell out, that Demetrius, collecting his forces against Lysimachus, would leave the lower country undefended. That very night he seemed in his sleep to be called by Alexander the Great, and approaching saw him sick abed, but was received with very kind words, and much respect, and promised zealous assistance. He making bold to reply, "How, Sir, can you, being sick, assist me?" "With my name," said he, and mounting Nisæan horse, seemed to lead the way. At the sight of this vision he was much assured, and with swift marches overrunning all the interjacent places, takes Berœa, and making his headquarters there, reduced the rest of the country by his commanders. When Demetrius received intelligence of this, and perceived likewise the Macedonians ready to mutiny in the army, he was afraid to advance further, lest coming near Lysimachus, a Macedonian king, and of great fame, they should revolt to him. So returning, he marched directly against Pyrrhus, as a stranger, and hated by the Macedonians. But while he lay encamped there near him, many who came out of Berœa infinitely praised Pyrrhus as invincible in arms a glorious warrior, who treated those he had taken kindly and humanely. Several of these Pyrrhus himself sent privately, pretending to be Macedonians, and saying, now was the time to be delivered from the severe government of Demetrius by coming over to Pyrrhus, a gracious prince and a lover of soldiers. By this artifice a great part of the army was in a state of excitement, and the soldiers began to look every way about inquiring for Pyrrhus. It happened he was without his helmet, till understanding they did not know him, he put it on again, and so was quickly recognized by his lofty crest, and the goat's horns he wore upon it. Then the Macedonians, running to him, desired to be told his password, and some put oaken boughs upon their heads, because they saw them worn by the soldiers about him. Some persons even took the confidence to say to Demetrius himself, that he would be well advised to withdraw, and lay down the government. And he, indeed, seeing the mutinous movements of the army to be only too consistent with what they said, privately got away, disguised in a broad hat, and a common soldier's coat. So Pyrrhus became master of the army without fighting, and was declared king of the Macedonians.

But Lysimachus now arriving, and claiming the defeat of Demetrius as the joint exploit of them both, and that therefore the kingdom should be shared between them, Pyrrhus, not as yet quite assured of the Macedonians, and in doubt of their faith, consented to the proposition of Lysimachus, and divided the country and cities between them accordingly. This was for the present useful, and prevented a war; but shortly after they found the partition not so much a peaceful settlement, as an occasion of further complaint and difference. For men whose ambition neither seas nor mountains, nor unpeopled deserts can limit, nor the bounds dividing Europe from Asia confine their vast desires, it would be hard to expect to forbear from injuring one another when they touch, and are close together. These are ever naturally at war, envying and seeking advantages of one another, and merely make use of those two words, peace and war, like current coin, to serve their occasions, not as justice but as expediency suggests, and are really better men when they openly enter on a war, than when they give to the mere forbearance from doing wrong, for want of opportunity, the sacred names of justice and friendship. Pyrrhus was an instance of this; for setting himself against the rise of Demetrius again, and en deavoring to hinder the recovery of his power, as it were from a kind of sickness, he assisted the Greeks, and came to Athens, where, having ascended the Acropolis, he offered sacrifice to the goddess, and the same day came down again, and told the Athenians he was much gratified by the good-will and the confidence they had shown to him; but if they were wise he advised them never to let any king come thither again, or open their city gates to him. He concluded also a peace with Demetrius, but shortly after he was gone into Asia, at the persuasion of Lysimachus, he tampered with the Thessalians to revolt, and besieged his cities in Greece; finding he could better preserve the attachment of the Macedonians in war than in peace, and being of his own inclination not much given to rest. At last, after Demetrius had been overthrown in Syria, Lysimachus, who had secured his affairs, and had nothing to do, immediately turned his whole forces upon Pyrrhus, who was in quarters at Edessa, and falling upon and seizing his convoy of provisions, brought first a great scarcity into the army; then partly by letters, partly by spreading rumors abroad, he corrupted the principal officers of the Macedonians, reproaching them that they had made one their master who was both a stranger and descended from those who had ever been servants to the Macedonians, and that they had thrust the old friends and familiars of Alexander out of the country. The Macedonian soldiers being much prevailed upon, Pyrrhus withdrew himself with his Epirots and auxiliary forces, relinquishing Macedon, just after the same manner he took it. So little reason have kings to condemn popular governments for changing sides as suits their interests, as in this they do but imitate them who are the great instructors of unfaithfulness and treachery · holding him the wisest that makes the least account of being an honest man.

Pyrrhus having thus retired into Epirus, and left Macedon, fortune gave him a fair occasion of enjoying himself in quiet, and peaceably governing his own subjects; but he who thought it a nauseous course of life not to be doing mischief to others, or receiving some from them, like Achilles, could not endure repose,

———But sad and languished far,
Desiring battle and the shout of war,

and gratified his inclination by the following pretext, for new troubles. The Romans were at war with the Tarentines, who, not being able to go on with the war, nor yet, through the foolhardiness, and the viciousness of their popular speakers to come to terms and give it up, proposed now to make Pyrrhus their general, and engage him in it, as of all the neighboring kings the most at leisure, and the most skilful as a commander. The more grave and discreet citizens opposing these counsels, were partly overborne by the noise and violence of the multitude; while others, seeing this, absented themselves from the assemblies; only one Meton, a very sober man, on the day this public decree was to be ratified, when the people were now seating themselves, came dancing into the assembly like one quite drunk, with a withered garland and a small lamp in his hand, and a woman playing on a flute before him. And as in great multitudes met at such popular assemblies, no decorum can be well observed, some clapped him, others laughed, none forbade him, but called to the woman to play, and to him to sing to the company, and when they thought he was going to do so, "'Tis right of you, O men of Tarentum," he said, "not to hinder any from making themselves merry, that have a mind to it, while it is yet in their power; and if you are wise, you will take out your pleasure of your freedom while you can, for you must change your course of life, and follow other diet when Pyrrhus comes to town." These words made a great impression upon many of the Tarentines, and a confused murmur went about, that he had spoken much to the purpose; but some who feared they should be sacrificed if a peace were made with the Romans, reviled the whole assembly for so tamely suffering themselves to be abused by a drunken sot, and crowding together upon Meton, thrust him out. So the public order was passed and ambassadors sent into Epirus, not only in their own names, but in those of all the Italian Greeks, carrying presents to Pyrrhus, and letting him know they wanted a general of reputation and experience; and that they could furnish him with large forces of Lucanians, Messapians, Samnites, and Tarentines, amounting to twenty thousand horse, and three hundred and fifty thousand foot. This did not only quicken Pyrrhus, but raised an eager desire, for the expedition in the Epirots.

There was one Cineas, a Thessalian, considered to be a man of very good sense, a disciple of the great orator Demosthenes, who of all that were famous at that time for speaking well most seemed, as in a picture, to revive in the minds of the audience the memory of his force and vigor of eloquence; and being always about Pyrrhus, and sent about in his service to several cities, verified the saying of Euripides, that

——————the force of words
Can do whate'er is done by conquering swords.

And Pyrrhus was used to say, that Cineas had taken more towns with his words, than he with his arms, and always did him the honor to employ him in his most important occasions. This person, seeing Pyrrhus eagerly preparing for Italy, led him one day when he was at leisure into the following reasonings: "The Romans, sir, are reported to be great warriors and conquerors of many warlike nations; if God permit us to overcome them, how should we use our victory?" "You ask," said Pyrrhus, "a thing evident of itself. The Romans once conquered, there is neither Greek nor barbarian city that will resist us, but we shall presently be masters of all Italy, the extent and resources and strength of which any one should rather profess to be ignorant of, than yourself." Cineas after a little pause, "And having subdued Italy, what shall we do next?" Pyrrhus not yet discovering his intention, "Sicily," he replied, "next holds out her arms, to receive us, a wealthy and populous island, and easy to be gained; for since Agathocles left it, only faction and anarchy, and the licentious violence of the demagogues prevail.' "You speak," said Cineas, "what is perfectly probable, but will the possession of Sicily put an end to the war?" "God grant us," answered Pyrrhus, "victory and success in that, and we will use these as forerunners of greater things; who could forbear from Libya and Carthage then within reach, which Agathocles, even when forced to fly from Syracuse, and passing the sea only with a few ships had all but surprised? These conquests once perfected, will any assert that of the enemies who now pretend to despise us, any one will dare to make further resistance?" "None," replied Cineas, "for then it is manifest we may with such mighty forces regain Macedon, and make an absolute conquest of Greece; and when all these are in our power what shall we do then?" Said Pyrrhus, smiling, "We will live at our ease, my dear friend, and drink all day, and divert ourselves with pleasant conversation." When Cineas had led Pyrrhus with his argument to this point: "And what hinders us now, sir, if we have a mind to be merry, and entertain one another, since we have at hand without trouble all those necessary things, to which through much blood and great labor, and infinite hazards and mischief done to ourselves and to others, we design at last to arrive?" Such reasonings rather troubled Pyrrhus with the thought of the happiness he was quitting, than any way altered his purpose, being unable to abandon the hopes of what he so much desired.

And first, he sent away Cineas to the Tarentines with three thousand men; presently after, many vessels for transport of horse, and galleys, and flat-bottomed boats of all sorts arriving from Tarentum, he shipped upon them twenty elephants, three thousand horse, twenty thousand foot, two thousand archers, and five hundred slingers. All being thus in readiness, he set sail, and being half way over, was driven by the wind, blowing, contrary to the season of the year, violently from the north, and carried from his course, but by the great skill and resolution of his pilots and seamen, he made the land with infinite labor, and beyond expectation. The rest of the fleet could not get up, and some of the dispersed ships, losing the coast of Italy, were driven into the Libyan and Sicilian Sea; others not able to double the cape of Japygium, were overtaken by the night; and, with a boisterous and heavy sea, throwing them upon a dangerous and rocky shore, they were all very much disabled except the royal galley. She, while the sea bore upon her sides, resisted with her bulk and strength, and avoided the force of it, till the wind coming about, blew directly in their teeth from the shore, and the vessel keeping up with her head against it, was in danger of going to pieces; yet on the other hand, to suffer themselves to be driven off to sea again, which was thus raging and tempestuous, with the wind shifting about every way, seemed to them the most dreadful of all their present evils. Pyrrhus, rising up, threw himself overboard. His friends and guards strove eagerly who should be most ready to help him, but night and the sea with its noise and violent surge, made it extremely difficult to do this; so that hardly, when with the morning the wind began to subside, he got ashore, breathless and weakened in body, but with high courage and strength of mind resisting his hard fortune. The Messapians, upon whose shore they were thrown by the tempest, came up eagerly to help them in the best manner they could; and some of the straggling vessels that had escaped the storm arrived; in which were a very few horse, and not quite two thousand foot, and two elephants.

With these Pyrrhus marched straight to Tarentum, where Cineas, being informed of his arrival, led out the troops to meet him. Entering the town, he did nothing unpleasing to

the Tarentines, nor put any force upon them, till the ships
were all in harbor, and the greatest part of the army got together ; but then perceiving that the people, unless some
strong compulsion was used to them, were not capable either
of saving others or being saved themselves, and were rather
in ending, while he engaged for them in the field, to remain
at home bathing and feasting themselves, he first shut up the
places of public exercise, and the walks, where, in their idle
way, they fought their country's battles and conducted her
campaigns in their talk ; he prohibited likewise all festivals,
revels, and drinking-parties as unseasonable, and summoning
them to arms, showed himself rigorous and inflexible in carrying out the conscription for service in the war. So that
many, not understanding what it was to be commanded, left
the town, calling it mere slavery not to do as they pleased.
He now received intelligence that Lævinus, the Roman consul, was upon his march with a great army, and plundering
Lucania as he went. The confederate forces were not come
up to him, yet he thought it impossible to suffer so near an
approach of an enemy, and drew out with his army, but first
sent an herald to the Romans to know if before the war they
would decide the differences between them and the Italian
Greeks by his arbitrament and mediation. But Lævinus returning answer, that the Romans neither accepted him as
arbitrator nor feared him as an enemy, Pyrrhus advanced, and
encamped in the plain between the cities of Pandosia and
Heraclea, and having notice the Romans were near, and lay
on the other side of the river Siris, he rode up to take a
view of them, and seeing their order, the appointment of the
watches, their method and the general form of their encampment, he was amazed, and addressing one of his friends next
to him : "This order," said he, "Magacles, of the barbarians,
is not at all barbarian in character ; we shall see presently
what they can do ; " and growing a little more thoughtful of
the event, resolved to expect the arriving of the confederate
troops. And to hinder the Romans, if in the mean time they
should endeavor to pass the river, he planted men all along the
bank to oppose them. But they, hastening to anticipate the
coming up of the same forces which he had determined to
wait for, attempted the passage with their infantry, where it
was fordable, and with the horse in several places, so that
the Greeks, fearing to be surrounded, were obliged to retreat,
and Pyrrhus, perceiving this, and being much surprised, bade
his foot officers draw their men up in line of battle, and con-

tinue in arms, while he himself with three thousand horse advanced, hoping to attack the Romans as they were coming over, scattered and disordered. But when he saw a vast number of shields appearing above the water, and the horse following them in good order, gathering his men in a closer body, himself at the head of them, he began the charge, conspicuous by his rich and beautiful armor, and letting it be seen that his reputation had not outgone what he was able effectually to perform. While exposing his hands and body in the fight, and bravely repelling all that engaged him, he still guided the battle with a steady and undisturbed reason, and such presence of mind, as if he had been out of the action and watching it from a distance, passing still from point to point, and assisting those whom he thought most pressed by the enemy. Here Leonnatus the Macedonian, observing one of the Italians very intent upon Pyrrhus, riding up towards him, and changing places as he did, and moving as he moved: "Do you see, Sir," said he, "that barbarian on the black horse with white feet? he seems to be one that designs some great and dangerous thing, for he looks constantly at you, and fixes his whole attention, full of vehement purpose, on you alone, taking no notice of others. Be on your guard, sir, against him." "Leonnatus," said Pyrrhus, "it is impossible for any man to avoid his fate; but neither he nor any other Italian shall have much satisfaction in engaging with me." While they were in this discourse, the Italian, lowering his spear and quickening his horse, rode furiously at Pyrrhus, and run his horse through with his lance; at the same instant Leonnatus ran his through. Both horses falling, Pyrrhus's friends surrounded him and brought him off safe, and killed the Italian, bravely defending himself. He was by birth a Frentanian, captain of a troop, and named Oplacus.

This made Pyrrhus use greater caution, and now seeing his horse give ground, he brought up the infantry against the enemy, and changing his scarf and his arms with Megacles, one of his friends, and obscuring himself, as it were, in his, charged upon the Romans, who received and engaged him, and a great while the success of the battle remained undetermined; and it is said there were seven turns of fortune both of pursuing and being pursued. And the change of his arms was very opportune for the safety of his person, but had like to have overthrown his cause and lost him the victory; for several falling upon Megacles, the first that gave him his mortal wound was one Dexous, who, snatching away his hel met and his robe, rode at once to Lævinus, holding them up, and saying aloud he had killed Pyrrhus. These spoils being carried about and shown among the ranks, the Romans were transported with joy, and shouted aloud; while equal discouragement and terror prevailed among the Greeks, until Pyrrhus, understanding what had happened, rode about the army with his face bare, stretching out his hand to his soldiers, and telling them aloud it was he. At last, the elephants more particularly began to distress the Romans, whose horses, before they came near, not enduring them, went back with their riders; and upon this, he commanded the Thessalian cavalry to charge them in their disorder, and routed them with great loss. Dionysius affirms near fifteen thousand of the Romans fell; Hieronymus, no more than seven thousand. On Pyrrhus's side, the same Dionysius makes thirteen thousand slain, the other under four thousand; but they were the flower of his men, and amongst them his particular friends as well as officers whom he most trusted and made use of. However, he possessed himself of the Romans' camp which they deserted, and gained over several confederate cities, and wasted the country round about, and advanced so far that he was within about thirty-seven miles of Rome itself. After the fight many of the Lucanians and Samnites came in and joined him, whom he chid for their delay, but yet he was evidently well pleased and raised in his thoughts, that he had defeated so great an army of the Romans with the assistance of the Tarentines alone.

The Romans did not remove Lævinus from the consulship; though it is told that Caius Fabricius said, that the Epirots had not beaten the Romans, but only Pyrrhus, Lævinus; insinuating that heir loss was not through want of valor but of conduct; but filled up their legions, and enlisted fresh men with all speed, talking high and boldly of war, which struck Pyrrhus with amazement. He thought it advisable by sending first to make an experiment whether they had any inclination to treat, thinking that to take the city and make an absolute conquest was no work for such an army as his was at that time, but to settle a friendship, and bring them to terms, would be highly honorable after his victory. Cineas was despatched away, and applied himself to several of the great ones, with presents for themselves and their ladies from the king; but not a person would receive any, and answered, as well men as women, that if an agreement were publicly concluded, they also should be ready, for their parts, to ex press their regard to the king. And Cineas, discoursing with the senate in the most persuasive and obliging manner in the world, yet was not heard with kindness or inclination, although Pyrrhus offered also to return all the prisoners he had taken in the fight without ransom, and promised his assistance for the entire conquest of all Italy, asking only their friendship for himself, and security for the Tarentines, and nothing further. Nevertheless, most were well-inclined to a peace, having already received one great defeat, and fearing another from an additional force of the native Italians, now joining with Pyrrhus. At this point Appius Claudius, a man of great distinction, but who, because of his great age and loss of sight, had declined the fatigue of public business, after these propositions had been made by the king, hearing a report that the senate was ready to vote the conditions of peace, could not forbear, but commanded his servants to take him up, was carried in his chair through the forum to the senate house. When he was set down at the door, his sons and sons-in-law took him up in their arms, and, walking close round about him, brought him into the senate. Out of reverence for so worthy a man, the whole assembly was respectfully silent.

And a little after raising up himself: "I bore," said he, "until this time, the misfortune of my eyes with some impatience, but now while I hear of these dishonorable motions and resolves of yours, destructive to the glory of Rome, it is my affliction, that being already blind, I am not deaf too. Where is now that discourse of yours that became famous in all the world, that if he, the great Alexander, had come into Italy, and dared to attack us when we were young men, and our fathers, who were then in their prime, he had not now been celebrated as invincible, but either flying hence, or falling here, had left Rome more glorious? You demonstrate now that all that was but foolish arrogance and vanity, by fearing Molossians and Chaonians, ever the Macedonian's prey, and by trembling at Pyrrhus who was himself but an humble servant to one of Alexander's life-guard, and comes here, not so much to assist the Greeks that inhabit among us, as to escape from his enemies at home, a wanderer about Italy, and yet dares to promise you the conquest of it all by that army which has not been able to preserve for him a little part of Macedon. Do not persuade yourselves that making him your friend is the way to send him back, it is the way rather to bring over other invaders from thence, contemning you as

easy to be reduced, if Pyrrhus goes off without punishment
for his outrages on you, but, on the contrary with the reward
of having enabled the Tarentines and Samnites to laugh at
the Romans." When Appius had done, eagerness for the
war seized on every man, and Cineas was dismissed with this
answer, that when Pyrrhus had withdrawn his forces out of
Italy, then, if he pleased, they would treat with him about
friendship and alliance, but while he stayed there in arms,
they were resolved to prosecute the war against him with all
their force, though he should have defeated a thousand
Lævinuses. It is said that Cineas, while he was managing
this affair, made it his business carefully to inspect the manners of the Romans, and to understand their methods of government, and having conversed with their noblest citizens, he
afterwards told Pyrrhus, among other things, that the senate
seemed to him an assembly of kings, and as for the people,
he feared lest it might prove that they were fighting with a
Lernæan hydra, for the consul had already raised twice as
large an army as the former, and there were many times over
the same number of Romans able to bear arms.

Then Caius Fabricius came in embassy from the Romans
to treat about the prisoners that were taken, one whom Cineas
had reported to be a man of highest consideration among
them as an honest man and a good soldier, but extremely
poor. Pyrrhus received him with much kindness, and privately would have persuaded him to accept of his gold, not for
any evil purpose, but calling it a mark of respect and hospitable kindness. Upon Fabricius's refusal, he pressed him no
further, but the next day, having a mind to discompose him,
as he had never seen an elephant before, he commanded one
of the largest, completely armed, to be placed behind the
hangings, as they were talking together. Which being done,
upon a sign given, the hangings was drawn aside, and the elephant, raising his trunk over the head of Fabricius, made an
horrid and ugly noise. He, gently turning about and smiling,
said to Pyrrhus, "neither your money yesterday, nor this
beast to-day make any impression upon me." At supper,
amongst all sorts of things that were discoursed of, but more
particularly Greece and the philosophers there. Cineas, by
accident, had occasion to speak of Epicurus, and explained
the opinions his followers hold about the gods and the commonwealth, and the objects of life, placing the chief happiness of man in pleasure, and declining public affairs as an
injury and disturbance of a happy life, removing the gods

afar aff both from kindness or anger, or any concern for us at all, to a life wholly without business and flowing in pleasures. Before he had done speaking, "O Hercules!" Fabricius cried out to Pyrrhus, "may Pyrrhus and the Samnites entertain themselves with this sort of opinions as long as they are in war with us." Pyrrhus, admiring the wisdom and gravity of the man, was the more transported with desire of making friendship instead of war with the city, and entreated him personally, after the peace should be concluded, to accept of living with him as the chief of his ministers and generals. Fabricius answered quietly, "Sir, this will not be for your advantage, for they who now honor and admire you, when they have had experience of me, will rather choose to be governed by me, than by you." Such was Fabricius. And Pyrrhus received his answer without any resentment or tyrannic passion; nay, among his friends he highly commended the great mind of Fabricius, and intrusted the prisoners to him alone, on condition that if the senate should not vote a peace, after they had conversed with their friends and celebrated the festival of Saturn, they should be remanded. And, accordingly, they were sent back after the holidays; it being decreed pain of death for any that stayed behind.

After this Fabricius taking the consulate, a person came with a letter to the camp written by the king's principal physician, offering to take off Pyrrhus by poison, and so end the war without further hazard to the Romans, if he might have a reward proportionable to his service. Fabricius, hating the villany of the man, and disposing the other consul to the same opinion, sent despatches immediately to Pyrrhus to caution him against the treason. His letter was to this effect: "Caius Fabricius and Quintus Æmilius, consuls of the Romans, to Pyrrhus the king, health. You seem to have made an ill judgment both of your friends and enemies; you will understand by reading this letter sent to us, that you are at war with honest men, and trust villains and knaves. Nor do we disclose this to you out of any favor to you, but lest your ruin might bring a reproach upon us, as if we had ended the war by treachery, as not able to do it by force." When Pyrrhus had read the letter, and made inquiry into the treason, he punished the physician, and as an acknowledgment to the Romans sent to Rome the prisoners without ransom, and again employed Cineas to negotiate a peace for him. But they, regarding it as at once too great a kindness from an enemy, and too great a reward for not doing an ill thing to accept their prisoners so, released in return an equal number of the Tarentines and Samnites, but would admit of no debate of alliance or peace until he had removed his arms and forces out of Italy, and sailed back to Epirus with the same ships that brought him over. Afterwards, his affairs demanding a second fight, when he had refreshed his men, he decamped, and met the Romans about the city Asculum, where, however, he was much incommoded by a woody country unfit for his horse, and a swift river, so that the elephants, for want of sure treading, could not get up with the infantry. After many wounded and many killed, night put an end to the engagement. Next day, designing to make the fight on even ground, and have the elephants among the thickest of the enemy, he caused a detachment to possess themselves of those incommodious grounds, and, mixing slingers and archers among the elephants, with full strength and courage, he advanced in a close and well-ordered body. The Romans, not having those advantages of retreating and falling on as they pleased, which they had before, were obliged to fight man to man upon plain ground, and, being anxious to drive back the infantry before the elephants could get up, they fought fiercely with their swords among the Macedonian spears, not sparing themselves, thinking only to wound and kill, without regard of what they suffered. After a long and obstinate fight, the first giving ground is reported to have been where Pyrrhus himself engaged with extraordinary courage; but they were most carried away by the overwhelming force of the elephants, not being able to make use of their valor, but overthrown as it were by the irruption of a sea or an earthquake, before which it seemed better to give way than to die without doing any thing, and not gain the least advantage by suffering the utmost extremity, the retreat to their camp not being far. Hieronymus says, there fell six thousand of the Romans, and of Pyrrhus's men, the king's own commentaries reported three thousand five hundred and fifty lost in this action. Dionysius, however, neither gives any account of two engagements at Asculum, nor allows the Romans to have been certainly beaten, stating that once only, after they had fought till sunset, both armies were unwillingly separated by the night, Pyrrhus being wounded by a javelin in the arm, and his baggage plundered by the Samnites, that in all there died of Pyrrhus's men and the Romans above fifteen thousand. The armies separated; and, it is said, Pyrrhus replied to one that gave him joy of his victory, that one other such would utterly undo him. For he had lost a great part of the forces he brought with him, and almost all his particular friends and principal commanders; there were no others there to make recruits, and he found the confederates in Italy backward. On the other hand, as from a fountain continually flowing out of the city, the Roman camp was quickly and plentifully filled up with fresh men, not at all abating in courage for the losses they sustained, but ever from their very anger gaining new force and resolution to go on with the war.

Among these difficulties he fell again into new hopes and projects distracting his purposes. For at the same time some persons arrived from Sicily, offering into his hands the cities of Agrigentum, Syracuse, and Leontini, and begging his assistance to drive out the Carthaginians, and rid the island of tyrants; and others brought him news out of Greece that Ptolemy, called Ceraunus, was slain in a fight, and his army cut in pieces by the Gauls, and that now, above all others, was his time to offer himself to the Macedonians, in great need of a king. Complaining much of fortune for bringing him so many occasions of great things all together at a time, and thinking that to have both offered to him, was to lose one of them he was doubtful, balancing in his thoughts. But the affairs of Sicily seeming to hold out the greater prospects, Africa lying so near, he turned himself to them, and presently despatched away Cineas, as he used to do, to make terms beforehand with the cities. Then he placed a garrison in Tarentum, much to the Tarentines' discontent, who required him either to perform what he came for, and continue with them in a war against the Romans, or leave the city as he found it. He returned no pleasing answer, but commanded them to be quiet and attend his time, and so sailed away. Being arrived in Sicily, what he had designed in his hopes was confirmed effectually, and the cities frankly surrendered to him; and wherever his arms and force were necessary, nothing at first made any considerable resistance. For advancing with thirty thousand foot, and twenty-five hundred horse, and two hundred ships, he totally routed the Phœnicians, and overran their whole province, and Eryx being the strongest town they held, and having a great garrison in it, he resolved to take it by storm. The army being in readiness to give the assault, he put on his arms, and coming to the head of his men made a vow of plays and sacrifices in honor to Hercules, if he signalized himself in that day's action before the Greeks that dwelt in Sicily, as became his great descent and his fortunes. The sign being given by sound of trumpet, he first scattered the barbarians with his shot, and then brought his ladders to the wall, and was the first that mounted upon it himself, and, the enemy appearing in great numbers, he beat them back; some he threw down from the walls on each side, others he laid dead in a heap round about him with his sword, nor did he receive the least wound, but by his very aspect inspired terror in the enemy; and gave a clear demonstration that Homer was in the right, and pronounced according to the truth of fact, that fortitude alone, of all the virtues, is wont to display itself in divine transports and frenzies. The city being taken, he offered to Hercules most magnificently, and exhibited all varities of shows and plays.

A sort of barbarous people about Messena, called Mamertines, gave much trouble to the Greeks, and put several of them under contribution. These being numerous and valiant (from whence they had their name, equivalent in the Latin tongue to *warlike*), he first intercepted the collectors of the contribution money, and cut them off, then beat them in open fight, and destroyed many of their places of strength. The Carthaginians being now inclined to composition, and offering him a round sum of money, and to furnish him with shipping, if a peace were concluded, he told them plainly, aspiring still to greater things, there was but one way for a friendship and right understanding between them, if they, wholly abandoning Sicily, would consent to make the African sea the limit between them and the Greeks. And being elevated with his good fortune, and the strength of his forces, and pursuing those hopes in prospect of which he first sailed thither, his immediate aim was at Africa; and as he had abundance of shipping, but very ill equipped, he collected seamen, not by fair and gentle dealing with the cities, but by force in a haughty and insolent way, and menacing them with punishments. And as at first he had not acted thus, but had been unusually indulgent and kind, ready to believe, and uneasy to none; now of a popular leader becoming a tyrant by these severe proceedings, he got the name of an ungrateful and a faithless man. However, they gave way to these things as necessary, although they took them very ill from him; and especially when he began to show suspicion of Thœnon and Sosistratus, men of the first position in Syracuse, who invited him over into Sicily, and when he was come, put the cities into his power, and were most instrumental in all he had done there since his arrival, whom he now would neither suffer to be about his person, nor leave at home; and when Sosistratus out of fear withdrew himself, and then he charged Thœnon, as in a conspiracy with the other, and put him to death, with this all his prospects changed, not by little and little, nor in a single place only, but a mortal hatred being raised in the cities against him, some fell off to the Carthaginians, others called in the Mamertines. And seeing revolts in all places, and desires of alteration, and a potent faction against him, at the same time he received letters from the Samnites and Tarentines, who were beaten quite out of the field, and scarce able to secure their towns against the war, earnestly begging his help. This served as a color to make his relinquishing Sicily no flight, nor a despair of good success; but in truth not being able to manage Sicily, which was as a ship laboring in a storm, and willing to be out of her, he suddenly threw himself over into Italy. It is reported that at his going off he looked back upon the island, and said to those about him, "How brave a field of war do we leave, my friends, for the Romans and Carthaginians to fight in," which, as he then conjectured, fell out indeed not long after.

When he was sailing off, the barbarians having conspired together, he was forced to a fight with the Carthaginians in the very road, and lost many of his ships; with the rest he fled into Italy. There, about one thousand Mamertines, who had crossed the sea a little before, though afraid to engage him in open field, setting upon him where the passages were difficult, put the whole army in confusion. Two elephants fell, and a great part of his rear was cut off. He, therefore, coming up in person, repulsed the enemy, but ran into great danger among men long trained and bold in war. His being wounded in the head with a sword, and retiring a little out of the fight, much increased their confidence, and one of them advancing a good way before the rest, large of body and in bright armor, with an haughty voice challenged him to come forth if he were alive. Pyrrhus, in great anger, broke away violently from his guards, and, in his fury, besmeared with blood, terrible to look upon, made his way through his own men, and struck the barbarian on the head with his sword such a blow, as with the strength of his arm, and the excellent temper of the weapon, passed downward so far that his body being cut asunder fell in two pieces. This stopped the course of the barbarians, amazed and confounded at Pyr rhus, as one more than man; so that continuing his march all the rest of the way undisturbed, he arrived at Tarentum with twenty thousand foot and three thousand horse, where, reinforcing himself with the choicest troops of the Tarentines, he advanced immediately against the Romans, who then lay encamped in the territories of the Samnites, whose affairs were extremely shattered, and their counsels broken, having been in many fights beaten by the Romans. There was also a discontent amongst them at Pyrrhus for his expedition into Sicily, so that not many came in to join him.

He divided his army into two parts, and despatched the first into Lucania to oppose one of the consuls there, so that he should not come in to assist the other; the rest he led against Manius Curius, who had posted himself very advantageously near Beneventum, and expected the other consul's forces, and partly because the priests had dissuaded him by unfavorable omens, was resolved to remain inactive. Pyrrhus, hastening to attack these before the other could arrive, with his best men, and the most serviceable elephants, marched in the night toward their camp. But being forced to go round about, and through a very woody country, their lights failed them, and the soldiers lost their way. A council of war being called, while they were in debate, the night was spent, and, at the break of day, his approach, as he came down the hills, was discovered by the enemy, and put the whole camp into disorder and tumult. But the sacrifices being auspicious, and the time absolutely obliging them to fight, Manius drew his troops out of the trenches, and attacked the vanguard, and, having routed them all, put the whole army into consternation, so that many were cut off, and some of the elephants taken. This success drew on Manius into the level plain, and here, in open battle, he defeated part of the enemy; but, in other quarters, finding himself overpowered by the elephants and forced back to his trenches, he commanded out those who were left to guard them, a numerous body, standing thick at the ramparts, all in arms and fresh. These coming down from their strong position, and charging the elephants, forced them to retire; and they in the flight turning back upon their own men, caused great disorder and confusion, and gave into the hands of the Romans the victory, and the future supremacy. Having obtained from these efforts, and these contests, the feeling as well as the fame of invincible strength, they at once reduced Italy under their power, and not long after Sicily too.

Thus fell Pyrrhus from his Italian and Sicilian hopes, after he had consumed six years in these wars, and though unsuccessful in his affairs, yet preserved his courage unconquerable among all these misfortunes, and was held, for military experience, and personal valor and enterprise, much the bravest of all the princes of his time, only what he got by great actions he lost again by vain hopes, and by new desires of what he had not, kept nothing of what he had. So that Antigonus used to compare him to a player with dice, who had excellent throws, but knew not how to use them. He returned into Epirus with eight thousand foot and five hundred horse, and for want of money to pay them, was fain to look out for a new war to maintain the army. Some of the Gauls joining him, he invaded Macedonia, where Antigonus, son of Demetrius, governed, designing merely to plunder and waste the country. But after he had made himself master of several towns, and two thousand men came over to him, he began to hope for something greater, and adventured upon Antigonus himself, and meeting him at a narrow passage, put the whole army in disorder. The Gauls, who brought up Antigonus's rear, were very numerous and stood firm, but after a sharp encounter, the greatest part of them were cut off, and they who had the charge of the elephants being surrounded every way, delivered up both themselves and the beasts, Pyrrhus, taking this advantage, and advising more with his good fortune than his reason, boldly set upon the main body of the Macedonian foot, already surprised with fear, and troubled at the former loss. They declined any action or engagement with him ; and he, holding out his hand and calling aloud both to the superior and under officers by name, brought over the foot from Antigonus, who, flying away secretly, was only able to retain some of the seaport towns. Pyrrhus, among all these kindnesses of fortune, thinking what he had effected against the Gauls the most advantageous for his glory, hung up their richest and goodliest spoils in the temple of Minerva Itonis, with this inscription :—

> Pyhrrus, descendant of Molossian kings,
> These shields to thee, Itonian goddess, brings,
> Won from the valiant Gauls when in the fight
> Antigonus and all his host took flight;
> 'Tis not to-day nor yesterday alone
> That for brave deeds the Æacidæ are known.

After this victory in the field, he proceeded to secure the cities, and having possessed himself of Aegæ, beside other hardships put upon the people there, he left in the town a garrison of Gauls, some of those in his own army, who, being insatiably desirous of wealth, instantly dug up the tombs of the kings that lay buried there, and took away the riches, and insolently scattered about their bones. Pyrrhus, in appearance, made no great matter of it, either deferring it on account of the pressure of other business, or wholly passing it by, out of fear of punishing those barbarians; but this made him very ill spoken of among the Macedonians, and his affairs being yet unsettled and brought to no firm consistence, he began to entertain new hopes and projects, and in raillery called Antigonus a shameless man, for still wearing his purple and not changing it for an ordinary dress; but upon Cleonymus, the Spartan, arriving and inviting him to Lacedæmon, he frankly embraced the overture. Cleonymus was of royal descent, but seeming too arbitrary and absolute, had no great respect nor credit at home; and Areus was king there. This was the occasion of an old and public grudge between him and the citizens; but, beside that, Cleonymus, in his old age, had married a young lady of great beauty and royal blood, Chilonis, daughter of Leotychides, who, falling desperately in love with Acrotatus, Areus's son, a youth in the flower of manhood, rendered this match both uneasy and dishonorable to Cleonymus, as there was none of the Spartans who did not very well know how much his wife slighted him; so these domestic troubles added to his public discontent. He brought Pyrrhus to Sparta with an army of twenty-five thousand foot, two thousand horse, and twenty-four elephants. So great a preparation made it evident to the whole world, that he came not so much to gain Sparta for Cleonymus, as to take all Peloponnesus for himself, although he expressly denied this to the Lacedæmonian ambassadors that came to him at Megalopolis, affirming he came to deliver the cities from the slavery of Antigonus, and declaring he would send his younger sons to Sparta, if he might, to be brought up in Spartan habits, that so they might be better bred than all other kings. With these pretensions amusing those who came to meet him in his march, as soon as ever he entered Laconia he began to plunder and waste the country, and on the ambassadors complaining that he began the war upon them before it was proclaimed: "We know," said he, "very well that neither do you Spartans, when you design any thing, talk of it beforehand." One Mandroclidas, then present, told him, in the broad Spartan dialect: "If you are a god, you

will do us no harm, we are wronging no man; but if you are
a man, there may be another stronger than you."

He now marched away directly for Lacedæmon, and being
advised by Cleonymus to give the assault as soon as he arrived, fearing, as it is said, lest the soldiers, entering by night,
should plunder the city, he answered, they might do it as well
next morning, because there were but few soldiers in town,
and those unprovided against his sudden approach, as Areus
was not there in person, but gone to aid the Gortynians in
Crete. And it was this alone that saved the town, because
he despised it as not tenable, and so immagining no defence
would be made, he sat down before it that night. Cleonymus's
friends, and the Helots, his domestic servants, had made
great preparation at his house, as expecting Pyrrhus there at
supper. In the night the Lacedæmonians held a consultation
to ship over all the women into Crete, but they unanimously
refused, and Archidamia came into the senate with a sword
in her hand, in the name of them all, asking if the men expected the women to survive the ruins of Sparta. It was next
resolved to draw a trench in a line directly over against the
enemy's camp, and, here and there in it, to sink wagons in
the ground, as deep as the naves of the wheels, that, so being
firmly fixed, they might obstruct the passage of the elephants.
When they had just begun the work, both maids and women
came to them, the married women with their robes tied like
girdles round their underfrocks, and the unmarried girls in
their single frocks only, to assist the elder men at the work.
As for the youth that were next day to engage, they left them
to their rest, and undertaking their proportion, they themselves
finished a third part of the trench, which was in breadth six
cubits, four in a depth, and eight hundred feet long, as Phylarchus says; Hieronymus makes it somewhat less. The enemy
beginning to move by break of day, they brought their arms
to the young men, and giving them also in charge the trench,
exhorted them to defend and keep it bravely, as it would be
happy for them to conquer in the view of their whole country,
and glorious to die in the arms of their mothers and wives,
falling as became Spartans. As for Chilonis, she retired
with a halter about her neck, resolving to die so rather than
fall into the hands of Cleonymus, if the city were taken.

Pyrrhus himself, in person, advanced with his foot to force
through the shields of the Spartans ranged against him, and
to get over the trench, which was scarce passable, because the
looseness of the fresh earth afforded no firm footing for the

soldiers. Ptolemy, his son, with two thousand Gauls, and some choice men of the Chaonians, went around the trench, and endeavored to get over where the wagons were. But they, being so deep in the ground, and placed close together, not only made his passage, but also the defence of the Lacedæmonians very troublesome. Yet now the Gauls had got the wheels out of the ground, and were drawing off the wagons toward the river, when young Acrotatus, seeing the danger, passing through the town with three hundred men, surrounded Ptolemy undiscerned, taking the advantage of some slopes of the ground, until he fell upon his rear, and forced him to wheel about. And thrusting one another into the ditch, and falling among the wagons, at last with much loss, not without difficulty, they withdrew. The elderly men and all the women saw this brave action of Acrotatus, and when he returned back into the town to his first post, all covered with blood and fierce and elate with victory, he seemed to the Spartan women to have become taller and more beautiful than before, and they envied Chilonis so worthy a lover. And some of the old men followed him, crying aloud, "Go on, Acrotatus, be happy with Chilonis, and beget brave sons for Sparta." Where Pyrrhus himself fought was the hottest of the action, and many of the Spartans did gallantly, but in particular one Phyllius signalized himself, made the best resistance, and killed most assailants; and when he found himself ready to sink with the many wounds he had received, retiring a little out of his place behind another, he fell down among his fellow-soldiers, that the enemy might not carry off his body. The fight ended with the day, and Pyrrhus, in his sleep, dreamed that he drew thunderbolts upon Lacedæmon, and set it all on fire, and rejoiced at the sight; and waking, in this transport of joy, he commanded his officers to get all things ready for a second assault, and relating his dream among his friends, supposing it to mean that he should take the town by storm, the rest assented to it with admiration, but Lysimachus was not pleased with the dream, and told him he feared lest as places struck with lightning are held sacred, and not to be trodden upon, so the gods might by this let him know the city should not be taken. Pyrrhus replied, that all these things were but idle talk, full of uncertainty, and only fit to amuse the vulgar; their thought, with their swords in their hands, should always be

The one good omen is king Pyrrhus's cause.

and so got up, and drew out his army to the walls by break of day. The Lacedæmonians, in resolution and courage, made a defence even beyond their power; the women were all by, helping them to arms, and bringing bread and drink to those that desired it, and taking care of the wounded. The Macedonians attempted to fill up the trench, bringing huge quantities of materials and throwing them upon the arms and dead bodies, that lay there and were covered over. While the Lacedæmonians opposed this with all their force, Pyrrhus, in person, appeared on their side of the trench and the wagons, pressing on horseback toward the city, at which the men who had that post calling out, and the women shrieking and running about, while Pyrrhus violently pushed on, and beat down all that disputed his way, his horse received a shot in the belly from a Cretan arrow, and, in his convulsions as he died, threw off Phyrrhus on slippery and steep ground. And all about him being in confusion at this, the Spartans came boldly up, and making good use of their missiles, forced them off again. After this Pyrrhus, in other quarters also, put an end to the combat, imagining the Lacedæmonians would be inclined to yield, as almost all of them were wounded, and very great numbers killed outright; but the good fortune of the city, either satisfied with the experiment upon the bravery of the citizens, or willing to prove how much even in the last extremities such interposition may effect, brought, when the Lacedæmonians had now but very slender hopes left, Aminias, the Phocian, one of Antigonus's commanders, from Corinth to their assistance, with a force of mercenaries; and they were no sooner received into the town, but Areus, their king, arrived there himself, too, from Crete, with two thousand men more. The women upon this went all home to their houses, finding it no longer necessary for them to meddle with the business of the war; and they also were sent back, who, though not of military age, were by necessity forced to take arms, while the rest prepared to fight Pyrrhus.

He, upon the coming of these additional forces, was indeed possessed with a more eager desire and ambition than before, to make himself master of the town; but his designs not succeeding, and receiving fresh losses every day, he gave over the siege, and fell to plundering the country, determining to winter thereabout. But fate is unavoidable, and a great feud happening at Argos between Aristeas and Aristippus, two principal citizens, after Aristippus had resolved to make use of the friendship of Antigonus, Aristeas to anticipate him invited Pyrrhus thither. And he always revolving hopes upon hopes, and treating all his successes as occasions of more, and his reverses as defects to be amended by new enterprises, allowed neither losses nor victories to limit him in his receiving or giving trouble, and so presently went for Argos. Areus, by frequent ambushes, and seizing positions where the ways were most unpracticable, harrassed the Gauls and Molossians that brought up the rear. It had been told Pyrrhus by one of the priests that found the liver of the sacrificed beast imperfect, that some of his near relations would be lost; in this tumult and disorder of his rear, forgetting the prediction, he commanded out his son Ptolemy with some of his guards to their assistance, while he himself led on the main body rapidly out of the pass. And the fight being very warm where Ptolemy was (for the most select men of the Lacedæmonians, commanded by Evalcus, were there engaged), one Oryssus of Aptera in Crete, a stout man and swift of foot, running on one side of the young prince, as he was fighting bravely, gave him a mortal wound and slew him. On his fall those about him turned their backs, and the Lacedæmonian horse, pursuing and cutting off many, got into the open plain, and found themselves engaged with the enemy before they were aware, without their infantry; Pyrrhus, who had received the ill news of his son, and was in great affliction, drew out his Molossian horse against them, and charging at the head of his men, satiated himself with the blood and slaughter of the Lacedæmonians, as indeed he always showed himself a terrible and invincible hero in actual fight, but now he exceeded all he had ever done before in courage and force. On his riding his horse up to Evalcus, he, by declining a little to one side, had almost cut off Pyrrhus's hand in which he held the reins, but lighting on the reins, only cut them; at the same instant Pyrrhus, running him through with his spear, fell from his horse, and there on foot as he was, proceeded to slaughter all those choice men that fought about the body of Evalcus; a severe additional loss to Sparta, incurred after the war itself was now at an end, by the mere animosity of the commanders. Pyrrhus having thus offered, as it were, a sacrifice to the ghost of his son, and fought a glorious battle in honor of his obsequies, and having vented much of his pain in action against the enemy, marched away to Argos. And having intelligence that Antigonus was already in possession of the high grounds, he encamped about Nauplia, and the next day despatched a herald to Antigonus, calling him a villain, and challenging him to descend into the plain field and fight with him for the kingdom. He answered, that his conduct should be measured by times as well as by arms, and that if Pyrrhus had no leisure to live, there were ways enough open to death. To both the kings, also, came ambassadors from Argos, desiring each party to retreat, and to allow the city to remain in friendship with both, without falling into the hands of either. Antigonus was persuaded, and sent his son as a hostage to the Argives; but Pyrrhus, although he consented to retire, yet, as he sent no hostage, was suspected. A remarkable portent happened at this time to Pyrrhus; the heads of the sacrificed oxen, lying apart from the bodies, were seen to thrust out their tongues and lick up their own gore. And in the city of Argos, the priestess of Apollo Lycius rushed out of the temple, crying she saw the city full of carcasses and slaughter, and an eagle coming out to fight, and presently vanishing again.

In the dead of the night, Pyrrhus, aproaching the walls, and finding the gate called Diamperes set open for them by Aristeas, was undiscovered long enough to allow all his Gauls to enter and take possession of the market-place. But the gate being too low to let in the elephants, they were obliged to take down the towers which they carried on their backs, and put them on again in the dark and in disorder, so that time being lost, the city took the alarm, and the people ran, some to Aspis the chief citadel, and others to other places of defence, and sent away to Antigonus to assist them. He, advancing within a short distance, made an halt, but sent in some of his principal commanders, and his son with a considerable force. Areus came thither, too, with one thousand Cretans, and some of the most active men among the Spartans, and all falling on at once upon the Gauls, put them in great disorder. Pyrrhus, entering in with noise and shouting near the Cylarabis, when the Gauls returned the cry, noticed that it did not express courage and assurance, but was the voice of men distressed, and that had their hands full. He, therefore, pushed forward in haste the van of his horse that marched but slowly and dangerously, by reason of the drains and sinks of which the city is full. In this night engagement, there was infinite uncertainty as to what was being done, or what orders were given; there was much mistaking and straggling in the narrow streets; all generalship was useless in that darkness and noise and pressure; so both sides continued without doing any thing, expecting daylight. At the first dawn, Pyrrhus, seeing the great citadel Aspis full of enemies, was disturbed, and remarking, among a variety of figures dedicated in the market-place, a wolf and bull of brass, as it were ready to attack one another, he was struck with alarm, recollecting an oracle that formerly predicted fate had determined his death when he should see a wolf fighting with a bull. The Argives say, these figures were set up in record of a thing that long ago had happened there. For Danaus, at his first landing in the country, near the Pyramia in Thyreatis, as he was on his way towards Argos, espied a wolf fighting with a bull, and conceiving the wolf to represent him (for this stranger fell upon a native as he designed to do), stayed to see the issue of the fight, and the wolf prevailing, he offered vows to Apollo Lycius, and thus made his attempt upon the town, and succeeded; Gelanor, who was then king, being displaced by a faction. And this was the cause of dedicating those figures.

Pyrrhus, quite out of heart at this sight, and seeing none of his designs succeed, thought best to retreat, but fearing the narrow passage at the gate, sent to his son Helenus, who was left without the town with a great part of his forces, commanding him to break down part of the wall, and assist the retreat if the enemy pressed hard upon them. But what with haste and confusion, the person that was sent delivered nothing clearly; so that quite mistaking, the young prince with the best of his men and the remaining elephants marched straight through the gates into the town to assist his father. Pyrrhus was now making good his retreat, and while the marketplace afforded them ground enough both to retreat and fight, frequently repulsed the enemy that bore upon him. But when he was forced out of that broad place into the narrow street leading to the gate, and fell in with those who came the other way to his assistance, some did not hear him call out to them to give back, and those who did, however eager to obey him, were pushed forward by others behind, who poured in at the gate. Besides, the largest of his elephants falling down on his side in the very gate, and lying roaring on the ground, was in the way of those that whould have got out. Another of the elephants already in the town, called Nicon, striving to take up his rider, who, after many wounds received, was fallen off his back, bore forward upon those that were retreating, and, thrusting upon friends as well as enemies, tumbled them all confusedly upon one another, till having found the body, and taken it up with his trunk, he carried it on his tusks, and, returning in a fury, trod down all before him. Being thus pressed and crowded together, not a man could do any thing for himself, but being wedged, as it were, together into one mass, the whole multitude rolled and swayed this way and that altogether, and did very little execution either upon the enemy in their rear, or on any of them who were intercepted in the mass, but very much harm to one another. For he who had either drawn his sword or directed his lance, could neither restore it again, nor put his sword up; with these weapons they wounded their own men, as they happened to come in the way, and they were dying by mere contact with each other.

Pyrrhus, seeing this storm and confusion of things, took off the crown he wore upon his helmet, by which he was distinguished, and gave it to one nearest his person, and trusting to the goodness of his horse, rode in among the thickest of the emeny, and being wounded with a lance through his breast-plate, but not dangerously, nor indeed very much, he turned about upon the man who struck him, who was an Argive, not of any illustrious birth, but the son of a poor old woman; she was looking upon the fight among other women from the top of a house, and perceiving her son engaged with Pyrrhus, and affrighted at the danger he was in, took up a tile with both hands and threw it at Pyrrhus. This falling on his head below the helmet, and bruising the vertebræ of the lower part of the neck, stunned and blinded him; his hands let go the reins, and sinking down from his horse, he fell just by the tomb of Licymnius. The common soldiers knew not who it was; but one Zopyrus, who served under Antigonus, and two or three others running thither, and knowing it was Pyrrhus, dragged him to a door-way hard by, just as he was recovering a little from the blow. But when Zopyrus drew out an Illyrian sword, ready to cut off his head, Pyrrhus gave him so fierce a look, that confounded with terror, and sometimes his hands trembling, and then again endeavoring to do it, full of fear and confusion, he could not strike him right, but cutting over his mouth and chin, it was a long time before he got off the head. By this time what had happened was known to a great many, and Alcyoneus hastening to the place, desired to look upon the head, and see whether he knew it, and taking it in his hand rode away to his father, and threw it at his feet, while he was sitting with some of his particular favorites. Antigonus, looking upon it, and knowing it, thrust his son from him, and struck him with his staff, calling him wicked and barbarous, and covering his eyes with his robe shed tears, thinking of his own father and grandfather, in stances in his own family of the changefulness of fortune, and caused the head and body of Pyrrhus to be burned with all due solemnity. After this, Alcyoneus, discovering Helenus under a mean disguise in a threadbare coat, used him very respectfully, and brought him to his father. When Antigonus saw him, "This, my son," said he, " is better; and yet even now you have not done wholly well in allowing these clothes to remain, to the disgrace of those who it seems now are the victors." And treating Helenus with great kindness, and as became a prince, restored him to his kingdom of Epirus, and gave the same obliging reception to all Pyrrhus's principal commanders, his camp and whole army having fallen into his hands.

CAIUS MARIUS.

WE are altogether ignorant of any third name of Caius Marius ; as also of Quintus Sertorius, that possessed himself of Spain; or of Lucius Mummius that destroyed Corinth, though this last was surnamed Achaicus from his conquests, as Scipio was called Africanus, and Metellus, Macedonicus. Hence Posidonius draws his chief argument to confute those that hold the third to be the Roman proper name, as Camillus, Marcellus, Cato; as in this case, those that had but two names would have no proper name at all. He did not, however, observe that by his own reasoning he must rob the women absolutely of their names ; for none of them have the first, which Posidonius imagines the proper name with the Romans. Of the other two, one was common to the whole family, Pompeii, Manlii, Cornelii (as with us Greeks, the Heraclidæ, and Pelopidæ), the other titular, and personal, taken either from their natures, or actions, or bodily characteristics, as Macrinus, Torquatus, Sylla ; such as are Mnemon, Grypus or Callinicus among the Greeks. On the subject of names, however, the irregularity of custom, would we insist upon it, might furnish us with discourse enough.

There is a likeness of Marius in stone at Ravenna, in Gaul, which I myself saw, quite corresponding with that roughness and harshness of character that is ascribed to him Being naturally valiant and warlike, and more acquainted also with the discipline of the camp than of the city, he could not moderate his passion when in authority. He is said never to have either studied Greek, or to have use of that language in any matter of consequence; thinking it ridiculous to bestow time in that learning, the teachers of which were little better than slaves. So after his second triumph, when at the dedication of a temple he presented some shows after the Greek fashion, coming into the theatre, he only sat down and immediately departed. And, accordingly, as Plato used to say to Xenocrates the philosopher, who was thought to show more than ordinary harshness of disposition, "I pray you, good Xenocrates, sacrifice to the Graces;" so if any could have persuaded Marius to pay his devotions to the Greek Muses and Graces, he had never brought his incomparable actions, both in war and peace, to so unworthy a conclusion, or wrecked himself, so to say, upon an old age of cruelty and vindictiveness, through passion, ill-timed ambition, and insatiable cupidity. But this will further appear by and by from the facts.

He was born of parents altogether obscure and indigent, who supported themselves by their daily labor; his father of the same name with himself, his mother called Fulcinia. He had spent a considerable part of his life before he saw and tasted the pleasures of the city; having passed previously in Cirrhæaton, a village of the territory of Arpinum, a life, compared with city delicacies, rude and unrefined, yet temperate, and conformable to the ancient Roman severity. He first served as a soldier in the war against the Celtiberians, when Scipio Africanus besieged Numantia; where he signalized himself to his general by courage far above his comrades, and particularly, by his cheerfully complying with Scipio's reformation of his army, being almost ruined by pleasures and luxury. It is stated, too, that he encountered and vanquished an enemy in single combat, in his general's sight. In consequence of all this he had several honors conferred upon him; and once when at an entertainment a question arose about commanders, and one of the company (whether really desirous to know, or only in complaisance) asked Scipio where the Romans, after him, should obtain such another general, Scipio, gently clapping Marius on the shoulder as he sat next him, replied, "Here, perhaps." So promising was his early youth of his future greatness, and so discerning was Scipio to detect the distant future in the present first beginnings. It was this speech of Scipio, we are told, which, like a divine admonition, chiefly emboldened Marius to aspire to a political career. He sought, and by the assistance of Cæcilius Metellus, of whose family he as well as his father were dependents, obtained the office of tribune of the people. In which place, when he brought forward a bill for the regulation of voting, which seemed likely to lessen the authority of the great men in the courts of justice, the consul Cotta opposed him, and persuaded the senate to declare against the law, and called Marius to account for it. He, however, when this decree was prepared coming into the senate, did not behave like a young man newly and undeservedly advanced to authority, but, assuming all the courage that his future actions would have warranted, threatened Cotta, unless he recalled the decree, to throw him into prison. And on his turning to Metellus, and asking his vote, and Metellus, rising up to concur with the consul, Marius, calling for the officer outside, commanded him to take Metellus into custody. He appealed to the other tribunes, but not one of them assisted him ; so that the senate, immediately complying, withdrew the decree. Marius came forth with glory to the people and confirmed his law, and was henceforth esteemed a man of undaunted courage and assurance, as well as a vigorous opposer of the senate in favor of the commons. But he immediately lost their opinion of him by a contrary action ; for when a law for the distribution of corn was proposed, he vigorously and successfully resisted it, making himself equally honored by both parties, in gratifying neither, contrary to the public interest.

After his tribuneship, he was candidate for the office of chief ædile ; there being two orders of them, one the curules, from the stool with crooked feet on which they sat when they performed their duty ; the other and inferior, called ædiles of the people. As soon as they have chosen the former, they give their voices again for the latter. Marius, finding he was likely to be put by for the greater, immediately changed and stood for the less ; but because he seemed too forward and hot, he was disappointed of that also. And yet though he was in one day twice frustrated of his desired preferment (which never happened to any before), yet he was not at all discouraged, but a little while after sought for the prætorship, and was nearly suffering a repulse, and then, too, though he was returned last of all, was nevertheless accused of bribery.

Cassius Sabaco's servant, who was observed within the rails among those who voted, chiefly occasioned the suspicion, as Sabaco was an intimate friend of Marius ; but on being called to appear before the judges, he alleged, that being thirsty by reason of the heat, he called for cold water, and that his servant brought him a cup, and as soon as he had drunk, departed; he was, however, excluded from the senate by the succeeding censors, and not undeservedly either, as was thought, whether it might be for his false evidence, or his want of temperance. Caius Herennius was also cited to appear as evidence, but pleaded that it was not customary for a patron (the Roman word for *protector*) to witness against his clients, and that the law excused them from that harsh duty; and both Marius and his parents had always been clients to the family of Herennii. And when the judges would have accepted of this plea, Marius himself opposed it, and told Herennius, that when he was first created magistrate he ceased to be his client; which was not altogether true. For 't is not every office that frees clients and their posterity from the observance due to their patrons, but only those to which the law has assigned a curule chair. Notwithstanding, though at the beginning of the suit it went somewhat hard with Marius, and he found the judges no way favorable to him, yet at last, their voices being equal, contrary to all expectation, he was acquitted.

In his prætorship he did not get much honor, yet after it he obtained the further Spain; which province he is said to have cleared of robbers, with which it was much infested, the old barbarous habits still prevailing, and the Spaniards, in those days, still regarding robbery as a piece of valor. In the city he had neither riches nor eloquence to trust to, with which the leading men of the time obtained power with the people, but his vehement disposition, his indefatigable labors, and his plain way of living, of themselves gained him esteem and influence; so that he made an honorable match with Julia, of the distinguished family of the Cæsars, to whom that Cæsar, was nephew who was afterwards so great among the Romans, and, in some degree, from his relationship, made Marius his example, as in his life we have observed.

Marius is praised for both temperance and endurance, of which latter he gave a decided instance in an operation of surgery. For having, as it seems, both his legs full of great tumors, and disliking the deformity, he determined to put himself into the hands of an operator; when, without being tied, he stretched out one of his legs, and silently, without changing countenance, endured most excessive torments in the cutting never either flinching or complaining; but when the surgeon went to the other, he declined to have it done, saying, "I see the cure is not worth the pain."

The consul Cæcilius Metellus, being declared general in the war against Jugurtha in Africa, took with him Marius for lieutenant; where, eager himself to do great deeds and services that would get him distinction, he did not, like others, consult Metellus's glory and the serving his interest, and attributing his honor of lieutenancy not to Metellus, but to fortune, which had presented him with a proper opportunity and theatre of great actions, he exerted his utmost courage. That war, too, affording several difficulties, he neither declined the greatest, nor disdained undertaking the least of them; but surpassing his equals in counsel and conduct, and matching the very common soldiers in labor and abstemiousness, he gained great popularity with them; as indeed any voluntary partaking with people in their labor is felt as an easing of that labor, as it seems to take away the constraint and necessity of it. It is the most obliging sight in the world to the Roman soldier to see a commander eat the same bread as himself, or lie upon an ordinary bed, or assist the work in the drawing a trench and raising a bulwark. For they do not so much admire those that confer honors and riches upon them, as those that partake of the same labor and danger with themselves; but love them better that will vouchsafe to join in their work, than those that encourage their idleness.

Marius thus employed, and thus winning the affections of the soldiers, before long filled both Africa and Rome with his fame, and some, too, wrote home from the army that the war with Africa would never be brought to a conclusion, unless they chose Caius Marius consul. All which was evidently unpleasing to Metellus; but what more especially grieved him was the calamity of Turpillius. This Turpillius had, from his ancestors, been a friend of Metellus, and kept up a constant hospitality with him, and was now serving in the war, in command of the smiths and carpenters of the army. Having the charge of a garrison in Vaga, a considerable city, and trusting too much to the inhabitants, because he treated them civilly and kindly, he unawares fell into the enemy's hands. They received Jugurtha into the city; yet nevertheless, at their request, Turpillius was dismissed safe and without receiving any injury; whereupon he was accused of betraying it to the enemy. Marius, being one of the council of war, was not only violent against him himself, but also incensed most of the others, so that Metellus was forced, much against his will, to put him to death. Not long after the accusation proved false, and when others were comforting

Metellus, who took heavily the loss of his friend, Marius, rather insulting and arrogating it to himself, boasted in all companies that he had involved Metellus in the guilt of putting his friend to death.

Henceforward they were at open variance; and it is reported that Metellus once, when Marius was present, said insultingly, "You, sir, design to leave us to go home and stand for the consulship, and will not be content to wait and be consul with this boy of mine?" Metellus's son being a mere boy at the time. Yet for all this Marius being very importunate to be gone, after several delays, he was dismissed about twelve days before the election of consuls; and performed that long journey from the camp to the seaport of Utica, in two days and a night, and there doing sacrifice before he went on ship-board, it is said the augur told him that heaven promised him some incredible good fortune, and such as was beyond all expectation. Marius, not a little elated with this good omen, began his voyage, and in four days, with a favorable wind, passed the sea; he was welcomed with great joy by the people, and being brought into the assembly by one of the tribunes, sued for the consulship, inveighing in all ways against Metellus, and promising either to slay Jugurtha or take him alive.

He was elected triumphantly, and at once proceeded to levy soldiers contrary both to law and custom, enlisting slaves and poor people; whereas former commanders never accepted of such, but bestowed arms, like other favors, as a matter of distinction, on persons who had the proper qualification, a man's property being thus a sort of security for his good behavior. These were not the only occasions of ill-will against Marius; some haughty speeches, uttered with great arrogance and contempt, gave great offence to the nobility; as, for example, his saying that he had carried off the consulship as a spoil from the effeminacy of the wealthy and high-born citizens, and telling the people that he gloried in wounds he had himself received for them, as much as others did in the monuments of dead men, and images of their ancestors. Often speaking of the commanders that had been unfortunate in Africa, naming Bestia, for example, and Albinus, men of very good families, but unfit for war, and who had miscarried through want of experience, he asked the people about him, if they did not think that the ancestors of these nobles had much rather have left a descendant like him, since they themselves grew famous not by nobility, but by their valor and great actions? This he did not say merely out of vanity and arrogance, or that he were willing, without any advantage, to offend the nobility; but the people always delighting in affronts and scurrilous contumelies against the senate, making boldness of speech their measure of greatness of spirit continually encouraged him in it, and strengthened his inclination not to spare persons of repute, so he might gratify the multitude.

As soon as he arrived again in Africa, Metellus, no longer able to control his feelings of jealousy, and his indignation that now when he had really finished the war, and nothing was left but to secure the person of Jugurtha, Marius grown great merely through his ingratitude to him, should come to bereave him both of his victory and triumph, could not bear to have any interview with him; but retired himself, whilst Rutilius, his lieutenant, surrendered up the army to Marius, whose conduct, however, in the end of the war, met with some sort of retribution, as Sylla deprived him of the glory of the action, as he had done Metellus. I shall state the circumstances briefly here, as they are given at large in the life of Sylla. Bocchus was king of the more distant barbarians, and was father-in-law to Jugurtha, yet sent him little or no assistance in his war, professing fears of his unfaithfulness, and really jealous of his growing power; but after Jugurtha fled, and in his distress came to him as his last hope, he received him as a suppliant, rather because ashamed to do otherwise, than out of real kindness; and when he had him in his power, he openly entreated Marius on his behalf, and interceded for him with bold words, giving out that he would by no means deliver him. Yet privately designing to betray him, he sent for Lucius Sylla, quæstor to Marius, and who had on a previous occasion befriended Bocchus in the war. When Sylla, relying on his word, came to him, the African began to doubt and repent of his purpose, and for several days was unresolved with himself, whether he should deliver Jugurtha or retain Sylla; at length he fixed upon his former treachery, and put Jugurtha alive into Sylla's possession. Thus was the first occasion given of that fierce and implacable hostility which so nearly ruined the whole Roman empire. For many that envied Marius, attributed the success wholly to Sylla; and Sylla himself got a seal made, on which was engraved Bocchus betraying Jugurtha to him, and constantly used it, irritating the hot and jealous temper of Marius, who was naturally greedy of distinction, and quick to resent any claim to share in his glory, and whose enemies took care to promote the quarrel, ascribing the beginning and chief business of the war to Metellus, and its conclusion to Sylla; that so the people might give over admiring and esteeming Marius as the worthiest person.

But these envyings and calumnies were soon dispersed and cleared away from Marius, by the danger that threatened Italy from the west; when the city, in great need of a good commander, sought about whom she might set at the helm, to meet the tempest of so great a war, no one would have any thing to say to any members of noble or potent families who offered themselves for the consulship, and Marius, though then absent, was elected.

Jugurtha's apprehension was only just known, when the news of the invasion of the Teutones and Cimbri began. The accounts at first exceeded all credit, as to the number and strength of the approaching army, but in the end, report proved much inferior to truth, as they were three hundred thousand effective fighting men, besides a far greater number of women and children. They professed to be seeking new countries to sustain these great multitudes, and cities where they might settle and inhabit, in the same way as they had heard the Celti before them had driven out the Tyrrhenians, and possessed themselves of the best part of Italy Having had no commerce with the southern nations, and travelling over a wide extent of country, no man knew what people they were, or whence they came, that thus like a cloud burst over Gaul and Italy; yet by their gray eyes and the largeness of their stature, they were conjectured to be some of the German races dwelling by the northern sea; besides that, the Germans call plunderers Cimbri.

There are some that say, that the country of the Celti, in its vast size and extent, reaches from the furthest sea and the arctic regions to the lake Mæotis eastward, and to that part of Scythia which is near Pontus, and that there the nations mingle together; that they did not swarm out of their country all at once, or on a sudden, but advancing by force of arms, in the summer season, every year, in the course of time they crossed the whole continent. And thus, though each party had several appellations, yet the whole army was called by the common name of Celto-Scythians. Others say that the Cimmerii, anciently known to the Greeks, were only a small part of the nation, who were driven out upon some quarrel among the Scythians, and passed all along from the lake Mæotis to Asia, under the conduct of one Lygdamis, and that the greater and more warlike part of them still inhabit the remotest regions lying upon the outer ocean. These, they say, live in a dark and woody country hardly penetrable by the sunbeams, the trees are so close and thick, extending into the interior as far as the Hercynian forest; and their position on the earth is under that part of heaven, where the pole is so elevated, that by the declination of the parallels, the zenith of the inhabitants seems to be but little distant from it ; and that their days and nights being almost of an equal length, they divide their year into one of each. This was Homer's occasion for the story of Ulysses calling up the dead, and from this region the people, anciently called Cimmerii, and afterwards, by an easy change, Cimbri, came into Italy. All this, however, is rather conjecture than an authentic history.

Their numbers, most writers agree, were not less, but rather greater than was reported. They were of invincible strength and fierceness in their wars, and hurried into battle with the violence of a devouring flame ; none could withstand them : all they assaulted became their prey. Several of the greatest Roman commanders with their whole armies, that advanced for the defence of Transalpine Gaul, were ingloriously overthrown, and, indeed, by their faint resistance, chiefly gave them the impulse of marching towards Rome. Having vanquished all they had met, and found abundance of plunder, they resolved to settle themselves nowhere till they should have razed the city, and wasted all Italy. The Romans, being from all parts alarmed with this news, sent for Marius to undertake the war, and nominated him the second time consul, though the law did not permit any one that was absent, or that had not waited a certain time after his first consulship, to be again created. But the people rejected all opposers for they considered this was not the first time that the law gave place to the common interest ; nor the present occasion less urgent than that when, contrary to law, they made Scipio consul, not in fear for the destruction of their own city, but desiring the ruin of that of the Carthaginians.

Thus it was decided ; and Marius, bringing over his legions out of Africa on the very first day of January, which the Romans count the beginning of the year, received the consulship, and then, also, entered in triumph, showing Jugurtha a prisoner to the people, a sight they had despaired of ever beholding, nor could any, so long as he lived, hope to reduce

Vol. II.—4

the enemy in Africa; so fertile in expedients was he to adapt himself to every turn of fortune, and so bold as well as subtle. When, however, he was led in triumph, it is said that he fell distracted, and when he was afterwards thrown into prison, where some tore off his clothes by force, and others, whilst they struggled for his golden ear-ring, with it pulled off the tip of his ear, and when he was, after this, cast naked into the dungeon, in his amazement and confusion, with a ghastly laugh, he cried out, "O Hercules! how cold your bath is!" Here for six days struggling with hunger, and to the very last minute desirous of life, he was overtaken by the just reward of his villanies. In this triumph was brought, as is stated, of gold three thousand and seven pounds weight, of silver bullion five thousand seven hundred and seventy-five, of money in gold and silver coin two hundred and eighty-seven thousand drachmas. After the solemnity, Marius called together the senate in the capitol, and entered, whether through inadvertency or unbecoming exultation with his good fortune, in his triumphal habit; but presently observing the senate offended at it, went out, and returned in his ordinary purple-bordered robe.

On the expedition he carefully disciplined and trained his army whilst they were on their way, giving them practice in long marches, and running of every sort, and compelling every man to carry his own baggage and prepare his own victuals; insomuch that thenceforward laborious soldiers, who did their work silently without grumbling, had the name of "Marius's mules." Some, however, think the proverb had a different occasion; that when Scipio beseiged Numantia, and was careful to inspect not only their horses and arms, but their mules and carriages too, and see how well equipped and in what readiness each one's was, Marius brought forth his horse which he had fed extremely well, and a mule in better case, stronger and gentler than those of others; that the general was very well pleased, and often afterwards mentioned Marius's beasts; and that hence the soldiers, when speaking jestingly in the praise of a drudging, laborious fellow, called him Marius's mule.

But to proceed; very great fortune seemed to attend Marius, for by the enemy in a manner changing their course, and falling first upon Spain, he had time to exercise his soldiers, and confirm their courage, and, which was most important, to show them what he himself was. For that fierce manner of his in command, and inexorableness in punishing, when his men became used not to do amiss or disobey was sent to be wholesome and advantageous, as well as just, and his violent spirit, stern voice, and harsh aspect, which in a little while grew familiar to them, they esteemed terrible not to themselves, but only to their enemies. But his uprightness in judging more especially pleased the soldiers, one remarkable instance of which is as follows. One Caius Lusius, his own nephew, had a command under him in the army, a man not in other respects of bad character, but shamefully licentious with young men. He had one young man under his command called Trebonius, with whom notwithstanding many solicitations he could never prevail. At length one night, he sent a messenger for him, and Trebonius came, as it was not lawful for him to refuse when he was sent for, and being brought into his tent, when Lusius began to use violence with him, he drew his sword and ran him through. This was done whilst Marius was absent. When he returned, he appointed Trebonius a time for his trial, where, whilst many accused him, and not any one appeared in his defence, he himself boldly related the whole matter, and brought witness of his previous conduct to Lusius, who had frequently offered him considerable presents. Marius, admiring his conduct and much pleased, commanded the garland, the usual Roman reward of valor, to be brought, and himself crowned Trebonius with it, as having performed an excellent action, at a time that very much wanted such good examples.

This being told at Rome, proved no small help to Marius towards his third consulship; to which also conduced the expectation of the barbarians at the summer season, the people being unwilling to trust their fortunes with any other general but him. However, their arrival was not so early as was imagined, and the time of Marius's consulship was again expired. The election coming on, and his colleague being dead, he left the command of the army to Manius Aquilius, and hastened to Rome, where, several eminent persons being candidates for the consulship, Lucius Saturninus, who more than any of the other tribunes swayed the populace and of whom Marius himself was very observant, exerted his eloquence with the people, advising them to choose Marius consul. He playing the modest part, and professing to the decline office, Saturninus called him traitor to his country, if, in such apparent danger, he would avoid command. And though it was not difficult to discover that he was merely helping Marius in putting this pretence upon the people yet, considering that the present juncture much re quired his skill, and his good fortune too, they voted him the fourth time consul, and made Catulus Lutatius his colleague, a man very much esteemed by the nobility, and not unagreeable to the commons.

Marius, having notice of the enemy's approach, with all expedition passed the Alps, and pitching his camp by the river Rhone, took care first for plentiful supplies of victuals: lest at any time he should be forced to fight at a disadvantage for want of necessaries. The carriage of provision for the army from the sea, which was formerly long and expensive, he made speedy and easy. For the mouth of the Rhone, by the influx of the sea, being barred and almost filled up with sand and mud mixed with clay, the passage there became narrow, difficult, and dangerous for the ships that brought their provisions. Hither, therefore, bringing his army, then at leisure, he drew a great trench; and by turning the course of a great part of the river brought it to a convenient point on the shore where the water was deep enough to receive ships of considerable burden, and where there was a calm and easy opening to the sea. And this still retains the name it took from him.

The enemy dividing themselves into two parts, the Cimbri arranged to go against Catulus higher up through the country of the Norici, and to force that passage; the Teutones and Ambrones to march against Marius by the sea-side through Liguria. The Cimbri were a considerable time in doing their part. But the Teutones and Ambrones with all expedition passing over the interjacent country, soon came in sight, in numbers beyond belief, of a terrible aspect, and uttering strange cries and shouts. Taking up a great part of the plain with their camp, they challenged Marius to battle; he seemed to take no notice of them, but kept his soldiers within their fortification, and sharply reprehended those that were too forward and eager to show their courage, and who, out of passion, would needs be fighting, calling them traitors to their country, and telling them they were not now to think of the glory of triumphs and trophies, but rather how they might repel such an impetuous tempest of war, and save Italy.

Thus he discoursed privately with his officers and equals, but placed the soldiers by turns upon the bulwarks to survey the enemy, and so made them familiar with their shape and voice, which were indeed altogether extravagant and barbarous, and he caused them to observe their arms, and the way of using them, so that in a little time what at first appeared terrible to their apprehensions, by often viewing, became familiar. For he very rationally supposed that the strangeness of things often makes them seem formidable when they are not so ; and that by our better acquaintance, even things which are really terrible, lose much of their frightfulness. This daily converse not only diminished some of the soldiers' fears, but their indignation warmed and inflamed their courage, when they heard the threats and insupportable insolence of their enemies ; who not only plundered and depopulated all the country round, but would even contemptuously and confidently attack the ramparts.

Complaints of the soldiers now began to come to Marius's ears. "What effeminacy does Marius see in us, that he should thus like women lock us up from encountering our enemies ? Come on, let us show ourselves men, and ask him if he expects others to fight for Italy ; and means merely to employ us in servile offices, when he would dig trenches, cleanse places of mud and dirt, and turn the course of the rivers ? It was to do such works as these, it seems, that he gave us all our long training ; he will return home, and boast of these great performances of his consulships to the people. Does the defeat of Carbo and Cæpio, who were vanquished by the enemy, affright him? Surely they were much inferior to Marius both in glory and valor, and commanded a much weaker army : at the worst, it is better to be in action, though we suffer for it like them, than to sit idle spectators of the destruction of our allies and companions." Marius, not a little pleased to hear this, gently appeased them, pretending that he did not distrust their valor, but that he took his measures as to the time and place of victory from some certain oracles.

And, in fact, he used solemnly to carry about in a litter, a Syrian woman, called Martha, a supposed prophetess, and to do sacrifice by her directions. She had formerly been driven away by the senate, to whom she addressed herself, offering to inform them about these affairs, and to foretell future events ; and after this betook herself to the women, and gave them proofs of her skill, especially Marius's wife, at whose feet she sat when she was viewing a contest of gladiators, and correctly foretold which of them should overcome. She was for this and the like predictings sent by her to Marius and the army, where she was very much looked up to, and, for the most part, carried about in a litter. When she went to sacrifice, she wore a purple robe lined and buckled up, and had in her hand a little spear trimmed with ribbons and garlands. This theatrical show made many question, whether Marius really gave any credit to her himself, or only played the counterfeit, when he showed her publicly to impose upon the soldiers.

What, however, Alexander the Myndian relates about the vultures, does really deserve admiration; that always before Marius's victories there appeared two of them, and accompanied the army which were known by their brazen collars (the soldiers having caught them and put these about their necks, and so let them go, from which time they in a manner knew and saluted the soldiers), and whenever these appeared in their marches, they used to rejoice at it, and thought themselves sure of some success. Of the many other prodigies that then were taken notice of, the greater part were but of the ordinary stamp; it was, however, reported that at Ameria and Tuder, two cities in Italy, there were seen at nights in the sky, flaming darts and shields, now waved about, and then again clashing against one another, all in accordance with the postures and motions soldiers use in fighting; that at length one party retreating, and the other pursuing, they all disappeared westward. Much about the same time came Bataces, one of Cybele's priests, from Pessinus, and reported how the goddess had declared to him out of her oracle, that the Romans should obtain the victory. The senate giving credit to him, and voting the goddess a temple to be built in hopes of the victory, Aulus Pompeius, a tribune, prevented Bataces, when he would have gone and told the people this same story, calling him imposter, and ignominiously pulling him off the hustings; which action in the end was the main thing that gained credit for the man's story, for Aulus had scarce dissolved the assembly, and returned home, when a violent fever seized him, and it was matter of universal remark, and in everybody's mouth, that he died within a week after.

Now the Teutones, whilst Marius lay quiet, ventured to attack his camp; from whence, however, being encountered with showers of darts, and losing several of their men, they determined to march forward, hoping to reach the other side of the Alps without opposition, and, packing up their baggage, passed securely by the Roman camp, where the greatness of their number was especially made evident by the long time they took in their march, for they were said to be six days continually going on in passing Marius's fortifications; they marched pretty near and revilingly asked the Romans if they would send any commands by them to their wives, for they would shortly be with them. As soon as they were passed and had gone on a little distance ahead, Marius began to move, and follow them at his leisure, always encamping at some small distance from them ; choosing also strong positions, and carefully fortifying them, that he might quarter with safety. Thus they marched till they came to the place called Sextilius's Waters, from whence it was but a short way before being amidst the Alps, and here Marius put himself in readiness for the encounter.

He chose a place for his camp of considerable strength, but where there was a scarcity of water ; designing, it is said, by this means, also, to put an edge on his soldiers' courage ; and when several were not a little distressed, and complained of thirst, pointing to a river that ran near the enemy's camp ; "There," said he, "you may have drink, if you will buy it with your blood." "Why, then," replied they, "do you not lead us to them, before our blood is dried up in us?" He answered, in a softer tone, "let us first fortify our camp," and the soldiers, though not without repining, proceeded to obey. Now a great company of their boys and camp followers, having neither drink for themselves nor for their horses, went down to that river ; some taking axes and hatchets, and some, too, swords and darts with their pitchers, resolving to have water though they fought for it. These were first encountered by a small party of the enemies ; for most of them had just finished bathing, and were eating and drinking, and several were still bathing, the country thereabouts abounding in hot springs ; so that the Romans partly fell upon them whilst they were enjoying themselves and occupied with the novel sights and pleasantness of the place. Upon hearing the shouts, greater numbers still joining in the fight, it was not a little difficult for Marius to contain his soldiers, who were afraid of losing the camp-servants ; and the more warlike part of the enemies, who had overthrown Manlius and Cæpio (they were called Ambrones, and were in number, one with another, above thirty thousand), taking the alarm, leaped up and hurried to arms.

These, though they had just been gorging themselves with food, and were excited and disordered with drink, nevertheless did not advance with an unruly step, or in mere senseless fury, nor were their shouts mere inarticulate cries ; but clasping their arms in concert and keeping time as they leapt and bounded onward, they continually repeated their own name, "Ambrones!" either to encourage one another, or to strike the greater terror into their enemies. Of all the Italians in Marius's army, the Ligurians were the first that charged; and when they caught the word of the enemy's confused shout, they, too, returned the same, as it was an ancient name also in their country, the Ligurians always using it when speaking of their descent. This acclamation, bandied from one army to the other before they joined, served to rouse and heighten their fury, while the men on either side strove, with all possible vehemence, the one to overshout the other.

The river disordered the Ambrones; before they could draw up all their army on the other side of it, the Ligurians presently fell upon the van, and began to charge them hand to hand. The Romans, too, coming to their assistance, and from the higher ground pouring upon the enemy, forcibly repelled them, and the most of them (one thrusting another into the river), were there slain, and filled it with their blood and dead bodies. Those that got safe over, not daring to make head, were slain by the Romans, as they fled to their camp and wagons; where the women meeting them with swords and hatchets, and making a hideous outcry, set upon those that fled as well as those that pursued, the one as traitors, the other as enemies, and mixing themselves with the combatants, with their bare arms pulling away the Romans' shields, and laying hold on their swords, endured the wounds and slashing of their bodies to the very last, with undaunted resolution. Thus the battle seems to have happened at that river rather by accident than by the design of the general.

After the Romans were retired from the great slaughter of the Ambrones, night came on; but the army was not indulged, as was the usual custom, with songs of victory, drinking in their tents, and mutual entertainments and (what is most welcome to soldiers after successful fighting) quiet sleep, but they passed that night, above all others, in fears and alarm. For their camp was without either rampart or palisade, and there remained thousands upon thousands of their enemies yet unconquered; to whom were joined as many of the Ambrones as escaped. There were heard from these all through the night, wild bewailings, nothing like the sighs and groans of men, but a sort of wild beast-like howling and cursing joined with threats and lamentations rising from the vast multitude, and echoed among the neighboring hills and hollow banks of the river. The whole plain was filled with hideous noise, insomuch that the Romans were not a little afraid, and Marius himself was apprehensive of a confused tumultuous night engagement. But the enemy did not stir either this night or the next day, but were employed in disposing and drawing themselves up to the greatest advantage.

Of this occasion Marius made good use; for there were beyond the enemies some wooded ascents and deep valleys thickly set with trees, whither he sent Claudius Marcellus, secretly, with three thousand regular soldiers, giving him orders to post them in ambush there, and show themselves at the rear of the enemies, when the fight was begun. The others, refreshed with victuals and sleep, as soon as it was day he drew up before the camp, and commanded the horse to sally out into the plain, at the sight of which the Teutones could not contain themselves till the Romans should come down and fight them on equal terms, but hastily arming themselves, charged in their fury up the hillside. Marius, sending officers to all parts, commanded his men to stand still and keep their ground; when they came within reach, to throw their javelins, then use their swords, and joining their shields, force them back; pointing out to them that the steepness of the ground would render the enemy's blows inefficient, nor could their shields be kept close together, the inequality of the ground hindering the stability of their footing.

This counsel he gave them, and was the first that followed it; for he was inferior to none in the use of his body, and far excelled all in resolution. The Romans accordingly stood for their approach, and, checking them in their advance upwards, forced them little by little to give way and yield down the hill, and here, on the level ground, no sooner had the Ambrones begun to restore their van into a posture of resistance, but they found their rear disordered. For Marcellus had not let slip the opportunity; but as soon as the shout was raised among the Romans on the hills, he, setting his men in motion, fell in upon the enemy behind, at full speed, and with loud cries, and routed those nearest him, and they, breaking the ranks of those that were before them, filled the whole army with confusion. They made no long resistance after they were thus broke in upon, but having lost all order, fled.

The Romans, pursuing them, slew and took prisoners above one hundred thousand, and possessing themselves of their spoil, tents, and carriages, voted all that was not purloined to Marius's share, which, though so magnificent a present, yet was generally thought less than his conduct deserved in so great a danger. Other authors give a different account, both about the division of the plunder and the number of the slain. They say, however, that the inhabitants of Massilia made fences round their vineyards with the bones, and that the ground, enriched by the moisture of the putrified bodies (which soaked with the rain of the following winter), yielded at the season a prodigious crop, and fully justified Archilochus, who said, that the fallows thus are fattened. It is an observation, also, that extraordinary rains pretty generally fall after great battles ; whether it be that some divine power thus washes and cleanses the polluted earth with showers from above, or that moist and heavy evaporations, steaming forth from the blood and corruption, thicken the air, which naturally is subject to alteration from the smallest causes.

After the battle, Marius chose out from amongst the barbarians' spoils and arms, those that were whole and handsome, and that would make the greatest show in his triumph ; the rest he heaped upon a large pile, and offered a very splendid sacrifice. Whilst the army stood round about with their arms and garlands, himself attired (as the fashion is on such occasions) in the purple-bordered robe, and taking a lighted torch, and with both hands lifting it up towards heaven, he was then going to put it to the pile, when some friends were espied with all haste coming towards him on horseback. Upon which every one remained in silence and expectation. They, upon their coming up, leapt off and saluted Marius, bringing him the news of his fifth consulship, and delivered him letters to that effect. This gave the addition of no small joy to the solemnity ; and while the soldiers clashed their arms and shouted, the officers again crowned Marius with a laurel wreath, and he thus set fire to the pile, and finished his sacrifice.

But whatever it be, which interferes to prevent the enjoyment of prosperity ever being pure and sincere, and still diversifies human affairs with the mixture of good and bad, whether fortune or divine displeasure, or the necessity of the nature of things, within a few days Marius received an account of his colleague, Catulus, which as a cloud in serenity and calm, terrified Rome with the apprehension of another imminent storm. Catulus, who marched against the Cimbri, despairing of being able to defend the passes of the Alps, lest, being compelled to divide his forces into several parties, he snould weaken himself, descended again into Italy, and posted his army behind the river Adige; where he occupied the passages with strong fortifications on both sides the river, and made a bridge, that so he might cross to the assistance of his men on the other side, if so be the enemy, having forced their way through the moun ain passes, should storm the fortresses. The barbarians, however, came on with such insolence and contempt of their enemies, that to show their strength and courage, rather than out of any necessity, they went naked in the showers of snow, and through the ice and deep snow climbed up to the tops of the hills, and from thence, placing their broad shields under their bodies, let themselves slide from the precipices along their vast slippery descents.

When they had pitched their camp at a little distance from the river, and surveyed the passage, they began to pile it up, giant-like, tearing down the neighboring hills; and brought trees pulled up by the roots, and heaps of earth to the river, damming up its course; and with great heavy materials which they rolled down the stream and dashed against the bridge, they forced away the beams which supported it; in consequence of which the greatest part of the Roman soldiers, much affrighted, left the large camp and fled. Here Catulus showed himself a generous and noble general, in preferring the glory of his people before his own; for when he could not prevail with his soldiers to stand to their colors, but saw how they all deserted them, he commanded his own standard to be taken up, and running to the foremost of those that fled, he led them forward, choosing rather that the disgrace should fall upon himself than upon his country, and that they should not seem to fly, but, fo lowing their captain, to make a retreat. The barbarians assaulted and took the fortress on the other side the Adige; where much admiring the few Romans there left, who had shown extreme courage, and had fought worthily of their country, they dismissed them upon terms, swearing them upon their brazen bull, which was afterwards taken in the battle, and carried, they say, to Catulus's house, as the chief trophy of victory.

Thus falling in upon the country destitute of defence, they wasted it on all sides. Marius was presently sent for to the city; where, when he arrived, every one supposing he would triumph, the senate, too, unanimously voting it, he himself did not think it convenient: whether that he were not willing to deprive his soldiers and officers of their share of the glory, or that to encourage the people in this juncture, he would leave the honor due to his past victory on trust, as it were, in the hands of the city and its future fortune; deferring it now to receive it afterwards with the greater splendor. Having left such orders as the occasion required, he hastened to Catulus, whose drooping spirits he much raised and sent for his own army from Gaul; and as soon as it came, passing the river Po, he endeavored to keep the barbarians out of that part of Italy which lies south of it.

They professed they were in expectation of the Teutones, and, saying they wondered they were so long in coming, deferred the battle; either that they were really ignorant of their defeat or were willing to seem so. For they certainly much maltreated those that brought them such news and, sending to Marius, required some part of the country for themselves and their brethren, and cities fit for them to inhabit. When Marius inquired of the ambassadors who their brethren were, upon their saying the Teutones, all that were present began to laugh; and Marius scoffingly answered them, "Do not trouble yourself for your brethren, for we have already provided lands for them, which they shall possess forever." The ambassadors, understanding the mockery, broke into insults, and threatened that the Cimbri would make him pay for this, and the Teutones, too, when they came. "They are not far off," replied Marius, "and it will be unkindly done of you to go away before greeting your brethren." Saying so, he commanded the kings of the Teutones to be brought out, as they were, in chains; for they were taken by the Sequani among the Alps, before they could make their escape. This was no sooner made known to the Cimbri, but they with all expedition came against Marius, who then lay still and guarded his camp.

It is said, that against this battle, Marius first altered the construction of the Roman javelins. For before, at the place where the wood was joined to the iron, it was made fast with two iron pins; but now Marius let one of them alone as it was, and pulling out the other, put a weak wooden peg in its place, thus contriving, that when it was driven into the enemy's shield, it should not stand right out, but the wooden peg breaking, the iron should bend, and so the javelin should hold fast by its crooked point, and drag. Bœorix, king of the Cimbri, came with a small party of horse to the Roman camp, and challenged Marius to appoint the time and place, where they might meet and fight for the country. Marius answered, that the Romans never consulted their enemies when to fight; however, he would gratify the Cimbri so far; and so they fixed upon the third day after, and for the place, the plain near Vercellæ, which was convenient enough for the Roman horse, and afforded room for the enemy to display their numbers.

They observed the time appointed, and drew out their forces against each other. Catulus commanded twenty thousand three hundred, and Marius thirty-two thousand, who were placed in the two wings, leaving Catulus the centre. Sylla, who was present at the fight, gives this account; saying, also, that Marius drew up his army in this order, because he expected that the armies would meet on the wings, since it generally happens that in such extensive fronts the centre falls back, and thus he would have the whole victory to himself and his soldiers, and Catulus would not be even engaged They tell us, also, that Catulus himself alleged this in vindication of his honor, accusing, in various ways, the enviousness of Marius. The infantry of the Cimbri marched quietly out of their fortifications, having their flanks equal to their front; every side of the army taking up thirty furlongs. Their horse, that were in number fifteen thousand, made a very splendid appearance. They wore helmets, made to resemble the heads and jaws of wild beasts, and other strange shapes, and heightening these with plumes of feathers, they made themselves appear taller than they were. They had breastplates of iron, and white glittering shields; and for their offensive arms every one had two darts, and when they came hand to hand, they used large and heavy swords.

The cavalry did not fall directly upon the front of the Romans, but, turning to the right, they endeavored to draw them on in that direction by little and little, so as to get them between themselves and their infantry, who were placed in the left wing. The Roman commanders soon perceived the design, but could not contain the soldiers; for one happening to shout out that the enemy fled, they all rushed to pursue them while the whole barbarian foot came on, moving like a great ocean. Here Marius, having washed his hands, and lifting them up towards heaven, vowed an hecatomb to the gods; and Catulus, too, in the same posture, solemnly promised to consecrate a temple to the "Fortune of that day." They say, too, that Marius, having the victim showed to him as he was sacrificing, cried out with a loud voice, "the victory is mine."

However, in the engagement, according to the accounts of Sylla and his friends, Marius met with what might be called a mark of divine displeasure. For a great dust being raised, which (as it might very probably happen) almost covered both the armies he, leading on his forces to the pursuit, missed the enemy, and having passed by their array, moved, for a good space, up and down the field; meanwhile the enemy, by chance, engaged with Catulus, and the heat of the battle was chiefly with him and his men, among whom Sylla says he was; adding, that the Romans had great advantage of the heat and sun that shone in the faces of the Cimbri. For they, well able to endure cold, and having been bred up (as we observed before) in cold and shady countries, were overcome with the excessive heat; they sweated extremely, and were much out of breath, being forced to hold their shields before their faces; for the battle was fought not long after the summer solstice, or as the Romans reckon, upon the third day before the new moon of the month now called August, and then Sextilis. The dust, too, gave the Romans no small addition to their courage, inasmuch as it hid the enemy. For afar off they could not discover their number; but every one advancing to encounter those that were nearest to them, they came to fight hand to hand, before the sight of so vast a multitude had struck terror into them. They were so much used to labor, and so well exercised, that in all the heat and toil of the encounter, not one of them was observed either to sweat, or to be out of breath; so much so, that Catulus himself, they say, recorded it in commendation of his soldiers.

Here the greatest part and most valiant of the enemies were cut in pieces; for those that fought in the front, that they might not break their ranks, were fast tied to one another, with long chains put through their belts. But as they pursued those that fled to their camp, they witnessed a most fearful tragedy; the women, standing in black clothes on their wagons, slew all that fled, some their husbands, some their brethren, others their fathers; and strangling their little children with their own hands, threw them under the wheels, and the feet of the cattle, and then killed themselves. They tell of one who hung herself from the end of the pole of a wagon, with her children tied dangling at her heels. The men, for want of trees, tied themselves, some to the horns of the oxen, others by the neck to their legs, that so pricking them on, by the starting and springing of the beasts, they might be torn and trodden to pieces. Yet for all they thus massacred themselves, above sixty thousand were taken prisoners, and those that were slain were said to be twice as many.

The ordinary plunder was taken by Marius's soldiers, but the other spoils, as ensigns, trumpets, and the like, they say, were brought to Catulus's camp; which he used for the best argument that the victory was obtained by himself and his army. Some dissensions arising, as was natural, among the soldiers, the deputies from Parma being then present, were made judges of the controversy; whom Catulus's men carried about among their slain enemies, and manifestly showed them that they were slain by their javelins, which were known by the inscriptions, having Catulus's name cut in the wood. Nevertheless, the whole glory of the action was ascribed to Marius, on account of his former victory, and under color of his present authority; the populace more especially styling him the third founder of their city, as having diverted a danger no less threatening than was that when the Gauls sacked Rome; and every one, in their feasts and rejoicings at home with their wives and children, made offerings and libations in honor of "*The Gods and Marius;*" and would have had him solely have the honor of both the triumphs. However, he did not do so, but triumphed together with Catulus, being desirous to show his moderation even in such great circumstances of good fortune; besides he was not a little afraid of the sodiers in Catulus's army, lest, if he should wholly bereave their general of the honor, they should endeavor to hinder him of his triumph.

Marius was now in his fifth consulship, and he sued for his sixth in such a manner as never any man before him had done, even for his first; he courted the people's favor and ingratiated himself with the multitude by every sort of complaisance; not only derogating from the state and dignity of his office, but also belying his own character, by attempting to seem popular and obliging, for which nature had never designed him. His passion for distinction did, indeed, they say, make him exceedingly timorous in any political matters, or in confronting public assemblies; and that undaunted presence of mind he always showed in battle against the enemy, forsook him when he was to address the people; he was easily upset by the most ordinary commendation or dispraise. It is told of him, that having at one time given the freedom of the city to one thousand men of Camerinum who had behaved valiantly in this war, and this seeming to be illegally done, upon some one or other calling him to an account for it, he answered, that the law spoke too softly to be heard in such a noise of war; yet he himself appeared to be more disconcerted and overcome by the clamor made in the assemblies. The need they had of him in time of war procured him power and dignity; but in civil affairs, when he despaired of getting the first place, he was forced to betake himself to the favor of the people, never caring to be a good man, so that he were but a great one.

He thus became very odious to all the nobility; and above all, he feared Metellus, who had been so ungratefully used by him, and whose true virtue made him naturally an enemy to those that sought influence with the people, not by the honorable course, but by subservience and complaisance. Marius, therefore, endeavored to banish him from the city, and for this purpose he contracted a close alliance with Glaucia and Saturninus, a couple of daring fellows, who had the great mass of the indigent and seditious multitude at their control; and by their assistance he enacted various laws, and bringing the soldiers, also, to attend the assembly, he was enabled to overpower Metellus. And as Rutilius relates (in all other respects a fair and faithful authority, but indeed, privately an enemy to Marius), he obtained his sixth consulship by distributing vast sums of money among the tribes, and by this bribery kept out Metellus, and had Valerius Flaccus given him as his instrument, rather than his colleague, in the consulship. The people had never before bestowed so many consulships on any one man, except on Valerius Corvinus only, and he, too, they say, was forty-five years between his first and last; but Marius, from his first, ran through five more, with one current of good fortune.

In the last, especially, he contracted a great deal of hatred, by committing several gross misdemeanors in compliance with the desires of Saturninus; among which was the murder of Nonius, whom Saturninus slew, because he stood in competition with him for the tribuneship. And when, afterwards, Saturninus, on becoming tribune, brought forward his law for the division of lands, with a clause enacting that the senate should publicly swear to confirm whatever the people should vote, and not to oppose them in any thing, Marius, in the senate, cunningly feigned to be against this provision, and said that he would not take any such oath, nor would any man, he thought, who was wise; for if there were no ill design in the law, still it would be an affront to the senate, to be compelled to give their approbation, and not to do it willingly and upon persuasion. This he said, not that it was agreeable to his own sentiments, but that he might entrap Metellus beyond any possibility of escape. For Marius, in whose ideas virtue and capacity consisted largely in deceit, made very little account of what he had openly professed to the senate ; and knowing that Metellus was one of a fixed resolution, and, as Pindar has it, esteemed "Truth the first principle of heroic virtue," he hoped to ensnare him into a declaration before the senate, and on his refusing, as he was sure to do, afterwards to take the oath, he expected to bring him into such odium with the people, as should never be wiped off. The design succeeded to his wish. As soon as Metellus had declared that he would not swear to it, the senate adjourned. A few days after, on Saturninus citing the senators to make their appearance, and take the oath before the people, Marius stepped forth, amidst a profound silence, every one being intent to hear him, and bidding farewell to those fine speeches he had before made in the senate, said, that his back was not so broad that he should think himself bound, once for all, by any opinion once given on so important a matter ; he would willingly swear and submit to the law, if so be it were one, a proviso which he added as a mere cover for his effrontery. The people, in great joy at his taking the oath, loudly clapped and applauded him, while the nobility stood by ashamed and vexed at his inconstancy ; but they submitted out of fear of the people, and all in order took the oath, till it came to Metellus's turn. But he, though his friends begged and entreated him to take it, and not to plunge himself irrecoverably into the penalties which Saturninus had provided for those that should refuse it, would not flinch from his resolution, nor swear ; but, according to his fixed custom, being ready to suffer any thing rather than do a base, unworthy action, he left the forum, telling those that were with him, that to do a wrong thing is base, and to do well where there is no danger, common ; the good man's characteristic is to do so, where there is danger.

Hereupon Saturninus put it to the vote, that the consuls should place Metellus under their interdict, and forbid him fire, water, and lodging. There were enough, too, of the basest of people ready to kill him. Nevertheless, when many of the better sort were extremely concerned, and gathered about Metellus, he would not suffer them to raise a sedition upon his account, but with this calm reflection left the city, "Either when the posture of affairs is mended and the people repent, I shall be recalled, or if things remain in their present condition, it will be best to be absent." But what great favor and honor Metellus received in his banishment, and in what

VOL. II.—5

manner he spent his time at Rhodes, in philosophy, will be more fitly our subject, when we write his life.

Marius, in return for this piece of service, was forced to connive at Saturninus, now proceeding to the very height of insolence and violence, and was, without knowing it, the instrument of mischief beyond endurance, the only course of which was through outrages and massacres to tyranny and the subversion of the government. Standing in some awe of the nobility, and, at the same time, eager to court the commonalty, he was guilty of a most mean and dishonest action. When some of the great men came to him at night to stir him up against Saturninus, at the other door, unknown to them, he let him in; then making the same pretence of some disorder of body to both, he ran from one party to the other, and staying at one time with them and another with him, he instigated and exasperated them one against another. At length when the senate and equestrian order concerted measures together, and openly manifested their resentment, he did bring his soldiers into the forum, and driving the insurgents into the capitol, and then cutting off the conduits, forced them to surrender by want of water. They, in this distress, addressing themselves to him, surrendered, as it is termed, on the *public faith*. He did his utmost to save their lives, but so wholly in vain, that when they came down into the forum, they were all basely murdered. Thus he had made himself equally odious both to the nobility and commons, and when the time was come to create censors, though he was the most obvious man, yet he did not petition for it; but fearing the disgrace of being repulsed, permitted others, his inferiors, to be elected, though he pleased himself by giving out, that he was not willing to disoblige too many by undertaking a severe inspection into their lives and conduct.

There was now an edict preferred to recall Metellus from banishment; this he vigorously, but in vain, opposed both by word and deed, and was at length obliged to desist. The people unanimously voted for it; and he, not able to endure the sight of Metellus's return, made a voyage to Cappadocia and Galatia; giving out that he had to perform the sacrifices, which he had vowed to Cybele; but actuated really by other less apparent reasons. For, in fact, being a man altogether ignorant of civil life and ordinary politics, he received all his advancement from war, and supposing his power and glory would by little and little decrease by his lying quietly out of action, he was eager by every means to excite some new commotions, and hoped that by setting at variance some of the kings, and by exasperating Mithridates, especially, who was then apparently making preparations for war, he himself should be chosen general against him, and so furnish the city with new matter of triumph, and his own house with the plunder of Pontus, and the riches of its king. Therefore, though Mithridates entertained him with all imaginable attention and respect, yet he was not at all wrought upon or softened by it; but said, "O king, either endeavor to be stronger than the Romans, or else quietly submit to their commands." With which he left Mithridates, as he indeed had often heard the fame of the bold speaking of the Romans, but now for the first time experienced it.

When Marius returned again to Rome, he built a house close by the forum, either, as he himself gave out, that he was not willing his clients should be tired with going far, or that he imagined distance was the reason why more did not come. This, however, was not so; the real reason was, that, being inferior to others in agreeableness of conversation and the arts of political life, like a mere tool and implement of war, he was thrown aside in time of peace. Amongst all those whose brightness eclipsed his glory, he was most incensed against Sylla, who had owed his rise to the hatred which the nobility bore Marius; and had made his disagreement with him the one principle of his political life. When Bocchus, king of Numidia, who was styled the associate of the Romans, dedicated some figures of Victory in the capitol, and with them a representation in gold, of himself delivering Jugurtha to Sylla, Marius upon this was almost distracted with rage and ambition, as though Sylla had arrogated this honor to himself and endeavored forcibly to pull down these presents; Sylla, on the other side, as vigorously resisted him; but the Social War, then on a sudden threatening the city, put a stop to this sedition, when just ready to break out. For the most warlike and best-peopled countries of all Italy formed a confederacy together against Rome, and were within a little of subverting the empire; as they were indeed strong, not only in their weapons and the valor of their soldiers, but stood nearly upon equal terms with the Romans, as to the skill and daring of their commanders.

As much glory and power as this war, so various in its events and so uncertain as to its success, conferred upon Sylla, so much it took away from Marius, who was thought tardy, unenterprising, and timid, whether it were that his age was now quenching his former heat and vigor (for he was above sixty-five years old), or that having, as he himself said some distemper that affected his muscles, and his body being unfit for action, he did service above his strength. Yet, for all this, he came off victor in a considerable battle, wherein he slew six thousand of the enemies, and never once gave them any advantage over him; and when he was surrounded by the works of the enemy, he contained himself, and though insulted over, and challenged, did no yield to the provocation. The story is told that when Publius Silo, a man of the greatest repute and authority among the enemies, said to him, "If you are indeed a great general, Marius, leave your camp and fight a battle," he replied, "If you are one, make me do so." And another time, when the enemy gave them a good opportunity of a battle, and the Romans through fear durst not charge, so that both parties retreated, he called an assembly of his soldiers, and said, "It is no small question whether I should call the enemies, or you, the greater cowards, for neither did they dare to face your backs, nor you to confront theirs." At length, professing to be worn out with the infirmity of his body, he laid down his command.

Afterwards when the Italians were worsted, there were several candidates suing with the aid of the popular leaders, for the chief command in the war with Mithridates. Sulpicius, tribune of the people, a bold and confident man, contrary to everybody's expectation, brought forward Marius, and proposed him as proconsul and general in that war. The people were divided; some were on Marius's side, others voted for Sylla, and jeeringly bade Marius go to the baths at Baiæ, to cure his body, worn out, as himself confessed, with age and catarrhs. Marius had indeed, there, about Misenum, a villa more effeminately and luxuriously furnished than seemed to become one that had seen service in so many and great wars and expeditions. This same house Cornelia bought for seventy-five thousand drachmas, and not long after Lucius Lucullus, for two million five hundred thousand; so rapid and so great was the growth of Roman sumptuosity. Yet, in spite of all this, out of a mere boyish passion for distinction, affecting to shake off his age and weakness, he went down daily to the Campus Martius, and exercising himself with the youth, showed himself still nimble in his armor, and expert in riding; though he was undoubtedly grown bulky in his old age, and inclining to excessive faintness and corpulency.

Some people were pleased with this, and went continually to see him competing and displaying himself in these exercises; but the better sort that saw him, pitied the cupidity and ambition that made one who had risen from utter poverty to extreme wealth, and out of nothing into greatness, unwilling to admit any limit to his high fortune, or to be content with being admired, and quietly enjoying what he had already got; why, as if he still were indigent, should he at so great an age leave his glory and his triumphs to go into Cappadocia and the Euxine Sea, to fight Archelaus and Neoptolemus, Mithridates's generals? Marius's pretences for this action of his seemed very ridiculous; for he said he wanted to go and teach his son to be a general.

The condition of the city, which had long been unsound and diseased, became hopeless now that Marius found so opportune an instrument for the public destruction as Sulpicius's insolence. This man professed, in all other respects, to admire and imitate Saturninus; only he found fault with him for backwardness and want of spirit in his designs. He, therefore, to avoid this fault, got six hundred of the equestrian order about him as his guard, whom he named anti-senators and with these confederates he set upon the consuls, whilst they were at the assembly, and took the son of one of them who fled from the forum, and slew him. Sylla, being hotly pursued, took refuge in Marius's house, which none could suspect, by that means escaping those that sought him, who hastily passed by there, and, it is said, was safely conveyed by Marius himself out at the other door, and came to the camp. Yet Sylla, in his memoirs, positively denies that he fled to Marius, saying he was carried thither to consult upon the matters to which Sulpicius would have forced him, against his will, to consent; that he, surrounding him with drawn swords, hurried him to Marius, and constrained him thus, till he went thence to the forum and removed, as they required him to do, the interdict on business.

Sulpicius, having thus obtained the mastery, decreed the command of the army to Marius, who proceeded to make preparations for his march, and sent two tribunes to receive the charge of the army from Sylla. Sylla hereupon exasperating his soldiers, who were about thirty-five thousand full-armed men, led them towards Rome. First falling upon the tribunes Marius had sent, they slew them; Marius having done as much for several of Sylla's friends in Rome, and now offering their freedom to the slaves on condition of their assistance in the war; of whom, however, they say, there were but three who accepted his proposal. For some small time he made head against Sylla's assault, but was soon overpowered and fled; those that were with him, as soon as he had escaped out of the city, were dispersed, and night coming on, he hastened to a country-house of his, called Solonium. Hence he sent his son to some neighboring farms of his father-in-law, Mucius, to provide necessaries; he went himself to Ostia, where his friend Numerius had prepared him a ship, and hence, not staying for his son, he took with him his son-in-law Granius, and weighed anchor.

Young Marius, coming to Mucius's farms, made his preparations; and the day breaking, was almost discovered by the enemy. For there came thither a party of horse that suspected some such matter; but the farm steward, foreseeing their approach, hid Marius in a cart full of beans, then yoking in his team and driving toward the city, met those that were in search of him. Marius, thus conveyed home to his wife, took with him some necessaries, and came at night to the sea-side; where, going on board a ship that was bound for Africa, he went away thither. Marius, the father, when he had put to sea, with a strong gale passing along the coast of Italy, was in no small apprehension of one Geminius, a great man at Terracina, and his enemy; and therefore bade the seaman hold off from that place. They were indeed willing to gratify him, but the wind now blowing in from the sea and making the waves swell to a great height, they were afraid the ship would not be able to weather out the storm, and Marius, too, being indisposed and sea-sick, they made for land, and not without some difficulty reached the shore near Circeium.

The storm now increasing and their victuals failing, they left their ship and wandered up and down without any certain purpose, simply as in great distresses people shun the present as the greatest evil, and rely upon the hopes of uncertainties. For the land and sea were both equally unsafe for them; it was dangerous to meet with people, and it was no less so to meet with none, on account of their want of necessaries. At length, though late, they lighted upon a few poor shepherds, that had not anything to relieve them; but knowing Marius, advised him to depart as soon as might be, for they had seen a little beyond that place a party of horse that were gone in search of him. Finding himself in a great straight, especially because those that attended him were not able to go further being spent with their long fasting, for the present he turned aside out of the road, and hid himself in a thick wood, where he passed the night in great wretchedness. The next day, pinched with hunger, and willing to make use of the little strength he had, before it were all exhausted, he travelled by the sea-side, encouraging his companions not to fall away from him before the fulfilment of his final hopes, for which in reliance on some old predictions, he professed to be sustaining himself. For when he was yet but very young, and lived in the country, he caught in the skirt of his garment an eagle's nest, as it was falling, in which were seven young ones, which his parents seeing and much admiring, consulted the augurs about it, who told them he should become the greatest man in the world, and that the fates had decreed he should seven times be possessed of the supreme power and authority. Some are of opinion that this really happened to Marius, as we have related it; others say, that those who then and through the rest of his exile heard him tell these stories, and believed him, have merely repeated a story that is altogether fabulous; for an eagle never hatches more than two; and even Musæus was deceived, who, speaking of the eagle, says that,—

"She lays three eggs, hatches two, and rears one."

However this be, it is certain Marius, in his exile and greatest extremities, would often say, that he should attain a seventh consulship.

When Marius and his company were now about twenty furlongs distant from Minturnæ, a city in Italy, they espied a troop of horse making up toward them with all speed, and by chance, also, at the same time, two ships under sail. Accordingly, they ran every one with what speed and strength they could to the sea, and plunging into it, swam to the ships. Those that were with Granius, reaching one of them, passed over to an island opposite, called Ænaria; Marius himself, whose body was heavy and unwieldy, was with great pains and difficulty kept above the water by two servants, and put into the other ship. The soldiers were by this time come to the sea-side, and from thence called out to the seamen to put to shore, or else to throw out Marius, and then they might go whither they would. Marius besought them with tears to the contrary, and the masters of the ship, after frequent changes, in a short space of time, of their purpose, inclining, first to one then to the other side resolved at length to answer the soldiers, that they would not give up Marius. As soon as they had ridden off in a rage, the seamen, again changing their resolution, came to land, and casting anchor at the mouth of the river Liris, where it overflows and makes a marsh, they advised him to land, refresh himself on shore, and take some care of his discomposed body, till the wind came fairer; which, said they, will happen at such an hour, when the wind from the sea will calm, and that from the marshes rise. Marius, following their advice, did so, and when the seamen had set him on shore, he laid him down in an adjacent field, suspecting nothing less than what was to befall him. They, as soon as they had got into the ship, weighed anchor and departed, as thinking it neither honorable to deliver Marius into the hands of those that sought him, nor safe to protect him.

He thus, deserted by all, lay a good while silently on the shore; at length collecting himself, he advanced with pain and difficulty, without any path, till, wading through deep bogs and ditches full of water and mud, he came upon the hut of an old man that worked in the fens, and falling at his feet besought him to assist and preserve one who, if he escaped the present danger, would make him returns beyond his expectation. The poor man, whether he had formerly known him, or were then moved with his superior aspect, told him that if he wanted only rest, his cottage would be convenient; but if he were flying from anybody's search, he would hide him in a more retired place. Marius desiring him to do so, he carried him into the fens and bade him hide himself in an hollow place by the river side, where he laid upon him a great many reeds, and other things that were light, and would cover, but not oppress him. But within a very short time he was disturbed with a noise and tumult from the cottage, for Geminius had sent several from Terracina in pursuit of him; some of whom happening to come that way, frightened and threatened the old man for having entertained and hid an enemy of the Romans. Whereupon Marius, arising and stripping himself, plunged into a puddle full of thick muddy water; and even there he could not escape their search, but was pulled out covered with mire, and carried away naked to Minturnæ, and delivered to the magistrates. For there had been orders sent through all the towns, to make public search for Marius, and if they found him to kill him; however, the magistrates thought convenient to consider a little better of it first, and sent him prisoner to the house of one Fannia.

This woman was supposed not very well affected towards him upon an old account. One Tinnius had formerly married this Fannia; from whom she afterwards, being divorced, demanded her portion, which was considerable, but her husband accused her of adultery; so the controversy was brought before Marius in his sixth consulship. When the case was examined thoroughly, it appeared both that Fannia had been incontinent, and that her husband knowing her to be so, had married and lived a considerable time with her. So that Marius was severe enough with both, commanding him to restore her portion, and laying a fine of four copper coins upon her by way of disgrace. But Fannia did not then behave like a woman that had been injured, but as soon as she saw Marius, remembered nothing less than old affronts; took care of him according to her ability, and comforted him. He made her his returns and told her he did not despair, for he had met with a lucky omen, which was thus. When he was brought to Fannia's house, as soon as the gate was opened, an ass came running out to drink at a spring hard by, and giving a bold and encouraging look, first stood still before him, then brayed aloud and pranced by him. From which Marius drew his conclusion, and said, that the fates designed his safety, rather by sea than land, because the ass neglected his dry fodder, and turned from it to the water. Having told Fannia this story, he bade the chamber door to be shut and went to rest.

Meanwhile the magistrates and councillors of Minturnæ consulted together, and determined not to delay any longer, but immediately to kill Marius; and when none of their citizens durst undertake the business, a certain soldier, a Gaulish or Cimbrian horseman (the story is told both ways), went in with his sword drawn to him. The room itself was not very light, that part of it especially where he then lay was dark, from whence Marius's eyes, they say, seemed to the fellow to dart out flames at him, and a loud voice to say, out of the dark, "Fellow, darest thou kill Caius Marius?" The barbarian hereupon immediately fled, and leaving his sword in the place, rushed out of doors, crying only this, "I cannot kill Caius Marius." At which they were all at first astonished, and presently began to feel pity, and remorse, and anger at themselves for making so unjust and ungrateful a decree against one who had preserved Italy, and whom it was bad enough not to assist. "Let him go," said they, "where he please to banishment, and find his fate somewhere else;

we only entreat pardon of the gods for thrusting Marius distressed and deserted out of our city."

Impelled by thoughts of this kind, they went in a body into the room, and taking him amongst them, conducted him towards the sea-side; on his way to which, though every one was very officious to him, and all made what haste they could, yet a considerable time was likely to be lost. For the grove of Marica (as she is called), which the people hold sacred, and make it a point of religion not to let any thing that is once carried into it be taken out, lay just in their road to the sea, and if they should go round about, they must needs come very late thither. At length one of the old men cried out and said, there was no place so sacred, but they might pass through it for Marius's preservation; and thereupon, first of all, he himself, taking up some of the baggage that was carried for his accommodation to the ship, passed through the grove, all the rest immediately, with the same readiness, accompanying him. And one Belæus (who afterwards had a picture of these things drawn, and put it in a temple at the place of embarkation), having by this time provided him a ship, Marius went on board, and hoisting sail, was by fortune thrown upon the island Ænaria, where meeting with Granius, and his other friends, he sailed with them for Africa. But their water failing them in the way, they were forced to put in near Eryx, in Sicily, where was a Roman quæstor on the watch, who all but captured Marius himself on his landing, and did kill sixteen of his retinue that went to fetch water. Marius, with all expedition loosing thence, crossed the sea to the isle of Meninx, where he first heard the news of his son's escape with Cethegus, and of his going to implore the assistance of Hiempsal, king of Numidia.

With this news, being somewhat comforted, he ventured to pass from that isle towards Carthage. Sextilius, a Roman, was then governor in Africa; one that had never received either any injury or any kindness from Marius; but who from compassion, it was hoped, might lend him some help. But he was scarce got ashore with a small retinue, when an officer met him, and said, "Sextilius, the governor, forbids you, Marius, to set foot in Africa; if you do, he says he will put the decree of the senate in execution, and treat you as an enemy to the Romans." When Marius heard this, he wanted words to express his grief and resentment, and for a good while held his peace, looking sternly upon the messenger, who asked him what he should say, or what answer he should re turn to the governor? Marius answered him with a deep sigh: "Go tell him that you have seen Caius Marius sitting in exile among the ruins of Carthage;" appositely applying the example of the fortune of that city to the change of his own condition.

In the interim, Hiempsal, king of Numidia, dubious of what he should determine to do, treated young Marius and those that were with him very honorably; but when they had a mind to depart, he still had some pretence or other to detain them, and it was manifest he made these delays upon no good design. However, there happened an accident that made well for their preservation. The hard fortune which attended young Marius, who was of a comely aspect, touched one of the king's concubines, and this pity of hers was the beginning and occasion of love for him. At first he declined the woman's solicitations, but when he perceived that there was no other way of escaping, and that her offers were more serious than for the gratification of intemperate passion, he accepted her kindness, and she finding means to convey them away, he escaped with his friends and fled to his father. As soon as they had saluted each other, and were going by the sea-side, they saw some scorpions fighting, which Marius took for an ill omen, whereupon they immediately went on board a little fisher-boat, and made towards Cercinas, an island not far distant from the continent. They had scarce put off from shore when they espied some horse, sent after them by the king, with all speed making towards that very place from which they were just retired. And Marius thus escaped a danger, it might be said, as great as any he ever incurred.

At Rome news came that Sylla was engaged with Mithridates's generals in Bœotia; the consuls, from factious opposition, were fallen to downright fighting, wherein Octavius prevailing, drove Cinna out of the city for attempting despotic government, and made Cornelius Merula consul in his stead; while Cinna, raising forces in other parts of Italy, carried the war against them. As soon as Marius heard of this he resolved, with all expedition, to put to sea again, and taking with him from Africa some Mauritanian horse, and a few of the refugees out of Italy, all together not above one thousand, he, with this handful, began his voyage. Arriving at Telamon, in Etruria, and coming ashore, he proclaimed freedom for the slaves; and many of the countrymen, also, and shepherds thereabouts, who were already freemen, at the hearing his name, flocked to him to the sea-side. He persuaded the youngest and strongest to join him, and in a small time got together a competent force with which he filled forty ships. Knowing Octavius to be a good man and willing to execute his office with the greatest justice imaginable, and Cinna to be suspected by Sylla, and in actual warfare against the established government, he determined to join himself and his forces with the latter. He therefore, sent a message to him, to let him know that he was ready to obey him as consul.

When Cinna had joyfully received his offer, naming him proconsul, and sending him the fasces and other ensigns of authority, he said that grandeur did not become his present fortune ; but wearing an ordinary habit, and still letting his hair grow as it had done, from that very day he first went into banishment, and being now above threescore and ten years old, he came slowly on foot, designing to move people's compassion ; which did not prevent, however, his natural fierceness of expression from still predominating, and his humiliation still let it appear that he was not so much dejected as exasperated, by the change of his condition. Having saluted Cinna and the soldiers, he immediately prepared for action, and soon made a considerable alteration in the posture of affairs. He first cut off the provision ships, and plundering all the merchants, made himself master of the supplies of corn ; then bringing his navy to the seaport towns, he took them, and at last, becoming master of Ostia by treachery, he pillaged that town, and slew a multitude of the inhabitants, and, blocking up the river, took from the enemy all hopes of supply by the sea ; then marched with his army toward the city, and posted himself upon the hill called Janiculum.

The public interest did not receive so great damage from Octavius's unskilfulness in his management of affairs, as from his omitting needful measures, through too strict observance of the law. As when several advised him to make the slaves free, he said that he would not give slaves the privilege of the country from which he then, in defence of the laws, was driving away Marius. When Metellus, son to that Metellus who was general in the war in Africa, and afterwards banished through Marius's means, came to Rome, being thought a much better commander than Octavius, the soldiers, deserting the consul, came to him and desired him to take the command of them and preserve the city ; that they when they had got an experienced valiant commander, should fight courageously, and come off conquerors. But when Metellus, offended at it, com

manded them angrily to return to the consul, they revolted to
the enemy. Metellus, too, seeing the city in a desperate condition, left it; but a company of Chaldæans, sacrificers, and
interpreters of the Sibyl's books, persuaded Octavius that
things could turn out happily, and kept him at Rome. He
was, indeed, of all the Romans the most upright and just, and
maintained the honor of the consulate, without cringing or
compliance, as strictly in accordance with ancient laws and
usages, as though they had been immutable mathematical
truths; and yet fell, I know not how, into some weaknesses,
giving more observance to fortune-tellers and diviners, than
to men skilled in civil and military affairs. He therefore,
before Marius entered the city, was pulled down from the
rostra, and murdered by those that were sent before by
Marius; and it is reported there was a Chaldæan writing found
in his gown, when he was slain. And it seemed a thing very
unaccountable, that of two famous generals, Marius should be
often successful by the observing divinations, and Octavius
ruined by the same means.

When affairs were in this posture, the senate assembled, and
sent a deputation to Cinna and Marius, desiring them to come
into the city peaceably and spare the citizens. Cinna, as
consul, received the embassy, sitting in the curule chair, and
returned a kind answer to the messengers; Marius stood by
him and said nothing, but gave sufficient testimony by the
gloominess of his countenance, and the sternness of his looks,
that he would in a short time fill the city with blood. As soon
as the council arose, they went toward the city, where Cinna
entered with his guards, but Marius stayed at the gates, and,
dissembling his rage, professed that he was then an exile and
banished his country by course of law; that if his presence
were necessary, they must, by a new decree, repeal the former
act by which he was banished; as though he were, indeed, a
religious observer of the laws, and as if he were returning to a
city free from fear or oppression. Hereupon the people were
assembled, but before three or four tribes had given their votes,
throwing up his pretences and his legal scruples about his
banishment, he came into the city with a select guard of the
slaves who had joined him, whom he called Bardyæi. These
proceeded to murder a number of citizens, as he gave command, partly by word of mouth, partly by the signal of his
nod. At length Ancharius, a senator, and one that had been
prætor, coming to Marius, and not being resaluted by him,
they with their drawn swords slew him before Marius's face;

and henceforth this was their token, immediately to kill all those who met Marius and saluting him were taken no notice of, nor answered with the like courtesy; so that his very friends were not without dreadful apprehensions and horror, whensoever they came to speak with him.

When they had now butchered a great number, Cinna, grew more remiss and cloyed with murders; but Marius's rage continued still fresh and unsatisfied, and he daily sought for all that were any way suspected by him. Now was every road and every town filled with those that pursued and hunted them that fled and hid themselves; and it was remarkable that there was no more confidence to be placed, as things stood, either in hospitality or friendship; for there were found but a very few that did not betray those that fled to them for shelter. And thus the servants of Cornutus deserve the greater praise and admiration, who, having concealed their master in the house, took the body of one of the slain, cut off the head, put a gold ring on the finger, and showed it to Marius s guards, and buried it with the same solemnity as if it had been their own master. This trick was perceived by nobody, and so Cornutus escaped, and was conveyed by his domestics into Gaul.

Marcus Antonius, the orator, though he, too, found a true friend, had ill-fortune. The man was but poor and a plebeian, and as he was entertaining a man of the greatest rank in Rome, trying to provide for him with the best he could, he sent his servant to get some wine of a neighboring vintner. The servant carefully tasting it and bidding him draw better the fellow asked him what was the matter, that he did not buy new and ordinary wine as he used to do, but richer and of a greater price; he without any designs, told him as his old friend and acquaintance that his master entertained Marcus Antonius, who was concealed with him. The villanous vintner, as soon as the servant was gone went himself to Marius, then at supper, and being brought into his presence, told him he would deliver Antonius into his hands. As soon as he heard it, it is said he gave a great shout, and clapped his hands for joy, and had very nearly risen up and gone to the place himself; but being detained by his friends, he sent Annius, and some soldiers with him, and commanded him to bring Antonius's head to him with all speed. When they came to the house, Annius stayed at the door, and the soldiers went up stairs into the chamber; where, seeing Antonius, they endeavored to shuffle off the murder from one another; for so great it seems were the graces and charms of his oratory, that as soon as he began to speak and beg his life, none of them durst touch or so much as look upon him; but hanging down their heads, every one fell a weeping, When their stay seemed something tedious, Annius came up himself and found Antonius discoursing, and the soldiers astonished and quite softened by it, and calling them cowards, went himself and cut off his head.

Catulus Lutatius, who was colleague with Marius, and his partner in the triumph over the Cimbri, when Marius replied to those that interceded for him and begged his life, merely with the words, " he must die," shut himself up in a room, and making a great fire, smothered himself. When maimed and headless carcasses were now frequently thrown about and trampled upon in the streets, people were not so much moved with compassion at the sight, as struck into a kind of horror and consternation. The outrages of those that were called Bardyæi, was the greatest grievance. These murdered the masters of families in their own houses, abused their children, and ravished their wives, and were uncontrollable in their rapine and murders, till those of Cinna's and Sertorius's party, taking counsel together, fell upon them in the camp and killed them every man.

In the interim, as if a change of wind was coming on, there came news from all parts that Sylla, having put an end to the war with Mithridates, and taken possession of the provinces, was returning into Italy with a great army. This gave some small respite and intermission to these unspeakable calamities. Marius and his friends believing war to be close at hand, Marius was chosen consul the seventh time, and appearing on the very calends of January, the beginning of the year, threw one Sextus Lucinus, from the Tarpeian precipice; an omen, as it seemed, portending the renewed misfortunes both of their party and of the city. Marius, himself now worn out with labor and sinking under the burden of anxieties, could not sustain his spirits, which shook within him with the apprehension of a new war and fresh encounters and dangers, the formidable character of which he knew by his own experience. He was not now to hazard the war with Octavius or Merula, commanding an inexperienced multitude or seditious rabble; but Sylla himself was approaching, the same who had formerly banished him, and since that, had driven Mithridates as far as the Euxine Sea.

Perplexed with such thoughts as these, and calling to mind

his banishment, and the tedious wanderings and dangers he underwent, both by sea and land, he fell into despondency, nocturnal frights, and unquiet sleep, still fancying that he heard some one telling him, that

>———the lion's lair
>Is dangerous, though the lion be not there.

Above all things fearing to lie awake, he gave himself up to drinking deep and besotting himself at night in a way most unsuitable to his age; by all means provoking sleep, as a diversion to his thoughts. At length on the arrival of a messenger from the sea, he was seized with new alarms, and so what with his fear for the future, and what with the burden and satiety of the present, on some slight predisposing cause, he fell into a pleurisy, as Posidonius the philosopher relates, who says he visited and conversed with him when he was sick, about some business relating to his embassy. Caius Piso, an historian, tells us, that Marius, walking after supper with his friends, fell into a conversation with them about his past life, and after reckoning up the several changes of his condition, that from the beginning had happened to him, said, that it did not become a prudent man to trust himself any longer with fortune; and, thereupon taking leave of those that were with him, he kept his bed seven days, and then died.

Some say his ambition betrayed itself openly in his sickness, and that he ran into an extravagant frenzy, fancying himself to be general in the war against Mithridates, throwing himself into such postures and motions of his body as he had formerly used when he was in battle, with frequent shouts and loud cries. With so strong and invincible a desire of being employed in that business had he been possessed through his pride and emulation. Though he had now lived seventy years, and was the first man that ever was chosen seven times consul, and had an establishment and riches sufficient for many kings, he yet complained of his ill fortune, that he must now die before he had attained what he desired. Plato, when he saw his death approaching, thanked the guiding providence and fortune of his life, first, that he was born a man and a Grecian, not a barbarian or a brute, and next, that he happened to live in Socrates's age. And so, indeed, they say Antipater of Tarsus, in like manner, at his death, calling to mind the happiness that he had enjoyed, did not so much as omit his prosperous voyage to Athens; thus recognizing every favor of his indulgent fortune with the greatest acknowledg ments, and carefully saving all to the last in that safest of human treasure-chambers, the memory. Unmindful and thoughtless persons, on the contrary, let all that occurs to them slip away from them as time passes on. Retaining and preserving nothing, they lose the enjoyment of their present prosperity by fancying something better to come; whereas by fortune we may be prevented to this, but that cannot be taken from us. Yet they reject their present success, as though it did not concern them, and do nothing but dream of future uncertainties; not indeed unnaturally; as till men have by reason and education laid a good foundation for external superstructures, in the seeking after and gathering them they can never satisfy the unlimited desires of their mind.

Thus died Marius on the seventeenth day of his seventh consulship, to the great joy and content of Rome, which thereby was in good hopes to be delivered from the calamity of a cruel tyranny; but in a small time they found that they had only changed their old and wornout master for another, young and vigorous; so much cruelty and savageness did his son Marius show in murdering the noblest and most approved citizens. At first, being esteemed resolute and daring against his enemies, he was named the son of Mars, but afterwards, his actions betraying his contrary disposition, he was called the son of Venus. At last, besieged by Sylla in Præneste, where he endeavored in many ways, but in vain, to save his life, when on the capture of the city there was no hope of escape, he killed himself with his own hand.

LYSANDER.

THE treasure-chamber of the Acanthians at Delphi has this inscription: "The spoils which Brasidas and the Acanthians took from the Athenians." And, accordingly, many take the marble statue, which stands within the building by the gates, to be Brasidas's; but, indeed, it is Lysander's, representing him with his hair at full length, after the old fashion, and with an ample beard. Neither is it true, as some give out, that because the Argives, after their great defeat, shaved themselves for sorrow, that the Spartans contrarywise triumphing in their achievements suffered their hair to grow; neither did the Spartans come to be ambitious of wearing long hair, because the Bacchiadæ, who fled from Corinth to Lacedæmon, looked mean and unsightly, having their heads all close cut. But this, also, is indeed one of the ordinances of Lycurgus, who, as it is reported, was used to say, that long hair made good-looking men more beautiful, and ill-looking men more terrible.

Lysander's father is said to have been Aristoclitus, who was not indeed of the royal family but yet of the stock of the Heraclidæ. He was brought up in poverty, and showed himself obedient and conformable, as ever any one did, to the customs of his country; of a manly spirit, also, and superior to all pleasures, excepting only that which their good actions bring to those who are honored and successful; and it is accounted no base thing in Sparta for their young men to be overcome with this kind of pleasure. For they are desirous, from the very first, to have their youth susceptible to good and bad repute, to feel pain at disgrace, and exultation at being commended; and any one who is insensible and unaffected in these respects is thought poor spirited and of no capacity for virtue. Ambition and the passion for distinction were thus implanted in his character by his Laconian education, nor, if they continued there, must we blame his natural disposition much for this. But he was submissive to great men, beyond what seems agreeable to the Spartan temper, and could easily bear the haughtiness of those who were in power, when it was any way for his advantage, which some are of opinion is no small part of political discretion. Aristotle, who says all great characters are more or less atrabilious, as Socrates and Plato and Hercules were, writes that Lysander, not indeed early in life, but when he was old, became thus affected. What is singular in his character is that he endured poverty very well, and that he was not at all enslaved or corrupted by wealth, and yet he filled his country with riches and the love of them, and took away from them the glory of not admiring money; importing amongst them an abundance of gold and silver after the Athenian war, though keeping not one drachma for himself. When Dionysius, the tyrant, sent his daughters some costly gowns of Sicilian manufacture, he would not receive them, saying he was afraid they would make them look more unhandsome. But a while after, being sent ambassador from the same city to the same tyrant, when he had sent him a couple of robes, and bade him choose which of them he would, and carry to his daughter: "She," said he, "will be able to choose best for herself," and taking both of them, went his way.

The Peloponnesian war having now been carried on a long time, and it being expected, after the disaster of the Athenians in Sicily, that they would at once lose the mastery of the sea, and ere long be routed everywhere, Alcibiades, returning from banishment, and taking the command, produced a great change, and made the Athenians again a match for their opponents by sea; and the Lacedæmonians, in great alarm at this, and calling up fresh courage and zeal for the conflict, feeling the want of an able commander and of a powerful armament, sent out Lysander to be admiral of the seas. Being at Ephesus, and finding the city well affected towards him, and favorable to the Lacedæmonian party, but in ill condition, and in danger to become barbarized by adopting the manners of the Persians, who were much mingled among them, the country of Lydia bordering upon them, and the king's generals being quartered there for a long time, he pitched his camp there, and commanded the merchant ships all about to put in thither, and proceeded to build ships of war there; and thus restored their ports by the traffic he created, and their market by the employment he gave, and filled their private houses and their workshops with wealth, so that from that time, the city began, first of all, by Lysander's means, to have some hopes of growing to that stateliness and grandeur which now it is at.

Understanding that Cyrus, the king's son, was come to Sardis, he went up to talk with him, and to accuse Tisaphernes, who, receiving a command to help the Lacedæmonians, and to drive the Athenians from the sea, was thought, on account of Alcibiades, to have become remiss and unwilling, and by paying the seamen slenderly to be ruining the fleet. Now Cyrus was willing that Tisaphernes might be found in blame, and be ill reported of, as being, indeed, a dishonest man, and privately at feud with himself. By these means, and by their daily intercourse together, Lysander, especially by the submissiveness of his conversation, won the affections of the young prince, and greatly roused him to carry on the war; and when he would depart, Cyrus gave him a banquet, and desired him not to refuse his good-will, but to speak and ask what ever he had a mind to, and that he should not be refused any thing whatsoever: "Since you are so very kind," replied Lysander, "I earnestly request you to add one penny to the seamen's pay, that instead of three pence, they may now receive four pence." Cyrus, delighted with his public spirit, gave him ten thousand darics, out of which he added the penny to the seamen's pay, and by the renown of this in a short time emptied the ships of the enemies, as many would come over to that side which gave the most pay, and those who remained, being disheartened and mutinous, daily created trouble to the captains. Yet for all Lysander had so distracted and weakened his enemies, he was afraid to engage by sea, Alcibiades being an energetic commander, and having the superior number of ships, and having been hitherto, in all battles, unconquered both by sea and land.

But afterwards, when Alcibiades sailed from Samos to Phocæa, leaving Antiochus, the pilot, in command of all his forces, this Antiochus, to insult Lysander, sailed with two galleys into the port of the Ephesians, and with mocking and laughter proudly rowed along before the place where the ships lay drawn up. Lysander, in indignation, launched at first a few ships only and pursued him, but as soon as he saw the Athenians come to his help, he added some other ships, and, at last, they fell to a set battle together; and Lysander won the victory, and taking fifteen of their ships, erected a trophy. For this, the people in the city being angry, put Alcibiades out of command, and finding himself despised by the soldiers in Samos, and ill spoken of, he sailed from the army into the Chersonese. And this battle, although not important in itself, was made remarkable by its consequences to Alcibiades.

Lysander, meanwhile, inviting to Ephesus such persons in the various cities as he saw to be bolder and haughtier-spirited than the rest, proceeded to lay the foundations of that government by bodies of ten, and those revolutions which afterwards came to pass, stirring up and urging them to unite in clubs, and apply themselves to public affairs, since as soon as ever the Athenians should be put down, the popular governments, he said, should be suppressed, and they should become supreme in their several countries. And he made them believe these things by present deeds, promoting those who were his friends already to great employments, honors, and offices, and, to gratify their covetousness, making himself a partner in injustice and wickedness. So much so, that all flocked to him, and courted and desired him, hoping, if he remained in power, that the highest wishes they could form would all be gratified. And therefore, from the very beginning, they could not look pleasantly upon Callicratidas, when he came to succeed Lysander as admiral; nor, afterwards, when he had given them experience that he was a most noble and just person, were they pleased with the manner of his government, and its straight forward, Dorian, honest character. They did, indeed, admire his virtue, as they might the beauty of some hero's image; but their wishes were for Lysander's zealous and profitable support of the interests of his friends and partisans, and they shed tears, and were much disheartened when he sailed from them. He himself made them yet more disaffected to Callicratidas; for what remained of the money which had been given him to pay the navy, he sent back again to Sardis, bidding them, if they would, apply to Callicratidas himself, and see how he was able to maintain the soldiers. And, at the last, sailing away, he declared to him that he delivered up the fleet in possession and command of the sea. But Callicratidas, to expose the emptiness of these high pretensions, said, "In that case, leave Samos on the left hand, and, sailing to Miletus, there deliver up the ships to me; for if we are masters of the sea, we need not fear sailing by our enemies in Samos." To which Lysander answering, that not himself, but he, commanded the ships, sailed to Peloponnesus, leaving Callicratidas in great perplexity. For neither had he brought any money from home with him, nor could he endure to tax the towns or force them, being in hardship enough. Therefore, the only course that was to be taken was to go and beg at the doors of the king's commanders, as Lysander had done; for which he was most unfit of any man, being of a generous and great spirit, and one who thought it more becoming for the Greeks to suffer any damage from one another, than to flatter and wait at the gates of barbarians, who, indeed, had gold enough, but nothing else that was commendable. But being compelled by necessity, he proceeded to Lydia, and went at once to Cyrus's house, and sent in word, that Callicratidas, the admiral, was there to speak with him; one of those who kept the gates replied, "Cyrus, O stranger, is not now at leisure, for he is drinking." To which Callicratidas answered, most innocently, "Very well, I will wait till he has done his draught." This time, therefore, they took him for some clownish fellow, and he withdrew, merely laughed at by the barbarians; but when, afterwards, he came a second time to the gate, and was not admitted, he took it hardly and set off for Ephesus, wishing a great many evils to those who first let themselves be insulted over by these barbarians, and taught them to be insolent because of their riches; and added vows to those who were present, that as soon as ever he came back to Sparta, he would do all he could to reconcile the Greeks, that they might be formidable to barbarians, and that they should cease henceforth to need their aid against one another. But Callicratdas, who entertained purposes worthy a Lacedæmonian, and showed himself worthy to compete with the very best of Greece, for his justice, his greatness of mind and courage, not long after, having been beaten in a seafight at Arginusæ, died.

And now, affairs going backwards, the associates in the war sent an embassy to Sparta, requiring Lysander to be their admiral, professing themselves ready to undertake the business much more zealously, if he was commander; and Cyrus, also sent to request the same thing. But because they had a law which would not suffer any one to be admiral twice, and wished nevertheless, to gratify their allies, they gave the title of admiral to one Aracus, and sent Lysander nominally as vice-admiral, but, indeed, with full powers. So he came out, long wished for by the greatest part of the chief persons and leaders in the towns, who hoped to grow to greater power still by his means, when the popular governments should be everywhere destroyed.

But to those who loved honest and noble behavior in their commanders, Lysander, compared with Callicratidas, seemed cunning and subtle, managing most things in the war by deceit, extolling what was just when it was profitable, and when it was not, using that which was convenient, instead of that which was good; and not judging truth to be in nature better than falsehood, but setting a value upon both according to interest. He would laugh at those who thought Hercules's posterity ought not to use deceit in war: "For where the lion's skin will not reach, you must patch it out with the fox's." Such is the conduct recorded of him in the business about Miletus; for when his friends and connections, whom he had promised to assist in suppressing popular government, and expelling their political opponents, had altered their minds, and were reconciled to their enemies, he pretended openly as if he was pleased with it, and was desirous to further the reconciliation, but privately he railed at and abused them, and provoked them to set upon the multitude. And as soon as ever he perceived a new attempt to be commencing, he at once came up and entered into the city, and the first of the conspirators he lit upon, he pretended to rebuke, and spoke roughly, as if he would punish them; but the others, meantime, he bade be courageous, and to fear nothing, now he was with them. And all this acting and dissembling was with the object that the most considerable men of the popular party might not fly away, but might stay in the city and be killed, which so fell out, for all who believed him were put to death.

There is a saying also, recorded by Androclides, which

makes him guilty of great indifference to the obligations of an oath. His recommendation, according to this account, was to "cheat boys with dice, and men with oaths," an imitation of Polycrates of Samos, not very honorable to a lawful commander to take example, namely, from a tyrant; nor in character with Laconian usages, to treat gods as ill as enemies, or indeed, even more injuriously; since he who overreaches by an oath admits that he fears his enemy, while he despises his God.

Cyrus now sent for Lysander to Sardis, and gave him some money, and promised him some more, youthfully protesting in favor to him, that if his father gave him nothing, he would supply him of his own; and if he himself should be destitute of all, he would cut up, he said, to make money, the very throne upon which he sat to do justice, it being made of gold and silver; and, at last, on going up into Media to his father, he ordered that he should receive the tribute of the towns, and committed his government to him, and so taking his leave, and desiring him not to fight by sea before he returned, for he would come back with a great many ships out of Phœnicia and Cilicia, departed to visit the king.

Lysander's ships were too few for him to venture to fight, and yet too many to allow of his remaining idle; he set out, therefore, and reduced some of the islands, and wasted Ægina and Salamis; and from thence landing in Attica, and saluting Agis, who came from Decelea to meet him, he made a display to the land forces of the strength of the fleet, as though he could sail where he pleased, and were absolute master by sea. But hearing the Athenians pursued him, he fled another way through the island into Asia. And finding the Hellespont without any defence, he attacked Lampsacus with his ships by sea; while Thorax, acting in concert with him with the land army, made an assault on the walls; and so having taken the city by storm, he gave it up to his soldiers to plunder. The fleet of the Athenians, a hundred and eighty ships, had just arrived at Elæus in the Chersonese; and hearing the news, that Lampsacus was destroyed, they presently sailed to Sestos; where, taking in victuals, they advanced to Ægos Potami, over against their enemies, who were still stationed about Lampsacus. Amongst other Athenian captains who were now in command was Philocles, he who persuaded the people to pass a decree to cut off the right thumb of the captives in the war, that they should not be able to hold the spear, though they might the oar.

Then they all rested themselves, hoping they should have battle the next morning. But Lysander had other things in his head; he commanded the mariners and pilots to go on board at dawn, as if there should be a battle as soon as it was day, and to sit there in order, and without any noise, excepting what should be commanded, and in like manner that the land army should remain quietly in their ranks by the sea But the sun rising, and the Athenians sailing up with their whole fleet in line, and challenging them to battle, he, though he had had his ships all drawn up and manned before daybreak, nevertheless did not stir. He merely sent some small boats to those who lay foremost, and bade them keep still and stay in their order; not to be disturbed, and none of them to sail out and offer battle. So about evening, the Athenians sailing back, he would not let the seamen go out of the ships before two or three, which he had sent to espy, were returned, after seeing the enemies disembark. And thus they did the next day, and the third, and so to the fourth. So that the Athenians grew extremely confident, and disdained their enemies as if they had been afraid and daunted. At this time, Alcibiades, who was in his castle in the Chersonese, came on horseback to the Athenian army, and found fault with their captains, first of all that they had pitched their camp neither well nor safely on an exposed and open beach, a very bad landing for the ships, and secondly, that where they were, they had to fetch all they wanted from Sestos, some considerable way off; whereas if they sailed round a little way to the town and harbor of Sestos, they would be at a safer distance from an enemy, who lay watching their movements, at the command of a single general, terror of whom made every order rapidly executed. This advice, however, they would not listen to; and Tydeus answered disdainfully, that not he, but others, were in office now. So Alcibiades who even suspected there must be treachery, departed.

But on the fifth day, the Athenians having sailed towards them, and gone back again as they were used to do, very proudly and full of contempt, Lysander sending some ships, as usual, to look out, commanded the masters of them that when they saw the Athenians go to land, they should row back again with all their speed, and that when they were about half-way across, they should lift up a brazen shield from the foredeck, as the sign of battle. And he himself sailing round, encouraged the pilots and masters of the ships, and exhorted them to keep all their men to their places, seamen and soldiers alike, and as soon as ever the sign should be given, to row up boldly to their enemies. Accordingly, when the shield had been lifted up from the ships, and the trumpet from the admiral's vessel had sounded for the battle, the ships rowed up, and the foot soldiers strove to get along by the shore to the promontory. The distance there between the two continents is fifteen furlongs, which, by the zeal and eagerness of the rowers, was quickly traversed. Conon, one of the Athenian commanders, was the first who saw from the land the fleet advancing, and shouted out to embark, and in the greatest distress bade some and entreated others, and some he forced to man the ships. But all his diligence signified nothing, because the men were scattered about; for as soon as they came out of the ships, expecting no such matter, some went to market, others walked about the country, or went to sleep in their tents, or got their dinners ready, being, through their commanders' want of skill, as far as possible from any thought of what was to happen; and the enemy now coming up with shouts and noise, Conon, with eight ships, sailed out, and making his escape, passed from thence to Cyprus, to Evagoras. The Peloponnesians falling upon the rest, some hey took quite empty, and some they destroyed while they vere filling; the men, meantime, coming unarmed and scat:ered to help, died at their ships, or, flying by land, were slain, their enemies disembarking and pursuing them. Lysander took three thousand prisoners, with the generals, and the whole fleet, excepting the sacred ship Paralus, and those which fled with Conon. So taking their ships in tow, and having plundered their tents, with pipe and songs of victory, he sailed back to Lampsacus, having accomplished a great work with small pains, and having finished in one hour, a war which had been protracted in its continuance, and diversified in its incidents and in its fortunes to a degree exceeding belief, compared with all before it. After altering its shape and character a thousand times, and after having been the destruction of more commanders than all the previous wars of Greece put together, it was now put an end to by the good counsel and ready conduct of one man.

Some, therefore, looked upon the result as a divine intervention, and there were certain who affirmed that the stars of Castor and Pollux were seen on each side of Lysander's ship, when he first set sail from the haven toward his enemies, shining about the helm; and some say the stone which fell down was a sign of this slaughter. For a stone of a great size did fall, according to the common belief from heaven, at Ægos Potami, which is shown to this day, and held in great esteem by the Chersonites. And it is said that Anaxagoras foretold, that the occurrence of a slip or shake among the bodies fixed in the heavens, dislodging any one of them, would be followed by the fall of the whole of them. For no one of the stars is now in the same place in which it was at first; for they, being according to him, like stones and heavy, shine by the refraction of the upper air round about them, and are carried along forcibly by the violence of the circular motion by which they were originally withheld from falling, when cold and heavy bodies were first separated from the general universe. But there is a more probable opinion than this maintained by some, who say that falling stars are no effluxes, or discharges of ethereal fire, extinguished almost at the instant of its igniting by the lower air; neither are they the sudden combustion and blazing up of a quantity of the lower air et loose in great abundance into the upper region; but the heavenly bodies, by a relaxation of the force of their circular movement, are carried by an irregular course, not in general into the inhabited part of the earth, but for the most part into the wide sea; which is the cause of their not being observed. Daimachus, in his treatise on Religion, supports the view of Anaxagoras. He says, that before this stone fell, for seventy-five days continually, there was seen in the heavens a vast fiery body, as if it had been a flaming cloud, not resting, but carried about with several intricate and broken movements, so that the flaming pieces, which were broken off by this commotion and running about, were carried in all directions, shining as falling stars do. But when it afterwards came down to the ground in this district, and the people of the place recovering from their fear and astonishment came together, there was no fire to be seen, neither any sign of it; there was only a stone lying, big indeed, but which bore no proportion, to speak of, to that fiery compass. It is manifest that Daimachus needs to have indulgent hearers; but if what he says be true, he altogether proves those to be wrong who say that a rock broken off from the top of some mountain, by winds and tempests, and caught and whirled about like a top, as soon as this impetus began to slacken and cease, was precipitated and fell to the ground. Unless, indeed, we choose to say that the phenomenon which was observed for so many days was really fire, and that the change in the atmosphere ensuing on its extinction was attended with violent winds and agitations, which might be the cause of this stone being carried off. The exacter treatment of this subject belongs, however, to a different kind of writing.

Lysander, after the three thousand Athenians whom he had taken prisoners were condemned by the commissioners to die, called Philocles the general, and asked him what punishment he considered himself to deserve, for having advised the citizens, as he had done, against the Greeks; but he, being nothing cast down at his calamity, bade him not to accuse him of matters of which nobody was a judge, but to do to him, now he was a conqueror, as he would have suffered, had he been overcome. Then washing himself, and putting on a fine cloak, he led the citizens the way to the slaughter, as Theophrastus writes in his history. After this Lysander, sailing about to the various cities, bade all the Athenians he met go into Athens, declaring that he would spare none, but kill every man whom he found out of the city, intending thus to cause immediate famine and scarcity there, that they might not make the siege laborious to him, having provisions sufficient to endure it. And suppressing the popular governments and all other constitutions, he left one Lacedæmonian chief officer in every city, with ten rulers to act with him, selected out of the societies which he had previously formed in the different towns. And doing thus as well in the cities of his enemies, as of his associates, he sailed leisurely on, establishing, in a manner, for himself supremacy over the whole of Greece. Neither did he make choice of rulers by birth or by wealth, but bestowed the offices on his own friends and partisans, doing every thing to please them, and putting absolute power of reward and punishment into their hands. And thus, personally appearing on many occasions of bloodshed and massacre, and aiding his friends to expel their opponents, he did not give the Greeks a favorable specimen of the Lacedæmonian government; and the expression of Theopompus, the comic poet, seemed but poor, when he compared the Lacedæmonians to tavern women, because when the Greeks had first tasted the sweet wine of liberty, they then poured vinegar into the cup; for from the very first it had a rough and bitter taste all government by the people being suppressed by Lysander, and the boldest and least scrupulous of the oligarchical party selected to rule the cities.

Having spent some little time about these things, and sent some before to Lacedæmon to tell them he was arriving with two hundred ships, he united his forces in Attica with those of the two kings Agis and Pausanias, hoping to take the city without delay. But when the Athenians defended themselves, he with his fleet passed again to Asia, and in like manner destroyed the forms of government in all the other cities, and placed them under the rule of ten chief persons, many in every one being killed, and many driven into exile; and n Samos, he expelled the whole people, and gave their cities to the exiles whom he brought back. And the Athenians still possessing Sestos, he took it from them, and suffered not the Sestians themselves to dwell in it, but gave the city and country to be divided out among the pilots and masters of the ships under him; which was his first act that was disallowed by the Lacedæmonians, who brought the Sestians back again into their country. All Greece, however, rejoiced to see the Ægi netans, by Lysander's aid, now again, after a long time, receiving back their cities, and the Melians and Scionæans restored, while the Athenians were driven out, and delivered up the cities.

But when he now understood they were in a bad case in the city because of the famine, he sailed to Piræus, and reduced the city, which was compelled to surrender on what conditions he demanded. One hears it said by Lacedæmonians that Lysander wrote to the Ephors thus: "Athens is taken;" and that these magistrates wrote back to Lysander, "Taken in enough." But this saying was invented for its neatness' sake; for the true decree of the magistrates was on this manner: "The government of the Lacedæmonians has made these orders; pull down the Piræus and the long walls; quit all the towns, and keep to your own land; if you do these things, you shall have peace, if you wish it, restoring also your exiles. As concerning the number of the ships, whatsoever there be judged necessary to appoint, that do.' This scroll of conditions the Athenians accepted, Theramenes, son of Hagnon, supporting it. At which time, too, they say that when Cleomenes, one of the young orators, asked him how he durst act and speak contrary to Themistocles, delivering up the walls to the Lacedæmonians, which he had built against the will of the Lacedæmonians, he said, "O young man, I do nothing contrary to Themistocles; for he raised these walls for the safety of the citizens, and we pull them down for their safety; and if walls make a city happy, then Sparta must be the most wretched of all, as it has none."

Lysander, as soon as he had taken all the ships except twelve, and the walls of the Athenians, on the sixteenth day of the month Munychion, the same on which they had overcome the barbarians at Salamis, then proceeded to take measures for altering the government. But the Athenians taking that very unwillingly, and resisting, he sent to the people and informed them, that he found that the city had broken the terms, for the walls were standing when the days were past within which they should have been pulled down. He should, therefore, consider their case anew, they having broken their first articles. And some state, in fact, the proposal was made in the congress of the allies, that the Athenians should all be sold as slaves; on which occasion, Erianthus, the Theban, gave his vote to pull down the city, and turn the country into sheep-pasture; yet afterwards, when there was a meeting of the captains together, a man of Phocis, singing the first chorus in Euripides's Electra, which begins,

> Electra, Agamemnon's child, I come
> Unto thy desert home,

they were all melted with compassion, and it seemed to be a cruel deed to destroy and pull down a city which had been so famous, and produced such men.

Accordingly Lysander, the Athenians yielding up every thing, sent for a number of flute-women out of the city, and collected together all that were in the camp, and pulled down the walls, and burnt the ships to the sound of the flute, the allies being crowned with garlands, and making merry together, as counting that day the beginning of their liberty. He proceeded also at once to alter the government, placing thirty rulers in the city, and ten in the Piræus: he put, also, a garrison into the Acropolis, and made Callibius, a Spartan, the governor of it; who afterwards taking up his staff to strike Autolycus, the athlete, about whom Xenophon wrote his "Banquet," on his tripping up his heels and throwing him to the ground, Lysander was not vexed at it, but chid Callibius, telling him he did not know how to govern freemen. The thirty rulers, however, to gain Callibius's favor, a little after killed Autolycus.

Lysander, after this, sails out to Thrace, and what remained of the public money, and the gifts and crowns which he had himself received, numbers of people, as might be expected, being anxious to make presents to a man of such great power, who was, in a manner, the lord of Greece, he sends to Lacedæmon by Gylippus, who had commanded formerly in Sicily. But he, it is reported, unsewed the sacks at the bottom, took a considerable amount of silver out of every one of them, and sewed them up again, not knowing there was a writing in every one stating how much there was. And coming into Sparta, what he had thus stolen away he hid under the tiles of his house, and delivered up the sacks to the magistrates, and showed the seals were upon them. But afterwards, on their opening the sacks and counting it, the quantity of the silver differed from what the writing expressed; and the matter causing some perplexity to the magistrates, Gylippus's servant tells them in a riddle, that under the tiles lay many owls; for, as it seems, the greatest part of the money then current bore the Athenian stamp of the owl. Gylippus having committed so foul and base a deed, after such great and distinguished exploits before, removed himself from Lacedæmon.

But the wisest of the Spartans, very much on account of this occurrence, dreading the influence of money, as being what had corrupted the greatest citizens, exclaimed against Lysander's conduct, and declared to the Ephors, that all the silver and gold should be sent away, as mere "alien mischiefs." These consulted about it; and Theopompus says, it was Sciraphidas, but Ephorus, that it was Phlogidas, who declared they ought not to receive any gold or silver into the city; but to use their own country coin which was iron, and was first of all dipped in vinegar when it was red hot, that it might not be worked up anew, but because of the dipping might be hard and unpliable. It was also, of course, very heavy and troublesome to carry, and a great deal of it in quantity and weight was but a little in value. And perhaps all the old money was so, coin consisting of iron, or in some countries, copper skewers, whence it comes that we still find a great number of small pieces of money retain the name of *obolus*, and the drachma is six of these, because so much may be grasped in one's hand. But Lysander's friends being against it, and endeavoring to keep the money in the city, it was resolved to bring in this sort of money to be used publicly, enacting, at the same time, that if any one was found in possession of any privately, he should be put to death, as if Lycurgus had feared the coin, and not the covetousness resulting from it, which they did not repress by letting no private man keep any, so much as they encouraged it, by allowing the state to possess it; attaching thereby a sort of dignity to it, over and above its ordinary utility. Neither was it possible, that what they saw was so much esteemed publicly they should privately despise as unprofitable; and that every one should think that thing could be nothing worth for his own personal use, which was so extremely valued and desired for the use of the state. And moral habits, induced by public practices, are far quicker in making their way into men's privates lives, than the failings and faults of individuals are in infecting the city at large. For it is probable that the parts will be rather corrupted by the whole if that grows bad; while the vices which flow from a part into the whole, find many correctives and remedies from that which remains sound. Terror and the law were now to keep guard over the citizens' houses, to prevent any money entering into them: but their minds could no longer be expected to remain superior to the desire of it when wealth in general was thus set up to be striven after, as a high and noble object. On this point, however, we have given our censure of the Lacedæmonians in one of our other writings.

Lysander erected out of the spoils brazen statues at Delphi of himself, and of every one of the masters of the ships, as also figures of the golden stars of Castor and Pollux, which vanished before the battle at Leuctra. In the treasury of Brasidas and the Acanthians, there was a trireme made of gold and ivory, of two cubits, which Cyrus sent Lysander in honor of his victory. But Alexandrides of Delphi writes, in his history, that there was also a deposit of Lysander's, a talent of silver, and fifty-two minas, besides eleven staters; a statement not consistent with the generally received account of his poverty. And at that time, Lysander, being in fact of greater power than any Greek before, was yet thought to show a pride, and to affect a superiority greater even than his power warranted. He was the first, as Duris says in his history, among the Greeks, to whom the cities reared altars as to a god, and sacrificed; to him were songs of triumph first sung, the beginning of one of which still remains recorded:—

> Great Greece's general from spacious Sparta we
> Will celebrate with songs of victory.

And the Samians decreed that their solemnities of Juno should be called the Lysandria; and out of the poets he had Chœrilus always with him, to extol his achievements in verse; and to Antilochus, who had made some verses in his commendation, being pleased with them, he gave a hat full of silver; and when Antimachus of Colophon, and one Niceratus of Heraclea, competed with each other in a poem on the deeds of Lysander, he gave the garland to Niceratus; at which

Antimachus, in vexation, suppressed his poem; but Plato, being then a young man, and admiring Antimachus for his poetry, consoled him for his defeat by telling him that it is the ignorant who are the sufferers by ignorance, as truly as the blind by want of sight. Afterwards, when Aristonus, the musician, who had been a conqueror six times at the Pythian games, told him as a piece of flattery, that if he were successful again, he would proclaim himself in the name of Lysander, "that is," he answered, "as his slave?"

This ambitious temper was indeed only burdensome to the highest personages and to his equals, but through having so many people devoted to serve him, an extreme haughtiness and contemptuousness grew up, together with ambition, in his character. He observed no sort of moderation, such as befitted a private man, either in rewarding or in punishing; the recompense of his friends and guests was absolute power over cities, and irresponsible authority, and the only satisfaction of his wrath was the destruction of his enemy; banishment would not suffice. As for example, at a later period, fearing lest the popular leaders of the Milesians should fly, and desiring also to discover those who lay hid, he swore he would do them no harm, and on their believing him and coming forth, he delivered them up to the oligarchical leaders to be slain, being in all no less than eight hundred. And, indeed, the slaughter in general of those of the popular party in the towns exceeded all computation; as he did not kill only for offences against himself, but granted these favors without sparing, and joined in the execution of them, to gratify the many hatreds, and the much cupidity of his friends everywhere round about him. From whence the saying of Eteocles, the Lacedæmonian, came to be famous, that "Greece could not have borne two Lysanders." Theophrastus says, that Archestratus said the same thing concerning Alcibiades. But in his case what had given most offence was a certain licentious and wanton self-will; Lysander's power was feared and hated because of his unmerciful disposition. The Lacedæmonians did not at all concern themselves for any other accusers; but afterwards, when Pharnabazus, having been injured by him, he having pillaged and wasted his country, sent some to Sparta to inform against him, the Ephors taking it very ill, put one of his friends and fellow-captains, Thorax, to death, taking him with some silver privately in his possession; and they sent him a scroll, commanding him to return home. This scroll is made up thus; when the Ephors send an admiral or general on his way, they take two round pieces of wood, both exactly of a length and thickness, and cut even to one another; they keep one themselves, and the other they give to the person they send forth; and these pieces of wood they call Scytales. When, therefore, they have occasion to communicate any secret or important matter, making a scroll of parchment long and narrow like a leathern thong, they roll it about their own staff of wood, leaving no space void between, but covering the surface of the staff with the scroll all over. When they have done this, they write what they please on the scroll, as it is wrapped about the staff; and when they have written, they take off the scroll, and send it to the general without the wood. He, when he has received it, can read nothing of the writing, because the words and letters are not connected, but all broken up; but taking his own staff, he winds the slip of the scroll about it, so that this folding, restoring all the parts into the same order that they were in before, and putting what comes first into connection with what follows, brings the whole consecutive contents to view round the outside. And this scroll is called a *staff*, after the name of the wood, as a thing measured is by the name of the measure.

But Lysander, when the staff came to him to the Hellespont, was troubled, and fearing Pharnabazus's accusations most, made haste to confer with him, hoping to end the difference by a meeting together. When they met, he desired him to write another letter to the magistrates, stating that he had not been wronged, and had no complaint to prefer. But he was ignorant that Pharnabazus, as it is in the proverb, played Cretan against Cretan; for pretending to do all that was desired, openly he wrote such a letter as Lysander wanted, but kept by him another, written privately; and when they came to put on the seals, changed the tablets, which differed not at all to look upon, and gave him the letter which had been written privately. Lysander, accordingly, coming to Lacedæmon, and going, as the custom is, to the magistrates' office, gave Pharnabazus's letter to the Ephors, being persuaded that the greatest accusation against him was now withdrawn; for Pharnabazus was beloved by the Lacedæmonians, having been the most zealous on their side in the war of all the king's captains. But after the magistrates had read the letter they showed it him, and he understanding now that

> Others beside Ulysses deep can be,
> Not the one wise man of the world is he,

in extreme confusion, left them at the time. But a few days after, meeting the Ephors, he said he must go to the temple of Ammon, and offer the god the sacrifices which he had vowed in war. For some state it as a truth, that when he was besieging the city of Aphytæ in Thrace, Ammon stood by him in his sleep; whereupon raising the siege, supposing the god had commanded it, he bade the Aphytæans sacrifice to Ammon, and resolved to make a journey into Libya to propitiate the god. But most were of opinion that the god was but the pretence, and that in reality he was afraid of the Ephors, and that impatience of the yoke at home, and dislike of living under authority, made him long for some travel and wandering, like a horse just brought in from open feeding and pasture to the stable, and put again to his ordinary work. For that which Ephorus states to have been the cause of this travelling about, I shall relate by and by.

And having hardly and with difficulty obtained leave of the magistrates to depart, he set sail. But the kings, while he was on his voyage, considering that keeping, as he did, the cities in possession by his own friends and partisans, he was in fact their sovereign and the lord of Greece, took measures for restoring the power to the people, and for throwing his friends out. Disturbances commencing again about these things, and, first of all, the Athenians from Phyle setting upon their thirty rulers and overpowering them, Lysander, coming home in haste, persuaded the Lacedæmonians to support the oligarchies and to put down the popular governments, and to the thirty in Athens, first of all, they sent a hundred talents for the war, and Lysander himself, as general, to assist them. But the kings envying him, and fearing lest he should take Athens again, resolved that one of themselves should take the command. Accordingly Pausanias went, and in words, indeed, professed as if he had been for the tyrant against the people, but in reality exerted himself for peace, that Lysander might not by the means of his friends become lord of Athens again. This he brought easily to pass; for, reconciling the Athenians, and quieting the tumults, he defeated the ambitious hopes of Lysander, though shortly after, on the Athenians rebelling again, he was censured for having thus taken, as it were, the bit out of the mouth of the people, which, being freed from the oligarchy, would now break out again into affronts and insolence; and Lysander regained the reputation of a person who employed his command not in gratification of others, not for applause, but strictly for the good of Sparta.

His speech, also, was bold and daunting to such as opposed him. The Argives, for example, contended about the bounds of their land, and thought they brought juster pleas than the Lacedæmonians ; holding out his sword, " He," said Lysander, " that is master of this, brings the best argument about the bounds of territory." A man of Megara, at some conference, taking freedom with him, " This language, my friend," said he, " should come from a city." To the Bœotians, who were acting a doubtful part, he put the question, whether he should pass through their country with spears upright, or levelled. After the revolt of the Corinthians, when, on coming to their walls, he perceived the Lacedæmonians hesitating to make the assault, and a hare was seen to leap through the ditch: " Are you not ashamed," he said, " to fear an enemy, for whose laziness, the very hares sleep upon their walls ? "

When king Agis died, leaving a brother Agesilaus, and Leontychides, who was supposed his son, Lysander, being attached to Agesilaus, persuaded him to lay claim to the kingdom, as being a true descendant of Hercules ; Leontychides lying under the suspicion of being the son of Alcibiades, who lived privately in familiarity with Timæa, the wife of Agis, at the time he was a fugitive in Sparta. Agis, they say, computing the time, satisfied himself that she could not have conceived by him, and had hitherto always neglected and manifestly disowned Leontychides ; but now when he was carried sick to Heræa, being ready to die, what by importunities of the young man himself, and of his friends, in the presence of many he declared Leontychides to be his ; and desiring those who were present to bear witness of this to the Lacedæmonians, died. They accordingly did so testify in favor of Leontychides. And Agesilaus, being otherwise highly reputed of, and strong in the support of Lysander, was, on the other hand, prejudiced by Diopithes, a man famous for his knowledge of oracles, who adduced this prophecy in reference to Agesilaus's lameness :—

> Beware, great Sparta, lest there come of thee,
> Though sound thyself, an halting sovereignty ;
> Troubles, both long and unexpected too,
> And storms of deadly warfare shall ensue.

When many, therefore, yielded to the oracle, and inclined to Leontychides, Lysander said that Diopithes did not take the prophecy rightly ; for it was not that the god would be offended if any lame person ruled over the Lacedæmonians, but that the kingdom would be a lame one, if bastards and false born should govern with the posterity of Hercules. By this argument, and by his great influence among them, he prevailed, and Agesilaus was made king.

Immediately, therefore, Lysander spurred him on to make an expedition into Asia, putting him in hopes that he might destroy the Persians, and attain the height of greatness. And he wrote to his friends in Asia, bidding them request to have Agesilaus appointed to command them in the war against the barbarians; which they were persuaded to, and sent ambassadors to Lacedæmon to entreat it. And this would seem to be a second favor done Agesilaus by Lysander, not inferior to his first in obtaining him the kingdom. But with ambitious natures, otherwise not ill qualified for command, the feeling of jealousy of those near them in reputation continually stands in the way of the performance of noble actions; they make those their rivals in virtue, whom they ought to use as their helpers to it. Agesilaus took Lysander, among the thirty counsellors that accompanied him, with intentions of using him as his especial friend; but when they were come into Asia, the inhabitants there, to whom he was but little known, addressed themselves to him but little and seldom; whereas Lysander, because of their frequent previous intercourse, was visited and attended by large numbers, by his friends out of observance, and by others out of fear; and just as in tragedies it not uncommonly is the case with the actors, the person who represents a messenger or servant is much taken notice of, and plays the chief part, while he who wears the crown and sceptre is hardly heard to speak, even so was it about the counsellor, he had all the real honors of the government, and to the king was left the empty name of power. This disproportionate ambition ought very likely to have been in some way softened down, and Lysander should have been reduced to his proper second place, but wholly to cast off and to insult and affront for glory's sake, one who was his benefactor and friend, was not worthy Agesilaus to allow in himself. For, first of all, he gave him no opportunity for any action, and never set him in any place of command; then, for whomsoever he perceived him exerting his interest, these persons he always sent away with a refusal, and with less attention than any ordinary suitors, thus silently undoing and weakening his influence.

Lysander, miscarrying in every thing, and perceiving that his diligence for his friends was but a hindrance to them

forebore to help them, entreating them that they would not
address themselves to, nor observe him, but that they would
speak to the king, and to those who could be of more service
to friends than at present he could; most, on hearing this,
forebore to trouble him about their concerns; but continued
their observances to him, waiting upon him in the walks and
places of exercise; at which Agesilaus was more annoyed
than ever, envying him the honor; and, finally, when he gave
many of the officers places of command and the governments
of cities, he appointed Lysander carver at his table, adding,
by way of insult to the Ionians, "Let them go now, and pay
their court to my carver." Upon this, Lysander thought fit
to come and speak with him; and a brief laconic dialogue
passed between them as follows: "Truly, you know very
well, O Agesilaus, how to depress your friends;" "Those
friends," replied he, "who would be greater than myself;
but those who increase my power, it is just should share in
it." "Possibly, O Agesilaus," answered Lysander, "in all
this there may be more said on your part than done on mine,
but I request you, for the sake of observers from without, to
place me in any command under you where you may judge
I shall be the least offensive, and most useful."

Upon this he was sent ambassador to the Hellespont; and
though angry with Agesilaus, yet did not neglect to perform
his duty, and having induced Spithridates the Persian, being
offended with Pharnabazus, a gallant man, and in command
of some forces, to revolt, he brought him to Agesilaus. He
was not, however, employed in any other service, but having
completed his time, returned to Sparta, without honor, angry
with Agesilaus, and hating more than ever the whole Spartan
government, and resolved to delay no longer, but while there
was yet time, to put into execution the plans which he appears
some time before to have concerted for a revolution
and change in the constitution. These were as follows. The
Heraclidæ who joined with the Dorians, and came into Peloponnesus,
became a numerous and glorious race in Sparta
but not every family belonging to it had the right of succession
in the kingdom, but the kings were chosen out of two
only, called the Eurypontidæ and the Agiadæ; the rest had
no privilege in the government by their nobility of birth, and
the honors which followed from merit lay open to all who
could obtain them. Lysander, who was born of one of these
families, when he had risen into great renown for his exploits,
and had gained great friends and power, was vexed to see

the city which had increased to what it was by him, ruled by others not at all better descended than himself, and formed a design to remove the government from the two families, and to give it in common to all the Heraclidæ; or, as some say, not to the Heraclidæ only, but to all the Spartans; that the reward might not belong to the posterity of Hercules, but to those who were like Hercules, judging by that personal merit which raised even him to the honor of the Godhead; and he hoped that when the kingdom was thus to be competed for, no Spartan would be chosen before himself.

Accordingly he first attempted and prepared to persuade the citizens privately, and studied an oration composed to this purpose by Cleon, the Halicarnassian. Afterwards perceiving so unexpected and great an innovation required bolder means of support, he proceeded as it might be on the stage, to avail himself of machinery, and to try the effects of divine agency upon his countrymen. He collected and arranged for his purpose, answers and oracles from Apollo, not expecting to get any benefit from Cleon's rhetoric, unless he should first alarm and overpower the minds of his fellow-citizens by religious and superstitious terrors, before bringing them to the consideration of his arguments. Ephorus relates, after he had endeavored to corrupt the oracle of Apollo, and had again failed to persuade the priestesses of Dodona by means of Pherecles, that he went to Ammon, and discoursed with the guardians of the oracle there, proffering them a great deal of gold, and that they, taking this ill, sent some to Sparta to accuse Lysander; and on his acquittal the Libyans, going away, said, "You will find us, O Spartans, better judges, when you come to dwell with us in Libya," there being a certain ancient oracle, that the Lacedæmonians should dwell in Libya. But as the whole intrigue and the course of the contrivance was no ordinary one, nor lightly undertaken, but depended as it went on, like some mathematical proposition, on a variety of important admissions, and proceeded through a series of intricate and difficult steps to its conclusion, we will go into it at length, following the account of one who was at once an historian and a philosopher.

There was a woman in Pontus, who professed to be pregnant by Apollo, which many, as was natural, disbelieved, and many also gave credit to, and when she had brought forth a man-child, several, not unimportant persons, took an interest in its rearing and bringing up. The name given the boy was Silenus, for some reason or other. Lysander, taking this for the groundwork, frames and devises the rest himself, making use of not a few, nor these insignificant champions of his story, who brought the report of the child's birth into credit without any suspicion. Another report, also, was procured from Delphi and circulated in Sparta, that there were some very old oracles which were kept by the priests in private writings; and they were not to be meddled with, neither was it lawful to read them, till one in after times should come, descended from Apollo, and, on giving some known token to the keepers, should take the books in which the oracles were. Things being thus ordered beforehand, Silenus, it was intended, should come and ask for the oracles, as being the child of Apollo, and those priests who were privy to the design, were to profess to search narrowly into all particulars, and to question him concerning his birth; and, finally, were to be convinced, and, as to Apollo's son, to deliver up to him the writings. Then he, in the presence of many witnesses, should read amongst other prophecies, that which was the object of the whole contrivance, relating to the office of the kings, that it would be better and more desirable to the Spartans to choose their kings out of the best citizens. And now, Silenus being grown up to a youth, and being ready for the action, Lysander miscarried in his drama through the timidity of one of his actors, or assistants, who just as he came to the point lost heart and drew back. Yet nothing was found out while Lysander lived, but only after his death.

He died before Agesilaus came back from Asia, being involved, or perhaps more truly having himself involved Greece, in the Boeotian war. For it is stated both ways; and the cause of it some make to be himself, others the Thebans, and some both together; the Thebans, on the one hand, being charged with casting away the sacrifices at Aulis, and that being bribed with the king's money brought by Androclides and Amphitheus, they had with the object of entangling the Lacedæmonians in a Grecian war, set upon the Phocians, and wasted their country; it being said, on the other hand, that Lysander was angry that the Thebans had preferred a claim to the tenth part of the spoils of the war, while the rest of the confederates submitted without complaint; and because they expressed indignation about the money which Lysander sent to Sparta, but most especially, because from them the Athenians had obtained the first opportunity of freeing themselves from the thirty tyrants, whom Lysander had made, and to support whom the Lacedæmo nians issued a decree that political refugees from Athens might be arrested in whatever country they were found, and that those who impeded their arrest should be excluded from the confederacy. In reply to this the Thebans issued counter decrees of their own, truly in the spirit and temper of the actions of Hercules and Bacchus, that every house and city in Bœotia should be opened to the Athenians who required it, and that he who did not help a fugitive who was seized, should be fined a talent for damages, and if any one should bear arms through Bœotia to Attica against the tyrants, that none of the Thebans should either see or hear of it. Nor did they pass these humane and truly Greek decrees, without at the same time making their acts conformable to their words. For Thrasybulus and those who with him occupied Phyle, set out upon that enterprise from Thebes, with arms and money, and secresy and a point to start from, provided for them by the Thebans. Such were the causes of complaint Lysander had against Thebes. And being now grown violent in his temper through the atrabilious tendency which increased upon him in his old age, he urged the Ephors and persuaded them to place a garrison in Thebes, and taking the commander's place, he marched forth with a body of troops. Pausanias, also the king, was sent shortly after with an army. Now Pausanias, going round by Cithæron, was to invade Bœotia; Lysander, meantime, advanced through Phocis to meet him, with a numerous body of soldiers. He took the city of the Orchomenians, who came over to him of their own accord, and plundered Lebadea. He despatched also letters to Pausanias, ordering him to move from Platæa to meet him at Haliartus, and that himself would be at the walls of Haliartus by break of day. These letters were brought to the Thebans, the carrier of them falling into the hands of some Theban scouts. They, having received aid from Athens, committed their city to the charge of the Athenian troops, and sallying out about the first sleep, succeeded in reaching Haliartus a little before Lysander, and part of them entered into the city. He upon this, first of all resolved posting his army upon a hill, to stay for Pausanias; then as the day advanced not being able to rest, he bade his men take up their arms, and encouraging the allies, led them in a column along the road to the walls. But those Thebans who had remained outside, taking the city on the left hand, advanced against the rear of their enemies, by the fountain which is called Cissusa; here they tell the story that the nurses washed the infant Bacchus after his birth; the water of it is of a bright wine color, clear, and most pleasant to drink; and not far off the Cretan storax grows all about, which the Haliartians adduce in token of Rhadamanthus having dwelt there, and they show his sepulchre, calling it Alea. And the monument also of Alcmena is hard by; for there as they say, she was bur'ed, having married Rhadamanthus after Amphitryon's death. But the Thebans inside the city forming in order of battle with the Haliartians stood still for some time, but on seeing Lysander with a party of those who were foremost approaching, on a sudden opening the gates and falling on, they killed him with the soothsayer at his side, and a few others; for the greater part immediately fled back to the main force. But the Thebans not slackening, but closely pursuing them, the whole body turned to fly towards the hills. There were one thousand of them slain; there died, also, of the Thebans three hundred, who were killed with their enemies, while chasing them into craggy and difficult places. These had been under suspicion of favoring the Lacedæmons, and in their eagerness to clear themselves in the eyes of their fellow-citizens, exposed themselves in the pursuit, and so met their death. News of the disaster reached Pausanias as he was on the way from Platæa to Thespiæ, and having set his army in order he came to Haliartus: Thrasybulus, also, came from Thebes, leading the Athenians.

Pausanias proposing to request the bodies of the dead under truce, the elders of the Spartans took it ill, and were angry among themselves, and coming to the king, declared that Lysander should not be taken away upon any conditions; if they fought it out by arms about his body, and conquered, then they might bury him; if they were overcome, it was glorious to die upon the spot with their commander When the elders had spoken these things, Pausanias saw it would be a difficult business to vanquish the Thebans, who had but just been conquerors; that Lysander's body also lay near the walls, so that it would be hard for them, though they overcame, to take it away without a truce; he therefore sent a herald, obtained a truce, and withdrew his forces, and carrying away the body of Lysander, they buried it in the first triendly soil they reached on crossing the Bœotian frontier, in the country of the Panopæans; where the monument still stands as you go on the road from Delphi to Chæronea. Now the army quartering there, it is said that a person of Phocis, relating the battle to one who was not in it, said, the enemies fell upon them just after Lysander had passed over the Hoplites; surprised at which a Spartan, a friend of Lysander, asked what Hoplites he meant, for he did not know the name "It was there," answered the Phocian, "that the enemy killed the first of us; the rivulet by the city is called Hoplites." On hearing which the Spartan shed tears and observed, how impossible it is for any man to avoid his appointed lot; Lysander, it appears, having received an oracle as follows:—

> Sounding Hoplites see thou bear in mind,
> And the earthborn dragon following behind.

Some, however, say that Hoplites does not run by Haliartus, but is a watercourse near Coronea, falling into the river Philarus, not far from the town in former times called Hoplias, and now Isomantus.

The man of Haliartus who killed Lysander, by name Neochorus, bore on his shield the device of a dragon; and this, it was supposed, the oracle signified. It is said also that at the time of the Peloponnesian war, the Thebans received an oracle from the sanctuary of Ismenus, referring at once to the battle at Delium, and to this which thirty years after took place at Haliartus. It ran thus:—

> Hunting the wolf, observe the utmost bound,
> And the hill Orchalides where foxes most are found.

By the words, "the utmost bound," Delium being intended, where Bœotia touches Attica, and by Orchalides, the hill now called Alopecus, which lies in the parts of Haliartus towards Helicon.

But such a death befalling Lysander, the Spartans took it so grievously at the time, that they put the king to a trial for his life, which he not daring to await, fled to Tegea, and there lived out his life in the sanctuary of Minerva. The poverty also of Lysander being discovered by his death, made his merit more manifest, since from so much wealth and power, from all the homage of the cities, and of the Persian kingdom, he had not in the least degree, so far as money goes, sought any private aggrandizement, as Theopompus in his history relates, whom any one may rather give credit to when he commends, than when he finds fault, as it is more agreeable to him to blame than to praise. But subsequently, Ephorus says, some controversy arising among the allies at Sparta, which made it necessary to consult the writings which Lysander had kept by him, Agesilaus came to his house, and finding the book in which the oration on the Spartan constitution was written at length, to the effect that the kingdom ought to be taken from the Eurypontidæ and Agiadæ, and to be offered in common, and a choice made out of the best citizens, at first he was eager to make it public, and to show his countrymen the real character of Lysander. But Lacratidas, a wise man, and at that time chief of the Ephors, hindered Agesilaus, and said they ought not to dig up Lysander again, but rather to bury with him a discourse, composed so plausibly and subtilly. Other honors, also, were paid him after his death; and amongst these they imposed a fine upon those who had engaged themselves to marry his daughters, and then when Lysander was found to be poor, after his decease, refused them; because when they thought him rich they had been observant of him, but now his poverty had proved him just and good, they forsook him. For there was, it seems, in Sparta, a punishment for not marrying, for a late, and for a bad marriage; and to the last penalty those were most especially liable, who sought alliances with the rich instead of with the good and with their friends. Such is the account we have found given of Lysander.

SYLLA.

Lucius Cornelius Sylla was descended of a patrician or noble family. Of his ancestors, Rufinus, it is said, had been consul, and incurred a disgrace more signal than his distinction. For being found possessed of more than ten pounds of silver plate, contrary to the law, he was for this reason put out of the senate. His posterity continued ever after in obscurity, nor had Sylla himself any opulent parentage. In his younger days he lived in hired lodgings, at a low rate, which in after-times was adduced against him as proof that he had been fortunate above his quality. When he was boasting and magnifying himself for his exploits in Libya, a person of noble station made answer, "And how can you be an honest man, who, since the death of a father who left you nothing, have become so rich?" The time in which he lived was no longer an age of pure and upright manners, but had already declined, and yielded to the appetite for riches and luxury; yet still, in the general opinion, they who deserted the hereditary poverty of their family were as much blamed as those who had run out a fair patrimonial estate And afterwards, when he had seized the power into his hands, and was putting many to death, a freedman, suspected of having concealed one of the proscribed, and for that reason sentenced to be thrown down the Tarpeian rock, in a reproachful way recounted how they had lived long together under the same roof, himself for the upper rooms paying two thousand sesterces, and Sylla for the lower three thousand; so that the difference between their fortunes then was no more than one thousand sesterces, equivalent in Attic coin to two hundred and fifty drachmas. And thus much of his early fortune.

His general personal appearance may be known by his statues; only his blue eyes, of themselves extremely keen and glaring, were rendered all the more forbidding and terrible by the complexion of his face, in which white was mixed with rough blotches of fiery red. Hence, it is said, he was surnamed Sylla, and in allusion to it one of the scurrilous jesters at Athens made the verse upon him,

> Sylla is a mulberry sprinkled o'er with meal.

Nor is it out of place to make use of marks of character like these, in the case of one who was by nature so addicted to raillery, that in his youthful obscure years he would converse freely with players and professed jesters, and join them in all their low pleasures. And when supreme master of all, he was often wont to muster together the most impudent players and stage-followers of the town, and to drink and bandy jests with them without regard to his age or the dignity of his place, and to the prejudice of important affairs that required his attention. When he was once at table, it was not in Sylla's nature to admit of any thing that was serious, and whereas at other times he was a man of business, and austere of countenance, he underwent all of a sudden, at his first entrance upon wine and good-fellowship, a total revolution, and was gentle and tractable with common singers and dancers, and ready to oblige any one that spoke with him. It seems to have been a sort of diseased result of this laxity, that he was so prone to amorous pleasures, and yielded without resistance to any temptation of voluptuousness, from which even in his old age he could not refrain. He had a long attachment for Metrobius, a player. In his first amours, it happened that he made court to a common but rich lady

Nicopolis by name, and, what by the air of his youth, and what by long intimacy, won so far on her affections, that she rather than he was the lover, and at her death she bequeathed him her whole property. He likewise inherited the estate of a step-mother who loved him as her own son. By these means he had pretty well advanced his fortunes.

He was chosen quæstor to Marius in his first consulship, and set sail with him for Libya, to war upon Jugurtha. Here, in general, he gained approbation; and more especially, by closing in dexterously with an accidental occasion, made a friend of Bocchus, king of Numidia. He hospitably entertained the king's embassadors, on their escape from some Numidian robbers, and after showing them much kindness, sent them on their journey with presents, and an escort to protect them. Bocchus had long hated and dreaded his son-in-law, Jugurtha, who had now been worsted in the field and had fled to him for shelter; and it so happened, he was at this time entertaining a design to betray him. He accordingly invited Sylla to come to him, wishing the seizure and surrender of Jugurtha to be effected rather through him, than directly by himself. Sylla, when he had communicated the business to Marius, and received from him a small detachment, voluntarily put himself into this imminent danger; and confiding in a barbarian, who had been unfaithful to his own relations, to apprehend another man's person, made surrender of his own. Bocchus, having both of them now in his power, was necessitated to betray one or other, and after long debate with himself, at last resolved on his first design, and gave up Jugurtha into the hands of Sylla.

For this Marius triumphed, but the glory of the enterprise, which, through people's envy of Marius was ascribed to Sylla, secretly grieved him. And the truth is, Sylla himself was by nature vainglorious, and this being the first time that from a low and private condition he had risen to esteem amongst the citizens and tasted of honor, his appetite for distinction carried him to such a pitch of ostentation, that he had a representation of this action engraved on a signet ring; which he carried about with him, and made use of ever after. The impress was Bocchus delivering, and Sylla receiving, Jugurtha. This touched Marius to the quick; however, judging Sylla to be beneath his rivalry, he made use of him as lieutenant, in his second consulship, and in his third, as tribune; and many considerable services were effected by his means. When acting as lieutenant he took Copillus, chief of the Tectosages prisoner, and compelled the Marsians, a great and populous nation, to become friends and confederates of the Romans.

Henceforward, however, Sylla, perceiving that Marius bore a jealous eye over him, and would no longer afford him opportunities of action, but rather opposed his advance, attached himself to Catulus, Marius's colleague, a worthy man, but not energetic enough as a general. And under this commander, who intrusted him with the highest and most important commissions, he rose at once to reputation and to power. He subdued by arms most part of the Alpine barbarians; and when there was a scarcity in the armies, he took that care upon himself and brought in such a store of provisions as not only to furnish the soldiers of Catulus with abundance, but likewise to supply Marius. This, as he writes himself, wounded Marius to the very heart. So slight and childish were the first occasions and motives of that enmity between them, which, passing afterwards through a long course of civil bloodshed and incurable divisions to find its end in tyranny, and the confusion of the whole State, proved Euripides to have been truly wise and thoroughly acquainted with the causes of disorders in the body politic, when he forewarned all men to beware of Ambition, as of all the higher Powers, the most destructive and pernicious to her votaries.

Sylla, by this time thinking that the reputation of his arms abroad was sufficient to entitle him to a part in the civil administration, betook himself immediately from the camp to the assembly, and offered himself as a candidate for a prætorship, but failed. The fault of this disappointment he wholly ascribes to the populace, who, knowing his intimacy with king Bocchus, and for that reason expecting, that if he was made ædile before his prætorship, he would then show them magnificent hunting-shows and combats between Libyan wild beasts, chose other prætors, on purpose to force him into the ædileship. The vanity of this pretext is sufficiently disproved by matter-of-fact. For the year following, partly by flatteries to the people, and partly by money, he got himself elected prætor. Accordingly, once while he was in office, on his angrily telling Cæsar that he should make use of his authority against him, Cæsar answered him with a smile, "You do well to call it your own, as you bought it." At the end of his prætorship he was sent over into Cappadocia, under the pretence of reestablishing Ariobarzanes in his kingdom, but in reality to keep in check the restless movements of Mithridates, who was gradually procuring himself as vast a new acquired power and dominion, as was that of his ancient inheritance. He carried over with him no great forces of his own, but making use of the cheerful aid of the confederates, succeeded, with considerable slaughter of the Cappadocians, and yet greater of the Armenian succors, in expelling Gordius and establishing Ariobarzanes as king

During his stay on the banks of the Euphrates, there came to him Orobazus, a Parthian, ambassador from king Arsaces, as yet there having been no correspondence between the two nations. And this also we may lay to the account of Sylla's felicity, that he should be the first Roman to whom the Parthians made address for alliance and friendship. At the time of which reception, the story is, that, having ordered three chairs of state to be set, one for Ariobarzanes, one for Orobazus, and a third for himself, he placed himself in the middle, and so gave audience. For this the king of Parthia afterwards put Orobazus to death. Some people commended Sylla for his lofty carriage towards the barbarians; others again accused him of arrogance and unseasonable display. It is reported that a certain Chaldæan, of Orobazus's retinue, looking Sylla wistfully in the face, and observing carefully the motions of his mind and body, and forming a judgment of his nature, according to the rules of his art, said that it was impossible for him not to become the greatest of men; it was rather a wonder how he could even then abstain from being head of all.

At his return, Censorinus impeached him of extortion, for having exacted a vast sum of money from a well-affected and associate kingdom. However, Censorinus did not appear at the trial, but dropped his accusation. His quarrel, meantime, with Marius began to break out afresh, receiving new material from the ambition of Bocchus, who, to please the people of Rome, and gratify Sylla, set up in the temple of Jupiter Capitolinus images bearing trophies, and a representation in gold of the surrender of Jugurtha to Sylla. When Marius, in great anger, attempted to pull them down, and others aided Sylla, the whole city would have been in tumult and commotion with this dispute, had not the Social War, which had long lain smouldering, blazed forth at last, and for the present put an end to the quarrel.

In the course of this war, which had many great changes of fortune, and which, more than any, afflicted the Romans, and, indeed, endangered the very being of the Commonwealth,

Marius was not able to signalize his valor in any action, but left behind him a clear proof, that warlike excellence requires a strong and still vigorous body. Sylla, on the other hand, by his many achievements, gained himself, with his fellow-citizens, the name of a great commander, while his friends thought him the greatest of all commanders, and his enemies called him the most fortunate. Nor did this make the same sort of impression on him, as it made on Timotheus the son of Conon, the Athenian; who, when his adversaries ascribed his successes to his good luck, and had a painting made, representing him asleep, and Fortune by his side, casting her nets over the cities, was rough and violent in his indignation at those who did it, as if, by attributing all to Fortune, they had robbed him of his just honors; and said to the people on one occasion at his return from war, "In this, ye men of Athens, Fortune had no part." A piece of boyish petulance, which the deity, we are told, played back upon Timotheus; who from that time was never able to achieve any thing that was great, but proving altogether unfortunate in his attempts, and falling into discredit with the people, was at last banished the city. Sylla, on the contrary, not only accepted with pleasure the credit of such divine felicities and favors, but joining himself and extolling and glorifying what was done, gave the honor of all to Fortune, whether it were out of boastfulness, or a real feeling of divine agency. He remarks, in his Memoirs, that of all his well-advised actions, none proved so lucky in the execution, as what he had boldly enterprised, not by calculation, but upon the moment. And, in the character which he gives of himself, that he was born for fortune rather than war, he seems to give Fortune a higher place than merit, and in short, makes himself entirely the creature of a superior power, accounting even his concord with Metellus, his equal in office, and his connection by marriage, a piece of preternatural felicity. For expecting to have met in him a a most troublesome, he found him a most accommodating colleague. Moreover, in the Memoirs which he dedicated to Lucullus, he admonished him to esteem nothing more trustworthy, than what the divine powers advise him by night. And when he was leaving the city with an army, to fight in the Social War, he relates, that the earth near the Laverna opened, and a quantity of fire came rushing out of it, shooting up with a bright flame into the heavens. The soothsayers upon this foretold, that a person of great qualities, and of a rare and singular aspect, should take the government in hand.

and quiet the present troubles of the city. Sylla affirms he was the man, for his golden head of hair made him an extraordinary-looking man, nor had he any shame, after the great actions he had done, in testifying to his own great qualities. And thus much of his opinion as to divine agency.

In general he would seem to have been of a very irregular character, full of inconsistencies with himself; much given to rapine, to prodigality yet more; in promoting or disgracing whom he pleased, alike unaccountable.; cringing to those he stood in need of, and domineering over others who stood in need of him, so that it was hard to tell, whether his nature had more in it of pride or of servility. As to his unequal distribution of punishments, as, for example, that upon slight grounds he would put to the torture, and again would bear patiently with the greatest wrongs; would readily forgive and be reconciled after the most heinous acts of enmity, and yet would visit small and inconsiderable offences with death, and confiscation of goods; one might judge that in himself he was really of a violent and revengeful nature, which, however, he could qualify, upon reflection, for his interest. In this very Social War, when the soldiers with stones and clubs had killed an officer of prætorian rank, his own lieutenant, Albinus by name, he passed by this flagrant crime without any inquiry, giving it out moreover in a boast, that the soldiers would behave all the better now, to make amends, by some special bravery, for their breach of discipline. He took no notice of the clamors of those that cried for justice, but designing already to supplant Marius, now that he saw the Social War near its end, he made much of his army, in hopes to get himself declared general of the forces against Mithridates.

At his return to Rome he was chosen Consul with Quintus Pompeius, in the fiftieth year of his age, and made a most distinguished marriage with Cæcilia, daughter of Metellus, the chief priest. The common people made a variety of verses in ridicule of the marriage, and many of the nobility also were disgusted at it, esteeming him, as Livy writes, unworthy of this connection, whom before they thought worthy of a consulship. This was not his only wife, for first, in his younger days, he was married to Ilia, by whom he had a daughter; after her to Ælia; and thirdly to Clœlia, whom he dismissed as barren, but honorably, and with professions of respect, adding, moreover, presents. But the match between him and Metella, falling out a few days after, occasioned suspicions that he had complained of Clœlia without due cause. To

Metella he always showed great deference, so much so that the people, when anxious for the recall of the exiles of Marius's party, upon his refusal, entreated the intercession of Metella. And the Athenians, it is thought, had harder measure, at the capture of their town, because they used insulting language to Metella in their jests from the walls during the seige. But of this hereafter.

At present esteeming the consulship but a small matter in comparison of things to come, he was impatiently carried away in thought to the Mithridatic War. Here he was withstood by Marius; who out of mad affectation of glory and thirst for distinction, those never dying passions, though he were now unweildy in body, and had given up service on account of his age, during the late campaigns, still coveted after command in a distant war beyond the seas. And whilst Sylla was departed for the camp, to order the rest of his affairs there, he sate brooding at home, and at last hatched that execrable sedition, which wrought Rome more mischief than all her enemies together had done, as was indeed foreshown by the gods. For a flame broke forth of its own accord, from under the staves of the ensigns, and was with difficulty extinguished. Three ravens brought their young into the open road, and ate them, carrying the relics into the nest again. Mice having gnawed the consecrated gold in one of the temples, the keepers caught one of them, a female, in a trap; and she bringing forth five young ones in the very trap, devoured three of them. But what was greatest of all, in a calm and clear sky there was heard the sound of a trumpet, with such a loud and dismal blast, as struck terror and amazement into the hearts of the people. The Etruscan sages affirmed that this prodigy betokened the mutation of the age, and a general revolution in the world. For according to them there are in all eight ages, differing one from another in the lives and the characters of men, and to each of these God has allotted a certain measure of time, determined by the circuit of the great year. And when one age is run out, at the approach of another, there appears some wonderful sign from earth or heaven, such as makes it manifest at once to those who have made it their business to study such things, that there has succeeded in the world a new race of men, differing in customs and institutes of life, and more or less regarded by the gods, than the preceding. Among other great changes that happen, as they say, at the turn of ages the art of divination, *** at one time rises in esteem, and is more successful in its predictions, clearer and surer tokens being sent from God, and then again, in another generation declines as low, becoming mere guesswork for the most part, and discerning future events by dim and uncertain intimations. This was the mythology of the wisest of the Tuscan sages, who were thought to possess a knowledge beyond other men. Whilst the Senate sat in consultation with the soothsayers, concerning these prodigies, in the temple of Bellona, a sparrow came flying in, before them all, with a grasshopper in its mouth, and letting fall one part of it, flew away with the remainder. The diviners foreboded commotions and dissentions between the great landed proprietors and the common city populace; the latter, like the grasshopper, being loud and talkative; while the sparrow might represent the "dwellers in the field."

Marius had taken into alliance Sulpicius, the tribune, a man second to none in any villanies, so that it was less the question what others he surpassed, but rather in what respects he most surpassed himself in wickedness. He was cruel, bold, rapacious, and in all these points utterly shameless and unscrupulous; not hesitating to offer Roman citizenship by public sale to freed slaves and aliens, and to count out the price on public money-tables in the forum. He maintained three thousand swordsmen, and had always about him a company of young men of the equestrian class ready for all occasions, whom he styled his Anti-Senate. Having had a law enacted, that no senator should contract a debt of above two thousand drachmas, he himself, after death, was found indebted three millions. This was the man whom Marius let in upon the Commonwealth, and who, confounding all things by force and the sword, made several ordinances of dangerous consequence, and amongst the rest, one giving Marius the conduct of the Mithridatic war. Upon this the consuls proclaimed a public cessation of business, but as they were holding an assembly near the temple of Castor and Pollux, he let loose the rabble upon them, and amongst many others slew the consul Pompeius's young son in the forum, Pompeius himself hardly escaping in the crowd. Sylla, being closely pursued into the house of Marius, was forced to come forth and dissolve the cessation; and for his doing this, Sulpicius, having deposed Pompeius, allowed Sylla to continue his consulship, only transferring the Mithridatic expedition to Marius.

There were immediately despatched to Nola tribunes to receive the army, and bring it to Marius; but Sylla, having got first to the camp, and the soldiers, upon hearing the news, having stoned the tribunes, Marius, in requital, proceeded to put the friends of Sylla in the city to the sword, and rifled their goods. Every kind of removal and flight went on, some hastening from the camp to the city, others from the city to the camp. The senate, no more in its own power, but wholly governed by the dictates of Marius and Sulpicius, alarmed at the report of Sylla's advancing with his troops towards the city, sent forth two of the prætors, Brutus and Servilius, to forbid his nearer approach. The soldiers would have slain these prætors in a fury, for their bold language to Sylla; contenting themselves, however, with breaking their rods, and tearing off their purple-edged robes, after much contumelious usage they sent them back, to the sad dejection of the citizens, who beheld their magistrates despoiled of their badges of office, and announcing to them, that things were now manifestly come to a rupture past all cure. Marius put himself in readiness, and Sylla with his colleague moved from Nola, at the head of six complete legions, all of them willing to march up directly against the city, though he himself as yet was doubtful in thought, and apprehensive of the danger. As he was sacrificing, Postumius the soothsayer, having inspected the entrails, stretching forth both hands to Sylla, required to be bound and kept in custody till the battle was over, as willing, if they had not speedy and complete success, to suffer the utmost punishment. It is said, also, that there appeared to Sylla himself in a dream, a certain goddess, whom the Romans learnt to worship from the Cappadocians, whether it be the Moon, or Pallas, or Bellona. This same goddess, to his thinking, stood by him, and put into his hand thunder and lightning, then naming his enemies one by one, bade him strike them, who, all of them, fell on the discharge and disappeared. Encouraged by this vision, and relating it to his colleague next day he led on towards Rome. About Picinæ being met by a deputation, beseeching him not to attack at once, in the heat of a march, for that the senate had decreed to do him all the right imaginable, he consented to halt on the spot, and sent his officers to measure out the ground, as is usual, for a camp; so that the deputation, believing it, returned. They were no sooner gone, but he sent a party on under the command of Lucius Basillus and Caius Mummius, to secure the city gate, and the walls on the side of the Esquiline hill and then close at their heels followed himself with all speed. Basillus made his way successfully into the city, but the unarmed multitude, pelting him with stones and tiles from off the houses, stopped his further progress, and beat him back to the wall. Sylla by this time was come up, and seeing what was going on, called aloud to his men to set fire to the houses, and taking a flaming torch, he himself led the way, and commanded the archers to make use of their fire-darts, letting fly at the tops of houses; all which he did, not upon any plan, but simply in his fury, yielding the conduct of that day's work to passion, and as if all he saw were enemies without respect or pity either to friends, relations, or acquaintance, made his entry by fire, which knows no distinction betwixt friend or foe.

In this conflict, Marius, being driven into the temple of Mother-Earth, thence invited the slaves by proclamation of freedom, but the enemy coming on he was overpowered and fled the city.

Sylla having called a senate, had sentence of death passed on Marius, and some few others, amongst whom was Sulpicius tribune of the people. Sulpicius was killed, being betrayed by his servant, whom Sylla first made free, and then threw him headlong down the Tarpeian rock. As for Marius, he set a price on his life, by proclamation, neither gratefully nor politically, if we consider into whose house, not long before, he put himself at mercy, and was safely dismissed. Had Marius at that time not let Sylla go, but suffered him to be slain by the hands of Sulpicius, he might have been lord of all; nevertheless he spared his life, and a few days after, when in a similar position himself, received a different measure.

By these proceedings, Sylla excited the secret distaste of the senate; but the displeasure and free indignation of the commonalty showed itself plainly by their actions. For they ignominiously rejected Nonius, his nephew, and Servius, who stood for offices of state by his interest, and elected others as magistrates, by honoring whom they thought they should most annoy him. He made semblance of extreme satisfaction at all this, as if the people by his means had again enjoyed the liberty of doing what seemed best to them. And to pacify the public hostility, he created Lucius Cinna consul, one of the adverse party, having first bound him under oaths and imprecations to be favorable to his interest. For Cinna, ascending the capitol with a stone in his hand, swore solemnly, and prayed with direful curses, that he himself, if he were not true to his friendship with Sylla, might be cast out of the city, as that stone out of his hand; and thereupon cast the stone to the ground. ir the presence of many people. Nevertheless

Cinna had no sooner entered on his charge, but he took measures to disturb the present settlement, having prepared an impeachment against Sylla, got Virginius, one of the tribunes of the people, to be his accuser; but Sylla, leaving him and the court of judicature to themselves, set forth against Mithridates.

About the time that Sylla was making ready to put off with his force from Italy, besides many other omens which befell Mithridates, then staying at Pergamus, there goes a story that a figure of Victory, with a crown in her hand, which the Pergamenians by machinery from above let down on him, when it had almost reached his head, fell to pieces, and the crown tumbling down into the midst of the theatre, there broke against the ground, occasioning a general alarm among the populace, and considerably disquieting Mithridates himself, although his affairs at that time were succeeding beyond expectation. For having wrested Asia from the Romans, and Bithynia and Cappadocia from their kings, he made Pergamus his royal seat, distributing among his friends riches, principalities, and kingdoms. Of his sons, one residing in Pontus and Bosporus held his ancient realm as far as the deserts beyond the lake Mæotis, without molestation; while Ariarathes, another, was reducing Thrace and Macedon, with a great army, to obedience. His generals, with forces under them, were establishing his supremacy in other quarters. Archelaus, in particular, with his fleet, held absolute mastery of the sea, and was bringing into subjection the Cyclades, and all the other islands as far as Malea, and had taken Eubœa itself. Making Athens his head-quarters, from thence as far as Thessaly he was withdrawing the States of Greece from the Roman allegiance, without the least ill success, except at Chæronea. For here Bruttius Sura, lieutenant to Sentius, governor of Macedon, a man of singular valor and prudence, met him, and, though he came like a torrent pouring over Bœotia, made stout resistance, and thrice giving him battle near Chæronea, repulsed and forced him back to the sea. But being commanded by Lucius Lucullus to give place to his successor, Sylla, and resign the war to whom it was decreed, he presently left Bœotia, and retired back to Sentius, although his success had outgone all hopes, and Greece was well disposed to a new revolution, upon account of his gallant behavior. These were the glorious actions of Bruttius.

Sylla, on his arrival, received by their deputations the compliments of all the cities of Greece, except Athens, against which, as it was compelled by the tyrant Aristion to hold for the king, he advanced with all his forces, and investing the Piræus, laid formal siege to it, employing every variety of engines, and trying every manner of assault; whereas, had he foreborne but a little while, he might without hazard have taken the Upper City by famine, it being already reduced to the last extremity through want of necessaries. But eager to return to Rome, and fearing innovation there, at great risk, with continual fighting and vast expense, he pushed on the war. Besides other equipage, the very work about the engines of battery was supplied with no less than ten thousand yoke of mules, employed daily in that service. And when timber grew scarce, for many of the works failed, some crushed to pieces by their own weight, others taking fire by the continual play of the enemy, he had recourse to the sacred groves, and cut down the trees of the Academy, the shadiest of all the suburbs, and the Lyceum. And a vast sum of money being wanted to carry on the war, he broke into the sanctuaries of Greece, that of Epidaurus and that of Olympia, sending for the most beautiful and precious offerings deposited there. He wrote, likewise, to the Amphictyons at Delphi, that it were better to remit the wealth of the god to him, for that he would keep it more securely or in case he made use of it, restore as much. He sent Caphis, the Phocian, one of his friends, with this message, commanding him to receive each item by weight. Caphis came to Delphi, but was loth to touch the holy things, and with many tears, in the presence of the Amphyctyons, bewailed the necessity. And on some of them declaring they heard the sound of a harp from the inner shrine, he, whether he himself believed it, or was willing to try the effect of religious fear upon Sylla, sent back an express. To which Sylla replied in a scoffing way, that it was surprising to him that Caphis did not know that music was a sign of joy, not anger; he should, therefore, go on boldly, and accept what a gracious and bountiful god offered.

Other things were sent away without much notice on the part of the Greeks in general, but in the case of the silver tun, that only relic of the regal donations, which its weight and bulk made it impossible for any carriage to receive, the Amphictyons were forced to cut it into pieces, and called to mind in so doing, how Titus Flamininus and Manius Acilius, and again Paulus Æmilius, one of whom drove Antiochus out of Greece, and the others subdued the Macedonian kings, had not only abstained from violating the Greek temples, but had even given them new gifts and honors, and increased the general veneration for them. They, indeed, the lawful commanders of temperate and obedient soldiers, and themselves great in soul, and simple in expenses, lived within the bounds of the ordinary established charges, accounting it a greater disgrace to seek popularity with their men, than to feel fear of their enemy. Whereas the commanders of these times, attaining to superiority by force, not worth, and having need of arms one against another, rather than against the public enemy, were constrained to temporize in authority, and in order to pay for the gratifications with which they purchased the labor of their soldiers, were driven, before they knew it, to sell the commonwealth itself, and, to gain the mastery over men better than themselves, were content to become slaves to the vilest of wretches. These practices drove Marius into exile, and again brought him in against Sylla. These made Cinna the assassin of Octavius, and Fimbria of Flaccus. To which courses Sylla contributed not the least; for to corrupt and win over those who were under the command of others, he would be munificent and profuse towards those who were under his own; and so, while tempting the soldiers of other generals to treachery, and his own to dissolute living, he was naturally in want of a large treasury, and especially during that siege.

Sylla had a vehement and an implacable desire to conquer Athens, whether out of emulation, fighting as it were against the shadow of the once famous city, or out of anger, at the foul words and scurrilous jests with which the tyrant Aristion, showing himself daily, with unseemly gesticulations, upon the walls, had provoked him and Metella.

The tyrant Aristion had his very being compounded of wantonness and cruelty, having gathered into himself all the worst of Mithridates's diseased and vicious qualities, like some fatal malady which the city, after its deliverance from innumerable wars, many tyrannies and seditions, was in its last days destined to endure. At the time when a medimnus of wheat was sold in the city for one thousand drachmas, and men were forced to live on the feverfew growing round the citadel, and to boil down shoes and oil-bags for their food, he, carousing and feasting in the open face of day, then dancing in armor, and making jokes at the enemy, suffered the holy lamp of the goddess to expire for want of oil, and to the chief priestess, who demanded of him the twelfth part of a medimnus of wheat, he sent the like quantity of pepper. The senators and priests, who came as suppliants to beg of him to take compassion on the city, and treat for peace with Sylla, he drove away and dispersed with a flight of arrows. At last with much ado, he sent forth two or three of his revelling companions to parley, to whom Sylla, perceiving that they made no serious overtures towards an accommodation, but went on haranguing in praise of Theseus, Eumolpus, and the Median trophies, replied, "My good friends, you may put up your speeches and be gone. I was sent by the Romans to Athens, not to take lessons, but to reduce rebels to obedience."

In the mean time news came to Sylla that some old men, talking in the Ceramicus, had been overheard to blame the tyrant for not securing the passages and approaches near the Heptachalcum, the one point where the enemy might easily get over. Sylla neglected not the report, but going in the night, and discovering the place to be assailable, set instantly to work. Sylla himself makes mention in his Memoirs, that Marcus Teius, the first man who scaled the wall, meeting with an adversary, and striking him on the headpiece a home stroke, broke his own sword, but, notwithstanding, did not give ground, but stood and held him fast. The city was certainly taken from that quarter, according to the tradition of the oldest of the Athenians.

When they had thrown down the wall, and made all level betwixt the Piraic and Sacred Gate, about midnight Sylla entered the breach, with all the terrors of trumpets and cornets sounding, with the triumphant shout and cry of an army let loose to spoil and slaughter, and scouring through the streets with swords drawn. There was no numbering the slain; the amount is to this day conjectured only from the space of ground overflowed with blood. For without mentioning the execution done in other quarters of the city, the blood that was shed about the market-place spread over the whole Ceramicus within the Double-gate, and, according to most writers, passed through the gate and overflowed the suburb. Nor did the multitudes which fell thus exceed the number of those, who, out of pity and love for their country, which they believed was now finally to perish, slew themselves; the best of them, through despair of their country's surviving, dreading themselves to survive, expecting neither humanity nor moderation in Sylla. At length, partly at the instance of Midias and Calliphon, two exiled men, beseeching and casting themselves at his feet, partly by the intercession of those senators who followed the camp, having had his fill of revenge, and making some honorable mention of the ancient Athenians, "I forgive," said he, "the many for the sake of the few, the living for the dead." He took Athens, according to his own Memoirs, on the calends of March, coinciding pretty nearly with the new moon of Anthesterion, on which day it is the Athenian usage to perform various acts in commemoration of the ruins and devastations occasioned by the deluge, that being supposed to be the time of its occurrence.

At the taking of the town, the tyrant fled into the citadel, and was there besieged by Curio, who had that charge given him. He held out a considerable time, but at last yielded himself up for want of water, and divine power immediately intimated its agency in the matter. For on the same day and hour that Curio conducted him down, the clouds gathered in a clear sky, and there came down a great quantity of rain and filled the citadel with water.

Not long after, Sylla won the Piræus, and burnt most of it; amongst the rest, Philo's arsenal, a work very greatly admired.

In the mean time Taxiles, Mithridates's general, coming down from Thrace and Macedon, with an army of one hundred thousand foot, ten thousand horse, and ninety chariots, armed with scythes at the wheels, would have joined Archelaus, who lay with a navy on the coast near Munychia, reluctant to quit the sea, and yet unwilling to engage the Romans in battle, but desiring to protract the war and cut off the enemy's supplies. Which Sylla perceiving much better than himself, passed with his forces into Bœotia, quitting a barren district which was inadequate to maintain an army even in time of peace. He was thought by some to have taken false measures in thus leaving Attica, a rugged country, and ill suited for cavalry to move in, and entering the plain and open fields of Bœotia, knowing as he did the barbarian strength to consist most in horses and chariots. But as was said before, to avoid famine and scarcity, he was forced to run the risk of a battle. Moreover he was in anxiety for Hortensius, a bold and active officer, whom on his way to Sylla with forces from Thessaly, the barbarians awaited in the straits. For these reasons Sylla drew off into Bœotia. Hortensius, meantime, was conducted by Caphis, our countryman, another way unknown to the barbarians, by Parnassus, just under Tithora, which was then not so large a town as it is now, but a mere fort, surrounded by steep precipices,

whither the Phocians also, in old time, when flying from the
invasion of Xerxes, carried themselves and their goods and
were saved. Hortensius, encamping here, kept off the enemy by day, and at night descending by difficult passages to
Patronis, joined the forces of Sylla, who came to meet him
Thus united they posted themselves on a fertile hill in the
middle of the plain of Elatea, shaded with trees and watered
at the foot. It is called Philobœotus, and its situation and
natural advantages are spoken of with great admiration by
Sylla.

As they lay thus encamped, they seemed to the enemy a
contemptible number, for there were not above fifteen hundred
horse, and less than fifteen thousand foot. Therefore the rest of
the commanders, overpersuading Archelaus, and drawing up
the army, covered the plain with horses, chariots, bucklers, targets. The clamor and cries of so many nations forming for
battle rent the air, nor was the pomp and ostentation of their
costly array altogether idle and unserviceable for terror; for
the brightness of their armor, embellished magnificently with
gold and silver, and the rich colors of their Median and
Scythian coats, intermixed with brass and shining steel, presented a flaming and terrible sight as they swayed about and
moved in their ranks, so much so that the Romans shrunk
within their trenches, and Sylla, unable by any arguments to
remove their fear, and unwilling to force them to fight against
their wills, was fain to sit down in quiet, ill-brooking to become the subject of barbarian insolence and laughter. This,
however, above all advantaged him, for the enemy, from contemning of him, fell into disorder amongst themselves, being
already less thoroughly under command, on account of the
number of their leaders. Some few of them remained within
the encampment, but others, the major part, lured out with
hopes of prey and rapine, strayed about the country many
days' journey from the camp, and are related to have destroyed the city of Panope, to have plundered Lebadea, and
robbed the oracle without any orders from their commanders.

Sylla, all this while, chafing and fretting to see the cities
all around destroyed, suffered not the soldiery to remain idle,
but leading them out, compelled them to divert the Cephisus
from its ancient channel by casting up ditches, and giving
respite to none, showed himself rigorous in punishing the
remiss, that, growing weary of labor, they might be induced
by hardship to embrace danger. Which fell out acccordingly,
for on the third day, being hard at work as Sylla passed by

they begged and clamored to be led against the enemy. Sylla replied, that this demand of war proceeded rather from a backwardness to labor than any forwardness to fight, but if they were in good earnest martially inclined, he bade them take their arms and get up thither, pointing to the ancient citadel of the Parapotamians, of which at present, the city being laid waste, there remained only the rocky hill itself, steep and craggy on all sides, and severed from Mount Hedylium by the breadth of the river Assus, which, running between, and at the bottom of the same hill falling into the Cephisus with an impetuous confluence, makes this eminence a strong position for soldiers to occupy. Observing that the enemy's division, called the Brazen Shields, were making their way up thither, Sylla was willing to take first possession, and by the vigorous efforts of the soldiers, succeeded Archelaus, driven from hence, bent his forces upon Chæronea The Chæroneans who bore arms in the Roman camp beseeching Sylla not to abandon the city, he despatched Gabinius, a tribune, with one legion, and sent out also the Chæroneans, who endeavored, but were not able to get in before Gabinius; so active was he, and more zealous to bring relief than those who had entreated it. Juba writes that Ericius was the man sent, not Gabinius. Thus narrowly did our native city escape.

From Lebadea and the cave of Trophonius there came favorable rumors and prophecies of victory to the Romans, of which the inhabitants of those places give a fuller account, but as Sylla himself affirms in the tenth book of his Memoirs, Quintus Titius, a man of some repute among the Romans who were engaged in mercantile business in Greece, came to him after the battle won at Chæronea, and declared that Trophonius had foretold another fight and victory on the place, within a short time. After him a soldier, by name Salvenius, brought an account from the god of the future issue of affairs in Italy. As to the vision, they both agreed in this, that they had seen one who in stature and in majesty was similar to Jupiter Olympius.

Sylla, when he had passed over the Assus, marching under the Mount Hedylium, encamped close to Archelaus, who had intrenched himself strongly between the mountains Acontium and Hedylium, close to what are called the Assia. The place of his intrenchment is to this day named from him, Archelaus. Sylla, after one day's respite, having left Murena behind him with one legion and two cohorts to amuse the enemy with continual alarms, himself went and sacrificed on the banks of Cephisus, and the holy rites ended, held on towards Chæronea to receive the forces there and view Mount Thurium, where a party of the enemy had posted themselves. This is a craggy height running up in a conical form to a point, called by us Orthopagus ; at the foot of it is the river Morius and the temple of Apollo Thurius. The god had his surname from Thuro, mother of Chæron, whom ancient record makes founder of Chæronea. Others assert that the cow, which Apollo gave to Cadmus for a guide, appeared there, and that the place took its name from the beast, Thor being the Phœnician word for cow.

At Sylla's approach to Chæronea, the tribune who had been appointed to guard the city led out his men in arms, and met him with a garland of laurel in his hand ; which Sylla accepting, and at the same time saluting the soldiers and animating them to the encounter, two men of Chæronea, Homoloichus and Anaxidamus, presented themselves before him, and offered, with a small party, to dislodge those who were posted on Thurium. For there lay a path out of sight of the barbarians, from what is called Petrochus along by the Museum, leading right down from above upon Thurium. By this way it was easy to fall upon them and either stone them from above or force them down into the plain. Sylla, assured of their faith and courage by Gabinius, bade them proceed with the enterprise, and meantime drew up the army, and disposing the cavalry on both wings, himself took command of the right ; the left being committed to the direction of Murena. In the rear of all, Galba and Hortensius, his lieutenants, planted themselves on the upper grounds with the cohorts of reserve, to watch the motions of the enemy, who with numbers of horse and swift-footed, light-armed infantry, were noticed to have so formed their wing as to allow it readily to change about and alter its position, and thus gave reason for suspecting that they intended to carry it far out and so to inclose the Romans.

In the mean while, the Chæroneans, who had Ericius for commander by appointment of Sylla, covertly making their way around Thurium, and then discovering themselves, occasioned a great confusion and rout among the barbarians, and slaughter, for the most part, by their own hands. For they kept not their place, but making down the steep descent, ran themselves on their own spears, and violently sent each other over the cliffs, the enemy from above pressing on and wounding them where they exposed their bodies; insomuch that there fell three thousand about Thurium. Some of those who escaped, being met by Murena as he stood in array, were cut off and destroyed. Others breaking through to their friends and falling pell-mell into the ranks, filled most part of the army with fear and tumult, and caused a hesitation and delay among the generals, which was no small disadvantage. For immediately upon the discomposure, Sylla coming full speed to the charge, and quickly crossing the interval between the armies, lost them the service of their armed chariots, which require a considerable space of ground to gather strength and impetuosity in their career, a short course being weak and ineffectual, like that of missiles without a full swing. Thus it fared with the barbarians at present, whose first chariots came feebly on and made but a faint impression; the Romans repulsing them with shouts and laughter, called out, as they do at the races in the circus, for more to come. By this time the mass of both armies met; the barbarians on one side fixed their long pikes, and with their shields locked close together, strove so far as in them lay to preserve their line of battle entire. The Romans, on the other side, having discharged their javelins, rushed on with their drawn swords, and struggled to put by the pikes to get at them the sooner, in the fury that possessed them at seeing in the front of the enemy fifteen thousand slaves, whom the royal commanders had set free by proclamation, and ranged amongst the men of arms. And a Roman centurion is reported to have said at this sight, that he never knew servants allowed to play the masters, unless at the Saturnalia. These men, by their deep and solid array, as well as by their daring courage, yielded but slowly to the legions, till at last by slinging engines, and darts, which the Romans poured in upon them behind, they were forced to give way and scatter.

As Archelaus was extending the right wing to encompass the enemy, Hortensius with his cohorts came down in force, with intention to charge him in the flank. But Archelaus wheeling about suddenly with two thousand horse, Hortensius, outnumbered and hard pressed, fell back towards the higher grounds, and found himself gradually getting separated from the main body and likely to be surrounded by the enemy. When Sylla heard this, he came rapidly up to his succor from the right wing, which as yet had not engaged. But Archelaus, guessing the matter by the dust of his troops, turned to the right wing, from whence Sylla came, in hopes to surprise it without a commander. At the same instant, likewise, Taxiles, with his Brazen Shields, assailed Murena, so that a cry coming from both places, and the hills repeating it around, Sylla stood in suspense which way to move. Deciding to resume his own station, he sent in aid to Murena four cohorts under Hortensius, and commanding the fifth to follow him, returned hastily to the right wing, which of itself held its ground on equal terms against Archelaus; and, at his appearance, with one bold effort forced them back, and, obtaining the mastery, followed them, flying in disorder to the river and Mount Acontium. Sylla, however, did not forget the danger Murena was in; but hasting thither and finding him victorious also, then joined in the pursuit. Many barbarians were slain in the field, many more were cut in pieces as they were making into the camp. Of all the vast multitude, ten thousand only got safe into Chalcis. Sylla writes that there were but fourteen of his soldiers missing, and that two of these returned towards evening; he, therefore, inscribed on the trophies the names of Mars, Victory, and Venus, as having won the day no less by good fortune than by management and force of arms. This trophy of the battle in the plain stands on the place where Archelaus first gave way, near the stream of the Molus; another is erected high on the top of Thurium, where the barbarians were environed, with an inscription in Greek, recording that the glory of the day belonged to Homoloichus and Anaxidamus. Sylla celebrated his victory at Thebes with spectacles, for which he erected a stage, near Œdipus's well. The judges of the performances were Greeks chosen out of other cities; his hostility to the Thebans being implacable, half of whose territory he took away and consecrated to Apollo and Jupiter, ordering that out of the revenue compensation should be made to the gods for the riches himself had taken from them.

After this, hearing that Flaccus, a man of the contrary faction, had been chosen consul, and was crossing the Ionian Sea with an army, professedly to act against Mithridates, but in reality against himself, he hastened towards Thessaly, designing to meet him, but in his march, when near Melitea, received advices from all parts that the countries behind him were overrun and ravaged by no less a royal army than the former. For Dorylaus, arriving at Chalcis with a large fleet, on board of which he brought over with him eighty thousand of the best appointed and best disciplined soldiers of Mithridates's army, at once invaded Bœotia, and occupied the country in hopes to bring Sylla to a battle, making no account of the dissuasions of Archelaus, but giving it out as to the last fight, that without treachery so many thousand men could never have perished. Sylla, however, facing about expeditiously, made it clear to him that Archelaus was a wise man, and had good skill in the Roman valor ; insomuch that he himself, after some small skirmishes with Sylla near Tilphossium, was the first of those who thought it not advisable to put things to the decision of the sword, but rather to wear out the war by expense of time and treasure. The ground, however, near Orchomenus, where they then lay encamped, gave some encouragement to Archelaus, being a battle field admirably suited for an army superior in cavalry. Of all the plains in Bœotia that are renowned for their beauty and extent, this alone, which commences from the city of Orchomenus, spreads out unbroken and clear of trees to the edge of the fens in which the Melas, rising close under Orchomenus, loses itself, the only Greek river which is a deep and navigable water from the very head, increasing also about the summer solstice like the Nile, and producing plants similar to those that grow there, only small and without fruit. It does not run far before the main stream disappears among the blind and woody marsh-grounds ; a small branch, however, joins the Cephisus, about the place where the lake is thought to produce the best flute-reeds.

Now that both armies were posted near each other, Archelaus lay still, but Sylla employed himself in cutting ditches from either side ; that if possible, by driving the enemies from the firm and open champaign, he might force them into the fens. They, on the other hand, not enduring this, as soon as their leaders allowed them the word of command, issued out furiously in large bodies ; when not only the men at work were dispersed, but most part of those who stood in arms to protect the work fled in disorder. Upon this, Sylla leaped from his horse, and snatching hold of an ensign, rushed through the midst of the rout upon the enemy, crying out aloud, " To me, O Romans, it will be glorious to fall here. As for you, when they ask you where you betrayed your general, remember and say, at Orchomenus." His men rallying again at these words, and two cohorts coming to his succor from the right wing, he led them to the charge and turned the day. Then retiring some short distance and refreshing his men, he proceeded again with his works to block up the enemy's camp. They again sallied out in better order than before. Here Diogenes, step-son to Archelaus, fighting on the right wing with much gallantry, made an honorable end. And the archers, being hard pressed by the Romans, and wanting space for a retreat, took their arrows by handfuls, and striking with these as with swords, beat them back. In the end, however, they were all driven into the intrenchment and had a sorrowful night of it with their slain and wounded. The next day again, Sylla, leading forth his men up to their quarters, went on finishing the lines of intrenchment, and when they issued out again with larger numbers to give him battle, fell on them and put them to the rout, and in the consternation ensuing, none daring to abide, he took the camp by storm. The marshes were filled with blood, and the lake with dead bodies, insomuch that to this day many bows, helmets, fragments of iron, breastplates, and swords of barbarian make, continue to be found buried deep in mud, two hundred years after the fight. Thus much of the actions of Chæronea and Orchomenus.

At Rome, Cinna and Carbo were now using injustice and violence towards persons of the greatest eminence, and many of them to avoid this tyranny repaired, as to a safe harbor, to Sylla's camp, where, in a short space, he had about him the aspect of a senate. Metella, likewise, having with difficulty conveyed himself and children away by stealth, brought him word that his houses, both in town and country, had been burnt by his enemies, and entreated his help at home. Whilst he was in doubt what to do, being impatient to hear of his country being thus outraged, and yet not knowing how to leave so great a work as the Mithridatic war unfinished, there comes to him Archelaus, a merchant of Delos, with hopes of an accommodation, and private instructions from Archelaus, the king's general. Sylla liked the business so well as to desire a speedy conference with Archelaus in person, and a meeting took place on the sea-coast near Delium, where the temple of Apollo stands. When Archelaus opened the conversation, and began to urge Sylla to abandon his pretensions to Asia and Pontus, and to set sail for the war in Rome, receiving money and shipping, and such forces as he should think fitting from the king, Sylla, interposing, bade Archelaus take no further care for Mithridates, but assume the crown to himself, and become a confederate of Rome, delivering up the navy. Archelaus professing his abhorrence of such treason, Sylla proceeded: "So you, Archelaus, a Cappadocian, and slave, or if it so please you friend, to a barbarian king, would not, upon such vast considerations, be guilty of what is dishonorable, and yet dare to talk to me, Roman general and Sylla, of treason ? as if you were not the selfsame Archelaus who ran away at Chæronea, with few remaining out of one hundred and twenty thousand men ; who lay for two days in the fens of Orchomenus, and left Bœotia impassable for heaps of dead carcasses." Archelaus, changing his tone at this, humbly besought him to lay aside the thoughts of war, and make peace with Mithridates. Sylla consenting to this request, articles of agreement were concluded on. That Mithridates should quit Asia and Paphlagonia, restore Bithynia to Nicomedes, Cappadocia to Ariobarzanes, and pay the Romans two thousand talents, and give him seventy ships of war with all their furniture. On the other hand, that Sylla should confirm to him his other dominions, and declare him a Roman confederate. On these terms he proceeded by the way of Thessaly and Macedon towards the Hellespont, having Archelaus with him, and treating him with great attention. For Archelaus being taken dangerously ill at Larissa, he stopped the march of the army, and took care of him, as if he had been one of his own captains, or his colleague in command. This gave suspicion of foul play in the battle of Chæronea ; as it was also observed that Sylla had released all the friends of Mithridates taken prisoners in war, except only Aristion the tyrant, who was at enmity with Archelaus, and was put to death by poison ; and, above all, ten thousand acres of land in Eubœa had been given to the Cappadocian, and he had received from Sylla the style of friend and ally of the Romans. On all which points Sylla defends himself in his Memoirs.

The ambassadors of Mithridates arriving and declaring that they accepted of the conditions, only Paphlagonia they could not part with ; and as for the ships, professing not to know of any such capitulation, Sylla in a rage exclaimed "What say you ? Does Mithridates then withhold Paphlagonia ? and as to the ships, deny that article ? I thought to have seen him prostrate at my feet to thank me for leaving him so much as that right hand of his, which has cut off so many Romans. He will shortly, at my coming over into Asia, speak another language ; in the mean time, let him at his ease in Pergamus sit managing a war which he never saw." The ambassadors in terror stood silent by, but Archelaus endeavored with humble supplications to assuage his wrath, laying hold on his right hand and weeping. In conclusion he obtained permission to go himself in person to Mithridates; for that he would either mediate a peace to the satisfaction of Sylla, or if not, slay himself. Sylla having thus despatched him away, made an inroad into Mædica, and after wide depopulations returned back again into Macedon, where he received Archelaus about Philippi, bringing word that all was well, and that Mithridates earnestly requested an interview. The chief cause of this meeting was Fimbria; for he, having assassinated Flaccus, the consul of the contrary faction, and worsted the Mithridatic commanders, was advancing against Mithridates himself, who, fearing this, chose rather to seek the friendship of Sylla.

And so met at Dardanus in the Troad, on one side Mithridates, attended with two hundred ships, and land forces consisting of twenty thousand men at arms, six thousand horse, and a large train of scythed chariots; on the other, Sylla with only four cohorts, and two hundred horse. As Mithridates drew near and put out his hand, Sylla demanded whether he was willing or no to end the war on the terms Archelaus had agreed to, but seeing the king made no answer, "How is this?" he continued, "ought not the petitioner to speak first, and the conqueror to listen in silence?" And when Mithridates, entering upon his plea, began to shift off the war, partly on the gods, and partly to blame the Romans themselves, he took him up, saying that he had heard, indeed, long since from others, and now he knew it himself for truth, that Mithridates was a powerful speaker, who in defence of the most foul and unjust proceedings, had not wanted for specious pretences. Then charging him with and inveighing bitterly against the outrages he had committed, he asked again whether he was willing or no to ratify the treaty of Archelaus? Mithridates answering in the affirmative, Sylla came forward, embraced and kissed him. Not long after he introduced Ariobarzanes and Nicomedes, the two kings, and made them friends. Mithridates, when he had handed over to Sylla seventy ships and five hundred archers, set sail for Pontus.

Sylla, perceiving the soldiers to be dissatisfied with the peace (as it seemed indeed a monstrous thing that they should see the king who was their bitterest enemy, and who had caused one hundred and fifty thousand Romans to be massacred in one day in Asia, now sailing off with the riches and spoils of Asia, which he had pillaged, and put under contribu tion for the space of four years), in his defence to them alleged, that he could not have made head against Fimbria and Mithridates, had they both withstood him in conjunction. Thence he set out and went in search of Fimbria, who lay with the army about Thyatira, and pitching his camp not far off, proceeded to fortify it with a trench. The soldiers of Fimbria came out in their single coats, and saluting his men, lent ready assistance to the work; which change Fimbria beholding, and apprehending Sylla as irreconcilable, laid violent hands on himself in the camp.

Sylla imposed on Asia in general a tax of twenty thousand talents, and despoiled individually each family by the licentious behavior and long residence of the soldiery in private quarters. For he ordained that every host should allow his guest four tetradrachms each day, and moreover entertain him, and as many friends as he should invite, with a supper; that a centurion should receive fifty drachmas a day, together with one suit of clothes to wear within doors, and another when he went abroad.

Having set out from Ephesus with the whole navy, he came the third day to anchor in the Piræus. Here he was initiated in the mysteries, and seized for his use the library of Apellicon the Teian, in which were most of the works of Theophrastus and Aristotle, then not in general circulation. When the whole was afterwards conveyed to Rome, there, it is said, the greater part of the collection passed through the hands of Tyrannion the grammarian, and that Andronicus the Rhodian, having through his means the command of numerous copies, made the treatises public, and drew up the catalogues that are now current. The elder Peripatetics appear themselves, indeed, to have been accomplished and learned men, but of the writings of Aristotle and Theophratus they had no large or exact knowledge, because Theophrastus bequeathing his books to the heir of Neleus of Scepsis, they came into careless and illiterate hands.

During Sylla's stay about Athens, his feet were attacked by a heavy benumbing pain, which Strabo calls the first inarticulate sounds of the gout. Taking, therefore, a voyage to Ædepsus, he made use of the hot waters there, allowing himself at the same time to forget all anxieties, and passing away his time with actors. As he was walking along the sea-shore, certain fishermen brought him some magnificent fish. Being much delighted with the gift, and understanding, on inquiry, that they were men of Halææ, "What," said he, "are there any men of Halææ surviving?" For after his victory at Orchomenus, in the heat of a pursuit, he had destroyed three cities of Bœotia, Anthedon, Larymna, and Halææ. The men not knowing what to say for fear, Sylla, with a smile bade them cheer up and return in peace, as they had brought with them no insignificant intercessors. The Halæans say that this first gave them courage to reunite and return to their city.

Sylla, having marched through Thessaly and Macedon to the sea-coast, prepared, with twelve hundred vessels, to cross over from Dyrrhachium to Brundisium. Not far from hence is Apollonia, and near it the Nymphæum, a spot of ground where, from among green trees and meadows, there are found at various points springs of fire continually streaming out. Here, they say, a satyr, such as statuaries and painters represent, was caught asleep, and brought before Sylla, where he was asked by several interpreters who he was, and, after much trouble, at last uttered nothing intelligible, but a harsh noise, something between the neighing of a horse and crying of a goat. Sylla, in dismay, and deprecating such an omen, bade it be removed.

At the point of transportation, Sylla being in alarm, lest at their first setting foot upon Italy, the soldiers should disband and disperse one by one among the cities, they of their own accord first took an oath to stand firm by him, and not of their good-will to injure Italy; then seeing him in distress for money, they made, so they say, a freewill offering, and contributed each man according to his ability. However Sylla would not accept of their offering, but praising their good-will, and arousing up their courage, went over (as he himself writes) against fifteen hostile generals in command of four hundred and fifty cohorts; but not without the most unmistakable divine intimations of his approaching happy successes. For when he was sacrificing at his first landing near Tarentum, the victim's liver showed the figure of a crown of laurel with two fillets hanging from it. And a little while before his arrival in Campania, near the mountain Hephæus, two stately goats were seen in the daytime, fighting together, and performing all the motions of men in battle. It proved to be an apparition, and rising up gradually from the ground, dispersed in the air, like fancied representations in the clouds, and so vanished out of sight. Not long after, in the selfsame place, when Marius the younger, and Norbanus the consul, attacked him with two great armies, without prescribing the order of battle, or arranging his men according to their divisions, by the sway only of one common alacrity and transport of courage, he overthrew the enemy, and shut up Norbanus into the city of Capua, with the loss of seven thousand of his men. And this was the reason, he says, that the soldiers did not leave him and disperse into the different towns, but held fast to him, and despised the enemy, though infinitely more in number.

At Silvium (as he himself relates it), there met him a servant of Pontius, in a state of divine possession, saying that he brought him the power of the sword and victory from Bellona, the goddess of war, and if he did not make haste, that the capitol would be burnt, which fell out on the same day the man foretold it, namely, on the sixth day of the month Quintilis, which we now call July.

At Fidentia, also, Marcus Lucullus, one of Sylla's commanders, reposed such confidence in the forwardness of the soldiers, as to dare to face fifty cohorts of the enemy, with only sixteen of his own: but because many of them were unarmed, delayed the onset. As he stood thus waiting, and considering with himself, a gentle gale of wind, bearing along with it from the neighboring meadows a quantity of flowers, scattered them down upon the army, on whose shields and helmets they settled, and arranged themselves spontaneously, so as to give the soldiers, in the eyes of the enemy, the appearance of being crowned with chaplets. Upon this, being yet further animated, they joined battle, and victoriously slaying eight thousand men, took the camp. This Lucullus was brother to that Lucullus who in after-times conquered Mithridates and Tigranes.

Sylla, seeing himself still surrounded by so many armies, and such mighty hostile powers, had recourse to art, inviting Scipio, the other consul, to a treaty of peace. The motion was willingly embraced, and several meetings and consultations ensued, in all which Sylla, still interposing matter of delay and new pretences, in the meanwhile debauched Scipio's men by means of his own, who were as well practised as the general himself, in all the artifices of inveigling. For entering into the enemy's quarters and joining in conversation, they gained some by present money, some by promises, others by fair words and persuasions; so that in the end, when Sylla with twenty cohorts drew near, on his men saluting Scipio's soldiers, they returned the greeting and came over, leaving Scipio behind them in his tent, where he was found all alone and dismissed. And having used his twenty cohorts as decoys to ensnare the forty of the enemy, he led them all back into the camp. On this occasion, Carbo was heard to say that he had both a fox and a lion in the breast of Sylla to deal with, and was most troubled with the fox.

Some time after, at Signa, Marius the younger, with eighty-five cohorts, offered battle to Sylla, who was extremely desirous to have it decided on that very day; for the night before he had seen a vision in his sleep, of Marius the elder, who had been some time dead, advising his son to beware of the following day, as of fatal consequence to him. For this reason, Sylla, longing to come to a battle, sent off for Dolabella, who lay encamped at some distance. But because the enemy had beset and blocked up the passes, his soldiers got tired with skirmishing and marching at once. To these difficulties was added, moreover, tempestuous rainy weather, which distressed them most of all. The principal officers therefore came to Sylla, and besought him to defer the battle that day, showing him how the soldiers lay stretched on the ground, where they had thrown themselves down in their weariness, resting their heads upon their shields to gain some repose. When, with much reluctance, he had yielded, and given orders for pitching the camp, they had no sooner begun to cast up the rampart and draw the ditch, but Marius came riding up furiously at the head of his troops, in hopes to scatter them in that disorder and confusion. Here the gods fulfilled Sylla's dream. For the soldiers, stirred up with anger, left off their work, and sticking their javelins into the bank, with drawn swords and a courageous shout, came to blows with the enemy, who made but small resistance, and lost great numbers in the flight. Marius fled to Præneste, but finding the gates shut, tied himself round by a rope that was thrown down to him, and was taken up on the walls. Some there are (as Fenestella for one) who affirm that Marius knew nothing of the fight, but, overwatched and spent with hard duty, had reposed himself, when the signal was given, beneath some shade, and was hardly to be awakened at the flight of his men. Sylla, according to his own account, lost only twenty-three men in this fight, having killed of the enemy twenty thousand, and taken alive eight thousand.

The like success attended his lieutenants, Pompey, Crassus, Metellus, Servilius, who with little or no loss cut off vast numbers of the enemy, insomuch that Carbo, the prime supporter of the cause, fled by night from his charge of the army, and sailed over into Libya.

In the last struggle, however, the Samnite Telesinus, like some champion, whose lot it is to enter last of all into the lists and take up the wearied conqueror, came nigh to have foiled and overthrown Sylla before the gates of Rome. For Telesinus with his second, Lamponius the Lucanian, having collected a large force, had been hastening towards Præneste, to relieve Marius from the siege ; but perceiving Sylla ahead of him, and Pompey behind, both hurrying up against him, straitened thus before and behind, as a valiant and experienced soldier, he arose by night, and marching directly with his whole army, was within a little of making his way unexpectedly into Rome itself. He lay that night before the city, at ten furlongs' distance from the Colline gate, elated and full of hope, at having thus out-generalled so many eminent commanders. At break of day, being charged by the noble youth of the city, among many others he overthrew Appius Claudius, renowned for high birth and character. The city, as is easy to imagine, was all in an uproar, the women shrieking and running about, as if it had already been entered forcibly by assault, till at last Balbus, sent forward by Sylla, was seen riding up with seven hundred horse at full speed. Halting only long enough to wipe the sweat from the horses, and then hastily bridling again, he at once attacked the enemy. Presently Sylla himself appeared, and commanding those who were foremost to take immediate refreshment, proceeded to form in order for battle. Dolabella and Torquatus were extremely earnest with him to desist awhile, and not with spent forces to hazard the last hope, having before them in the field, not Carbo or Marius, but two warlike nations bearing immortal hatred to Rome, the Samnities and Lucanians, to grapple with. But he put them by, and commanded the trumpets to sound a charge, when it was now about four o'clock in the afternoon. In the conflict which followed, as sharp a one as ever was, the right wing where Crassus was posted had clearly the advantage; the left suffered and was in distress, when Sylla came to its succor, mounted on a white courser, full of mettle and exceedingly swift, which two of the enemy knowing him by, had their lances ready to throw at him ; he himself observed nothing, but his attendant behind him giving the horse a touch, he was, unknown to himself, just so far carried forward, that the points, falling beside the horse's tail, stuck in the ground. There is a story that he had a small golden image of Apollo from Delphi, which he was always wont in battle to carry about him in his bosom, and that he then kissed it with these words, ' O Apollo Pythius, who in so many battles hast raised to honor and greatness the Fortunate Cornelius Sylla, wilt thou now cast him down, bringing him before the gate of his country, to perish shamefully with his fellow-citizens?" Thus, they say, addressing himself to the god, he entreated some of his men, threatened some, and seized others with his hand, till at length the left wing being wholly shattered, he was forced, in the general rout, to betake himself to the camp, having lost many of his friends and acquaintances. Many, likewise, of the city spectators, who had come out, were killed or trodden under foot. So that it was generally believed in the city that all was lost, and the siege of Præneste was all but raised; many fugitives from the battle making their way thither, and urging Lucretius Ofella, who was appointed to keep on the siege, to rise in all haste, for that Sylla had perished, and Rome fallen into the hands of the enemy.

About midnight there came into Sylla's camp messengers from Crassus, to fetch provision for him and his soldiers; for having vanquished the enemy, they had pursued him to the walls of Antemna, and had sat down there. Sylla, hearing this, and that most of the enemy were destroyed, came to Antemna by break of day, where three thousand of the besieged having sent forth a herald, he promised to receive them to mercy, on condition they did the enemy some mischief in their coming over. Trusting to his word, they fell foul on the rest of their companions, and made a great slaughter one of another. Nevertheless, Sylla gathered together in the circus, as well these as other survivors of the party, to the number of six thousand, and just as he commenced speaking to the senate, in the temple of Bellona, proceeded to cut them down, by men appointed for that service. The cry of so vast a multitude put to the sword, in so narrow a space, was naturally heard some distance, and startled the senators. He, however, continuing his speech with a clam and unconcerned countenance, bade them listen to what he had to say, and not busy themselves with what was doing out of doors; he had given directions tor the chastisement of some offenders. This gave the most stupid of the Romans to understand, that they had merely exchanged, not escaped, tyranny. And Marius, being of a naturally harsh temper, had not altered, but merely continued what he had been, in authority; whereas Sylla, using his fortune moderately and unambitiously at first, and giving good hopes of a true patriot, firm to the interests both of the nobility and commonalty, being, moreover, of a gay and cheerful temper from his youth, and so easily moved to pity as to shed tears readily, has, perhaps deservedly, cast a blemish upon offices of great authority, as if they deranged men's former habits and character, and gave rise to violence, pride, and inhumanity. Whether this be a real change and revolution in the mind, caused by fortune, or rather a lurking viciousness of nature, discovering itself in authority, it were matter of another sort of disquisition to decide.

Sylla being thus wholly bent upon slaughter, and filling the city with executions without number or limit, many wholly uninterested persons falling a sacrifice to private enmity, through his permission and indulgence to his friends, Caius Metellus, one of the younger men, made bold in the senate to ask him what end there was of these evils, and at what point he might be expected to stop? "We do not ask you," said he, "to pardon any whom you have resolved to destroy, but to free from doubt those whom you are pleased to save." Sylla answering, that he knew not as yet whom to spare, "Why then," said he, "tell us whom you will punish." This Sylla said he would do. These last words, some authors say, were spoken not by Metellus, but by Afidius, one of Sylla's fawning companions. Immediately upon this, without communicating with any of the magistrates, Sylla proscribed eighty persons, and notwithstanding the general indignation, after one day's respite, he posted two hundred and twenty more, and on the third again, as many. In an address to the people on this occasion, he told them he had put up as many names as he could think of; those which had escaped his memory, he would publish at a future time. He issued an edict likewise, making death the punishment of humanity, proscribing any who should dare to receive and cherish a proscribed person without exception to brother, son, or parents. And to him who should slay any one proscribed person, he ordained two talents reward, even were it a slave who had killed his master, or a son his father. And what was thought most unjust of all, he caused the attainder to pass upon their sons, and son's sons, and made open sale of all their property. Nor did the proscription prevail only at Rome, but throughout all the cities of Italy the effusion of blood was such, that neither sanctuary of the gods, nor hearth of hospitality, nor ancestral home escaped. Men were butchered in the embraces of their wives, children in the arms of their mothers. Those who perished through public animosity or private enmity, were nothing in comparison of the numbers of those who suffered for their riches. Even the murderers began to say, that "his fine house killed this man, a garden that, a third, his hot baths." Quintus Aurelius, a quiet, peaceable man, and one who thought all his part in the common calamity consisted in condoling with the misfortunes of others coming into the forum to read the list, and finding himself among the proscribed, cried out, "Woe is me, my Alban farm has informed against me." He had not gone far before he was dispatched by a ruffian, sent on that errand.

In the mean time, Marius, on the point of being taken, killed himself; and Sylla, coming to Præneste, at first proceeded judicially against each particular person, till at last, finding it a work of too much time, he cooped them up together in one place, to the number of twelve thousand men, and gave order for the execution of them all, his own host alone excepted. But he, brave man, telling him he could not accept the obligation of life from the hands of one who had been the ruin of his country, went in among the rest, and submitted willingly to the stroke. What Lucius Catilina did was thought to exceed all other acts. For having, before matters came to an issue, made away with his brother, he besought Sylla to place him in the list of proscription, as though he had been alive, which was done; and Catiline, to return the kind office, assassinated a certain Marcus Marius, one of the adverse party, and brought the head to Sylla, as he was sitting in the forum, and then going to the holy water of Apollo, which was nigh, washed his hands.

There were other things, besides this bloodshed, which gave offence. For Sylla had declared himself dictator, an office which had then been laid aside for the space of one hundred and twenty years. There was, likewise, an act of grace passed on his behalf, granting indemnity for what was passed, and for the future intrusting him with the power of life and death, confiscation, division of lands, erecting and demolishing of cities, taking away of kingdoms, and bestowing them at pleasure. He conducted the sale of confiscated property after such an arbitrary, imperious way, from the tribunal, that his gifts excited greater odium even than his usurpations, women, mimes, and musicians, and the lowest of the freed slaves had presents made them of the territories of nations, and the revenues of cities: and women of rank were married against their will to some of them. Wishing to insure the fidelity of Pompey the Great, by a nearer tie of blood, he bade him divorce his present wife, and forcing Æmilia, the daughter of Scaurus and Metella, his own wife, to leave her husband, Manius Glabrio, he bestowed her, though then with child, on Pompey, and she died in childbirth at his house.

When Lucretius Ofella, the same who reduced Marius by siege, offered himself for the consulship, he first forbade him; then, seeing he could not restrain him, on his coming down into the forum with a numerous train of followers, he sent one of the centurions who were immediately about him, and slew him, himself sitting on the tribunal in the temple of Castor, and beholding the murder from above. The citizens apprehending the centurion, and dragging him to the tribunal, he bade them cease their clamoring and let the centurion go, for he had commanded it.

His triumph was, in itself, exceedingly splendid, and distinguished by the rarity and magnificence of the royal spoils; but its yet greatest glory was the noble spectacle of the exiles. For in the rear followed the most eminent and most potent of the citizens, crowned with garlands, and calling Sylla savior and father, by whose means they were restored to their own country, and again enjoyed their wives and children. When the solemnity was over, and the time come to render an account of his actions, addressing the public assembly, he was as profuse in enumerating the lucky chances of war, as any of his own military merits. And, finally, from this felicity, he requested to receive the surname of Felix. In writing and transacting business with the Greeks, he styled himself Epaphroditus, and on his trophies which are still extant with us the name is given Lucius Cornelius Sylla Epaphroditus. Moreover, when his wife had brought him forth twins, he named the male Faustus, and the female Fausta, the Roman words for what is auspicious and of happy omen. The confidence which he reposed in his good genius, rather than in any abilities of his own, emboldened him, though deeply involved in bloodshed, and though he had been the author of such great changes and revolutions of State, to lay down his authority, and place the right of consular elections once more in the hands of the people. And when they were held, he not only declined to seek that office, but in the forum exposed his person publicly to the people, walking up and down as a private man. And contrary to his will, a certain bold man and his enemy, Marcus Lepidus, was expected to become consul, not so much by his own interest, as by the power and solicitation of Pompey, whom the people were willing to oblige. When the business was over, seeing Pompey going home overjoyed with the success, he called him to him and said, "What a politic act, young man, to pass by Catulus, the best of men, and choose Lepidus, the worst! It will be well for you to be vigilant, now that you have strengthened your opponent against yourself." Sylla spoke this, it may seem, by a prophetic instinct, for, not long after, Lepidus grew insolent, and broke into open hostility to Pompey and his friends.

Sylla, consecrating the tenth of his whole substance to Hercules, entertained the people with sumptuous feastings. The provision was so much above what was necessary, that they were forced daily to throw great quantities of meat into the river, and they drank wine forty years old and upwards. In the midst of the banqueting, which lasted many days, Metella died of a disease. And because that the priest forbade him to visit the sick, or suffer his house to be polluted with mourning, he drew up an act of divorce, and caused her to be removed into another house whilst alive. Thus far, out of religious apprehension, he observed the strict rule to the very letter, but in the funeral expenses he transgressed the law he himself had made, limiting the amount, and spared no cost. He transgressed, likewise, his own sumptuary laws respecting expenditure in banquets, thinking to allay his grief by luxurious drinking parties and revellings with common buffoons.

Some few months after, at a show of gladiators, when men and women sat promiscuously in the theatre, no distinct places being as yet appointed, there sat down by Sylla a beautiful woman of high birth, by name Valeria, daughter of Messala, and sister to Hortensius the orator. Now it happened that she had been lately divorced from her husband. Passing along behind Sylla, she leaned on him with her hand, and plucking a bit of wool from his garment, so proceeded to her seat. And on Sylla looking up and wondering what it meant, "What harm, mighty Sir," said she, "if I also was desirous to partake a little in your felicity?" It appeared at once that Sylla was not displeased, but even tickled in his fancy, for he sent out to inquire her name, her birth, and past life. From this time there passed between them many side glances, each continually turning round to look at the other, and frequently interchanging smiles. In the end, overtures were made, and a marriage concluded on. All which was innocent, perhaps, on the lady's side, but, though she had been never so modest and virtuous, it was scarcely a temperate and worthy occasion of marriage on the part of Sylla, to take fire, as a boy might, at a face and a bold look, incentives not seldom to the most disorderly and shameless passions

Notwithstanding this marriage, he kept company with actresses, musicians, and dancers, drinking with them on couches night and day. His chief favorites were Roscius the comedian, Sorex the arch mime, and Metrobius the player, for whom, though past his prime, he still professed a passionate fondness. By these courses he encouraged a disease which had begun from unimportant cause; and for a long time he failed to observe that his bowels were ulcerated, till at length the corrupted flesh broke out into lice. Many were employed day and night in destroying them, but the work so multiplied under their hands, that not only his clothes, baths, basins, but his very meat was polluted with that flux and contagion, they came swarming out in such numbers. He went frequently by day into the bath to scour and cleanse his body, but all in vain; the evil generated too rapidly and too abundantly for any ablutions to overcome it. There died of this disease, amongst those of the most ancient times, Acastus, the son of Pelias; of later date, Alcman the poet, Pherecydes the theologian, Callisthenes the Olynthian, in the time of his imprisonment, as also Mucius the lawyer; and if we may mention ignoble, but notorious names, Eunus the fugitive, who stirred up the slaves of Sicily to rebel against their masters, after he was brought captive to Rome, died of this creeping sickness.

Sylla not only foresaw his end, but may be also said to have written of it. For in the two and twentieth book of his Memoirs, which he finished two days before his death, he writes that the Chaldeans foretold him, that after he had led a life of honor, he should conclude it in fulness of prosperity. He declares, moreover, that in a vision he had seen his son, who had died not long before Metella, stand by in mourning attire, and beseech his father to cast off further care, and come along with him to his mother Metella, there to live at ease and quietness with her. However, he could not refrain from intermeddling in public affairs. For, ten days before his decease, he composed the differences of the people of Dicæarchia, and prescribed laws for their better government. And the very day before his end, it being told him that the magistrate Granius deferred the payment of a public debt, in expectation of his death, he sent for him to his house, and placing his attendants about him, caused him to be strangled; but through the straining of his voice and body, the imposthume breaking, he lost a great quantity of blood. Upon this, his strength failing him, after spending a troublesome night, he died, leaving behind him two young children by Metella. Valeria was afterwards delivered of a daughter, named Posthuma ; for so the Romans call those who are born after the father's death.

Many ran tumultuously together, and joined with Lepidus, to deprive the corpse of the accustomed solemnities ; but Pompey, though offended at Sylla (for he alone of all his friends was not mentioned in his will), having kept off some by his interest and entreaty, others by menaces, conveyed the body to Rome, and gave it a secure and honorable burial. It is said that the Roman ladies contributed such vast heaps of spices, that besides what was carried on two hundred and ten litters, there was sufficient to form a large figure of Sylla himself, and another representing a lictor, out of the costly frankincense and cinnamon. The day being cloudy in the morning, they deferred carrying forth the corpse till about three in the afternoon, expecting it would rain. But a strong wind blowing full upon the funeral pile, and setting it all in a bright flame, the body was consumed so exactly in good time, that the pyre had begun to smoulder, and the fire was upon the point of expiring, when a violent rain came down, which continued till night. So that his good fortune was firm even to the last, and did as it were officiate at his funeral. His monument stands in the Campus Martius, with an epitaph of his own writing ; the substance of it being, that he had not been outdone by any of his friends in doing good turns, nor by any of his foes in doing bad.

COMPARISON OF LYSANDER WITH SYLLA.

HAVING completed this Life also, come we now to the comparison. That which was common to them both, was that they were founders of their own greatness, with this difference, that Lysander had the consent of his fellow-citizens, in times of sober judgment, for the honors he received ; nor did he force any thing from them against their good-will, **nor hold any power** contrary to the laws.

In civil strife e'en villains rise to fame.

And so then at Rome, when the people were distempered, and the government out of order, one or other was still raised to despotic power ; no wonder, then, if Sylla reigned, when the Glauciæ and Saturnini drove out the Metelli, when sons of consuls were slain in the assemblies, when silver and gold purchased men and arms, and fire and sword enacted new laws, and put down lawful opposition. Nor do I blame any one, in such circumstances, for working himself into supreme power, only I would not have it thought a sign of great goodness to be head of a State so wretchedly discomposed. Lysander, being employed in the greatest commands and affairs of State by a sober and well-governed city, may be said to have had repute as the best and most virtuous man, in the best and most virtuous commonwealth. And thus, often returning the government into the hands of the citizens, he received it again as often, the superiority of his merit still awarding him the first place. Sylla, on the other hand, when he had once made himself general of an army, kept his command for ten years together, creating himself sometimes consul, sometimes proconsul, and sometimes dictator, but always remaining a tyrant.

It is true Lysander, as was said, designed to introduce a new form of government; by milder methods, however, and more agreeably to law than Sylla, not by force of arms, but persuasion, nor by subverting the whole State at once, but simply by amending the succession of the kings; in a way, moreover, which seemed the naturally just one, that the most deserving should rule, especially in a city which itself exercised command in Greece, upon account of virtue, not nobility. For as the hunter considers the whelp itself, not the bitch, and the horse-dealer the foal, not the mare (for what if the foal should prove a mule?), so likewise were that politician extremely out, who, in the choice of a chief magistrate, should inquire, not what the man is, but how descended. The very Spartans themselves have deposed several of their kings for want of kingly virtues, as degenerated and good for nothing. As a vicious nature, though of an ancient stock, is dishonorable, it must be virtue itself, and not birth, that makes virtue honorable. Furthermore, the one committed his acts of injustice for the sake of his friends; the other extended his to his friends themselves. It is confessed on all hands, that Lysander offended most commonly for the sake of his companions, committing several slaughters to uphold their power and dominion; but as for Sylla, he, out of envy, reduced Pompey's command by land, and Dolabella's by sea, although he himself had given them those places; and ordered Lucretius Ofella, who sued for the consulship as the reward of many great services, to be slain before his eyes, exciting horror and alarm in the minds of all men, by his cruelty to his dearest friends.

As regards the pursuit of riches and pleasures, we yet further discover in one a princely, in the other a tyrannical disposition. Lysander did nothing that was intemperate or licentious, in that full command of means and opportunity, but kept clear, as much as ever man did, of that trite saying:

Lions at home, but foxes out of doors;

and ever maintained a sober, truly Spartan, and well-disciplined course of conduct. Whereas Sylla could never moderate his unruly affections, either by poverty when young, or by years when grown old, but would be still prescribing laws to the citizens concerning chastity and sobriety, himself living all that time, as Sallust affirms, in lewdness and adultery. By these ways he so impoverished and drained the city of her treasures, as to be forced to sell privileges and immunities to allied and friendly cities for money, although he daily gave up the wealthiest and the greatest families to public sale and confiscation. There was no end of his favors vainly spent and thrown away on flatterers; for what hope could there be, or what likelihood of forethought or economy, in his more private moments over wine, when, in the open face of the people, upon the auction of a large estate, which he would have passed over to one of his friends at a small price, because another bid higher, and the officer announced the advance, he broke out into a passion, saying: "What a strange and unjust thing is this, O citizens, that I cannot dispose of my own booty as I please!" But Lysander, on the contrary, with the rest of the spoil, sent home for public use even the presents which were made him. Nor do I commend him for it, for he, perhaps, by excessive liberality, did Sparta more harm than ever the other did Rome by rapine; I only use it as an argument of his indifference to riches. They exercised a strange influence on their respective cities. Sylla, a profuse debauchee, endeavored to restore sober living amongst the citizens; Lysander, temperate himself, filled Sparta with the luxury he disregarded. So that both were blameworthy, the one for raising himself above his own laws, the other for causing his fellow-citizens to fall beneath his own example. He taught Sparta to want the very things which he himself had learned to do without. And thus much of their civil administration.

As for feats of arms, wise conduct in war, innumerable victories, perilous adventures, Sylla was beyond compare. Lysander, indeed, came off twice victorious in two battles by sea; I shall add to that the siege of Athens, a work of greater fame than difficulty. What occurred in Bœotia, and at Haliartus, was the result, perhaps, of ill-fortune; yet it certainly looks like ill counsel, not to wait for the king's forces, which had all but arrived from Platæa, but out of ambition and eagerness to fight, to approach the walls at disadvantage, and so to be cut off by a sally of inconsiderable men. He received his death-wound, not as Cleombrotus, at Leuctra, resisting manfully the assault of an enemy in the field; not as Cyrus or Epaminondas, sustaining the declining battle, or making sure the victory; all these died the death of kings and generals; but he, as it had been some common skirmisher or scout, cast away his life ingloriously, giving testimony to the wisdom of the ancient Spartan maxim, to avoid attacks on walled cities, in which the stoutest warrior may chance to fall by the hand, not only of a man utterly his inferior, but by that of a boy or woman, as Achilles, they say, was slain by Paris in the gates. As for Sylla, it were hard to reckon up how many set battles he won, or how many thousand he slew; he took Rome itself twice, as also the Athenian Piræus, not by famine, as Lysander did, but by a series of great battles, driving Archelaus into the sea. And what is most important, there was a vast difference between the commanders they had to deal with. For I look upon it as an easy task or rather sport, to beat Antiochus, Alcibiades's pilot, or to circumvent Philocles, the Athenian demagogue,

Sharp only at the inglorious point of tongue,

whom Mithridates would have scorned to compare with his groom, or Marius with his lictor. But of the potentates, consuls, commanders, and demagogues, to pass by all the rest who opposed themselves to Sylla, who amongst the Romans so formidable as Marius, what king more powerful than Mithridates? who of the Italians more warlike than Lamponius and Telesinus? yet of these, one he drove into banishment, one he quelled, and the others he slew.

And what is more important, in my judgment, than any thing yet adduced, is that Lysander had the assistance of the State in all his achievements; whereas Sylla, besides that he was a banished person, and overpowered by a faction, at a time when his wife was driven from home, his houses demolished, adherents slain, himself then in Bœotia, stood embatt'ed against countless numbers of the public enemy, and, endangering himself for the sake of his country, raised a trophy of victory; and not even when Mithridates came with proposals

of alliance and aid against his enemies, would he show any
sort of compliance, or even clemency; did not so much as
address him, or vouchsafe him his hand, until he had it from
the king's own mouth, that he was willing to quit Asia, surrender the navy, and restore Bithynia and Cappadocia to
the two kings. Than which action, Sylla never performed
a braver, or with a nobler spirit, when preferring the public
good to the private, and like good hounds, where he had once
fixed, never letting go his hold, till the enemy yielded, then,
and not until then, he set himself to revenge his own private
quarrels. We may perhaps let ourselves be influenced, moreover, in our comparison of their characters, by considering
their treatment of Athens. Sylla, when he had made himself
master of the city, which then upheld the dominion and
power of Mithridates in opposition to him, restored her to
liberty and the free exercise of her own laws; Lysander, on
the contrary, when she had fallen from a vast height of dignity and rule, showed her no compassion, but abolishing her
democratic government, imposed on her the most cruel and
lawless tyrants. We are now qualified to consider whether
we should go far from the truth or no, in pronouncing that
Sylla performed the more glorious deeds, but Lysander committed the fewer faults, as, likewise, by giving to one the pre-
eminence for moderation and self-control, to the other for
conduct and valor.

CIMON.

PERIPOLTAS, the prophet, having brought the king Opheltas,
and those under his command, from Thessaly into Bœotia,
left there a family, which flourished a long time after; the
greatest part of them inhabiting Chæronea, the first city out
of which they expelled the barbarians. The descendants of
this race, being men of bold attempts and warlike habits, exposed themselves to so many dangers in the invasions of the
Mede, and in battles against the Gauls, that at last they were
almost wholly consumed.

There was left one orphan of this house, called Damon,
surnamed Peripoltas, in beauty and greatness of spirit surpassing all of his age, but rude and undisciplined in temper.
A Roman captain of a company that wintered in Chæronea

became passionately fond of this youth, who was now pretty nearly grown a man. And finding all his approaches, his gifts, his entreaties alike repulsed, he showed violent inclinations to assault Damon. Our native Chæronea was then in a distressed condition, too small and too poor to meet with anything but neglect. Damon, being sensible of this, and looking upon himself as injured already, resolved to inflict punishment. Accordingly, he and sixteen of his companions conspired against the captain; but that the design might be managed without any danger of being discovered, they all daubed their faces at night with soot. Thus disguised and inflamed with wine, they set upon him by break of day, as he was sacrificing in the market-place; and having killed him, and several others that were with him, they fled out of the city, which was extremely alarmed and troubled at the murder. The council assembled immediately, and pronounced sentence of death against Damon and his accomplices. This they did to justify the city to the Romans. But that evening, as the magistrates were at supper together, according to the custom, Damon and his confederates breaking into the hall, killed them, and then again fled out of the town. About this time, Lucius Lucullus chanced to be passing that way with a body of troops, upon some expedition, and this disaster having but recently happened, he stayed to examine the matter. Upon inquiry, he found the city was in no wise faulty, but rather that they themselves had suffered; therefore he drew out the soldiers, and carried them away with him. Yet Damon continuing to ravage the country all about, the citizens, by messages and decrees, in appearance favorable, enticed him into the city, and upon his return, made him Gymnasiarch; but afterwards as he was anointing himself in the vapor baths, they set upon him and killed him. For a long while after apparitions continuing to be seen, and groans to be heard in that place, so our fathers have told us, they ordered the gates of the baths to be built up; and even to this day those who live in the neighborhood believe that they sometimes see spectres, and hear alarming sounds. The posterity of Damon, of whom some still remain, mostly in Phocis, near the town of Stiris, are called Asbolomeni, that is, in the Æolian idiom, men daubed with soot: because Damon was thus besmeared when he committed this murder.

But there being a quarrel between the people of Chæronea and the Orchomenians, their neighbors, these latter hired an informer, a Roman, to accuse the community of Chæronea as if it had been a single person of the murder of the Romans, of which only Damon and his companions were guilty; accordingly, the process was commenced, and the cause pleaded before the Prætor of Macedon, since the Romans as yet had not sent governors into Greece.

The advocates who defended the inhabitants appealed to the testimony of Lucullus, who, in answer to a letter the Prætor wrote to him, returned a true account of the matter-of-fact. By this means the town obtained its acquittal, and escaped a most serious danger. The citizens, thus preserved, erected a statue to Lucullus in the market-place, near that of the god Bacchus.

We also have the same impressions of gratitude; and though removed from the events by the distance of several generations, we yet feel the obligation to extend to ourselves; and as we think an image of the character and habits to be a greater honor than one merely representing the face and the person, we will put Lucullus's life amongst our parallels of illustrious men, and without swerving from the truth, will record his actions. The commemoration will be itself a sufficient proof of our grateful feeling, and he himself would not thank us, if in recompense for a service which consisted in speaking the truth, we should abuse his memory with a false and counterfeit narration. For as we would wish that a painter who is to draw a beautiful face, in which there is yet some imperfection, should neither wholly leave out, nor yet too pointedly express what is defective, because this would deform it, and that spoil the resemblance; so since it is hard, or indeed perhaps impossible, to show the life of a man wholly free from blemish, in all that is excellent we must follow truth exactly, and give it fully; any lapses or faults that occur, through human passions or political necessities, we may regard rather as the shortcomings of some particular virtue, than as the natural effects of vice; and may be content without introducing them, curiously and officiously, into our narrative, if it be but out of tenderness to the weakness of nature, which has never succeeded in producing any human character so perfect in virtue as to be pure from all admixture, and open to no criticism. On considering with myself to whom I should compare Lucullus I find none so exactly his parallel as Cimon.

They were both valiant in war, and successful against the barbarians; both gentle in political life, and more than any others gave their countrymen a respite from civil troubles at home, while abroad, each of them raised trophies and gained famous victories. No Greek before Cimon, nor Roman before Lucullus, ever carried the scene of war so far from their own country; putting out of the question the acts of Bacchus and Hercules, and any exploit of Perseus against the Ethiopians, Medes, and Armenians, or again of Jason, of which any record that deserves credit can be said to have come down to our days. Moreover in this they were alike, that they did not finish the enterprises they undertook. They brought their enemies near their ruin, but never entirely conquered them. There was yet a great conformity in the free good-will and lavish abundance of their entertainments and general hospitalities, and in the youthful laxity of their habits. Other points of resemblance, which we have failed to notice, may be easily collected from our narrative itself.

Cimon was the son of Miltiades and Hegesipyle, who was by birth a Thracian, and daughter to the king Olorus, as appears from the poem of Melanthius and Archelaus, written in praise of Cimon. By this means the historian Thucydides was his kinsman by the mother's side; for his father's name also, in remembrance of this common ancestor, was Olorus, and he was the owner of the gold mines in Thrace, and met his death, it is said, by violence, in Scapte Hyle, a district of Thrace; and his remains having afterwards been brought into Attica, a monument is shown as his among those of the family of Cimon, near the tomb of Elpinice, Cimon's sister. But Thucydides was of the township of Halimus, and Miltiades and his family were Laciadæ. Miltiades, being condemned in a fine of fifty talents of the State, and unable to pay it, was cast into prison, and there died. Thus Cimon was left an orphan very young, with his sister Elpinice, who was also young and unmarried. And at first he had but an indifferent reputation, being looked upon as disorderly in his habits, fond of drinking, and resembling his grandfather, also called Cimon, in character, whose simplicity got him the surname of Coalemus. Stesimbrotus of Thasos, who lived near about the same time with Cimon, reports of him that he had little acquaintance either with music, or any of the other liberal studies and accomplishments, then common among the Greeks; that he had nothing whatever of the quickness and the ready speech of his countrymen in Attica; that he had great nobleness and candor in his disposition, and in his character in general, resembled rather a native of Peloponnesus than of Athens; as Euripides describes Hercules,

> Rude
> And unrefined, for great things well-endued:

for this may fairly be added to the character which Stesimbrotus has given of him.

They accused him, in his younger years, of cohabiting with his own sister Elpinice, who, indeed, otherwise had no very clear reputation, but was reported to have been over intimate with Polygnotus, the painter; and hence, when he painted the Trojan women in the porch, then called the Plesianactium, and now the Pœcile, he made Laodice a portrait of her. Polygnotus was not an ordinary mechanic, nor was he paid for this work, but out of a desire to please the Athenians, painted the portico for nothing. So it is stated by the historians, and in the following verses by the poet Melanthius:—

> Wrought by his hand the deeds of heroes grace
> At his own charge our temples and our Place.

Some affirm that Elpinice lived with her brother, not secretly, but as his married wife, her poverty excluding her from any suitable match. But afterwards, when Callias, one of the richest men of Athens, fell in love with her, and proffered to pay the fine the father was condemned in, if he could obtain the daughter in marriage, with Elpinice's own consent, Cimon betrothed her to Callias. There is no doubt but that Cimon was, in general, of an amorous temper. For Melanthius, in his elegies, rallies him on his attachment for Asteria of Salamis, and again for a certain Mnestra. And there can be no doubt of his unusually passionate affection for his lawful wife Isodice, the daughter of Euryptolemus, the son of Megacles; nor of his regret, even to impatience, at her death, if any conclusion may be drawn from those elegies of condolence, addressed to him upon his loss of her. The philosopher Panætius is of opinion, that Archelaus, the writer on physics, was the author of them, and indeed the time seems to favor that conjecture. All the other points of Cimon's character were noble and good. He was as daring as Miltiades, and not inferior to Themistocles in judgment, and was incomparably more just and honest than either of them. Fully their equal in all military virtues, in the ordinary duties of a citizen at home he was immeasurably their superior. And this, too, when he was very young, his years not yet strengthened by any experience. For when Themistocles, upon the Median invasion, advised the Athenians to forsake their city and their country, and to carry all their arms on shipboard, and fight the enemy by sea, in the straits of Salamis; when all the people stood amazed at the confidence and rashness of this advice, Cimon was seen, the first of all men, passing with a cheerful countenance through the Ceramicus, on his way with his companions to the citadel, carrying a bridle in his hand to offer to the goddess, intimating that there was no more need of horsemen now, but of mariners. There, after he had paid his devotions to the goddess, and offered up the bridle, he took down one of the bucklers that hung upon the walls of the temple, and went down to the port; by this example giving confidence to many of the citizens. He was also of a fairly handsome person, according to the poet Ion, tall and large, and let his thick and curly hair grow long. After he had acquitted himself gallantly in this battle of Salamis, he obtained great repute among the Athenians, and was regarded with affection, as well as admiration. He had many who followed after him, and bade him aspire to actions not less famous than his father's battle of Marathon. And when he came forward in political life, the people welcomed him gladly, being now weary of Themistocles; in opposition to whom, and because of the frankness and easiness of his temper, which was agreeable to every one, they advanced Cimon to the highest employments in the government. The man that contributed most to his promotion was Aristides, who early discerned in his character his natural capacity, and purposely raised him, that he might be a counterpoise to the craft and boldness of Themistocles.

After the Medes had been driven out of Greece, Cimon was sent out as an admiral, when the Athenians had not yet attained their dominion by sea, but still followed Pausanias and the Lacedæmonians; and his fellow-citizens under his command were highly distinguished, both for the excellence of their discipline, and for their extraordinary zeal and readiness. And further, perceiving that Pausanias was carrying on secret communications with the barbarians, and writing letters to the king of Persia to betray Greece, and puffed up with authority and success, was treating the allies haughtily, and committing many wanton injustices, Cimon, taking this advantage, by acts of kindness to those who were suffering wrong, and by his general humane bearing, robbed him of the command of the Greeks, before he was aware, not by arms, but by his mere language and character. The greatest part of the allies, no longer able to endure the harshness and pride of Pausanias, revolted from him to Cimon and Aristides, who accepted the duty, and wrote to the Ephors of Sparta, desiring them to recall a man who was causing dishonor to Sparta, and trouble to Greece. They tell of Pausanias, that when he was in Byzantium, he solicited a young lady of a noble family in the city, whose name was Cleonice, to debauch her. Her parents, dreading his cruelty, were forced to consent, and so abandoned their daughter to his wishes. The daughter asked the servants outside the chamber to put out all the lights; so that approaching silently and in the dark towards his bed, she stumbled upon the lamp which she overturned. Pausanias, who was fallen asleep, awakened and, startled with the noise, thought an assassin had taken that dead time of night to murder him, so that hastily snatching up his poniard that lay by him, he struck the girl, who fell with the blow, and died. After this, he never had rest, but was continually haunted by her, and saw an apparition visiting him in his sleep, and addressing him with these angry words:—

> Go on thy way, unto the evil end,
> That doth on lust and violence attend.

This was one of the chief occasions of indignation against him among the confederates, who now, joining their resentments and forces with Cimon's, besieged him in Byzantium. He escaped out of their hands, and, continuing, as it is said, to be disturbed by the apparition, fled to the oracle of the dead at Heraclea, raised the ghost of Cleonice, and entreated her to be reconciled. Accordingly she appeared to him, and answered that as soon as he came to Sparta, he should speedily be freed from all evils; obscurely foretelling, it would seem, his imminent death. This story is related by many authors.

Cimon, strengthened with the accession of the allies, went as general into Thrace. For he was told that some great men among the Persians, of the king's kindred, being in possession of Eion, a city situated upon the river Strymon, infested the neighboring Greeks. First he defeated these Persians in battle, and shut them up within the walls of their town. Then he fell upon the Thracians of the country beyond the Strymon, because they supplied Eion with victuals, and driving them entirely out of the country, took possession of it as conqueror, by which means he reduced the besieged to such straits, that Butes, who commanded there for the king, in desperation set fire to the town, and burned himself, his goods, and all his relations, in one common flame. By this means, Cimon got the town, but no great booty; as the barbarians had not only consumed themselves in the fire, but the richest of their effects. However, he put the country about into the hands of the Athenians, a most advantageous and desirable situation for a settlement. For this action, the people permitted him to erect the stone Mercuries, upon the first of which was this inscription:—

> Of bold and patient spirit, too, were those,
> Who, where the Strymon under Eion flows,
> With famine and the sword, to utmost need
> Reduced at last the children of the Mede.

Upon the second stood this:—

> The Athenians to their leaders this reward
> For great and useful service did accord;
> Others hereafter, shall, from their applause,
> Learn to be valiant in their country's cause.

and upon the third, the following:—

> With Atreus' sons, this city sent of yore
> Divine Menestheus to the Trojan shore;
> Of all the Greeks, so Homer's verses say,
> The ablest man an army to array:
> So old the title of her sons the name
> Of chiefs and champions in the field to claim.

Though the name of Cimon is not mentioned in these inscriptions, yet his contemporaries considered them to be the very highest honors to him; as neither Miltiades nor Themistocles ever received the like. When Miltiades claimed a garland, Sochares of Decelea stood up in the midst of the assembly and opposed it, using words which, though ungracious, were received with applause by the people, "When you have gained a victory by yourself, Miltiades, then you may ask to triumph so too." What then induced them so particularly to honor Cimon? Was it that under other commanders they stood upon the defensive? but by his conduct, they not only attacked their enemies, but invaded them in their own country, and acquired new territory, becoming masters of Eion and Amphipolis, where they planted colonies, as also they did in the isle of Scyros, which Cimon had taken on the following occasion. The Dolopians were the inhabitants of this isle, a people who neglected all husbandry, and had, for many generations, been devoted to piracy; this they practised to that degree, that at last they began to plunder foreigners that brought merchandise into their ports. Some merchants of Thessaly, who had come to shore near to Ctesium, were not only spoiled of their goods, but themselves put it to confinement. These men afterwards escaping from their prison, went and obtained sentence against the Scyrians in a court of Amphictyons, and when the Scyrian people declined to make public restitution, and called upon the individuals who had got the plunder to give it up, these persons, in alarm, wrote to Cimon to succor them, with his fleet, and declared themselves ready to deliver the town into his hands. Cimon, by these means, got the town, expelled the Dolopian pirates, and so opened the traffic of the Ægean sea. And, understanding that the ancient Theseus, the son of Ægeus, when he fled from Athens and took refuge in this isle, was here treacherously slain by king Lycomedes who feared him, Cimon endeavored to find out where he was buried. For an oracle had commanded the Athenians to bring home his ashes, and pay him all due honors as a hero; but hitherto they had not been able to learn where he was interred, as the people of Scyros dissembled the knowledge of it, and were not willing to allow a search. But now, great inquiry being made, with some difficulty he found out the tomb and carried the relics into his own galley, and with great pomp and show brought them to Athens, four hundred years, or thereabouts, after his expulsion. This act got Cimon great favor with the people, one mark of which was the judgment, afterwards so famous, upon the tragic poets. Sophocles, still a young man, had just brought forward his first plays; opinions were much divided, and the spectators had taken sides with some heat. So, to determine the case, Apsephion, who was at that time archon, would not cast lots who should be judges; but when Cimon and his brother commanders with him, came into the theatre, after they had performed the usual rites to the god of the festival, he would not allow them to retire, but came forward and made them swear (being ten in all, one from each tribe,) the usual oath; and so being sworn judges, he made them sit down to give sentence. The eagerness for victory grew all the warmer, from the ambition to get the suffrages of such honorable judges. And the victory was at last adjudged to Sophocles, which Æschylus is said to have taken so ill, that he left Athens shortly after, and went in anger to Sicily, where he died, and was buried near the city of Gela.

Ion relates that when he was a young man, and recently come from Chios to Athens, he chanced to sup with Cimon at Laomedon's house. After supper, when they had, according to custom, poured out wine to the honor of the gods,

Cimon was desired by the company to give them a song, which he did with sufficient success, and received the commendations of the company, who remarked on his superiority to Themistocles, who, on a like occasion, had declared he had never learnt to sing, nor to play, and only knew how to make a city rich and powerful. After talking of things incident to such entertainments, they entered upon the particulars of the several actions for which Cimon had been famous. And when they were mentioning the most signal, he told them they had omitted one, upon which he valued himself most for address and good contrivance. He gave this account of it. When the allies had taken a great number of the barbarians prisoners in Sestos and Byzantium, they gave him the preference to divide the booty; he accordingly put the prisoners in one lot, and the spoils of their rich attire and jewels in the other. This the allies complained of as an unequal division; but he gave them their choice to take which lot they would, for that the Athenians should be content with that which they refused. Herophytus of Samos advised them to take the ornaments for their share, and leave the slaves to the Athenians; and Cimon went away, and was much laughed at for his ridiculous division. For the allies carried away the golden bracelets, and armlets, and collars, and purple robes, and the Athenians had only the naked bodies of the captives, which they could make no advantage of, being unused to labor. But a little while after, the friends and kinsmen of the prisoners coming from Lydia and Phrygia, redeemed every one his relations at a high ransom; so that by this means Cimon got so much treasure that he maintained his whole fleet of galleys with the money for four months; and yet there was some left to lay up in the treasury at Athens.

Cimon now grew rich, and what he gained from the barbarians with honor, he spent yet more honorably upon the citizens. For he pulled down all the enclosures of his gardens and grounds, that strangers, and the needy of his fellow-citizens, might gather of his fruits freely. At home he kept a table, plain, but sufficient for a considerable number; to which any poor townsman had free access, and so might support himself without labor, with his whole time left free for public duties. Aristotle states, however, that this reception did not extend to all the Athenians, but only to his own fellow-townsmen, the Laciadæ. Besides this, he always went attended by two or three young companions, very well clad; and if he met with an elderly citizen in a poor habit, one of these would change clothes with the decayed citizen, which was looked upon as very nobly done. He enjoined them, likewise, to carry a considerable quantity of coin about them, which they were to convey silently into the hands of the better class of poor men, as they stood by them in the market-place. This, Cratinus the poet speaks of in one of his comedies, the Archilochi:—

> For I, Metrobius too, the scrivener poor,
> Of ease and comfort in my age secure
> By Greece's noblest son in life's decline,
> Cimon, the generous-hearted, the divine,
> Well-fed and feasted hoped till death to be,
> Death which, alas! has taken him ere me.

Gorgias the Leontine gives him this character, that he got riches that he might use them, and used them that he might get honor by them. And Critias, one of the thirty tyrants, makes it, in his elegies, his wish to have

> The Scopads' wealth, and Cimon's nobleness,
> And king Agesilaus's success.

Lichas, we know, became famous in Greece, only because on the days of the sports, when the young boys run naked, he used to entertain the strangers that came to see these diversions. But Cimon's generosity outdid all the old Athenian hospitality and good-nature. For though it is the city's just boast that their forefathers taught the rest of Greece to sow corn, and how to use springs of water, and to kindle fire, yet Cimon, by keeping open house for his fellow-citizens, and giving travellers liberty to eat the fruits which the several seasons produced in his land, seemed to restore to the world that community of goods, which mythology says existed in the reign of Saturn. Those who object to him that he did this to be popular, and gain the applause of the vulgar, are confuted by the constant tenor of the rest of his actions, which all tended to uphold the interests of the nobility and the Spartan policy, of which he gave instances, when together with Aristides, he opposed Themistocles, who was advancing the authority of the people beyond its just limits, and resisted Ephialtes, who, to please the multitude, was for abolishing the jurisdiction of the court of Areopagus. And when all of his time, except Aristides and Ephialtes, enriched themselves out of the public money, he still kept his hands clean and untainted, and to his last day never acted or spoke for his own private gain or emolument. They tell us that Rhœsaces, a

Persian, who had traitorously revolted from the king his master, fled to Athens, and there, being harassed by sycophants, who were still accusing him to the people, he applied himself to Cimon for redress, and, to gain his favor, laid down in his doorway two cups, the one full of gold, and the other of silver Darics. Cimon smiled and asked him whether he wished to have Cimon's hired service or his friendship. He replied, his friendship. "If so," said he, "take away these pieces, for, being your friend, when I shall have occasion for them, I will send and ask for them."

The allies of the Athenians began now to be weary of of war and military service, willing to have repose, and to look after their husbandry and traffic. For they saw their enemies driven out of the country, and did not fear any new vexations from them. They still paid the tax they were assessed at, but did not send men and galleys, as they had done before. This the other Athenian generals wished to constrain them to, and by judicial proceedings against defaulters, and penalties which they inflicted on them, made the government uneasy, and even odious. But Cimon practiced a contrary method; he forced no man to go that was not willing, but of those that desired to be excused from service he took money and vessels unmanned, and let them yield to the temptation of staying at home, to attend to their private business. Thus they lost their military habits and luxury, and their own folly quickly changed them into unwarlike husbandmen and traders; while Cimon, continually embarking large numbers of Athenians on board his galleys, thoroughly disciplined them in his expeditions, and ere long made them the lords of their own paymasters. The allies, whose indolence maintained them, while they thus went sailing about everywhere, and incessantly bearing arms and acquiring skill, began to fear and flatter them, and found themselves after a while allies no longer, but unwittingly become tributaries and slaves.

Nor did any man ever do more than Cimon did to humble the pride of the Persian king. He was not content with getting rid of him out of Greece; but following close at his heels, before the barbarians could take breath and recover themselves, he was already at work, and what with his devastations, and his forcible reduction of some places, and the revolts and voluntary accession of others in the end from Ionia to Pamphylia, all Asia was clear of Persian soldiers. Word being brought him that the royal commanders were lying in wait upon the coast of Pamphylia with a numerous land army, and

a large fleet, he determined to make the whole sea on his side
the Chelidonian islands so formidable to them that they should
never dare to show themselves in it; and setting off from
Cnidos and the Triopian headland with two hundred galleys,
which had been originally built with particular care by Themistocles, for speed and rapid evolutions, and to which he now
gave greater width and roomier decks along the sides to move
to and fro upon, so as to allow a great number of full-armed
soldiers to take part in the engagements and fight from them,
he shaped his course first of all against the town of Phaselis,
which though inhabited by Greeks, yet would not quit the in
terests of Persia, but denied his galleys entrance into their
port. Upon this he wasted the country, and drew up his
army to their very walls; but the soldiers of Chios, who were
then serving under him, being ancient friends to the Phase-
lites, endeavoring to propitiate the general in their behalf, at
the same time shot arrows into the town, to which were fastened letters conveying intelligence. At length he concluded
peace with them, upon the conditions that they should pay
down ten talents, and follow him against the barbarians.
Ephorus says the admiral of the Persian fleet was Tithraustes,
and the general of the land army Pherendates; but Callisthenes is positive that Ariomandes, the son of Gobryas, had
the supreme command of all the forces. He lay waiting
with the whole fleet at the mouth of the river Eurymedon,
with no design to fight, but expecting a reinforcement of
eighty Phœnician ships on their way from Cyprus. Cimon,
aware of this, put out to sea, resolved, if they would not fight
a battle willingly, to force them to it. The barbarians, seeing
this, retired within the mouth of the river to avoid being
attacked; but when they saw the Athenians come upon them,
notwithstanding their retreat, they met them with six hundred
ships, as Phanodemus relates, but according to Ephorus,
only with three hundred and fifty. However, they did nothing worthy such mighty forces, but immediately turned the
prows of their galleys toward the shore, where those that came
first threw themselves upon the land, and fled to their army
drawn up thereabout, while the rest perished with their vessels, or were taken. By this, one may guess at their number,
for though a great many escaped out of the fight, and a great
many others were sunk, yet two hundred galleys were taken
by the Athenians.

When their land army drew toward the seaside, Cimon
was in suspense whether he should venture to try and force

his way on shore ; as he should thus expose his Greeks, wearied with slaughter in the first engagement, to the swords of the barbarians, who were all fresh men, and many times their number. But seeing his men resolute, and flushed with victory, he bade them land, though they were not yet cool from their first battle. As soon as they touched ground, they set up a shout and ran upon the enemy, who stood firm and sustained the first shock with great courage, so that the fight was a hard one, and some principal men of the Athenians in rank and courage were slain. At length, though with much ado, they routed the barbarians, and killing some, took others prisoners, and plundered all their tents and pavilions, which were full of rich spoil. Cimon, like a skilled athlete at the games, having in one day carried off two victories wherein he surpassed that of Salamis by sea, and that of Platæa by land, was encouraged to try for yet another success. News being brought that the Phœnician succors, in number eighty sail, had come in sight at Hydrum, he set off with all speed to find them, while they as yet had not received any certain account of the larger fleet, and were in doubt what to think ; so that thus surprised, they lost all their vessels and most of their men with them. This success of Cimon so daunted the king of Persia, that he presently made that celebrated peace, by which he engaged that his armies should come no nearer the Grecian sea than the length of a horse's course ; and that none of his galleys or vessels of war should appear between the Cyanean and Chelidonian isles. Callisthenes, however, says that he did not agree to any such articles, but that, upon the fear this victory gave him, he did in reality thus act, and kept off so far from Greece, that when Pericles with fifty, and Ephialtes with thirty galleys, cruised beyond the Chelidonian isles, they did not discover one Persian vessel. But in the collection which Craterus made of the public acts of the people, there is a draft of this treaty given. And it is told, also, that at Athens they erected the altar of Peace upon this occasion, and decreed particular honors to Callias, who was employed as ambassador to procure the treaty.

The people of Athens raised so much money from the spoils of this war, which were publicly sold, that besides other expenses, and raising the south wall of the citadel, they laid the foundation of the long walls, not, indeed, finished till at a later time, which were called the Legs. And the place where they built them being soft and marshy ground, they were forced to sink great weights of stone and rubble to secure the foundation, and did all this out of the money Cimon supplied them with. It was he, likewise, who first embellished the upper city with those fine and ornamental places of exercise and resort, which they afterwards so much frequented and delighted in. He set the market-place with plane trees; and the Academy, which was before a bare, dry, and dirty spot, he converted into a well-watered grove, with shady alleys to walk in, and open courses for races.

When the Persians who had made themselves masters of the Chersonese, so far from quitting it, called in the people of the interior of Thrace to help them against Cimon, whom they despised for the smallness of his forces, he set upon them with only four galleys, and took thirteen of theirs; and having driven out the Persians, and subdued the Thracians, he made the whole Chersonese the property of Athens. Next he attacked the people of Thasos, who had revolted from the Athenians; and, having defeated them in a fight at sea, where he took thirty-three of their vessels, he took their town by siege, and acquired for the Athenians all the mines of gold on the opposite coast, and the territory dependent on Thasos. This opened him a fair passage into Macedon, so that he might, it was thought, have acquired a good portion of that country; and because he neglected the opportunity, he was suspected of corruption, and of having been bribed off by king Alexander. So, by the combination of his adversaries, he was accused of being false to his country. In his defence he told the judges, that he had always shown himself in his public life the friend, not, like other men, of rich Ionians and Thessalians, to be courted, and to receive presents, but of the Lacedæmonians; for as he admired, so he wished to imitate the plainness of their habits, their temperance, and simplicity of living, which he preferred to any sort of riches; but that he always had been, and still was proud to enrich his country with the spoils of her enemies. Stesimbrotus, making mention of this trial, states that Elpinice, in behalf of her brother, addressed herself to Pericles, the most vehement of his accusers, to whom Pericles answered, with a smile, "You are old, Elpinice, to meddle with affairs of this nature." However, he proved the mildest of his prosecutors, and rose up but once all the while, almost as a matter of form, to plead against him. Cimon was acquitted.

In his public life after this, he continued, whilst at home, to control and restrain the common people, who would have trampled upon the nobility, and drawn all the power and sov-

VOL. II.—11

ereignty to themselves. But when he afterwards was sent out to war, the multitude broke loose, as it were, and overthrew all the ancient laws and customs they had hitherto observed, and, chiefly at the instigation of Ephialtes, withdrew the cognizance of almost all causes from the Areopagus ; so that all jurisdiction now being transferred to them, the government was reduced to a perfect democracy, and this by the help of Pericles, who was already powerful, and had pronounced in favor of the common people. Cimon, when he returned, seeing the authority of this great council so upset, was exceedingly troubled, and endeavored to remedy these disorders by bringing the courts of law to their former state, and restoring the old aristocracy of the time of Clisthenes. This the others declaimed against with all the vehemence possible, and began to revive those stories concerning him and his sister, and cried out against him as the partisan of the Lacedæmonians. To these calumnies the famous verses of Eupolis, the poet, upon Cimon refer :—

> He was as good as others that one sees,
> But he was fond of drinking and of ease ;
> And would at nights to Sparta often roam,
> Leaving his sister desolate at home.

But if, though slothful and a drunkard, he could capture so many towns, and gain so many victories, certainly if he had been sober and minded his business, there had been no Grecian commander, either before or after him, that could have surpassed him for exploits of war.

He was, indeed, a favorer of the Lacedæmonians, even from his youth, and he gave the names of Lacedæmonius and Eleus to two sons, twins, whom he had, as Stesimbrotus says, by a woman of Clitorium, whence Pericles often upbraided them with their mother's blood. But Diodorus, the geographer, asserts that both these, and another son of Cimon's, whose name was Thessalus, were born of Isodice, the daughter of Euryptolemus, the son of Megacles.

However, this is certain, that Cimon was countenanced by the Lacedæmonians in opposition to Themistocles, whom they disliked ; and while he was yet very young, they endeavored to raise and increase his credit in Athens. This the Athenians perceived at first with pleasure, and the favor the Lacedæmonians showed him was in various ways advantageous to them and their affairs ; as at that time they were just rising to power, and were occupied in winning the allies to their side. So they seemed not at all offended with the honor and kindness shown to Cimon, who then had the chief management of all the affairs of Greece, and was acceptable to the Lacedæmonians, and courteous to the allies. But afterwards the Athenians, grown more powerful, when they saw Cimon so entirely devoted to the Lacedæmonians, began to be angry, for he would always in his speeches prefer them to the Athenians, and upon every occasion, when he would reprimand them for a fault, or incite them to emulation, he would exclaim, " The Lacedæmonians would not do thus." This raised the discontent, and got him in some degree the hatred of the citizens; but that which ministered chiefly to the accusation against him fell out upon the following occasion.

In the fourth year of the reign of Archidamus, the son of Zeuxidamus, king of Sparta, there happened in the country of Lacedæmon the greatest earthquake that was known in the memory of man; the earth opened into chasms, and the nountain Taygetus was so shaken, that some of the rocky points of it fell down, and except five houses, all the town of Sparta was shattered to pieces. They say that a little before any motion was perceived, as the young men and the boys just grown up were exercising themselves together in the middle of the portico, a hare, of a sudden, started out just by them, which the young men, though all naked and daubed with oil, ran after for sport. No sooner were they gone from the place, than the gymnasium fell down upon the boys who had stayed behind, and killed them all. Their tomb is to this day called Sismatias. Archidamus, by the present danger made apprehensive of what might follow, and seeing the citizens intent upon removing the most valuable of their goods out of their houses, commanded an alarm to be sounded, as if an enemy were coming upon them, in order that they should collect about him in a body, with arms. It was this alone that saved Sparta at that time, for the Helots were got together from the country about, with design to surprise the Spartans, and overpower those whom the earthquake had spared. But finding them armed and well prepared, they retired into the towns and openly made war with them, gaining over a number of the Laconians of the country districts; while at the same time the Messenians, also, made an attack upon the Spartans, who therefore despatched Periclidas to Athens to solicit succors, of whom Aristophanes says in mockery that he came and

> In a red jacket, at the altars seated,
> With a white face, for men and arms entreated.

This Ephialtes opposed, protesting that they ought not to raise up or assist a city that was a rival to Athens ; but that being down, it were best to keep her so, and let the pride and arrogance of Sparta be trodden under. But Cimon, as Critias says, preferring the safety of Lacedæmon to the aggrandizement of his own country, so persuaded the people, that he soon marched out with a large army to their relief. Ion records, also, the most successful expression which he used to move the Athenians. "They ought not to suffer Greece to be lamed, nor their own city to be deprived of her yokefellow."

In his return from aiding the Lacedæmonians, he passed with his army through the territory of Corinth ; whereupon Lachartus reproached him for bringing his army into the country without first asking leave of the people. For he that knocks at another man's door ought not to enter the house till the master gives him leave. "But you Corinthians, O Lachartus," said Cimon, "did not knock at the gates of the Cleonæans and Megarians, but broke them down, and entered by force, thinking that all places should be open to the stronger." And having thus rallied the Corinthian, he passed on with his army. Some time after this, the Lacedæmonians sent a second time to desire succors of the Athenians against the Messenians and Helots, who had seized upon Ithome. But when they came, fearing their boldness and gallantry, of all that came to their assistance, they sent them only back, alleging they were designing innovations. The Atheians returned home, enraged at this usage, and vented their anger upon all those who were favorers of the Lacedæmonians, and seizing some slight occasion, they banished Cimon for ten years, which is the time prescribed to those that are banished by the ostracism. In the mean time, the Lacedæmonians, on their return after freeing Delphi from the Phocians, encamped their army at Tanagra, whither the Athenians presently marched with design to fight them.

Cimon, also, came thither armed, and ranged himself among those of his own tribe which was the Œneis, desirous of fighting with the rest against the Spartans ; but the council of five hundred being informed of this, and frighted at it, his adversaries crying out he would disorder the army, and bring the Lacedæmonians to Athens, commanded the officers not to receive him. Wherefore Cimon left the army, conjuring Euthippus, the Anaphlystian, and the rest of his companions, who were most suspected as favoring the Lacedæmonians, to behave themselves bravely against their enemies, and by their actions make their innocence evident to their countrymen. These, being in all a hundred, took the arms of Cimon, and followed his advice; and making a body by themselves, fought so desperately with the enemy, that they were all cut off, leaving the Athenians deep regret for the loss of such brave men, and repentance for having so unjustly suspected them. Accordingly, they did not long retain their severity toward Cimon, partly upon remembrance of his former services, and partly, perhaps, induced by the juncture of the times. For being defeated at Tanagra in a great battle, and fearing the Peloponnesians would come upon them at the opening of the spring, they recalled Cimon by a decree, of which Pericles himself was author. So reasonable were men's resentments in those times, and so moderate their anger, that it always gave way to the public good. Even ambition, the least governable of all human passions, could then yield to the necessities of the State.

Cimon, as soon as he returned, put an end to the war, and reconciled the two cities. Peace thus established, seeing the Athenians impatient of being idle, and eager after the honor and aggrandizement of war, lest they should set upon the Greeks themselves, or with so many ships cruising about the isles and Peloponnesus, they should give occasions to intestine wars, or complaints of their allies against them, he equipped two hundred galleys, with design to make an attempt upon Egypt and Cyprus; purposing, by this means, to accustom the Athenians to fight against the barbarians, and enrich themselves honestly by spoiling those who were the natural enemies to Greece. But when all things were prepared, and the army ready to embark, Cimon had this dream. It seemed to him that there was a furious bitch barking at him, and mixed with the barking, a kind of human voice uttered these words —

> Come on, for thou shalt shortly be
> A pleasure to my whelps and me.

This dream was hard to interpret, yet Astyphilus of Posidonia, a man skilled in divinations, and intimate with Cimon, told him that his death was presaged by this vision, which he thus explained. A dog is enemy to him he barks at; and one is always most a pleasure to one's enemies, when one is dead; the mixture of human voice with barking signifies the Medes, for the army of the Medes is mixed up of Greeks and barba rians. After this dream, as he was sacrificing to Bacchus, and the priest cutting up the victim, a number of ants, taking up the congealed particles of the blood laid them about Cimon's great toe. This was not observed for a good while, but at the very time when Cimon spied it, the priest came and showed him the liver of the sacrifice imperfect, wanting that part of it called the head. But he could not then recede from the enterprise, so he set sail. Sixty of his ships he sent toward Egypt; with the rest he went and fought the king of Persia's fleet, composed of Phœnician and Cilician galleys, recovered all the cities thereabout, and threatened Egypt; designing no less than the entire ruin of the Persian empire. And the rather, for that he was informed Themistocles was in great repute among the barbarians, having promised the king to lead his army, whenever he should make war upon Greece. But Themistocles it is said, abandoning all hopes of compassing his designs, very much out of the despair of overcoming the valor and good-fortune of Cimon, died a voluntary death. Cimon, intent on great designs, which he was now to enter upon, keeping his navy about the isle of Cyprus, sent messengers to consult the oracle of Jupiter Ammon upon some secret matter. For it is not known about what they were sent, and the god would give them no answer, but commanded them to return again, for that Cimon was already with him. Hearing this, they returned to sea, and as soon as they came to the Grecian army, which was then about Egypt, they understood that Cimon was dead; and computing the time of the oracle, they found that his death had been signified, he being then already with the gods.

He died, some say, of sickness, while besieging Citium, in Cyprus; according to others, of a wound he received in a skirmish with the barbarians. When he perceived he should die, he commanded those under his charge to return, and by no means to let the news of his death be known by the way; this they did with such secrecy that they all came home safe, and neither their enemies nor the allies knew what had happened. Thus, as Phanodemus relates, the Grecian army was, as it were, conducted by Cimon thirty days after he was dead. But after his death there was not one commander among the Greeks that did any thing considerable against the barbarians, and instead of uniting against their common enemies, the popular leaders and partisans of war animated them against one another to that degree, that none could interpose their good offices to reconcile them. And while, by their mutual discord, they ruined the power of Greece, they gave the Persians time to recover breath, and repair all their losses. It is true, indeed, Agesilaus carried the arms of Greece into Asia, but it was a long time after; there were, indeed, some brief appearances of a war against the king's lieutenants in the maritime provinces, but they all quickly vanished; before he could perform any thing of moment, he was recalled by fresh civil dissensions and disturbances at home. So that he was forced to leave the Persian king's officers to impose what tribute they pleased on the Greek cities in Asia, the confederates and allies of the Lacedæmonians. Whereas, in the time of Cimon, not so much as a letter-carrier, or a single horseman, was ever seen to come within four hundred furlongs of the sea.

The monuments, called Cimonian to this day, in Athens, show that his remains were conveyed home, yet the inhabitants of the city Citium pay particular honor to a certain tomb which they call the tomb of Cimon, according to Nausicrates, the rhetorician, who states that in a time of famine, when the crops of their land all failed, they sent to the oracle, which commanded them not to forget Cimon, but give him the honors of a superior being. Such was the Greek commander.

LUCULLUS.

LUCULLUS's grandfather had been consul; his uncle by the mother's sisters was Metellus, surnamed Numidicus. As for his parents his father was convicted of extortion, and his mother Cæcilia's reputation was bad. The first thing that Lucullus did before ever he stood for any office, or meddled with the affairs of state, being then but a youth, was to accuse the accuser of his father, Servilius the augur, having caught him in offence against the state. This thing was much taken notice of among the Romans, who commended it as an act of high merit. Even without the provocation the accusation was esteemed no unbecoming action, for they delighted to see young men as eagerly attacking injustice, as good dogs do wild beasts. But when great animosities ensued, insomuch that some were wounded and killed in the fray, Servilius escaped. Lucullus followed his studies and became a competent speaker, in both Greek and Latin, insomuch that Sylla, when composing the commentaries of his own life and actions, dedicated them to him, as one who could have performed the task better himself. His speech was not only elegant and ready for purposes of mere business, like the ordinary oratory which will in the public market-place,

> Lash as a wounded tunny does the sea,

but on every other occasion shows itself

> Dried up and perished with the want of wit;

but even in his younger days he addicted himself to the study, simply for its own sake, of the liberal arts ; and when advanced in years, after a life of conflicts, he gave his mind, as it were, its liberty, to enjoy in full leisure the refreshment of philosophy; and summoning up his contemplative faculties, administered a timely check, after his difference with Pompey, to his feelings of emulation and ambition. Besides what has been said of his love of learning already, one instance more was, that in his youth, upon a suggestion of writing the Marsian war in Greek and Latin verse and prose, arising out of some pleasantry that passed into a serious proposal, he agreed with Hortensius the lawyer, and Sisenna the historian, that he would take his lot ; and it seems that the lot directed him to the Greek tongue, for a Greek history of that war is still extant.

Among the many signs of the great love which he bore to his brother Marcus, one in particular is commemorated by the Romans. Though he was elder brother, he would not step into authority without him, but deferred his own advance until his brother was qualified to bear a share with him, and so won upon the people, as when absent to be chosen Ædile with him.

He gave many and early proofs of his valor and conduct in the Marsian war, and was admired by Sylla for his constancy and mildness, and always employed in affairs of importance, especially in the mint ; most of the money for carrying on the Mithridatic war being coined by him in Peloponnesus which, by the soldiers' wants, was brought into rapid circulation and long continued current under the name of Lucullean coin. After this, when Sylla conquered Athens, and was victorious by land, but found the supplies for his army cut off, the enemy being master at sea, Lucullus was the man whom he sent into Libya and Egypt, to procure him shipping It was the depth of winter when he ventured with but three small Greek vessels, and as many Rhodian galleys, not only into the main sea, but also among multitudes of vessels belonging to the enemies who were cruising about as absolute masters. Arriving at Crete, he gained it, and finding the Cyrenians harassed by long tyrannies and wars, he composed their troubles, and settled their government; putting the city in mind of that saying which Plato once had oracularly uttered of them, who being requested to prescribe laws to them, and mould them into some sound form of government, made an swer that it was a hard thing to give laws to the Cyrenians, abounding, as they did, in wealth and plenty. For nothing is more intractable than man when in felicity, nor any thing more docile, when he has been reduced and humbled by fortune. This made the Cyrenians so willingly submit to the laws which Lucullus imposed upon them. From thence sailing into Egypt, and pressed by pirates, he lost most of his vessels; but he himself narrowly escaping, made a magnificent entry into Alexandria. The whole fleet, a compliment due only to royalty, met him in full array, and the young Ptolemy showed wonderful kindness to him, appointing him lodging and diet in the palace, where no foreign commander before him had been received. Besides, he gave him gratuities and presents, not such as were usually given to men of his condition, but four times as much; of which, however, he took nothing more than served his necessity and accepted of no gift, though what was worth eighty talents was offered him. It is reported he neither went to see Memphis, nor any of the celebrated wonders of Egypt. It was for a man of no business and much curiosity to see such things, not for him who had left his commander in the field lodging under the ramparts of his enemies.

Ptolemy, fearing the issue of that war, deserted the confederacy, but nevertheless sent a convoy with him as far as Cyprus, and at parting, with much ceremony, wishing him a good voyage, gave him a very precious emerald set in gold. Lucullus at first refused it, but when the king showed him his own likeness cut upon it, he thought he could not persist in a denial, for had he parted with such open offence, it might have endangered his passage. Drawing a considerable squadron together, which he summoned as he sailed by, out of all the maritime towns except those suspected of piracy, he sailed for Cyprus; and there understanding that the enemy lay in wait under the promontories for him, he laid up his fleet, and sent to the cities to send in provisions for his wintering among them. But when time served, he launched his ships suddenly, and went off, and hoisting all his sails in the night, while he kept them down in the day, thus came safe to Rhodes. Being furnished with ships at Rhodes, he also prevailed upon the inhabitants of Cos and Cnidus, to leave the king's side, and join in an expedition against the Samians. Out of Chios he himself drove the king's party, and set the Colophonians at liberty, having seized Epigonus the tyrant, who oppressed them.

About this time Mithridates left Pergamus, and retired to Pitane, where being closely besieged by Fimbria on the land, and not daring to engage with so bold and victorious a commander, he was concerting means for escape by sea, and sent for all his fleets from every quarter to attend him. Which when Fimbria perceived, having no ships of his own, he sent to Lucullus, entreating him to assist him with his, in subduing the most odious and warlike of kings, lest the opportunity of humbling Mithridates, the prize which the Romans had pursued with so much blood and trouble, should now at last be lost, when he was within the net, and easily to be taken. And were he caught, no one would be more highly commended than Lucullus, who stopped his passage and seized him in his flight. Being driven from the land by the one, and met in the sea by the other, he would give matter of renown and glory to them both, and the much applauded actions of Sylla at Orchomenus and about Chæronea, would no longer be thought of by the Romans. The proposal was no unreasonable thing; it being obvious to all men, that if Lucullus had hearkened to Fimbria, and with his navy, which was then near at hand, had blocked up the haven, the war soon had been brought to an end, and infinite numbers of mischiefs prevented thereby. But he, whether from the sacredness of friendship between himself and Sylla, reckoning all other considerations of public or of private advantage inferior to it, or out of detestation of the wickedness of Fimbria, whom he abhorred for advancing himself by the late death of his friend and the general of the army, or by a divine fortune sparing Mithridates then, that he might have him an adversary for a time to come, for whatever reason, refused to comply, and suffered Mithridates to escape and laugh at the attempts of Fimbria. He himself alone first, near Lectum, in Troas, in a sea fight, overcame the king's ships; and afterwards, discovering Neoptolemus lying in wait for him near Tenedos, with a greater fleet, he went aboard a Rhodian quinquereme galley, commanded by Damagoras, a man of great experience at sea, and friendly to the Romans, and sailed before the rest. Neoptolemus made up furiously at him, and commanded the master, with all imaginable might, to charge; but Damagoras, fearing the bulk and massy stem of the admiral, thought it dangerous to meet him prow to prow, and, rapidly wheeling round, bid his men back water, and so received him astern; in which place, though violently borne upon, he received no manner of harm, the blow being defeated by falling on those parts of the ship which lay under water. By which time, the rest of the fleet coming up to him, Lucullus gave order to turn again, and vigorously falling upon the enemy, put them to flight, and pursued Neoptolemus. After this he came to Sylla, in Chersonesus, as he was preparing to pass the strait, and brought timely assistance for the safe transportation of the army.

Peace being presently made, Mithridates sailed off to the Euxine sea, but Sylla taxed the inhabitants of Asia twenty thousand talents, and ordered Lucullus to gather and coin the money. And it was no small comfort to the cities under Sylla's severity, that a man of not only incorrupt and just behavior, but also of moderation, should be employed in so heavy and odious an office. The Mitylenæans, who absolutely revolted, he was willing should return to their duty, and submit to a moderate penalty for the offence they had given in the case of Marius. But finding them bent upon their own destruction, he came up to them, defeated them at sea, blocked them up in their city and besieged them; then sailing off from them openly in the day to Elæa, he returned privately, and posting an ambush near the city, lay quiet himself. And on the Mitylenæans coming out eagerly and in disorder to plunder the deserted camp, he fell upon them, took many of them, and slew five hundred, who stood upon their defence. He gained six thousand slaves, and a very rich booty.

He was no way engaged in the great and general troubles of Italy which Sylla and Marius created, a happy providence at that time detaining him in Asia upon business. He was as much in Sylla's favor, however, as any of his other friends; Sylla, as was said before, dedicated his Memoirs to him as a token of kindness, and at his death, passing by Pompey, made him guardian to his son; which seems, indeed, to have been the rise of the quarrel and jealousy between them two, being both young men, and passionate for honor.

A little after Sylla's death he was made consul with Marcus Cotta, about the one hundred and seventy-sixth

Olympiad. The Mithridatic war being then under debate, Marcus declared that it was not finished, but only respited for a time, and therefore, upon choice of provinces, the lot falling to Lucullus to have Gaul within the Alps, a province where no great action was to be done, he was ill-pleased. But chiefly, the success of Pompey in Spain fretted him, as, with the renown he got there, if the Spanish war were finished in time, he was likely to be chosen general before any one else against Mithridates. So that when Pompey sent for money and signified by letter that, unless it were sent him, he would leave the country and Sertorius, and bring his forces home to Italy, Lucullus most zealously supported his request, to prevent any pretence of his returning home during his own consulship; for all things would have been at his disposal, at the head of so great an army. For Cethegus, the most influential popular leader at that time, owing to his always both acting and speaking to please the people, had, as it happened, a hatred to Lucullus, who had not concealed his disgust at his debauched, insolent, and lawless life. Lucullus, therefore, was at open warfare with him. And Lucius Quintius, also, another demagogue, who was taking steps against Sylla's constitution, and endeavoring to put things out of order, by private exhortations and public admonitions he checked in his designs, and repressed his ambition, wisely and safely remedying a great evil at the very outset.

At this time news came that Octavius, the governor of Cilicia, was dead, and many were eager for the place, courting Cethegus, as the man best able to serve them. Lucullus set little value upon Cilicia itself, no otherwise than as he thought, by his acceptance of it, no other man besides himself might be employed in the war against Mithridates, by reason of its nearness to Cappadocia. This made him strain every effort that that province might be allotted to himself, and to none other; which led him at last into an expedient not so honest or commendable, as it was serviceable for compassing his design, submitting to necessity against his own inclination There was one Præcia, a celebrated wit and beauty, but r other respects nothing better than an ordinary harlot; who, however, to the charms of her person adding the reputation of one that loved and served her friends, by making use of those who visited her to assist their designs and promote their interests, had thus gained great power. She had seduced Cethegus, the first man at that time in reputation and authority of all the city, and enticed him to her love, and so had made all author ity follow her. For nothing of moment was done in which Cethegus was not concerned, and nothing by Cethegus without Præcia. This woman Lucullus gained to his side by gifts and flattery (and a great price it was in itself to so stately and magnificent a dame, to be seen engaged in the same cause with Lucullus), and thus he presently found Cethegus his friend, using his utmost interest to procure Cilicia for him; which when once obtained, there was no more need of applying himself either of Præcia, or Cethegus; for all unanimously voted him to the Mithridatic war, by no hands likely to be so successfully managed as his. Pompey was still contending with Sertorius, and Metellus by age unfit for service; which two alone were the competitors who could prefer any claim with Lucullus for that command. Cotta, his colleague, after much ado in the senate, was sent away with a fleet to guard the Propontis, and defend Bithynia.

Lucullus carried with him a legion under his own orders and crossed over into Asia and took the command of the forces there, composed of men who were all thoroughly disabled by dissoluteness and rapine, and the Fimbrians, as they were called, utterly unmanageable by long want of any sort of discipline. For these were they who under Fimbria had slain Flaccus, the consul and general, and afterwards betrayed Fimbria to Sylla; a wilful and lawless set of men, but warlike, expert and hardy in the field. Lucullus in a short time took down the courage of these, and disciplined the others, who then first, in all probability, knew what a true commander and governor was; whereas in former times they had been courted to service, and took up arms at nobody's command, but their own wills.

The enemy's provisions for war stood thus; Mithridates, like the Sophists, boastful and haughty at first, set upon the Romans, with a very inefficient army, such, indeed, as made a good show, but was nothing for use; but being shamefully routed, and taught a lesson for a second engagement, he reduced his forces to a proper, serviceable shape. Dispensing with the mixed multitudes, and the noisy menaces of barbarous tribes of various languages, and with the ornaments of gold and precious stones, a greater temptation to the victors, than security to the bearers, he gave his men broad swords like the Romans', and massy shields; chose horses better for service than show, drew up an hundred and twenty thousand foot in the figure of the Roman phalanx, and had sixteen thousand horse, besides chariots armed with scythes, no less than a hundred. Besides which, he set out a fleet not at all cumbered with gilded cabins, luxurious baths, and women's furniture, but stored with weapons and darts, and other necessaries, and thus made a descent upon Bithynia. Not only did these parts willingly receive him again, but almost all Asia regarded him as their salvation from the intolerable miseries which they were suffering from the Roman money-lenders, and revenue farmers. These, afterwards, who like harpies stole away their very nourishment, Lucullus drove away, and at this time by reproving them, did what he could to make them more moderate, and to prevent a general secession, then breaking out in all parts. While Lucullus was detained in rectifying these matters, Cotta, finding affairs ripe for action, prepared for battle with Mithridates; and news coming from all hands that Lucullus had already entered Phrygia, on his march against the enemy, he, thinking he had a triumph all but actually in his hands, lest his colleague should share in the glory of it, hasted to battle without him. But being routed, both by sea and land, he lost sixty ships with their men, and four thousand foot, and himself was forced into and besieged in Chalcedon, there waiting for relief from Lucullus. There were those about Lucullus who would have had him leave Cotta, and go forward, in hope of surprising the defenceless kingdom of Mithridates. And this was the feeling of the soldiers in general, who were indignant that Cotta should by his ill-counsel not only lose his own army, but hinder them also, from conquest, which at that time, without the hazard of a battle, they might have obtained. But Lucullus, in a public address, declared to them that he would rather save one citizen from the enemy, than be master of all that they had.

Archelaus, the former commander in Bœotia under Mithridates, who afterwards deserted him and accompanied the Romans, protested to Lucullus that, upon his bare coming, he would possess himself of all Pontus. But he answered, that it did not become him to be more cowardly than huntsmen, to leave the wild beasts abroad and seek after sport in their deserted dens. Having so said, he made towards Mithridates with thirty thousand foot, and two thousand five hundred horse. But on being come in sight of his enemies, he was astonished at their numbers, and thought to forbear fighting, and wear out time. But Marius, whom Sertorius had sent out of Spain to Mithridates with forces under him, stepping out and challenging him, he prepared for battle. In the very instant before joining battle, without any perceptible alteration preceding, on a sudden the sky opened, and a large luminous body fell down in the midst between the armies, in shape like a hogshead, but in color like melted silver, insomuch that both armies in alarm withdrew. This wonderful prodigy happened in Phrygia, near Otryæ. Lucullus after this began to think with himself that no human power and wealth could suffice to sustain such great numbers as Mithridates had, for any long time in the face of an enemy, and commanded one of the captives to be brought before him, and first of all asked him, how many companions had been quartered with him and how much provision he had left behind him, and when he had answered him, commanded him to stand aside; then asked a second and a third the same question; after which, comparing the quantity of provision with the men, he found that in three or four days' time, his enemies would be brought to want. This all the more determined him to trust to time, and he took measures to store his camp with all sorts of provision, and thus living in plenty, trusted to watch the necessities of his hungry enemy.

This made Mithridates set out against the Cyzicenians, miserably shattered in the fight at Chalcedon, where they lost no less than three thousand citizens and ten ships. And that he might the safer steal away unobserved by Lucullus, immediately after supper by the help of a dark and wet night, he went off, and by the morning gained the neighborhood of the city, and sat down with his forces upon the Adrastean mount. Lucullus, on finding him gone, pursued, but was well pleased not to overtake him with his own forces in disorder; and he sat down near what is called the Thracian village, an admirable position for commanding all the roads and the places whence, and through which the provisions for Mithridates's camp must of necessity come. And judging now of the event, he no longer kept his mind from his soldiers, but when the camp was fortified and their work finished, called them together, and with great assurance told them that in a few days, without the expense of blood, he would give them victory.

Mithridates besieged the Cyzicenians with ten camps by land, and with his ships occupied the strait that was betwixt their city and the main land, and so blocked them up on all sides; they, however, were fully prepared stoutly to receive him, and resolved to endure the utmost extremity, rather than forsake the Romans. That which troubled them most was, that they knew not where Lucullus was, and heard nothing of him, though at that time his army was visible before them

But they were imposed upon by the Mithridatians, who, showing them the Romans encamped on the hills, said, "Do ye see those? those are the auxiliary Armenians and Medes, whom Tigranes has sent to Mithridates." They were thus overwhelmed with thinking of the vast numbers round them, and could not believe any way of relief was left them, even if Lucullus should come up to their assistance. Demonax, a messenger sent in by Archelaus, was the first who told them of Lucullus's arrival; but they disbelieved his report, and thought he came with a story invented merely to encourage them. At which time it happened that a boy, a prisoner who had run away from the enemy, was brought before them; who, being asked where Lucullus was, laughed at their jesting, as he thought, but, finding them in earnest, with his finger pointed to the Roman camp; upon which they took courage. The lake Dascylitis was navigated with vessels of some little size; one, the biggest of them, Lucullus drew ashore, and carrying her across in a wagon to the sea, filled her with soldiers, who, sailing along unseen in the dead of the night, came safe into the city.

The gods themselves, too, in admiration of the constancy of the Cyzicenians, seems to have animated them with manifest signs, more especially now in the festival of Proserpine, where a black heifer being wanting for sacrifice, they supplied it by a figure made of dough, which they set before the altar. But the holy heifer set apart for the goddess, and at that time grazing with the other herds of the Cyzicenians on the other side of the strait, left the herd and swam over to the city alone, and offered herself for sacrifice. By night, also, the goddess appearing to Aristagoras, the town clerk, "I am come," said she, "and have brought the Libyan piper against the Pontic trumpeter; bid the citizens, therefore, be of good courage." While the Cyzicenians were wondering what the words could mean, a sudden wind sprung up and caused a considerable motion on the sea. The king's battering engines, the wonderful contrivance of Niconides of Thessaly then under the walls, by their cracking and rattling soon demonstrated what would follow; after which an extraordinarily tempestuous south wind succeeding shattered, in a short space of time, all the rest of the works, and by a violent concussion, threw down the wooden tower a hundred cubits high. It is said that in Ilium Minerva appeared to many that night in their sleep, with the sweat running down her person, and showed them her robe torn in one place, telling them that she had just arrived from relieving the Cyzicenians ; and the inhabitants to this day show a monument with an inscription, including a public decree, referring to the fact.

Mithridates, through the knavery of his officers, not knowing for some time the want of provision in his camp, was troubled in mind that the Cyzicenians should hold out against him. But his ambition and anger fell, when he saw his soldiers in the extremity of want, and feeding on man's flesh ; as in truth, Lucullus was not carrying on the war as mere matter of show and stage-play, but according to the proverb, made the seat of war in the belly, and did every thing to cut off their supplies of food. Mithridates, therefore, took advantage of the time while Lucullus was storming a tort, and sent away almost all his horse to Bithynia, with the sumpter cattle, and as many of the foot as were unfit for service. On intelligence of which, Lucullus, while it was yet night, came to his camp, and in the morning, though it was stormy weather, took with him ten cohorts of foot, and the horse, and pursued them under falling snow and in cold so severe that many of his soldiers were unable to proceed ; and with the rest coming upon the enemy, near the river Rhyndacus, he overthrew them with so great a slaughter that the very women of Apollonia came out to seize on the booty and strip the slain. Great numbers, as we may suppose, were slain ; six thousand horses were taken, with an infinite number of beasts of burden, and no less than fifteen thousand men. All which he led along by the enemy's camp. I cannot but wonder on this occasion at Sallust, who says that this was the first time camels were seen by the Romans, as if he thought those who, long before, under Scipio, defeated Antiochus, or those who lately had fought against Archelaus near Orchomenus and Chæronea, had not known what a camel was. Mithridates himself, fully determined upon flight, as mere delays and diversions for Lucullus, sent his admiral Aristonicus to the Greek sea ; who, however, was betrayed in the very instant of going off, and Lucullus became master of him, and ten thousand pieces of gold which he was carrying with him to corrupt some of the Roman army. After which, Mithridates himself made for the sea, leaving the foot officers to conduct the army, upon whom Lucullus fell, near the river Granicus, where he took a vast number alive, and slew twenty thousand. It is reported that the total number killed, of fighting men and of others who followed the camp, amounted to something not far short of three hundred thousand.

VOL. II.—

Lucullus first went to Cyzicus, where he was received with all the joy and gratitude suiting the occasion, and then collected a navy, visiting the shores of the Hellespont. And arriving at Troas, he lodged in the temple of Venus, where, in the night, he thought he saw the goddess coming to him, and saying,

> Sleep'st thou, great lion, when the fawns are nigh?

Rising up hereupon, he called his friends to him, it being yet night, and told them his vision; at which instant some Ilians came up and acquainted him that thirteen of the king's quinqueremes were seen off the Achæan harbor, sailing for Lemnos. He at once put to sea, took these, and slew their Admiral Isidorus. And then he made after another squadron, who were just come into port, and were hauling their vessels ashore, but fought from the decks, and sorely galled Lucullus's men; there being neither room to sail round them, nor to bear upon them for any damage, his ships being afloat, while theirs stood secure and fixed on the sand. After much ado, at the only landing-place of the island, he disembarked the choicest of his men, who, falling upon the enemy behind, killed some, and forced others to cut their cables, and thus making from the shore, they fell foul upon one another, or came within the reach of Lucullus's fleet. Many were killed in the action. Among the captives was Marius, the commander sent by Sertorius, who had but one eye. And it was Lucullus's strict command to his men before the engagement, that they should kill no man who had but one eye, that he might rather die under disgrace and reproach.

This being over, he hastened his pursuit after Mithridates, whom he hoped to find still in Bithynia, intercepted by Voconius, whom he sent out before to Nicomedia with part of the fleet, to stop his flight. But Voconius, loitering in Samothrace to get initiated and celebrate a feast, let slip his opportunity, Mithridates being passed by with all his fleet. He, hastening into Pontus before Lucullus should come up to him, was caught in a storm, which dispersed his fleet and sunk several ships. The wreck floated on all the neighboring shore for many days after. The merchant ship, in which he himself was, could not well in that heavy swell be brought ashore by the masters for its bigness, and it being heavy with water and ready to sink, he left it and went aboard a pirate vessel, delivering himself into the hands of pirates, and thus unexpectedly and wonderfully came safe to Heraclea, in Pontus.

Thus the proud language Lucullus had used to the senate, ended without any mischance. For they having decreed him three thousand talents to furnish out a navy, he himself was against it, and sent them word that without any such great and costly supplies, by the confederate shipping alone, he did not in the least doubt but to rout Mithridates from the sea And so he did, by divine assistance, for it is said that the wrath of Diana of Priapus brought the great tempest upon the men of Pontus, because they had robbed her temple, and removed her image.

Many were persuading Lucullus to defer the war, but he rejected their counsel, and marched through Bithynia and Galatia into the king's country, in such great scarcity of provision at first, that thirty thousand Galatians followed, every man carrying a bushel of wheat at his back. But subduing all in his progress before him, he at last found himself in such great plenty, that an ox was sold in the camp for a single drachma, and a slave 10r four. The other booty they made no account of, but left it behind or destroyed it; there being no disposing of it, where all had such abundance. But when they had made frequent incursions with their cavalry, and had advanced as far as Themiscyra, and the plains of the Thermodon, merely laying waste the country before them, they began to find fault with Lucullus, asking "why he took so many towns by surrender, and never one by storm, which might enrich them with the plunder? and now, forsooth, leaving Amisus behind, a rich and wealthy city, of easy conquest, if closely besieged, he will carry us into the Tibarenian and Chaldean wilderness, to fight with Mithridates." Lucullus, little thinking this would be of such dangerous consequence as it afterwards proved, took no notice and slighted it; and was rather anxious to excuse himself to those who blamed his tardiness, in losing time about small, pitiful places not worth the while, and allowing Mithridates opportunity to recruit. "That is what I design," said he, "and sit here contriving by my delay, that he may grow great again, and gather a considerable army, which may induce him to stand, and not fly away before us. For do you not see the wide and unknown wilderness behind? Caucasus is not far off, and a multitude of vast mountains, enough to conceal ten thousand kings that wished to avoid a battle. Besides this, a journey but of few days leads from Cabira to Armenia, where Tigranes reigns, king of kings, and holds in his hands a power that has enabled him to keep the Parthians in narrow bounds, to remove Greek cities bodily into Media, to conquer Syria and Palestine, to put to death the kings of the royal line of Seleucus, and carry away their wives and daughters by violence. This same is relation and son-in-law to Mithridates, and cannot but receive him upon entreaty, and enter into war with us to defend him; so that, while we endeavor to dispose Mithridates, we shall endanger the bringing in of Tigranes against us, who already has sought occasion to fall out with us, but can never find one so justifiable as the succor of a friend and prince in his necessity. Why, therefore, should we put Mithridates upon this resource, who as yet does not see how he may best fight with us, and disdains to stoop to Tigranes; and not rather allow him time to gather a new army and grow confident again, that we may thus fight with Colchains, and Tibarenians, whom we have often defeated already, and not with Medes and Armenians."

Upon these motives, Lucullus sat down before Amisus, and slowly carried on the siege. But the winter being well spent, he left Murena in charge of it, and went himself against Mithridates, then rendezvousing at Cabira, and resolving to await the Romans, with forty thousand foot about him, and fourteen thousand horse, on whom he chiefly confided. Passing the river Lycus, he challenged the Romans into the plains, where the cavalry engaged, and the Romans were beaten. Pomponius, a man of some note, was taken wounded; and sore, and in pain as he was, was carried before Mithridates, and asked by the king if he would become his friend, if he saved his life. He answered, "yes, if you become reconciled to the Romans; if not, your enemy." Mithridates wondered at him, and did him no hurt. The enemy being with their cavalry master of the plains, Lucullus was something afraid, and hesitated to enter the mountains, being very large, woody, and almost inaccessible, when, by good luck, some Greeks who had fled into a cave were taken, the eldest of whom, Artemidorus by name, promised to bring Lucullus, and seat him in a place of safety for his army, where there was a fort that overlooked Cabira. Lucullus, believing him, lighted his fires, and marched in the night; and safely passing the defile, gained the place, and in the morning was seen above the enemy, pitching his camp in a place advantageous to descend upon them if he desired to fight, and secure from being forced, if he preferred to lie still. Neither side was willing to engage at present. But it is related that some of the king's party were hunting a stag, and some Ro mans wanting to cut them off, came out and met them Whereupon they skirmished, more still drawing together to each side, and at last the king's party prevailed, on which the Romans, from their camp seeing their companions fly, were enraged, and ran to Lucullus with entreaties to lead them out, demanding that the sign might be given for battle. But he, that they might know of what consequence the presence and appearance of a wise commander is in time of conflict and danger, ordered them to stand still. But he went down himself into the plains, and meeting with the foremost that fled, commanded them to stand and turn back with him. These obeying, the rest also turned and formed again in a body, and thus, with no great difficulty, drove back the enemies, and pursued them to their camp. After his return, Lucullus inflicted the customary punishment upon the fugitives, and made them dig a trench of twelve foot, working in their frocks unfastened, while the rest stood by and looked on.

There was in Mithridates's camp, one Olthacus, a chief of the Dandarians, a barbarous people living near the lake Mæotis, a man remarkable for strength and courage in fight, wise in council, and pleasant and ingratiating in conversation. He, out of emulation, and a constant eagerness which possessed him to outdo one of the other chiefs of his country, promised a great piece of service to Mithridates, no less than the death of Lucullus. The king commended his resolution, and, according to agreement, counterfeited anger, and put some disgrace upon him; whereupon he took horse, and fled to Lucullus, who kindly received him, being a man of great name in the army. After some short trial of his sagacity and perseverance, he found way to Lucullus's board and council. The Dandarian, thinking he had a fair opportunity, commanded his servants to lead his horse out of the camp, while he himself, as the soldiers were refreshing and resting themselves, it being then high noon, went to the general's tent, not at all expecting that entrance would be denied to one who was so familiar with him, and came under pretence of extraordinary business with him. He had certainly been admitted had not sleep, which has destroyed many captains, saved Lucullus. For so it was, and Menedemus, one of the bedchamber, was standing at the door, who told Olthacus that it was altogether unseasonable to see the general, since, after long watching and hard labor, he was but just before laid down to repose himself. Olthacus would not go away upon this denial, but still persisted, saying that he must go in to speak of some necessary affairs, whereupon Menedemus grew angry, and replied that nothing was more necessary than the safety of Lucullus and forced him away with both hands. Upon which, out of fear, he straightway left the camp, took horse, and without effect returned to Mithridates. Thus in action as in physic, it is the critical moment that gives both the fortunate and the fatal effect.

After this, Sornatius being sent out with ten companies for forage, and pursued by Menander, one of Mithridates's captains, stood his ground, and after a sharp engagement, routed and slew a considerable number of the enemy. Adrianus being sent afterward, with some forces, to procure food enough and to spare for the camp, Mithridates did not let the opportunity slip, but despatched Menemachus and Myro, with a great force, both horse and foot, against him, all which except two men, it is stated, were cut off by the Romans. Mithridates concealed the loss, giving it out that it was a small defeat, nothing near so great as reported, and occasioned by the unskilfulness of the leaders. But Adrianus in great pomp passed by his camp, having many wagons full of corn and other booty, filling Mithridates with distress, and the army with confusion and consternation. It was resolved, therefore, to stay no longer. But when the king's servants sent away their own goods quietly, and hindered others from doing so too, the soldiers in great fury thronged and crowded to the gates, seized on the king's servants and killed them, and plundered the baggage. Dorylaus, the general, in this confusion, having nothing else besides his purple cloak, lost his life for that, and Hermæus, the priest, was trod underfoot in the gate.

Mithridates, having not one of his guards, nor even a groom remaining with him, got out of the camp in the throng, but had none of his horses with him; until Ptolemy, the eunuch, some little time after, seeing him in the press making his way among the others, dismounted and gave his horse to the king. The Romans were already close upon him in their pursuit nor was it through want of speed that they failed to catch him, but they were as near as possible doing so. But greediness and a petty military avarice hindered them from acquiring that booty which in so many fights and hazards they had sought after, and lost Lucullus the prize of his victory. For the horse which carried the king was within reach, but one of the mules that carried the treasure either by accident stepping in, or by order of the king so appointed to go between him and the pursuers, they seized and pilfered the gold, and fall ing out among themselves about the prey, let slip the great prize. Neither was their greediness prejudical to Lucullus in this only, but also they slew Callistratus, the king's confidential attendant, under suspicion of having five hundred pieces of gold in his girdle; whereas Lucullus had specially ordered that he should be conveyed safe into the camp. Notwithstanding all which, he gave them leave to plunder the camp.

After this, in Cabira, and other strongholds which he took, he found great treasures, and private prisons, in which many Greeks and many of the king's relations had been confined, who, having long since counted themselves no other than dead men, by the favor of Lucullus, met with relief so truly as with a new life and second birth. Nyssa, also, sister of Mithridates, enjoyed the like fortunate captivity; while those who seemed to be most out of danger, his wives and sisters at Phernacia, placed in safety as they thought, miserably perished, Mithridates in his flight sending Bacchides the eunuch to them. Among others there were two sisters of the king, Roxana and Statira, unmarried women forty years old, and two Ionian wives, Berenice of Chios, and Monime of Miletus. This latter was the most celebrated among the Greeks, because she so long withstood the king in his courtship to her, though he presented her with fifteen thousand pieces of gold, until a covenant of marriage was made, and a crown was sent her, and she was saluted queen. She had been a sorrowful woman before, and often bewailed her beauty, that had procured her a keeper, instead of a husband, and a watch of barbarians, instead of the home and attendance of a wife; and, removed far from Greece, she enjoyed the pleasure which she proposed to herself, only in a dream, being in the mean time robbed of that which is real. And when Bacchides came and bade them prepare for death, as every one thought most easy and painless, she took the diadem from her head, and fastening the string to her neck, suspended herself with it; which soon breaking, "O wretched headband!" said she, "not able to help me even in this small thing!" And throwing it away she spat on it, and offered her throat to Bacchides. Berenice had prepared a potion for herself, but at her mother's entreaty, who stood by, she gave her part of it. Both drank of the potion, which prevailed over the weaker body. But Berenice, having drunk too little, was not released by it, but lingering on unable to die, was strangled by Bacchides for haste. It is said that one of the unmarried sisters drank the poison, with bitter execrations and curses; but Statira uttered nothing ungentle or reproachful, but on the contrary, commended her brother, who in his own danger neglected not theirs, but carefully provided that they might go out of the world without shame or disgrace.

Lucullus, being a good and humane man, was concerned at these things. However, going on he came to Talaura, from whence four days before his arrival Mithridates had fled, and was got to Tigranes in Armenia. He turned off, therefore, and subdued the Chaldeans and Tibarenians, with the lesser Armenia, and having reduced all their forts and cities, he sent Appius to Tigranes to demand Mithridates. He himself went to Amisus, which still held out under the command of Callimachus, who, by his great engineering skill, and his dexterity at all the shifts and subtleties of a siege, had greatly incommoded the Romans. For which afterward he paid dear enough, and was now out-manœuvred by Lucullus, who, unexpectedly coming upon him at the time of the day when the slodiers used to withdraw and rest themselves, gained part of the wall, and forced him to leave the city, in doing which he fired it; either envying the Romans the booty, or to secure his own escape the better. No man looked after those who went off in the ships, but as soon as the fire had seized on most part of the wall, the soldiers prepared themselves for plunder; while Lucullus, pitying the ruin of the city, brought assistance from without, and encouraged his men to extinguish the flames. But all, being intent upon the prey, and giving no heed to him, with loud outcries, beat and clashed their arms together, until he was compelled to let them plunder, that by that means he might at least save the city from fire. But they did quite the contrary, for in searching the houses with lights and torches everywhere, they were themselves the cause of the destruction of most of the buildings, inasmuch that when Lucullus the next day went in, he shed tears, and said to his friends, that he had often before blessed the fortune of Sylla, but never so much admired it as then, because when he was willing, he was also able to save Athens, "but my infelicity is such, that while I endeavor to imitate him, I become like Mummius." Nevertheless, he endeavored to save as much of the city as he could, and at the same time, also, by a happy providence a fall of rain concurred to extinguish the fire. He himself while present repaired the ruins as much as he could, receiving back the inhabitants who had fled, and settling as many other Greeks as were willing to live there adding a hundred furlongs of ground to the place.

This city was a colony of Athens, built at that time when she flourished and was powerful at sea, upon which account many who fled from Aristion's tyranny settled here, and were admitted as citizens. but had the ill-luck to fly from evils at home, into greater abroad. As many of these as survived Lucullus furnished every one with clothes, and two hundred drachmas, and sent them away into their own country. On this occasion, Tyrannion the grammarian was taken. Murena begged him of Lucullus, and took him and made him a freedman; but in this he abused Lucullus's favor who by no means liked that a man of high repute for learning should be first made a slave, and then freed; for freedom thus speciously granted again, was a real deprivation of what he had before. But not in this case alone Murena showed himself far inferior in generosity to the general.

Lucullus was now busy in looking after the cities of Asia, and having no war to divert his time, spent it in the administration of law and justice, the want of which had for a long time left the province a prey to unspeakable and incredible miseries; so plundered and enslaved by tax-farmers and usurers, that private people were compelled to sell their sons in the flower of their youth, and their daughters in their virginity, and the States publicly to sell their consecrated gifts, pictures and statues In the end their lot was to yield themselves up slaves to their creditors, but before this, worse troubles befel them, tortures, inflicted with ropes and by horses, standing abroad to be scorched when the sun was hot, and being driven into ice and clay in the cold; insomuch that slavery was no less than a redemption and joy to them. Lucullus in a short time freed the cities from all these evils and oppressions; for, first of all, he ordered there should be no more taken than one per cent. Secondly, where the interest exceeded the principal, he struck it off. The third, and most considerable order was, that the creditor should receive the fourth part of the debtor's income; but if any lender had added the interest to the principal, it was utterly disallowed. Insomuch, that in the space of four years all debts were paid, and lands returned to their right owners. The public debt was contracted when Asia was fined twenty thousand talents by Sylla, but twice as much was paid to the collectors who by their usury had by this time advanced it to a hundred and twenty thousand talents. And accordingly they inveighed against Lucullus at Rome, as grossly injured by him, and by their money's help (as indeed, they were very powerful, and had many of the statesmen in their debt), they stirred up several leading men against him. But Lucullus was not only beloved by the cities which he obliged, but was also wished for by other provinces, who blessed the good-luck of those who had such a governor over them.

Appius Clodius, who was sent to Tigranes (the same Clodius was brother to Lucullus's wife), being led by the king's guides, a roundabout way, unnecessarily long and tedious, through the upper country, being informed by his freedman, a Syrian by nation, of the direct road, left that lengthy and fallacious one; and bidding the barbarians, his guides, adieu, in a few days passed over Euphrates, and came to Antioch upon Daphne. There being commanded to wait for Tigranes, who at that time was reducing some towns in Phœnicia, he won over many chiefs to his side, who unwillingly submitted to the king of Armenia, among whom was Zarbienus, king of the Gordyenians; also many of the conquered cities corresponded privately with him, whom he assured of relief from Lucullus, but ordered them to lie still at present. The Armenian government was an oppressive one, and intolerable to the Greeks, especially that of the present king, who growing insolent and overbearing with his success, imagined all things valuable and esteemed among men not only were his in fact, but had been purposely created for him alone. From a small and inconsiderable beginning, he had gone on to be the conqueror of many nations, had humbled the Parthian power more than any before him, and filled Mesopotamia with Greeks, whom he carried in numbers out of Cilicia and Cappadocia. He transplanted also the Arabs, who lived in tents, from their country and home, and settled them near him, that by their means he might carry on the trade.

He had many kings waiting on him, but four he always carried with him as servants and guards, who, when he rode, ran by his horse's side in ordinary under-frocks, and attended him, when sitting on his throne, and publishing his decrees to the people, with their hands folded together; which posture of all others was that which most expressed slavery, it being that of men who had bidden adieu to liberty, and had prepared their bodies more for chastisement, than the service of their masters. Appius, nothing dismayed or surprised at this theatrical display, as soon as audience was granted him, said he came to demand Mithridates for Lucullus's triumph, otherwise to denounce war against Tigranes: insomuch that though Tigranes endeavored to receive him with a smooth countenance and a forced smile, he could not dissemble his discomposure to those who stood about him, at the bold language of the young man; for it was the first time, perhaps, in twenty-five years, the length of his reign, or, more truly, of his tyranny, that any free speech had been uttered to him. However, he made answer to Appius, that he would not desert Mithridates, and would defend himself, if the Romans attacked him. He was angry, also, with Lucullus for calling him only king in his letter, and not king of kings, and, in his answer, would not give him his tittle of imperator. Great gifts were sent to Appius, which he refused; but on their being sent again and augmented, that he might not seem to refuse in anger, he took one goblet and sent the rest back, and without delay went off to the general.

Tigranes before this neither vouchsafed to see nor speak with Mithridates, though a near kinsman, and forced out of so considerable a kingdom, but proudly and scornfully kept him at a distance, as a sort of prisoner, in a marshy and unhealthy district; but now, with much profession of respect and kindness, he sent for him, and at a private conference between them in the palace, they healed up all private jealousies between them, punishing their favorites, who bore all the blame; among whom Metrodorus of Scepsis was one, an eloquent and learned man, and so close an intimate as commonly to be called the king's father. This man, as it happened, being employed in an embassy by Mithridates to solicit help against the Romans, Tigranes asked him, "what would you, Metrodorus, advise me to in this affair?" In return to which, either out of good-will to Tigranes, or a want of solicitude for Mithridates, he made answer, that as ambassador he counselled him to it, but as a friend dissuaded him from it. This Tigranes reported, and affirmed to Mithridates, thinking that no irreparable harm would come of it to Metrodorus. But upon this he was presently taken off, and Tigranes was sorry for what he had done, though he had not, indeed, been absolutely the cause of his death; yet he had given the fatal turn to the anger of Mithridates, who had privately hated him before, as appeared from his cabinet papers when taken, among which there was an order that Metrodorus should die. Tigranes buried him splendidly, sparing no cost to his dead body, whom he betrayed when alive. In Tigranes's court died, also, Amphicrates the orator (if for the sake of Athens, we may also mention him), of whom it is told that he left his country and fled to Seleucia, upon the river Tigris, and, being desired to teach logic among them, arrogantly replied, that the dish was too little to hold a dolphin. He, therefore, came to Cleopatra, daughter of Mithridates, and queen to Tigranes, but being accused of misdemeanors, prohibited all commerce with his countrymen, ended his days by starving himself. He, in like manner, received from Cleopatra an honorable burial, near Sapha, a place so called in that country.

Lucullus, when he had reëstablished law and a lasting peace in Asia, did not altogether forget pleasure and mirth, but, during his residence at Ephesus, gratified the cities with sports, festival triumphs, wrestling games, and single combats of gladiators. And they, in requital, instituted others, called Lucullean games, in honor to him, thus manifesting their love to him, which was of more value to him than all the honor. But when Appius came to him and told him he must prepare for war with Tigranes, he went again into Pontus, and, gathering together his army, besieged Sinope, or rather the Cilicians of the king's side who held it ; who thereupon killed a number of the Sinopians, and set the city on fire, and by night endeavored to escape. Which when Lucullus perceived, he entered the city, and killed eight thousand of them who were still left behind ; but restored to the inhabitants what was their own, and took special care for the welfare of the city. To which he was chiefly prompted by this vision. One seemed to come to him in his sleep, and say, "Go on a little further, Lucullus, for Autolycus is coming to see thee." When he arose he could not imagine what the vision meant. The same day he took the city, and as he was pursuing the Cilicians, who were flying by sea, he saw a statue lying on the shore, which the Cilicians carried so far, but had not time to carry aboard. It was one of the masterpieces of Sthenis. And one told him that it was the statue of Autoycus, the founder of the city. This Autolycus is reported to have been son to Deimachus, and one of those who, under Hercules, went on the expedition out of Thessaly against the Amazons ; from whence in his return with Demoleon and Phlogius, he lost his vessel on a point of the Chersonesus, called Pedalium. He himself, with his companions and their weapons, being saved, came to Sinope, and dispossessed the Syrians there. The Syrians held it, descended from Syrus, as is the story, the son of Apol'o, and Sinope, the daughter of

Æsopus. Which as soon as Lucullus heard, he remembered the admonition of Sylla, whose advice it is in his Memoirs to treat nothing as so certain and so worthy of reliance as an intimation given in dreams.

When it was now told him that Mithridates and Tigranes were just ready to transport their forces into Lycaonia and Cilicia, with the object of entering Asia before him, he wondered much why the Armenian, supposing him to entertain any real intention to fight with the Romans, did not assist Mithridates in his flourishing condition, and join forces when he was fit for service, instead of suffering him to be vanquished and broken in pieces, and now at last beginning the war, when its hopes were grown cold, and throwing himself down headlong with them, who were irrevocably fallen already. But when Machares, the son of Mithridates, and governor of Bosporus, sent him a crown, valued at a thousand pieces of gold, and desired to be enrolled as a friend and confederate of the Romans, he fairly reputed that war at an end, and left Sornatius, his deputy, with six thousand soldiers, to take care of Pontus. He himself with twelve thousand foot, and a little less than three thousand horse, went forth to the second war, advancing, it seemed very plain, with too great and ill-advised speed, into the midst of warlike nations and many thousands upon thousands of horse, into an unknown extent of country, every way inclosed with deep rivers and mountains, never free from snow; which made the soldiers, already far from orderly, follow him with great unwillingness and opposition. For the same reason, also, the popular leaders at home publicly inveighed and declaimed against him, as one that raised up war after war, not so much for the interest of the republic, as that he himself, being still in commission, might not lay down arms, but go on enriching himself by the public dangers. These men, in the end, effected their purpose. But Lucullus by long journeys, came to the Euphrates, where, finding the waters high and rough from the winter, he was much troubled for fear of delay and difficulty while he should procure boats and make a bridge of them. But in the evening the flood beginning to retire, and decreasing all through the night, the next day they saw the river far down within his banks, so much so that the inhabitants, discovering the little islands in the river, and the water stagnating among them, a thing which had rarely happened before, made obeisance to Lucullus, before whom the very river was humble and submissive, and yielded an easy and swift passage. Making use ot the opportunity, he carried over his army, and met with a lucky sign at landing. Holy heifers are pastured on purpose for Diana Persia, whom, of all the gods, the barbarians beyond Euphrates chiefly adore. They use these heifers only for her sacrifices. At other times they wander up and down undisturbed, with the mark of the goddess, a torch, branded on them; and it is no such light or easy thing, when occasion requires, to seize one of them. But one of these, when the army had passed the Euphrates, coming to a rock consecrated to the goddess, stood upon it, and then laying down her neck, like others that are forced down with a rope, offered herself to Lucullus for sacrifice. Besides which, he offered also a bull to Euphrates, for his safe passage. That day he tarried there, but on the next, and those that followed, he travelled through Sophene, using no manner of violence to the people who came to him, and willingly received his army. And when the soldiers were desirous to plunder a castle that seemed to be well stored within, "That is the castle," said he, "that we must storm," showing them Taurus at a distance; "the rest is reserved for those who conquer there." Wherefore hastening his march, and passing the Tigris, he came over into Armenia.

The first messenger that gave notice of Lucullus's coming was so far from pleasing Tigranes, that he had his head cut off for his pains; and no man daring to bring further information, without any intelligence at all, Tigranes sat while war was already blazing around him, giving ear only to those who flattered him, by saying that Lucullus would show himself a great commander, if he ventured to wait for Tigranes at Ephesus, and did not at once fly out of Asia, at the mere sight of the many thousands that were come against him. He is a man of a strong body that can carry off a great quantity of wine, and of a powerful constitution of mind that can sustain felicity. Mithrobarzanes, one of his chief favorites, first dared to tell him the truth, but had no more thanks for his freedom of speech, than to be immediately sent out against Lucullus with three thousand horse, and a great number of foot, with peremptory demands to bring him alive, and trample down his army. Some of Lucullus's men were then pitching their camp, and the rest were coming up to them, when the scouts gave notice that the enemy was approaching, whereupon he was in fear lest they should fall upon him, while his men were divided and unarranged; which made him stay to pitch the camp himself, and send out Sextilius, the legate, with sixteen hundred horse, and about as many heavy and light arms, with orders to advance towards the enemy, and wait until intelligence came to him that the camp was finished. Sextilius designed to have kept this order; but Mithrobarzanes coming furiously upon him, he was forced to fight. In the engagement, Mithrobarzanes himself was slain, fighting, and all his men, except a few who ran away, were destroyed. After this, Tigranes left Tigranocerta, a great city built by himself, and retired to Taurus, and called all his forces about him.

But Lucullus, giving him no time to rendezvous, sent out Murena, to harass and cut off those who marched to Tigranes, and Sextilius, also, to disperse a great company of Arabians then on the way to the king. Sextilius fell upon the Arabians in their camp, and destroyed most of them, and also Murena, in his pursuit after Tigranes through a craggy and narrow pass, opportunely fell upon him. Upon which Tigranes, abandoning all his baggage, fled; many of the Armenians were killed, and more taken. After this success, Lucullus went to Tigranocerta, and sitting down before the city, besieged it. In it were many Greeks carried away out of Cilicia, and many barbarians in like circumstances with the Greeks, Adiabenians, Assyrians, Gordyenians, and Cappadocians, whose native cities he had destroyed, and forced away the inhabitants to settle here. It was a rich and beautiful city, every common man, and every man of rank, in imitation of the king, studied to enlarge and adorn it. This made Lucullus more vigorously press the siege, in the belief that Tigranes would not patiently endure it, but even against his own judgment would come down in anger to force him away; in which he was not mistaken. Mithridates earnestly dissuaded him from it, sending messengers and letters to him not to engage, but rather with his horse to try and cut off the supplies. Taxiles, also, who came from Mithridates, and who stayed with his army, very much entreated the king to 'orbear, and to avoid the Roman arms, things it was not safe to meddle with. To this he hearkened at first, but when the Armenians and Gordyenians in a full body, and the whole forces of Medes and Adiabenians, under their respective kings, joined him; when many Arabians came up from the sea beyond Babylon; and from the Caspian sea, the Albanians and the Iberians their neighbors, and not a few of the free people, without kings, living about the Araxes, by entreaty and hire also came together to him; and all the king's feasts and councils rang of nothing but expectations, boastings, and barbaric threatenings, Taxiles went in danger of his life, for giving council against fighting, and it was imputed to envy in Mithridates thus to discourage him from so glorious an enterprise. Therefore Tigranes would by no means tarry for him for fear he should share in the glory, but marched on with all his army, lamenting to his friends, as it is said, that he should fight with Lucullus alone, and not with all the Roman generals together. Neither was his boldness to be accounted wholly frantic or unreasonable, when he had so many nations and kings attending him, and so many tens of thousands of well armed foot and horse about him. He had twenty thousand archers and slingers, fifty-five thousand horse, of which seventeen thousand were in complete armor, as Lucullus wrote to the senate, a hundred and fifty thousand heavy-armed men, drawn up partly into cohorts, partly into phalanxes, besides various divisions of men appointed to make roads and lay bridges, to drain off waters and cut wood, and to perform other necessary services, to the number of thirty-five thousand, who, being quartered behind the army, added to its strength, and made it the more formidable to behold.

As soon as he had passed Taurus, and appeared with his forces, and saw the Romans beleaguering Tigranocerta, the barbarous people within, with shoutings and acclamations, received the sight, and threatening the Romans from the wall, pointed to the Armenians. In a council of war, some advised Lucullus to leave the siege, and march up to Tigranes, others that it would not be safe to leave the siege, and so many enemies behind. He answered that neither side by itself was right, but together both gave sound advice; and accordingly he divided his army, and left Murena with six thousand foot in charge of the siege, and himself went out with twenty-four cohorts, in which were no more than ten thousand men at arms, and with all the horse and slingers and archers and about a thousand sitting down by the river in a large plain, he appeared, indeed, very inconsiderable to Tigranes, and a fit subject for the flattering wits about him. Some of whom jeered, others cast lots for the spoil, and every one of the kings and commanders came and desired to undertake the engagement alone, and that he would be pleased to sit still and behold. Tigranes himself wishing to be witty and pleasant upon the occasion, made use of the well-known saying, that they were too many for ambassadors, and too few for soldiers. Thus they continued sneering and scoffing. As soon as day came, Lucullus brought out his forces under arms. The barbarian army stood on the eastern side of the river, and there being a bend of the river westward in that part of it, where it was easiest forded, Lucullus, while he led his army on in haste, seemed to Tigranes to be flying; who thereupon called Taxiles, and in derision said, "Do you not see these invincible Romans flying?" But Taxiles replied, "Would, indeed, O king, that some such unlikely piece of fortune might be destined you; but the Romans do not, when going on a march, put on their best clothes, nor use bright shields, and naked head-pieces, as now you see them, with the leathern coverings all taken off, but this is a preparation for war of men just ready to engage with their enemies." While Taxiles was thus speaking, as Lucullus wheeled about, the first eagle appeared, and the cohorts, according to their divisions and companies, formed in order to pass over, when with much ado, and like a man that is just recovering from a drunken fit, Tigranes cried out twice or thrice, "What, are they upon us?" In great confusion, therefore, the army got in array, the king keeping the main body to himself, while the left wing given in charge to the Adiabenian, and the right to the Mede, in the front of which latter were posted most of the heavy-armed cavalry. Some officers advised Lucullus, just as he was going to cross the river, to lie still, that day being one of the unfortunate ones which they call black days, for on it the army under Cæpio, engaging with the Cimbrians, was destroyed. But he returned the famous answer, "I will make it a happy day to the Romans." It was the day before the nones of October.

Having so said, he bade them take courage, passed over the river, and himself first of all led them against the enemy, clad in a coat of mail, with shining steel scales and a fringed mantle; and his sword might already be seen out of the scabbard, as if to signify that they must without delay come to a hand-to-hand combat with an enemy whose skill was in distant fighting, and by the speed of their advance curtail the space that exposed them to the archery. But when he saw the heavy-armed horse, the flower of the army, drawn up under a hill, on the top of which was a broad and open plain about four furlongs distant, and of no very difficult or troublesome access, he commanded his Thracian and Galatian horse to fall upon their flank, and beat down their lances with their swords. The only defence of these horse men-at-arms are their lances; they have nothing else that they can use to protect themselves, or annoy their enemy, on account of the weight and stiffness of their armor, with which they are, as it were, built up. He himself, with two cohorts, made to the mountain, the soldiers briskly following, when they saw him in arms afoot first toiling and climbing up. Being on the top and standing in an open place, with a loud voice he cried out, "We have overcome, we have overcome, fellow-soldiers!" And having so said, he marched against the armed horsemen, commanding his men not to throw their javelins, but coming up hand to hand with the enemy, to hack their shins and thighs, which parts alone were unguarded in these heavy-armed horsemen. But there was no need of this way of fighting, for they stood not to receive the Romans, but with great clamor and worse flight they and their heavy horses threw themselves upon the ranks of the foot, before ever these could so much as begin the fight, insomuch that without a wound or bloodshed, so many thousands were overthrown. The greatest slaughter was made in the flight, or rather in the endeavoring to fly away, which they could not well do by reason of the depth and closeness of their own ranks, which hindered them. Tigranes at first fled with a few, but seeing his son in the same misfortune, he took the diadem from his head, and with tears gave it him, bidding him save himself by some other road if he could. But the young man, not daring to put it on, gave it to one of his trustiest servants to keep for him. This man, as it happened, being taken, was brought to Lucullus, and so, among the captives, the crown, also, of Tigranes was taken. It is stated that above a hundred thousand foot were lost, and that of the horse but very few escaped at all. Of the Romans, a hundred were wounded, and five killed. Antiochus the philosopher, making mention of this fight in his book about the gods, says that the sun never saw the like. Strabo, a second philosopher, in his historical collection says, that the Romans could not but blush and deride themselves, for putting on armor against such pitiful slaves. Livy also says, that the Romans never fought an enemy with such unequal forces, for the conquerors were not so much as one twentieth part of the number of the conquered. The most sagacious and experienced Roman commanders made it a chief commendation of Lucullus, that he had conquered two great and potent kings by two most opposite ways, haste and delay. For he wore out the flourishing power of Mithridates by delay and time, and crushed that of Tigranes by haste ; being one of the rare examples of generals who made use of delay for active achievement, and speed for security.

On this account it was that Mithridates had made no haste to come up to fight, imagining Lucullus would, as he had done before, use caution and delay, which made him march at his leisure to join Tigranes. And first, as he began to meet some straggling Armenians in the way, making off in great fear and consternation, he suspected the worst, and when greater numbers of stripped and wounded men met him and assured him of the defeat, he set out to seek for Tigranes. And finding him destitute and humiliated, he by no means requited him with insolence, but alighting from his horse, and condoling with him on their common loss, he gave him his own royal guard to attend him, and animated him for the future. And they together gathered fresh forces about them. In the city Tigranocerta, the Greeks meantime, dividing from the barbarians, sought to deliver it up to Lucullus, and he attacked and took it. He seized on the treasure himself but gave the city to be plundered by the soldiers, in which were found, amongst other property, eight thousand talents of coined money. Besides this, also, he distributed eight hundred drachmas to each man, out of the spoils. When he understood that many players were taken in the city, whom Tigranes had invited from all parts for opening the theatre which he had built, he made use of them for celebrating his triumphal games and spectacles. The Greeks he sent home, allowing them money for their journey, and the barbarians also, as many as had been forced away from their own dwellings. So that by this one city being dissolved, many, by the restitution of their former inhabitants, were restored. By all of which Lucullus was beloved as a benefactor and founder. Other successes, also, attended him, such as he well deserved, desirous as he was far more of praise for acts of justice and clemency, than for feats in war, these being due partly to the soldiers, and very greatly to fortune, while those are the sure proofs of a gentle and liberal soul ; and by such aids Lucullus, at that time, even without the help of arms, succeeded in reducing the barbarians. For the kings of the Arabians came to him, tendering what they had, and with them the Sophenians also submitted. And he so dealt with the Gordyenians that they were willing to leave their own habitations, and to follow him with their wives and children. Which was for this cause. Zarbienus, king of the Gordyenians, as has been told, being impatient under the tyranny of Tigranes, had by Appius secretly made overtures of confederacy with Lucullus, but, being discovered, was executed, and his wife and children with him, before the Romans entered Armenia. Lucullus forgot not this, but coming to the Gordyenians made a solemn interment in honor of Zarbienus, and adorning the funeral pile with royal robes, and gold, and the spoils of Tigranes, he himself in person kindled the fire, and poured in perfumes with the friends and relations of the deceased, calling him his companion and the confederate of the Romans. He ordered, also, a costly monument to be built for him. There was a large treasure of gold and silver found in Zarbienus's palace, and no less than three million measures of corn, so that the soldiers were provided for, and Lucullus had the high commendation of maintaining the war at its own charge, without receiving one drachma from the public treasury.

After this came an embassy from the king of Parthia to him, desiring amity and confederacy; which being readily embraced by Lucullus, another was sent by him in return to the Parthian, the members of which discovered him to be a double-minded man, and to be dealing privately at the same time with Tigranes, offering to take part with him, upon condition Mesopotamia were delivered up to him. Which as soon as Lucullus understood, he resolved to pass by Tigranes and Mithridates as antagonists already overcome, and to try the power of Parthia, by leading his army against them, thinking it would be a glorious result, thus in one current of war, like an athlete in the games, to throw down three kings one after another, and successively to deal as a conqueror with three of the greatest powers under heaven. He sent, therefore, into Pontus to Sornatius and his colleagues, bidding them bring the army thence, and join with him in his expedition out of Gordyene. The soldiers there, however, who had been restive and unruly before, now openly displayed their mutinous temper. No manner of entreaty or force availed with them, but they protested and cried out that they would stay no longer even there, but would go away and desert Pontus. The news of which, when reported to Lucullus, did no small harm to the soldiers about him, who were already corrupted with wealth and plenty, and desirous of ease. And on hearing the boldness of the others, they called them men, and declared they themselves ought to follow their example, for the actions which they had done did now well deserve release from service, and repose.

Upon these and worse words, Lucullus gave up the thoughts of invading Parthia, and in the height of summer time, went against Tigranes. Passing over Taurus, he was filled with apprehension at the greenness of the fields before him, so long is the season deferred in this region by the coldness of the air. But nevertheless, he went down, and twice or thrice putting to flight the Armenians who dared to come out against him, he plundered and burnt their villages, and seizing on the provision designed for Tigranes, reduced his enemies to the necessity which he had feared for himself. But when, after doing all he could to provoke the enemy to fight, by drawing entrenchments round their camp and by burning the country before them, he could by no means bring them to venture out, after their frequent defeats before he rose up and marched to Artaxata, the royal city of Tigranes, where his wives and young children were kept, judging that Tigranes would never suffer that to go without the hazard of a battle. It is related that Hannibal the Carthaginian, after the defeat of Antiochus by the Romans, coming to Artaxas, king of Armenia, pointed out to him many other matters to his advantage, and observing the great natural capacities and the pleasantness of the site, then lying unoccupied and neglected, drew a model of a city for it, and bringing Artaxas thither, showed it to him and encouraged him to build. At which the king being pleased, and desiring him to oversee the work, erected a large and stately city which was called after his own name, and made metropolis of Armenia.

And in fact, when Lucullus proceeded against it, Tigranes no longer suffered it, but came with his army, and on the fourth day sat down by the Romans, the river Arsanias lying between them, which of necessity Lucullus must pass in his march to Artaxata. Lucullus, after sacrifice to the Gods, as if victory were already obtained, carried over his army, having twelve cohorts in the first division in front, the rest being disposed in the rear to prevent the enemy's in closing them. For there were many choice horse drawn up against him; in the front stood the Mardian horse-archers, and Iberians with long spears, in whom, being the most warlike, Tigranes more confided than in any other of his foreign troops. But nothing of moment was done by them, for though they skirmished with the Roman horse at a distance, they were not able to stand when the foot came up to them; but being broken, and flying on both sides, drew the horse in pursuit after them. Though these were routed, yet Lucullus

was not without alarm when he saw the cavalry about Tigranes with great bravery and in large numbers coming upon
him ; he recalled his horse from pursuing, and he himself,
first of all, with the best of his men, engaged the Satrapenians
who were opposite him, and before ever they came to close
fight, routed them with the mere terror. Of three kings
in battle against him, Mithridates of Pontus fled away the
most shamefully, being not so much as able to endure the
shout of the Romans. The pursuit reached a long way, and
all through the night the Romans slew and took prisoners,
and carried off spoils and treasure, till they were weary.
Livy says there were more taken and destroyed in the first
battle, but in the second, men of greater distinction.

Lucullus, flushed and animated by this victory, determined
to march on into the interior and there complete his conquests
over the barbarians, but winter weather came on, contrary to
expectation, as early as the autumnal equinox, with storms
and frequent snows, and, even in the most clear days, hoar
frost and ice, which made the waters scarcely drinkable for
the horses by their exceeding coldness, and scarcely passable
through the ice breaking and cutting the horses' sinews. The
country for the most part being quite uncleared, with difficult
passes, and much wood, kept them continually wet, the snow
falling thickly on them as they marched in the day, and the
ground that they lay upon at night being damp and watery.
After the battle they followed not Lucullus many days before
they began to be refractory, first of all entreating and sending
the tribunes to him, but presently they tumultuously gathered
together, and made a shouting all night long in their tents, a
plain sign of a mutinous army. But Lucullus as earnestly
entreated them, desiring them to have patience, but till they
took the Armenian Carthage, and overturned the work of
their great enemy, meaning Hannibal. But when he could
not prevail, he led them back, and crossing Taurus by
another road, came into the fruitful and sunny country of
Mygdonia, where was a great and populous city, by the barbarians called Nisibis, by the Greeks Antioch of Mygdonia.
This was defended by Guras, brother of Tigranes, with the
dignity of governor and by the engineering skill and dexterity
of Callimachus, the same who so much annoyed the Romans
at Amisus. Lucullus, however, brought his army up to it, and
laying close siege, in a short time took it by storm. He used
Guras, who surrendered himself, kindly, but gave no attention
to Callimachus, though he offered to make discovery of hid

den treasures, commanding him to be kept in chains, to be punished for firing the city of Amisus, which had disappointed his ambition of showing favor and kindness to the Greeks.

Hitherto, one would imagine fortune had attended and fought with Lucullus, but afterwards, as if the wind had failed of a sudden, he did all things by force, and as it were, against the grain ; and showed certainly the conduct and patience of a wise captain, but in the results met with no fresh honor or reputation ; and inded, by bad success and vain embarrassments with his soldiers, he came within a little of losing even what he had before. He himself was not the least cause of all this, being far from inclined to seek popularity with the mass of the soldiers, and more ready to think any indulgence shown to them an invasion of his own authority. But what was worst of all he was naturally unsociable to his great officers in commission with him, despising others and thinking them worthy of nothing in comparison with himself. These faults, we are told, he had with all his many excellencies; he was of a large and noble person, an eloquent speaker, and a wise counseller, both in the forum and the camp. Sallust says, the soldiers were ill affected to him from the beginning of the war, because they were forced to keep the field two winters at Cyzicus, and afterwards at Amisus. Their other winters, also, vexed them, for they either spent them in an enemy's country, or else were confined to their tents in the open field among their confederates ; for Lucullus not so much as once went into a Greek confederate town with his army. To this ill affection abroad, the tribunes yet more contributed at home, invidiously accusing Lucullus, as one who for empire and riches prolonged the war, holding, it might almost be said, under his sole power Cilicia, Asia, Bithynia, Paphlagonia, Pontus, Armenia, all as far as the river Phasis ; and now of late had plundered the royal city of Tigranes, as if he had been commissioned not so much to subdue, as to strip kings. This is what we are told was said by Lucius Quintius, one of the prætors, at whose instance, in particular, the people determined to send one who should succeed Lucullus in his province, and voted, also, to relieve many of the soldiers under him from further service.

Besides these evils, that which most of all prejudiced Lucullus, was Publius Clodius, an insolent man, very vicious and bold, brother to Lucullus's wife, a woman of bad conduct, with whom Clodius was himself suspected of criminal intercourse. Being then in the army under Lucullus, but not in as great authority as he expected (for he would fain have been the chief of all, but on account of his character was postponed to many), he ingratiated himself secretly with the Fimbrian troops, and stirred them up against Lucullus, using fair speeches to them, who of old had been used to be flattered in such a manner. These were those whom Fimbria before had persuaded to kill the consul Flaccus, and choose him their leader. And so they listened not unwillingly to Clodius, and called him the soldiers' friend, for the concern he professed for them, and the indignation he expressed at the prospect that "there must be no end of wars and toils, but in fighting with all nations, and wandering throughout all the world they must wear out their lives receiving no other reward for their service than to guard the carriages and camels of Lucullus, laden with gold and precious goblets; while as for Pompey's soldiers, they were all citizens, living safe at home with their wives and children, on fertile lands, or in towns, and that, not after driving Mithridates and Tigranes into wild deserts, and overturning the royal cities of Asia, but after having merely reduced exiles in Spain, or fugitive slaves in Italy. Nay, if indeed we must never have an end of fighting, should we not rather reserve the remainder of our bodies and souls for a general who will reckon his chiefest glory to be the wealth of his soldiers."

By such practices the army of Lucullus, being corrupted, neither followed him against Tigranes, nor against Mithridates, when he now at once returned into Pontus out of Armenia, and was recovering his kingdom, but under pretence of the winter, sat idle in Gordyene, every minute expecting either Pompey, or some other general, to succeed Lucullus. But when news came that Mithridates had defeated Fabius, and was marching against Sornatius and Triarius, out of shame they followed Lucullus. Triarius, ambitiously aiming at victory before ever Lucullus came to him, though he was then very near, was defeated in a great battle, in which it is said that above seven thousand Romans fell, among whom were a hundred and fifty centurions, and four and twenty tribunes, and that the camp itself was taken. Lucullus, coming up a few days after, concealed Triarius from the search of the angry soldiers. But when Mithridates declined battle, and waited for the coming of Tigranes, who was then on his march with great forces, he resolved before they joined their forces to turn once more and engage with Tigranes. But in the way the mutinous Fimbrians deserted their ranks professing themselves released from service by a decree, and that Lucullus, the provinces being allotted to others, had no longer any right to command them. There was nothing beneath the dignity of Lucullus which he did not now submit to bear, entreating them one by one, from tent to tent, going up and down humbly and in tears, and even taking some like a suppliant, by the hand. But they turned away from his salutes, and threw down their empty purses, bidding him engage alone with the enemy, as he alone made advantage of it At length by the entreaty of the other soldiers, the Fimbrians, being prevailed upon, consented to tarry that summer under him, but if during that time no enemy came to fight them, to be free. Lucullus of necessity was forced to comply with this, or else to abandon the country to the barbarians. He kept them, indeed, with him, but without urging his authority upon them; nor did he lead them out to battle, being contented if they should but stay with him, though he then saw Cappadocia wasted by Tigranes, and Mithridates again triumphing, whom not long before he reported to the senate to be wholly subdued; and commissioners were now arrived to settle the affairs of Pontus, as if all had been quietly in his possession. But when they came, they found him not so much as master of himself, but contemned and derided by the common soldiers, who arrived at that height of insolence against their general, that at the end of summer they put on their armor and drew their swords, and defied their enemies then absent and gone off a long while before, and with great outcries and waving their swords in the air, they quitted the camp, proclaiming that the time was expired which they promised to stay with Lucullus. The rest were summoned by letters from Pompey to come and join him; he by the favor of the people and by flattery of their leaders, having been chosen general of the army against Mithridates and Tigranes, though the senate and the nobility all thought that Lucullus was injured, having those put over his head who succeeded rather to his triumph, than to his commission, and that he was not so truly deprived of his command, as of the glory he had deserved in his command, which he was forced to yield to another.

It was yet more of just matter of pity and indignation, to those who were present; for Lucullus remained no longer master of rewards or punishments for any actions done in the war; neither would Pompey suffer any man to go to him, or pay any respect to the orders and arrangements he made with advice of his ten commissioners, but expressly issued edicts to the contrary, and could not but be obeyed by reason of his greater power. Friends, however, on both sides, thought it desirable to bring them together, and they met in a village of Galatia, and saluted each other in a friendly manner, with congratulations on each other's successes. Lucullus was the elder, but Pompey the more distinguished by his more numerous commands and his two triumphs. Both had rods dressed with laurel carried before them for their victories, and as Pompey's laurels were withered with passing through hot and droughty countries, Lucullus's lictors courteously gave Pompey's some of the fresh and green ones which they had, which Pompey's friends counted a good omen, as indeed of a truth, Lucullus's actions furnished the honors of Pompey's command. The interview, however, did not bring them to any amicable agreement; they parted even less friends than they met. Pompey repealed all the acts of Lucullus, drew off his soldiers, and left him no more than sixteen hundred for his triumph, and even those unwilling to go with him. So wanting was Lucullus, either through natural constitution or adverse circumstances, in that one first and most important requisite of a general, which had he but added to his other many and remarkable virtues, his fortitude, vigilance, wisdom, justice, the Roman empire had not had Euphrates for its boundary, but the utmost ends of Asia and the Hyrcanian sea; as other nations were then disabled by the late conquests of Tigranes, and the power of Parthia had not in Lucullus's time shown itself so formidable as Crassus afterwards found it, nor had as yet gained that consistency, being crippled by wars at home, and on its frontiers, and unable even to make head against the encroachments of the Armenians. And Lucullus, as it was, seems to me through others' agency to have done Rome greater harm, than he did her advantage by his own. For the trophies in Armenia, near the Parthian frontier, and Tigranocerta, and Nisibis, and the great wealth brought from thence to Rome, with the captive crown of Tigranes carried in triumph, all helped to puff up Crassus, as if the barbarians had been nothing else but spoil and booty, and he, falling among the Parthian archers, soon demonstrated that Lucullus's triumphs were not beholden to the inadvertency and effeminacy of his enemies, but to his own courage and conduct. But of this afterwards.

Lucullus upon his return to Rome, found his brother Marcus accused by Caius Memmius for his acts as quæstor, done by Sylla's orders; and on his acquittal, Memmius changed the scene, and animated the people against Lucullus himself, urging them to deny him a triumph for appropriating the spoils and prolonging the war. In this great struggle, the nobility and chief men went down and mingling in person among the tribes, with much entreaty and labor, scarce at length prevailed upon them to consent to his triumph. The pomp of which proved not so wonderful or so wearisome with the length of the procession and the number of things carried in it, but consisted chiefly in vast quantities of arms and machines of the king's with which he adorned the Flaminian circus, a spectacle by no means despicable. In his progress there passed by a few horsemen in heavy armor, ten chariots armed with scythes, sixty friends and officers of the king's, and a hundred and ten brazen-beaked ships of war, which were conveyed along with them, a golden image of Mithridates six feet high, a shield set with precious stones, twenty loads of silver vessels, and thirty-two of golden cups, armor, and money, all carried by men. Besides which, eight mules were laden with golden couches, fifty six with bullion, and a hundred and seven with coined silver, little less than two million seven hundred thousand pieces. There were tablets, also, with inscriptions, stating what moneys he gave Pompey for prosecuting the piratic war, what he delivered into the treasury, and what he gave to every soldier, which was nine hundred and fifty drachmas each. After all which he nobly feasted the city and adjoining villages or *vici*.

Being divorced from Clodia, a dissolute and wicked woman, he married Servilia, sister to Cato. This also proved an unfortunate match, for she only wanted one of all of Clodia's vices, the criminality she was accused of with her brothers. Out of reverence to Cato, he for a while connived her impurity and immodesty, but at length dismissed her. When the senate expected great things from him, hoping to find in him a check to the usurpations of Pompey, and that with the greatness of his station and credit he would come forwards as the champion of the nobility, he retired from business and abandoned public life; either because he saw the State to be in a difficult and diseased condition, or, as others say, because he was as great as he could well be, and inclined to a quiet and easy life, after those many labors and toils which had ended with him so far from fortunately. There are those who highly commend his change of life, saying that he thus avoided the rock on which Marius split. For he, after the great and glorious deeds of his Cimbrian victories, was not contented to retire upon his honors, but out of an insatiable desire of glory and power, even in his old age, headed a political party against young men, and let himself fall into miserable actions, and yet more miserable sufferings. Better in like manner, they say, had it been for Cicero, after Catiline's conspiracy, to have retired and grown old, and for Scipio, after his Numantine and Carthaginian conquests, to have sat down contented. For the administration of public affairs has, like other things, its proper term, and statesmen, as well as wrestlers, will break down, when strength and youth fail. But Crassus and Pompey, on the other hand, laughed to see Lucullus abandoning himself to pleasure and expense, as if luxurious living were not a thing that as little became his years as government of affairs at home, or of an army abroad.

And, indeed, Lucullus's life, like the Old Comedy, presents us at the commencement with acts of policy, and of war, at the end offering nothing but good eating and drinking, feastings and revellings, and mere play. For I give no higher name to his sumptuous buildings, porticos and baths, still less to his paintings and sculptures, and all his industry about these curiosities, which he collected with vast expense, lavishly bestowing all the wealth and treasure which he got in the war upon them, insomuch that even now, with all the advance of luxury, the Lucullean gardens are counted the noblest the emperor has. Tubero the stoic, when he saw his buildings at Naples, where he suspended the hills upon vast tunnels, brought in the sea for moats and fish-ponds round his house, and built pleasure-houses in the waters, called him Xerxes in a gown. He had also fine seats in Tusculum, belvederes, and large open balconies for men's apartments, and porticos to walk in, where Pompey coming to see him, blamed him for making a house which would be pleasant in summer, but uninhabitable in winter; whom he answered with a smile, "You think me, then, less provident than cranes and storks, not to change my home with the season." When a prætor, with great expense and pains, was preparing a spectacle for the people, and asked him to lend him some purple robes for the performers in a chorus, he told him he would go home and see, and if he had got any, would let him have them; and the next day asking how many he wanted, and being told that a hundred would suffice, bade him to take twice as many: on which the poet Horace observes, that a house is but a poor one, where the valuables unseen and unthought of do not exceed all those that meet the eye.

Lucullus's daily entertainments were ostentatiously extravagant, not only with purple coverlets, and plate adorned with precious stones, and dancings, and interludes, but with the greatest diversity of dishes and the most elaborate cookery, for the vulgar to admire and envy. It was a happy thought of Pompey in his sickness, when his physician prescribed a thrush for his dinner, and his servants told him that in summer time thrushes were not to be found anywhere but in Lucullus's fattening coops, that he would not suffer them to fetch one thence, but observing to his physician, "So if Lucullus had not been an epicure, Pompey had not lived," ordered some thing else that could easily be got to be prepared for him. Cato was his friend and connection, but, nevertheless, so hated his life and habits, that when a young man in the senate made a long and tedious speech in praise of frugality and temperance, Cato got up and said, "How long do you mean to go on making money like Crassus, living like Lucullus and talking like Cato?" There are some, however, who say the words were said but not by Cato.

It is plain from the anecdotes on record of him, that Lucullus was not only pleased with, but even gloried in his way of living. For he is said to have feasted several Greeks upon their coming to Rome day after day, who of a true Grecian principal, being ashamed, and declining the invitations, where so great an expense was every day incurred for them, he with a smile told them, "Some of this, indeed, my Grecian friends, is for your sakes, but more for that of Lucullus." Once when he supped alone, there being only one course, and that but moderately furnished, he called his steward and reproved him, who professing to have supposed that there would be no need of any great entertainment, when nobody was invited, was answered, "What, did not you know, then, that to-day Lucullus dines with Lucullus?" Which being much spoken of about the city, Cicero and Pompey one day met him loitering in the forum, the former his intimate friend and familiar, and, though there had been some ill-will between Pompey and him about the command in the war, still they used to see each other and converse on easy terms together. Cicero accordingly saluted him, and asked him whether to-day were a good time for asking a favor of him, and on his answering, "Very much so," and begging to hear what it was, "Then," said Cicero, "we should like to dine with you to-day, just on the dinner that is prepared for yourself." Lucullus being surprised, and requesting a day's time they refused to grant it, neither suffered him to talk with his servants, for fear he should give order for more than was appointed before. But thus much they consented to, that before their faces he might tell his servants, that to-day he would sup in the Apollo (for so one of his best dining rooms was called), and by this evasion he outwitted his guests. For every room, as it seems, had its own assessment of expenditure, dinner at such a price, and all else in accordance; so that the servants, on knowing where he would dine, knew also how much was to be expended, and in what style and form dinner was to be served. The expense for the Apollo was fifty thousand drachmas, and thus much being that day laid out, the greatness of the cost did not so much amaze Pompey and Cicero, as the rapidity of the outlay. One might believe Lucullus thought his money really captive and barbarian, so wantonly and contumeliously did he treat it.

His furnishing a library, however, deserves praise and record, for he collected very many choice manuscripts; and the use they were put to was even more magnificent than the purchase, the library being always open, and the walks and reading-rooms about it free to all Greeks, whose delight it was to leave their other occupations and hasten thither as to the habitation of the Muses, there walking about, and diverting one another. He himself often passed his hours there, disputing with the learned in the walks, and giving his advice to statesmen who required it, insomuch that his house was altogether a home, and in a manner a Greek prytaneum for those that visited Rome. He was fond of all sorts of philosophy, and was well-read and expert in them all. But he always from the first specially favored and valued the Academy; not the New one, which at that time under Philo flourished with the precepts of Carneades, but the Old one, then sustained and represented by Antiochus of Ascalon, a learned and eloquent man. Lucullus with great labor made him his friend and champion, and set him up against Philo's auditors, among whom Cicero was one, who wrote an admirable treatise in defence of his sect, in which he puts the argument in favor of *comprehension* in the mouth of Lucullus, and the opposite argument in his own. The book is called Lucullus. For as has been said, they were great friends, and took the same side in politics. For Lucullus did not wholly retire from the republic, but only from ambition, and from the dangerous and often lawless struggle for political preëminence, which he left to Crassus and Cato, whom the senators, jealous of Pompey's greatness, put forward as their champions, when Lucullus refused to head them. For his friends' sake he came into the forum and into the senate, when occasion offered to humble the ambition and pride of Pompey, whose settlement, after his conquests over the kings, he got cancelled, and by the assistance of Cato, hindered a division of lands to his soldiers, which he proposed. So Pompey went over to Crassus and Cæsar's alliance, or rather conspiracy, and filling the city with armed men, procured the ratification of his decrees by force, and drove Cato and Lucullus out of the forum. Which being resented by the nobility, Pompey's party produced one Vettius, pretending they apprehended him in a design against Pompey's life. Who in the senate-house accused others, but before the people named Lucullus, as if he had been suborned by him to kill Pompey. Nobody gave heed to what he said, and it soon appeared that they had put him forward to make false charges and accusations. And after a few days the whole intrigue became yet more obvious, when the dead body of Vettius was thrown out of the prison, he being reported, indeed, to have died a natural death, but carrying marks of a halter and blows about him, and seeming rather to have been taken off by those who suborned him. These things kept Lucullus at a greater distance from the republic.

But when Cicero was banished the city, and Cato sent to Cyprus, he quitted public affairs altogether. It is said, too, that before his death, his intellects failed him by degrees. But Cornelius Nepos denies that either age or sickness impaired his mind, which was rather affected by a potion, given him by Callisthenes his freedman. The potion was meant by Callisthenes to strengthen his affection for him, and was supposed to have that tendency, but it stood quite otherwise, and so disabled and unsettled his mind, that while he was yet alive, his brother took charge of his affairs. At his death, as though it had been the death of one taken off in the very height of military and civil glory, the people were much concerned, and flocked together, and would have forcibly taken his corps, as it was carried into the market-place by young men of the highest rank, and have buried it in the field of Mars, where they buried Sylla. Which being altogether unexpected, and necessaries not easily to be procured on a sudden, his brother, after much entreaty and solicitation, prevailed upon them to suffer him to be buried on his Tuscular estate as had been appointed. He himself survived him but a short time, coming not far behind in death, as he did 'n age and renown, in all respects, a most loving brother.

COMPARISON OF LUCULLUS WITH CIMON.

One might bless the end of Lucullus, which was so timed as to let him die before the great revolution, which fate, by intestine wars, was already effecting against the established government, and to close his life in a free, though troubled commonwealth. And in this, above all other things, Cimon and he are alike. For he died also when Greece was as yet undisordered, in its highest felicity; though in the field at the head of his army, not recalled, nor out of his mind, nor sullying the glory of his wars, engagements, and conquests, by making feastings and debauches seem the apparent end and aim of them all; as Plato says scornfully of Orpheus, that he makes an eternal debauch hereafter, the reward of those who lived well here. Indeed, ease and quiet, and the study of pleasant and speculative learning, to an old man retiring from command and office, is a most suitable and becoming solace; but to misguide virtuous actions to pleasure as their utmost end, and as the conclusion of campaigns and commands, to keep the feast of Venus, did not become the noble Academy, and the follower of Xenocrates, but rather one that inclined to Epicurus. And this is one surprising point of contrast between them; Cimon's youth was ill-reputed and intemperate, Lucullus's well disciplined and sober. Undoubtedly we must give the preference to the change for good, for it argues the better nature, where vice declines and virtue grows. Both had great wealth, but employed it in different ways; and there is no comparison between the south wall of the acropolis built by Cimon, and the chambers and galleries, with their sea-views, built at Naples by Lucullus, out of the spoils of the barbarians. Neither can we compare Cimon's popular and liberal table with the sumptuous oriental one of Lucullus, the former receiving a great many guests every day at small cost, the latter expensively spread for a few men of pleasure, unless you will say that different times made the alteration. For who can tell but that Cimon, if he had retired in his old age from business and war to quiet and solitude, might have lived a more luxurious and self-indulgent life, as he was fond of wine and company, and accused, as has been said, of laxity with women? The better pleasures gained in successful action and effort leave the baser appetites no time or place, and makes active and heroic men forget them. Had but Lucullus ended his days in the field, and in command, envy and detraction itself could never have accused him. So much for their manner of life.

In war, it is plain they were both soldiers of excellent conduct, both at land and sea. But as in the games they honor those champions who on the same day gain the garland, both in wrestling and in the pancratium, with the name of "Victors and more," so Cimon, honoring Greece with a sea and land victory on the same day, may claim a certain preëminence among commanders. Lucullus received command from his country, whereas Cimon brought it to his. He annexed the territories of enemies to her, who ruled over confederates before, but Cimon made his country, which when he began was a mere follower of others, both rule over confederates, and conquer enemies too, forcing the Persians to relinquish the sea, and inducing the Lacedæmonians to surrender their command. If it be the chiefest thing in a general to obtain the obedience of his soldiers by good-will, Lucullus was despised by his own army, but Cimon highly prized even by others. His soldiers deserted the one, the confederates came over to the other. Lucullus came home without the forces which he led out; Cimon, sent out at first to serve as one confederate among others, returned home with authority even over these also, having successfully effected for his city three most difficult services, establishing peace with the enemy, dominion over confederates, and concord with Lacedæmon. Both aiming to destroy great kingdoms, and subdue all Asia, failed in their enterprise, Cimon by a simple piece of ill-fortune, for he died when general, in the height of success; but Lucullus no man can wholly acquit of being in fault with his soldiers, whether it were he did not know, or would not comply with the distastes and complaints of his army, which brought him at last into such extreme unpopularity among them. But did not Cimon also suffer like him in this? For the citizens arraigned him, and did not leave off till they had banished him, that, as Plato says, they might not hear him for the space of ten years. For high and noble minds seldom please the vulgar, or are acceptable to them; for the force they use to straighten their distorted actions gives the same pain as surgeons' bandages do in bringing dislocated bones to their natural position. Both of them, perhaps, come off pretty much with an equal acquittal on this count.

Lucullus very much outwent him in war, being the first Roman who carried an army over Taurus, passed the Tigris, took and burnt the royal palaces of Asia in the sight of the kings, Tigranocerta, Cabira, Sinope, and Nisibis, seizing and overwhelming the northern parts as far as the Phasis, the east as far as Media, and making the South and Red Sea his own through the kings of the Arabians. He shattered the power of the kings, and narrowly missed their persons, while like wild beasts they fled away into deserts and thick and impassable woods. In demonstration of this superiority, we see that the Persians, as if no great harm had befallen them under Cimon, soon after appeared in arms against the Greeks, and overcame and destroyed their numerous forces in Egypt. But after Lucullus, Tigranes and Mithridates were able to do nothing; the latter, being disabled and broken in the former wars, never dared to show his army to Pompey outside the camp, but fled away to Bosporus, and there died. Tigranes threw himself, naked and unarmed, down before Pompey, and taking his crown from his head, laid it at his feet, complimenting Pompey with what was not his own, but, in real truth, the conquest already effected by Lucullus. And when he received the ensigns of majesty again, he was well pleased, evidently because he had forfeited them before. And the commander, as the wrestler, is to be accounted to have done most who leaves an adversary almost conquered for his successor. Cimon, moreover, when he took the command, found the power of the king broken, and the spirits of the Persians humbled by their great defeats and incessant routs under Themistocles, Pausanias, and Leontychides, and thus easily overcame the bodies of men whose souls were quelled and defeated beforehand. But Tigranes had never yet in many combats been beaten, and was flushed with success when he engaged with Lucullus. There is no comparison between the numbers, which came against Lucullus, and those subdued by Cimon. All which things being rightly considered, it is a hard matter to give judgment. For supernatural favor also appears to have attended both of them, directing the one what to do, the other what to avoid, and thus they have, both of them, so to say, the vote of the gods, to declare them noble and divine characters.

NICIAS.

CRASSUS, in my opinion, may most p operly be set against Nicias, and the Parthian disaster compared with that in Sicily. But here it will be well for me to entreat the reader, in all courtesy, not to think that I contend with Thucydides in matters so pathetically, vividly, and eloquently, beyond all imitation, and even beyond himself, expressed by him ; nor to believe me guilty of the like folly with Timæus, who, hoping in his history to surpass Thucydides in art, and to make Philistus appear a trifler and a novice, pushes on in his descriptions, through all the battles, sea-fights, and public speeches, in recording which they have been most successful, without meriting so much as to be compared in Pindar's phrase, to

> One that on his feet
> Would with the Lydian cars compete.

He simply shows himself all along a half-lettered, childish writer; in the words of Diphilus,

> ——— of wit obese,
> O'erlarded with Sicilian grease.

Often he sinks to the very level of Xenarchus, telling us that he thinks it ominous to the Athenians, that their general, who had victory in his name, was unwilling to take command in the expedition ; and that the defacing of the Hermæ was a divine intimation that they should suffer much in the war by Hermocrates, the son of Hermon ; and, moreover, how it was likely that Hercules should aid the Syracusans for the sake of Proserpine, by whose means he took Cerberus, and should be angry with the Athenians for protecting the Egesteans, descended from Trojan ancestors, whose city he, for an injury of their king Laomedon, had overthrown. However, all these may be merely other instances of the same happy taste that makes him correct the diction of Philistus, and abuse Plato and Aristotle. This sort of contention and rivalry with others in matter of style, to my mind, in any case, seems petty and pedantic, but when its objects are works of inimitable excellence, it is absolutely senseless. Such actions in Nicias's life as Thucydides and Philistus have related, since they cannot be passed by, illustrating as they do most espe cially his character and temper, under his many and great troubles, that I may not seem altogether negligent, I shall briefly run over. And such things as are not commonly known, and lie scattered here and there in other men's writings, or are found amongst the old monuments and archives, I shall endeavor to bring together; not collecting mere useless pieces of learning, but adducing what may make his disposition and habit of mind understood.

First of all, I would mention what Aristotle has said of Nicias, that there had been three good citizens eminent above the rest for their hereditary affection and love to the people, Nicias the son of Niceratus, Thucydides the son of Melesias, and Theramenes the son of Hagnon, but the last less than the others; for he had his dubious extraction cast in his teeth, as a foreigner from Ceos, and his inconstancy which made him side sometimes with one party, sometimes with another in public life, and which obtained him the nickname of the Buskin.

Thucydides came earlier, and, on the behalf of the nobility, was a great opponent of the measures by which Pericles courted the favor of the people.

Nicias was a younger man, yet was in some reputation even whilst Pericles lived; so much so as to have been his colleague in the office of general, and to have held command by himself more than once. But on the death of Pericles, he presently rose to the highest place, chiefly by the favor of the rich and eminent citizens, who set him up for their bulwark against the presumption and insolence of Cleon; nevertheless, he did not forfeit the good-will of the commonalty, who, likewise, contributed to his advancement. For though Cleon got great influence by his exertions

——— to please
The old men, who trusted him to find them fees.

Yet even those, for whose interest, and to gain whose favor he acted, nevertheless observing the avarice, the arrogance, and the presumption of the man, many of them supported Nicias. For his was not that sort of gravity which is harsh and offensive, but he tempered it with a certain caution and deference, winning upon the people, by seeming afraid of them. And being naturally diffident and unhopeful in war, his good fortune surplied his want of courage, and kept it from being detected, as in all his commands he was constantly successful. And his timorousness in civil life, and his extreme dread of accusers, was thought very suitable in a citizen of a free State; and from the people's good-will towards him, got him no small power over them, they being fearful of all that despised them, but willing to promote one who seemed to be afraid of them; the greatest compliment their betters could pay them being not to contemn them.

Pericles, who by solid virtue and the pure force of argument ruled the commonwealth, had stood in need of no disguises nor persuasions with the people. Nicias, inferior in these respects, used his riches, of which he had abundance, to gain popularity. Neither had he the nimble wit of Cleon, to win the Athenians to his purposes by amusing them with bold jests; unprovided with such qualities, he courted them with dramatic exhibitions, gymnastic games, and other public shows, more sumptuous and more splendid than had been ever known in his, or in former ages. Amongst his religious offerings, there was extant, even in our days, the small figure of Minerva in the citadel, having lost the gold that covered it; and a shrine in the temple of Bacchus, under the tripods, that were presented by those who won the prize in the shows or plays. For at these he had often carried off the prize, and never once failed. We are told that on one of these occasions, a slave of his appeared in the character of Bacchus, of a beautiful person and noble stature, and with as yet no beard upon his chin; and on the Athenians being pleased with the sight, and applauding a long time, Nicias stood up, and said he could not in piety keep as a slave one whose person had been consecrated to represent a god. And forthwith he set the young man free. His performances at Delos are, also, on record, as noble and magnificent works of devotion. For whereas the choruses which the cities sent to sing hymns to the god were wont to arrive in no order, as it might happen, and, being there met by a crowd of people crying out to them to sing, in their hurry to begin, used to disembark confusedly, putting on their garlands, and changing their dresses as they left the ships, he, when he had to convoy the sacred company, disembarked the chorus at Rhenea, together with the sacrifice, and other holy appurtenances. And having brought along with him from Athens a bridge fitted by measurement for the purpose, and magnificently adorned with gilding and coloring, and with garlands and tapestries; this he laid in the night over the channel betwixt Rhenea and Delos, being no great distance. And at break of day he marched forth with all the procession to the god, and led chorus, sumptuously ornamented, and singing their hymns along over the bridge. The sacrifices, the games, and the feast being over, he set up a palm-tree of brass for a present to the god, and bought a parcel of land with ten thousand drachmas which he consecrated; with the revenue the inhabitants of Delos were to sacrifice and to feast, and to pray the gods for many good things to Nicias. This he engraved on a pillar, which he left in Delos to be a record of his bequest. This same palm-tree, afterwards broken down by the wind, fell on the great statue which the men of Naxos presented, and struck it to the ground.

It is plain that much of this might be vainglory, and the mere desire of popularity and applause; yet from other qualities and carriages of the man, one might believe all this cost and public display to be the effect of devotion. For he was one of those who dreaded the divine powers extremely, and, as Thucydides tells us, was much given to arts of divination. In one of Pasiphon's dialogues, it is stated that he daily sacrificed to the gods, and keeping a diviner at his house, professed to be consulting always about the commonwealth, but for the most part, inquired about his own private affairs, more especially concerning his silver mines; for he owned many works at Laurium, of great value, but somewhat hazardous to carry on. He maintained there a multitude of slaves, and his wealth consisted chiefly in silver. Hence he had many hangers-on about him, begging and obtaining. For he gave to those who could do him mischief, no less than to those who deserved well. In short, his timidity was a revenue to rogues, and his humanity to honest men. We find testimony in the comic writers, as when Teleclides, speaking of one of the professed informers, says:—

> Charicles gave the man a pound, the matter not to name,
> That from inside a money-bag into the world he came;
> And Nicias, also, paid him four; I know the reason well.
> But Nicias is a worthy man, and so I will not tell.

So, also, the informer whom Eupolis introduces in his Maricas, attacking a good, simple, poor man:—

> How long ago did you and Nicias meet?
>
> I did but see him just now in the street.
>
> The man has seen him and denies it not,
> 'Tis evident that they are in a plot.
>
> See you, O citizens! 't is fact,
> Nicias is taken in the act.

> Taken, Fools! take so good a man
> In aught that's wrong none will or can.

Cleon, in Aristophanes, makes it one of his threats:—

> I'll outscream all the speakers, and make Nicias stand aghast.

Phrynichus also implies his want of spirit, and his easiness to be intimidated in the verses,

> A noble man he was, I well can say,
> Nor walked like Nicias, cowering on his way.

So cautious was he of informers, and so reserved, that he never would dine out with any citizen, nor allowed himself to indulge in talk and conversation with his friends, nor give himself any leisure for such amusements; but when he was general he used to stay at the office till night, and was the first that came to the council-house, and the last that left it. And if no public business engaged him, it was very hard to have access, or to speak with him, he being retired at home and locked up. And when any came to the door, some friend of his gave them good words, and begged them to excuse him, Nicias was very busy; as if affairs of State and public duties still kept him occupied. He who principally acted this part for him, and contributed most to this state and show, was Hiero, a man educated in Nicias's family, and instructed by him in letters and music. He professed to be the son of Dionysius, surnamed Chalcus, whose poems are yet extant, and had led out the colony to Italy, and founded Thurii. This Hiero transacted all his secrets for Nicias with the diviners; and gave out to the people, what a toilsome and miserable life he led, for the sake of the commonwealth. "He," said Hiero, "can never be either at the bath or at his meat, but some public business interferes. Careless of his own and zealous for the public good, he scarcely ever goes to bed till after others have had their first sleep. So that his health is impaired, and his body out of order, nor is he cheerful or affable with his friends, but loses them as well as his money in the service of the State, while other men gain friends by public speaking, enrich themselves, fare delicately and make government their amusement." And in fact this was Nicias's manner of life, so that he well might apply to himself the words of Agamemnon:—

> Vain pomp's the ruler of the life we live,
> And a slave's service to the crowd we give.

He observed that the people, in the case of men of eloquence, or of eminent parts, make use of their talents upon occasion, but were always jealous of their abilities, and held a watchful eye upon them, taking all opportunities to humble their pride and abate their reputation; as was manifest in their condemnation of Pericles, their banishment of Damon, their distrust of Antiphon the Rhamnusian, but especially in the case of Paches who took Lesbos, who, having to give an account of his conduct, in the very court of justice unsheathed his sword and slew himself. Upon such considerations, Nicias declined all difficult and lengthy enterprises; if he took a command, he was for doing what was safe; and if, as thus was likely, he had for the most part success, he did not attribute it to any wisdom, conduct, or courage of his own, but, to avoid envy, he thanked fortune for all, and gave the glory to the divine powers. And the actions themselves bore testimony in his favor; the city met at that time with several considerable reverses, but he had not a hand in any of them. The Athenians were routed in Thrace by the Chalcidians, Calliades and Xenophon commanding in chief. Demosthenes was the general when they were unfortunate in Ætolia. At Delium, they lost a thousand citizens under the conduct of Hippocrates; the plague was principally laid to the charge of Pericles, he to carry on the war, having shut up close together in the town the crowd of people from the country, who, by the change of place, and of their usual course of living, bred the pestilence. Nicias stood clear of all this; under his conduct was taken Cythera, an island most commodious against Laconia, and occupied by the Lacedæmonian settlers; many places, likewise, in Thrace, which had revolted, were taken or won over by him; he shutting up the Megarians within their town, seized upon the isle of Minoa; and soon after, advancing from thence to Nisæa, made himself master there, and then making a descent upon the Corinthian territory, fought a successful battle, and slew a great number of the Corinthians with their captain Lycophron. There it happened that two of his men were left by an oversight, when they carried off the dead, which when he understood, he stopped the fleet, and sent a herald to the enemy for leave to carry off the dead; though by law and custom, he that by a truce craved leave to carry off the dead, was hereby supposed to give up all claim to the victory. Nor was it lawful for him that did this to erect a trophy, for his is the victory who is master of the field, and he is not master who asks leave, as wanting power to take. But he chose rather to renounce his victory and his glory, than to let two citizens lie unburied. He scoured the coast of Laconia all along, and beat the Lacedæmonians that made head against him. He took Thyrea, occupied by the Æginetans, and carried the prisoners to Athens.

When Demosthenes had fortified Pylos, and the Peloponnesians brought together both their sea and land forces before it, after the fight, about the number of four hundred native Spartans were left ashore in the isle Sphacteria. The Athenians thought it a great prize, as indeed it was, to take these men prisoners. But the siege, in places that wanted water, being very difficult and untoward, and to convey necessaries about by sea in summer tedious and expensive, in winter doubtful, or plainly impossible, they began to be annoyed, and to repent their having rejected the embassy of the Lacedæmonians, that had been sent to propose a treaty of peace, which had been done at the importunity of Cleon, who opposed it chiefly out of a pique to Nicias; for, being his enemy, and observing him to be extremely solicitous to support the offers of the Lacedæmonians, he persuaded the people to refuse them.

Now, therefore, that the siege was protracted, and they heard of the difficulties that pressed their army, they grew enraged against Cleon. But he turned all the blame upon Nicias, charging it on his softness and cowardice, that the besieged were not yet taken. "Were I general," said he, "they should not hold out so long." The Athenians not unnaturally asked the question, "Why, then, as it is, do not you go with a squadron against them?" And Nicias standing up resigned his command at Pylos to him, and bade him take what forces he pleased along with him, and not be bold in words, out of harm's way, but go forth and perform some real service for the commonwealth. Cleon, at the first, tried to draw back, disconcerted at the proposal, which he had never expected; but the Athenians insisting, and Nicias loudly upbraiding him, he thus provoked, and fired with ambition, took upon him the charge, and said further, that within twenty days after he embarked, he would either kill the enemy upon the place, or bring them alive to Athens. This the Athenians were readier to laugh at than to believe, as on other occasions, also, his bold assertions and extravagances used to make them sport, and were pleasant enough. As, for instance, it is reported that once when the people were assembled, and had waited his coming a long time, at last he appeared with a garland on his head, and prayed them to adjourn to the next day. "For," said he, "I am not at leisure to-day; I have sacrificed to the gods, and am to entertain some strangers." Whereupon the Athenians, laughing, rose up, and dissolved the assembly. However, at this time he had good fortune, and in conjunction with Demosthenes, conducted the enterprise so well, that within the time he had limited, he carried captive to Athens all the Spartans that had not fallen in battle.

This brought great disgrace on Nicias; for this was not to throw away his shield, but something yet more shameful and ignominious, to quit his charge voluntarily out of cowardice, and voting himself, as it were, out of his command of his own accord, to put into his enemy's hand the opportunity of achieving so brave an action. Aristophanes has a jest against him on this occasion in the Birds :—

> Indeed, not now the word that must be said
> Is, do like Nicias, or retire to bed.

And, again, in his Husbandmen :—

> I wish to stay at home and farm,
> What then?
> Who should prevent you?
> You, my countrymen;
> Whom I would pay a thousand drachmas down,
> To let me give up office and leave town.
>
> Enough; content; the sum two thousand is,
> With those that Nicias paid to give up his.

Besides all this, he did great mischief to the city by suffering the accession of so much reputation and power to Cleon, who now assumed such lofty airs, and allowed himself in such intolerable audacity, as led to many unfortunate results, a sufficient part of which fell to his own share. Amongst other things, he destroyed all the decorum of public speaking; he was the first who ever broke out into exclamations, flung open his dress, smote his thigh, and ran up and down whilst he was speaking, things which soon after introduced, amongst those who managed the affairs of State, such license and contempt of decency, as brought all into confusion.

Already, too, Alcibiades was beginning to show his strength at Athens, a popular leader, not, indeed, as utterly violent as Cleon, but as the land of Egypt, through the richness of its soil, is said,

> ——— great plenty to produce,
> Both wholesome herbs and drugs of deadly juice.

so the nature of Alcibiades was strong and luxuriant in both kinds, and made way for many serious innovations. Thus it fell out that after Nicias had got his hands clear of Cleon, he had not opportunity to settle the city perfectly into quietness. For having brought matters to a pretty hopeful condition, he found every thing carried away and plunged again into confusion by Alcibiades, through the wildness and vehemence of his ambition, and all embroiled again in war worse than ever. Which fell out thus. The persons who had principally hindered the peace were Cleon and Brasidas. War setting off the virtue of the one and hiding the villany of the other, gave to the one occasions of achieving brave actions, to the other opportunity of committing equal dishonesties. Now when these two were in one battle both slain near Amphipolis, Nicias was aware that the Spartans had long been desirous of a peace, and that the Athenians had no longer the same confidence in the war. Both being alike tired, and, as it were by consent, letting fall their hands, he, therefore, in this nick of time, employed his efforts to make a friendship betwixt the two cities, and to deliver the other States of Greece from the evils and calamities they labored under, and so establish his own good name for success as a statesman for all future time. He found the men of substance, the elder men, and the land-owners and farmers, pretty generally all inclined to peace. And when, in addition to these, by conversing and reasoning, he had cooled the wishes of a good many others for war, he now encouraged the hopes of the Lacedæmonians, and counselled them to seek peace. They confided in him, as on account of his general character for moderation and equity, so, also, because of the kindness and care he had shown to the prisoners taken at Pylos and kept in confinement, making their misfortune the more easy to them.

The Athenians and the Spartans had before this concluded a truce for a year, and during this, by associating with one another, they had tasted again the sweets of peace and security, and unimpeded intercourse with friends and connections, and thus longed for an end of that fighting and bloodshed, and heard with delight the chorus sing such verses as

—————— my lance I'll leave
Laid by, for spiders to o'erweave,

and remembered with joy the saying, In peace, they who sleep are awaked by the cock-crow, not by the trumpet. So shutting their ears, with loud reproaches, to the forebodings of those who said that the Fates decreed this to be a war of thrice nine years, the whole question having been debated, they made a peace. And most people thought, now, indeed, they had got an end of all their evils. And Nicias was in every man's mouth, as one especially beloved of the gods, who, for his piety and devotion, had been appointed to give a name to the fairest and greatest of all blessings. For in fact they considered the peace Nicias's work, as the war the work of Pericles; because he, on light occasions, seemed to have plunged the Greeks into great calamities, while Nicias had induced them to forget all the evils they had done each other and to be friends again; and so to this day it is called the Peace of Nicias.

The articles being, that the garrisons and towns taken on either side, and the prisoners should be restored, and they to restore the first to whom it should fall by lot. Nicias, as Theophrastus tells us, by a sum of money procured that the lot should fall for the Lacedæmonians to deliver the first. Afterwards, when the Corinthians and the Bœotians showed their dislike of what was done, and by their complaints and accusations were well nigh bringing the war back again, Nicias persuaded the Athenians and the Lacedæmonians, besides the peace, to make a treaty of alliance, offensive and defensive, as a tie and confirmation of the peace, which would make them more terrible to those that held out, and the firmer to each other. Whilst these matters were on foot, Alcibiades, who was no lover of tranquillity, and who was offended with the Lacedæmonians because of their applications and attentions to Nicias, while they overlooked and despised himself, from first to last, indeed, had opposed the peace though all in vain, but now finding that the Lacedæmonians did not altogether continue to please the Athenians, but were thought to have acted unfairly in having made a league with the Bœotians, and had not given up Panactum, as they should have done, with its fortifications unrazed, nor yet Amphipolis, he laid hold on these occasions for his purpose, and availed himself of every one of them to irritate the people. And, at length, sending for ambassadors from the Argives, he exerted himself to effect a confederacy between the Athenians and them. And now, when Lacedæmonian ambassadors were come with full powers, and at their preliminary audience by the council seemed to come in all points with just proposals, he, fearing that the over general assembly, also, would be won to their offers, overreached them with false professions and oaths of assistance, on the condition that they would not avow that they came with full powers this, he said, being the only way for them to attain their desires. They being overpersuaded and decoyed from Nicias to follow him, he introduced them to the assembly, and asked them presently whether or no they came in all points with full powers, which, when they denied, he, contrary to their expectation, changing his countenance, called the council to witness their words, and now bade the people beware how they trust or transact any thing with such manifest liars, who say at one time one thing, and at another the very opposite upon the same subject. These plenipotentiaries were, as well they might be, confounded at this, and Nicias, also being at a loss what to say, and struck with amazement and wonder, the assembly resolved to send immediately for the Argives, to enter into a league with them. An earthquake, which interrupted the assembly, made for Nicias's advantage; and the next day the people being again assembled, after much speaking and soliciting, with great ado he brought it about that the treaty with the Argives should be deferred, and he be sent to the Lacedæmonians, in full expectation that so all would go well.

When he arrived at Sparta, they received him there as a good man, and one well inclined towards them; yet he effected nothing, but, baffled by the party that favored the Bœotians, he returned home, not only dishonored and hardly spoken of, but likewise in fear of the Athenians, who were vexed and enraged that through his persuasions they had released so many and such considerable persons, their prisoners, for the men who had been brought from Pylos were of the chiefest families of Sparta, and had those who were highest there in place and power for their friends and kindred. Yet did they not in their heat proceed against him, otherwise than that they chose Alcibiades general, and took the Mantineans and Eleans, who had thrown up their alliance with the Lacedæmonians, into the league, together with the Argives, and sent to Pylos freebooters to infest Laconia, whereby the war began to break out afresh.

But the enmity betwixt Nicias and Alcibiades running higher and higher, and the time being at hand for decreeing the ostracism or banishment, for ten years, which the people, putting the name on a sherd, where wont to inflict at certain times on some person suspected or regarded with jealousy for his popularity or wealth, both were now in alarm and apprehension one of them, in all likelihood, being to undergo this ostracism; as the people abominated the life of Alcibiades, and stood in fear of his boldness and resolution, as is shown particularly in the history of him; while as for Nicias, his riches made him envied, and his habits of living, in particular, his unsociable and exclusive ways, not like those of a fellow-citizen, or even a fellow-man, went against him, and having many times opposed their inclinations, forcing them against their feelings to do what was their interest, he had got himself disliked.

To speak plainly, it was a contest of the young men who were eager for war, against the men of years and lovers of peace, they turning the ostracism upon the one, these upon the other. But

> In civil strife e'en villains rise to fame.

And so now it happened that the city, distracted into two actions, allowed free course to the most impudent and profligate persons, among whom was Hyperbolus of the Perithœdæ, one who could not, indeed, be said to be presuming upon any power, but rather by his presumption rose into power, and by the honor he found in the city, became the scandal of it. He, at this time, thought himself far enough from the ostracism, as more properly deserving the slave's gallows, and made account, that one of these men being despatched out of the way, he might be able to play a part against the other that should be left, and openly showed his pleasure at the dissension, and his desire to inflame the people against both of them. Nicias and Alcibiades, perceiving his malice, secretly combined together, and setting both their interests jointly at work, succeeded in fixing the ostracism not on either of them, but even on Hyperbolus. This, indeed, at the first made sport, and raised laughter among the people; but afterwards it was felt as an affront, that the thing should be dishonored by being employed upon so unworthy a subject; punishment, also, having its proper dignity, and ostracism being one that was appropriate rather for Thucydides, Aristides, and such like persons; whereas for Hyperbolus it was a glory, and a fair ground for boasting on his part, when for his villany he suffered the same with the best men. As Plato, the comic poet, said of him,

> The man deserved the fate, deny who can;
> Yes, but the fate did not deserve the man;
> Not for the like of him and his slave-brands,
> Did Athens put the sherd into our hands.

And, in fact, none ever afterwards suffered this sort of punishment, but Hyperbolus was the last, as Hipparchus the Cholargian, who was kin to the tyrant, was the first.

There is no judgment to be made of fortune ; nor can any reasoning bring us to a certainty about it. If Nicias had run the risk with Alcibiades, whether of the two should undergo the ostracism, he had eiher prevailed, and, his rival being expelled the city, he had remained secure ; or, being overcome, he had avoided the utmost disasters, and preserved the reputation of a most excellent commander. Meantime I am not ignorant that Theophrastus says, that when Hyperbolus was banished, Phæax, not Nicias, contested it with Alcibiades ; but most authors differ from him.

It was Alcibiades, at any rate, whom when the Ægestean and Leontine ambassadors arrived and urged the Athenians to make an expedition against Sicily, Nicias opposed, and by whose persuasions and ambition he found himself overborne, who, even before the people could be assembled, had preoccupied and corrupted their judgment with hopes and with speeches ; insomuch that the young men at their sports, and the old men in their workshops, and sitting together on the benches, would be drawing maps of Sicily, and making charts showing the seas, the harbors, and general character of the coast of the island opposite Africa. For they made not Sicily the end of the war but rather its starting point and head-quarters from whence they might carry it to the Carthaginians, and possess themselves of Africa, and of the seas as far as the pillars of Hercules. The bulk of the people, therefore, pressing this way, Nicias, who opposed them, found but few supporters, nor those of much influence ; for the men of substance, fearing lest they should seem to shun the public charges and ship-money, were quiet against their inclination ; nevertheless he did not tire nor give it up, but even after the Athenians decreed a war and chose him in the first place general, together with Alcibiades and Lamachus, when they were again assembled, he stood up, dissuaded them, and protested against the decision, and laid the blame on Alcibiades, charging him with going about to involve the city in foreign dangers and difficulties, merely with a view to his own private lucre and ambition. Yet it came to nothing. Nicias, because of his experience, was looked upon as the fitter for the employment, and his wariness with the bravery of Alcibiades, and the easy temper of Lamachus, all compounded together, promised such security, that he did but confirm the resolution. Demostratus, who, of the popular leaders, was the one who chiefly pressed the Athenians to the expedition, stood up and said he would stop the mouth of Nicias from urging any more excuses, and moved that the generals should have absolute power both at home and abroad, to order and to act as they thought best ; and this vote the people passed.

The priests, however, are said to have very earnestly opposed the enterprise. But Alcibiades had his diviners of another sort, who from some old prophecies announced that "there shall be great fame of the Athenians in Sicily," and messengers came back to him from Jupiter Ammon, with oracles importing that "the Athenians shall take all the Syracusans." Those, meanwhile, who knew any thing that boded ill, concealed it lest they might seem to forespeak ill-luck. For even prodigies that were obvious and plain would not deter them ; not the defacing of the Hermæ, all maimed in one night except one, called the Hermes of Andocides, erected by the tribe of Ægeus, placed directly before the house then occupied by Andocides ; nor what was perpetrated on the altar of the twelve gods, upon which a certain man leaped suddenly up, and then turning round mutilated himself with a stone. Likewise at Delphi, there stood a golden image of Minerva, set on a palm-tree of brass, erected by the city of Athens, from the spoils they won from the Medes ; this was pecked at several days together by crows flying upon it, who, also, plucked off and knocked down the fruit, made of gold, upon the palm-tree. But the Athenians said these were all but inventions of the Delphians, corrupted by the men of Syracuse. A certain oracle bade them bring from Claz omenæ the priestess of Minerva there ; they sent for the woman and found her named *Hesychia*, *Quietness*, this being, it would seem, what the divine powers advised the city at this time, to be quiet. Whether, therefore, the astrologer Meton feared these presages, or that from human reason he doubted its success (for he was appointed to a command in it), feigning himself mad, he set his house on fire. Others say he did not counterfeit madness, but set his house on fire in the night, and the next morning came before the assembly in great distress, and besought the people, in consideration of the sad disaster, to release his son from the service, who was about to go captain of a galley for Sicily. The genius, also, of the philosopher Socrates, on this occasion, too, gave him intimation by the usual tokens, that the expedition would prove the ruin of the commonwealth ; this he imparted to his friends and familiars, and by them it was mentioned to a number of people. Not a few were troubled because the days on which the fleet set sail happened to be the time when the women celebrated the death of Adonis ; there being everywhere then exposed to view images of dead men, carried about with mourning and lamentation, and women beating their breasts. So that such as laid any stress on these matters were extremely troubled, and feared lest that all this warlike preparation, so splendid and so glorious, should suddenly, in a little time, be blasted in its very prime of magnificence, and come to nothing.

Nicias, in opposing the voting of this expedition, and neither being puffed up with hopes, nor transported with the honor of his high command so as to modify his judgment, showed himself a man of virtue and constancy. But when his endeavors could not diverge the people from the war, nor get leave for himself to be discharged of the command, but the people, as it were, violently took him up and carried him, and against his will put him in the office of general, this was no longer now a time for his excessive caution and his delays, nor was it for him, like a child, to look back from the ship, often repeating and reconsidering over and over again how that his advice had not been overruled by fair arguments, thus blunting the courage of his fellow commanders and spoiling the season of action. Whereas, he ought speedily to have closed with the enemy and brought the matter to an issue, and put fortune immediately to the test in battle. But, on the contrary, when Lamachus counselled to sail directly to Syracuse, and fight the enemy under their city walls, and Alcibiades advised to secure the friendship of the other towns, and then to march against them, Nicias dissented from them both, and insisted that they should cruise quietly around the island and display their armament, and having landed a small supply of men for the Egesteans, return to Athens, weakening at once the resolution and casting down the spirits of the men. And when, a little while after, the Athenians called home Alcibiades in order to his trial, he being, though joined nominally with another in commission, in effect the only general, made now no end of loitering, of cruising, and considering, till their hopes were grown stale, and all the disorder and consternation which the first approach and view of their forces had cast amongst the enemy was worn off, and had left them.

Whilst yet Alcibiades was with the fleet, they went before

Syracuse with a squadron of sixty galleys, fifty of them lying in array without the harbor, while the other ten rowed in to reconnoitre, and by a herald called upon the citizens of Leontini to return to their own country. These scouts took a galley of the enemy's, in which they found certain tablets, on which was set down a list of all the Syracusans, according to their tribes. These were wont to be laid up at a distance from the city, in the temple of Jupiter Olympius, but were now brought forth for examination to furnish a muster-roll of young men for the war. These being so taken by the Athenians, and carried to the officers, and the multitude of names appearing, the diviners thought it unpropitious, and were in apprehension lest this should be the only destined fulfilment of the prophecy, that "the Athenians shall take all the Syracusans." Yet, indeed, this was said to be accomplished by the Athenians at another time, when Callippus the Athenian, having slain Dion, became master of Syracuse. But when Alcibiades shortly after sailed away from Sicily, the command fell wholly to Nicias. Lamachus was, indeed, a brave and honest man, and ready to fight fearlessly with his own hand in battle, but so poor and ill off, that whenever he was appointed general, he used always, in accounting for his outlay of public money, to bring some little reckoning or other of money for his very clothes and shoes. On the contrary, Nicias, as on other accounts, so, also, because of his wealth and station, was very much thought of. The story is told that once upon a time the commission of generals being in consultation together in their public office, he bade Sophocles the poet give his opinion first, as the senior of the board. "I," replied Sophocles, "am the older, but you are the senior." And so now, also, Lamachus, who better understood military affairs, being quite his subordinate, he himself, evermore delaying and avoiding risk, and faintly employing his forces, first by his sailing about Sicily at the greatest distance aloof from the enemy, gave them confidence, then by afterwards attacking Hybla, a petty fortress, and drawing off before he could take it, made himself utterly despised. At the last he retreated to Catana without having achieved any thing, save that he demolished Hyccara, an humble town of the barbarians, out of which, the story goes, that Lais the courtesan, yet a mere girl, was sold amongst the other prisoners, and carried thence away to Peloponnesus.

But when the summer was spent, after reports began to reach him that the Syracusans were grown so confident that they would come first to attack him, and troopers skirmishing to the very camp twitted his soldiers, asking whether they came to settle with the Catanians, or to put the Leontines in possession of their city, at last, with much ado, Nicias resolved to sail against Syracuse. And wishing to form his camp safely and without molestation, he procured a man to carry from Catana intelligence to the Syracusans that they might seize the camp of the Athenians unprotected, and all their arms, if on such a day they should march with all their forces to Catana ; and that, the Athenians living mostly in the town, the friends of the Syracusans had concerted, as soon as they should perceive them coming, to possess themselves of one of the gates, and to fire the arsenal, that many now were in the conspiracy and awaited their arrival. This was the ablest thing Nicias did in the whole of his conduct of the expedition. For having drawn out all the strength of the enemy, and made the city destitute of men, he set out from Catana, entered the harbor, and chose a fit place for his camp, where the enemy could least incommode him with the means in which they were superior to him, while with the means in which he was superior to them, he might expect to carry on the war without impediment.

When the Syracusans returned from Catana, and stood in battle array before the city gates, he rapidly led up the Athenians and fell on them and defeated them, but did not kill many, their horse hindering the pursuit. And his cutting and breaking down the bridges that lay over the river gave Hermocrates, when cheering up the Syracusans, occasion to say, that Nicias was ridiculous, whose great aim seemed to be to avoid fighting, as if fighting were not the thing he came for. However, he put the Syracusans into a very great alarm and consternation, so that instead of fifteen generals then in service, they chose three others, to whom the people engaged by oath to allow absolute authority.

There stood near them the temple of Jupiter Olympius, which the Athenians (there being in it many consecrated things of gold and silver) were eager to take, but were purposely withheld from it by Nicias, who let the opportunity slip, and allowed a garrison of the Syracusans to enter it, judging that if the soldiers should make booty of that wealth, it would be no advantage to the public, and he should bear the guilt of the impiety. Not improving in the least this success, which was everywhere famous, after a few days' stay, away he goes to Naxos, and there winters, spending largely for the maintenance of so great an army, and not doing any thing except some matters of little consequence with some native Sicilians that revolted to him. Insomuch, that the Syracusans took heart again, made excursions to Catana, wasted the country, and fired the camp of the Athenians. For which everybody blamed Nicias, who, with his long reflection, his deliberateness, and his caution, had let slip the time for action. None ever found fault with the man when once at work, for in the brunt he showed vigor and activity enough, but was slow and wanted assurance to engage.

When, therefore, he brought again the army to Syracuse, such was his conduct, and with such celerity, and at the same time security, he came upon them, that nobody knew of his approach, when already he had come to shore with his galleys at Thapsus, and had landed his men; and before any could help it, he had surprised Epipolæ, had defeated the body of picked men that came to its succor, took three hundred prisoners, and routed the cavalry of the enemy, which had been thought invincible. But what chiefly astonished the Syracusans, and seemed incredible to the Greeks, was in so short a space of time the walling about of Syracuse, a town not less than Athens, and far more difficult, by the unevenness of the ground, and the nearness of the sea and the marshes adjacent, to have such a wall drawn in a circle round it; yet this, all within a very little, finished by a man that had not even his health for such weighty cares, but lay ill of the stone, which may justly bear the blame for what was left undone. I admire the industry of the general, and the bravery of the soldiers for what they succeeded in. Euripides, after their ruin and disaster, writing their funeral elegy, said that

> Eight victories over Syracuse they gained,
> While equal yet to both the gods remained.

And in truth one shall not find eight, but many more victories won by these men against the Syracusans, till the gods, in real truth, or fortune intervened to check the Athenians in this advance to the height of power and greatness.

Nicias, therefore, doing violence to his body, was present in most actions. But once, when his disease was the sharpest upon him, he lay in the camp with some few servants to attend him. And Lamachus having the command fought the Syracusans, who were bringing a cross-wall from the city along to that of the Athenians, to hinder them from carrying it round; and in the victory, the Athenians hurrying in some disorder to the pursuit, Lamachus getting separated from his men, had to resist the Syracusan horse that came upon him. Before the rest advanced Callicrates, a man of good courage and skill in war. Lamachus, upon a challenge, engaged with him in single combat, and receiving the first wound, returned it so home to Callicrates, that they both fell and died together. The Syracusans took away his body and arms, and at full speed advanced to the wall of the Athenians, where Nicias lay without any troops to oppose to them, yet roused by this necessity, and seeing the danger, he bade those about him go and set on fire all the wood and materials that lay provided before the wall for the engines, and the engines themselves; this put a stop to the Syracusans, saved Nicias, saved the walls and all the money of the Athenians. For when the Syracusans saw such a fire blazing up between them and the wall, they retired.

Nicias now remained sole general, and with great prospects; for cities began to come over to alliance with him, and ships laden with corn from every coast came to the camp, every one favoring when matters went well. And some proposals from among the Syracusans despairing to defend the city, about a capitulation, were already conveyed to him. And in fact Gylippus, who was on his way with a squadron to their aid from Lacedæmon, hearing, on his voyage, of the wall surrounding them, and of their distress, only continued his enterprise thenceforth, that, giving Sicily up for lost, he might, if even that should be possible, secure the Italians their cities. For a strong report was everywhere spread about that the Athenians carried all before them, and had a general alike for conduct and for fortune invincible.

And Nicias himself, too, now against his nature grown bold in his present strength and success, especially from the intelligence he received under hand of the Syracusans, believing they would almost immediately surrender the town upon terms, paid no manner of regard to Gylippus coming to their assistance, nor kept any watch of his approach, so that, neglected altogether and despised, Gylippus went in a long boat ashore without the knowledge of Nicias, and, having landed in the remotest parts from Syracuse, mustered up a considerable force, the Syracusans not so much as knowing of his arrival nor expecting him; so that an assembly was summoned to consider the terms to be arranged with Nicias, and some were actually on the way, thinking it essential to have all despatched before the town should be quite walled round, for now there remained very little to be done, and the materials for the building lay all ready along the line.

In this very nick of time and danger arrived Gongylus in one galley from Corinth, and every one, as may be imagined, flocking about him, he told them that Gylippus would be with them speedily, and that other ships were coming to relieve them. And, ere yet they could perfectly believe Gongylus, an express was brought from Gylippus, to bid them go forth to meet him. So now taking good heart, they armed themselves; and Gylippus at once led on his men from their march in battle array against the Athenians, as Nicias also embattled these. And Gylippus, piling his arms in view of the Athenians, sent a herald to tell them he would give them leave to depart from Sicily without molestation. To this Nicias would not vouchsafe any answer, but some of his soldiers laughing, asked if with the sight of one coarse coat and Laconian staff the Syracusan prospects had become so brilliant that they could despise the Athenians, who had released to the Lacedæmonians three hundred, whom they held in chains, bigger men than Gylippus, and longer-haired? Timæus, also, writes that even the Syracusans made no account of Gylippus, at the first sight mocking at his staff and long hair, as afterwards they found reason to blame his covetousness and meanness. The same author, however, adds that on Gylippus's first appearance, as it might have been at the sight of an owl abroad in the air, there was a general flocking together of men to serve in the war. And this is the truer saying of the two; for in the staff and the cloak they saw the badge and authority of Sparta, and crowded to him accordingly. And not only Thucydides affirms that the whole thing was done by him alone, but so, also, does Philistus, who was a Syracusan and an actual witness of what happened.

However, the Athenians had the better in the first encounter, and slew some few of the Syracusans, and amongst them Gongylus of Corinth. But on the next day Gylippus showed what it is to be a man of experience; for with the same arms, the same horses, and on the same spot of ground, only employing them otherwise, he overcame the Athenians; and they fleeing to their camp, he set the Syracusans to work, and with the stone and materials that had been brought together for finishing the wall of the Athenians, he built a crosswall to intercept theirs and break it off, so that even if they were successful in the field, they would not be able to do any thing. And after this the Syracusans taking courage manned their galleys, and with their horse and followers ranging about took a good many prisoners; and Gylippus going himself to the cities, called upon them to join with him, and was listened to and supported vigorously by them. So that Nicias fell back again to his old views, and, seeing the face of affairs change, desponded, and wrote to Athens, bidding them either send another army, or recall this out of Sicily, and that he might, in any case, be wholly relieved of the command, because of his disease.

Before this the Athenians had been intending to send another army to Sicily, but envy of Nicias's early achievements and high fortune had occasioned, up to this time, many delays; but now they were all eager to send off succors. Eurymedon went before, in midwinter, with money, and to announce that Euthydemus and Menander were chosen out of those that served there under Nicias, to be joint commanders with him. Demosthenes was to go after in the spring with a great armament. In the mean time Nicias was briskly attacked, both by sea and land; in the beginning he had the disadvantage on the water, but in the end repulsed and sunk many galleys of the enemy. But by land he could not provide succor in time, so Gylippus surprised and captured Plemmyrium, in which the stores for the navy, and a great sum of money being there kept, all fell into his hands, and many were slain, and many taken prisoners. And what was of greatest importance, he now cut off Nicias's supplies, which had been safely and readily conveyed to him under Plemmyrium, while the Athenians still held it, but now that they were beaten out, he could only procure them with great difficulty, and with opposition from the enemy, who lay in wait with their ships under that fort. Moreover, it seemed manifest to the Syracusans that their navy had not been beaten by strength, but by their disorder in the pursuit. Now, therefore, all hands went to work to prepare for a new attempt, that should succeed better than the former. Nicias had no wish for a sea-fight, but said it was mere folly for them, when Demosthenes was coming in all haste with so great a fleet and fresh forces to their succor, to engage the enemy with a less number of ships and ill provided. But, on the other hand, Menander and Euthydemus, who were just commencing their new command, prompted by a feeling of rivalry and emulation of both the generals were eager to gain some great success before Demosthenes came, and to prove themselves superior to Nicias They urged the honor of the city, which, said they, would be blemished and utterly lost, if they should decline a challenge from the Syracusans. Thus they forced Nicias to a sea-fight; and by the stratagem of Ariston, the Corinthian pilot (his trick, described by Thucydides, about the men's dinners), they were worsted, and lost many of their men, causing the greatest dejection to Nicias, who had suffered so much from having the sole command, and now again miscarried through his colleagues.

But now by this time, Demosthenes with his splendid fleet came in sight outside the harbor, a terror to the enemy. He brought along, in seventy-three galleys, five thousand men at arms; of darters, archers, and slingers, not less than three thousand; with the glittering of their armor, the flags waving from the galleys, the multitude of coxswains and flute players giving time to the rowers, setting off the whole with all possible warlike pomp and ostentation to dismay the enemy. Now one may believe the Syracusans were again in extreme alarm, seeing no end or prospect of release before them, toiling, as it seemed, in vain, and perishing to no purpose. Nicias, however, was not long overjoyed with the reinforcement, for the first time he conferred with Demosthenes, who advised forthwith to attack the Syracusans, and to put all to the speediest hazard, to win Syracuse, or else return home, afraid, and wondering at his promptness and audacity, he besought him to do nothing rashly and desperately, since delay would be the ruin of the enemy, whose money would not hold out, nor their confederates be long kept together; that when once they came to be pinched with want, they would presently come again to him for terms, as formerly. For, indeed, many in Syracuse held secret correspondence with him, and urged him to stay, declaring that even now the people were quite worn out with the war, and weary of Gylippus. And if their necessities should the least sharpen upon them they would give up all.

Nicias glancing darkly at these matters, and unwilling to speak out plainly, made his colleagues imagine that it was cowardice which made him talk in this manner. And saying that this was the old story over again, the well-known procrastinations and delays and refinements with which at first he let slip the opportunity in not immediately falling on the enemy, but suffering the armament to become a thing of yesterday, that nobody was alarmed with, they took the side of Demosthenes, and with much ado forced Nicias to comply. And so Demosthenes, taking the land forces, by night made an assault upon Epipolæ; part of the enemy he slew ere they took the alarm, the rest defending themselves he put to flight. Nor was he content with this victory there, but pushed on further, till he met the Bœotians. For these were the first that made head against the Athenians, and charged them with a shout, spear against spear, and killed many on the place. And now at once there ensued a panic and confusion throughout the whole army; the victorious portion got infected with the fears of the flying part, and those who were still disembarking and coming forward, falling foul of the retreaters, came into conflict with their own party, taking the fugitives for pursuers, and treating their friends as if they were the enemy.

Thus huddled together in disorder, distracted with fear and uncertainties, and unable to be sure of seeing anything, the night not being absolutely dark, nor yielding any steady light, the moon then towards setting, shadowed with the many weapons and bodies that moved to and fro, and glimmering so as not to show an object plain, but to make friends through fear suspected for foes, the Athenians fell into utter perplexity and desperation. For, moreover, they had the moon at their backs, and consequently their own shadows fell upon them, and both hid the number and the glittering of their arms; while the reflection of the moon from the shields of the enemy made them show more numerous and better appointed than, indeed, they were. At last, being pressed on every side, when once they had given way, they took to rout, and in their flight were destroyed, some by the enemy, some by the hand of their friends, and some tumbling down the rocks, while those that were dispersed and straggled about were picked off in the morning by the horsemen and put to the sword. The slain were two thousand; and of the rest few came off safe with their arms.

Upon this disaster, which to him was not wholly an unexpected one, Nicias accused the rashness of Demosthenes; but he, making his excuses for the past, now advised to be gone in all haste, for neither were other forces to come, nor could the enemy be beaten with the present. And, indeed, even supposing they were yet too hard for the enemy in any case, they ought to remove and quit a situation which they understood to be always accounted a sickly one, and dangerous for an army, and was more particularly unwholesome now, as they could see themselves, because of the time of year. It was the beginning of autumn, and many now lay sick, and all were out of heart.

It grieved Nicias to hear of flight and departing home, not that he did not fear the Syracusans, but he was worse afraid of the Athenians, their impeachments and sentences; he professed that he apprehended no further harm there, or if it must be, he would rather die by the hand of an enemy than by his fellow-citizens. He was not of the opinion which Leo of Byzantium declared to his fellow-citizens: "I had rather," said he, "perish by you, than with you." As to the matter of place and quarter whither to remove their camp that, he said, might be debated at leisure. And Demosthenes, his former counsel having succeeded so ill, ceased to press him further; others thought Nicias had reasons for expectation, and relied on some assurance from people within the city, and that this made him so strongly oppose their retreat, so they acquiesced. But fresh forces now coming to the Syracusans and the sickness growing worse in his camp, he, also, now approved of their retreat, and commanded the soldiers to make ready to go abroad.

And when all were in readiness, and none of the enemy had observed them, not expecting such a thing, the moon was eclipsed in the night, to the great fright of Nicias and others, who, for want of experience, or out of superstition, felt alarm at such appearances. That the sun might be darkened about the close of the month, this even ordinary people now understood pretty well to be the effect of the moon; but the moon itself to be darkened, how that could come about, and how, on the sudden, a broad full moon should lose her light, and show such various colors, was not easy to be comprehended; they concluded it to be ominous, and a divine intimation of some heavy calamities. For he who the first, and the most plainly of any, and with the greatest assurance committed to writing how the moon is enlightened and overshadowed, was Anaxagoras; and he was as yet but recent, nor was his argument much known, but was rather kept secret, passing only amongst a few, under some kind of caution and confidence. People would not then tolerate natural philosophers, and theorists, as they then called them, about things above; as lessening the divine power, by explaining away its agency into the operation of irrational causes and senseless forces acting by necessity, without any thing of Providence, or a free agent. Hence it was that Protagoras was banished, and Anaxagoras cast in prison, so that Pericles had much difficulty to procure his liberty; and Socrates, though he had no concern whatever with this sort of learning, yet was put to death for philosophy. It was only afterwards that the reputation of Plato, shining forth by his life, and because he subjected natural necessity to divine and more excellent principles, took away the obloquy and scandal that had attached to such contemplations, and obtained these studies currency among all people. So his friend Dion, when the moon, at the time he was to embark from Zacynthus to go against Dionysius, was eclipsed, was not in the least disturbed, but went on, and arriving at Syracuse, expelled the tyrant. But it so fell out with Nicias, that he had not at this time a skilful diviner with him; his former habitual adviser who used to moderate much of his superstition, Stilbides, had died a little before. For in fact, this prodigy, as Philochorus observes, was not unlucky for men wishing to fly, but on the contrary very favorable; for things done in fear require to be hidden, and the light is their foe. Nor was it usual to observe signs in the sun or moon more than three days, as Autoclides states in his Commentaries. But Nicias persuaded them to wait another full course of the moon, as if he had not seen it clear again as soon as ever it had passed the region of shadow where the light was obstructed by the earth.

In a manner abandoning all other cares, he betook himself wholly to his sacrifices, till the enemy came upon them with their infantry, besieging the forts and camp, and placing their ships in a circle about the harbor. Nor did the men in the galleys only, but the little boys everywhere got into the fishing-boats and rowed up and challenged the Athenians, and insulted over them. Amongst these a youth of noble parentage, Heraclides by name, having ventured out beyond the rest, an Athenian ship pursued and wellnigh took him. His uncle Pollichus, in fear for him, put out with ten galleys which he commanded, and the rest, to relieve Pollichus, in like manner drew forth; the result of it being a very sharp engagement, in which the Syracusans had the victory, and slew Eurymedon, with many others. After his the Athenian soldiers had no patience to stay longer, but raised an outcry against their officers, requiring them to depart by land; for the Syracusans, upon their victory, immediately shut and blocked up the entrance of the harbor; but Nicias would not consent to this, as it was a shameful thing to leave behind so many ships of burden, and galleys little less than two hundred. Putting, therefore, on board the best of the foot, and the most serviceable darters, they filled one hundred and ten galleys; the rest wanted oars. The remainder of his army

Nicias posted along by the sea-side, abandoning the great camp and the fortifications adjoining the temple of Hercules ; so the Syracusans, not having for a long time performed their usual sacrifice to Hercules, went up now, both priests and captains, to sacrifice.

And their galleys being manned, the diviners predicted from their sacrifices victory and glory to the Syracusans, provided they would not be the aggressors, but fight upon the defensive ; for so Hercules overcame all, by only defending himself when set upon. In this confidence they set out ; and this proved the hottest and fiercest of all their sea-fights, raising no less concern and passion in the beholders than in the actors ; as they could oversee the whole action with all the various and unexpected turns of fortune which, in a short space, occurred in it ; the Athenians suffering no less from their own preparations, than from the enemy ; for they fought against light and nimble ships, that could attack from any quarter, with theirs laden and heavy. And they were thrown at with stones that fly indifferently any way, for which they could only return darts and arrows, the direct aim of which the motion of the water disturbed, preventing their coming true, point foremost to their mark. This the Syracusans had learned from Ariston the Corinthian pilot, who, fighting stoutly, fell himself in this very engagement, when the victory had already declared for the Syracusans.

The Athenians, their loss and slaughter being very great, their flight by sea cut off, their safety by land so difficult, did not attempt to hinder the enemy towing away their ships, under their eyes, nor demanded their dead, as, indeed, their want of burial seemed a less calamity than the leaving behind the sick and wounded which they now had before them. Yet more miserable still than those did they reckon themselves, who were to work on yet, through more such sufferings, after all to reach the same end.

They prepared to dislodge that night. And Gylippus and his friends seeing the Syracusans engaged in their sacrifices and at their cups, for their victories, and it being also a holiday, did not expect either by persuasion or by force, to rouse them up and carry them against the Athenians as they decamped. But Hermocrates, of his own head, put a trick upon Nicias, and sent some of his companions to him, who pretended they came from those that were wont to hold secret intelligence with him, and advised him not to stir that night, the Syracusans having laid ambushes and beset the ways. Nicias, caught with this stratagem, remained, to encounter presently in reality, what he had feared when there was no occasion. For they, the next morning, marching before, seized the defiles, fortified the passes where the rivers were fordable, cut down the bridges, and ordered their horsemen to range the plains and ground that lay open, so as to leave no part of the country where the Athenians could move without fighting. They stayed both that day and another night, and then went along as if they were leaving their own, not an enemy's country, lamenting and bewailing for want of necessaries, and for their parting from friends and companions that were not able to help themselves; and, nevertheless, judging the present evils lighter than those they expected to come. But among the many miserable spectacles that appeared up and down in the camp, the saddest sight of all was Nicias himself, laboring under his malady, and unworthily reduced to the scantiest supply of all the accommodations necessary for human wants, of which he in his condition required more than ordinary, because of his sickness; yet bearing up under all this illness, and doing and undergoing more than many in perfect health. And it was plainly evident that all this toil was not for himself, or from any regard to his own life, but that purely for the sake of those under his command he would not abandon hope. And, indeed, the rest were given over to weeping and lamentation through fear or sorrow, but he, whenever he yielded to any thing of the kind, did so, it was evident, from reflection upon the shame and dishonor of the enterprise, contrasted with the greatness and glory of the success he had anticipated, and not only the sight of his person, but, also, the recollection of the arguments and the dissuasions he used to prevent this expedition enhanced their sense of the undeservedness of his sufferings, nor had they any heart to put their trust in the gods, considering that a man so religious, who had performed to the divine powers so many and so great acts of devotion, should have no more favorable treatment than the wickedest and meanest of the army.

Nicias, however, endeavored all the while by his voice, his countenance, and his carriage, to show himself undefeated by these misfortunes. And all along the way shot at, and receiving wounds eight days continually from the enemy, he yet preserved the forces with him in a body entire, till that Demosthenes was taken prisoner with the party that he led, whilst they fought and made a resistance, and so got behind and were surrounded near the country house of Polyzelus. Demosthenes thereupon drew his sword, and wounded but did not kill himself, the enemy speedily running in and seizing upon him. So soon as the Syracusans had gone and informed Nicias of this, and he had sent some horsemen, and by them knew the certainty of the defeat of that division, he then vouchsafed to sue to Gylippus for a truce for the Athenians to depart out of Sicily, leaving hostages for payment of money that the Syracusans had expended in the war.

But now they would not hear of these proposals, but threatening and reviling them, angrily and insultingly continued to ply their missiles at them, now destitute of every necessary. Yet Nicias still made good his retreat all that night, and the next day, through all their darts, made his way to the river Asinarus. There, however, the enemy encountering them, drove some into the stream, while others, ready to die for thirst, plunged in headlong, while they drank at the same time, and were cut down by their enemies. And here was the cruellest and the most immoderate slaughter. Till at last Nicias falling down to Gylippus, "Let pity, O Gylippus," said he, "move you in your victory; not for me, who was destined, it seems, to bring the glory I once had to this end, but for the other Athenians; as you well know that the chances of war are common to all, and the Athenians used them moderately and mildly towards you in their prosperity."

At these words, and at the sight of Nicias, Gylippus was somewhat troubled, for he was sensible that the Lacedæmonians had received good offices from Nicias in the late treaty, and he thought it would be a great and glorious thing for him to carry off the chief commanders of the Athenians alive. He therefore raised Nicias with respect, and bade him be of good cheer, and commanded his men to spare the lives of the rest. But the word of command being communicated slowly, the slain were a far greater number than the prisoners. Many, however, were privately conveyed away by particular soldiers. Those taken openly were hurried together in a mass; their arms and spoils hung up on the finest and largest trees along the river. The conquerors, with garlands on their heads, with their own horses splendidly adorned, and cropping short the manes and tails of those of their enemies, entered the city, having, in the most signal conflict ever waged by Greeks against Greeks, and with the greatest strength and the utmost effort of valor and manhood won a most entire victory.

And a general assembly of the people of Syracuse and their confederates sitting, Eurycles, the popular leader moved; first, that the day on which they took Nicias should from thence forward be kept holiday by sacrificing and forbearing all manner of work, and from the river be called the Asinarian Feast. This was the twenty-sixth day of the month Carneus, the Athenian Metagitnion. And that the servants of the Athenians with the other confederates be sold for slaves, and they themselves and the Sicilian auxiliaries be kept and employed in the quarries, except the generals, who should be put to death. The Syracusans favored the proposal, and when Hermocrates said, that to use well a victory was better than to gain a victory, he was met with great clamor and outcry. When Gylippus, also, demanded the Athenian generals to be delivered to him, that he might carry them to the Lacedæmonians, the Syracusans, now insolent with their good fortune, gave him ill words. Indeed, before this, even in the war, they had been impatient at his rough behavior and Lacedæmonian haughtiness, and had, as Timæus tells us, discovered sordidness and avarice in his character, vices which may have descended to him from his father Cleandrides, who was convicted of bribery and banished. And the very man himself, of the one thousand talents which Lysander sent to Sparta, embezzled thirty, and hid them under the tiles of his house, and was detected and shamefully fled his country. But this is related more at large in the life of Lysander. Timæus says that Demosthenes and Nicias did not die, as Thucydides and Philistus have written, by the order of the Syracusans, but that upon a message sent them from Hermocrates, whilst yet the assembly were sitting, by the connivance of some of their guards, they were enabled to put an end to themselves. Their bodies, however, were thrown out before the gates and offered for a public spectacle. And I have heard that to this day in a temple at Syracuse is shown a shield, said to have been Nicias's, curiously wrought and embroidered with gold and purple intermixed. Most of the Athenians perished in the quarries by diseases and ill diet, being allowed only one pint of barley every day, and one half pint of water. Many of them, however, were carried off by stealth, or, from the first, were supposed to be servants, and were sold as slaves. These latter were branded on their foreheads with the figure of a horse. There were, however Athenians, who, in addition to slavery, had to endure even this. But their discreet and orderly conduct was an advantage to them ; they were either soon set free, or won the respect of their masters with whom they continued to live. Several were saved for the sake of Euripides, whose poetry, it appears, was in request among the Sicilians more than among any of the settlers out of Greece. And when any travellers arrived that could tell them some passage, or give them any specimen of his verses, they were delighted to be able to communicate them to one another. Many of the captives who got safe back to Athens are said, after they reached home, to have gone and made their acknowledgments to Euripides, relating how that some of them had been released from their slavery by teaching what they could remember of his poems, and others, when straggling after the fight, been relieved with meat and drink for repeating some of his lyrics. Nor need this be any wonder, for it is told that a ship of Caunus fleeing into one of their harbors for protection, pursued by pirates, was not received, but forced back, till one asked if they knew any of Euripides's verses, and on their saying they did, they were admitted, and their ship brought into harbor.

It is said that the Athenians would not believe their loss, in a great degree because of the person who first brought them news of it. For a certain stranger, it seems, coming to Piræus, and there sitting in a barber's shop, began to talk of what had happened, as if the Athenians already knew all that had passed ; which the barber hearing, before he acquainted anybody else, ran as fast as he could up into the city, addressed himself to the Archons, and presently spread it about in the public Place. On which, there being everywhere, as may be imagined, terror and consternation, the Archons summoned a general assembly, and there brought in the man and questioned him how he came to know. And he, giving no satisfactory account, was taken for a spreader of false intelligence and a disturber of the city, and was, therefore, fastened to the wheel and racked a long time, till other messengers arrived that related the whole disaster particularly. So hardly was Nicias believed to have suffered the calamity which he had ofter predicted.

CRASSUS.

MARCUS CRASUS, whose father had borne the office of a censor, and received the honor of a triumph, was educated in a little house together with his two brothers, who both married in their parents' lifetime ; they kept but one table amongst them ; all which, perhaps, was not the least reason of his own temperance and moderation in diet. One of his brothers dying, he married his widow, by whom he had his children ; neither was there in these respects any of the Romans who lived a more orderly life than he did, though later in life he was suspected to have been too familiar with one of the vestal virgins, named Licinia, who was, nevertheless, acquitted, upon an impeachment brought against her by one Plotinus. Licinia stood possessed of a beautiful property in the suburbs, which Crassus desiring to purchase at a low price, for this reason was frequent in his attentions to her which gave occasion to the scandal, and his avarice, so to say, serving to clear him of the crime, he was acquitted. Nor did he leave the lady till he had got the estate.

People were wont to say that the many virtues of Crassus were darkened by the one vice of avarice, and indeed he seemed to have no other but that ; for it being the most predominant, obscured others to which he was inclined. The arguments in proof of his avarice were the vastness of his estate, and the manner of raising it ; for whereas at first he was not worth above three hundred talents, yet, though in the course of his political life he dedicated the tenth of all he had to Hercules, and feasted the people, and gave to every citizen corn enough to serve him three months, upon casting up his accounts, before he went upon his Parthian expedition, he found his possessions to amount to seven thousand one hundred talents ; most of which, if we may scandal him with a truth, he got by fire and rapine, making his advantages of the public calamities. For when Sylla seized the city, and exposed to sale the goods of those that he had caused to be slain, accounting them booty and spoils, and, indeed, calling them so too, and was desirous of making as many, and as eminent men as he could, partakers in the crime, Crassus never was the man that refused to accept, or give money for them. Moreover observing how extremely subject the city

VOL. II.—16

was to fire, and falling down of houses, by reason of their height and their standing so near together, he bought slaves that were builders and architects, and when he had collected these to the number of more than five hundred, he made it his practice to buy houses that were on fire, and those in the neighborhood, which, in the immediate danger and uncertainty the proprietors were willing to part with for little or nothing; so that the greatest part of Rome, at one time or other, came into his hands. Yet for all he had so many workmen, he never built any thing but his own house, and used to say that those that were addicted to building would undo themselves soon enough without the help of other enemies. And though he had many silver mines, and much valuable land, and laborers to work in it, yet all this was nothing in comparison of his slaves, such a number and variety did he possess of excellent readers, amanuenses, silversmiths, stewards and table-waiters, whose instruction he always attended to himself, superintending in person while they learned, and teaching them himself, accounting it the main duty of a master to look over the servants that are, indeed, the living tools of housekeeping; and in this, indeed, he was in the right, in thinking, that is, as he used to say, that servants ought to look after all other things, and the master after them. For economy, which in things inanimate is but money-making, when exercised over men becomes policy. But it was surely a mistaken judgment, when he said no man was to be accounted rich that could not maintain an army at his own cost and charges, for war, as Archidamus well observed, is not fed at a fixed allowance, so that there is no saying what wealth suffices for it, and certainly it was one very far removed from that of Marius; for when he had distributed fourteen acres of land a man, and understood that some desired more, "God forbid," said he, "that any Roman should think that too little which is enough to keep him alive and well."

Crassus, however, was very eager to be hospitable to strangers; he kept open house, and to his friends he would lend money without interest, but called it in precisely at the time; so that his kindness was often thought worse than the paying the interest would have been. His entertainments were, for the most part, plain and citizenlike, the company general and popular; good taste and kindness made them pleasanter than sumptuosity would have done. As for learning, he chiefly cared for rhetoric, and what would be serviceable with large numbers; he became one of the best speakers a. Rome, and by his pains and industry outdid the best natural orators. For there was no trial how mean and contemptible soever that he came to unprepared ; nay, several times he undertook and concluded a cause, when Pompey and Cæsar and Cicero refused to stand up, upon which account particularly he got the love of the people, who looked upon him as a diligent and careful man, ready to help and succor his fellow-citizens. Besides, the people were pleased with his courteous and unpretending salutations and greetings, for he never met any citizen however humble and low, but he returned him his salute by name. He was looked upon as a man well-read in history, and pretty well versed in Aristotle's philosophy, in which one Alexander instructed him, a man whose intercourse with Crassus gave a sufficient proof of his good-nature, and gentle disposition ; for it is hard to say, whether he was poorer when he entered into his service, or while ne continued in it ; for being his only friend that used to accompany him when travelling, he used to receive from him a cloak for the journey, and when he came home had it demanded from him again ; poor, patient sufferer, when even the philosophy he professed did not look upon poverty as a thing indifferent. But of this hereafter.

When Cinna and Marius got the power in their hands it was soon perceived that they had not come back for any good they intended to their country, but to effect the ruin and utter destruction of the nobility. And as many as they could lay their hands on they slew, amongst whom were Crassus's father and brother ; he himself, being very young, for the moment escaped the danger ; but understanding that he was every way beset and hunted after by the tyrants, taking with him three friends and ten servants, with all possible speed he fled into Spain, having formerly been there and secured a great number of friends, while his father was prætor of that country. But finding all people in a consternation, and trembling at the cruelty of Marius, as if he was already standing over them in person, he durst not discover himself to anybody, but hid himself in a large cave which was by the sea-shore, and belonged to Vibius Pacianus, to whom he sent one of his servants to sound him, his provisions, also, beginning to fail. Vibius was well pleased at his escape and inquiring the place of his abode and the number of his companions, he went not to him himself, but commanded his steward to provide every day a good meal's meat, and carry it and leave it near such a rock and to return without taking any further notice or being in quisitive, promising him his liberty if he did as he commanded, and that he would kill him if he intermeddled. The cave is not far from the sea ; a small and insignificant looking opening in the cliffs conducts you in ; when you are entered, a wonderfully high roof spreads above you, and large chambers open out one beyond another, nor does it lack either water or light for a very pleasant and wholesome spring runs at the foot of the cliffs, and natural chinks, in the most advantageous place, let in the light all day long, and the thickness of the rock makes the air within pure and clear, all the wet and moisture being carried off into the spring.

While Crassus remained here, the steward brought them what was necessary, but never saw them, nor knew any thing of the matter, though they within saw, and expected him at the customary times. Neither was their entertainment such as just to keep them alive, but given them in abundance and for their enjoyment ; for Pacianus resolved to treat him with all imaginable kindness, and considering that he was a young man, thought it well to gratify a little his youthful inclinations ; for to give just what is needful, seems rather to come from necessity than from a hearty friendship. Once taking with him two female servants, he showed them the place and bade them go in boldly, whom when Crassus and his friends saw, they were afraid of being betrayed, and demanded what they were, and what they would have. They, according as they were instructed, answered, they came to wait upon their master who was hid in that cave. And so Crassus perceiving it was a piece of pleasantry and of good-will on the part of Vibius, took them in and kept them there with him as long as he stayed, and employed them to give information to Vibius of what they wanted, and how they were. Fenestella says he saw one of them, then very old, and often heard her speak of the time and repeat the story with pleasure.

After Crassus had lain concealed there eight months, on hearing that Cinna was dead, he appeared abroad, and a great number of people flocking to him, out of whom he selected a body of two thousand five hundred, he visited many cities, and, as some write, sacked Malaca, which he himself, however, always denied, and contradicted all who said so. Afterwards, getting together some ships, he passed into Africa, and joined with Metellus Pius, an eminent person that had raised a very considerable force ; but upon some difference between him and Metellus, he stayed not long there, but went over to Sylla, by whom he was very much esteemed. When Sylla passed over into Italy, he was anxious to put all the young men that were with him in employment; and as he despatched some one way, and some another, Crassus, on its falling to his share to raise men among the Marsians, demanded a guard, being to pass through the enemy's country, upon which Sylla replied sharply, "I give you for guard your father, your brother, your friends and kindred, whose unjust and cruel murder I am now going to revenge;" and Crassus, being nettled, went his way, broke boldly through the enemy, collected a considerable force, and in all Sylla's wars acted with great zeal and courage. And in these times and occasions, they say, began the emulation and rivalry for glory between him and Pompey; for though Pompey was the younger man, and had the disadvantage to be descended of a father that was disesteemed by the citizens, and hated as much as ever man was, yet in these actions he shone out and was proved so great, that Sylla always used, when he came in, to stand up and uncover his head, an honor which he seldom showed to older men and his own equals, and always saluted him *Imperator*. This fired and stung Crassus, though, indeed he could not with any fairness claim to be preferred; for he both wanted experience, and his two innate vices, sordidness and avarice, tarnished all the lustre of his actions. For when he had taken Tudertia, a town of the Umbrians, he converted, it was said, all the spoils to his own use, for which he was complained of to Sylla. But in the last and greatest battle before Rome itself, where Sylla was worsted, some of his battalions giving ground, and others being quite broken, Crassus got the victory on the right wing, which he commanded, and pursued the enemy till night, and then sent Sylla to acquaint him with his success, and demand provision for his soldiers. In the time, however, of the proscriptions and sequestrations, he lost his repute again, by making great purchases for little or nothing, and asking for grants. Nay, they say he proscribed one of the Bruttians without Sylla's order, only for his own profit, and that, on discovering this, Sylla never after trusted him in any public affairs. As no man was more cunning than Crassus to ensnare others by flattery, so no man lay more open to it, or swallowed it more greedily than himself. And this particularly was observed of him, that though he was the most covetous man in the world, yet he habitually disliked and cried out against others who were so.

It troubled him to see Pompey so successful in all his un

dertakings; that he had had a triumph before he was capable to sit in the senate, and that the people had surnamed him Magnus, or the great. When somebody was saying Pompey the Great was coming, he smiled, and asked him, "How big is he?" Despairing to equal him by feats of arms, he betook himself to civil life, where by doing kindnesses, pleading, lending money, by speaking and canvassing among the people for those who had objects to obtain from them, he gradually gained as great honor and power as Pompey had from his many famous expeditions. And it was a curious thing in their rivalry, that Pompey's name and interests in the city was greatest when he was absent, for his renown in war, but when present he was often less successful than Crassus, by reason of his superciliousness and haughty way of living, shunning crowds of people, and appearing rarely in the forum, and assisting only some few, and that not readily, that his interests might be the stronger when he came to use it for himself. Whereas Crassus, being a friend always at hand, ready to be had and easy of access, and always with his hands full of other people's business, with his freedom and courtesy, got the better of Pompey's formality. In point of dignity of person, eloquence of language, and attractiveness of countenance, they were pretty equally excellent. But, however, this emulation never transported Crassus so far as to make him bear enmity, or any ill-will; for though he was vexed to see Pompey and Cæsar preferred to him, yet he never mingled any hostility or malice with his jealousy; though Cæsar, when he was taken captive by the corsairs in Asia, cried out, "O Crassus, how glad you will be at the news of my captivity!" Afterwards they lived together on friendly terms, for when Cæsar was going prætor into Spain, and his creditors, he being then in want of money, came upon him and seized his equipage, Crassus then stood by him and relieved him, and was his security for eight hundred and thirty talents And in general, Rome being divided into three great interests, those of Pompey, Cæsar, and Crassus (for as for Cato, his fame was greater than his power, and he was rather admired than followed), the sober and quiet part were for Pompey, the restless and hot-headed followed Cæsar's ambition, but Crassus trimmed between them, making advantages of both, and changed sides continually, being neither a trusty friend nor an implacable enemy, and easily abandoned both his attachments and his animosities, as he found it for his advantage, so that in short spaces of time, the same men and the same measures had him both as their supporter and as their opponent. He was much liked, but was feared as much or even more. At any rate, when Sicinius, who was the greatest troubler of the magistrates and ministers of his time, was asked how it was he let Crassus alone, "Oh," said he, "he carries hay on his horns," alluding to the custom of tying hay to the horns of a bull that used to butt, that people might keep out of his way.

The insurrection of the gladiators and the devastation of Italy, commonly called the war of Spartacus, began upon this occasion. One Lentulus Batiates trained up a great many gladiators in Capua, most of them Gauls and Thracians, who, not for any fault by them committed, but simply through the cruelty of their master, were kept in confinement for this object of fighting one with another. Two hundred of these formed a plan to escape, but being discovered, those of them who became aware of it in time to anticipate their master, being seventy-eight, got out of a cook's shop chopping-knives and spits, and made their way through the city, and lighting by the way on several wagons that were carrying gladiators' arms to another city, they seized upon them and armed themselves. And seizing upon a defensible place, they chose three captains, of whom Spartacus was chief, a Thracian of one of the nomad tribes, and a man not only of high spirit and valiant, but in understanding, also, and in gentleness, superior to his condition, and more of a Grecian than the people of his country usually are. When he first came to be sold at Rome, they say a snake coiled itself upon his face as he lay asleep, and his wife, who at this latter time also accompanied him in his flight, his country-woman, a kind of prophetess, and one of those possessed with the bacchanal frenzy, declared that it was a sign portending great and formidable power to him with no happy event.

First, then, routing those that came out of Capua against them, and thus procuring a quantity of proper soldiers' arms, they gladly threw away their own as barbarous and dishonorable. Afterwards Clodius, the prætor, took the command against them with a body of three thousand men from Rome, and besieged them within a mountain, accessible only by one narrow and difficult passage, which Clodius kept guarded, encompassed on all other sides with steep and slippery precipices. Upon the top, however, grew a great many wild vines, and cutting down as many of their boughs as they had need of, they twisted them into strong ladders long enough to reach from thence to the bottom, by which, without any danger, they got down all but one, who stayed there to throw them down their arms, and after this succeeded in saving himself. The Romans were ignorant of all this, and, therefore, coming upon them in the rear, they assaulted them unawares and took their camp. Several, also, of the shepherds and herdsmen that were there, stout and nimble fellows, revolted over to them, to some of whom they gave complete arms, and made use of others as scouts and light-armed soldiers. Publius Varinus, the prætor, was now sent against them, whose lieutenant, Furius, with two thousand men, they fought and routed. Then Cossinius was sent with considerable forces, to give his assistance and advice, and him Spartacus missed but very little of capturing in person, as he was bathing at Salinæ; for he with great difficulty made his escape, while Spartacus possessed himself of his baggage, and following the chase with a great slaughter, stormed his camp and took it, where Cossinius himself was slain. After many successful skirmishes with the prætor himself, in one of which he took his lictors and his own horse, he began to be great and terrible; but wisely considering that he was not to expect to match the force of the empire, he marched his army towards the Alps, intending, when he had passed them, that every man should go to his own home, some to Thrace, some to Gaul. But they, grown confident in their numbers, and puffed up with their success, would give no obedience to him, but went about and ravaged Italy; so that now the senate was not only moved at the indignity and baseness, both of the enemy and of the insurrection, but, looking upon it as a matter of alarm and of dangerous consequence, sent out both the consuls to it, as to a great and difficult enterprise. The consul Gellius, falling suddenly upon a party of Germans, who through contempt and confidence had straggled from Spartacus, cut them all to pieces. But when Lentulus with a large army besieged Spartacus, he sallied out upon him, and, joining battle, defeated his chief officers, and captured all his baggage. As he made toward the Alps, Cassius, who was prætor of that part of Gaul that lies about the Po, met him with ten thousand men, but being overcome in battle, he had much ado to escape himself, with the loss of a great many of his men.

When the senate understood this, they were displeased at the consuls, and ordering them to meddle no further, they appointed Crassus general of the war, and a great many of the nobility went volunteers with him, partly out of friendship, and partly to get honor. He stayed himself on the borders of Picenum, expecting Spartacus would come that way, and sent his lieutenant, Mummius, with two legions, to wheel about and observe the enemy's motions, but upon no account to engage or skirmish. But he, upon the first opportunity, joined battle, and was routed, having a great many of his men slain, and a great many only saving their lives with the loss of their arms. Crassus rebuked Mummius severely, and arming the soldiers again, he made them find sureties for their arms, that they would part with them no more, and five hundred that were the beginners of the flight, he divided into fifty tens, and one of each was to die by lot, thus reviving the ancient Roman punishment of decimation, where ignominy is added to the penalty of death, with a variety of appalling and terrible circumstances, presented before the eyes of the whole army, assembled as spectators. When he had thus reclaimed his men, he led them against the enemy; but Spartacus retreated through Lucania toward the sea, and in the straits meeting with some Cilician pirate ships, he had thoughts of attempting Sicily, where, by landing two thousand men, he hoped to new kindle the war of the slaves, which was but lately extinguished, and seemed to need but little fuel to set it burning again. But after the pirates had struck a bargain with him, and received his earnest, they deceived him and sailed away. He thereupon retired again from the sea, and established his army in the peninsula of Rhegium; there Crassus came upon him, and considering the nature of the place, which of itself suggested the undertaking, he set to work to build a wall across the isthmus; thus keeping his soldiers at once from idleness, and his foes from forage. This great and difficult work he perfected in a space of time short beyond all expectation, making a ditch from one sea to the other, over the neck of land, three hundred furlongs long, fifteen feet broad, and as much in depth, and above it built a wonderfully high and strong wall. All which Spartacus at first slighted and despised, but when provisions began to fail, and on his proposing to pass further, he found he was walled in, and no more was to be had in the peninsula, taking the opportunity of a snowy, stormy night, he filled up part of the ditch with earth and boughs of trees, and so passed the third part of his army over.

Crassus was afraid lest he should march directly to Rome, but was soon eased of that fear when he saw many of his men break out in a mutiny and quit him, and encamped by themselves upon the Lucanian lake. This lake they say changes at intervals of time, and is sometimes sweet, and somtimes so salt that it cannot be drunk. Crassus falling upon these beat them from the lake, but he could not pursue the slaughter, because of Spartacus suddenly coming up, and checking the flight. Now he began to repent that he had previously written to the senate to call Lucullus out of Thrace, and Pompey out of Spain ; so that he did all he could to finish the war before they came, knowing that the honor of the action would redound to him that came to his assistance. Resolving, therefore, first to set upon those that had mutinied and encamped apart, whom Caius Cannicius and Castus commanded, he sent six thousand men before to secure a little eminence, and to do it as privately as possible, which that they might do, they covered their helmets, but being discovered by two women that were sacrificing for the enemy, they had been in great hazard, had not Crassus immediately appeared, and engaged in a battle which proved a most bloody one. Of twelve thousand three hundred whom he killed, two only were found wounded in their backs, the rest all having died standing in their ranks, and fighting bravely. Spartacus, after this discomfiture, retired to the mountains of Petelia, but Quintius, one of Crassus's officers, and Scrofa, the quæstor, pursued and overtook him. But when Spartacus rallied and faced them, they were utterly routed and fled, and had much ado to carry off their quæstor, who was wounded. This success, however, ruined Spartacus, because it encouraged the slaves, who now disdained any longer to avoid fighting, or to obey their officers, but as they were upon the march, they came to them with their swords in their hand, and compelled them to lead them back again through Lucania, against the Romans, the very thing which Crassus was eager for. For news was already brought that Pompey was at hand ; and people began to talk openly, that the honor of this war was reserved to him, who would come and at once oblige the enemy to fight and put an end to the war. Crassus, therefore, eager to fight a decisive battle, encamped very near the enemy, and began to make lines of circumvallation ; but the slaves made a sally, and attacked the pioneers. As fresh supplies came in on either side, Spartacus, seeing there was no avoiding it, set all his army in array, and when his horse was brought him, he drew out his sword and killed him, saying, if he got the day he should have a great many better horses of the enemies' and if he lost it, he should have no need of this. And so making directly towards Crassus himself, through the midst of arms and wounds, he missed him, but slew two centurions that fell upon him together. At last being deserted by those that were about him, he himself stood his ground, and, surrounded by the enemy, bravely defending himself, was cut in pieces. But though Crassus had good fortune, and not only did the part of a good general, but gallantly exposed his person, yet Pompey had much of the credit of the action. For he met with many of the fugitives, and slew them, and wrote to the senate that Crassus indeed had vanquished the slaves in a pitched battle, but that he had put an end to the war. Pompey was honored with a magnificent triumph for his conquest over Sertorius and Spain, while Crassus could not himself so much as desire a triumph in its full form, and indeed it was thought to look but meanly in him to accept of the lesser honor, called the ovation, for a servile war, and perform a procession on foot. The difference between this and the other, and the origin of the name, are explained in the life of Marcellus.

And Pompey being immediately invited to the consulship, Crassus, who had hoped to be joined with him, did not scruple to request his assistance. Pompey most readily seized the opportunity, as he desired by all means to lay some obligation upon Crassus, and zealously promoted his interest; and at last he declared in one of his speeches to the people, that he should be not less beholden to them for his colleague, than for the honor of his own appointment. But once entered upon the employment, this amity continued not long; but differing almost in every thing, disagreeing, quarrelling, and contending, they spent the time of their consulship, without effecting any measure of consequence, except that Crassus made a great sacrifice to Hercules, and feasted the people at ten thousand tables, and measured them out corn for three months. When their command was now ready to expire, and they were, as it happened, addressing the people, a Roman knight, one Onatius Aurelius, an ordinary private person, living in the country, mounted the hustings, and declared a vision he had in his sleep: "Jupiter," said he, "appeared to me and commanded me to tell you, that you should not suffer your consuls to lay down their charge before they are made friends." When he had spoken, the people cried out that they should be reconciled. Pompey stood still and said nothing, but Crassus, first offering him his hand, said, "I cannot think, my countrymen, that I do any thing humiliating or unworthy of myself, if I make the first offers of accommodation and friendship with Pompey, whom you yourselves styled the Great, before he was of man's estate, and decreed him a triumph before he was capable of sitting in the senate."

This is what was memorable in Crassus's consulship, but as for his censorship, that was altogether idle and inactive, for he neither made a scrutiny of the senate, nor took a review of the horsemen, nor a census of the people, though he had as mild a man as could be desired for his colleague, Lutatius Catulus. It is said, indeed, that when Crassus intended a violent and unjust measure, which was the reducing Egypt to be tributary to Rome, Catulus strongly opposed it, and falling out about it, they laid down their office by consent. In the great conspiracy of Catiline, which was very near subverting the government, Crassus was not without some suspicion of being concerned, and one man came forward and declared him to be in the plot; but nobody credited him. Yet Cicero, in one of his orations, clearly charges both Crassus and Cæsar with the guilt of it, though that speech was not published till they were both dead. But in his speech upon his consulship, he declares that Crassus came to him by night, and brought a letter concerning Catiline, stating the details of the conspiracy. Crassus hated him ever after, but was hindered by his son from doing him any injury; for Publius was a great lover of learning and eloquence, and a constant follower of Cicero, insomuch that he put himself into mourning when he was accused, and induced the other young men to do the same. And at last he reconciled him to his father.

Cæsar now returning from his command, and designing to get the consulship, and seeing that Crassus and Pompey were again at variance, was unwilling to disoblige one by making application to the other, and despaired of success without the help of one of them; he therefore made it his business to reconcile them, making it appear that by weakening each other's influence, they were promoting the interest of the Ciceros, the Catuli, and the Catos, who would really be of no account if they would join their interests and their factions, and act together in public with one policy and one united power. And so reconciling them by his persuasions out of the three parties he set up one irresistible power, which utterly subverted the government both of senate and people. Not that he made either Pompey or Crassus greater than they were before, but by their means made himself greatest of all ; for by the help of the adherents of both, he was at once gloriously declared consul, which office when he administered with credit, they decreed him the command of an army, and allotted him Gaul for his province, and so placed him as it were in the citadel, not doubting but they should divide the rest at their pleasure between themselves, when they had confirmed him in his allotted command Pompey was actuated in all this by an immoderate desire of ruling, but Crassus, adding to his old disease of covetousness, a new passion after trophies and triumphs, emulous of Cæsar's exploits, not content to be beneath him in these points, though above him in all others, could not be at rest, till it ended in an ignominious overthrow, and a public calamity. When Cæsar came out of Gaul to Lucca, a great many went thither from Rome to meet him. Pompey and Crassus had various conferences with him in secret, in which they came to the resolution to proceed to still more decisive steps, and to get the whole management of affairs into their hands, Cæsar to keep his army, and Pompey and Crassus to obtain new ones and new provinces. To effect all which there was but one way, the getting the consulate a second time, which they were to stand for, and Cæsar to assist them by writing to his friends and sending many of his soldiers to vote.

But when they returned to Rome, their design was presently suspected, and a report was soon spread that this interview had been for no good. When Marcellinus and Domitius asked Pompey in the senate if he intended to stand for the consulship, he answered, perhaps he would, perhaps not ; and being urged again, replied, he would ask it of the honest citizens, but not of the dishonest. Which answer appearing too haughty and arrogant, Crassus said, more modestly, that he would desire it if it might be for the advantage of the public, otherwise he would decline it. Upon this some others took confidence and came forward as candidates, among them Domitius. But when Pompey and Crassus now openly appeared for it, the rest were afraid and drew back ; only Cato encouraged Domitius, who was his friend and relation, to proceed, exciting him to persist, as though he was now defending the public liberty, as these men, he said, did not so much aim at the consulate, as at arbitrary government, and it was not a petition for office, but a seizure of provinces and armies. Thus spoke and thought Cato, and almost forcibly compelled Domitius to appear in the forum, where many sided with them. For there was, indeed, much wonder and question among the people, "Why should Pompey and Crassus want another consulship? and why they two together, and not with some third person? We have a great many men not unworthy to be fellow-consuls with either the one or the other." Pompey's party, being apprehensive of this, committed all manner of indecencies and violences, and amongst other things ay in wait for Domitius, as he was coming thither before daybreak with his friends; his torch-bearer they killed, and wounded several others, of whom Cato was one. And these being beaten back and driven into a house, Pompey and Crassus were proclaimed consuls. Not long after, they surrounded the house with armed men, thrust Cato out of the forum, killed some that made resistance, and decreed Cæsar his command for five years longer, and provinces for themselves, Syria, and both the Spains, which being divided by lots, Syria fell to Crassus, and the Spains to Pompey.

All were well pleased with the change, for the people were desirous that Pompey should not go far from the city, and he, being extremely fond of his wife, was very glad to continue there; but Crassus was so transported with his fortune, that it was manifest he thought he had never had such good luck befall him as now, so that he had much to do to contain himself before company and strangers; but amongst his private friends he let fall many vain and childish words, which were unworthy of his age, and contrary to his usual character, for he had been very little given to boasting hitherto. But then being strangely puffed up, and his head heated, he would not limit his fortune with Parthia and Syria; but looking on the actions of Lucullus against Tigranes and the exploits of Pompey against Mithridates as but child's play, he proposed to himself in his hopes to pass as far as Bactria and India, and the utmost ocean. Not that he was called upon by the decree which appointed him to his office to undertake any expedition against the Parthians, but it was well known that he was eager for it, and Cæsar wrote to him out of Gaul, commending his resolution, and inciting him to the war. And when Ateius, the tribune of the people, designed to stop his journey, and many others murmured that one man should undertake a war against a people that had done them no injury, and were at amity with them, he desired Pompey to stand by him and accompany him out of the town, as he had a great name amongst the common people. And when several were ready prepared to interfere and raise an outcry, Pompey appeared with a pleasing countenance, and so mollified the people, that they let Crassus pass quietly. Ateius, however, met him, and first by word of mouth warned and conjured him not to proceed, and then commanded his attendant officer to seize him and detain him; but the other tribunes not permitting it, the officer released Crassus. Ateius, therefore, running to the gate, when Crassus was come thither, set down a chafing-dish with lighted fire in it, and burning incense and pouring libations on it, cursed him with dreadful imprecations, calling upon and naming several strange and horrible deities. In the Roman belief there is so much virtue in these sacred and ancient rites, that no man can escape the effects of them, and that the utterer himself seldom prospers; so that they are not often made use of, and but upon a great occasion. And Ateius was blamed at the time for resorting to them, as the city itself, in whose cause he used them, would be the first to feel the ill effects of these curses and supernatural terrors.

Crassus arrived at Brundusium, and though the sea was very rough, he had not patience to wait, but went on board, and lost many of his ships. With the remnant of his army he marched rapidly through Galatia, where meeting with king Deiotarus, who, though he was very old, was about building a new city, Crassus scoffingly told him, "Your majesty begins to build at the twelfth hour." "Neither do you," said he, "O general, undertake your Parthian expedition very early." For Crassus was then sixty years old, and he seemed older than he was. At his first coming, things went as he would have them, for he made a bridge over the Euphrates without much difficulty, and passed over his army in safety, and occupied many cities of Mesopotamia, which yielded voluntarily. But a hundred of his men were killed in one, in which Apollonius was tyrant; therefore, bringing his forces against it, he took it by storm, plundered the goods, and sold the inhabitants. The Greeks call this city Zenodotia, upon the taking of which, he permitted the army to salute him Imperator, but this was very ill thought of, and it looked as if he despaired a nobler achievement, that he made so much of this little success. Putting garrisons of seven thousand foot and one thousand horse in the new conquests, he returned to take up his winter-quarters in Syria, where his son was to meet him coming from Cæsar out of Gaul, decorated with rewards for his valor, and bringing with him one thousand select horse. Here Crassus seemed to commit his first error, and except, indeed, the whole expedition, his greatest; for, whereas he ought to have gone forward and seized Babylon and Seleucia, cities that were ever at enmity with the Parthians, he gave the enemy time to provide against him. Besides, he spent his time in Syria more like an usurer than a general, not in taking an account of the arms, and in improving the skill and discipline of his soldiers, but in computing the revenue of the cities, wasting many days in weighing by scale and balance the treasure that was in the temple of Hierapolis, issuing requisitions for levies of soldiers upon particular towns and kingdoms and then again withdrawing them on payment of sums of money, by which he lost his credit and became despised. Here, too, he met with the first ill-omen from that goddess, whom some call Venus, others Juno, others Nature, or the Cause that produces out of moisture the first principles and seeds of all things, and gives mankind their earliest knowledge of all that is good for them. For as they were going out of the temple, young Crassus stumbled, and his father fell upon him.

When he drew his army out of winter-quarters, ambassadors came to him from Arsaces, with this short speech : If the army was sent by the people of Rome, he denounced mortal war, but if, as he understood was the case, against the consent of his country, Crassus for his own private profit had invaded his territory, then their king would be more merciful, and taking pity upon Crassus's dotage, would send those soldiers back who had been left not so truly to keep guard on him as to be his prisoners. Crassus boastfully told them he would return his answer at Seleucia, upon which Vagises, the eldest of them, laughed and showed the palm of his hand, saying, "Hair will grow here before you will see Seleucia ;" so they returned to their king, Hyrodes, telling him it was war. Several of the Romans that were in garrison in Mesopotamia with great hazard made their escape, and brought word that the danger was worth consideration, urging their own eye-witness of the numbers of the enemy, and the manner of their fighting, when they assaulted their towns ; and, as men's manner is, made all seem greater than really it was. By flight it was impossible to escape them, and as impossible to overtake them when they fled, and they had a new and strange sort of darts, as swift as sight, for they pierced whatever they met with, before you could see who threw them ; their men-at-arms were so provided that their weapons would cut through any thing, and their armor give way to nothing. All which when the soldiers heard, their hearts failed them · for till now they thought there was no difference between the Parthians and the Armenians or Cappadocians, whom Lucullus grew weary with plundering, and had been persuaded that the main difficulty of the war consisted only in the tediousness of the march and the trouble of chasing men that durst not come to blows, so that the danger of a battle was beyond their expectation; accordingly, some of the officers advised Crassus to proceed no further at present, but reconsider the whole enterprise, amongst whom in particular was Cassius, the quæstor. The soothsayers, also, told him privately the signs found in the sacrifices were continually adverse and unfavorable. But he paid no heed to them, or to anybody who gave any other advice than to proceed. Nor did Artabazes, king of Armenia, confirm him a little, who came to his aid with six thousand horse; who, however, were said to be only the king's life-guard and suite, for he promised ten thousand cuirassiers more, and thirty thousand foot, at his own charge. He urged Crassus to invade Parthia by the way of Armenia, for not only would he be able there to supply his army with abundant provision, which he would give him, but his passage would be more secure in the mountains and hills, with which the whole country was covered, making it almost impassable to horse, in which the main strength of the Parthians consisted. Crassus returned him but cold thanks for his readiness to serve him, and for the splendor of his assistance, and told him he was resolved to pass through Mesopotamia, where he had left a great many brave Roman soldiers; whereupon the Armenian went his way. As Crassus was taking the army over the river at Zeugma, he encountered preternaturally violent thunder, and the lightning flashed in the faces of the troops, and during the storm a hurricane broke upon the bridge, and carried part of it away; two thunderbolts fell upon the very place where the army was going to encamp; and one of the general's horses, magnificently caparisoned, dragged away the groom into the river and was drowned. It is said, too, that when they went to take up the first standard, the eagle of itself turned its head backward; and after he had passed over his army, as they were distributing provisions, the first thing they gave was lentils and salt, which with the Romans are the food proper to funerals, and are offered to the dead. And as Crassus was haranguing his soldiers, he let fall a word which was thought very ominous in the army; for "I am going," he said, "to break down the bridge, that none of you may return;" and whereas he ought, when he had perceived his blunder, to have corrected himself, and explained his meaning, seeing the men alarmed at the expression, he would not do it out of mere stubbornness. And when at the last general sacrifice the priest gave him the entrails, they slipt out of his hand, and when he saw the standers-by concerned at it, he laughed and said, "See what it is to be an old man but I shall hold my sword fast enough."

So he marched his army along the river with seven legions, little less than four thousand horse, and as many light-armed soldiers, and the scouts returning declared that not one man appeared, but that they saw the footing of a great many horses which seemed to be retiring in flight, whereupon Crassus conceived great hopes, and the Romans began to despise the Parthians, as men that would not come to combat, hand to hand. But Cassius spoke with him again, and advised him to refresh his army in some of the garrison towns, and remain there till they could get some certain intelligence of the enemy, or at least to make toward Seleucia, and keep by the river, that so they might have the convenience of having provision constantly supplied by the boats, which might always accompany the army, and the river would secure them from being environed, and, if they should fight, it might be upon equal terms.

While Crassus was still considering, and as yet undetermined, there came to the camp an Arab chief named Ariamnes, a cunning and wily fellow, who, of all the evil chances which combined to lead them on to destruction, was one chief and the most fatal. Some of Pompey's old soldiers knew him, and remembered him to have received some kindnesses of Pompey, and to have been looked upon as a friend to the Romans, but he was now suborned by the king's generals, and sent to Crassus to entice him if possible from the river and hills into the wide open plain, where he might be surrounded. For the Parthians desired any thing, rather than to be obliged to meet the Romans face to face. He, therefore, coming to Crassus (and he had a persuasive tongue), highly commended Pompey as his benefactor, and admired the forces that Crassus had with him, but seemed to wonder why he delayed and made preparations, as if he should not use his feet more than any arms, against men that, taking with them their best goods and chattels, had designed long ago to fly for refuge to the Scythians or Hyrcanians. "If you meant to fight, you should have made all possible haste, before the king should recover courage, and collect his forces together; at present you see

Surena and Sillaces opposed to you, to draw you off in pursuit of them, while the king himself keeps out of the way." But this was all a lie, for Hyrodes had divided his army in two parts, with one he in person wasted Armenia, revenging himself upon Artavasdes, and sent Surena against the Romans, not out of contempt, as some pretend, for there is no likelihood that he should despise Crassus, one of the chiefest men of Rome, to go and fight with Artavasdes, and invade Armenia; but much more probably he really apprehended the danger, and therefore waited to see the event, intending that Surena should first run the hazard of a battle, and draw the enemy on. Nor was this Surena an ordinary person, but in wealth, family, and reputation, the second man in the kingdom, and in courage and prowess the first, and for bodily stature and beauty no man like him. Whenever he travelled privately, he had one thousand camels to carry his baggage, two hundred chariots for his concubines, one thousand completely armed men for his life-guards, and a great many more light-armed; and he had at least ten thousand horsemen altogether, of his servants and retinue. The honor had long belonged to his family, that at the king's coronation he put the crown upon his head, and when this very king Hyrodes had been exiled, he brought him in; it was he, also, that took the great city of Seleucia, was the first man that scaled the walls, and with his own hand beat off the defenders. And though at this time he was not above thirty years old, he had a great name for wisdom and sagacity, and, indeed, by these qualities chiefly, he overthrew Crassus, who first through his overweening confidence, and afterwards because he was cowed by his calamities, fell a ready victim to his subtlety. When Ariamnes had thus worked upon him, he drew him from the river into vast plains, by a way that at first was pleasant and easy but afterwards very troublesome by reason of the depth of the sand; no tree, nor any water, and no end of this to be seen; so that they were not only spent with thirst, and the difficulty of the passage, but were dismayed with the uncomfortable prospect of not a bough, not a stream, not a hillock, not a green herb, but in fact a sea of sand, which encompassed the army with its waves. They began to suspect some treachery, and at the same time came messengers from Artavasdes, that he was fiercely attacked by Hyrodes, who had invaded his country, so that now it was impossible for him to send any succors, and that he therefore advised Crassus to turn back, and with joint forces to give Hyrodes battle, or ai least that he should march and encamp where horses could not easily come, and keep to the mountains. Crassus, out of anger and perverseness, wrote him no answer, but told them, at present he was not at leisure to mind the Armenians, but he would call upon them another time, and revenge himself upon Artavasdes for his treachery. Cassius and his friends began again to complain, but when they perceived that it merely displeased Crassus, they gave over, but privately railed at the barbarian, "What evil genius, O thou worst of men, brought thee to our camp, and with what charms and potions hast thou bewitched Crassus, that he should march his army through a vast and deep desert, through ways which are rather fit for a captain of Arabian robbers, than for the general of a Roman army?" But the barbarian, being a wily fellow, very submissively exhorted them, and encouraged them to sustain it a little further, and ran about the camp, and, professing to cheer up the soldiers, asked them, jokingly, "What, do you think you march through Campania, expecting everywhere to find springs, and shady trees, and baths, and inns of entertainment? Consider you now travel through the confines of Arabia and Assyria." Thus he managed them like children, and before the cheat was discovered, he rode away; not but that Crassus was aware of his going, but he had persuaded him that he would go and contrive how to disorder the affairs of the enemy.

It is related that Crassus came abroad that day not in his scarlet robe, which Roman generals usually wear, but in a black one, which, as soon as he perceived, he changed. And the standard-bearers had much ado to take up their eagles, which seemed to be fixed to the place. Crassus laughed at it, and hastened their march, and compelled his infantry to keep pace with his cavalry, till some few of the scouts returned and told them that their fellows were slain and they hardly escaped, that the enemy was at hand in full force, and resolved to give them battle. On this all was in an uproar; Crassus was struck with amazement, and for haste could scarcely put his army in good order. First, as Cassius advised, he opened their ranks and files that they might take up as much space as could be, to prevent their being surounded, and distributed the horse upon the wings, but afterwards changing his mind, he drew up his army in a square, and made a front every way, each of which consisted of twelve cohorts, to every one of which he allotted a troop of horse, that no part might be destitute of the assistance that the horse might give, and that they might be ready to assist everywhere, as need should require. Cassius commanded one of the wings, young Crassus the other, and he himself was in the middle. Thus they marched on till they came to a little river named Balissus, a very inconsiderable one in itself, but very grateful to the soldiers, who had suffered so much by drouth and heat all along their march. Most of the commanders were of the opinion that they ought to remain there that night, and to inform themselves as much as possible of the number of the enemies, and their order, and so march against them at break of day; but Crassus was so carried away by the eagerness of his son, and the horsemen that were with him, who desired and urged him to lead them on and engage, that he commanded those that had a mind to it to eat and drink as they stood in their ranks, and before they had all well done, he led them on, not leisurely and with halts to take breath, as if he was going to battle, but kept on his pace as if he had been in haste, till they saw the enemy, contrary to their expectation, neither so many nor so magnificently armed as the Romans expected. For Surena had hid his main force behind the first ranks, and ordered them to hide the glittering of their armor with coats and skins. But when they approached and the general gave the signal, immediately all the field rung with a hideous noise and terrible clamor. For the Parthians do not encourage themselves to war with cornets and trumpets, but with a kind of kettle-drum, which they strike all at once in various quarters. With these they make a dead, hollow noise, like the bellowing of beasts, mixed with sounds resembling thunder, having, it would seem, very correctly observed that of all our senses hearing most confounds and disorders us, and that the feelings excited through it most quickly disturb, and most entirely overpower the understanding.

When they had sufficiently terrified the Romans with their noise, they threw off the covering of their armor, and shone like lightning in their breastplates and helmets of polished Margianian steel, and with their horses covered with brass and steel trappings. Surena was the tallest and finest looking man himself, but the delicacy of his looks and effeminacy of his dress did not promise so much manhood as he really was master of; for his face was painted, and his hair parted after the fashion of the Medes, whereas the other Parthians made a more terrible appearance, with their shaggy hair gathered in a mass upon their foreheads after the Scythian mode. Their first design was with their lances to beat down and force back the first ranks of the Romans, but when they perceived the depth of their battle, and that the soldiers firmly kept their ground, they made a retreat, and pretending to break their order and disperse, they encompassed the Roman square before they were aware of it. Crassus commanded his light-armed soldiers to charge, but they had not gone far before they were received with such a shower of arrows that they were glad to retire amongst the heavy-armed, with whom this was the first occasion of disorder and terror, when they perceived the strength and force of their darts, which pierced their arms, and passed through every kind of covering, hard and soft alike. The Parthians now placing themselves at distances began to shoot from all sides, not aiming at any particular mark (for, indeed, the order of the Romans was so close, that they could not miss if they would), but simply sent their arrows with great force out of strong bent bows, the strokes from which came with extreme violence. The position of the Romans was a very bad one from the first; for if they kept their ranks, they were wounded, and if they tried to charge, they hurt the enemy none the more, and themselves suffered none the less. For the Parthians threw their darts as they fled an art in which none but the Scythians excel them, and it is, indeed, a cunning practice, for while they thus fight to make their escape, they avoid the dishonor of a flight.

However, the Romans had some comfort to think that when they had spent all their arrows, they would either give over or come to blows; but when they presently understood that there were numerous camels loaded with arrows, and that when the first ranks had discharged those they had, they wheeled off and took more, Crassus seeing no end of it, was out of all heart, and sent to his son that he should endeavor to fall in upon them before he was quite surrounded; for the enemy advanced most upon that quarter, and seemed to be trying to ride round and come upon the rear. Therefore the young man, taking with him thirteen hundred horse, one thousand of which he had from Cæsar, five hundred archers, and eight cohorts of the full-armed soldiers that stood next him, led them up with design to charge the Parthians. Whether it was that they found themselves in a piece of marshy ground, as some think, or else designing to entice young Crassus as far as they could from his father, they turned and began to fly; whereupon he crying out that they durst not stand, pursued them, and with him Censorinus and Megabacchus, both famous the latter for his courage and prowess, the other for being of a senator's family, and an excellent orator, both intimates of Crassus, and of about the same age The horse thus pushing on, the infantry stayed a little behind, being exalted with hopes and joy, for they supposed they had already conquered, and now were only pursuing; till when they were gone too far, they perceived the deceit, for they that seemed to fly, now turned again, and a great many fresh ones came on. Upon this they made a halt, for they doubted not but now the enemy would attack them, because they were so few. But they merely placed their cuirassiers to face the Romans, and with the rest of their horse rode about scouring the field, and thus stirring up the sand, they raised such a dust that the Romans could neither see nor speak to one another, and being driven in upon one another in one close body, they were thus hit and killed, dying, not by a quick and easy death, but with miserable pains and convulsions; for writhing upon the darts in their bodies, they broke them in their wounds, and when they would by force pluck out the barbed points, they caught the nerves and veins, so that they tore and tortured themselves. Many of them died thus, and those that survived were disabled for any service, and when Publius exhorted them to charge the cuirassiers, they showed him their hands nailed to their shields, and their feet stuck to the ground, so that they could neither fly nor fight. He charged in himself boldly, however, with his horse, and came to close quarters with them, but was very unequal, whether as to the offensive or defensive part; for with his weak and little javelins, he struck against targets that were of tough raw hides and iron, whereas the lightly clad bodies of his Gaulish horsemen were exposed to the strong spears of the enemy. For upon these he mostly depended, and with them he wrought wonders; for they would catch hold of the great spears, and close upon the enemy, and so pull them off from their horses, where they could scarce stir by reason of the heaviness of their armor, and many of the Gauls quitting their own horses, would creep under those of the enemy, and stick them in the belly; which, growing unruly with the pain, trampled upon their riders and upon the enemies promiscuously. The Gauls were chiefly tormented by the heat and drouth, being not accustomed to either, and most of their horses were slain by being spurred on against the spears, so that they were forced to retire among the foot, bearing off Publius grievously wounded. Observing a sandy hillock not far off, they made to it, and tying their horses to one another, and placing them in the midst, and joining all their shields together before them, they thought they might make some defence against the barbarians. But it fell out quite contrary, for when they were drawn up in a plain, the front in some measure secured those that were behind; but when they were upon the hill, one being of necessity higher up than another, none were in shelter, but all alike stood equally exposed, bewailing their inglorious and useless fate. There were with Publius two Greeks that lived near there at Carrhæ, Hieronymus and Nicomachus; these men urged him to retire with them and fly to Ichnæ, a town not far from thence, and friendly to the Romans. "No," said he, "there is no death so terrible, for the fear of which Publius would leave his friends that die upon his account;" and bidding them to take care of themselves, he embraced them and sent them away, and, because he could not use his arm, for he was run through with a dart, he opened his side to his armor-bearer, and commanded him to run him through. It is said that Censorinus fell in the same manner. Megabacchus slew himself, as did also the rest of best note. The Parthians coming upon the rest with their lances, killed them fighting, nor were there above five hundred taken prisoners. Cutting off the head of Publius, they rode off directly towards Crassus.

His condition was thus. When he had commanded his son to fall upon the enemy, and word was brought him that they fled and that there was a distant pursuit, and perceiving also that the enemy did not press upon him so hard as formerly, for they were mostly gone to fall upon Publius, he began to take heart a little; and drawing his army towards some sloping ground, expected when his son would return from the pursuit. Of the messengers whom Publius sent to him (as soon as he saw his danger), the first were intercepted by the enemy, and slain; the last hardly escaping, came and declared that Publius was lost, unless he had speedy succors. Crassus was terribly distracted, not knowing what counsel to take, and indeed no longer capable of taking any; overpowered now by fear for the whole army, now by desire to help his son. At last he resolved to move with his forces. Just upon this, up came the enemy with their shouts and noises more terrible than before, their drums sounding again in the ears of the Romans, who now feared a fresh engagement. And they who brought Publius's head upon the point of a spear, riding up near enough that it could be known, scoffingly inquired where were his parents, and what family he was of, for it was im possible that so brave and gallant a warrior should be the son of so pitiful a coward as Crassus. This sight above all the rest dismayed the Romans, for it did not incite them to anger as it might have done, but to horror and trembling, though they say Crassus outdid himself in this calamity, for he passed through the ranks and cried out to them, " This, O my countrymen, is my own peculiar loss, but the fortune and the glory of Rome is safe and untainted so long as you are safe. But if any one be concerned for my loss of the best of sons, let him show it in revenging him upon the enemy. Take away their joy, revenge their cruelty, nor be dismayed at what is past; for whoever tries for great objects must suffer something. Neither did Lucullus overthrow Tigranes without bloodshed, nor Scipio Antiochus; our ancestors lost one thousand ships about Sicily, and how many generals and captains in Italy? no one of which losses hindered them from overthrowing their conquerors; for the State of Rome did not arrive to this height by fortune, but by perseverance and virtue in confronting danger."

While Crassus thus spoke exhorting them, he saw but few that gave much heed to him, and when he ordered them to shout for battle, he could no longer mistake the despondency of his army, which made but a faint and unsteady noise, while the shout of the enemy was clear and bold. And when they came to the business, the Parthian servants and dependents riding about shot their arrows, and the horsemen in the foremost ranks with their spears drove the Romans close together, except those who rushed upon them for fear of being killed by their arrows. Neither did these do much execution, being quickly despatched: for the strong, thick spear made large and mortal wounds, and often run through two men at once. As they were thus fighting, the night coming on parted them, the Parthians boasting that they would indulge Crassus with one night to mourn his son, unless upon better consideration he would rather go to Arsaces, than be carried to him. These, therefore, took up their quarters near them, being flushed with their victory. But the Romans had a sad night of it; for neither taking care for the burial of their dead, nor the cure of the wounded, nor the groans of the expiring, every one bewailed his own fate. For there was no means of escaping, whether they should stay for the light, or venture to retreat into the vast desert in the dark. And now the wounded men gave them new trouble, since to take them with them would retard their flight, and if they should leave them, they might serve as guides to the enemy by their cries. However, they were all desirous to see and hear Crassus, though they were sensible that he was the cause of all their mischief. But he wrapped his cloak around him, and hid himself, where he lay as an example, to ordinary minds, of the caprice of fortune, but to the wise, of inconsiderateness and ambition ; who, not content to be superior to so many millions of men, being inferior to two, esteemed himself as the lowest of all. Then came Octavius, his lieutenant, and Cassius, to comfort him, but he being altogether past helping, they themselves called together the centurions and tribunes, and agreeing that the best way was to fly, they ordered the army out, without sound of trumpet, and at first with silence. But before long, when the disabled men found they were left behind, strange confusion and disorder, with an outcry and lamentation, seized the camp, and a trembling and dread presently fell upon them, as if the enemy were at their heels. By which means, now and then turning out of their way, now and then standing to their ranks, sometimes taking up the wounded that followed, sometimes laying them down, they wasted the time, except three hundred horse, whom Egnatius brought safe to Carrhæ about midnight ; where calling, in the Roman tongue, to the watch, as soon as they heard him, he bade them tell Coponius, the governor, that Crassus had fought a very great battle with the Parthians ; and having said but this, and not so much as telling his name, he rode away at full speed to Zeugma. And by this means he saved himself and his men, but lost his reputation by deserting his general. However, his message to Coponius was for the advantage of Crassus ; for he, suspecting by this hasty and confused delivery of the message that all was not well, immediately ordered the garrison to be in arms, and as soon as he understood that Crassus was upon the way towards him, he went out to meet him, and received him with his army into the town.

The Parthians, although they perceived their dislodgement in the night, yet did not pursue them, but as soon as it was day, they came upon those that were left in the camp, and put no less than four thousand to the sword, and with their light horse picked up a great many stragglers. Varguntinus, the lieutenant, while it was yet dark, had broken off from the main body with four cohorts which had strayed out of the way ; and the Parthians encompassing these on a small hill, slew every man of them excepting twenty, who with their drawn swords forced their way through the thickest, and they admiring their courage, opened their ranks to the right and left, and let them pass without molestation to Carrhæ.

Soon after a false report was brought to Surena, that Crassus, with his principal officers, had escaped, and that those who were got into Carrhæ were but a confused rout of insignificant people, not worth further pursuit. Supposing therefore, that he had lost the very crown and glory of his victory, and yet being uncertain whether it were so or not, and anxious to ascertain the fact, that so he should either stay and besiege Carrhæ or follow Crassus, he sent one of his interpreters to the walls, commanding him in Latin to call for Crassus or Cassius, for that the general, Surena, desired a conference. As soon as Crassus heard this, he embraced the proposal, and soon after there came up a band of Arabians, who very well knew the faces of Crassus and Cassius, as having been frequently in the Roman camp before the battle. They having espied Cassius from the wall, told him that Surena desired a peace, and would give them safe convoy, if they would make a treaty with the king his master, and withdraw all their troops out of Mesopotamia; and this he thought most advisable for them both, before things came to the last extremity. Cassius, embracing the proposal, desired that a time and place might be appointed where Crassus and Surena might have an interview. The Arabians, having charged themselves with the message, went back to Surena, who was not a little rejoiced that Crassus was there to be besieged.

Next day, therefore, he came up with his army, insulting over the Romans, and haughtily demanded of them Crassus and Cassius bound, if they expected any mercy. The Romans, seeing themselves deluded and mocked, were much troubled at it, but advising Crassus to lay aside his distant and empty hopes of aid from the Armenians, resolved to fly for it; and this design ought to have been kept private, till they were upon their way, and not have been told to any of the people of Carrhæ. But Crassus let this also be known to Andromachus, the most faithless of men, nay, he was so infatuated as to choose him for his guide. The Parthians then, to be sure, had punctual intelligence of all that passed; but it being contrary to their usage, and also difficult for them to fight by night, and Crassus having chosen that time to set out, Andromachus, lest he should get the start too far of his pursuers, led him hither and thither, and at last conveyed him into the midst of morasses and places full of ditches, so that the Romans had a troublesome and perplexing journey of it, and some there were who, supposing by these windings and turnings of Adromachus hat no good was intended, resolved to follow him no further. And at last Cassius himself returned to Carrhæ, and his guides, the Arabians, advising him to tarry there till the moon was got out of Scorpio, he told them that he was most afraid of Sagittarius, and so with five hundred horse went off to Syria. Others there were, who having got honest guides, took their way by the mountains called Sinnaca, and got into places of security by daybreak; these were five thousand under the command of Octavius, a very gallant man. But Crassus fared worse; day overtook him still deceived by Andromachus, and entangled in the fens and the difficult country. There were with him four cohorts of legionary soldiers, a very few horsemen, and five lictors, with whom having with great difficulty got into the way, and not being a mile and a half from Octavius, instead of going to join him, although the enemy were already upon him, he retreated to another hill, neither so defensible nor impassable for the horse, but lying under the hills at Sinnaca, and continued so as to join them in a long ridge through the plain. Octavius could see in what danger the general was, and himself, at first but slenderly followed, hurried to the rescue. Soon after, the rest, unbraiding one another with baseness in forsaking their officers, marched down, and falling upon the Parthians, drove them from the hill, and compassing Crassus about, and fencing him with their shields, declared proudly, that no arrow in Parthia should ever touch their general, so long as there was a man of them left alive to protect him.

Surena, therefore, perceiving his soldiers less inclined to expose themselves, and knowing that if the Romans should prolong the battle till night, they might then gain the mountains and be out of his reach, betook himself to his usual craft. Some of the prisoners were set free, who had, as it was contrived, been in hearing, while some of the barbarians spoke a set purpose in the camp to the effect that the king did not design the war to be pursued to extremity against the Romans, but rather desired, by his general treatment of Crassus, to make a step towards reconciliation. And the barbarians desisted from fighting, and Surena himself, with his chief officers, riding gently to the hill, unbent his bow and held out his hand, inviting Crassus to an agreement, and saying that it was beside the king's intentions, that they had thus had experience of the courage and the strength of his soldiers; that now he desired no other contention but that of kindness and friendship, by making a truce, and permitting them to go away in safety. These words of Surena the rest received joyfully, and were eager to accept the offer; but Crassus, who had had sufficient experience of their perfidiousness, and was unable to see any reason for the sudden change, would give no ear to them, and only took time to consider. But the soldiers cried out and advised him to treat, and then went on to unbraid and affront him, saying that it was very unreasonable that he should bring them to fight with such men armed, whom himself, without their arms, durst not look in the face. He tried first to prevail with them by entreaties, and told them that if they would have patience till evening, they might get into the mountains and passes, inaccessible for horse, and be out of danger, and withal he pointed out the way with his hand, entreating them not to abandon their preservation, now close before them. But when they mutined and clashed their targets in a threatening manner, he was overpowered and forced to go, and only turning about at parting, said, " You, Octavius and Petronius, and the rest of the officers who are present, see, the necessity of going which I lie under, and cannot but be sensible of the indignities and violence offered to me. Tell all men when you have escaped, that Crassus perished rather by the subtilty of his enemies, than by the disobedience of his countrymen."

Octavius, however, would not stay there, but with Petronius went down from the hill; as for the lictors, Crassus bade them be gone. The first that met him were two half-blood Greeks, who, leaping from their horses, made a profound reverence to Crassus, and desired him, in Greek, to send some before him, who might see that Surena himself was coming towards them, his retinue disarmed, and not having so much as their wearing swords along with them. But Crassus answered, that if he had the least concern for his life, he would never have intrusted himself in their hands, but sent two brothers of the name of Roscius to inquire on what terms, and in what numbers they should meet. These Surena ordered immediately to be seized, and himself with his principal officers came up on horseback, and greeting him, said, " How is this, then ? A Roman commander is on foot, whilst I and my train are mounted." But Crassus replied, that there was no error committed on either side, for they both met according to the custom of their own country. Surena told him that from that time there was a league between the king his master and the Romans, but that Crassus must go with him to the river to sign it, "for you Romans," said he, "have not good memories for conditions," and so saying, reached out his hand to him. Crassus, therefore, gave order that one of his horses should be brought; but Surena told him there was no need, "the king, my master, presents you with this;" and immediately a horse with a golden bit was brought up to him, and himself was forcibly put into the saddle by the grooms, who ran by the side and struck the horse to make the more haste. But Octavius running up, got hold of the bridle, and soon after one of the officers, Petronius, and the rest of the company came up, striving to stop the horse, and pulling back those who on both sides of him forced Crassus forward. Thus from pulling and thrusting one another, they came to a tumult, and soon after to blows. Octavius, drawing his sword, killed a groom of one of the barbarians, and one of them, getting behind Octavius, killed him. Petronius was not armed, but being struck on the breastplate, fell down from his horse, though without hurt. Crassus was killed by a Parthian, called Pomaxathres; others say by a different man, and that Pomaxathres only cut off his head and right hand after he had fallen. But this is conjecture rather than certain knowledge, for those that were by had not leisure to observe particulars, and were either killed fighting about Crassus, or ran off at once to get to their comrades on the hill. But the Parthians coming up to them, and saying that Crassus had the punishment he justly deserved, and that Surena bade the rest come down from the hill without fear, some of them came down and surrendered themselves, others were scattered up and down in the night, a very few of whom got safe home, and others the Arabians, beating through the country, hunted down and put to death. It is generally said, that in all twenty thousand men were slain, and ten thousand taken prisoners.

Surena sent the head and hand of Crassus to Hyrodes the king, into Armenia, but himself by his messengers scattering a report that he was bringing Crassus alive to Seleucia, made a ridiculous procession, which, by way of scorn he called a triumph. For one Caius Paccianus, who of all the prisoners was most like Crassus, being put into a woman's dress of the fashion of the barbarians, and instructed to answer to the title of Crassus and Imperator, was brought sitting upon his horse, while before him went a parcel of trumpeters and lictors upon camels. Purses were hung at the end of the bundles of rods, and the heads of the slain fresh bleeding at the end of their axes. After them followed the Seleucian singing women, repeating scurrilous and abusive songs upon the effeminacy and cowardliness of Crassus. This show was seen by everybody; but Surena, calling together the senate of Seleucia, laid before them certain wanton books, of the writings of Aristides, his Milesiaca ; neither, indeed, was this any forgery, for they had been found among the baggage of Rustius, and were a good subject to supply Surena with insulting remarks upon the Romans, who were not able even in the time of war to forget such writings and practices. But the people of Seleucia had reason to commend the wisdom of Æsop's fable of the wallet, seeing their general Surena carrying a bag full of loose Milesian stories before him, but keeping behind him a whole Parthian Sybaris in his many wagons full of concubines ; like the vipers and asps people talk of, all the foremost and more visible parts fierce and terrible with spears and arrows and horsemen, but the rear terminating in loose women and castanets, music of the lute, and midnight revellings. Rustius, indeed, is not to be excused, but the Parthians had forgot, when they mocked at the Milesian stories, that many of the royal line of their Arsacidæ had been born of Milesian and Ionian mistresses.

Whilst these things were doing, Hyrodes had struck u, peace with the king of Armenia, and made a match between his son Pacorus and the king of Armenia's sister. Their feastings and entertainments in consequence were very sumptuous, and various Grecian compositions, suitable to the occasion, were recited before them. For Hyrodes was not ignorant of the Greek language and literature, and Artavasdes was so expert in it, that he wrote tragedies and orations and histories, some of which are still extant. When the head of Crassus was brought to the door, the tables were just taken away, and one Jason, a tragic actor, of the town of Tralles, was singing the scene in the Bacchæ of Euripides concerning Agave. He was receiving much applause, when Sillaces, coming to the room, and having made obeisance to the king, threw down the head of Crassus into the midst of the company. The Parthians receiving it with joy and acclamations, Sillaces, by the king's command, was made to sit down, while Jason handed over the costume of Pentheus to one of the dancers in the chorus, and taking up the head of Crassus, and acting the part of a bacchante in her frenzy, in a rapturous impassioned manner, sang the lyric passages,

> We've hunted down a mighty chase to-day,
> And from the mountain bring the noble prey;

to the great delight of all the company; but when the verses of the dialogue followed,

> What happy hand the glorious victim slew?
> I claim that honor to my courage due;

Pomaxathres, who happened to be there at the supper, started up and would have got the head into his own hands, "for it is my due," said he, "and no man's else." The king was greatly pleased, and gave presents, according to the custom of the Parthians, to them, and to Jason, the actor, a talent. Such was the burlesque that was played, they tell us, as the afterpiece to the tragedy of Crassus's expedition. But divine justice failed not to punish both Hyrodes, for his cruelty, and Surena for his perjury; for Surena not long after was put to death by Hyrodes, out of mere envy to his glory; and Hyrodes himself, having lost his son Pacorus, who was beaten in a battle with the Romans, falling into a disease which turned to a dropsy, had aconite given him by his second son, Phraates; but the poison working only upon the disease, and carrying away the dropsical matter with itself, the king began suddenly to recover, so that Phraates at length was forced to take the shortest course, and strangled him.

COMPARISON OF CRASSUS WITH NICIAS.

In the comparison of these two, first, if we compare the estate of Nicias with that of Crassus, we must acknowledge Nicias's to have been more honestly got. In itself, indeed, one cannot much approve of gaining riches by working mines, the greatest part of which is done by malefactors and barbarians, some of them, too, bound, and perishing in those close and unwholesome places. But if we compare this with the sequestrations of Sylla, and the contracts for houses ruined by fire, we shall then think Nicias came very honestly by his money. For Crassus publicly and avowedly made use of these arts, as other men do of husbandry, and putting out money to interest; while as for other matters which he used to deny, when taxed with them, as, namely, selling his voice in the senate for gain's sake, and injuring allies, and courting women, and conniving at criminals, these are things which Nicias was never so much as falsely accused of; nay, he was rather laughed at for giving money to those who made a trade of impeachments, merely out of timorousness, a course, indeed, that would by no means become Pericles and Aristides, but necessary for him who by nature was wanting in assurance, even as Lycurgus, the orator, frankly acknowledged to the people; for when he was accused for buying off an evidence, he said that he was very much pleased that having administered their affairs for so long a time, he was at last accused, rather for giving, than receiving. Again, Nicias, in his expenses, was of a more public spirit than Crassus, priding himself much on the dedication of gifts in temples, on presiding at gymnastic games, and furnishing choruses for the plays, and adorning processions, while the expenses of Crassus, in feasting and afterwards providing food for so many myriads of people, were much greater than all that Nicias possessed as well as spent, put together. So that one might wonder at any one's failing to see that vice is a certain inconsistency and incongruity of habit, after such an example of money dishonorably obtained, and wastefully lavished away.

Let so much be said of their estates; as for their management of public affairs, I see not that any dishonesty, injustice, or arbitrary action can be objected to Nicias, who was rather the victim of Alcibiades's tricks, and was always careful and scrupulous in his dealings with the people. But Crassus is very generally blamed for his changeableness in his friendships and enmities, for his unfaithfulness, and his mean and underhand proceedings; since he himself could not deny that to compass the consulship, he hired men to lay violent hands upon Domitius and Cato. Then at the assembly held for assigning the provinces, many were wounded and four actually killed, and he himself, which I had omitted in the narrative of his life, struck with his fist one Lucius Analius, a senator, for contradicting him, so that he left the place bleeding. But as Crassus was to be blamed for his violent and arbitrary courses, so is Nicias no less to be blamed for his timorousness and meanness of spirit, which made him submit and give in to the basest people, whereas in this respect Crassus showed himself lofty-spirited and magnanimous, who having to do not with such as Cleon or Hyperbolus, but with the splendid acts of Cæsar and the three triumphs of

Pompey, would not stoop, but bravely bore up against their joint interests, and in obtaining the office of censor, surpassed even Pompey himself. For a statesman ought not to regard how invidious the thing is, but how noble, and by his greatness to overpower envy; but if he will be always aiming at security and quiet, and dread Alcibiades upon the hustings, and the Lacedæmonians at Pylos, and Perdiccas in Thrace, there is room and opportunity enough for retirement and he may sit out of the noise of business, and weave himself, as one of the sophists says, his triumphal garland of inactivity. His desire of peace, indeed, and of finishing the war, was a divine and truly Grecian ambition, nor in this respect would Crassus deserve to be compared to him, though he had enlarged the Roman empire to the Caspian Sea or the Indian Ocean.

In a State where there is a sense of virtue, a powerful man ought not to give way to the ill-affected, or expose the government to those that are incapable of it, nor suffer high trusts to be committed to those who want common honesty. Yet Nicias, by his connivance, raised Cleon, a fellow remarkable for nothing but his loud voice and brazen face, to the command of an army. Indeed, I do not commend Crassus, who in the war with Spartacus was more forward to fight than became a discreet general, though he was urged into it by a point of honor, lest Pompey by his coming should rob him of the glory of the action, as Mummius did Metellus at the taking of Corinth, but Nicias's proceedings are inexcusable. For he did not yield up a mere opportunity of getting honor and advantage to his competitor, but believing that the expedition would be very hazardous, was thankful to take care of himself, and left the Commonwealth to shift for itself. And whereas Themistocles, lest a mean and incapable fellow should ruin the State by holding command in the Persian war, bought him off, and Cato, in a most dangerous and critical conjuncture, stood for the tribuneship for the sake of his country, Nicias, reserving himself for trifling expeditions against Minoa and Cythera, and the miserable Melians, if there be occasion to come to blows with the Lacedæmonians, slips off his general's cloak and hands over to the unskilfulness and rashness of Cleon, fleet, men, and arms, and the whole command, where the utmost possible skill was called for. Such conduct, I say, is not to be thought so much carelessness of his own fame, as of the interest and preservation of his country. By this means it came to pass he was com pelled to the Sicilian war, men generally believing that he was not so much honestly convinced of the difficulty of the enterprise, as ready out of mere love of ease and cowardice to lose the city the conquest of Sicily. But yet it is a great sign of his integrity, that though he was always averse from war, and unwilling to command, yet they always continued to appoint him as the best experienced and ablest general they had. On the other hand Crassus, though always ambitious of command, never attained to it, except by mere necessity in the servile war, Pompey and Metellus and the two brothers Lucullus being absent, although at that time he was at his highest pitch of interest and reputation. Even those who thought most of him, seem to have thought him, as the comic poet says:—

A brave man anywhere but in the field.

There was no help, however, for the Romans, against his passion for command and for distinction. The Athenians sent out Nicias against his will to the war, and Crassus led out the Romans against theirs; Crassus brought misfortune on Rome, as Athens brought it on Nicias.

Still this is rather ground for praising Nicias, than for finding fault with Crassus. His experience and sound judgment as a general saved him from being carried away by the delusive hopes of his fellow-citizens, and made him refuse to entertain any prospect of conquering Sicily. Crassus, on the other hand, mistook, in entering on a Parthian war as an easy matter. He was eager, while Caesar was subduing the west, Gaul, Germany, and Britain, to advance for his part to the east and the Indian Sea, by the conquest of Asia, to complete the incursions of Pompey and the attempts of Lucullus, men of prudent temper and of unimpeachable worth, who nevertheless, entertained the same projects as Crassus, and acted under the same convictions. When Pompey was appointed to the like command, the senate was opposed to it; and after Caesar had routed three hundred thousand Germans, Cato recommended that he should be surrendered to the defeated enemy, to expiate in his own person the guilt of breach of faith. The people, meantime (their service to Cato!), kept holiday for fifteen days, and were overjoyed. What would have been their feelings, and how many holidays would they have celebrated, if Crassus had sent news from Babylon of victory, and thence marching onward had converted Media and Persia. the Hyrcanians, Susa and Bactra, into Roman provinces?

If wrong we must do, as Euripides says, and cannot be content with peace and present good things, let it not be for such results as destroying Mende or Scandea, or beating up the exiled Æginetans in the coverts to which like hunted birds they had fled, when expelled from their homes, but let it be for some really great remuneration; nor let us part with justice, like a cheap and common thing, for a small and trifling price. Those who praise Alexander's enterprise and blame that of Crassus, judge of the beginning unfairly by the results.

In actual service, Nicias did much that deserves high praise. He frequently defeated the enemy in battle, and was on the very point of capturing Syracuse; nor should he bear the whole blame of the disaster, which may fairly be ascribed in part to his want of health and to the jealousy entertained of him at home. Crassus, on the other hand, committed so many errors as not to leave fortune room to show him favor. It is no surprise to find such imbecility fall a victim to the power of Parthia; the only wonder is to see it prevailing over the wonted good-fortune of Rome. One scrupulously observed, the other entirely slighted the arts of divination: and as both equally perished, it is difficult to see what inference we should draw. Yet the fault of over-caution, supported by old and general opinion, better deserves forgiveness than that of self-willed and lawless transgression.

In his death, however, Crassus has the advantage, as he did not surrender himself, nor submit to bondage, or let himself be taken in by trickery, but was the victim only of the entreaties of his friends and the perfidy of his enemies; whereas Nicias enhanced the shame of his death by yielding himself up in the hope of a disgraceful and inglorious escape.

SERTORIUS.

It is no great wonder if in long process of time, while fortune takes her course hither and thither, numerous coincidences should spontaneously occur. If the number and variety of subjects to be wrought upon be infinite, it is all the more easy for fortune, with such an abundance of material, to effect this similarity of results. Or if, on the other hand, events are limited to the combinations of some finite number

then of necessity the same must often recur, and in the same
sequence. There are people who take a pleasure in making
collections of all such fortuitous occurrences that they have
heard or read of, as look like works of a rational power and
design; they observe, for example, that two eminent persons
whose names were Attis, the one a Syrian, the other of Arcadia, were both slain by a wild boar; that of two whose names
were Actæon, the one was torn in pieces by his dogs the other
by his lovers; that of two famous Scipios, the one overthrew
the Carthaginians in war, the other totally ruined and destroyed them; the city of Troy was the first time taken by Hercules for the horses promised him by Laomedon, the second
time by Agamemnon, by means of the celebrated great
wooden horse, and the third time by Charidemus, by occasion
of a horse falling down at the gate, which hindered the
Trojans, so that they could not shut them soon enough; and
of two cities which take their names from the most agreeable
odoriferous plants, Ios and Smyrna, the one from a violet, the
other from myrrh, the poet Homer is reported to have been
born in the one and to have died in the other. And so to
these instances let us further add, that the most warlike commanders, and most remarkable for exploits of skilful stratagem, have had but one eye; as Philip, Antigonus, Hannibal,
and Sertorius, whose life and actions we describe at present;
of whom, indeed, we might truly say, that he was more continent than Philip, more faithful to his friends than Antigonus,
and more merciful to his enemies than Hannibal; and that
for prudence and judgment he gave place to none of them,
but in fortune was inferior to them all. Yet though he had
continually in her a far more difficult adversary to contend
against than his open enemies, he nevertheless maintained
his ground, with the military skill of Metellus, the boldness
of Pompey, the success of Sylla, and the power of the Roman
people all to be encountered by one who was a banished man
and a stranger at the head of a body of barbarians. Among
Greek commanders, Eumenes of Cardia may be best compared
with him; they were both of them men born for command, for
warfare, and for stratagem; both banished from their countries, and holding command over strangers; both had fortune
for their adversary, in their last days so harshly so, that they
were both betrayed, and murdered by those who served
them and with whom they had formerly overcome their enemies.

Quintus Sertorius was of a noble family, born in the city

of Nursia, in the country of the Sabines; his father died when he was young, and he was carefully and decently educated by his mother, whose name was Rhea, and whom he appears to have extremely loved and honored. He pa'd some attention to the study of oratory and pleading in his youth, and acquired some reputation and influence in Rome by his eloquence; bu. the splendor of his actions in arms, and his successful achievements in the wars, drew off his ambition in that direction.

At his first beginning, he served under Cæpio, when the Cimbri and Teutones invaded Gaul; where the Romans fighting unsuccessfully, and being put to flight, he was wounded in many parts of his body, and lost his horse, yet, nevertheless, swam across the river Rhone in his armor, with his breastplate and shield, bearing himself up against the violence of the current; so strong and so well inured to hardship was his body.

The second time that the Cimbri and Teutones came down with some hundreds of thousands, threatening death and destruction to all, when it was no small piece of service for a Roman soldier to keep his ranks and obey his commander, Sertorius undertook, while Marius led the army, to spy out the enemy's camp. Procuring a Celtic dress, and acquainting himself with the ordinary expressions of their language requisite for common intercourse, he threw himself in amongst the barbarians; where having carefully seen with his own eyes, or having been fully informed by persons upon the place of all their most important concerns, he returned to Marius, from whose hands he received the rewards of valor; and afterwards giving frequent proof both of conduct and courage in all the following war, he was advanced to places of honor and trust under his general. After the wars with the Cimbri and Teutones, he was sent into Spain, having the command of a thousand men under Didius, the Roman general, and wintered in the country of the Celtiberians, in the city of Castulo, where the soldiers enjoying great plenty, and growing insolent and continually drinking, the inhabitants despised them and sent for aid by night to the Gyriscœnians, their near neighbors, who fell upon the Romans in their lodgings and slew a great number of them. Sertorius, with a few of his soldiers, made his way out, and rallying together the rest who escaped, he marched round about the walls, and finding the gate open, by which the Gyriscœnians had made their secret entrance, he gave not them the same opportunity, but placing a guard at the gate, and seizing upon all quarters of the city, he slew all who were of age to bear arms, and then ordering his soldiers to lay aside their weapons and put off their own clothes, and put on the accoutrements of the barbarians, he commanded them to follow him to the city from whence the men came who had made this night attack upon the Romans. And thus deceiving the Gyriscenians with the sight of their own armor he found the gates of their city open, and took a great number prisoners, who came out thinking to meet their friends and fellow-citizens come home from a successful expedition. Most of them were thus slain by the Romans at their own gates, and the rest within yielded up themselves and were sold for slaves.

This action made Sertorius highly renowned throughout all Spain, and as soon as he returned to Rome he was appointed quæstor of Cisalpine Gaul, at a very seasonable moment for his country, the Marsian war being on the point of breaking out. Sertorius was ordered to raise soldiers and provide arms, which he performed with a diligence and alacrity, so contrasting with the feebleness and slothfulness of other officers of his age, that he got the repute of a man whose life would be one of action. Nor did he relinquish the part of a soldier, now that he had arrived at the dignity of a commander, but performed wonders with his own hands, and never sparing himself, but exposing his body freely in all conflicts, he lost one of his eyes. This he always esteemed an honor to him; observing that others do not continually carry about with them the marks and testimonies of their valor, but must often lay aside their chains of gold, their spears and crowns; whereas his ensigns of honor, and the manifestations of his courage, always remained with him, and those who beheld his misfortune, must at the same time recognize his merits. The people also paid him the respect he deserved, and when he came into the theatre, received him with plaudits and joyful acclamations, an honor rarely bestowed even on persons of advanced standing and established reputation. Yet, notwithstanding this popularity, when he stood to be tribune of the people, he was disappointed, and lost the place, being opposed by the party of Sylla, which seems to have been the principal cause of his subsequent enmity to Sylla.

After that Marius was overcome by Sylla and fled into Africa, and Sylla had left Italy to go to the wars against Mithridates, and of the two consuls Octavius and Cinna, Octavius remained steadfast to the policy of Sylla, but Cinna, desirous of a new revolution, attempted to recall the lost interest of Marius, Sertorius joined Cinna's party, more particularly as he saw that Octavius was not very capable, and was also suspicious of any one that was a friend to Marius. When a great battle was fought between the two consuls in the forum, Octavius overcame, and Cinna and Sertorius, having lost not less than ten thousand men, left the city, and gaining over most part of the troops who were dispersed about and remained still in many parts of Italy, they in a short time mustered up a force against Octavius sufficient to give him battle again, and Marius, also, now coming by sea out of Africa, proffered himself to serve under Cinna, as a private soldier under his consul and commander.

Most were for the immediate reception of Marius, but Sertorius openly declared against it, whether he thought that Cinna would not now pay as much attention to himself, when a man of higher military repute was present, or feared that the violence of Marius would bring all things to confusion, by his boundless wrath and vengeance after victory. He insisted upon it with Cinna that they were already victorious, that there remained little to be done, and that if they admitted Marius, he would deprive them of the glory and advantage of the war, as there was no man less easy to deal with, or less to be trusted in, as a partner in power. Cinna answered, that Sertorius rightly judged the affair, but that he himself was at a loss, and ashamed, and knew not how to reject him, after he had sent for him to share in his fortunes. To which Sertorius immediately replied, that he had thought that Marius came into Italy of his own accord, and therefore had deliberated as to what might be most expedient, but that Cinna ought not so much as to have questioned whether he should accept him whom he had already invited, but should have honorably received and employed him, for his word once passed left no room for debate. Thus Marius being sent for by Cinna, and their forces being divided into three parts, under Cinna, Marius, and Sertorius, the war was brought to a successful conclusion; but those about Cinna and Marius committing all manner of insolence and cruelty, made the Romans think the evils of war a golden time in comparison. On the contrary it is reported of Sertorius, that he never slew any man in his anger, to satisfy his own private revenge, nor ever insulted over any one whom he had overcome, but was much offended with Marius, and often privately entreated Cinna to use his power more moderately. And in the end, when the slaves whom Marius had freed at his landing to increase his army, being made not only his fellow-soldiers in the war, but also now his guard in his usurpation, enriched and powerful by his favor, either by the command or permission of Marius, or by their own lawless violence, committed all sorts of crimes, killed their masters, ravished their masters' wives, and abused their children, their conduct appeared so intolerable to Sertorius that he slew the whole body of them, four thousand in number, commanding his soldiers to shoot them down with their javelins, as they lay encamped together.

Afterwards, when Marius died, and Cinna shortly after was slain, when the younger Marius made himself consul against Sertorius's wishes and contrary to law, when Carbo, Norbanus, and Scipio fought unsuccessfully against Sylla, now advancing to Rome, when much was lost by the cowardice and remissness of the commanders, but more by the treachery of their party, when with the want of prudence in the chief leaders, all went so ill that his presence could do no good, in the end when Sylla had placed his camp near to Scipio, and by pretending friendship, and putting him in hopes of a peace, corrupted his army, and Scipio could not be made sensible of this, although often forewarned of it by Sertorius,—at last he utterly despaired of Rome, and hasted into Spain, that by taking possession there beforehand, he might secure a refuge to his friends, from their misfortunes at home. Having bad weather in his journey, and travelling through mountainous countries, and the inhabitants stopping the way, and demanding a toll and money for passage, those who were with him were out of all patience at the indignity and shame it would be for a proconsul of Rome to pay tribute to a crew of wretched barbarians. But he little regarded their censure, and slighting that which had only the appearance of an indecency, told them he must buy time, the most precious of all things to those who go upon great enterprises; and pacifying the barbarous people with money, he hastened his journey, and took possession of Spain, a country flourishing and populous, abounding with young men fit to bear arms; but on account of the insolence and covetousness of the governors from time to time sent thither from Rome, they had generally an aversion to Roman supremacy. He, however, soon gained the affection of their nobles by intercourse with them, and the good opinion of the people by remitting their taxes. But that which won him most popularity, was his exempting them from finding lodgings for the soldiers, when he commanded his army to take up their winter-quarters outside the cities, and to pitch their camp in the suburbs; and when he himself, first of all, caused his own tent to be raised without the walls. Yet not being willing to rely totally upon the good inclination of the inhabitants, he armed all the Romans who lived in those countries that were of military age, and undertook the building of ships and the making of all sorts of warlike engines, by which means he kept the cities in due obedience, showing himself gentle in all peaceful business, and at the same time formidable to his enemies by his great preparations for war.

As soon as he was informed that Sylla had made himself master of Rome, and that the party which sided with Marius and Carbo was going to destruction, he expected that some commander with a considerable army would speedily come against him, and therefore sent away Julius Salinator immediately, with six thousand men fully armed, to fortify and defend the passes of the Pyrenees. And Caius Annius not long after being sent out by Sylla, finding Julius unassailable, sat down short at the foot of the mountains in perplexlity. But a certain Calpurnius, surnamed Lanarius, having treacherously slain Julius, and his soldiers then forsaking the heights of the Pyrenees, Caius Annius advanced with large numbers and drove before him all who endeavored to hinder his march. Sertorius, also, not being strong enough to give him battle, retreated with three thousand men into New Carthage, where he took shipping, and crossed the seas into Africa. And coming near the coast of Mauritania, his men went on shore to water, and straggling about negligently, the natives fell upon them and slew a great number. This new misfortune forced him to sail back again into Spain, whence he was also repulsed, and, some Cilician pirate ships joining with him, they made for the island of Pityussa, where they landed and overpowered the garrison placed there by Annius, who, however, came not long after with a great fleet of ships, and five thousand soldiers. And Sertorius made ready to fight him by sea, although his ships were not built for strength, but for lightness and swift sailing; but a violent west wind raised such a sea that many of them were run aground and shipwrecked, and he himself, with a few vessels, being kept from putting further out to sea by the fury of the weather, and from landing by the power of his enemies, was tossed about painfully for ten days together, amidst the boisterous and adverse waves.

He escaped with difficulty, and after the wind ceased, ran for certain desert islands scattered in those seas, affording no water, and after passing a night there, making out to sea again, he went through the straits of Cadiz, and sailing outward, keeping the Spanish shore on his right hand, he landed a little above the mouth of the river Bætis, where it falls into the Atlantic sea, and gives the name to that part of Spain Here he met with seamen recently arrived from the Atlantic islands, two in number, divided from one another only by a narrow channel, and distant from the coast of Africa ten thousand furlongs. These are called the Islands of the Blest; rains fall there seldom, and in moderate showers, but for the most part they have gentle breezes, bringing along with them soft dews, which render the soil not only rich for ploughing and planting, but so abundantly fruitful that it produces spontaneously an abundance of delicate fruits, sufficient to feed the inhabitants, who may here enjoy all things without trouble or labor. The seasons of the year are temperate, and the transitions from one to another so moderate, that the air is almost always serene and pleasant. The rough northerly and easterly winds which blow from the coasts of Europe and Africa, dissipated in the vast open space, utterly lose their force before they reach the islands. The soft western and southerly winds which breathe upon them sometimes produce gentle sprinkling showers, which they convey along with them from the sea, but more usually bring days of moist, bright weather, cooling and gently fertilizing the soil, so that the firm belief prevails, even among the barbarians, that this is the seat of the blessed, and that these are the Elysian Fields celebrated by Homer.

When Sertorius heard this account, he was seized with a wonderful passion for these islands, and had an extreme desire to go and live there in peace and quietness, and safe from oppression and unending wars; but his inclinations being perceived by the Cilician pirates, who desired not peace nor quiet, but riches and spoils, they immediately forsook him and sailed away into Africa to assist Ascalis, the son of Iphtha, and to help to restore him to his kingdom of Mauritania. Their sudden departure noways discouraged Sertorius; he presently resolved to assist the enemies of Ascalis, and by this new adventure trusted to keep his soldiers together, who from this might conceive new hopes, and a prospect of a new scene of action. His arrival in Mauritania being very acceptable to the Moors, he lost no time, but immediately giving battle to Ascalis, beat him out of the field and besieged him; and Paccianus being sent by Sylla, with a powerful supply, to raise the siege, Sertorius slew him in the field, gained over all his forces, and took the city of Tingis, into which Ascalis and his brothers were fled for refuge. The Africans tell that Antæus was buried in this city, and Sertorius had the grave opened, doubting the story because of the prodigious size, and finding there his body, in effect, it is said, full sixty cubits long, he was infinitely astonished, offered sacrifice, and heaped up the tomb again, gave his confirmation to the story, and added new honors to the memory of Antæus. The Africans tell that after the death of Antæus, his wife Tinga lived with Hercules, and had a son by him called Sophax, who was king of these countries, and gave his mother's name to this city, whose son, also, was Diodorus, a great conqueror, who brought the greatest part of the Libyan tribes under his subjection, with an army of Greeks, raised out of the colonies of the Olbians and Myceneans placed here by Hercules. Thus much I may mention for the sake of king Juba, of all monarchs the greatest student of history, whose ancestors are said to have sprung from Diodorus and Sophax.

When Sertorius had made himself absolute master of the whole country, he acted with great fairness to those who had confided in him, and who yielded to his mercy; he restored to them their property, cities, and government, accepting only of such acknowledgments as they themselves freely offered. And whilst he considered which way next to turn his arms, the Lusitanians sent ambassadors to desire him to be their general; for being terrified with the Roman power, and finding the necessity of having a commander of great authority and experience in war, being also sufficiently assured of his worth and valor by those who had formerly known him, they were desirous to commit themselves especially to his care And in fact Sertorius is said to have been of a temper unassailable either by fear or pleasure, in adversity and dangers undaunted, and noways puffed up with prosperity. In straight forward fighting, no commander in his time was more bold and daring, and in whatever was to be performed in war by stratagem, secrecy, or surprise, if any strong place was to be secured, any pass to be gained speedily, for deceiving and overreaching an enemy, there was no man equal to him in subtlety and skill. In bestowing rewards and conferring honors upon those who had performed good service in the wars, he was bountiful and magnificent, and was no less sparing and moderate in inflicting punishment. It is true that that piece of harshness and cruelty which he executed in the latter part of his days upon the Spanish hostages, seems to argue that his clemency was not natural to him, but only worn as a dress, and employed upon calculation, as his occasion or necessity required. As to my own opinion, I am persuaded that pure virtue, established by reason and judgment, can never be totally perverted or changed into its opposite, by any misfortune whatever. Yet I think it at the same time possible, that virtuous inclinations and natural good qualities may, when unworthily oppressed by calamities, show, with change of fortune, some change and alteration of their temper; and thus I conceive it happened to Sertorius, who when prosperity failed him, became exasperated by his disasters against those who had done him wrong.

The Lusitanians having sent for Sertorius, he left Africa, and being made general with absolute authority, he put all in order amongst them, and brought the neighboring parts of Spain under subjection. Most of the tribes voluntarily submitted themselves, won by the fame of his clemency and of his courage, and, to some extent, also, he availed himself of cunning artifices of his own devising to impose upon them and gain influence over them. Amongst which, certainly, that of the hind was not the least. Spanus, a countryman who lived in those parts, meeting by chance a hind that had recently calved, flying from the hunters, let the dam go, and pursuing the fawn, took it, being wonderfully pleased with the rarity of the color, which was all milk white. And as at that time Sertorius was living in the neighborhood, and accepted gladly any presents of fruit, fowl, or venison, that the country afforded, and rewarded liberally those who presented them, the countryman brought him his young hind, which he took and was well pleased with at the first sight, but when in time he had made it so tame and gentle that it would come when he called, and follow him wheresoever he went, and could endure the noise and tumult of the camp, knowing well that uncivilized people are naturally prone to superstition, by little and little he raised it into something preternatural, saying that it was given him by the goddess Diana, and that it revealed to him many secrets. He added, also, further contrivances. If he had received at any time private intelligence that the enemies had made an incursion into any part of the districts under his command, or had solicited any city to revolt, he pretended that the hind had informed him of it in his sleep, and charged him to keep his forces in readiness. Or if again he had notice that any of the commanders under him had got a victory, he would hide the messengers and bring forth the hind crowned with flowers, for joy of the good news that was to come, and would encourage them to rejoice and sacrifice to the gods for the good account they should soon receive of their prosperous success.

By such practices, he brought them to be more tractable and obedient in all things; for now they thought themselves no longer to be led by a stranger, but rather conducted by a god, and the more so, as the facts themselves seemed to bear witness to it, his power contrary to all expectation or probability, continually increasing. For with two thousand six hundred men, whom for honor's sake he called Romans, combined with seven hundred Africans, who landed with him when he first entered Lusitania, together with four thousand targeteers, and seven hundred horse of the Lusitanians themselves, he made war against four Roman generals, who commanded a hundred and twenty thousand foot, six thousand horse, two thousand archers and slingers, and had cities innumerable in their power; whereas at the first he had not above twenty cities in all. And from this weak and slender beginning, he raised himself to the command of large nations of men, and the possession of numerous cities; and of the Roman commanders who were sent against him, he overthrew Cotta in a sea-fight, in the channel near the town of Mellaria; he routed Fufidius, the governor of Bætica, with the loss of two thousand Romans, near the banks of the river Bætis; Lucius Domitius, proconsul of the other province of Spain, was overthrown by one of his lieutenants; Thoranius, another commander sent against him by Metellus with a great force, was slain, and Metellus, one of the greatest and most approved Roman generals then living, by a series of defeats, was reduced to such extremities, that Lucius Manlius came to his assistance out of Gallia Narbonensis, and Pompey the Great was sent from Rome itself in all haste, with considerable forces. Nor did Metellus know which way to turn himself, in a war with such a bold and ready commander, who was continually molesting him, and yet could not be brought to a set battle, but by the swiftness and dexterity of his Spanish soldiery, was enabled to shift and adapt himself to any change of circumstances. Metellus had had experience in battles fought by regular legions of soldiers, fully armed and drawn up in due order into a heavy standing phalanx, admirably trained for encountering and overpowering an enemy who came to close combat, hand to hand, but entirely unfit for climbing among the hills, and competing incessantly with the swift attacks and retreats of a set of fleet mountaineers, or to endure hunger and thirst, and live exposed like them to the wind and weather, without fire or covering.

Besides, being now in years, and having been formerly engaged in many fights and dangerous conflicts, he had grown inclined to a more remiss, easy, and luxurious life, and was the less able to contend with Sertorius, who was in the prime of his strength and vigor, and had a body wonderfully fitted for war, being strong, active, and temperate, continually accustomed to endure hard labor, to take long, tedious journeys, to pass many nights together without sleep, to eat little, and to be satisfied with very coarse fare, and who was never stained with the least excess in wine, even when he was most at leisure. What leisure time he allowed himself, he spent in hunting and riding about, and so made himself thoroughly acquainted with every passage for escape when he would fly, and for overtaking and intercepting in pursuit, and gained a perfect knowledge of where he could and where he could not go. Insomuch that Metellus suffered all the inconveniences of defeat, although he earnestly desired to fight, and Sertorius, though he refused the field, reaped all the advantages of a conqueror. For he hindered them from foraging, and cut them off from water; if they advanced, he was nowhere to be found; if they stayed in any place and encamped, he continually molested and alarmed them; if they besieged any town, he presently appeared and besieged them again, and put them to extremities for want of necessaries. And thus he so wearied out the Roman army, that when Sertorius challenged Metellus to fight singly with him, they commended it, and cried out, it was a fair offer, a Roman to fight against a Roman, and a general against a general; and when Metellus refused the challenge, they reproached him. Metellus derided and contemned this, and rightly so; for, as Theophrastus observes, a general should die like a general, and not like a skirmisher. But perceiving that the town of the Langobritæ, who gave great assistance to Sertorius, might easily be taken for want of water, as there was but one well within the walls, and the besieger would be master of the springs and fountains in the suburbs, he advanced against the place, expecting to carry it in two days' time, there being no more water, and gave command to his soldiers to take five days' provision only. Sertorius, however, resolving to send speedy relief, ordered two thousand skins to be filled with water, naming a considerable sum of money for the carriage of every skin ; and many Spaniards and Moors undertaking the work, he chose out those who were the strongest and swiftest of foot, and sent them through the mountains, with order that when they had delivered the water, they should convey away privately all those who would be least serviceable in the siege, that there might be water sufficient for the defendants. As soon as Metellus understood this, he was disturbed, as he had already consumed most part of the necessary provisions for his army, but he sent out Aquinus with six thousand soldiers to fetch in fresh supplies. But Sertorius having notice of it, laid an ambush for him, and having sent out beforehand three thousand men to take post in a thickly wooded water-course, with these he attacked the rear of Aquinus in his return, while he himself, charging him in the front, destroyed part of his army, and took the rest prisoners, Aquinus only escaping, after the loss of both his horse and his armor. And Metellus, being forced shamefully to raise the siege, withdrew amidst the laughter and contempt of the Spaniards; while Sertorius became yet more the object of their esteem and admiration.

He was also highly honored for his introducing discipline and good order amongst them, for he altered their furious savage manner of fighting, and brought them to make use of the Roman armor, taught them to keep their ranks, and observe signals and watchwords ; and out of a confused number of thieves and robbers, he constituted a regular, well-disciplined army. He bestowed silver and gold upon them liberally to gild and adorn their helmets, he had their shields worked with various figures and designs, he brought them into the mode of wearing flowered and embroidered cloaks and coats, and by supplying money for these purposes, and joining with them in all improvements, he won the hearts of all. That, however, which delighted them most, was the care that he took of their children. He sent for all the boys of noblest parentage out of all their tribes, and placed them in the great city of Osca, where he appointed masters to instruct them in the Grecian and Roman learning that when they came to be men, they might, as he professed, be fitted to share with him in authority, and in conducting the government, although under this pretext he really made them hostages However, their fathers were wonderfully pleased to see their children going daily to the schools in good order, handsomely dressed in gowns edged with purple, and that Sertorius paid for their lessons, examined them often, distributed rewards to the most deserving, and gave them the golden bosses to hang about their necks, which the Romans called bullæ.

There being a custom in Spain, that when a commander was slain in battle, those who attended his person fought it out till they all died with him, which the inhabitants of those countries called an *offering*, or libation, there were few commanders that had any considerable guard or number of attendants; but Sertorius was followed by many thousands who offered themselves, and vowed to spend their blood with his. And it is told that when his army was defeated near a city in Spain, and the enemy pressed hard upon them, the Spaniards, with no care for themselves, but being totally solicitous to save Sertorius, took him up on their shoulders and passed him from one to another, till they carried him into the city, and only when they had thus placed their general in safety, provided afterwards each man for his own security.

Nor were the Spaniards alone ambitious to serve him, but the Roman soldiers, also, that came out of Italy, were impatient to be under his command; and when Perpenna Vento, who was of the same faction with Sertorius, came into Spain with a quantity of money and a large number of troops, and designed to make war against Metellus on his own account, his own soldiers opposed it, and talked continually of Sertorius, much to the mortification of Perpenna, who was puffed up with the grandeur of his family and his riches. And when they afterwards received tidings that Pompey was passing the Pyrenees, they took up their arms, laid hold on their ensigns, called upon Perpenna to lead them to Sertorius, and threatened him that if he refused they would go without him, and place themselves under a commander who was able to defend himself and those that served him. And so Perpenna was obliged to yield to their desires, and joining Sertorius, added to his army three and fifty cohorts.

And when now all the cities on this side of the river Ebro also united their forces together under his command, his army grew great, for they flocked together and flowed in upon him from all quarters. But when they continually cried out to attack the enemy, and were impatient of delay, their inexperienced, disorderly rashness caused Sertorius much trouble, who at first strove to restrain them with reason and good counsel, but when he perceived them refractory and unseasonably violent, he gave way to their impetuous desires, and permitted them to engage with the enemy, in such sort that they might, being repulsed, yet not totally routed, become more obedient to his commands for the future. Which happening as he had anticipated, he soon rescued them, and brought them safe into his camp. And after a few days, being willing to encourage them again, when he had called all his army together, he caused two horses to be brought into the field, one old, feeble, lean animal, the other a lusty, strong horse, with a remarkable thick and long tail. Near the lean one he placed a tall, strong man, and near the strong young horse a weak, despicable-looking fellow; and at a sign given, the strong man took hold of the weak horse's tail with both his hands, and drew it to him with his whole force, as if he would pull it off; the other, the weak man, in the mean time, set to work to pluck off hair by hair from the great horse's tail. And when the strong man had given trouble enough to himself in vain, and sufficient diversion to the company, and had abandoned his attempt, whilst the weak, pitiful fellow in a short time and with little pains had left not a hair on the great horse's tail, Sertorius rose up and spoke to his army. "You see, fellow-soldiers, that perseverance is more prevailing than violence, and that many things which cannot be overcome when they are together, yield themselves up when taken little by little. Assiduity and persistence are irresistible, and in time overthrow and destroy the greatest powers whatever. Time being the favorable friend and assistant of those who use their judgment to await his occasions, and the destructive enemy of those who are unseasonably urging and pressing forward." With a frequent use of such words and such devices, he soothed the fierceness of the barbarous people, and taught them to attend and watch for their opportunities.

Of all his remarkable exploits, none raised greater admiration than that which he put in practice against the Characitanians. These are a people beyond the river Tagus, who inhabit neither cities nor towns, but live in a vast high hill, within the deep dens and caves of the rocks, the mouths of which open all towards the north. The country below is of a soil resembling a light clay, so loose as easily to break into powder, and is not firm enough to bear any one that treads upon it, and if you touch it in the least it flies about like ashes or unslacked lime. In any danger of war, these people descended into their caves, and carrying in their booty and prey along with them, stay quietly within, secure from every attack. And when Sertorius, leaving Metellus some distance off, had placed his camp near this hill, they slighted and despised him, imagining that he retired into these parts, being overthrown by the Romans. And whether out of anger or resentment, or out of his unwillingness to be thought to fly from his enemies, early in the morning he rode up to view the situation of the place. But finding there was no way to come at it, as he rode about, threatening them in vain and disconcerted, he took notice that the wind raised the dust and carried it up towards the caves of the Characitanians, the mouths of which, as I said before, opened towards the north; and the northerly wind, which some call Cæcias, prevailing most in those parts, coming up out of moist plains or mountains covered with snow, at this particular time, in the heat of summer, being further supplied and increased by the melting of the ice in the northern regions, blew a delightful fresh gale, cooling and refreshing the Characitanians and their cattle all the day long. Sertorius, considering well all circumstances in which either the information of the inhabitants, or his own experience had instructed him, commanded his soldiers to shovel up a great quantity of this light, dusty earth, to heap it up together, and make a mount of it over against the hill in which those barbarous people resided, who, imagining that all this preparation was for raising a mound to get at them, only mocked and laughed at it. However, he continued the work till the evening, and brought his soldiers back into their camp. The next morning a gentle breeze at first arose, and moved the lightest parts of the earth and dispersed it about as the chaff before the wind; but when the sun coming to be higher, the strong northerly wind had covered the hills with the dust, the soldiers came and turned this mound of earth over and over, and broke the hard clods in pieces, whilst others on horseback rode through it backward and forward, and raised a cloud of dust into the air: there with the wind the whole of it was carried away and blown into the dwellings of the Characitanians, all lying open to the north. And there being no other vent or breathing place than that through which the Cæcias rushed in upon them, it quickly blinded their eyes and filled their lungs, and all but choked them, whilst they strove to draw in the rough air mingled with dust and powdered earth. Nor were they able, with all they could do, to hold out above two days, but yielded up themselves on the third, adding, by their defeat, not so much to the power of Sertorius, as to his renown, in proving that he was able to conquer places by art, which were impregnable by the force of arms.

So long as he had to do with Metellus, he was thought to owe his successes to his opponent's age and slow temper, which were ill-suited for coping with the daring and activity of one who commanded a light army more like a band of robbers than regular soldiers. But when Pompey also passed over the Pyrenees, and Sertorius pitched his camp near him, and offered and himself accepted every occasion by which military skill could be put to the proof, and in this contest of dexterity was found to have the better, both in baffling his enemy's designs and in counter-scheming himself, the fame of him now spread even to Rome itself, as the most expert commander of his time. For the renown of Pompey was not small, who had already won much honor by his achievements in the wars of Sylla, from whom he received the title of Magnus, and was called Pompey the Great; and who had risen to the honor of a triumph before the beard had grown on his face. And many cities which were under Sertorius were on the very eve of revolting and going over to Pompey, when they were deterred from it by that great action, amongst others, which he performed near the city of Lauron, contrary to the expectation of all.

For Sertorius had laid siege to Lauron, and Pompey came with his whole army to relieve it; and there being a hill near this city very advantageously situated, they both made haste to take it. Sertorius was beforehand, and took possession of it first, and Pompey, having drawn down his forces, was not sorry that it had thus happened, imagining that he had hereby enclosed his enemy between his own army and the city, and sent in a messenger to the citizens of Lauron, to bid them be of good courage, and to come upon their walls, where they might see their besieger besieged. Sertorius, perceiving their intentions, smiled, and said, he would now teach Sylla's scholar, for so he called Pompey in derision, that it was the part of a general to look as well behind him as before him, and at the same time showed them six thousand soldiers, whom he had left in his former camp, from whence he marched out to take the hill, where if Pompey should assault him, they might fall upon his rear. Pompey discovered this too late, and not daring to give battle, for fear of being encompassed, and yet being ashamed to desert his friends and confederates in their extreme danger, was thus forced to sit still, and see them ruined before his face. For the besieged despaired of relief, and delivered up themselves to Sertorius, who spared their lives and granted them their liberty, but burnt their city, not out of anger or cruelty, for ot all commanders that ever were, Sertorius seemed least of all to have indulged these passions, but only for the greater shame and confusion of the admirers of Pompey, and that it might be reported amongst the Spaniards, that though he had been so close to the fire which burnt down the city of his confederates as actually to feel the heat of it, he still had not dared to make any opposition.

Sertorius, however, sustained many losses; but he always maintained himself and those immediately with him undefeated, and it was by other commanders under him that he suffered; and he was more admired for being able to repair his losses, and for recovering the victory, than the Roman generals against him for gaining these advantages; as at the battle of the Sucro against Pompey, and at the battle near Tuttia, against him and Metellus together. The battle near the Sucro was fought, it is said, through the impatience of Pompey, lest Metellus should share with him in the victory, Sertorius being also willing to engage Pompey before the arrival of Metellus. Sertorius delayed the time till the evening, considering that the darkness of the night would be a disadvantage to his enemies, whether flying or pursuing, being strangers, and having no knowledge of the country. When the fight began, it happened that Sertorius was not placed directly against Pompey, but against Afranius, who had command of the left wing of the Roman army, as he commanded the right wing of his own; but when he understood that his left wing began to give way, and yield to the assault of Pompey, he committed the care of his right wing to other commanders, and made haste to relieve those in distress; and rallying some that were flying, and encouraging others that still kept their ranks, he renewed the fight, and attacked the enemy in their pursuit so effectively as to cause a considerable rout, and brought Pompey into great danger of his life. For after being wounded and losing his horse, he escaped unexpectedly. For the Africans with Sertorius, who took Pompey's horse, set out with gold, and covered with rich trappings, fell out with one another; and upon the dividing of the spoil, gave over the pursuit. Afranius, in the mean time, as soon as Sertorius had left his right wing, to assist the other part of his army, overthrew all that opposed him; and pursuing them to their camp, fell in together with them, and plundered them till it was dark night; knowing nothing of Pompey's overthrow, nor being unable to restrain his soldiers from pillaging; when Sertorius, returning with victory fell upon him and upon his men, who were all in disorder, and slew many of them. And the next morning he came into the field again well armed, and offered battle, but perceiving that Metellus was near, he drew off, and returned to his camp, saying, "If this old woman had not come up, I would have whipped that boy soundly, and sent him to Rome."

He was much concerned that his white hind could no where be found; as he was thus destitute of an admirable contrivance, to encourage the barbarous people, at a time when he most stood in need of it. Some men, however, wandering in the night, chanced to meet her, and knowing her by her color, took her; to whom Sertorius promised a good reward, if they would tell no one of it; and immediately shut her up. A few days after, he appeared in public with a very cheerful look, and declared to the chief men of the country that the gods had foretold him in a dream that some great good fortune should shortly attend him; and, taking his seat, proceeded to answer the petitions of those who applied themselves to him. The keepers of the hind, who were not far off, now let her loose, and she no sooner espied Sertorius, but she came leaping with great joy to his feet, laid her head upon his knees, and licked his hands, as she formerly used to do. And Sertorius stroking her, and making much of her again, with that tenderness that the tears stood in his eyes, all that were present were immediately filled with wonder and astonishment, and accompanying him to his house with loud shouts for joy, looked upon him as a person above the rank of mortal men, and highly beloved by the gods; and were in great courage and hope for the future.

When he had reduced his enemies to the last extremity, for want of provision, he was forced to give them battle, in the plains near Saguntum, to hinder them from foraging, and plundering the country. Both parties fought gloriously. Memmius, the best commander in Pompey's army, was slain in the heat of the battle. Sertorius overthrew all before him, and with great slaughter of his enemies pressed forward towards Metellus. This old commander, making a resistance beyond what could be expected from one of his years, was wounded with a lance; an occurrence which filled all who either saw it or heard of it, with shame, to be thought to have left their general in distress, but at the same time to provoke them to revenge and fury against their enemies; they covered Metellus with their shields, and brought him off in safety and then valiantly repulsed the Spaniards; and so victory changed sides, and Sertorius, that he might afford a more secure retreat to his army, and that fresh forces might more easily be raised, retired into a strong city in the mountains. And though it was the least of his intention to sustain a long siege, yet he began to repair the walls, and to fortify the gates, thus deluding his enemies, who came and sat down before the town, hoping to take it without much resistance; and meantime gave over the pursuit of the Spaniards, and allowed opportunity for raising new forces for Sertorius, to which purpose he had sent commanders to all their cities, with orders, when they had sufficiently increased their numbers, to send him word of it. This news he no sooner received, but he sallied out and forced his way through his enemies, and easily joined them with the rest of his army. And having received this considerable reinforcement, he set upon the Romans again, and by rapidly assaulting them, by alarming them on all sides, by ensnaring, circumventing, and laying ambushes for them, he cut off all provisions by land, while with his piratical vessels, he kept all the coast in awe, and hindered their supplies by sea. He thus forced the Roman generals to dislodge, and to separate from one another: Metellus departed into Gaul, and Pompey wintered among the Vaccæans, in a wretched condition, where, being in extreme want of money, he wrote a letter to the senate, to let them know that if they did not speedily supply him, he must draw off his army; for he had already spent his own money in the defence of Italy. To these extremities, the chiefest and the most powerful commanders of the age were reduced by the skill of Sertorius; and it was the common opinion in Rome, that he would be in Italy before Pompey.

How far Metellus was terrified, and at what rate he esteemed him, he plainly declared, when he offered by proclamation an hundred talents, and twenty thousand acres of land to any Roman that should kill him, and leave, if he were banished, to return; attempting villanously to buy his life by treachery, when he despaired of ever being able to overcome him in open war. And when once he gained the advantage in a battle against Sertorius, he was so pleased and transported with his good fortune, that he caused himself to be publicly proclaimed imperator; and all the cities which he visited received him with altars and sacrifices; he allowed himself, it is said, to have garlands placed on his head, and accepted sumptuous entertainments, at which he sat drinking in triumphal robes, while images and figures of victory were introduced by the motion of machines, bringing in with them crowns and trophies of gold to present to him, and companies of young men and women danced before him, and sang to him songs of joy and triumph. By all which he rendered himself deservedly ridiculous, for being so excessively delighted and puffed up with the thoughts of having followed one who was retiring of his own accord, and for having once had the better of him whom he used to call Sylla's runaway slave, and his forces, the remnant of the defeated troops of Carbo.

Sertorius, meantime, showed the loftiness of his temper in calling together all the Roman senators who had fled from Rome, and had come and resided with him, and giving them the name of a senate; and out of these he chose prætors and quæstors, and adorned his government with all the Roman laws and institutions. And though he made use of the arms, riches, and cities of the Spaniards, yet he would never, even in word, remit to them the imperial authority, but set Roman officers and commanders over them, intimating his purpose to restore liberty to the Romans, not to raise up the Spaniard's power against them. For he was a sincere lover of his country, and had a great desire to return home; but in his adverse fortune he showed undaunted courage, and behaved himself towards his enemies in a manner free from all dejection and mean-spiritedness; and when he was in his prosperity, and in the height of his victories, he sent word to Metellus and Pompey, that he was ready to lay down his arms, and live a private life, if he were allowed to return home, declaring that he had rather live as the meanest citizen in Rome, than, exiled from it, be supreme commander of all other cities together. And it is thought that his great desire for his country was in no small measure promoted by the tenderness he had for his mother, under whom he was brought up after the death of his father, and upon whom he had placed his entire affection. And after that his friends had sent for him into Spain to be their general, as soon as he heard of his mother's death, he had almost cast away himself and died for grief; for he lay seven days together continually in his tent, without giving the word, or being seen by the nearest of his friends; and when the chief commanders of the army, and persons of the greatest note came about his tent, with great difficulty they prevailed with him at last to come abroad, and speak to his soldiers, and to take upon him the management of affairs, which were in a prosperous condition. And thus, to many men's judgment, he seemed to have been in himself of a mild and compassionate temper, and naturally given to ease and quietness and to have accepted of the command of military forces contrary to his own inclination, and not being able to live in safety otherwise, to have been driven by his enemies to have recourse to arms, and to espouse the wars as a necessary guard for the defence of his person.

His negotiations with king Mithridates further argue the greatness of his mind. For when Mithridates recovering himself from his overthrow by Sylla, like a strong wrestler that gets up to try another fall, was again endeavoring to reestablish his power in Asia, at this time the great fame of Sertorius was celebrated in all places; and when the merchants who came out of the western parts of Europe, bringing these, as it were, among their other foreign wares, had filled the kingdom of Pontus with their stories of his exploits in war, Mithridates was extremely desirous to send an embassy to him, being also highly encouraged to it by the boastings of his flattering courtiers, who, comparing Mithridates to Pyrrhus, and Sertorius to Hannibal, professed that the Romans would never be able to make any considerable resistance against such great forces, and such admirable commanders, when they should be set upon on both sides at once, on one by the most warlike general, and on the other by the most powerful prince in existence.

Accordingly, Mithridates sends ambassadors into Spain to Sertorius with letters and instructions, and commission to promise ships and money towards the charge of the war, if Sertorius would confirm his pretensions upon Asia, and authorize him to possess all that he had surrendered to the Romans in his treaty with Sylla. Sertorius summoned a full council which he called a senate where, when others joyfully approved of the conditions, and were desirous immediately to accept of his offer, seeing that he desired nothing of them but a name, and an empty title to places not in their power to dispose of, in recompense of which they should be supplied with what they then stood most in need of, Sertorius would by no means agree to it; declaring that he was willing that king Mithridates should exercise all royal power and authority over Bithynia and Cappadocia, countries accustomed to a monarchical government, and not belonging to Rome, but he could never consent that he should seize or detain a province, which, by the justest right and title, was possessed by the Romans, which Mithridates had formerly taken away from them, and had afterwards lost in open war to Fimbria, and quitted upon a treaty of peace with Sylla. For he looked upon it as his duty to enlarge the Roman possessions by his conquering arms, and not to increase his own power by the diminution of the Roman territories. Since a noble-minded man, though he willingly accepts of victory when it comes with honor, will never so much as endeavor to save his own life upon any dishonorable terms.

When this was related to Mithridates, he was struck with amazement, and said to his intimate friends, "What will Sertorius enjoin us to do when he comes to be seated in the Palatium in Rome, who at present, when he is driven out to the borders of the Atlantic sea, sets bounds to our kingdoms in the east, and threatens us with war, if we attempt the recovery of Asia?" However, they solemnly, upon oath, concluded a league between them, upon these terms : that Mithridates should enjoy the free possession of Cappadocia, and Bithynia, and that Sertorius should send him soldiers, and a general for his army, in recompense of which the king was to supply him with three thousand talents and forty ships. Marcus Marius, a Roman senator who had quitted Rome to follow Sertorius, was sent general into Asia, in company with whom, when Mithridates had reduced divers of the Asian cities, Marius made his entrance with rods and axes carried before him, and Mithridates followed in the second place, voluntarily waiting upon him. Some of these cities he set at liberty, and others he freed from taxes, signifying to them that these privileges were granted to them by the favor of Sertorius, and hereby Asia, which had been miserably tormented by the revenue-farmers, and oppressed by the insolent pride and covetousness of the soldiers, began to rise again to new hopes, and to look forward with joy to the expected change of government.

But in Spain, the senators about Sertorius, and others of the nobility, finding themselves strong enough for their enemies, no sooner laid aside fear, but their minds were possessed by envy and irrational jealousies of Sertorius's power. And chiefly Perpenna, elevated by the thoughts of his noble birth, and carried away with a fond ambition of commanding the army, threw out villanous discourses in private amongst his acquaintance. "What evil genius," he would say, "hurries us perpetually from worse to worse? We who disdained to obey the dictates of Sylla, the ruler of the sea and land, and thus to live at home in peace and quiet, are come hither to our destruction, hoping to enjoy our liberty, and have made ourselves slaves of our own accord ; and are become the contemptible guards and attendants of the banished Sertorius. who, that he may expose us the further, gives us a name that renders us ridiculous to all that hear it, and calls us the Senate, when at the same time he makes us undergo as much hard labor, and forces us to be as subject to his haughty commands and insolences, as any Spaniards and Lusitanians." With these mutinous discourses, he seduced them; and though the greater number could not be led into open rebellion against Sertorius, fearing his power, they were prevailed with to endeavor to destroy his interest secretly. For by abusing the Lusitanians and Spaniards, by inflicting severe punishments upon them, by raising exorbitant taxes, and by pretending that all this was done by the strict command of Sertorius, they caused great troubles, and made many cities to revolt ; and those who were sent to mitigate and heal these differences, did rather exasperate them, and increase the number of his enemies, and left them at their return more obstinate and rebellious than they found them. And Sertorius, incensed with all this, now so far forgot his former clemency and goodness, as to lay hands on the sons of the Spaniards, educated in the city of Osca ; and, contrary to all justice, he cruelly put some of them to death, and sold others.

In the mean time, Perpenna, having increased the number of his conspirators, drew in Manlius, a commander in the army, who, at that time being attached to a youth, to gain his affections the more, discovered the confederacy to him, bidding him neglect others, and be constant to him alone ; who, in a few days, was to be a person of great power and authority. But the youth having a greater inclination for Aufidius, disclosed all to him, which much surprised and amazed him. For he was also one of the confederacy, but knew not that Manlius was anyways engaged in it ; but when the youth began to name Perpenna, Gracinus, and others, whom he knew very well to be sworn conspirators, he was very much terrified and astonished ; but made light of it to the youth, and bade him not regard what Manlius said, a vain, boasting fellow. However, he went presently to Perpenna, and giving him notice of the danger they were in, and of the shortness of their time, desired him immediately to put their designs in execution. And when all the confederates had consented to it, they provided a messenger who brought feigned letters to Sertorius, in which he had notice of a victory obtained, it said, by one of his lieutenants, and of the great slaughter of his enemies; and as Sertorius being extremely well pleased, was sacrificing and giving thanks to the gods for his prosperous success, Perpenna invited him, and those with him, who were also of the conspiracy, to an entertainment, and being very importunate prevailed with him to come. At all suppers and entertainments where Sertorius was present, great order and decency was wont to be observed, for he would not endure to hear or see any thing that was rude or unhandsome, but made it the habit of all who kept his company, to entertain themselves with quiet and inoffensive amusements. But in the middle of this entertainment, those who sought occasion to quarrel, fell into dissolute discourse openly, and making as if they were very drunk, committed many insolences on purpose to provoke him. Sertorius, being offended with their ill behavior, or perceiving the state of their minds by their way of speaking and their unusually disrespectful manner, changed the posture of his lying, and leaned backward, as one that neither heard nor regarded them. Perpenna now took a cup full of wine, and, as he was drinking, let it fall out of his hand and made a noise, which was the sign agreed upon amongst them; and Antonius, who was next to Sertorius, immediately wounded him with his sword. And whilst Sertorius, upon receiving the wound, turned himself, and strove to get up, Antonius threw himself upon his breast, and held both his hands, so that he died by a number of blows, without being able even to defend himself.

Upon the first news of his death, most of the Spaniards left the conspirators, and sent ambassadors to Pompey and Metellus, and yielded themselves up to them. Perpenna attempted to do something with those that remained, but he made only so much use of Sertorius's arms and preparations for war, as to disgrace himself in them, and to let it be evident to all, that he understood no more how to command, than he knew how to obey; and when he came against Pompey, he was soon overthrown, and taken prisoner. Neither did he bear this last affliction with any bravery, but having Sertorius's papers and writings in his hands, he offered to show Pompey letters from persons of consular dignity, and of the highest quality in Rome, written with their own hands, expressly to call Sertorius into Italy, and to let him know

what great numbers there were that earnestly desired to alter
the present state of affairs, and to introduce another manner
of government. Upon this occasion, Pompey behaved not
like a youth, or one of a light inconsiderate mind, but as a
man of a confirmed, mature, and solid judgment; and so freed
Rome from great fears and dangers of change. For he put
all Sertorius's writings and letters together and read not one
of them, nor suffered any one else to read them, but burnt
them all, and caused Perpenna immediately to be put to death.
lest by discovering their names, further troubles and revolutions might ensue.

Of the rest of the conspirators with Perpenna, some were
taken and slain by the command of Pompey, others fled into
Africa, and were set upon by the Moors, and run through
with their darts: and in a short time, not one of them was
left alive, except only Aufidius, the rival of Manlius, who,
hiding himself, or not being much inquired after, died an old
man, in an obscure village in Spain, in extreme poverty, and
hated by all.

EUMENES.

Duris reports that Eumenes, the Cardian, was the son of
a poor wagoner in the Thracian Chersonesus, yet liberally
educated, both as a scholar and a soldier; and that while he
was but young, Philip, passing through Cardia, diverted himself with a sight of the wrestling-matches and other exercises
of the youth of that place, among whom Eumenes pertorming
with success, and showing signs of intelligence and bravery,
Philip was so pleased with him, as to take him into his service. But they seem to speak more probably, who tell us
that Philip advanced Eumenes for the friendship he bore to
his father, whose guest he had sometime been. After the
death of Philip, he continued in the service of Alexander, with
the title of his principal secretary, but in as great favor as the
most intimate of his familiars, being esteemed as wise and faithful as any person about him, so that he went with troops under
his immediate command as general in the expedition against
India, and succeeded to the post of Perdiccas, when Perdiccas
was advanced to that of Hephæstion, then newly deceased
And therefore, after the death of Alexander, when Neoptole

mus. who had been captain of his lifeguard, said that he had followed Alexander with shield and spear, but Eumenes only with pen and paper, the Macedonians laughed at him, as knowing very well that besides other marks of favor, the king had done him the honor to make him a kind of kinsman to himself by marriage. For Alexander's first mistress in Asia, by whom he had his son Hercules, was Barsine the daughter of Artabazus; and in the distribution of the Persian ladies amongst his captains, Alexander gave Apame, one of her sisters, to Ptolemy, and another, also called Barsine, to Eumenes.

Notwithstanding, he frequently incurred Alexander's displeasure, and put himself into some danger, through Hephæstion. The quarters that had been taken up for Eumenes, Hephæstion assigned to Euius, the flute-player. Upon which, in great anger, Eumenes and Mentor came to Alexander, and loudly complained, saying that the way to be regarded was to throw away their arms, and turn flute-players or tragedians; so much so that Alexander took their part and chid Hephæstion; but soon after changed his mind again, and was angry with Eumenes, and accounted the freedom he had taken to be rather an affront to the king, than a reflection upon Hephæstion. Afterwards, when Nearchus, with a fleet, was to be sent to the Southern Sea, Alexander borrowed money of his friends, his own treasury being exhausted, and would have had three hundred talents of Eumenes, but he sent a hundred only, pretending that it was not without great difficulty he had raised so much from his stewards. Alexander neither complained nor took the money, but gave private order to set Eumenes's tent on fire, designing to take him in a manifest lie, when his money was carried out. But before that could be done, the tent was consumed, and Alexander repented of his orders, all his papers being burnt; the gold and silver, however, which was melted down in the fire, being afterwards collected, was found to be more than one thousand talents; yet Alexander took none of it, and only wrote to the several governors and generals to send new copies of the papers that were burnt, and ordered them to be delivered to Eumenes.

Another difference happened between him and Hephæstion concerning a gift, and a great deal of ill language passed between them, yet Eumenes still continued in favor. But Hephæstion dying soon after, the king, in his grief, presuming all those that differed with Hephæstion in his lifetime were now rejoicing at his death, showed much harshness and severity in his behavior with them, especially towards Eumenes, whom he often upbraided with his quarrels and ill language to Hephæstion. But he, being a wise and dexterous courtier, made advantage of what had done him prejudice, and struck in with the king's passion for glorifying his friend's memory, suggesting various plans to do him honor, and contributing largely and readily towards erecting his monument.

After Alexander's death, when the quarrel broke out between the troops of the phalanx and the officers, his companions, Eumenes, though in his judgment he inclined to the latter, yet in his professions stood neuter, as if he thought it unbecoming him, who was a stranger, to interpose in the private quarrels of the Macedonians. And when the rest of Alexander's friends left Babylon, he stayed behind, and did much to pacify the foot-soldiers, and to dispose them towards an accommodation. And when the officers had agreed among themselves, and, recovering from the first disorder, proceeded to share out the several commands and provinces, they made Eumenes governor of Cappadocia and Paphlagonia, and all the coast upon the Pontic Sea as far as Trebizond, which at that time was not subject to the Macedonians, for Ariarathes kept it as king, but Leonnatus and Antigonus, with a large army, were to put him in possession of it. Antigonus, already filled with hopes of his own, and despising all men, took no notice of Perdiccas's letters; but Leonnatus with his army came down into Phrygia to the service of Eumenes. But being visited by Hecatæus, the tyrant of the Cardians, and requested rather to relieve Antipater and the Macedonians that were besieged in Lamia, he resolved upon that expedition, inviting Eumenes to a share in it, and endeavoring to reconcile him to Hecatæus. For there was an hereditary feud between them, arising out of political differences, and Eumenes had more than once been known to denounce Hecatæus as a tyrant, and to exhort Alexander to restore the Cardians their liberty. Therefore at this time, also, he declined the expedition proposed, pretending that he feared lest Antipater, who already hated him, should for that reason, and to gratify Hecatæus, kill him. Leonnatus so far believed, as to impart to Eumenes his whole design, which, as he had pretended and given out, was to aid Antipater, but in truth was to seize the kingdom of Macedon; and he showed him letters from Cleopatra, in which, it appeared, she invited him to Pella, with promises to marry him. But Eumenes, whether fearing Antipater, or looking upon Leonnatus as a rash, headstrong, and unsafe man, stole away from him by night, taking with him all his men, namely, three hundred horse, and two hundred of his own servants armed, and all his gold, to the value of five thousand talents of silver, and fled to Perdiccas, discovered to him Leonnatus's design, and thus gained great interest with him, and was made of the council. Soon after, Perdiccas, with a great army, which he led himself, conducted Eumenes into Cappadocia, and, having taken Ariarathes prisoner, and subdued the whole country, declared him governor of it. He accordingly proceeded to dispose of the chief cities among his own friends, and made captains of garrisons, judges, receivers, and other officers, of such as he thought fit himself, Perdiccas not at all interposing. Eumenes, however, still continued to attend upon Perdiccas, both out of respect to him, and a desire not to be absent from the royal family.

But Perdiccas, believing he was able enough to attain his own further objects without assistance, and that the country he left behind him might stand in need of an active and faithful governor, when he came into Cilicia, dismissed Eumenes, under color of sending him to his command, but in truth to secure Armenia, which was on its frontier, and was unsettled through the practices of Neoptolemus. Him, a proud and vain man, Eumenes exerted himself to gain by personal attentions; but to balance the Macedonian foot, whom he found insolent and self-willed, he contrived to raise an army of horse, excusing from tax and contribution all those of the country that were able to serve on horseback, and buying up a number of horses, which he distributed among such of his own men as he most confided in, stimulating the courage of his new soldiers by gifts and honors, and inuring their bodies to service, by frequent marching and exercising; so that the Macedonians were some of them astonished, others overjoyed to see that in so short a time he had got together a body of no less than six thousand three hundred horsemen.

But when Craterus and Antipater, having subdued the Greeks, advanced into Asia, with intentions to quell the power of Perdiccas, and were reported to design an invasion of Cappadocia, Perdiccas, resolving himself to march against Ptolemy, made Eumenes commander-in-chief of all the forces of Armenia and Cappadocia, and to that purpose wrote letters, requiring Alcetas and Neoptolemus to be obedient to Eumenes, and giving full commission to Eumenes to dispose and order all things as he thought fit. Alcetas flatly refused to serve, because his Macedonians, he said, were ashamed to fight against Antipater, and loved Craterus so well, they were ready to receive him for their commander. Neoptolemus designed treachery against Eumenes, but was discovered; and being summoned, refused to obey, and put himself in a posture of defence. Here Eumenes first found the benefit of his own foresight and contrivance, for his foot being beaten, he routed Neoptolemus with his horse, and took all his baggage; and coming up with his whole force upon the phalanx while broken and disordered in its flight, obliged the men to lay down their arms, and take an oath to serve under him. Neoptolemus, with some few stragglers whom he rallied, fled to Craterus and Antipater. From them had come an embassy to Eumenes, inviting him over to their side, offering to secure him in his present government and to give him additional command, both of men and of territory, with the advantage of gaining his enemy Antipater to become his friend, and keeping Craterus his friend from turning to be his enemy. To which Eumenes replied, that he could not so suddenly be reconciled to his old enemy Antipater, especially at a time when he saw him use his friends like enemies, but was ready to reconcile Craterus to Perdiccas, upon any just and equitable terms; but in case of any aggression, he would resist the injustice to his last breath, and would rather lose his life than betray his word.

Antipater, receiving this answer, took time to consider upon the whole matter; when Neoptolemus arrived from his defeat and acquainted them with the ill success of his arms, and urged them to give him assistance, to come, both of them, if possible, but Craterus at any rate, for the Macedonians loved him so excessively, that if they saw but his hat, or heard his voice, they would all pass over in a body with their arms. And in truth, Craterus had a mighty name among them, and the soldiers after Alexander's death were extremely fond of him, remembering how he had often for their sakes incurred Alexander's displeasure, doing his best to withhold him when he began to follow the Persian fashions, and always maintaining the customs of his country, when, through pride and luxuriousness, they began to be disregarded. Craterus, therefore, sent on Antipater into Cilicia, and himself and Neoptolemus marched with a large division of the army against Eumenes; expecting to come upon him unawares, and to find his army disordered with revelling after the late victory. Now that Eumenes should suspect his coming, and be prepared to receive him, is an argument of his vigilance, but not perhaps a proof of any extraordinary sagacity, but that he should contrive both to conceal from his enemies the disadvantages of his position, and from his own men whom they were to fight with, so that he led them on against Craterus himself, without their knowing that he commanded the enemy, this, indeed, seems to show peculiar address and skill in the general. He gave out that Neoptolemus and Pigres were approaching with some Cappadocian and Paphlagonian horse. And at night, having resolved on marching, he fell asleep, and had an extraordinary dream. For he thought he saw two Alexanders ready to engage, each commanding his several phalanx, the one assisted by Minerva, the other by Ceres; and that after a hot dispute, he on whose side Minerva was, was beaten, and Ceres, gathering ears of corn, wove them into a crown for the victor. This vision Eumenes interpreted at once as boding success to himself, who was to fight for a fruitful country, and at that very time covered with the young ears, the whole being sowed with corn, and the fields so thick with it, that they made a beautiful show of a long peace. And he was further emboldened, when he understood that the enemy's password was Minerva and Alexander. Accordingly he also gave out as his, Ceres and Alexander, and gave his men orders to make garlands for themselves, and to dress their arms with wreaths of corn. He found himself under many temptations to discover to his captains and officers whom they were to engage with, and not to conceal a secret of such moment in his own breast alone, yet he kept to his first resolutions, and ventured to run the hazard of his own judgment.

When he came to give battle, he would not trust any Macedonian to engage Craterus, but appointed two troops of foreign horse, commanded by Pharnabazus, son to Artabazus and Phœnix of Tenedos, with order to charge as soon as ever they saw the enemy, without giving them leisure to speak or retire, or receiving any herald or trumpet from them. For he was exceedingly afraid about his Macedonians, lest, if they found out Craterus to be there, they should go over to his side. He himself, with three hundred of his best horse, led the right wing against Neoptolemus. When having passed a little hill they came in view, and were seen advancing with more than ordinary briskness, Craterus was amazed, and bitterly reproached Neoptolemus for deceiving him with hopes of the Macedonians' revolt, but he encouraged his men to do bravely, and forthwith charged. The first engagement was very fierce, and the spears being soon broken to pieces, they came to close fighting with their swords; and here Craterus did by no means dishonor Alexander, but slew many of his enemies, and repulsed many assaults, but at last received a wound in his side from a Thracian, and fell off his horse. Being down, many not knowing him went past him, but Gorgias, one of Eumenes's captains, knew him, and alighting from his horse, kept guard over him, as he lay badly wounded and slowly dying. In the mean time Neoptolemus and Eumenes were engaged; who, being inveterate and mortal enemies, sought for one another, but missed for the two first courses but in the third discovering one another, they drew their swords, and with loud shouts immediately charged. And their horses striking against one another like two galleys, they quitted their reins, and taking mutual hold pulled at one another's helmets, and at the armor from their shoulders. While they were thus struggling, their horses went from under them, and they fell together to the ground, there again still keeping their hold and wrestling. Neoptolemus was getting up first, but Eumenes wounded him in the ham, and got upon his feet before him. Neoptolemus supporting himself upon one knee, the other leg being disabled, and himself undermost, fought courageously, though his blows were not mortal, but receiving a stroke in the neck he fell and ceased to resist. Eumenes, transported with passion and his inveterate hatred to him, fell to reviling and stripping him, and perceived not that his sword was still in his hand. And with this he wounded Eumenes under the bottom of his corslet in the groin, but in truth more frightened than hurt him; his blow being faint for want of strength. Having stript the dead body, ill as he was with the wounds he had received in his legs and arms, he took horse again, and hurried towards the left wing of his army, which he supposed to be still engaged. Hearing of the death of Craterus, he rode up to him, and finding there was yet some life in him, alighted from his horse and wept, and laying his right hand upon him, inveighed bitterly against Neoptolemus, and lamented both Craterus's misfortune and his own hard fate, that he should be necessitated to engage against an old friend and acquaintance, and either do or suffer so much mischief.

This victory Eumenes obtained about ten days after the former, and got great reputation alike for his conduct and his valor in achieving it. But on the other hand, it created him great envy both among his own troops and his enemies, that he, a stranger and a foreigner, should employ the forces and arms of Macedon, to cut off the bravest and most an proved man among them. Had the news of this defeat come timely enough to Perdiccas, he had doubtless been the greatest of all the Macedonians; but now, he being slain in a mutiny in Egypt, two days before the news arrived, the Macedonians in a rage decreed Eumenes's death, giving joint commission to Antigonus and Antipater to prosecute the war against him. Passing by Mount Ida, where there was a royal establishment of horses, Eumenes took as many as he had occasion for, and sent an account of his doing so to the overseers, at which Antipater is said to have laughed, calling it truly laudable in Eumenes thus to hold himself prepared for giving in to them (or would it be taking from them?) strict account of all matters of administration. Eumenes had designed to engage in the plains of Lydia, near Sardis, both because his chief strength lay in horse, and to let Cleopatra see how powerful he was. But at her particular request, for she was afraid to give any umbrage to Antipater, he marched into the upper Phrygia, and wintered in Celænæ; when Alcetas, Polemon, and Docimus disputing with him who should command in chief, "You know," said he, "the old saying, That destruction regards no punctilios." Having promised his soldiers pay within three days, he sold them all the farms and castles in the country, together with the men and beasts with which they were filled; every captain or officer that bought, received from Eumenes the use of his engines to storm the place, and divided the spoil among his company, proportionably to every man's arrears. By this Eumenes came again to be popular, so that when letters were found thrown about the camp by the enemy, promising one hundred talents, besides great honors, to any one that should kill Eumenes, the Macedonians were extremely offended, and made an order that from that time forward one thousand of their best men should continually guard his person, and keep strict watch about him by night in their several turns. This order was cheerfully obeyed, and they gladly received of Eumenes the same honors which the kings used to confer upon their favorites. He now had leave to bestow purple hats and cloaks, which among the Macedonians is one of the greatest honors the king can give.

Good fortune will elevate even petty minds, and give them the appearance of a certain greatness and stateliness, as from their high place they look down upon the world; but the truly noble and resolved spirit raises itself, and becomes more conspicuous in times of disaster and ill fortune, as was now the case with Eumenes. For having by the treason of one of his own men lost the field to Antigonus at Orcynii, in Cappadocia, in his flight he gave the traitor no opportunity to escape to the enemy, but immediately seized and hanged him. Then in his flight, taking a contrary course to his pursuers, he stole by them unawares, returned to the place where the battle had been fought, and encamped. There he gathered up the dead bodies and burnt them with the doors and windows of the neighboring villages, and raised heaps of earth upon their graves; insomuch that Antigonus, who came thither soon after, expressed his astonishment at his courage and firm resolution. Falling afterwards upon the baggage of Antigonus, he might easily have taken many captives, both bond and freemen, and much wealth collected from the spoils of so many wars; but he feared lest his men, overladen with so much booty, might become unfit for rapid retreat, and too fond of their ease to sustain the continual marches and endure the long waiting on which he depended for success, expecting to tire Antigonus into some other course. But then considering it would be extremely difficult to restrain the Macedonians from plunder, when it seemed to offer itself, he gave them order to refresh themselves, and bait their horses, and then attack the enemy. In the mean time he sent privately to Menander, who had care of all this baggage, professing a concern for him upon the score of old friendship and acquaintance; and therefore advising him to quit the plain and secure himself upon the sides of the neighboring hills, where the horse might not be able to hem him in. When Menander, sensible of his danger, had speedily packed up his goods and decamped, Eumenes openly sent his scouts to discover the enemy's posture, and commanded his men to arm, and bridle their horses, as designing immediately to give battle; but the scouts returning with news that Menander had secured so difficult a post it was impossible to take him, Eumenes, pretending to be grieved with the disappointment, drew off his men another way. It is said that when Menander reported this afterwards to Antigonus, and the Macedonians commended Eumenes, imputing it to his singular good-nature, that having it in his power to make slaves of their children, and outrage their wives, he forbore and spared them all, Antigonus replied, "Alas, good friends, he had no regard to us, but to himself, being loath to wear so many shackles when he designed to fly."

From this time Eumenes, daily flying and wandering

about, persuaded many of his men to disband, whether out of kindness to them, or unwillingness to lead about such a body of men as were too few to engage, and too many to fly undiscovered. Taking refuge at Nora, a place on the confines of Lycaonia and Cappadocia, with five hundred horse, and two hundred heavy-armed foot, he again dismissed as many of his friends as desired it, through fear of the probable hardships to be encountered there, and embracing them with all demonstrations of kindness, gave them license to depart. Antigonus, when he came before this fort, desired to have an interview with Eumenes before the siege; but he returned answer, that Antigonus had many friends who might command in his room; but they whom Eumenes defended, had nobody to substitute if he should miscarry; therefore, if Antigonus thought it worth while to treat with him, he should first send him hostages. And when Antigonus required that Eumenes should first address himself to him as his superior, he replied, "While I am able to wield a sword, I shall think no man greater than myself." At last, when according to Eumenes's demand, Antigonus sent his own nephew Ptolemy to the fort, Eumenes went out to him, and they mutually embraced with great tenderness and friendship, as having formerly been very intimate. After long conversation, Eumenes making no mention of his own pardon and security, but requiring that he should be confirmed in his several governments, and restitution be made him of the rewards of his service, all that were present were astonished at his courage and gallantry. And many of the Macedonians flocked to see what sort of person Eumenes was, for since the death of Craterus, no man had been so much talked of in the army. But Antigonus, being afraid lest he might suffer some violence, first commanded the soldiers to keep off, calling out and throwing stones at those who pressed forwards. At last, taking Eumenes in his arms, and keeping off the crowd with his guards, not without great difficulty, he returned him safe into the fort.

Then Antigonus, having built a wall round Nora, left a force sufficient to carry on the siege, and drew off the rest of his army; and Eumenes was beleaguered and kept garrison, having plenty of corn and water and salt, but no other thing, either for food, or delicacy; yet with such as he had, he kept a cheerful table for his friends, inviting them severally in their turns, and seasoning his entertainment with a gentle and affable behavior. For he had a pleasant countenance, and looked not like an old and practised soldier, but was smooth and florid, and his shape as delicate as if his limbs had been carved by art in the most accurate proportions He was not a great orator, but winning and persuasive, as may be seen in his letters. The greatest distress of the besieged was the narrowness of the place they were in, their quarters being very confined, and the whole place but two furlongs in compass; so that both they and their horses fed without exercise. Accordingly, not only to prevent the listlessness of such inactive living but to have them in condition to fly if occasion required, he assigned a room one and twenty feet long, the largest in all the fort, for the men to walk in, directing them to begin their walk gently, and so gradually mend their pace. And for the horses, he tied them to the roof with great halters, fastening which about their necks, with a pulley he gently raised them, till standing upon the ground with their hinder feet, they just touched it with the very ends of their fore feet. In this posture the grooms plied them with whips and shouts, provoking them to curvet and kick out with their hind legs, struggling and stamping at the same time to find support for their fore feet, and thus their whole body was exercised, till they were all in a foam and sweat; excellent exercise, whether for strength or speed; and then he gave them their corn already coarsely ground, that they might sooner despatch, and better digest it.

The siege continuing long, Antigonus received advice that Antipater was dead in Macedon, and that affairs were embroiled by the differences of Cassander and Polysperchon, upon which he conceived no mean hopes, purposing to make himself master of all, and, in order to his design, thought to bring over Eumenes, that he might have his advice and assistance. He, therefore, sent Hieronymus to treat with him, proposing a certain oath, which Eumenes first corrected, and then referred himself to the Macedonians themselves that besieged him, to be judged by them, which of the two forms were the most equitable. Antigonus in the beginning of his had slightly mentioned the kings as by way of ceremony, while all the sequel referred to himself alone; but Eumenes changed the form of it to Olympias and the kings, and proceeded to swear not to be true to Antigonus, only, but to them, and to have the same friends and enemies, not with Antigonus, but with Olympias and the kings. This form the Macedonians thinking the more reasonable, swore Eumenes according to it, and raised the siege, sending also to Antigonus, that he should swear in the same form to Eumenes. Meantime, all the hostages of the Cappadocians whom Eumenes had in Nora he returned, obtaining from their friends war horses, beasts of carriage, and tents in exchange. And collecting again all the soldiers who had dispersed at the time of his flight, and were now wandering about the country, he got together a body of near a thousand horse, and with them fled from Antigonus, whom he justly feared. For he had sent orders not only to have him blocked up and besieged again, but had given a very sharp answer to the Macedonians, for admitting Eumenes's amendment of the oath.

While Eumenes was flying, he received letters from those in Macedonia, who were jealous of Antigonus's greatness, from Olympias, inviting him thither, to take the charge and protection of Alexander's infant son, whose person was in danger, and other letters from Polysperchon, and Philip the king, requiring him to make war upon Antigonus, as general of the forces in Cappadocia, and empowering him out of the treasure at Quinda to take five hundred talents, compensation for his own losses, and to levy as much as he thought necessary to carry on the war. They wrote also to the same effect to Antigenes and Teutamus, the chief officers of the Argyraspids; who, on receiving these letters, treated Eumenes with a show of respect and kindness; but it was apparent enough that they were full of envy and emulation, disdaining to give place to him. Their envy Eumenes moderated, by refusing to accept the money, as if he had not needed it; and their ambition and emulation, who were neither able to govern nor willing to obey, he conquered by help of superstition. For he told them that Alexander had appeared to him in a dream, and showed him a regal pavilion richly furnished, with a throne in it; and told him if they would sit in council there, he himself would be present, and prosper all the consultations and actions upon which they should enter in his name. Antigenes and Teutamus were easily prevailed upon to believe this, being as little willing to come and consult Eumenes, as he himself was to be seen waiting at other men's doors. Accordingly, they erected a tent royal, and a throne, called Alexander's, and there they met to consult upon all affairs of moment.

Afterwards they advanced into the interior of Asia, and in their march met with Peucestes, who was friendly to them, and with the other satraps, who joined forces with them, and greatly encouraged the Macedonians with the number and appearance of their men. But they themselves, having since Alexander's decease become imperious and ungoverned in their tempers, and luxurious in their daily habits, imagining themselves great princes, and pampered in their conceit by the flattery of the barbarians, when all these conflicting pretensions now came together, were soon found to be exacting and quarrelsome one with another, while all alike unmeasurably flattered the Macedonians, giving them money for revels and sacrifices till in a short time they brought the camp to be a dissolute place of entertainment, and the army a mere multitude of voters, canvassed as in a democracy for the election of this or that commander. Eumenes, perceiving they despised one another, and all of them feared him, and sought an opportunity to kill him, pretended to be in want of money, and borrowed many talents, of those especially who most hated him, to make them at once confide in him, and forbear all violence to him for fear of losing their own money. Thus his enemies' estates were the guard of his person, and by receiving money he purchased safety, for which it is more common to give it.

The Macedonians, also, while there was no show of danger, allowed themselves to be corrupted, and made all their court to those who gave them presents, who had their bodyguards, and affected to appear generals-in-chief. But when Antigonus came upon them with a great army, and their affairs themselves seemed to call out for a true general, then not only the common soldiers cast their eyes upon Eumenes, but these men, who had appeared so great in a peaceful time of ease, submitted all of them to him, and quietly posted themselves severally as he appointed them. And when Antigonus attempted to pass the river Pasitigris, all the rest that were appointed to guard the passes were not so much as aware of his march; only Eumenes met and encountered him, slew many of his men, and filled the river with the dead, and took four thousand prisoners. But it was most particularly when Eumenes was sick, that the Macedonians let it be seen how in their judgment, while others could feast them handsomely and make entertainments, he alone knew how to fight and lead an army. For Peucestes, having made a splendid entertainment in Persia, and given each of the soldiers a sheep to sacrifice with, made himself sure of being commander-in-chief. Some few days after, the army was to march, and Eumenes, having been dangerously ill was carried in a litter apart from the body of the army, that any rest he got might not be disturbed. But when they were a little advanced, unexpectedly they had a view of the enemy, who had passed the hills that lay between them, and was marching down into the plain At the sight of the golden armor glittering in the sun as they marched down in their order, the elephants with their castles on their backs, and the men in their purple, as their manner was when they were going to give battle, the front stopped their march, and called out for Eumenes, for they would not advance a step but under his conduct; and fixing their arms in the ground gave the word among themselves to stand, requiring their officers also not to stir or engage or hazard themselves without Eumenes. News of this being brought to Eumenes, he hastened those that carried his litter, and drawing back the curtains on both sides, joyfully put forth his right hand. As soon as the soldiers saw him they saluted him in their Macedonian dialect, and took up their shields, and striking them with their pikes, gave a great shout; inviting the enemy to come on, for now they had a leader.

Antigonus understanding by some prisoners he had taken that Eumenes was out of health, to that degree that he was carried in a litter, presumed it would be no hard matter to crush the rest of them, since he was ill. He therefore made the greater haste to come up with them and engage. But being come so near as to discover how the enemy was drawn up and appointed, he was astonished, and paused for some time; at last he saw the litter carrying from one wing of the army to the other, and, as his manner was, laughing aloud, he said to his friends, "That litter there, it seems, is the thing that offers us battle;" and immediately wheeled about, retired with all his army, and pitched his camp. The men on the other side, finding a little respite, returned to their former habits, and allowing themselves to be flattered, and making the most of the indulgence of their generals, took up for their winter-quarters near the whole country of the Gabeni, so that the front was quartered nearly a thousand furlongs from the rear; which Antigonus understanding, marched suddenly towards them, taking the most difficult road through a country that wanted water; but the way was short though uneven; hoping, if he should surprise them thus scattered in their winter quarters, the soldiers would not easily be able to come up time enough and join with their officers. But having to pass through a country uninhabited, where he met with violent winds and severe frosts, he was much checked in his march, and his men suffered exceedingly. The only possible relief was making numerous fires, by which his enemies got notice of his coming. For the barbarians who dwelt on the mountains overlooking the desert, amazed at the multitude of fires they saw, sent messengers upon dromedaries to acquaint Peucestes. He being astonished and almost out of his senses with the news, and finding the rest in no less disorder, resolved to fly, and collect what men he could by the way. But Eumenes relieved him from his fear and trouble, undertaking so to stop the enemy's advance, that he should arrive three days later than he was expected. Having persuaded them, he immediately despatched expresses to all the officers to draw the men out of their winter-quarters, and muster them with all speed. He himself, with some of the chief officers, rode out, and chose an elevated tract within view, at a distance, of such as travelled the desert; this he occupied and quartered out, and commanded many fires to be made in it, as the custom is in a camp. This done, and the enemies seeing the fire upon the mountains, Antigonus was filled with vexation and despondency, supposing that his enemies had been long since advertised of his march, and were prepared to receive him. Therefore, lest his army, now tired and wearied out with their march, should be immediately forced to encounter with fresh men, who had wintered well and were ready for him, quitting the near way, he marched slowly through the towns and villages to refresh his men. But meeting with no such skirmishes as are usual when two armies lie near one another, and being assured by the people of the country that no army had been seen, but only continual fires at that place, he concluded he had been outwitted by a stratagem of Eumenes, and, much troubled, advanced to give open battle.

By this time, the greater part of the forces were come together to Eumenes, and admiring his sagacity, declared him alone commander-in-chief of the whole army; upon which Antigenes and Teutamus, the commanders of the Argyraspids, being very much offended, and envying Eumenes, formed a conspiracy against him; and assembling the greater part of the satraps and officers, consulted when and how to cut him off. When they had unanimously agreed, first to use his service in the next battle, and then to take an occasion to destroy him, Eudamus, the master of the elephants, and Phædimus, gave Eumenes private advice of this design, not out of kindness or good-will to him, but lest they should lose the money they had lent him. Eumenes, having commended them, retired to his tent, and telling his friends he lived among a herd of wild beasts, made his will, and tore up all his letters, lest his correspondents after his death should be questioned or punished on account of any thing in his secret papers. Having thus disposed of his affairs, he thought of letting the enemy win the field, or of flying through Media and Armenia and seizing Cappadocia, but came to no resolution while his friends stayed with him. After turning to many expedients in his mind, which his changeable fortune had made versatile, he at last put his men in array, and encouraged the Greeks and barbarians; as for the phalanx and the Argyraspids, they encouraged him, and bade him be of good heart, for the enemy would never be able to stand them. For indeed they were the oldest of Philip's and Alexander's soldiers, tried men, that had long made war their exercise, that had never been beaten or foiled; most of them seventy, none less than sixty years old. And so when they charged Antigonus's men, they cried out, "You fight against your fathers, you rascals," and furiously falling on, routed the whole phalanx at once, nobody being able to stand them, and the greatest part dying by their hands. So that Antigonus's foot was routed, but his horse got the better, and he became master of the baggage, through the cowardice of Peucestes, who behaved himself negligently and basely; while Antigonus used his judgment calmly in the danger, being aided moreover by the ground. For the place where they fought was a large plain, neither deep, nor hard under foot, but, like the sea-shore, covered with a fine soft sand, which the treading of so many men and horses in the time of battle, reduced to a small white dust, that like a cloud of lime darkened the air, so that one could not see clearly at any distance, and so made it easy for Antigonus to take the baggage unperceived.

After the battle, Teutamus sent a message to Antigonus to demand the baggage. He made answer, he would not only restore it to the Argyraspids, but serve them further in other things if they would but deliver up Eumenes. Upon which the Argyraspids took a villanous resolution to deliver him up alive into the hands of his enemies. So they came to wait upon him, being unsuspected by him, but watching their opportunity, some lamenting the loss of the baggage, some encouraging him as if he had been victor, some accusing the other commanders, till at last they all fell upon him, and seizing his sword, bound his hands behind him with his own girdle. When Antigonus had sent Nicanor to receive him he begged he might be led through the body of he Macedonians, and have liberty to speak to them, neither to request nor deprecate any thing, but only to advise them what would be for their interest. A silence being made, as he stood upon a rising ground, he stretched out his hands bound, and said, "What trophy, O ye basest of all the Macedonians, could Antigonus have wished for so great as you yourselves have erected for him, in delivering up your general captive into his hands? You are not ashamed, when you are conquerors, to own yourselves conquered, for the sake only of your baggage, as if it were wealth, not arms, wherein victory consisted; nay, you deliver up your general to redeem your stuff. As for me, I am unvanquished, though a captive, conqueror of my enemies, and betrayed by my fellow-soldiers. For you, I adjure you by Jupiter, the protector of arms, and by all the gods that are the avengers of perjury, to kill me here with your own hands; for it is all one; and if I am murdered yonder, it will be esteemed your act, nor will Antigonus complain, for he desires not Eumenes alive, but dead. Or if you withhold your own hands, release but one of mine, it shall suffice to do the work; and if you dare not trust me with a sword, throw me bound as I am under the feet of the wild beasts. This if you do I shall freely acquit you from the guilt of my death, as the most just and kind of men to their general."

While Eumenes was thus speaking, the rest of the soldiers wept for grief, but the Argyraspids shouted out to lead him on, and give no attention to his trifling. For it was no such great matter if this Chersonesian pest should meet his death, who in thousands of battles had annoyed and wasted the Macedonians; it would be a much more grievous thing for the choicest of Philip's and Alexander's soldiers to be defrauded of the fruits of so long service, and in their old age to come to beg their bread, and to leave their wives three nights in the power of their enemies. So they hurried him on with violence. But Antigonus, fearing the multitude, for nobody was left in the camp, sent ten of his strongest elephants with divers of his Mede and Parthian lances to keep off the press. Then he could not endure to have Eumenes brought into his presence, by reason of their former intimacy and friendship; but when they that had taken him inquired how he would have him kept, "As I would," said he, "an elephant, or a lion." A little after, being moved with compassion, he commanded the heaviest of his irons to be knocked off, one of his servants to be admitted to anoint him, and that any of his friends that were willing should have liberty to visit him, and bring him what he wanted. Long time he deliberated what to do with him, sometimes inclining to the advice and promises of Nearchus of Crete, and Demetrius his son, who were very earnest to preserve Eumenes, whilst all the rest were unanimously instant and importunate to have him taken off. It is related that Eumenes inquired of Onomarchus, his keeper, why Antigonus, now he had his enemy in his hands, would not forthwith despatch or generously release him? And that Onomarchus contumeliously answered him, that the field had been a more proper place than this to show his contempt of death. To whom Eumenes replied, "And by heavens, I showed it there; ask the men else that engaged me, but I could never meet a man that was my superior." "Therefore," rejoined Onomarchus, "now you have found such a man, why don't you submit quietly to his pleasure?"

When Antigonus resolved to kill Eumenes, he commanded to keep his food from him, and so with two or three days' fasting he began to draw near his end; but the camp being on a sudden to remove, an executioner was sent to despatch him. Antigonus granted his body to his friends, permitted them to burn it, and having gathered his ashes into a silver urn, to send them to his wife and children.

Eumenes was thus taken off; and Divine Providence assigned to no other man the chastisement of the commanders and soldiers that had betrayed him; but Antigonus himself, abominating the Argyraspids as wicked and inhuman villains, delivered them up to Sibyrtius, the governor of Arachosia, commanding him by all ways and means to destroy and exterminate them, so that not a man of them might ever come to Macedon, or so much as within sight of the Greek sea.

COMPARISON OF SERTORIUS WITH EUMENES.

These are the most remarkable passages that are come to our knowledge concerning Eumenes and Sertorius. In comparing their lives, we may observe that this was common to them both; that being aliens, strangers, and banished men, they came to be commanders of powerful forces, and had the leading of numerous and warlike armies, made up of divers nations. This was peculiar to Sertorius, that the chief command was, by his whole party, freely yielded to him, as to the person of the greatest merit and renown, whereas Eumenes had many who contested the office with him, and only by his actions obtained the superiority. They followed the one honestly, out of desire to be commanded by him; they submitted themselves to the other for their own security, because they could not command themselves. The one, being a Roman, was the general of the Spaniards and Lusitanians, who for many years had been under the subjection of Rome; and the other, a Chersonesian, who was chief commander of the Macedonians, who were the great conquerors of mankind, and were at that time subduing the world. Sertorius, being already in high esteem for his former services in the wars, and his abilities in the senate, was advanced to the dignity of a general; whereas Eumenes obtained this honor from the office of a writer, or secretary, in which he had been despised. Nor did he only at first rise from inferior opportunities, but afterwards, also, met with greater impediments in the progress of his authority, and that not only from those who publicly resisted him, but from many others that privately conspired against him. It was much otherwise with Sertorius, not one of whose party publicly opposed him, only late in life, and secretly, a few of his acquaintance entered into a conspiracy against him. Sertorius put an end to his dangers as often as he was victorious in the field, whereas the victories of Eumenes were the beginning of his perils, through the malice of those that envied him.

Their deeds in war were equal and parallel, but their general inclinations different. Eumenes naturally loved war and contention, but Sertorius esteemed peace and tranquillity; when Eumenes might have lived in safety, with honor, if he would have quietly retired out of their way, he persisted in a dangerous contest with the greatest of the Macedonian leaders; but Sertorius, who was unwilling to trouble himself with any public disturbances, was forced, for the safety of his person, to make war against those who would not suffer him to live in peace. If Eumenes could have contented himself with the second place, Antigonus, freed from his competition for the first, would have used him well, and shown him favor, whereas Pompey's friends would never permit Sertorius so much as to live in quiet. The one made war of his own accord, out of a desire for command; and the other was con strained to accept of command, to defend himself from war that was made against him. Eumenes was certainly a true lover of war, for he preferred his covetous ambition before his own security; but Sertorius was truly warlike, who procured his own safety by the success of his arms.

As to the manner of their deaths, it happened to one without the least thought or surmise of it; but to the other when he suspected it daily; which in the first, argues an equitable temper, and a noble mind, not to distrust his friends; but in the other, it showed some infirmity of spirit, for Eumenes intended to fly and was taken. The death of Sertorius dishonored not his life; he suffered that from his companions which none of his enemies were ever able to perform. The other, not being able to deliver himself before his imprisonment, being willing also to live in captivity, did neither prevent nor expect his fate with honor or bravery; for by meanly supplicating and petitioning, he made his enemy, that pretended only to have power over his body, to be lord and master of his body and mind.

AGESILAUS.

ARCHIDAMUS, the son of Zeuxidamus, having reigned gloriously over the Lacedæmonians, left behind him two sons, Agis the elder, begotten of Lampido, a noble lady, Agesilaus, much the younger, born of Eupolia, the daughter of Melesippidas. Now the succession belonging to Agis by law, Agesilaus, who in all probability was to be but a private man, was educated according to the usual discipline of the country, hard and severe, and meant to teach young men to obey their superiors. Whence it was that, men say, Simonides called Sparta "the tamer of men," because by early strictness of education, they, more than any nation, trained the citizens to obedience to the laws, and made them tractable and patient of subjection, as horses that are broken in while colts. The law did not impose this harsh rule on the heirs apparent of the kingdom. But Agesilaus, whose good fortune it was to be born a younger brother, was consequently bred to all the arts of obedience, and so the better fitted for the government, when it fell to his share; hence it was that he proved the most popular-tempered of the Spartan kings, his early life having added to his natural kingly and commanding qualities, the gentle and humane feelings of a citizen.

While he was yet a boy, bred up in one of what are called the *flocks*, or classes, he attracted the attachment of Lysander, who was particularly struck with the orderly temper that he manifested. For though he was one of the highest spirits, emulous above any of his companions, ambitious of preeminence in every thing, and showed an impetuosity and fervor of mind which irresistibly carried him through all opposition or difficulty he could meet with; yet on the other side, he was so easy and gentle in his nature, and so apt to yield to authority, that though he would do nothing on compulsion, upon ingenuous motives he would obey any commands, and was more hurt by the least rebuke or disgrace, than he was distressed by any toil or hardship.

He had one leg shorter than the other, but this deformity was little observed in the general beauty of his person in youth. And the easy way in which he bore it (he being the first always to pass a jest upon himself), went far to make it disregarded. And indeed his high spirit and eagerness to distinguish himself were all the more conspicuous by it, since he never let his lameness withhold him from any toil or any brave action. Neither his statue nor picture are extant, he never allowing them in his life, and utterly forbidding them to be made after his death. He is said to have been a little man, of a contemptible presence; but the goodness of his humor, and his constant cheerfulness and playfulness of temper, always free from any thing of moroseness or haughtiness, made him more attractive, even to his old age, than the most beautiful and youthful men of the nation. Theophrastus writes, that the Ephors laid a fine upon Archidamus for marrying a little wife, "For," said they, "she will bring us a race of kinglets, instead of kings."

Whilst Agis, the elder brother, reigned, Alcibiades, being then an exile from Athens, came from Sicily to Sparta; nor had he stayed long there, before his familiarity with Timæa, the king's wife, grew suspected, insomuch that Agis refused to own a child of hers, which, he said, was Alcibiades's, not his. Nor, if we may believe Duris, the historian, was Timæa much concerned at it, being herself forward enough to whisper among her helot maid servants, that the infant's true name was Alcibiades, not Leotychides. Meanwhile it was believed, that the amour he had with her was not the effect of his love but of his ambition, that he might have Spartan kings of his posterity. This affair being grown public, it became needful for Alcibiades to withdraw from Sparta. But the child Leotychides had not the honors due to a legitimate son paid him, nor was he ever owned by Agis, till by his prayers and tears he prevailed with him to declare him his son before several witnesses upon his death-bed. But this did not avail to fix him in the throne of Agis, after whose death Lysander, who had lately achieved his conquest of Athens by sea, and was of the greatest power in Sparta, promoted Agesilaus, urging Leotychides's bastardy as a bar to his pretensions. Many of the other citizens, also, were favorable to Agesilaus, and zealously joined his party, induced by the opinion they had of his merits, of which they themselves had been spectators, in the time that he had been bred up among them. But there was a man, named Diopithes, at Sparta, who had a great knowledge of ancient oracles, and was thought particularly skilful and clever in all points of religion and divination. He alleged, that it was unlawful to make a lame man king of Lacedæmon, citing in the debate the following oracle:—

> Beware, great Sparta, lest there come of thee
> Though sound thyself, an halting sovereignty;
> Troubles, both long and unexpected too,
> And storms of deadly warfare shall ensue.

But Lysander was not wanting with an evasion, alleging, that if the Spartans were really apprehensive of the oracle, they must have a care of Leotychides; for it was not the limping foot of a king that the gods cared about, but the purity of the Herculean family, into whose rights, if a spurious issue were admitted, it would make the kingdom to halt indeed. Agesilaus likewise alleged, that the bastardy of Leotychides was witnessed to by Neptune, who threw Agis out of bed by a violent earthquake, after which time he ceased to visit his wife, yet Leotychides was born above ten months after this

Agesilaus was upon these allegations declared king, and soon possessed himself of the private estate of Agis, as well as his throne, Leotychides being wholly rejected as a bastard. He now turned his attention to his kindred by the mother's side, persons of worth and virtue, but miserably poor. To them he gave half his brother's estate, and by this popular act gained general good-will and reputation, in the place of the envy and ill-feeling which the inheritance might otherwise have procured him. What Xenophon tells us of him, that by complying with, and, as it were, being ruled by his conntry, he grew into such great power with them, that he could do what he pleased, is meant to apply to the power he gained in the following manner with the Ephors and Elders. These were at that time of the greatest authority in the State; the former, officers annually chosen; the Elders, holding their places during life; both instituted, as already told in the life of Lycurgus, to restrain the power of the kings. Hence it was that there was always from generation to generation, a feud and contention between them and the kings. But Agesilaus took another course. Instead of contending with them, he courted them; in all proceedings he commenced by taking their advice, was always ready to go, nay almost run, when they called him; if he were upon his royal seat, hearing causes, and the Ephors came in, he rose to them; whenever any man was elected into the Council of Elders, he presented him with a gown and an ox. Thus, whilst he made a show of deference to them, and of a desire to extend their authority, he secretly advanced his own, and enlarged the prerogatives of the kings by several liberties which their friendship to his person conceded.

To other citizens he so behaved himself, as to be less blamable in his enmities than in his friendships; for against his enemy he forbore to take any unjust advantage, but his friends he would assist, even in what was unjust. If an enemy had done any thing praiseworthy, he felt it shameful to detract from his due, but his friends he knew not how to reprove when they did ill, nay, he would eagerly join with them, and assist them in their misdeed, and thought all offices of friendship commendable let the matter in which they were employed be what it would. Again, when any of his adversaries was overtaken in a fault, he would be the first to pity him; and be soon entreated to procure his pardon, by which he won the hearts of all men. Insomuch that his popularity grew at last suspected by the Ephors, who laid a fine on him, professing that he was appropriating the citizens to himself, who ought to be the common property of the State. For as it is the opinion of philosophers, that could you take away strife and opposition out of the universe, all the heavenly bodies would stand still, generation and motion would cease in the mutual concord and agreement of all things, so the Spartan legislator seems to have admitted ambition and emulation, among the ingredients of his Commonwealth, as the incentives of virtue, distinctly wishing that there should be some dispute and competition among his men of worth, and pronouncing the mere idle, uncontested, mutual compliance to unproved deserts to be but a false sort of concord. And some think Homer had an eye to this, when he introduces Agamemnon well pleased with the quarrel arising between Ulysses and Achilles, and with the "terrible words" that passed between them, which he would never have done, unless he had thought emulations and dissensions between the noblest men to be of great public benefit. Yet this maxim is not simply to be granted, without restriction, for if animosities go too far, they are very dangerous to cities, and of most pernicious consequence.

When Agesilaus was newly entered upon the government, there came news from Asia, that the Persian king was making great naval preparations, resolving with a high hand to dispossess the Spartans of their maritime supremacy. Lysander was eager for the opportunity of going over and succoring his friends in Asia, whom he had there left governors and masters of the cities, whose maladministration and tyrannical behavior was causing them to be driven out, and in some cases put to death. He therefore persuaded Agesilaus to claim the command of the expedition, and by carrying the war far from Greece into Persia, to anticipate the designs of the barbarian. He also wrote to his friends in Asia, that by embassy they should demand Agesilaus for their captain. Agesilaus, therefore, coming into the public assembly, offered his service, upon condition that he might have thirty Spartans for captains and counsellors; two thousand chosen men of the newly enfranchised helots, and allies to the number of six thousand. Lysander's authority and assistance soon obtained his request, so that he was sent away with the thirty Spartans, of whom Lysander was at once the chief, not only because of his power and reputation, but also on account of his friendship with Agesilaus, who esteemed his procuring him this charge a greater obligation, than that of preferring him to the kingdom.

Whilst the army was collecting to the rendezvous at Geræstus, Agesilaus went with some of his friends to Aulis, where in a dream he saw a man approach him, and speak to him after this manner: "O king of the Lacedæmonians, you cannot but know that, before yourself, there hath been but one general captain of the whole of the Greeks, namely, Agamemnon; now, since you succeed him in the same office and command the same men, since you war against the same enemies, and begin your expedition from the same place, you ought also to offer such a sacrifice as he offered before he weighed anchor." Agesilaus at the same moment remembered that the sacrifice which Agamemnon offered was his own daughter, he being so directed by the oracle. Yet was he not at all disturbed by it, but as soon as he arose, he told his dream to his friends, add'ng, that he would propitiate the goddess with the sacrifices a goddess must delight in, and would not follow the ignorant example of his predecessor. He therefore ordered an hind to be crowned with chaplets and bade his own soothsayer perform the rite, not the usual person whom the Bœotians, in ordinary course, appointed to that office. When the Bœotian magistrates understood it, they were much offended, and sent officers to Agesilaus, to forbid his sacrificing contrary to the laws of the country. These having delivered their message to him, immediately went to the altar, and threw down the quarters of the hind that lay upon it. Agesilus took this very ill, and without further sacrifice immediately sailed away, highly displeased with the Bœotians, and much discouraged in his mind at the omen, boding to himself an unsuccessful voyage and an imperfect issue of the whole expedition.

When he came to Ephesus, he found the power and inter es of Lysander, and the honors paid to him, insufferably great; all applications were made to him, crowds of suitors attended at his door, and followed upon his steps, as if nothing but the mere name of commander belonged, to satisfy the usage, to Agesilaus, the whole power of it being devolved upon Lysander. None of all the commanders that had been sent into Asia was either so powerful or so formidable as he ; no one had rewarded his friends better, or had been more severe against his enemies ; which things having been lately done, made the greater impression on men's minds, especially when they compared the simple and popular behavior of Agesilaus, with the harsh and violent and brief-spoken demeanor which Lysander still retained Universal preference was yielded to this, and little regard shown to Agesilaus. This first occasioned offence to the other Spartan captains, who resented that they should rather seem the attendants of Lysander, than the councillors of Agesilaus. And at length Agesilaus himself, though not perhaps an envious man in his nature, nor apt to be troubled at the honors redounding upon other men, yet eager for honor and jealous of his glory, began to apprehend that Lysander's greatness would carry away from him the rep utation of whatever great action should happen. He therefore went this way to work. He first opposed him in all his counsels; whatever Lysander specially advised was rejected, and other proposals followed. Then whoever made any address to him, if he found him attached to Lysander, certainly lost his suit. So also in judicial cases, any one whom he spoke strongly against was sure to come off with success, and any man whom he was particularly solicitous to procure some benefit for, might think it well if he got away without an actual loss. These things being clearly not done by chance, but constantly and of a set purpose, Lysander was soon sensible of them, and hesitated not to tell his friends, that they suffered for his sake, bidding them apply themselves to the king, and such as were more powerful with him than he was. Such sayings of his seeming to be designed purposely to excite ill feeling, Agesilaus went on to offer himself a more open affront, appointing him his meat-carver, and would in public companies scornfully say, " Let them go now and pay their court to my carver." Lysander, no longer able to brook these indignities, complained at last to Agesilaus himself, telling him, that he knew very well how to humble his friends. Agesilaus answered, " I know certainly how to humble those who pretend to more power than myself." "That," replied Lysander, "is perhaps rather said by you, than done by me: I desire only, that you will assign me some office and place, in which I may serve you without incurring your displeasure."

Upon this Agesilaus sent him to the Hellespont, whence he procured Spithridates, a Persian of the province of Pharnabazus, to come to the assistance of the Greeks with two hundred horse, and a great supply of money. Yet his anger did not so come down, but he thenceforward pursued the design of wresting the kingdom out of the hands of the two families which then enjoyed it, and making it wholly elective; and it is thought that he would on account of this quarrel have excited a great commotion in Sparta, if he had not died in the Bœotian war. Thus ambitious spirits in a commonwealth, when they transgress their bounds, are apt to do more harm than good. For though Lysander's pride and assumption was most ill-timed and insufferable in its display, yet Agesilaus surely could have found some other way of setting him right, less offensive to a man of his reputation and ambitious temper. Indeed they were both blinded with the same passion, so as one not to recognize the authority of his superior, the other not to bear with the imperfections of his friend.

Tisaphernes being at first afraid of Agesilaus, treated with him about setting the Grecian cities at liberty, which was agreed on. But soon after finding a sufficient force drawn together, he resolved upon war, for which Agesilaus was not sorry. For the expectation of this expedition was great, and he did not think it for his honor, that Xenophon with ten thousand men should march through the heart of Asia to the sea, beating the Persian forces when and how he pleased, and that he at the head of the Spartans, then sovereigns both at sea and land, should not achieve some memorable action for Greece. And so to be even with Tisaphernes, he requites his perjury by a fair stratagem. He pretends to march into Caria, whither when he has drawn Tisaphernes and his army, he suddenly turns back, and falls upon Phrygia, takes many of their cities, and carries away great booty, showing his allies, that to break a solemn league was a downright contempt of the gods, but the circumvention of an enemy in war was not only just but glorious, a gratification at once and an advantage.

Being weak in horse, and discouraged by ill omens in the sacrifices, he retired to Ephesus, and there raised cavalry. He obliged the rich men, that were not inclined to serve in person, to find each of them a horseman armed and mounted; and there being many who preferred doing this, the army was quickly reinforced by a body, not of unwilling recruits for the infantry, but of brave and numerous horsemen. For those that were not good at fighting themselves, hired such as were more military in their inclinations, and such as loved not horse-service substituted in their places such as did. Agamemnon's example had been a good one, when he took the present of an excellent mare, to dismiss a rich coward from the army.

When by Agesilaus's order the prisoners he had taken in Phrygia were exposed to sale, they were first stripped of their garments, and then sold naked. The clothes found many customers to buy them, but the bodies being, from the want of all exposure and exercise, white and tender-skinned, were derided and scorned as unserviceable. Agesilaus, who stood by at the auction, told his Greeks, "These are the men against whom ye fight, and these the things you will gain by it."

The season of the year being come, he boldly gave out that he would invade Lydia; and this plain dealing of his was now mistaken for a stratagem by Tisaphernes, who by not believing Agesilaus, having been already deceived by him, overreached himself. He expected that he should have made choice of Caria, as a rough country, not fit for horse, in which he deemed Agesilaus to be weak, and directed his own marches accordingly. But when he found him to be as good as his word, and to have entered into the country of Sardis, he made great haste after him, and by great marches of his horse, overtaking the loose stragglers who were pillaging the country, he cut them off. Agesilaus meanwhile, considering that the horse had outridden the foot, but that he himself had the whole body of his own army entire, made haste to engage them. He mingled his light-armed foot, carrying targets, with the horse, commanding them to advance at full speed and begin the battle, whilst he brought up the heavier-armed men in the rear. The success was answerable to the design; the barbarians were put to the rout, the Grecians pursued hard, took their camp, and put many of them to the sword. The consequence of this victory was very great; for they had not only the liberty of foraging the Persian country, and plundering at pleasure, but also saw Tisaphernes pay dearly for all the cruelty he had showed the Greeks, to whom he was a professed enemy. For the king of Persia sent Tithraustes, who took off his head, and presently dealt with Agesilaus about his return into Greece, sending to him ambassadors to that purpose, with commission to offer him great sums of money. Agesilaus's answer was, that the making of peace belonged to the Lacedæmonians, not to him; as for wealth, he had rather see it in his soldiers' hands than his own; that the Grecians thought it not honorable to enrich themselves with the bribes of their enemies, but with their spoils only. Yet, that he might gratify Tithraustes for the justice he had done upon Tisaphernes, the common enemy of the Greeks, he removed his quarters into Phrygia, accepting thirty talents for his expenses. Whilst he was upon his march, he received a *staff* from the government at Sparta, appointing him admiral as well as general. This was an honor which was never done to any but Agesilaus, who being now undoubtedly the greatest and most illustrious man of his time, still as Theopompus has said, gave himself more occasion of glory in his own virtue and merit than was given him in this authority and power. Yet he committed a fault in preferring Pisander to the command of the navy, when there were others at hand both older and more experienced; in this not so much consulting the public good, as the gratification of his kindred, and especially his wife whose brother Pisander was.

Having removed his camp into Pharnabazus's province, he not only met with great plenty of provisions, but also raised great sums of money, and marching on to the bounds of Paphlagonia, he soon drew Cotys, the king of it, into a league, to which he of his own accord inclined, out of the opinion he had of Agesilaus's honor and virtue. Spithridates, from the time of his abandoning Pharnabazus, constantly attending Agesilaus in the camp whithersoever he went. This Spithridates had a son, a very handsome boy, called Megabates, of whom Agesilaus was extremely fond, and also a very beautiful daughter that was marriageable. Her Agesilaus matched to Cotys, and taking of him a thousand horse, with two thousand light-armed foot, he returned into Phrygia, and there pillaged the country of Pharnabazus, who durst not meet him in the field, nor yet trust to his garrisons, but getting his valuables together, got out of the way and moved about up and down with a flying army, till Spithridates joining with Herippidas the Spartan, took his camp, and all his property. Herippidas being too severe an inquirer into the plunder with which the barbarian soldiers had enriched themselves, and forcing them to deliver it up with too much strictness, so disobliged Spithridates with his questioning and examining, that he changed sides again, and went off with the Paphlagonians to Sardis. This was a very great vexation to Agesilaus, not only that he had lost the friendship of a gallant commander, and with him a considerable part of his army, but still more that it had been done with the disrepute of a sordid and petty covetousness, of which he always had made it a point of honor to keep both himself and his country clear. Besides these public causes, he had a private one, his excessive fondness for the son, which touched him to the quick, though he endeavored to master it, and, especially in presence of the boy, to suppress all appearance of it; so much so that when Megabates, for that was his name, came once to receive a kiss from him, he declined it. At which when the young boy blushed and drew back, and afterward saluted him at a more reserved distance, Agesilaus soon repenting his coldness, and changing his mind, pretended to wonder why he did not salute him with the same familiarity as formerly. His friends about him answered, "You are in the fault, who would not accept the kiss of the boy, but turned away in alarm; he would come to you again, if you would have the courage to let him do so." Upon this Agesilaus paused a while, and at length answered, 'you need not encourage him to it; I think I had rather be master of myself in that refusal, than see all things that are now before my eyes turned into gold." Thus he demeaned himself to Megabates when present, but he had so great a passion for him in his absence, that it may be questioned whether, if the boy had returned again, all the courage he had would have sustained him in such another refusal.

After this Pharnabazus sought an opportunity of conferring with Agesilaus, which Apollophanes of Cyzicus, the common host of them both, procured for him. Agesilaus coming first to the appointed place, threw himself down upon the grass under a tree, lying there in expectation of Pharnabazus, who, bringing with him soft skins and wrought carpets to lie down upon, when he saw Agesilaus's posture, grew ashamed of his luxuries, and made no use of them, but laid himself down upon the grass also, without regard for his delicate and richly dyed clothing. Pharnabazus had matter enough of complaint against Agesilaus, and therefore, after the mutual civilities were over, he put him in mind of the great services he had done the Lacedæmonians in the Attic war, of which he thought it an ill recompense to have his country thus harassed and spoiled, by those men who owed so much to him. The Spartans that were present hung down their heads, as conscious of the wrong they had done to their ally. But Agesilaus said, "We, O Pharnabazus, when we were in amity with your master the king, behaved ourselves like friends, and now that we are at war with him, we behave ourselves as enemies. As for you, we must look upon you as a part of his property, and must do these outrages upon you, not intending the harm to you, but to him whom we wound through you. But whenever you will choose rather to be a friend to the Grecians, than a slave of the king of Persia, you may then reckon this army and navy to be all at your command, to defend both you, your country, and your liberties, without which there is nothing honorable, or indeed desirable among men." Upon this Pharnabazus discovered his mind, and answered, "If the king sends another governor in my room, I will certainly come over to you, but as long as he trusts me with the government, I shall be just to him, and not fail to do my utmost endeavors in opposing you." Agesilaus was taken with the answer and shook hands with him; and rising, said, "How much rather had I have so brave a man my friend than my enemy."

Pharnabazus being gone off, his son staying behind, ran up to Agesilaus, and smilingly said, Agesilaus, I make you my guest;" and thereupon presented him with a javelin which he had in his hand. Agesilaus received it, and being much taken with the good mien and courtesy of the youth, looked about to see if there were any thing in his train fit to offer him in return; and observing the horse of Idæus, the secretary, to have very fine trappings on, he took them off, and bestowed them upon the young gentleman. Nor did his kindness rest there, but he continued ever after to be mindful of him, so that when he was driven out of his country by his brothers, and lived an exile in Peloponnesus, he took great care of him and condescended even to assist him in some love-matters. He had an attachment for a youth of Athenian birth, who was bred up as an athlete; and when at the Olympic games this boy, on account of his great size and general strong and full-grown appearance, was in some danger of not being admitted into the list, the Persian betook himself to Agesilaus, and made use of his friendship. Agesilaus readily assisted him, and not without a great deal of difficulty effected his desires. He was in all other things a man of great and exact justice, but when the case concerned a friend, to be strait-laced in point of justice, he said, was only a colorable pretence of denying him. There is an epistle written to Idrieus, prince of Caria, that is ascribed to Agesilaus; it is this; "If Nicias be innocent, absolve him; if he be guilty, absolve him upon my account; however, be sure to absolve him." This was his usual character in his deportment towards his friends. Yet his rule was not without exception; for sometimes he considered the necessity of his affairs more than his friend, of which he once gave an example, when upon a sudden and disorderly removal of his camp, he left a sick friend behind him, and when he called loudly after him, and implored his help, turned his back, and said it was hard to be compassionate and wise too. This story is related by Hieronymus, the philosopher.

Another year of the war being spent, Agesilaus's fame still increased, insomuch that the Persian king received daily information concerning his many virtues, and the great esteem the world had of his temperance, his plain living, and his moderation. When he made any journey, he would usually take up his lodging in a temple, and there make the gods witnesses of his most private actions, which others would scarce permit men to be acquainted with. In so great an army, you should scarce find a common soldier lie on a coarser mattress, than Agesilaus he was so indifferent to the varieties of heat and cold, that all the seasons, as the gods sent them, seemed natural to him. The Greeks that inhabited Asia were much pleased to see the great lords and governors of Persia, with all the pride, cruelty, and luxury in which they lived, trembling and bowing before a man in a poor threadbare cloak, and at one laconic word out of his mouth, obsequiously deferring and changing their wishes and purposes. So that it brought to the minds of many the verses of Timotheus.

> Mars is the tyrant, gold Greece does not fear.

Many parts of Asia now revolting from the Persians, Agesilaus restored order in the cities, and without bloodshed or banishment of any of their members, re-established the proper constitution in the governments, and now resolved to carry away the war from the seaside, and to march further up into the country, and to attack the king of Persia himself in his own home in Susa and Ecbatana; not willing to let the monarch sit idle in his chair, playing umpire in the conflicts of the Greeks, and bribing their popular leaders. But these great thoughts were interrupted by unhappy news from Sparta; Epicydidas is from thence sent to remand him home, to assist his own country, which was then involved in a great war;

> Greece to herself doth a barbarian grow,
> Others could not, she doth herself o'erthrow.

What better can we say of those jealousies, and that league and conspiracy of the Greeks for their own mischief, which arrested fortune in full career, and turned back arms that were already uplifted against the barbarians, to be used upon themselves, and recalled into Greece the war which had been banished out of her? I by no means assent to Demaratus, of Corinth, who said that those Greeks lost a great satisfaction, that did not live to see Alexander sit in the throne of Darius. That sight should rather have drawn tears from them, when they considered that they had left that glory to Alexander and the Macedonians, whilst they spent all their own great commanders in playing them against each other in the fields of Leuctra, Coronea, Corinth, and Arcadia.

Nothing was greater or nobler than the behavior of Agesilaus on this occasion, nor can a nobler instance be found in story, of a ready obedience and just deference to orders. Hannibal, though in a bad condition himself, and almost driven out of Italy, could scarcely be induced to obey, when he was called home to serve his country. Alexander made a jest of the battle between Agis and Antipater, laughing and saying, "So, whilst we were conquering Darius in Asia, it seems there was a battle of mice in Arcadia." Happy Sparta, meanwhile, in the justice and modesty of Agesilaus, and in the deference he paid to the laws of his country; who, immediately upon receipt of his orders, though in the midst of his high fortune and power, and in full hope of great and glorious success, gave all up and instantly departed, "his object unachieved," leaving many regrets behind him among his allies in Asia, and proving by his example the falseness of that saying of Demostratus, the son of Phæax, "That the Lacedæmonians were better in public, but the Athenians in private." For while approving himself an excellent king and general, he likewise showed himself in private an excellent friend, and a most agreeable companion.

The coin of Persia was stamped with the figure of an archer; Agesilaus said, That a thousand Persian archers had driven him out of Asia; meaning the money that had been laid out in bribing the demagogues and the orators in Thebes and Athens, and thus inciting those two States to hostility against Sparta.

Having passed the Hellespont, he marched by land through Thrace, not begging or entreating a passage anywhere, only he sent his messengers to them, to demand whether they would have him pass as a friend or as an enemy. All the rest received him as a friend, and assisted him on his journey. But the Trallians, to whom Xerxes also is said to have given money, demanded a price of him, namely, one hundred talents of silver, and one hundred women. Agesilaus in scorn asked, Why they were not ready to receive them? He marched on, and finding the Trallians in arms to oppose him, fought them, and slew great numbers of them. He sent the like embassy to the king of Macedonia, who replied, He would take time to deliberate: "Let him deliberate," said Agesilaus, "we will go forward in the mean time." The Macedonian, being surprised and daunted at the resolution of the Spartan, gave orders to let him pass as a friend. When he came into Thessaly, he wasted the country, because they were in league with the enemy. To Larissa, the chief city of Thessaly, he sent Xenocles and Scythes to treat of a peace, whom when the Larissæans had laid hold of, and put into custody, others were enraged, and advised the siege of the town; but he answered, That he valued either of those men at more than the whole country of Thessaly. He therefore made terms with them, and received his men again upon composition. Nor need we wonder at this saying of Agesilaus, since when he had news brought him from Sparta, of several great captains slain in a battle near Corinth, in which the slaughter fell upon other Greeks, and the Lacedæmonians obtained a great victory with small loss, he did not appear at all satisfied; but with a great sigh cried out, "O Greece, how many brave men hast thou destroyed; who, if they had been preserved to so good an use, had sufficed to have conquered all Persia!" Yet when the Pharsalians grew troublesome to him, by pressing upon his army, and incommoding his passage, he led out five hundred horse, and in person fought and routed them, setting up a trophy under the mount Narthacius. He valued himself very much upon that victory, that with so small a number of his own training, he had vanquished a body of men that thought themselves the best horsemen of Greece.

Here Diphridas, the Ephor, met him, and delivered his message from Sparta, which ordered him immediately to make an inroad into Bœotia; and though he thought this fitter to have been done at another time, and with greater force, he yet obeyed the magistrates. He thereupon told his soldiers that the day was come, on which they were to enter upon that employment, for the performance of which they were brought out of Asia. He sent for two divisions of the army near Corinth to his assistance. The Lacedæmonians at home, in honor to him, made proclamations for volunteers that would serve under the king, to come in and be enlisted. Finding all the young men in the city ready to offer themselves, they chose fifty of the strongest, and sent them.

Agesilaus having gained Thermopylæ, and passed quietly through Phocis, as soon as he had entered Bœotia, and pitched his camp near Chæronea, at once met with an eclipse of the sun, and with ill news from the navy, Pisander, the Spartan admiral, being beaten and slain at Cnidos, by Pharnabazus and Conon. He was much moved at it, both upon his own and the public account. Yet lest his army, being now near engaging, should meet with any discouragement, he ordered the messengers to give out that the Spartans were the conquerors, and he himself putting on a garland, solemnly sacrificed for the good news, and sent portions of the sacrifices to his friends.

When he came near to Coronea, and was within view of the

enemy, he drew up his army, and giving the left wing to the Orchomenians, he himself led the right. The Thebans took the right wing of their army, leaving the left to the Argives Xenophon, who was present, and fought on Agesilaus's side, reports it to be the hardest fought battle that he had seen The beginning of it was not so, for the Thebans soon put the Orchomenians to rout, as also did Agesilaus the Argives. But both parties having news of the misfortune of their left wings, they betook themselves to their relief. Here Agesilaus might have been sure of his victory, had he contented himself not to charge them in the front, but in the flank or rear; but being angry and heated in the fight, he would not wait the opportunity, but fell on at once, thinking to bear them down before him. The Thebans were not behind him in courage, so that the battle was fiercely carried on on both sides, especially near Agesilaus's person, whose new guard of fifty volunteers stood him in great stead that day, and saved his life. They fought with great valor, and interposed their bodies frequently between him and danger, yet could they not so preserve him, but that he received many wounds through his armor with lances and swords, and was with much difficulty gotten off alive by their making a ring about him, and so guarding him, with the slaughter of many of the enemy and the loss of many of their own number. At length, finding it too hard a task to break the front of the Theban troops, they opened their own files, and let the enemy march through them (an artifice which in the beginning they scorned), watching in the mean time the posture of the enemy, who, having passed through, grew careless, as esteeming themselves past danger; in which position they were immediately set upon by the Spartans. Yet were they not then put to rout, but marched on to Helicon, proud of what they had done, being able to say that they themselves, as to their part of the army, were not worsted.

Agesilaus, sore wounded as he was, would not be borne to his tent, till he had been first carried about the field, and had seen the dead conveyed within his encampment. As many of his enemies as had taken sanctuary in the temple, he dismissed. For there stood near the battle-field, the temple of Minerva the Itonian, and before it a trophy erected by the Bœotians, for the victory which, under the conduct of Sparton, their general, they obtained over the Athenians under Tolmides, who himself fell in the battle. And next morning early, to make trial of the Theban courage, whether they had any mind to a second encounter, he commanded his soldiers to put on garlands on their heads, and play with their flutes, and raise a trophy before their faces; but when they, instead of fighting sent for leave to bury their dead, he gave it them; and having so assured himself of the victory, after this he went to Delphi, to the Pythian games, which were then celebrating, at which feast he assisted, and there solemnly offered the tenth part of the spoils he had brought from Asia, which amounted to a hundred talents.

Thence he returned to his own country, where his way and habits of life quickly excited the affection and admiration of the Spartans; for, unlike other generals, he came home from foreign lands the same man that he went out, having not so learned the fashions of other countries, as to forget his own, much less to dislike or despise them. He followed and respected all the Spartan customs, without any change either in the manner of his supping, or bathing, or his wife's apparel, as if he had never travelled over the river Eurotas. So also with his household furniture and his own armor, nay, the very gates of his house were so old, that they might well be thought of Aristodemus's setting up. His daughter's *Canathrum* says Xenophon, was no richer than that of ary one else. The Canathrum, as they call it, is a chair or chariot made of wood, in the shape of a Griffin, or tragelaphus, on which the children and young virgins are carried in processions. Xenophon has not left us the name of this daughter of Agesilaus; and Dicæarchus expresses some indignation, because we do not know, he says, the name of Agesilaus's daughter, nor of Epaminondas's mother. But in the records of Laconia, we ourselves found his wife's name to have been Cleora, and his two daughters to have been called Eupolia and Prolyta. And you may also to this day see Agesilaus's spear kept in Sparta, nothing differing from that of other men.

There was a vanity he observed among the Spartans, about keeping running horses for the Olympic games, upon which he found they much valued themselves. Agesilaus regarded it as a display not of any real virtue, but of wealth and expense; and to make this evident to the Greeks, induced his sister, Cynisca, to send a chariot into the course. He kept with him Xenophon, the philosopher, and made much of him, and proposed to him to send for his children, and educate them at Sparta, where they would be taught the best of all learning; how to obey, and how to command. Finding on Lysander's death a large faction formed, which he on his return from Asia had established against Agesilaus, he thought it advisable to expose both him and it, by showing what manner of a citizen he had been whilst he lived. To that end, finding among his writings an oration, composed by Cleon the Halicarnassean, but to have been spoken by Lysander in a public assembly, to excite the people to innovations and changes in the government, he resolved to publish it as an evidence of Lysander's practices. But one of the Elders having the perusal of it, and finding it powerfully written, advised him to have a care of digging up Lysander again, and rather bury that oration in the grave with him; and this advice he wisely hearkened to, and hushed the whole thing up; and ever after forebore publicly to affront any of his adversaries, but took occasions of picking out the ringleaders, and sending them away upon foreign services. He thus had means for exposing the avarice and the injustice of many of them in their employments; and again when they were by others brought into question, he made it his business to bring them off, obliging them, by that means, of enemies to become his friends, and so by degrees left none remaining.

Agesipolis, his fellow king, was under the disadvantage of being born of an exiled father, and himself young, modest, and inactive, meddled not much in affairs. Agesilaus took a course of gaining him over, and making him entirely tractable. According to the custom of Sparta, the kings, if they were in town, always dined together. This was Agesilaus's opportunity of dealing with Agesipolis, whom he found quick, as he himself was, in forming attachments for young men, and accordingly talked with him always on such subjects, joining and aiding him, and acting as his confidant, such attachments in Sparta being entirely honorable, and attended always with lively feelings of modesty, love of virtue, and a noble emulation; of which more is said in Lycurgus's life.

Having thus established his power in the city, he easily obtained that his half-brother Teleutias might be chosen admiral, and thereupon making an expedition against the Corinthians, he made himself master of the long walls by land, through the assistance of his brother at sea. Coming thus upon the Argives, who then held Corinth, in the midst of their Isthmian festival, he made them fly from the sacrifice they had just commenced, and leave all their festive provision behind them. The exiled Corinthians that were in the Spartan army, desired him to keep the feast, and to preside in the celebration of it. This he refused, but gave them leave to carry on the solemnity if they pleased, and he in the mean time stayed and guarded them. When Agesilaus marched off, the Argives returned and celebrated the games over again, when some who were victors before, became victors a second time, others lost the prizes which before they had gained. Agesilaus thus made it clear to everybody, that the Argives must in their own eyes have been guilty of great cowardice, since they set such a value on presiding at the games, and yet had not dared to fight for it. He himself was of opinion, that to keep a mean in such things was best; he assisted at the sports and dances usual in his own country, and was always ready and eager to be present at the exercises either of the young men, or of the girls, but things that many men used to be highly taken with, he seemed not at all concerned about. Callippides, the tragic actor, who had a great name in all Greece and was made much of, once met and saluted him; of which when he found no notice taken, he confidently thrust himself into his train, expecting that Agesilaus would pay him some attention. When all that failed, he boldly accosted him, and asked him whether he did not remember him? Agesilaus turned, and looking him in the face, " Are you not," said he, " Callippides the showman?" Being invited once to hear a man who admirably imitated the nightingale, he declined, saying he had heard the nightingale itself. Menecrates, the physician, having had great success in some desperate diseases, was by way of flattery called Jupiter; he was so vain as to take the name, and having occasion to write a letter to Agesilaus, thus addressed it: " Jupiter Menecrates to King Agesilaus, greeting." The king returned answer: " Agesilaus to Menecrates, health and a sound mind."

Whilst Agesilaus was in the Corinthian territories, having just taken the Heræum, he was looking on while his soldiers were carrying away the prisoners and the plunder, when ambassadors from Thebes came to him to treat of peace. Having a great aversion for that city, and thinking it then advantageous to his affairs publicly to slight them, he took the opportunity, and would not seem either to see them, or hear them speak. But as if on purpose to punish him in his pride, before they parted from him, messengers came with news of the complete slaughter of one of the Spartan divisions by Iphicrates, a greater disaster than had befallen them for many years; and that the more grievous, because it was a choice regiment of full-armed Lacedæmonians overthrown by a parcel of mere mercenary targeteers. Agesilaus leapt from his seat, to go at once to their rescue, but found it too late, the business being over. He therefore returned to the Heræum, and sent for the Theban ambassadors to give them audience. They now resolved to be even with him for the affront he gave them, and without speaking one word of the peace, only desired leave to go into Corinth. Agesilaus, irritated with this proposal, told them in scorn, that if they were anxious to go and see how proud their friends were of their success, they should do it to-morrow with safety. Next morning, taking the ambassadors with him, he ravaged the Corinthian territories, up to the very gates of the city, where, having made a stand, and let the ambassadors see that the Corinthians durst not come out to defend themselves, he dismissed them. Then gathering up the small remainders of the shattered regiment, he marched homewards, always removing his camp before day, and always pitching his tents after night, that he might prevent their enemies among the Arcadians from taking any opportunity of insulting over their loss.

After this, at the request of the Achæans, he marched with them into Acarnania, and there collected great spoils, and defeated the Acarnanians in battle. The Achæans would have persuaded him to keep his winter quarters there, to hinder the Acarnanians from sowing their corn; but he was of the contrary opinion, alleging that they would be more afraid of a war next summer, when their fields were sown, than they would be if they lay fallow. The event justified his opinion; for next summer, when the Achæans began their expedition again, the Acarnanians immediately made peace with them.

When Conon and Pharnabazus with the Persian navy were grown masters of the sea, and had not only infested the coast of Laconia, but also rebuilt the walls of Athens at the cost of Pharnabazus, the Lacedæmonians thought fit to treat of peace with the king of Persia. To that end, they sent Antalcidas to Tiribazus, basely and wickedly betraying the Asiatic Greeks, on whose behalf Agesilaus had made the war. But no part of this dishonor fell upon Agesilaus, the whole being transacted by Antalcidas, who was his bitter enemy, and was urgent for peace upon any terms, because war was sure to increase his power and reputation. Nevertheless, once being told by way of reproach, that the Lacedæmonians had gone over to the Medes, he replied, "No, the Medes had come over to the Lacedæmonians." And when the Greeks were backward to submit to the agreement, he threat ened them with war, unless they fulfilled the king of Persia's conditions, his particular end in this being to weaken the Thebans; for it was made one of the articles of peace, that the country of Bœotia should be left independent. This feeling of his to Thebes appeared further afterwards, when Phœbidas, in full peace, most unjustifiably seized upon the Cadmea. The thing was much resented by all Greece, and not well liked by the Lacedæmonians themselves; those especially who were enemies to Agesilaus, required an account of the action, and by whose authority it was done, laying the suspicion of it at his door. Agesilaus resolutely answered, on the behalf of Phœbidas, that the profitableness of the act was chiefly to be considered; if it were for the advantage of the commonwealth, it was no matter whether it were done with or without authority. This was the more remarkable in him, because in his ordinary language, he was always observed to be a great maintainer of justice, and would commend it as the chief of virtues, saying, that valor without justice was useless, and if all the world were just, there would be no need of valor. When any would say to him, the Great King will have it so; he would reply, "How is he greater than I, unless he be juster?" nobly and rightly taking, as a sort of royal measure of greatness, justice, and not force. And thus when, on the conclusion of the peace, the King of Persia wrote to Agesilaus, desiring a private friendship and relations of hospitality, he refused it, saying that the public friendship was enough; whilst that lasted there was no need of private. Yet in his acts he was not constant to his doctrine, but sometimes out of ambition, and sometimes out of private pique, he let himself be carried away; and particularly in this case of the Thebans, he not only saved Phœbidas, but persuaded the Lacedæmonians to take the fault upon themselves, and to retain the Cadmea, putting a garrison into it, and to put the government of Thebes into the hands of Archias and Leontidas, who had been betrayers of the castle to them.

This excited strong suspicion that what Phœbidas did was by Agesilaus's order, which was corroborated by after-occurrences. For when the Thebans had expelled the garrison, and asserted their liberty, he, accusing them of the murder of Archias and Leontidas, who indeed were tyrants, though in name holding the office of Polemarchs, made war upon them. He sent Cleombrotus on that errand, who was now his fellow king, in the place of Agesipolis, who was dead, excusing

himself by reason of his age; for it was forty years since he
had first borne arms, and he was consequently exempt by the
law; meanwhile the true reason was, that he was ashamed,
having so lately fought against tyranny in behalf of the Phil
iasians, to fight now in defence of a tyranny against the The
bans.

One Sphodrias, of Lacedæmon, of the contrary faction to
Agesilaus, was governor in Thespiæ, a bold and enterprising
man, though he had perhaps more of confidence than wisdom.
This action of Phœbidas fired him, and incited his ambition
to attempt some great enterprise, which might render him as
famous as he perceived the taking of the Cadmea had made
Phœbidas. He thought the sudden capture of the Piræus,
and the cutting off thereby the Athenians from the sea,
would be a matter of far more glory. It is said, too, that
Pelopidas and Melon, the chief captains of Bœotia, put him
upon it; that they privily sent men to him, pretending to be
of the Spartan faction, who, highly commending Sphodrias,
filled him with a great opinion of himself, protesting him to
be the only man in the world that was fit for so great an enterprise. Being thus stimulated, he could hold no longer,
but hurried into an attempt as dishonorable and treacherous
as that of the Cadmea, but executed with less valor and less
success; for the day broke whilst he was yet in the Thria-
sian plain, whereas he designed the whole exploit to have
been done in the night. As soon as the soldiers perceived
the rays of light reflecting from the temples of Eleusis, upon
the first rising of the sun, it is said that their hearts failed
them; nay, he himself, when he saw that he could not have
the benefit of the night, had not courage enough to go on
with his enterprise; but having pillaged the country, he returned with shame to Thespiæ. An embassy was upon this
sent from Athens to Sparta, to complain of the breach of
peace; but the ambassadors found their journey needless,
Sphodrias being then under process by the magistrates of
Sparta. Sphodrias durst not stay to expect judgment,
which he found would be capital, the city being highly incensed against him, out of the shame they felt at the busi
ness, and their desire to appear in the eyes of the Athenians
as fellow-sufferers in the wrong, rather than accomplices in its
being done.

This Sphodrias had a son of great beauty named Cleonymus, to whom Archidamus, the son of Agesilaus was ex
remely attached. Archidamus, as became him, was con

cerned for the danger of his friend's father, but yet he durst not do any thing openly for his assistance, he being one of the professed enemies of Agesilaus. But Cleonymus having solicited him with tears about it, as knowing Agesilaus to be of all his father's enemies the most formidable, the young man for two or three days followed after his father with such fear and confusion, that he durst not speak to him. At last, the day of sentence being at hand, he ventured to tell him that Cleonymus had entreated him to intercede for his father Agesilaus, though well aware of the love between the two young men, yet did not prohibit it, because Cleonymus from his earliest years had been looked upon as a youth of very great promise ; yet he gave not his son any kind or hopeful answer in the case, but coldly told him, that he would consider what he could honestly and honorably do in it, and so dismissed him. Archidamus being ashamed of his want of success, forebore the company of Cleonymus, whom he usually saw several times every day. This made the friends of Sphodrias to think his case desperate, till Etymocles, one of Agesilaus's friends discovered to them the king's mind ; namely, that he abhorred the fact, but yet he thought Sphodrias a gallant man such as the commonwealth much wanted at that time. For Agesilaus used to talk thus concerning the cause, out of a desire to gratify his son. And now Cleonymus quickly understood that Archidamus had been true to him, in using all his interests with his father ; and Sphodrias's friend ventured to be forward in his defence. The truth is, that Agesilaus was excessively fond of his children ; and it is to him the story belongs, that when they were little ones, he used to make a horse of a stick, and ride with them ; and being caught at this sport by a friend, he desired him not to mention it till he himself were the father of children.

Meanwhile, Sphodrias being acquitted, the Athenians betook themselves to arms, and Agesilaus fell into disgrace with the people ; since to gratify the whims of a boy he had been willing to pervert justice, and make the city accessory to the crimes of private men, whose most unjustifiable actions had broken the peace of Greece. He also found his colleague, Cleombrotus, little inclined to the Theban war ; so that it became necessary for him to waive the privilege of his age, which he before had claimed, and to lead the army himself into Bœotia ; which he did with variety of success, sometimes conquering, and sometimes conquered ; insomuch that receiving a wound in a battle, he was reproached by Antal cidas, that the Thebans had paid him well for the lessons he had given them in fighting. And, indeed, they were now grown far better soldiers than ever they had been, being so continually kept in training, by the frequency of the Lacedæmonian expeditions against them. Out of the foresight of which it was, that anciently Lycurgus, in three several laws forbade them to make any wars with the same nation, as this would be to instruct their enemies in the art of it. Mean while, the allies of Sparta were not a little discontented at Agesilaus, because this war was commenced not upon any fair public ground of quarrel, but merely out of his private hatred to the Thebans; and they complained with indignation that they, being the majority of the army, should from year to year be thus exposed to danger and hardship here and there, at the will of a few persons. It was at this time, we are told, that Agesilaus, to obviate the objection, devised this expedient, to show the allies were not the greater number. He gave orders that all the allies, of whatever country, should sit down promiscuously on one side, and all the Lacedæmonians on the other: which being done, he commanded a herald to proclaim, that all the potters of both divisions should stand out; then all the blacksmiths; then all the masons; next the carpenters; and so he went through all the handicrafts. By this time almost all the allies were risen, but of the Lacedæmonians not a man, they being by law forbidden to learn any mechanical business; and now Agesilaus laughed and said, "You see, my friends, how many more soldiers we send out than you do."

When he brought back his army from Bœotia through Megara, as he was going up to the magistrate's office in the Acropolis, he was suddenly seized with pain and cramp in his sound leg, and great swelling and inflammation ensued. He was treated by a Syracusan physician, who let him blood below the ankle; this soon eased his pain, but then the blood could not be stopped, till the loss of it brought on fainting and swooning; at length, with much trouble, he stopped it. Agesilaus was carried home to Sparta in a very weak condition, and did not recover strength enough to appear in the field for a long time after.

Meanwhile, the Spartan fortune was but ill; they received many losses both by sea and land; but the greatest was that at Tegyræ, when for the first time they were beaten by the Thebans in a set battle.

All the Greeks were, accordingly, disposed to a general

peace, and to that end ambassadors came to Sparta. Among these was Epaminondas, the Theban, famous at that time for his philosophy and learning, but he had not yet given proof of his capacity as a general. He, seeing all the others crouch to Agesilaus, and court favor with him, alone maintained the dignity of an ambassador, and with that freedom that became his character, made a speech in behalf not of Thebes only, from whence he came, but of all Greece, remonstrating, that Sparta alone grew great by war, to the distress and suffering of all her neighbors. He urged, that a peace should be made upon just and equal terms, such as alone would be a lasting one, which could not otherwise be done, than by reducing all to equality. Agesilaus, perceiving all the other Greeks to give much attention to this discourse, and to be pleased with it, presently asked him whether he thought it a part of this justice and equality that the Bœotian towns should enjoy their independence. Epaminondas instantly and without wavering asked him in return, whether he thought it just and equal that the Laconian towns should enjoy theirs. Agesilaus started from his seat and bade him once for all speak out and say whether or not Bœotia should be independent. And when Epaminondas replied once again with the same inquiry, whether Laconia should be so, Agesilaus was so enraged that, availing himself of the pretext, he immediately struck the name of the Thebans out of the league, and declared war against them. With the rest of the Greeks he made a peace, and dismissed them with this saying, that what could be peaceably adjusted, should; what was otherwise incurable, must be committed to the success of war, it being a thing of two great difficulty to provide for all things by treaty.

The Ephors upon this despatched their orders to Cleombrotus, who was at that time in Phocis, to march directly into Bœotia, and at the same time sent to their allies for aid. The confederates were very tardy in their business and unwilling to engage, but as yet they feared the Spartans too much to dare to refuse. And although many portents, and prodigies of ill presage, which I have mentioned in the life of Epaminondas, had appeared; and though Prothous, the Laconian, did all he could to hinder it, yet Agesilaus would needs go forward, and prevailed so, that the war was decreed. He thought the present juncture of affairs very advantageous for their revenge, the rest of Greece being wholly free, and the Thebans excluded from the peace. But that this war was undertaken more upon passion than judgment, the event may prove ; for the treaty was finished but the fourteenth of Scirophorion, and the Lacedæmonians received their great overthrow at Leuctra, on the fifth of Hecatombæon, within twenty days. There fell at that time a thousand Spartans, and Cleombrotus their king, and around him the bravest men of the nation ; particularly, the beautiful youth, Cleonymus, the son of Sphodrias, who was thrice struck down at the feet of the king, and as often rose, but was slain at the last.

This unexpected blow, which fell so heavy upon the Lacedæmonians, brought greater glory to Thebes than ever was acquired by any other of the Grecian republics, in their civil wars against each other. The behavior, notwithstanding, of the Spartans, though beaten, was as great, and as highly to be admired, as that of the Thebans. And indeed, if, as Xenophon says, in conversation good men even in their sports and at their wine let fall many sayings that are worth the preserving ; how much more worthy to be recorded is an exemplary constancy of mind, as shown both in the words and in the acts of brave men, when they are pressed by adverse fortune ! It happened that the Spartans were celebrating a solemn feast, at which many strangers were present from other countries, and the town full of them, when this news of the overthrow came. It was the gymnopædiæ, and the boys were dancing in the theatre, when the messengers arrived from Leuctra. The Ephors, though they were sufficiently aware that this blow had ruined the Spartan power, and that their primacy over the rest of Greece was gone forever, yet gave orders that the dances should not break off, nor any of the celebration of the festival abate ; but privately sending the names of the slain to each family, out of which they were lost, they continued the public spectacles. The next morning, when they had full intelligence concerning it, and everybody knew who were slain, and who survived, the fathers, relatives, and friends of the slain came out rejoicing in the market-place, saluting each other with a kind of exultation ; on the contrary, the fathers of the survivors hid themselves at home among the women. If necessity drove any of them abroad they went very dejectedly, with downcast looks, and sorrowful countenances. The women outdid the men in it ; those whose sons were slain, openly rejoicing, cheerfully making visits to one another, and meeting triumphantly in the temples ; they who expected their children home, being very silent, and much troubled.

But the people in general, when their allies now began to desert them, and Epaminondas, in all the confidence of victory, was expected with an invading army in Peloponnesus, began to think again of Agesilaus's lameness, and to entertain feelings of religious fear and despondency, as if their having rejected the sound-footed, and having chosen the halting king which the oracle had specially warned them against, was the occasion of all their distresses. Yet the regard they had to the merit and reputation of Agesilaus, so far stilled this murmuring of the people, that, notwithstanding it, they intrusted themselves to him in this distress, as the only man that was fit to heal the public malady, the arbiter of all their difficulties, whether relating to the affairs of war or peace. One great one was then before them, concerning the runaways (as their name is for them) that had fled out of the battle, who being many and powerful, it was feared that they might make some commotion in the republic, to prevent the execution of the law upon them for their cowardice. The law in that case was very severe; for they were not only to be debarred from all honors, but also it was a disgrace to intermarry with them; whoever met any of them in the streets, might beat him if he chose, nor was it lawful for him to resist; they, in the meanwhile, were obliged to go about unwashed and meanly dressed, with their clothes patched with divers colors, and to wear their beards half shaved, half unshaven. To execute so rigid a law as this, in a case where the offenders were so many, and many of them of such distinction, and that in a time when the commonwealth wanted soldiers so much as then it did, was of dangerous consequence. Therefore they chose Agesilaus as a sort of new law-giver for the occasion. But he, without adding to or diminishing from or any way changing the law, came out into the public assembly, and said that the law should sleep for to-day, but from this day forth be vigorously executed. By this means he at once preserved the law from abrogation, and the citizens from infamy; and that he might alleviate the despondency and self-distrust of the young men, he made an inroad into Arcadia, where, carefully avoiding all fighting, he contented himself with spoiling the territory, and taking a small town belonging to the Mantineans, thus reviving the hearts of the people, letting them see that they were not everywhere unsuccessful.

Epaminondas now invaded Laconia with an army of forty thousand, besides light-armed men and others that followed the camp only for plunder, so that in all they were at least seventy thousand. It was now six hundred years since the Dorians had possessed Laconia, and in all that time the face of an enemy had not been seen within their territories, no man daring to invade them; but now they made their entrance, and burnt and plundered without resistance the hitherto untouched and sacred territory, up to Eurotas, and the very suburbs of Sparta; for Agesilaus would not permit them to encounter so impetuous a torrent, as Theopompus calls it, of war. He contented himself with fortifying the chief parts of the city, and with placing guards in convenient places, enduring meanwhile the taunts of the Thebans, who reproached him by name as the kindler of the war, and the author of all that mischief to his country, bidding him defend himself if he could. But this was not all; he was equally disturbed at home with the tumults of the city, the outcries and running about of the old men, who were enraged at their present condition, and the women yet worse, out of their senses with the clamors, and the fires of the enemy in the field. He was also himself afflicted by the sense of his lost glory; who, having come to the throne of Sparta when it was in its most flourishing and powerful condition, now lived to see it laid low in esteem, and all its great vaunts cut down, even that which he himself had been accustomed to use, that the women of Sparta had never seen the smoke of the enemy's fire. As it is said, also that when Antalcidas, once being in dispute with an Athenian about the valor of the two nations, the Athenian boasted, that they had often driven the Spartans from the river Cephisus, "Yes," said Antalcidas, "but we never had occasion to drive you from Eurotas." And a common Spartan of less note, being in company with an Argive, who was bragging how many Spartans lay buried in the fields of Argos, replied, "None of you are buried in the country of Laconia." Yet now the case was so altered, that Antalcidas, being one of the Ephors, out of fear sent away his children privately to the island of Cythera.

When the enemy essayed to get over the river and thence to attack the town, Agesilaus, abandoning the rest, betook himself to the high places and strongholds of it. But it happened, Eurotas at that time was swollen to a great height with snow that had fallen and made the passage very difficult to the Thebans, not only by its depth, but much more by its extreme coldness. Whilst this was doing, Epaminondas was seen in the front of the phalanx, and was pointed out to Agesilaus, who looked long at him, and said but these words, "O bold man!" But when he came to the city, and would have fain attempted something within the limits of it that might raise him a trophy there, he could not tempt Agesilaus out of his hold, but was forced to march off again, wasting the country as he went.

Meanwhile, a body of long discontented and bad citizens, about two hundred in number, having got into a strong part of the town called the Issorion, where the temple of Diana stands, seized and garrisoned it. The Spartans would have fallen upon them instantly; but Agesilaus, not knowing how far the sedition might reach, bade them forbear, and going himself in his ordinary dress, with but one servant, when he came near the rebels, called out, and told them that they mistook their orders; this was not the right place; they were to go, one part of them thither showing them another place in the city, and part to another which he also showed. The conspirators gladly heard this, thinking themselves unsuspected of treason, and readily went off to the places which he showed them. Whereupon Agesilaus placed in their room a guard of his own; and of the conspirators he apprehended fifteen, and put them to death in the night. But after this, a much more dangerous conspiracy was discovered of Spartan citizens, who had privately met in each other's houses, plotting a revolution. These were men whom it was equally dangerous to prosecute publicly according to law, and to connive at. Agesilaus took council with the Ephors, and put these also to death privately without process; a thing never before known in the case of any born Spartan.

At this time, also, many of the Helots and country people, who were in the army, ran away to the enemy, which was a matter of great consternation to the city. He therefore caused some officers of his, every morning before day, to search the quarters of the soldiers, and where any man was gone, to hide his arms, that so the greatness of the number might not appear.

Historians differ about the cause of the Thebans' depart ure from Sparta. Some say, the winter forced them; as also that the Arcadian soldiers disbanding, made it necessary for the rest to retire. Others say that they stayed there three months, till they had laid the whole country waste. Theopompus is the only author who says that when the Bœotian generals had already resolved upon the retreat, Phrixus, the Spartan, came to them, and offered them from Agesilaus ten talents to be gone, so hiring them to do what they were al ready doing of their own accord. How he alone should come to be aware of this, I know not; only in this all authors agree, that the saving of Sparta from ruin was wholly due to the wisdom of Agesilaus, who in this extremity of affairs quitted all his ambition and his haughtiness, and resolved to play a saving game. But all his wisdom and courage was not sufficient to recover the glory of it, and to raise it to its ancient greatness. For as we see in human bodies, long used to a very strict and too exquisitely regular diet, any single great disorder is usually fatal; so here one stroke overthrew the whole State's long prosperity. Nor can we be surprised at this. Lycurgus had formed a polity admirably designed for the peace, harmony, and virtuous life of the citizens; and their fall came from their assuming foreign dominion and arbitrary sway, things wholly undesirable, in the judgment of Lycurgus, for a well-conducted and happy State.

Agesilaus being now in years, gave over all military employments; but his son, Archidamus, having received help from Dionysius of Sicily, gave a great defeat to the Arcadians, in the fight known by the name of the Tearless Battle, in which there was a great slaughter of the enemy without the loss of one Spartan. Yet this victory, more than anything else, discovered the present weakness of Sparta; for heretofore victory was esteemed so usual a thing with them, that for their greatest successes, they merely sacrificed a cock to the gods. The soldiers never vaunted, nor did the citizens display any great joy at the news; even when the great victory, described by Thucydides, was obtained at Mantinea, the messenger that brought the news had no other reward than a piece of meat, sent by the magistrates from the common table. But at the news of this Arcadian victory, they were not able to contain themselves; Agesilaus went out in procession with tears of joy in his eyes, to meet and embrace his son, and all the magistrates and public officers attended him. The old men and the women marched out as far as the river Eurotas, lifting up their hands, and thanking the gods that Sparta was now cleared again of the disgrace and indignity that had befallen her, and once more saw the light of day. Since before, they tell us, the Spartan men, out of shame at their disasters, did not dare so much as to look their wives in the face.

When Epaminondas restored Messene, and recalled from all quarters the ancient citizens to inhabit it, they were not able to obstruct the design, being not in condition of appearing in the field against hem. But it went greatly against Agesilaus in the minds of his countrymen, when they found so large a territory, equal to their own in compass, and for fertility the richest of all Greece, which they had enjoyed so long, taken from them in his reign. Therefore it was that the king broke off treaty with the Thebans, when they offered him peace, rather than set his hand to the passing away of that country, though it was already taken from him. Which point of honor had like to have cost him dear; for not long after he was overreached by a stratagem, which had almost amounted to the loss of Sparta. For when the Mantineans again revolted from Thebes to Sparta, and Epaminondas understood that Agesilaus was come to their assistance with a powerful army, he privately in the night quitted his quarters at Tegea, and, unknown to the Mantineans, passing by Agesilaus, marched toward Sparta, insomuch that he failed very little of taking it empty and unarmed. Agesilaus had intelligence sent him by Euthynus, the Thespian, as Callisthenes says, but Xenophon says by a Cretan; and immediately despatched a horseman to Lacedæmon, to apprise them of it, and to let them know that he was hastening to them. Shortly after his arrival the Thebans crossed the Eurotas. They made an assault upon the town, and were received by Agesilaus with great courage, and with exertions beyond what was to be expected at his years. For he did not now fight with that caution and cunning which he formerly made use of, but put all upon a desperate push; which, though not his usual method, succeeded so well, that he rescued the city out of the very hands of Epaminondas, and forced him to retire, and, at the erection of a trophy, was able, in the presence of their wives and children, to declare that the Lacedæmonians had nobly paid their debt to their country, and particularly his son Archidamus, who had that day made himself illustrious, both by his courage and agility of body, rapidly passing about by the short lanes to every endangered point, and everywhere maintaining the town against the enemy with but few to help him. Isadas, however, the son of Phœbidas, must have been, I think, the admiration of the enemy as well as of his friends. He was a youth of remarkable beauty and stature, in the very flower of the most attractive time of life, when the boy is just rising into the man. He had no arms upon him, and scarcely clothes; he had just anointed himself at home, when, upon the alarm, without further awaiting in that undress, he snatched a spear in one hand, and a sword in the other, and broke his way through the combatants to the enemies, striking at all he met. He received no wound, whether it were that a special divine care rewarded his valor with an extraordinary protection, or whether his shape being so large and beautiful, and his dress so unusual, they thought him more than a man. The Ephors gave him a garland; but as soon as they had done so, they fined him a thousand drachmas, for going out to battle unarmed.

A few days after this there was another battle fought near Mantinea, in which Epaminondas, having routed the van of the Lacedæmonians, was eager in the pursuit of them, when Anticrates, the Laconian, vounded him with a spear, says Dioscorides; but the Spartans to this day call the posterity of this Anticrates, swordsmen, because he wounded Epaminondas with a sword. They so dreaded Epaminondas when living, that the slayer of him was embraced and admired by all; they decreed honors and gifts to him, and an exemption from taxes to his posterity, a privilege enjoyed at this day by Callicrates, one of his descendants.

Epaminondas being slain, there was a general peace again concluded, from which Agesilaus's party excluded the Messenians, as men that had no city, and therefore would not let them swear to the league; to which when the rest of the Greeks admitted them, the Lacedæmonians broke off, and continued the war alone, in hopes of subduing the Messenians. In this Agesilaus was esteemed a stubborn and head strong man, and insatiable of war, who took such pains to undermine the general peace, and to protract the war at a time when he had not money to carry it on with, but was forced to borrow of his friends and raise subscriptions, with much difficulty, while the city, above all things, needed repose. And all this to recover the one poor town of Messene, after he had lost so great an empire both by sea and land, as the Spartans were possessed of, when he began to reign.

But it added still more to his ill-repute when he put himself into the service of Tachos, the Egyptian. They thought it too unworthy of a man of his high station, who was then looked upon as the first commander in all Greece, who had filled all countries with his renown, to let himself out to hire to a barbarian, an Egyptian rebel (for Tachos was no better), and to fight for pay, as captain only of a band of mercenaries. If they said, at those years of eighty and odd, after his body had been worn out with age, and enfeebled with wounds, he had resumed that noble undertaking, the liberation of the

Greeks from Persia, i. had been worthy of some reproof. To make an action honorable, it ought to be agreeable to the age, and other circumstances of the person; since it is circumstance and proper measure that give an action its character, and make it either good or bad. But Agesilaus valued not other men's discourses; he thought no public employment dishonorable; the ignoblest thing in his esteem, was for a man to sit idle and useless at home, waiting for his death to come and take him. The money, therefore, that he received from Tachos, he laid out in raising men, with whom, having filled his ships, he took also thirty Spartan counsellors with him, as formerly he had done in his Asiatic expedition, and set sail for Egypt.

As soon as he arrived in Egypt, all the great officers of the kingdom came to pay their compliments to him at his landing. His reputation being so great, had raised the expectation of the whole country, and crowds flocked in to see him; but when they found, instead of the splendid prince whom they looked for, a little old man of contemptible appearance, without all ceremony lying down upon the grass, in coarse and threadbare clothes, they fell into laughter and scorn of him, crying out, that the old proverb was now made good, "The mountain had brought forth a mouse." They were yet more astonished at his stupidity, as they thought it, who, when presents were made him of all sorts of provisions, took only the meal, the calves, and the geese, but rejected the sweatmeats, the confections and perfumes; and when they urged him to the acceptance of them, took them and gave them to the helots in his army. Yet he was taken, Theophrastus tells us, with the garlands they made of the papyrus, because of their simplicity, and when he returned home, he demanded one of the king, which he carried with him.

When he joined with Tachos, he found his expectation of being general-in-chief disappointed. Tachos reserved that place for himself, making Agesilaus only captain of the mercenaries, and Chabrias, the Athenian, commander of the fleet. This was the first occasion of his discontent, but there followed others; he was compelled daily to submit to the insolence and vanity of this Egyptian, and was at length forced to attend him into Phœnicia, in a condition much below his character and dignity, which he bore and put up with for a time, till he had opportunity of showing his feelings. It was afforded him by Nectanabis, the cousin of Tachos, who commanded a large force under him, and shortly after de

serted him, and was proclaimed king by the Egyptians. Th
man invited Agesilaus to join his party, and the like he did
to Chabrias, offering great rewards to both. Tachos, suspecting it, immediately applied himself both to Agesilaus and
Chabrias, with great humility beseeching their continuance in
his friendship. Chabrias consented to it, and did what he
could by persuasion and good words to keep Agesilaus with
them. But he gave this short reply, "You, O Chabrias, came
hither a volunteer, and may go and stay as you see cause;
but I am the servant of Sparta, appointed to head the Egyptians, and therefore I cannot fight against whose to whom I
was sent as a friend, unless I am commanded to do so by my
country." This being said, he despatched messengers to
Sparta, who were sufficiently supplied with matter both for
dispraise of Tachos, and commendation of Nectanabis. The
two Egyptians also sent their ambassadors to Lacedæmon
the one to claim continuance of the league already made, the
other to make great offers for the breaking of it, and making
a new one. The Spartans having heard both sides, gave in
their public answer, that they referred the whole matter to
Agesilaus; but privately wrote to him, to act as he should
find it best for the profit of the commonwealth. Upon receipt of his orders, he at once changed sides, carrying all the
mercenaries with him to Nectanabis, covering with the plausible pretence of acting for the benefit of his country, a most
questionable piece of conduct, which, stripped of that disguise, in real truth was no better than downright treachery.
But the Lacedæmonians, who make it their first principle of
action to serve their country's interest, know not any thing to
be just or unjust by any measure but that.

Tachos, being thus deserted by the mercenaries, fled for
it; upon which a new king of the Mendesian province was
proclaimed his successor, and came against Nectanabis with
an army of one hundred thousand men. Nectanabis, in his
talk with Agesilaus, professed to despise them as newly
raised men, who, though many in number, were of no skill in
war, being most of them mechanics and tradesmen, never
bred to war. To whom Agesilaus answered, that he did not
fear their numbers, but did fear their ignorance, which gave
no room for employing stratagem against them. Stratagem
only avails with men who are alive to suspicion, and, expecting to be assailed, expose themselves by their attempts at defence; but one who has no thought or expectation of any
thing, gives as little opportunity to the enemy, as he who

stands stock-still does to a wrestler. The Mendesian was not wanting in solicitations of Agesilaus, insomuch that Nectanabis grew jealous. But when Agesilaus advised to fight the enemy at once, saying it was folly to protract the war and rely on time, in a contest with men who had no experience in fighting battles, but with their great numbers might be able to surround them, and cut off their communications by intrenchments, and anticipate them in many matters of advantage, this altogether confirmed him in his fears and suspicions. He took quite the contrary course, and retreated into a large and strongly fortified town. Agesilaus, finding himself mistrusted, took it very ill, and was full of indignation, yet was ashamed to changes sides back again, or to go away without effecting any thing, so that he was forced to follow Nectanabis into the town.

When the enemy came up, and began to draw lines about the town, and to intrench, the Egyptian now resolved upon a battle, out of fear of a siege. And the Greeks were eager for it, provisions growing already scarce in the town. When Agesilaus opposed it, the Egyptians then suspected him much more, publicly calling him the betrayer of the king. But Agesilaus, being now satisfied within himself, bore these reproaches patiently, and followed the design which he had laid, of overreaching the enemy, which was this.

The enemy were forming a deep ditch and high wall, resolving to shut up the garrison and starve it. When the ditch was brought almost quite round and the two ends had all but met, he took the advantage of the night, and armed all his Greeks. Then going to the Egyptian, "This, young man, is your opportunity," said he, " of saving yourself, which I all this while durst not announce, lest discovery should prevent it; but now the enemy has, at his own cost, and the pains and labor of his own men, provided for our security. As much of this wall as is built will prevent them from surrounding us with their multitude, the gap yet left will be sufficient for us to sally out by; now play the man, and follow the example the Greeks will give you, and by fighting valiantly, save yourself and your army; their front will not be able to stand against us, and their rear we are sufficiently secured from by a wall of their own making." Nectanabis, admiring the sagacity of Agesilaus, immediately placed himself in the middle of the Greek troops, and fought with them; and upon the first charge soon routed the enemy. Agesilaus having now gained credit with the king, proceeded to use, like a trick in wrestling, the same stratagem over again. He sometimes pretended a retreat, at other times advanced to attack their flanks, and by this means at last drew them into a place inclosed between two ditches that were very deep, and full of water. When he had them at this advantage, he soon charged them, drawing up the front of his battle equal to the space between the two ditches, so that they had no way of surrounding him, being inclosed themselves on both sides. They made but little resistance; many fell, others fled and were dispersed.

Nectanabis, being thus settled and fixed in his kingdom, with much kindness and affection invited Agesilaus to spend his winter in Egypt, but he made haste home to assist in wars of his own country, which was, he knew, in want of money, and forced to hire mercenaries, whilst their own men were fighting abroad. The king, therefore, dismissed him very honorably, and among other gifts presented him with two hundred and thirty talents of silver, toward the charge of the war. But the weather being tempestuous, his ships kept in shore, and passing along the coast of Africa he reached an uninhabited spot called the Port of Menelaus, and here, when his ships were just upon landing, he expired, being eighty-four years old, and having reigned in Lacedæmon forty-one. Thirty of which years he passed with the reputation of being the greatest and most powerful man of all Greece, and was looked upon as, in a manner, general and king of it, until the battle of Leuctra. It was the custom of the Spartans to bury their common dead in the place where they died, whatsoever country it was, but their kings they carried home. The followers of Agesilaus, for want of honey, inclosed his body in wax, and so conveyed him to Lacedæmon.

His son, Archidamus, succeeded him on his throne; so did his posterity successively to Agis, the fifth from Agesilaus; who was slain by Leonidas, while attempting to restore the ancient discipline of Sparta.

POMPEY.

The people of Rome seem to have entertained for Pompey from his childhood the same affection that Prometheus, in the tragedy of Æschylus, expresses for Hercules, speaking of him as the author of his deliverance, in these words,

> Ah cruel Sire! how dear thy son to me!
> The generous offspring of my enemy!

For on the one hand, never did the Romans give such demonstrations of a vehement and fierce hatred against any of their generals, as they did against Strabo, the father of Pompey ; during whose lifetime, it is true, they stood in awe of his military power, as indeed he was a formidable warrior, but immediately upon his death, which happened by a stroke of thunder, they treated him with the utmost contumely, dragging his corpse from the bier, as it was carried to his funeral. On the other side, never had any Roman the people's goodwill and devotion more zealous throughout all the changes of fortune, more early in its first springing up, or more steadily rising with his prosperity, or more constant in his adversity, than Pompey had. In Strabo, there was one great cause of their hatred, his insatiable covetousness ; in Pompey, there were many that helped to make him the object of their love ; his temperance, his skill, and exercise in war, his eloquence of speech, integrity of mind, and affability in conversation and address ; insomuch that no man ever asked a favor with less offence, or conferred one with a better grace. When he gave, it was without assumption; when he received, it was with dignity and honor.

In his youth, his countenance pleaded for him, seeming to anticipate his eloquence, and win upon the affections of the people before he spoke. His beauty even in his bloom of youth had something in it at once of gentleness and dignity ; and when his prime of manhood came, the majesty and kingliness of his character at once became visible in it. His hair sat somewhat hollow or rising a little ; and this, with the languishing motion of his eyes, seemed to form a resemblance in his face, though perhaps more talked of than really apparent, to the statues of the king Alexander. And because many applied that name to him in his youth, Pompey himself did not decline it, insomuch that some called him so in derision. And Lucius Philippus, a man of consular dignity, when he was pleading in favor of him, thought it not unfit to say, that people could not be surprised if Philip was a lover of Alexander.

It is related of Flora, the courtesan, that when she was now pretty old, she took great delight in speaking of her early familiarity with Pompey, and was wont to say that she could never part after being with him without a bite. She would further tell, that Geminius a companion of Pompey's, fell in love with her, and made his court with great importunity; and on her refusing, and telling him, however her inclinations were, yet she could not gratify his desires for Pompey's sake, he therefore made his request to Pompey, and Pompey frankly gave his consent, but never afterwards would have any converse with her, notwithstanding that he seemed to have a great passion for her; and Flora, on this occasion, showed none of the levity that might have been expected of her, but languished for some time after under a sickness brought on by grief and desire. This Flora, we are told, was such a celebrated beauty, that Cæcilius Metellus, when he adorned the temple of Castor and Pollux with paintings and statues, among the rest dedicated hers for her singular beauty. In his conduct also to the wife of Demetrius, his freed servant (who had great influence with him in his lifetime, and left an estate of four thousand talents), Pompey acted contrary to his usual habits, not quite fairly or generously, fearing lest he should fall under the common censure of being enamored and charmed with her beauty, which was irresistible, and became famous everywhere. Nevertheless, though he seemed to be so extremely circumspect and cautious, yet even in matters of this nature, he could not avoid the calumnies of his enemies, but upon the score of married women, they accused him, as if he had connived at many things, and embezzled the public revenue to gratify their luxury.

Of his easiness of temper and plainness, in what related to eating and drinking, the story is told, that once in a sickness, when his stomach nauseated common meats, his physician prescribed him a thrush to eat; but upon search, there was none to be bought, for they were not then in season, and one telling him they were to be had at Lucullus's, who kept them all the year round, "So then," said he, "if it were not for Lucullus's luxury, Pompey should not live;" and thereupon not minding the prescription of the physician, he contented himself with such meat as could easily be procured. But this was at a later time.

Being as yet a very young man, and upon an expedition in which his father was commanding against Cinna, he had in his tent with him one Lucius Terentius, as his companion and comrade, who, being corrupted by Cinna, entered into an engagement to kill Pompey, as others had done to set the general's tent on fire. This conspiracy being discovered to Pompey at supper, he showed no discomposure at it, but on the contrary drank more liberally than usual, and expressed great kindness to Terentius; but about bedtime, pretending to go to his repose, he stole away secretly out of the tent, and setting a guard about his father, quietly expected the event. Terentius, when he thought the proper time come, rose with his naked sword and coming to Pompey's bedside, stabbed several strokes through the bed-clothes, as if he were lying there. Immediately after this there was a great uproar throughout all the camp, arising from the hatred they bore to the general, and an universal movement of the soldiers to revolt, all tearing down their tents, and betaking themselves to their arms. The general himself all this while durst not venture out because of the tumult; but Pompey, going about in the midst of them, besought them with tears; and at last threw himself prostrate upon his face before the gate of the camp, and lay there in the passage at their feet, shedding tears, and bidding those that were marching off, if they would go, trample upon him. Upon which, none could help going back again, and all, except eight hundred, either through shame or compassion, repented, and were reconciled to the general.

Immediately upon the death of Strabo, there was an action commenced against Pompey, as his heir, for that his father had embezzled the public treasure. But Pompey, having traced the principal thefts, charged them upon one Alexander, a freed slave of his father's, and proved before the judges that he had been the appropriator. But he himself was accused of having in his possession some hunting tackle, and books, that were taken at Asculum. To this he confessed thus far, that he received them from his father when he took Asculum, but pleaded further, that he had lost them since, upon Cinna's return to Rome, when his house was broken open and plundered by Cinna's guards. In this cause he had a great many preparatory pleadings against his accuser, in which he showed an activity and steadfastness beyond his years, and gained great reputation and favor, insomuch that Antistius, the prætor and judge of the cause, took a great liking to him, and offered him his daughter in marriage, having had some communications with his friends about it. Pompey accepted the proposal, and they were privately contracted; however, the secret was not so closely kept as to escape the multitude, but it was discernible enough, from the favor shown him by Antistius in his cause. And at last, when Antistius pronounced the absolutory sentence of the judges, the people, as if it had been upon a signal given, made the acclamation used according to ancient custom, at marriages, *Talasio.* The origin of which custom is related to be this. At the time when the daughters of the Sabines came to Rome, to see the shows and sports there, and were violently seized upon by the most distinguished and bravest of the Romans for wives, it happened that some goatswains and herdsmen of the meaner rank were carrying off a beautiful and tall maiden; and lest any of their betters should meet them, and take her away, as they ran, they cried out with one voice, *Talasio*, Talasius being a well known and popular person among them, in so much that all that heard the name, clapped their hands for joy, and joined with them in the shout, as applauding and congratulating the chance. Now, say they, because this proved a fortunate match to Talasius, hence it is that this acclamation is sportively used as a nuptial cry at all weddings. This is the most credible of the accounts that are given of the Talasio. And some few days after this judgment, Pompey married Antistia.

After this he went to Cinna's camp, where, finding some false suggestions and calumnies prevailing against him, he began to be afraid, and presently withdrew himself secretly; which sudden disappearance occasioned great suspicion. And there went a rumor and speech through all the camp, that Cinna had murdered the young man; upon which all that had been anyways disobliged, and bore any malice to him, resolved to make an assault upon him. He, endeavoring to make his escape, was seized by a centurion, who pursued him with his naked sword. Cinna, in this distress, fell upon his knees, and offered him his seal-ring, of great value, for his ransom; but the centurion repulsed him insolently, saying, "I did not come to seal a covenant, but to be revenged upon a lawless and wicked tyrant;" and so dispatched him immediately.

Thus Cinna being slain, Carbo, a tyrant yet more senseless than he, took the command and exercised it, while Sylla meantime was approaching, much to the joy and satisfaction of most people, who in their present evils were ready to find some comfort if it were but in the exchange of a master. For the city was brought to that pass by oppression and calamities, that, being utterly in despair of liberty, men were only anxious for the mildest and most tolerable bondage. At that time Pompey was in Picenum in Italy, where he spent some time amusing himself, as he had estates in the country there though the chief motive of his stay was the liking he felt for the towns of that district, which all regarded him with hereditary feelings of kindness and attachment. But when he now saw that the noblest and best of the city began to forsake their homes and property, and fly from all quarters to Sylla's camp, as to their haven, he likewise was desirous to go; not, however, as a fugitive, alone and with nothing to offer, but as a friend rather than a suppliant, in a way that would gain him honor, bringing help along with him, and at the head of a body of troops. Accordingly he solicited the Picentines for their assistance, who as cordially embraced his motion, and rejected the messengers sent from Carbo; insomuch that a certain Vindius taking upon him to say that Pompey was come from the school-room to put himself at the head of the people, they were so incensed that they fell forthwith upon this Vindius and killed him. From henceforward Pompey, finding a spirit of government upon him, though not above twenty-three years of age, nor deriving an authority by commission from any man, took the privilege to grant himself full power, and, causing a tribunal to be erected in the market-place of Auximum, a populous city, expelled two of their principal men, brothers, of the name of Ventidius, who were acting against him in Carbo's interest, commanding them by a public edict to depart the city; and then proceeded to levy soldiers, issuing out commissions to centurions and other officers, according to the form of military discipline. And in this manner he went round all the rest of the cities in the district. So that those of Carbo's faction flying, and all others cheerfully submitting to his command, in a little time he mustered three entire legions, having supplied himself besides with all manner of provisions, beasts of burden, carriages, and other necessaries of war. And with this equipage he set forward on his march towards Sylla, not as if he were in haste, or desirous of escaping observation, but by small journeys, making several halts upon the road, to distress and annoy the enemy, and exerting himself to detach from Carbo's interest every part of Italy that he passed through.

Three commanders of the enemy encountered him at once, Carinna, Cloelius, and Brutus, and drew up their forces, not all in the front, nor yet together on any one part, but encamping three several armies in a circle about him, they resolved to encompass and overpower him. Pompey was no way alarmed at this, but collecting all his troops into one body, and placing his horse in the front of the battle, where he himself was in person, he singled out and bent all his forces against Brutus, and when the Celtic horsemen from the enemy's side rode out to meet him, Pompey himself encountering hand to hand with the foremost and stoutest among them, killed him with his spear. The rest seeing this turned their backs, and fled, and breaking the ranks of their own foot, presently caused a general rout; whereupon the commanders fell out among themselves, and marched off, some one way, some another, as their fortunes led them, and the towns round about came in and surrendered themselves to Pompey, concluding that the enemy was dispersed for fear. Next after these, Scipio, the consul, came to attack him, and with as little success; for before the armies could join, or be within the throw of their javelins, Scipio's soldiers saluted Pompey's, and came over to them, while Scipio made his escape by flight. Last of all, Carbo himself sent down several troops of horse against him by the river Arsis, which Pompey assailed with the same courage and success as before; and having routed and put them to flight, he forced them in the pursuit into difficult ground, unpassable for horse, where, seeing no hopes of escape, they yielded themselves with their horses and armor, all to his mercy.

Sylla was hitherto unacquainted with all these actions; and on the first intelligence he received of his movements was in great anxiety about him, fearing lest he should be cut off among so many and such experienced commanders of the enemy, and marched therefore with all speed to his aid. Now Pompey, having advice of his approach, sent out orders to his officers, to marshal and draw up all his forces in full array, that they might make the finest and noblest appearance before the commander-in-chief; for he expected indeed great honors from him, but met with even greater. For as soon as Sylla saw him thus advancing, his army so well appointed, his men so young and strong, and their spirits so high and hopeful with their successes, he alighted from his horse, and being first, as was his due, saluted by them with the title of Imperator, he returned the salutation upon Pompey, in the same term and style of Imperator, which might well cause surprise, as none could have ever anticipated that he would have imparted, to one so young in years and not yet a senator, a title which was the object of contention between him and the Scipios and Marii. And indeed all the rest of his deportment was agreeable to this first compliment; whenever Pompey came into his presence, he paid some sort of respect to him, either in rising and being uncovered, or the like, which he was rarely seen to do with any one else, notwithstanding that there were many about him of great rank and honor.

Yet Pompey was not puffed up at all, or exalted with these favors. And when Sylla would have sent him with all expedition into Gaul, a province in which it was thought Metellus who commanded in it had done nothing worthy of the large forces at his disposal, Pompey urged that it could not be fair or honorable for him to take a province out of the hands of his senior in command and his superior in reputation; however, if Metellus were willing, and should request his service, he should be very ready to accompany and assist him in the war. Which when Metellus came to understand, he approved of the proposal, and invited him over by letter. And on this Pompey fell immediately into Gaul, where he not only achieved wonderful exploits of himself, but also fired up and kindled again that bold and warlike spirit, which old age had in a manner extinguished in Metellus, into a new heat; just as molten copper, they say, when poured upon that which is cold and solid, will dissolve and melt it faster than fire itself. But as when a famous wrestler has gained the first place among men, and borne away the prizes at all the games, it is not usual to take account of his victories as a boy, or to enter them upon record among the rest; so with the exploits of Pompey in his youth, though they were extraordinary in themselves, yet because they were obscured and buried in the multitude and greatness of his later wars and conquests, I dare not be particular in them, lest, by trifling away time in the lesser moments of his youth, we should be driven to omit those greater actions and fortunes which best illustrate his character.

Now, when Sylla had brought all Italy under his dominion, and was proclaimed dictator, he began to reward the rest of his followers, by giving them wealth, appointing them to offices in the state, and granting them freely and without restriction any favors they asked for. But as for Pompey, admiring his valor and conduct, and thinking that he might prove a great stay and support to him hereafter in his affairs, he sought means to attach him to himself by some personal alliance, and his wife Metella joining in his wishes, they two persuaded Pompey to put away Antistia, and marry Æmilia, the stepdaughter of Sylla, born by Metella to Scaurus, her former husband, she being at that very time the wife of another man, living with him, and with child by him. These were the very tyrannies of marriage, and much more agreeable to the times under Sylla, than to the nature and habits of Pompey; that Æmilia great with child should be, as it were, ravished from the embraces of another for him, and that Antistia should be divorced with dishonor and misery, by him, for whose sake she had been but just before bereft of her father. For Antistius was murdered in the senate, because he was suspected to be a favorer of Sylla for Pompey's sake; and her mother likewise, after she had seen all these indignities, made away with herself, a new calamity to be added to the tragic accompaniments of this marriage, and that there might be nothing wanting to complete them, Æmilia herself died, almost immediately after entering Pompey's house in childbed.

About this time news came to Sylla, that Perpenna was fortifying himself in Sicily, that the island was now become a refuge and receptacle for the relics of the adverse party, that Carbo was hovering about those seas with a navy, that Domitius had fallen in upon Africa, and that many of the exiled men of note who had escaped from the proscriptions were daily flocking into those parts. Against these, therefore, Pompey was sent with a large force; and no sooner was he arrived in Sicily, but Perpenna immediately departed, leaving the whole island to him. Pompey received the distressed cities into favor, and treated all with great humanity, except the Mamertines in Messena; for when they protested against his court and jurisdiction, alleging their privilege and exemption founded upon an ancient charter or grant of the Romans, he replied sharply, "What! will you never cease prating of laws to us that have swords by our sides?" It was thought, likewise, that he showed some inhumanity to Carbo, seeming rather to insult over his misfortunes, than to chastise his crimes. For if there had been a necessity, as perhaps there was, that he should be taken off, that might have been done at first, as soon as he was taken prisoner, for then it would have been the act of him that commanded it. But here Pompey commanded a man that had been thrice consul of Rome, to be brought in fetters to stand at the bar, he himself sitting upon the bench in judgment, examining the cause with the formalities of law, to the offence and indignation of all that were present, and afterwards ordered him to be taken away and put to death. It is related, by the way, of Carbo, that as soon as he was brought to the place, and saw the sword drawn for execution, he was suddenly seized with a looseness or pain in his bowels, and desired a little respite of the executioner, and a convenient place to relieve himself. And yet further, Caius Oppius, the friend of Cæsar, tells us, that Pompey dealt cruelly with Quintus Valerius, a man of singular learning and science. For when he was brought to him, he walked aside, and drew him into conversation, and after putting a variety of questions to him, and receiving answers from him, he ordered his officers to take him away, and put him to death. But we must not be too credulous in the case of narratives told by Oppius, especially when he undertakes to relate any thing touching the friends or foes of Cæsar. This is certain, that there lay a necessity upon Pompey to be severe upon many of Sylla's enemies, those at least that were eminent persons in themselves, and notoriously known to be taken; but for the rest, he acted with all the clemency possible for him, conniving at the concealment of some, and himself being the instrument in the escape of others. So in the case of the Himeræans; for when Pompey had determined on severely punishing their city, as they had been abettors of the enemy, Sthenis, the leader of the people there, craving liberty of speech, told him, that what he was about to do was not at all consistent with justice, for that he would pass by the guilty, and destroy the innocent; and on Pompey demanding who that guilty person was that would assume the offences of them all, Sthenis replied, it was himself, who had engaged his friends by persuasion to what they had done, and his enemies by force; whereupon Pompey being much taken with the frank speech and noble spirit of the man, first forgave his crime, and then pardoned all the rest of the Himeræans. Hearing, likewise, that his soldiers were very disorderly in their march, doing violence upon the roads, he ordered their swords to be sealed up in their scabbards, and whosoever kept them not so, were severely punished.

Whilst Pompey was thus busy in the affairs and government of Sicily, he received a decree of the senate, and a commission from Sylla, commanding him forthwith to sail into Africa, and make war upon Domitius with all his forces: for Domitius had rallied up a far greater army than Marius had had not long since, when he sailed out of Africa into Italy, and caused a revolution in Rome, and himself, of a fugitive outlaw, became a tyrant. Pompey, therefore, having prepared every thing with the utmost speed, left Memmius, his sister's husband, governor of Sicily, and set sail with one hundred and twenty galleys, and eight hundred other vessels laden with provisions, money, ammunition, and engines of battery. He arrived with his fleet, part at the port of Utica, part at Carthage; and no sooner was he landed, but seven thousand of the enemy revolted and came over to him, while his own forces that he brought with him consisted of six entire legions.

Here they tell us of a pleasant incident that happened to him at his first arrival. For some of his soldiers having by accident stumbled upon a treasure, by which they got a good sum of money, the rest of the army hearing this, began to fancy that the field was full of gold and silver, which had been hid there of old by the Carthaginians in the time of their calamities, and thereupon fell to work, so that the army was useless to Pompey for many days, being totally engaged in digging for the fancied treasure, he himself all the while walking up and down only, and laughing to see so many thousands together, digging and turning up the earth Until at last, growing weary and hopeless, they came to themselves and returned to their general, begging him to lead them where he pleased, for that they had already received the punishment of their folly. By this time Domitius had prepared himself and drawn out his army in array against Pompey; but there was a watercourse betwixt them, craggy, and difficult to pass over; and this, together with a great storm of wind and rain pouring down even from break of day, seemed to leave but little possibility of their coming together; so that Domitius, not expecting any engagement that day, commanded his forces to draw off and retire to the camp. Now Pompey, who was watchful upon every occasion, making use of the opportunity ordered a march forthwith, and having passed over the torrent, fell in immediately upon their quarters. The enemy was in a great disorder and tumult, and in that confusion attempted a resistance; but they neither were all there, nor supported one another; besides, the wind having veered about, beat the rain full in their faces. Neither indeed was the storm less troublesome to the Romans, for that they could not clearly discern one another, insomuch that even Pompey himself, being unknown, escaped narrowly; for when one of his soldiers demanded of him the word of battle, it happened that he was somewhat slow in his answer, which might have cost him his life.

The enemy being routed with a great slaughter (for it is said, that of twenty thousand there escaped but three thousand), the army saluted Pompey by the name of Imperator; but he declined it, telling them that he could not by any means accept of that title, as long as he saw the camp of the enemy standing; but if they designed to make him worthy of the honor, they must first demolish that. The soldiers on hearing this, went at once and made an assault upon the works and trenches, and there Pompey fought without his helmet, in memory of his former danger, and to avoid the like. The camp was thus taken by storm, and among the rest, Domitius was slain. After that overthrow, the cities of the country thereabouts were all either secured by surrender, or taken by storm. King Iarbas, likewise, a confederate and auxiliary of Domitius, was taken prisoner, and his kingdom was given to Hiempsal.

Pompey could not rest here, but being ambitious to follow the good fortune and use the valor of his army, entered Numidia; and marching forward many days' journey up into the country, he conquered all wherever he came. And having revived the terror of the Roman power, which was now almost obliterated among the barbarous nations, he said likewise, that the wild beasts of Africa ought not to be left without some experience of the courage and success of the Romans; and therefore he bestowed some few days in hunting lions and elephants. And it is said, that it was not above the space of forty days at the utmost, in which he gave a total overthrow to the enemy, reduced Africa, and established the affairs of the kings and kingdoms of all that country, being then in the twenty-fourth year of his age.

When Pompey returned back to the city of Utica, there were presented to him letters and orders from Sylla, commanding him to disband the rest of his army, and himself with one legion only to wait there the coming of another general, to succeed him in the government. This, inwardly, was extremely grievous to Pompey, though he made no show of it. But the army resented it openly, and when Pompey besought them to depart and go home before him, they began to revile Sylla, and declared broadly, that they were resolved not to forsake him, neither did they think it safe for him to trust the tyrant. Pompey at first endeavored to appease and pacify them by fair speeches; but when he saw that his persuasions were vain, he left the bench, and retired to his tent with tears in his eyes. But the soldiers followed him, and seizing upon him, by force brought him again, and placed him in his tribunal; where great part of that day was spent in dispute, they on their part persuading him to stay and command them, he, on the other side, pressing upon them obedience, and the danger of mutiny. At last, when they grew yet more importunate and clamorous, he swore that he would kill himself if they attempted to force him; and scarcely even thus appeased them. Nevertheless, the first tidings brought to Sylla were, that Pompey was up in rebellion; on which he remarked to some of his friends, "I see, then, it is my destiny to contend with children in my old age;" alluding at the same time to Marius, who, being but a mere youth, had given him great trouble, and brought him into extreme danger. But being undeceived afterwards by better intelligence, and finding the whole city prepared to meet Pompey, and receive him with every display of kindness and honor, he resolved to exceed them all. And, therefore, going out foremost to meet him, and embracing him with great cordiality, he gave him his welcome aloud in the title of Magnus, or the Great, and bade all that were present call him by that name. Others say that he had this title first given him by a general acclamation of all the army in Africa, but that it was fixed upon him by this ratification of Sylla. It is certain that he himself was the last that owned the title; for it was a long time after, when he was sent proconsul into Spain against Sertorius, that he began to write himself in his letters and commissions by the name of Pompeius Magnus; common and familiar use having then worn off the invidiousness of the title. And one cannot but accord respect and admiration to the ancient Romans, who did not reward the successes of action and conduct in war alone with such honorable titles, but adorned likewise the virtues and services of eminent men in civil government with the same distinctions and marks of honor. Two persons received from the people the name of Maximus, or the Greatest, Valerius, for reconciling the senate and people, and Fabius Rullus, because he put out of the senate certain sons of freed slaves who had been admitted into it because of their wealth.

Pompey now desired the honor of a triumph, which Sylla opposed, alleging that the law allowed that honor to none but consuls and prætors, and therefore Scipio the elder, who subdued the Carthaginians in Spain in far greater and nobler conflicts, never petitioned for a triumph, because he had never been consul or prætor; and if Pompey, who had scarcely yet fully grown a beard, and was not of age to be a senator, should enter the city in triumph, what a weight of envy would it bring, he said, at once upon his government and Pompey's honor. This was his language to Pompey, intimating that he could not by any means yield to his request, but if he would persist in his ambition, that he was resolved to interpose his power to humble him. Pompey, however, was not daunted; but bade Sylla recollect, that more worshipped the rising than the setting sun; as if to tell him that his power was increasing, and Sylla's in the wane. Sylla did not perfectly hear the words, but observing a sort of amazement and wonder in the looks and gestures of those that did hear them, he asked what it was that he said. When it was told him, he seemed astounded at Pompey's boldness, and cried out twice together, "Let him triumph," and when others began to show their disapprobation and offence at it, Pompey, it is said, to gall and vex them the more, designed to have his triumphant chariot drawn with four elephants (having brought over several which belonged to the African kings), but the gates of the city being too narrow, he was forced to desist from that project, and be content with horses. And when his soldiers, who had not received as large rewards as they had expected, began to clamor, and interrupt the triumph, Pompey regarded these as little as the rest and plainly told them that he had rather lose the honor of his triumph, than flatter them. Upon which Servilius, a man of great distinction, and at first one of the chief opposers of Pompey's triumph, said, he now perceived that Pompey was truly great and worthy of a triumph. It is clear that he might easily have been a senator, also, if he had wished, but he did not sue for that, being ambitious, it seems, only of unusual honors. For what wonder had it been for Pompey to sit in the senate before his time? But to triumph before he was in the senate, was really an excess of glory.

And, moreover, it did not a little ingratiate him with the people; who were much pleased to see him after his triumph take his place again among the Roman knights. On the other side, it was no less distasteful to Sylla to see how fast he came on, and to what a height of glory and power he was advancing; yet being ashamed to hinder him, he kept quiet. But when, against his direct wishes, Pompey got Lepidus made consul, having openly joined in the canvass and, by the goodwill the people felt for himself, conciliated their favor for Lepidus, Sylla could forbear no longer; but when he saw him coming away from the election through the forum with a great train ofter him, cried out to him, "Well, young man, I see you rejoice in your victory. And, indeed, is it not a most generous and worthy act, that the consulship should be given to Lepidus, the vilest of men, in preference to Catulus, the best and most deserving in the city, and all by your influence with the people? It will be well, however, for you to be wakeful and look to your interests; as you have been making your enemy stronger than yourself." But that which gave the clearest demonstration of Sylla's ill-will to Pompey, was his last will and testament; for whereas he had bequeathed several legacies to all the rest of his friends, and appointed some of them guardians to his son, he passed by Pompey without the least remembrance. However, Pompey bore this with great moderation and temper; and when Lepidus and others were disposed to obstruct his interment in the Campus Martius, and to prevent any public funeral taking place, came forward in support of it, and saw his obsequies performed with all honor and security.

Shortly after the death of Sylla, his prophetic words were fulfilled; and Lepidus proposing to be the successor to all his power and authority, without any ambiguities or pretences, immediately appeared in arms, rousing once more and gathering about him all the long dangerous remains of the old factions, which had escaped the hand of Sylla. Catulus, his colleague, who was followed by the sounder part of the senate and people, was a man of the greatest esteem among the Romans for wisdom and justice; but his talent lay in the government of the city rather than the camp, whereas the exigency required the skill of Pompey. Pompey, therefore, was not long in suspense which way to dispose of himself, but joining with the nobility, was presently appointed general of the army against Lepidus, who had already raised up war in great part of Italy, and held Cisalpine Gaul in subjection with an army under Brutus. As for the rest of his garrisons, Pompey subdued them with ease in his march, but Mutina in Gaul resisted in a formal siege, and he lay here a long time encamped against Brutus. In the mean time Lepidus marched in all haste against Rome, and sitting down before it with a crowd of followers, to the terror of those within, demanded a second consulship. But that fear quickly vanished upon letters sent from Pompey, announcing that he had ended the war without a battle; for Brutus, either betraying his army, or being betrayed by their revolt, surrendered himself to Pompey, and receiving a guard of horse, was conducted to a little town upon the river Po, where he was slain the next day by Geminius, in execution of Pompey's commands. And for this Pompey was much censured; for, having at the beginning of the revolt written to the senate that Brutus had voluntarily surrendered himself, immediately afterward he sent other letters, with matter of accusation against the man after he was taken off. Brutus who, with Cassius, slew Cæsar, was son to this Brutus; neither in war nor in his death like his father, as appears at large in his life. Lepidus upon this being driven out of Italy, fled to Sardinia, where he fell sick and died of sorrow, not for his public misfortunes, as they say, but upon the discovery of a letter proving his wife to have been unfaithful to him

There yet remained Sertorius, a very different general from Lepidus, in possession of Spain, and making himself formidable to Rome; the final disease, as it were, in which the scattered evils of the civil wars had now collected. He had already cut off various inferior commanders, and was at this time coping with Metellus Pius, a man of repute and a good soldier, though perhaps he might now seem too slow, by reason of his age, to second and improve the happier moments of war, and might be sometimes wanting to those advantages which Sertorius, by his quickness and dexterity, would wrest out of his hands. For Sertorius was always hovering about, and coming upon him unawares, like a captain of thieves rather than soldiers, disturbing him perpetually with ambuscades and light skirmishes; whereas Metellus was accustomed to regular conduct, and fighting in battle array with full-armed soldiers. Pompey, therefore, keeping his army in readiness, made it his object to be sent in aid to Metellus; neither would he be induced to disband his forces, notwithstanding that Catulus called upon him to do so, but by some colorable device or other he still kept them in arms about the city, until the senate at last thought fit, upon the report of Lucius Philippus, to decree him that government. At that time, they say, one of the senators there expressing his wonder and demanding of Philippus whether his meaning was that Pompey should be sent into Spain as proconsul, "No," replied Philippus, "but as pro-*consuls*," as if both consuls for that year were in his opinion wholly useless.

When Pompey was arrived in Spain, as is usual upon the fame of a new leader, men began to be inspired with new hopes, and those nations that had not entered into a very strict alliance with Sertorius, began to waver and revolt; whereupon Sertorius uttered various arrogant and scornful speeches against Pompey, saying in derision, that he should want no other weapon but a ferula and rod to chastise this boy with, if he were not afraid of that old woman, meaning Metellus. Yet in deed and reality he stood in awe of Pompey, and kept on his guard against him, as appeared by his whole management of the war, which he was observed to conduct much more warily than before; for Metellus, which one would not have imagined, was grown excessively luxurious in his habits, hav ing given himself over to self-indulgence and pleasure, and from a moderate and temperate, became suddenly a sumptuous and ostentatious liver, so that this very thing gained Pompey great reputation and good-will, as he made himself somewhat specially an example of frugality, although that virtue was habitual in him, and required no great industry to exercise it, as he was naturally inclined to temperance, and no ways inordinate in his desires. The fortune of the war was very various; nothing, however, annoyed Pompey so much as the taking of the town of Lauron by Sertorius. For when Pompey thought he had him safe inclosed, and had boasted somewhat largely of raising the siege, he found himself all of a sudden encompassed; insomuch that he durst not move out of his camp, but was forced to sit still whilst the city was taken and burnt before his face. However, afterwards in a battle near Valentia, he gave a great defeat to Herennius and Perpenna, two commanders among the refugees who had fled to Sertorius, and now lieutenants under him, in which he slew above ten thousand men.

Pompey, being elated and filled with confidence by this victory, made all haste to engage Sertorius himself, and the rather lest Metellus should come in for a share in the honor of the victory. Late in the day towards sunset, they joined battle near the river Sucro, both being in fear lest Metellus should come: Pompey, that he might engage alone, Sertorius, that he might have one alone to engage with. The issue of the battle proved doubtful, for a wing of each side had the better, but of the generals, Sertorius had the greater honor, for that he maintained his post, having put to flight the entire division that was opposed to him, whereas Pompey was himself almost made a prisoner; for being set upon by a strong man at arms that fought on foot (he being on horseback), as they were closely engaged hand to hand, the strokes of their swords chanced to light upon their hands, but with a different success; for Pompey's was a slight wound only, whereas he cut off the others hand. However, it happened so, that many now falling upon Pompey together, and his own forces there being put to the rout, he made his escape beyond expectation, by quitting his horse, and turning him out among the enemy. For the horse being richly adorned with golden trappings, and having a caparison of great value, the soldiers quarrelled among themselves for the booty, so that while they were fighting with one another, and dividing the spoil, Pompey made his escape

By break of day the next morning, each drew out his forces into the field to claim the victory; but Metellus coming up, Sertorius vanished, having broken up and dispersed his army. For this was the way in which he used to raise and disband his armies, so that sometimes he would be wandering up and down all alone, and at other times again he would come pouring into the field at the head of no less than one hundred and fifty thousand fighting men, swelling of a sudden like a winter torrent.

When Pompey was going, after the battle, to meet and welcome Metellus, and when they were near one another, he commanded his attendants to lower their rods in honor of Metellus, as his senior and superior. But Metellus on the other side forbade it, and behaved himself in general very obligingly to him, not claiming any prerogative either in respect of his consular rank or seniority; excepting only that when they encamped together, the watchword was given to the whole camp by Metellus. But generally they had their camps asunder, being divided and distracted by the enemy, who took all shapes, and being always in motion, would by some skilful artifice appear in a variety of places almost in the same instant, drawing them from one attack to another, and at last keeping them from foraging, wasting the country, and holding the dominion of the sea, Sertorius drove them both out of that part of Spain which was under his control, and forced them, for want of necessaries, to retreat into provinces that did not belong to them.

Pompey, having made use of and expended the greatest part of his own private revenues upon the war, sent and demanded moneys of the senate, adding, that in case they did not furnish him speedily, he should be forced to return into Italy with his army. Lucullus being consul at that time, though at variance with Pompey, yet in consideration that he himself was a candidate for the command against Mithridates, procured and hastened these supplies, fearing lest there should be any pretence, or occasion given to Pompey of returning home, who of himself was no less desirous of leaving Sertorius, and of undertaking the war against Mithridates, as an enterprise which by all appearance would prove much more honorable and not so dangerous. In the meantime Sertorius died, being treacherously murdered by some of his own party; and Perpenna, the chief among them, took the command, and attempted to carry on the same enterprises with Sertorius, having indeed the same forces and the same means, only wanting the same skill and conduct in the use of them. Pompey therefore marched directly against Perpenna, and finding him acting merely at random in his affairs, had a decoy ready for him, and sent out a detachment of ten cohorts into the level country with orders to range up and down and disperse themselves abroad. The bait took accordingly, and no sooner had Perpenna turned upon the prey and had them in chase, but Pompey appeared suddenly with all his army and joining battle, gave him a total overthrow. Most of his officers were slain in the field, and he himself being brought prisoner to Pompey, was by his order put to death. Neither was Pompey guilty in this of ingratitude or unmindfulness of what had occurred in Sicily, which some have laid to his charge, but was guided by a high-minded policy and a deliberate counsel for the security of his country. For Perpenna, having in his custody all Sertorius's papers, offered to produce several letters from the greatest men in Rome, who, desirous of a change and subversion of the government, had invited Sertorius into Italy. And Pompey, fearing that these might be the occasion of worse wars than those which were now ended, thought it advisable to put Perpenna to death, and burnt the letters without reading them.

Pompey continued in Spain after this so long a time as was necessary for the suppression of all the greatest disorders in the province ; and after moderating and allaying the more violent heats of affairs there, returned with his army into Italy, where he arrived, as chance would have it, in the height of the servile war. Accordingly, upon his arrival, Crassus, the commander in that war, at some hazard, precipitated a battle, in which he had great success, and slew upon the place twelve thousand three hundred of the insurgents. Nor yet was he so quick, but that fortune reserved to Pompey some share of honor in the success of this war, for five thousand of those that had escaped out of the battle fell into his hands ; and when he had totally cut them off, he wrote to the senate that Crassus had overthrown the slaves in battle, but that he had plucked up the whole war by the roots. And it was agreeable in Rome both thus to say, and thus to hear said, because of the general favor of Pompey. But of the Spanish war and the conquest of Sertorius, no one, even in jest, could have ascribed the honor to any one else. Nevertheless, all this high respect for him, and this desire to see him come home, were not unmixed with apprehensions and suspicions that he might perhaps not disband his army, but take his way by the force of arms and a supreme command to the seat of Sylla. And so in the number of all those that ran out to meet him and congratulate his return, as many went out of fear as affection. But after Pompey had removed this alarm, by declaring beforehand that he would discharge the army after his triumph, those that envied him could now only complain that he affected popularity, courting the common people more than the nobility, and that whereas Sylla had abolished the tribuneship of the people, he designed to gratify the people by restoring that office, which was indeed the fact. For there was not any one thing that the people of Rome were more wildly eager for, or more passionately desired, than the restoration of that office, insomuch that Pompey thought himself extremely fortunate in this opportunity, despairing (if he were anticipated by some one else in this) of ever meeting with any other sufficient means of expressing his gratitude for the favors which he had received from the people.

Though a second triumph was decreed him, and he was declared consul, yet all these honors did not seem so great an evidence of his power and glory, as the ascendant which he had over Crassus; for he, the wealthiest among all the statesmen of his time, and the most eloquent and greatest too, who had looked down on Pompey himself, and on all others beneath him, durst not appear a candidate for the consulship before he had applied to Pompey. The request was made accordingly, and was eagerly embraced by Pompey, who had long sought an occasion to oblige him in some friendly office; so that he solicited for Crassus, and entreated the people heartily, declaring, that their favor would be no less to him in choosing Crassus his colleague, than in making himself consul. Yet for all this, when they were created consuls, they were always at variance, and opposing one another. Crassus prevailed most in the senate, and Pompey's power was no less with the people, he having restored to them the office of tribune, and having allowed the courts of judicature to be transferred back to the knights by a new law. He himself in person, too, afforded them a most grateful spectacle, when he appeared and craved his discharge from the military service. For it is an ancient custom among the Romans, that the knights, when they had served out their legal time in the wars, should lead their horses into the market-place before the two officers, called censors, and having given an account of the commanders and generals under whom they served, as also of the places and actions of their service, should be discharged, every man with honor or disgrace, according to his deserts. There were then sitting in state upon the bench two censors, Gellius and Lentulus, inspecting the knights, who were passing by in muster before them, when Pompey was seen coming down into the forum, with all the ensigns of a consul, but leading his horse in his hand. When he came up, he bade his lictors make way for him, and so he led his horse to the bench; the people being all this while in a sort of a maze, and all in silence, and the censors themselves regarding the sight with a mixture of respect and gratification. Then the senior censor examined him: "Pompeius Magnus, I demand of you whether you have served the full time in the wars that is prescribed by the law?" "Yes," replied Pompey, with a loud voice, "I have served all, and all under myself as general." The people hearing this gave a great shout, and made such an outcry for delight, that there was no appeasing it; and the censors rising from their judgment-seat accompanied him home to gratify the multitude, who followed after, clapping their hands and shouting.

Pompey's consulship was now expiring, and yet his difference with Crassus increasing, when one Caius Aurelius, a knight, a man who had declined public business all his lifetime, mounted the hustings, and addressed himself in an oration to the assembly, declaring that Jupiter had appeared to him in a dream, commanding him to tell the consuls, that they should not give up office until they were friends. After this was said, Pompey stood silent, but Crassus took him by the hand, and spoke in this manner: "I do not think, fellow-citizens, that I shall do any thing mean or dishonorable, in yielding first to Pompey, whom you were pleased to ennoble with the title of Great, when as yet he scarce had a hair on his face; and granted the honor of two triumphs, before he had a place in the senate." Hereupon they were reconciled and laid down their office. Crassus resumed the manner of life which he had always pursued before; but Pompey in the great generality of causes for judgment declined appearing on either side, and by degrees withdrew himself totally from the forum, showing himself but seldom in public; and whenever he did, it was with a great train after him. Neither was it easy to meet or visit him without a crowd of people about him; he was most pleased to make his appearance before large numbers at once, as though he wished to maintain in this way his state and majesty, and as if he held himself bound to preserve his dignity from contact with the addresses and conversation of common people. And life in the robe of peace is only too apt to lower the reputation of men that have grown great by arms, who naturally find difficulty in adapting themselves to the habits of civil equality. They expect to be treated as the first in the city, even as they were in the camp; and on the other hand, men who in war were nobody think it intolerable if in the city at any rate they are not to take the lead. And so when a warrior renowned for victories and triumphs shall turn advocate and appear among them in the forum, they endeavor their utmost to obscure and depress him; whereas, if he gives up any pretensions here and retires, they will maintain his military honor and authority beyond the reach of envy. Events themselves not long after showed the truth of this.

The power of the pirates first commenced in Cilicia, having in truth but a precarious and obscure beginning, but gained life and boldness afterwards in the wars of Mithridates, where they hired themselves out and took employment in the king's service. Afterwards, whilst the Romans were embroiled in their civil wars, being engaged against one another even before the very gates of Rome, the seas lay waste and unguarded, and by degrees enticed and drew them on not only to seize upon and spoil the merchants and ships upon the seas, but also to lay waste the islands and seaport towns. So that now there embarked with these pirates men of wealth and noble birth and superior abilities, as if it had been a natural occupation to gain distinction in. They had divers arsenals, or piratic harbors, as likewise watch towers and beacons, all along the sea-coast; and fleets were here received that were well manned with the finest mariners, and well served with the expertest pilots, and composed of swift-sailing and light-built vessels adapted for their special purpose. Nor was it merely their being thus formidable that excited indignation; they were even more odious for their ostentation than they were feared for their force. Their ships had gilded masts at their stems; the sails woven of purple, and the oars plated with silver, as if their delight were to glory in their iniquity. There was nothing but music and dancing, banqueting and revels, all along the shore. Officers in command were taken prisoners, and cities put under contribution, to the reproach and dishonor of the Roman supremacy. There were of these corsairs above one thousand sail, and they had taken no less than four hundred cities committing sacrilege upon the temples of the gods, and enriching themselves with the spoils of many never violated before, such as were those of Claros, Didyma, and Samothrace ; and the temple of the Earth in Hermione, and that of Æsculapius in Epidaurus, those of Neptune at the Isthmus, at Tænarus, and at Calauria ; those of Apollo at Actium and Leucas, and those of Juno, in Samos, at Argos, and at Lacinium. They themselves offered strange sacrifices upon Mount Olympus, and performed certain secret rites or religious mysteries, among which those of Mithras have been preserved to our own time, having received their previous institution from them. But besides these insolencies by sea, they were also injurious to the Romans by land ; for they would often go inland up the roads, plundering and destroying their villages and country-houses. And once they seized upon two Roman prætors, Sextilius and Bellinus, in their purple-edged robes, and carried them off together with their officers and lictors. The daughter also of Antonius, a man that had had the honor of a triumph, taking a journey into the country, was seized, and redeemed upon payment of a large ransom. But it was most abusive of all, that when any of the captives declared himself to be a Roman and told his name, they affected to be surprised, and feigning fear, smote their thighs and fell down at his feet, humbly beseeching him to be gracious and forgive them. The captive seeing them so humble and suppliant, believed them to be in earnest ; and some of them now would proceed to put Roman shoes on his feet, and to dress him in a Roman gown to prevent, they said, his being mistaken another time. After all this pageantry, when they had thus deluded and mocked him long enough, at last putting out a ship's ladder, when they were in the midst of the sea, they told him he was free to go, and wished him a pleasant journey ; and if he resisted they themselves threw him overboard and drowned him.

This piratic power having got the dominion and control of all the Mediterranean there was left no place for navigation or commerce. And this it was which most of all made the Romans, finding themselves to be extremely straitened in their markets, and considering that if it should continue, there would be a dearth and famine in the land, determine at last to send out Pompey to recover the seas from the pirates Gabinius, one of Pompey's friends, preferred a law, whereby there was granted to him, not only the government of the seas as admiral, but in direct words, sole and irresponsible sovereignty over all men For the decree gave him absolute power and authority in a l the seas within the pillars of Hercules, and in the adjacent mainland for the space of four hundred furlongs from the sea. Now there were but few regions in the Roman empire out of that compass; and the greatest of the nations and most powerful of the kings were included in the limit. Moreover, by this decree he had a power of selecting fifteen lieutenants out of the senate, and of assigning to each his province in charge; then he might take likewise out of the treasury and out of the hands of the revenue-farmers what moneys he pleased; as also two hundred sail of ships, with a power to press and levy what soldiers and seamen he thought fit. When this law was read, the common people approved of it exceedingly, but the chief men and most important among the senators looked upon it as an exorbitant power, even beyond the reach of envy, but well deserving their fears. Therefore concluding with themselves that such unlimited authority was dangerous, they agreed unanimously to oppose the bill, and all went against it, except Cæsar, who gave his vote for the law, not to gratify Pompey, but the people, whose favor he had courted underhand from the beginning, and hoped to compass for himself. The rest inveighed bitterly against Pompey, insomuch that one of the consuls told him, that if he was ambitious of the place of Romulus, he would scarce avoid his end, but he was in danger of being torn in pieces by the multitude for his speech. Yet when Catulus stood up to speak against the law, the people in reverence to him were silent and attentive. And when, after saying much in the most honorable terms in favor of Pompey, he proceeded to advise the people in kindness to spare him, and not to expose a man of his value to such a succession of dangers and wars, " For," said he, " where could you find another Pompey, or whom would you have in case you should chance to lose him?" they all cried out with one voice, "Yourself." And so Catulus, finding all his rhetoric ineffectual, desisted. Then Roscius attempted to speak, but could obtain no hearing, and made signs with his fingers, intimating, " Not him alone," but that there might be a second Pompey or colleague in authority with him. Upon this, it is said, the multitude being extremely incensed, made such a loud outcry, that a crow flying over the marketplace at that instant was struck, and dropt down among the crowd; whence it would appear that the cause of birds falling down to the ground, is not any rupture or division of the air causing a vacuum, but purely the actual stroke of the voice which when carried up in a great mass and with violence, raises a sort of tempest and billow, as it were, in the air.

The assembly broke up for that day; and when the day was come, on which the bill was to pass by suffrage into a decree, Pompey went privately into the country; but hearing that it was passed and confirmed, he returned again into the city by night, to avoid the envy that might be occasioned by the concourse of people that would meet and congratulate him. The next morning he came aboard and sacrificed to the gods, and having audience at an open assembly, so handled the matter that they enlarged his power, giving him many things besides what was already granted, and almost doubling the preparation appointed in the former decree. Five hundred ships were manned for him, and an army raised of one hundred and twenty thousand foot, and five thousand horse. Twenty-four senators that had been generals of armies were appointed to serve as lieutenants under him, and to these were added two quæstors. Now it happened within this time that the prices of provisions were much reduced, which gave an occasion to the joyful people of saying that the very name of Pompey had ended the war. However, Pompey, in pursuance of his charge, divided all the seas, and the whole Mediterranean into thirteen parts, allotting a squadron to each, under the command of his officers; and having thus dispersed his power into all quarters, and encompassed the pirates everywhere, they began to fall into his hands by whole shoals which he seized and brought into his harbors. As for those that withdrew themselves betimes, or otherwise escaped his general chase, they all made to Cilicia, where they hid themselves as in their hives; against whom Pompey now proceeded in person with sixty of his best ships, not, however, until he had first scoured and cleared all the seas near Rome, the Tyrrhenian, and the African, and all the waters of Sardinia, Corsica, and Sicily; all which he performed in the space of forty days, by his own indefatigable industry, and the zeal of his lieutenants.

Pompey met with some interruption in Rome, through the malice and envy of Piso, the consul, who had given some check to his proceedings by withholding his stores and discharging his seamen; whereupon he sent his fleet round to Brundusium, himself going the nearest way by land through Tuscany to Rome; which was no sooner known by the people, than they all flocked out to meet him upon the way as if they had not sent him out but a few days before. What chiefly excited their joy, was the unexpectedly rapid change in the markets, which abounded now with the greatest plenty, so that Piso was in great danger to have been deprived of his consulship, Gabinius having a law ready prepared for that purpose ; but Pompey forbade it, behaving himself as in that, so in all things else, with great moderation, and when he had made sure of all that he wanted or desired, he departed for Brundusium, whence he set sail in pursuit of the pirates. And though he was straitened in time, and his hasty voyage forced him to sail by several cities without touching, yet he would not pass by the city of Athens unsaluted ; but landing there, after he had sacrified to the gods, and made an address to the people, as he was returning out of the city, he read at the gates two epigrams, each in a single line, written in his own praise ; one within the gate :—

Thy humbler thoughts make thee a god the more:

the other without :—

Adieu we bid, who welcome bade before.

Now because Pompey had shown himself merciful to some of these pirates that were yet roving in bodies about the seas, having upon their supplication ordered a seizure of their ships and persons only, without any further process or severity, therefore the rest of their comrades in hopes of mercy too, made their escape from his other commanders, and surrendered themselves with their wives and children into his protection. He continued to pardon all that came in, and the rather because by them he might make discovery of those who fled from his justice, as conscious that their crimes were beyond an act of indemnity. The most numerous and important part of these conveyed their families and treasures, with all their people that were unfit for war, into castles and strong forts about Mount Taurus ; but they themselves having well manned their galleys, embarked for Coracesium in Cilicia, where they received Pompey and gave him battle. Here they had a final overthrow, and retired to the land, where they were besieged. At last, having despatched their heralds to him with a submission, they delivered up to his mercy themselves, their towns, islands, and strong holds, all which they had so fortified that they were almost impregnable, and scarcely even accessible.

Thus was this war ended, and the whole power of the

pirates at sea dissolved everywhere in the space of three months, wherein, besides a great number of other vessels, he took ninety men-of-war with brazen beaks; and likewise pris oners of war to the number of no less than twenty thousand.

As regarded the disposal of these prisoners, he never so much as entertained the thought of putting them to death; and yet it might be no less dangerous on the other hand to disperse them, as they might reunite and make head again, being numerous, poor, and warlike. Therefore wisely weighing with himself, that man by nature is not a wild or unsocial creature, neither was he born so, but makes himself what he naturally is not, by vicious habit; and that again on the other side, he is civilized and grows gentle by a change of place, occupation, and manner of life, as beasts themselves that are wild by nuture, become tame and tractable by housing and gentler usage, upon this consideration he determined to translate these pirates from sea to land, and give them a taste of an honest and innocent course of life, by living in towns, and tilling the ground. Some therefore were admitted into the small and half-peopled towns of the Cilicians, who, for an enlargement of their territories, were willing to receive them. Others he planted in the city of the Solians, which had been lately laid waste by Tigranes, king of Armenia, and which he now restored. But the largest number were settled in Dyme, the town of Achæa, at that time extremely depopulated, and possessing an abundance of good land.

However, these proceedings could not escape the envy and censure of his enemies; and the course he took against Metellus in Crete was disapproved of even by the chiefest of his friends. For Metellus, a relation of Pompey's former colleague in Spain, had been sent prætor into Crete, before this province of the seas was assigned to Pompey. Now Crete was the second source of pirates next to Cilicia, and Metellus having shut up a number of them in their strongholds there was engaged in reducing and extirpating them. Those that were yet remaining and besieged sent their supplications to Pompey, and invited him into the island as a part of his province, alleging it to fall, every part of it, within the distance from the sea specified in his commission, and so within the precincts of his charge. Pompey receiving the submission, sent letters to Metellus, commanding him to leave off the war; and others in like manner to the cities, in which he charged them not to yield any obedience to the commands of Metellus. And after these he sent Lucius Octavius, one of his lieutenants, to act as general, who entering the besieged fortifications, and fighting in defence of the pirates, rendered Pompey not odious only, but even ridiculous too; that he should lend his name as a guard to a nest of thieves, that knew neither god nor law, and make his reputation serve as a sanctuary to them, only out of pure envy and emulation to Meteilus. For neither was Achilles thought to act the part of a man, but rather of a mere boy, mad after glory, when by signs he forbade the rest of the Greeks to strike at Hector:—

"for fear
Some other hand should give the blow, and he
Lose the first honor of the victory."

Whereas Pompey even sought to preserve the common enemies of the world, only that he might deprive a Roman prætor, after all his labors, of the honor of a triumph. Metellus, however, was not daunted, but prosecuted the war against the pirates, expelled them from their strongholds and punished them; and dismissed Octavius with the insults and reproaches of the whole camp.

When the news came to Rome that the war with the pirates was at an end, and that Pompey was unoccupied, diverting himself in visits to the cities for want of employment, one Manlius, a tribune of the people, preferred a law that Pompey should have all the forces of Lucullus, and the provinces under his government, together with Bithynia, which was under the command of Glabrio; and that he should forthwith conduct the war against the two kings, Mithridates and Tigranes, retaining still the same naval forces and the sovereignty of the seas as before. But this was nothing less than to constitute one absolute monarch of all the Roman empire. For the provinces which seemed to be exempt from his commission by the former decree, such as were Phrygia, Lycaonia, Galatia, Cappadocia, Cilicia, the upper Colchis, and Armenia, were all added in by this latter law, together with all the troops and forces with which Lucullus had defeated Mithridates and Tigranes. And though Lucullus was thus simply robbed of the glory of his achievements in having a successor assigned him, rather to the honor of his triumph, than the danger of the war; yet this was of less moment in the eyes of the aristocratical party, though they could not but admit the injustice and ingratitude to Lucullus. But their great grievance was, that the power of Pompey should be converted into a manifest tyranny; and they therefore exhorted and encour aged one another privately to bend all their forces in opposition to this law, and not tamely to cast away their liberty, yet when the day came on which it was to pass into a decree, their hearts failed them for fear of the people, and all were silent except Catulus, who boldly inveighed against the law and its proposer, and when he found that he could do nothing with the people, turned to the senate, crying out and bidding them seek out some mountain as their forefathers had done, and fly to the rocks where they might preserve their iberty. The law passed into a decree, as it is said, by the suffrages of all the tribes. And Pompey, in his absence, was made lord of almost all that power which Sylla only obtained by force of arms, after a conquest of the very city itself. When Pompey had advice by letters of the decree, it is said that in the presence of his friends, who came to give him joy of his honor, he seemed displeased, frowning and smiting his thigh, and exclaimed as one overburdened, and weary of government, " Alas, what a series of labors upon labors ! If I am never to end my service as a soldier, nor to escape from this invidious greatness, and live at home in the country with my wife, I had better have been an unknown man." But all this was looked upon as mere trifling, neither indeed could the best of his friends call it anything else, well knowing that his enmity with Lucullus, setting a flame just now to his natural passion for glory and empire, made him feel more than usually gratified.

As indeed appeared not long afterwards by his actions, which clearly unmasked him ; for in the first place, he sent out his proclamations into all quarters, commanding the soldiers to join him, and summoned all the tributary kings and princes within his charge ; and in short, as soon as he had entered upon his province, he left nothing unaltered that had been done and established by Lucullus. To some he remitted their penalties, and deprived others of their rewards, and acted in all respects as if with the express design that the admirers of Lucullus might know that all his authority was at an end. Lucullus expostulated by friends, and it was thought fitting that there should be a meeting betwixt them ; and accordingly they met in the country of Galatia. As they were both great and successful generals, their officers bore their rods before them all wreathed with branches of laurel ; Lucullus came through a country full of green trees and shady woods, but Pompey's march was through a cold and barren district. Therefore the lictors of Lucullus, perceiving that Pompey's laurels were withered and dry, helped him to some of their own, and adorned and crowned his rods with fresh laurels. This was thought ominous, and looked as if Pompey came to take away the reward and honor of Lucullus's victories. Lucullus had the priority in the order of consulships, and also in age; but Pompey's two triumphs made him the greater man. Their first addresses in this interview were dignified and friendly, each magnifying the other's actions, and offering congratulations upon his success. But when they came to the matter of their conference or treaty, they could agree on no fair or equitable terms of any kind, but even came to harsh words against each other, Pompey upbraiding Lucullus with avarice, and Lucullus retorting ambition upon Pompey, so that their friends could hardly part them. Lucullus remaining in Galatia, made a distribution of the lands within his conquests, and gave presents to whom he pleased; and Pompey encamping not far distant from him, sent out his prohibitions, forbidding the execution of any of the orders of Lucullus, and commanded away all his soldiers, except sixteen hundred, whom he thought likely to be unserviceable to himself, being disorderly and mutinous, and whom he knew to be hostile to Lucullus; and to these acts he added satirical speeches, detracting openly from the glory of his actions, and giving out, that the battles of Lucullus had been but with the mere stage-shows and idle pictures of royal pomp, whereas the real war against a genuine army, disciplined by defeat, was reserved to him, Mithridates having now begun to be in earnest, and having betaken himself to his shields, swords, and horses. Lucullus, on the other side, to be even with him, replied, that Pompey came to fight with the mere image and shadow of war, it being his usual practice, like a lazy bird of prey, to come upon the carcass, when others had slain the dead, and to tear in pieces the relics of a war. Thus he had appropriated to himself the victories over Sertorius, over Lepidus, and over the insurgents under Spartacus; whereas this last had been achieved by Crassus, that obtained by Catulus, and the first won by Metellus. And therefore it was no great wonder, that the glory of the Pontic and Armenian war should be usurped by a man who had condescended to any artifices to work himself into the honor of a triumph over a few runaway slaves.

After this Lucullus went away, and Pompey having placed his whole navy in guard upon the seas betwixt Phœnicia and

Bosphorus, himself marched against Mithridates, who had a phalanx of thirty thousand foot, with two thousand horse, yet durst not bid him battle. He had encamped upon a strong mountain where it would have been hard to attack him, but abandoned it in no long time, as destitute of water. No sooner was he gone but Pompey occupied it, and observing the plants that were thriving there, together with the hollows which he found in several places, conjectured that such a plot could not be without springs, and therefore ordered his men to sink wells in every corner. After which there was, in a little time, great plenty of water throughout all the camp, insomuch that he wondered how it was possible for Mithridates to be ignorant of this, during all that time of his encampment there. After this Pompey followed him to his next camp, and there drawing lines round about him, shut him in. But he, after having endured a siege of forty-five days, made his escape secretly, and fled away with all the best part of his army, having first put to death all the sick and unserviceable. Not long after Pompey overtook him again near the banks of the river Euphrates, and encamped close by him; but fearing lest he should pass over the river and give him the slip there too, he drew up his army to attack him at midnight. And at that very time Mithridates, it is said, saw a vision in his dream foreshowing what should come to pass. For he seemed to be under sail in the Euxine Sea with a prosperous gale, and just in view of Bosphorus, discoursing pleasantly with the ship's company, as one overjoyed for his past danger and present security, when on a sudden he found himself deserted of all, and floating upon a broken plank of the ship at the mercy of the sea. Whilst he was thus laboring under these passions and phantasms, his friends came and awaked him with the news of Pompey's approach; who was now indeed so near at hand, that the fight must be for the camp itself, and the commanders accordingly drew up the forces in battle array. Pompey perceiving how ready they were and well prepared for defence, began to doubt with himself whether he should put it to the hazard of a fight in the dark, judging it more prudent to encompass them only at present, least they should fly, and to give them battle with the advantage of numbers the next day. But his oldest officers were of another opinion, and by entreaties and encouragements obtained permission that they might charge them immediately. Neither was the night so very dark, but that, though the moon was going down, it yet gave light enough to discern a body

And indeed this was one especial disadvantage to the king's army. For the Romans coming upon them with the moon on their backs, the moon, being very low, and just upon setting, cast the shadows a long way before their bodies, reaching almost to the enemy, whose eyes were thus so much deceived that not exactly discerning the distance, but imagining them to be near at hand, they threw their darts at the shadows without the least execution. The Romans therefore perceiving this, ran in upon them with a great shout; but the barbarians, all in a panic, unable to endure the charge, turned and fled, and were put to great slaughter, above ten thousand being slain; the camp also was taken. As for Mithridates himself, he at the beginning of the onset, with a body of eight hundred horse, charged through the Roman army, and made his escape. But before long all the rest dispersed, some one way, some another, and he was left only with three persons, among whom was his concubine, Hypsicratia, a girl always of a manly and daring spirit, and the king called her on that account Hypsicrates. She being attired and mounted like a Persian horseman, accompanied the king in all his flight, never weary even in the longest journey, nor ever failing to attend the king in person, and look after his horse too, until they came to Inora, a castle of the king's, well stored with gold and treasure. From thence Mithridates took his richest apparel, and gave it among those that had resorted to him in their flight; and so to every one of his friends he gave a deadly poison, that they might not fall into the power of the enemy against their wills. From thence he designed to have gone to Tigranes in Armenia, but being prohibited by Tigranes, who put out a proclamation with a reward of one hundred talents to any one that should apprehend him, he passed by the head-waters of the river Euphrates, and fled through the country of Colchis.

Pompey in the mean time made an invasion into Armenia, upon the invitation of young Tigranes, who was now in rebellion against his father, and gave Pompey a meeting about the river Araxes, which rises near the head of Euphrates, but turning its course and bending towards the east, falls into the Caspian Sea. They two, therefore, marched together through the country, taking in all the cities by the way, and receiving their submission. But king Tigranes, having lately suffered much in the war with Lucullus, and understanding that Pompey was of a kind and gentle disposition, admitted Roman troops into his royal palaces, and taking along with him his friends and relations, went in person to surrender himself into the hands of Pompey. He came as far as the trenches on horseback, but there he was met by two of Pompey's lictors, who commanded him to alight and walk on foot, for no man ever was seen on horseback within a Roman camp. Tigranes submitted to this immediately, and not only so, but loosing his sword, delivered up that too ; and last of all, as soon as he appeared before Pompey, he pulled off his royal turban, and attempted to have laid it at his feet. Nay, worst of all, even he himself had fallen prostrate as an humble suppliant at his knees, had not Pompey prevented it, taking him by the hand and placing him near him, Tigranes himself on one side of him and his son upon the other. Pompey now told him that the rest of his losses were chargeable upon Lucullus, by whom he had been dispossessed of Syria, Phœnicia, Cilicia, Galatia, and Sophene ; but all that he had preserved to himself entire till that time he should peaceably enjoy, paying the sum of six thousand talents as a fine or penalty for injuries done to the Romans, and that his son should have the kingdom of Sophene. Tigranes himself was well pleased with these conditions of peace, and when the Romans saluted him king, seemed to be overjoyed, and promised to every common soldier half a mina of silver, to every centurion ten minas, and to every tribune a talent ; but the son was displeased, insomuch that when he was invited to supper he replied, that he did not stand in need of Pompey for that sort of honor, for he would find out some other Roman to sup with. Upon this he was put into close arrest, and reserved for the triumph.

Not long after this Phraates, king of Parthia, sent to Pompey, and demanded to have young Tigranes, as his son-in-law, given up to him, and that the river Euphrates should be the boundary of the empires. Pompey replied, that for Tigranes, he belonged more to his own natural father than his father-in-law, and for the boundaries, he would take care that they should be according to right and justice.

So Pompey, leaving Armenia in the custody of Afranius, went himself in chase of Mithridates ; to do which he was forced of necessity to march through several nations inhabiting about Mount Caucasus. Of these the Albanians and Iberians were the two chiefest. The Iberians stretch out as far as the Moschian mountains and the Pontus ; the Albanians lie more eastwardly, and towards the Caspian Sea. These Albanians at first permitted Pompey, upon his request, to pass through the country, but when winter had stolen upon the

Romans whilst they were still in the country, and they were busy celebrating the festival of Saturn, they mustered a body of no less than forty thousand fighting men, and set upon them, having passed over the river Cyrnus, which rising from the mountains of Iberia, and receiving the river Araxes in its course from Armenia, discharges itself by twelve mouths into the Caspian. Or, according to others, the Araxes does not fall into it, but they flow near one another, and so discharge themselves as neighbors into the same sea. It was in the power of Pompey to have obstructed the enemy's passage over the river, but he suffered them to pass over quietly; and then leading on his forces and giving battle, he routed them, and slew great numbers of them in the field. The king sent ambassadors with his submission, and Pompey upon his supplication pardoned the offence, and making a treaty with him, he marched directly against the Iberians, a nation no less in number than the other, but much more warlike, and extremely desirous of gratifying Mithridates, and driving out Pompey. These Iberians were never subject to the Medes or Persians, and they happened likewise to escape the dominion of the Macedonians, because Alexander was so quick in his march through Hyrcania. But these also Pompey subdued in a great battle, where there were slain nine thousand upon the spot, and more than ten thousand taken prisoners. From thence he entered into the country of Colchis, where Servilius met him by the river Phasis, bringing the fleet with which he was guarding the Pontus.

The pursuit of Mithridates, who had thrown himself among the tribes inhabiting Bosphorus and the shores of the Mæotian Sea, presented great difficulties. News was also brought to Pompey that the Albanians had again revolted. This made him turn back, out of anger and determination not to be beaten by them, and with difficulty and great danger passed back over the Cyrnus, which the barbarous people had fortified a great way down the banks with palisadoes. And after this, having a tedious march to make through a waterless and difficult country, he ordered ten thousand skins to be filled with water, and so advanced towards the enemy, whom he found drawn up in order of battle near the river Abas, to the number of sixty thousand horse, and twelve thousand foot, ill armed generally, and most of them covered only with the skins of wild beasts. Their general was Cosis, the king's brother, who, as soon as the battle was begun, singled out Pompey, and rushing in upon him darted his javelin into the joints of his breastplate; while Pompey, in return, struck him through the body with his lance, and slew him. It is related that in this battle there were Amazons fighting as auxiliaries with the barbarians, and that they came down from the mountains by the river Thermodon. For that after the battle, when the Romans were taking the spoil and plunder of the field, they met with several targets and buskins of the Amazons; but no woman's body was found among the dead. They inhabit the parts of Mount Caucasus that reach down to the Hyrcanian Sea, not immediately bordering upon the Albanians, for the Gelæ and the Leges lie betwixt; and they keep company with these people yearly, for two months only, near the river Thermodon; after which they retire to their own habitations, and live alone all the rest of the year.

After this engagement, Pompey was eager to advance with his forces upon the Hyrcanian and Caspian Sea, but was forced to retreat at a distance of three days' march from it, by the number of venomous serpents, and so he retreated into Armenia the Less. Whilst he was there, the kings of the Elymæans and Medes sent ambassadors to him, to whom he gave friendly answer by letter; and sent against the king of Parthia, who had made incursions upon Gordyene, and despoiled the subjects of Tigranes, an army under the command of Afranius, who put him to the rout, and followed him in chase as far as the district of Arbela.

Of the concubines of king Mithridates that were brought before Pompey, he took none to himself, but sent them all away to their parents and relations; most of them being either the daughters or wives of princes and great commanders. Stratonice, however, who had the greatest power and influence with him, and to whom he had committed the custody of his best and richest fortress, had been, it seems, the daughter of a musician, an old man, and of no great fortune, and happening to sing one night before Mithridates at a banquet, she struck his fancy so, that immediately he took her with him, and sent away the old man much dissatisfied, the king having not so much as said one kind word to himself. But when he rose in the morning, and saw tables in his house richly covered with gold and silver plate, a great retinue of servants, eunuchs, and pages, bringing him rich garments, and a horse standing before the door richly caparisoned, in all respects as was usual with the king's favorites, he looked upon it all as a piece of mockery, and thinking himself trifled with, attempted to make off and run away. But the servants laying hold upon him,

and informing him really that the king had bestowed on him
the house and furniture of a rich man lately deceased, and
that these were but the first-fruits or earnests of greater riches
and possessions that were to come, he was persuaded at last
with much difficulty to believe them. And so putting on his
purple robes, and mounting his horse, he rode through the
city, crying out, "All this is mine;" and to those that laughed
at him, he said, there was no such wonder in this, but it was
a wonder rather that he did not throw stones at all he met,
he was so transported with joy. Such was the parentage and
blood of Stratonice. She now delivered up this castle into
the hands of Pompey, and offered him many presents of
great value, of which he accepted only such as he thought
might serve to adorn the temples of the gods, and add to the
splendor of his triumph: the rest he left to Stratonice's disposal, bidding her please herself in the enjoyment of them.

And in the same manner he dealt with the presents offered
him by the king of Iberia, who sent him a bedstead, table,
and a chair of state, all of gold, desiring him to accept of
them; but he delivered them all into the custody of the public
treasurers, for the use of the Commonwealth.

In another castle called Cænum, Pompey found and read
with pleasure several secret writings of Mithridates, containing
much that threw light on his character. For there were
memoirs by which it appeared that besides others, he had
made away with his son Ariarathes by poison, as also with
Alcæus the Sardian, for having robbed him of the first honors
in a horse-race. There were several judgments upon the
interpretation of dreams, which either he himself or some of his
mistresses had had; and besides these, there was a series of
wanton letters to and from his concubine Monime. Theophanes tells us that there was found also an address by Rutilius,
in which he attempted to exasperate him to the slaughter of
all the Romans in Asia; though most men justly conjecture
this to be a malicious invention of Theophanes, who probably
hated Rutilius because he was a man in nothing like himself;
or perhaps it might be to gratify Pompey, whose father is
described by Rutilius in his history, as the vilest man alive.

From thence Pompey came to the city of Amisus, where
his passion for glory put him into a position which might be
called a punishment on himself. For whereas he had often
sharply reproached Lucullus, in that while the enemy was
still living, he had taken upon him to issue decrees, and distribute rewards and honors, as conquerors usually do only

when the war is brought to an end, yet now was he himself, while Mithridates was paramount in the kingdom of Bosphorus, and at the head of a powerful army, as if all were ended, just doing the same thing, regulating the provinces, and distributing rewards, many great commanders and princes having flocked to him, together with no less than twelve barbarian kings; insomuch that to gratify these other kings, when he wrote to the king of Parthia, he would not condescend, as others used to do, in the superscription of his letter, to give him his title of king of kings.

Moreover, he had a great desire and emulation to occupy Syria, and to march through Arabia to the Red Sea, that he might thus extend his conquests every way to the great ocean that encompasses the habitable earth; as in Africa he was the first Roman that advanced his victories to the ocean; and again in Spain he made the Atlantic Sea the limit of the empire; and then thirdly, in his late pursuit of the Albanians, he had wanted but little of reaching the Hyrcanian Sea. Accordingly he raised his camp, designing to bring the Red Sea within the circuit of his expedition; especially as he saw how difficult it was to hunt after Mithridates with an army, and that he would prove a worse enemy flying than fighting. But yet he declared that he would leave a sharper enemy behind him than himself, namely, famine; and therefore he appointed a guard of ships to lie in wait for the merchants that sailed to Bosphorus, death being the penalty for any who should attempt to carry provisions thither.

Then he set forward with the greatest part of his army and in his march casually fell in with several dead bodies still uninterred, of those soldiers who were slain with Triarius in his unfortunate engagement with Mithridates: these he, buried splendidly and honorably. The neglect of whom, it is thought, caused, as much as any thing, the hatred that was felt against Lucullus, and alienated the affections of the soldiers from him. Pompey having now by his forces under the command of Afranius, subdued the Arabians about the mountain Amanus, himself entered Syria, and finding it destitute of any natural and lawful prince, reduced it into the form of a province, as a possession of the people of Rome. He conquered also Judæa, and took its king, Aristobulus, captive. Some cities he built anew, and to others he gave their liberty, chastising their tyrants. Most part of the time that he spent there was employed in the administration of justice, in deciding controversies of kings and States; and where he himself could not be present in person, he gave commissions to his friends, and sent them. Thus when there arose a difference betwixt the Armenians and Parthians about some territory, and the judgment was referred to him, he gave a power by commission to three judges and arbiters to hear and determine the controversy. For the reputation of his power was great; nor was the fame of his justice and clemency inferior to that of his power, and served indeed as a veil for a multitude of faults committed by his friends and familiars. For although it was not in his nature to check or chastise wrongdoers, yet he himself always treated those that had to do with him in such a manner, that they submitted to endure with patience the acts of covetousness and oppression done by others.

Among these friends of his, there was one Demetrius, who had the greatest influence with him of all; he was a freed slave, a youth of good understanding, but somewhat too insolent in his good fortune, of whom there goes this story. Cato, the philosopher, being as yet a very young man, but of great repute and a noble mind, took a journey of pleasure to Antioch, at a time when Pompey was not there, having a great desire to see the city. He, as his custom was, walked on foot, and his friends accompanied him on horseback; and seeing before the gates of the city a multitude dressed in white, the young men on one side of the road, and the boys on the other, he was somewhat offended at it, imagining that it was officiously done in honor of him, which was more than he had any wish for. However, he desired his companions to alight and walk with him; but when they drew near, the master of the ceremonies in this procession came out with a garland and a rod in his hand, and met them, inquiring where they had left Demetrius, and when he would come? Upon which Cato's companions burst out into laughter, but Cato said only, "Alas, poor city!" and passed by without any other answer. However, Pompey rendered Demetrius less odious to others by enduring his presumption and impertinence to himself. For it is reported how that Pompey, when he had invited his friends to an entertainment, would be very ceremonious in waiting till they all came and were placed, while Demetrius would be already stretched upon the couch as if he cared for no one, with his dress over his ears, hanging down from his head. Before his return into Italy, he had purchased the pleasantest country-seat about Rome, with the finest walks and places for exercise, and there were sumptuous gardens, called by the name of Demetrius while Pompey his master, up to his third triumph, was contented with an ordinary and simple habitation. Afterwards, it is true, when he had erected his famous and stately theatre for the people of Rome, he built as a sort of appendix to it, a house for himself, much more splendid than his former, and yet no object even this to excite men's envy, since he who came to be master of it after Pompey could not but express wonder and inquire where Pompey the Great used to sup. Such is the story told us.

The king of the Arabs near Petra, who had hitherto despised the power of the Romans, now began to be in great alarm at it, and sent letters to him promising to be at his commands, and to do whatever he should see fit to order. However, Pompey having a desire to confirm and keep him in the same mind, marched forwards for Petra, an expedition not altogether irreprehensible in the opinion of many; who thought it a mere running away from their proper duty, the pursuit of Mithridates, Rome's ancient and inveterate enemy, who was now rekindling the war once more, and taking preparations, it was reported, to lead his army through Scythia and Pæonia, into Italy. Pompey, on the other side, judging it easier to destroy his forces in battle, than to seize his person in flight, resolved not to tire himself out in a vain pursuit, but rather to spend his leisure upon another enemy, as a sort of digression in the mean while. But fortune resolved the doubt; for when he was now not far from Petra, and had pitched his tents and encamped for that day, as he was taking exercise with his horse outside the camp, couriers came riding up from Pontus, bringing good news, as was known at once by the heads of their javelins, which it is the custom to carry crowned with branches of laurel. The soldiers, as soon as they saw them, flocked immediately to Pompey, who, notwithstanding was minded to finish his exercise; but when they began to be clamorous and importunate, he alighted from his horse, and taking the letters went before them into the camp. Now there being no tribunal erected there, not even that military substitute for one which they make by cutting up thick turfs of earth, and piling them one upon another, they, through eagerness and impatience, heaped up a pile of pack-saddles, and Pompey standing upon that, told them the news of Mithridates's death, how that he had himself put an end to his life upon the revolt of his son Pharnaces, and that Pharnacus had taken all things there into his hands and possession, which he did, his letters said, in right of himself and the Romans. Upon this news, the whole army expressing their joy, as was to be expected, fell to sacrificing to the gods, and fasting as if in the person of Mithridates alone there had died many thousands of their enemies.

Pompey by this event having brought this war to its completion, with much more ease than was expected, departed forthwith out of Arabia, and passing rapidly through the intermediate provinces, he came at length to the city Amisus. There he received many presents brought from Pharnaces with several dead bodies of the royal blood, and the corpse of Mithridates himself, which was not easy to be known by the face, for the physicians that embalmed him had not dried up his brain, but those who were curious to see him knew him by the scars there. Pompey himself would not endure to see him, but to deprecate the divine jealousy, sent it away to the city of Sinope. He admired the richness of his robes no less than the size and splendor of his armor. His sword belt, however, which had cost four hundred talents, was stolen by Publius, and sold to Ariarathes; his tiara also, a piece of admirable workmanship, Gaius, the foster-brother of Mithridates, gave secretly to Faustus, the son of Sylla, at his request. All which Pompey was ignorant of, but afterwards, when Pharnaces came to understand it, he severely punished those that embezzled them.

Pompey now having ordered all things, and established that province, took his journey homewards in greater pomp and with more festivity. For when he came to Mitylene, he gave the city their freedom upon the intercession of Theophanes, and was present at the contest, there periodically held, of the poets, who took at that time no other theme or subject than the actions of Pompey. He was extremely pleased with the theatre itself, and had a model of it taken, intending to erect one in Rome on the same design, but larger and more magnificent. When he came to Rhodes, he attended the lectures of all the philosophers there, and gave to every one of them a talent. Posidonius has published the disputation which he held before him against Hermagoras the rhetorician, upon the subject of Invention in general. At Athens, also, he showed similar munificence to the philosophers, and gave fifty talents towards the repairing and beautifying the city. So that now by all these acts he well hoped to return into Italy in the greatest splendor and glory possible to man, and find his family as desirous to see him, as he felt himself to come home to them. But that supernatural agency, whose province and charge it is always to mix some ingredient of evil with the greatest and most glorious goods of fortune, had for some time back been busy in his household, preparing him a sad welcome. For Mucia during his absence had dishonored his bed. Whilst he was abroad at a distance, he had refused all credence to the report; but when he drew nearer to Italy, where his thoughts were more at leisure to give consideration to the charge, he sent her a bill of divorce; but neither then in writing, nor afterwards by word of mouth, did he ever give a reason why he discharged her; the cause of it is mentioned in Cicero's epistles.

Rumors of every kind were scattered abroad about Pompey, and were carried to Rome before him, so that there was a great tumult and stir, as if he designed forthwith to march with his army into the city, and establish himself securely as sole ruler. Crassus withdrew himself, together with his children and property, out of the city, either that he was really afraid, or that he counterfeited rather, as is most probable, to give credit to the calumny and exasperate the jealousy of the people. Pompey, therefore, as soon as he entered Italy, called a general muster of the army; and having made a suitable address and exchanged a kind farewell with his soldiers, he commanded them to depart every man to his country and place of habitation, only taking care that they should not fail to meet again at his triumph. Thus the army being disbanded, and the news commonly reported, a wonderful result ensued. For when the cities saw Pompey the Great passing through the country unarmed, and with a small train of familiar friends only, as if he was returning from a journey of pleasure, not from his conquests, they came pouring out to display their affection for him, attending and conducting him to Rome with far greater forces than he disbanded; insomuch that if he had designed any movement or innovation in the State, he might have done it without his army.

Now, because the law permitted no commander to enter into the city before his triumph, he sent to the senate, entreating them as a favor to him to prorogue the election of consuls, that thus he might be able to attend and give countenance to Piso, one of the candidates. The request was resisted by Cato, and met with a refusal. However, Pompey could not but admire the liberty and boldness of speech which Cato alone had dared to use in the maintenance of law and justice. He therefore had a great desire to win him over, and purchase his friendship at any rate; and to that end, Cato having two nieces, Pompey asked for one in marriage for himself, the other for his son. But Cato looked unfavorably on the proposal, regarding it as a design for undermining his honesty, and in a manner bribing him by a family alliance; much to the displeasure of his wife and sister, who were indignant that he should reject a connection with Pompey the Great. About that time Pompey having a design of setting up Afranius for the consulship, gave a sum of money among the tribes for their votes, and people came and received it in his own gardens, a proceeding which, when it came to be generally known, excited great disapprobation, that he should thus for the sake of men who could not obtain the honor by their own merits, make merchandise of an office which had been given to himself as the highest reward of his services. "Now" said Cato, to his wife and sister, "had we contracted an alliance with Pompey, we had been allied to this dishonor, too," and this they could not but acknowledge, and allow his judgment of what was right and fitting to have been wiser and better than theirs.

The splendor and magnificence of Pompey's triumph was such that though it took up the space of two days, yet they were extremely straitened in time, so that of what was prepared for that pageantry, there was as much withdrawn as would have set out and adorned another triumph. In the first place, there were tables carried, inscribed with the names and titles of the nations over whom he triumphed, Pontus, Armenia, Cappadocia, Paphlagonia, Media, Colchis, the Iberians, the Albanians, Syria, Cilicia, and Mesopotamia, together with Phœnicia and Palestine, Judæa, Arabia, and all the power of the pirates subdued by sea and land. And in these different countries there appeared the capture of no less than one thousand fortified places, nor much less than nine hundred cities, together with eight hundred ships of the pirates, and the foundation of thirty-nine towns. Besides, there was set forth in these tables an account of all the tributes throughout the empire, and how that before these conquests the revenue amounted but to fifty millions, whereas from his acquisitions they had a revenue of eighty-five millions; and that in present payment he was bringing into the common treasury ready money, and gold and silver plate, and ornaments, to the value of twenty thousand talents, over and above what had been distributed among the soldiers, of whom he that had least had fifteen hundred drachmas for his share. The prisoners o war that were led in triumph, besides the chief pirates, were the son of Tigranes, king of Armenia, with his wife and daughter; as also Zosime, wife of king Tigranes himself, and Aristobulus, king of Judæa, the sister of king Mithridates, and her five sons, and some Scythian women. There were likewise the hostages of the Albanians and Iberians, and of the king of Commagene, besides a vast number of trophies, one for every battle in which he was conqueror, either himself in person, or by his lieutenants. But that which seemed to be his greatest glory, being one which no other Roman ever attained to, was this, that he made his third triumph over the third division of the world. For others among the Romans had the honor of triumphing thrice, but his first triumph was over Africa, his second over Europe, and this last over Asia; so that he seemed in these three triumphs to have led the whole world captive.

As for his age, those who affect to make the parallel exact in all things betwixt him and Alexander the Great, do not allow him to have been quite thirty-four, whereas in truth at that time he was near forty. And well had it been for him had he terminated his life at this date, while he still enjoyed Alexander's fortune, since all his after-time served only either to bring him prosperity that made him odious, or calamities too great to be retrieved. For that great authority which he had gained in the city by his merits, he made use of only in patronizing the iniquities of others, so that by advancing their fortunes, he detracted from his own glory, till at last he was overthrown even by the force and greatness of his own power. And as the strongest citadel or fort in a town, when it is taken by an enemy, does then afford the same strength to the foe, as it had done to friends before, so Cæsar, after Pompey's aid had made him strong enough to defy his country, ruined and overthrew at last the power which had availed him against the rest. The course of things was as follows. Lucullus, when he returned out of Asia, where he had been treated with insult by Pompey, was received by the senate with great honor, which was yet increased when Pompey came home; to check whose ambition they encouraged him to assume the administration of the government, whereas he was now grown cold and disinclined to business, having given himself over to the pleasures of ease and the enjoyment of a splendid fortune. However, he began for the time to exert himself against Pompey, attacked him sharply, and succeeeded in having his own acts and decrees, which were repealed by Pompey, reestablished, and with the assistance of Cato, gained the superiority in the senate. Pompey having fallen from his hopes in such an unworthy repulse, was forced to fly to the tribunes of the people for refuge, and to attach himself to the young men, among whom was Clodius, the vilest and most impudent wretch alive, who took him about, and exposed him as a tool to the people, carrying him up and down among the throngs in the market place, to countenance those laws and speeches which he made to cajole the people and ingratiate himself. And at last for his reward, he demanded of Pompey, as if he had not disgraced, but done him a great kindness, that he should forsake (as in the end he did forsake) Cicero, his friend, who on many public occasions had done him the greatest service. And so when Cicero was in danger, and implored his aid, he would not admit him into his presence, but shutting up his gates against those that came to mediate for him, slipt out at a back door, whereupon Cicero fearing the result of his trial, departed privately from Rome.

About that time Cæsar, returning from military service, started a course of policy which brought him great present favor, and much increased his power for the future, and proved extremely destructive both to Pompey and the commonwealth. For now he stood candidate for his first consulship, and well observing the enmity betwixt Pompey and Crassus, and finding that by joining with one he should make the other his enemy, he endeavored by all means to reconcile them, an object in itself honorable and tending to the public good, but as he undertook it, a mischievous and subtle intrigue. For he well knew that opposite parties or factions in a commonwealth, like passengers in a boat, serve to trim and balance the unsteady motions of power there; whereas if they combine and come all over to one side, they cause a shock which will be sure to overset the vessel and carry down every thing. And therefore Cato wisely told those who charged all the calamities of Rome upon the disagreement betwixt Pompey and Cæsar, that they were in error in charging all the crime upon the last cause; for it was not their discord and enmity, but their unanimity and friendship, that gave the first and greatest blow to the commonwealth.

Cæsar being thus elected consul, began at once to make an interest with the poor and meaner sort, by preferring and establishing laws for planting colonies and dividing lands, lowering the dignity of his office, and turning his consulship into a sort of tribuneship rather. And when Bibulus, his col league, opposed him, and Cato was prepared to second Bibulus, and assist him vigorously, Cæsar brought Pompey upon the hustings, and addressing him in the sight of the people demanded his opinion upon the laws that were proposed. Pompey gave his approbation. "Then," said Cæsar, "in case any man should offer violence to these laws, will you be ready to give assistance to the people?" "Yes," replied Pompey, "I shall be ready, and against those that threaten the sword, I will appear with sword and buckler." Nothing ever was said or done by Pompey up to that day, that seemed more insolent or overbearing; so that his friends endeavored to apologize for it as a word spoken inadvertently; but by his actions afterwards it appeared plainly that he was totally devoted to Cæsar's service. For on a sudden, contrary to all expectation, he married Julia, the daughter of Cæsar, who had been affianced before and was to be married within a few days to Cæpio. And to appease Cæpio's wrath, he gave him his own daughter in marriage, who had been espoused before to Faustus, the son of Sylla. Cæsar himself married Calpurnia, the daughter of Piso.

Upon this Pompey, filling the city with soldiers, carried all things by force as he pleased. As Bibulus, the consul, was going to the forum, accompanied by Lucullus and Cato, they fell upon him on a sudden and broke his rods; and somebody threw a vessel of ordure upon the head of Bibulus himself; and two tribunes of the people, who escorted him, were desperately wounded in the fray. And thus having cleared the forum of all their adversaries, they got their bill for the division of lands established and passed into an act; and not only so, but the whole populace being taken with this bait, became totally at their devotion, inquiring into nothing and without a word giving their suffrages to whatever they propounded. Thus they confirmed all those acts and decrees of Pompey, which were questioned and contested by Lucullus; and to Cæsar they granted the provinces of Gaul, both within and without the Alps, together with Illyricum, for five years, and likewise an army of four entire legions; then they created consuls for the year ensuing, Piso, the father-in-law of Cæsar, and Gabinius, the most extravagant of Pompey's flatterers.

During all these transactions, Bibulus kept close within doors. nor did he appear publicly in person for the space of eight months together, notwithstanding he was consul, but sent out proclamations full of bitter invectives and accusations against them both. Cato turned prophet, and as if he had been possessed with a spirit of divination, did nothing else in the senate but foretell what evils should befall the Commonwealth and Pompey. Lucullus pleaded old age, and retired to take his ease, as superannuated for affairs of State; which gave occasion to the saying of Pompey, that the fatigues of luxury were not more seasonable for an old man than those of government. Which in truth proved a reflection upon himself; for he not long after let his fondness for his young wife seduce him also into effeminate habits. He gave all his time to her, and passed his days in her company in country-houses and gardens, paying no heed to what was going on in the forum. Insomuch that Clodius, who was then tribune of the people, began to despise him, and engage in the most audacious attempts. For when he had banished Cicero, and sent away Cato into Cyprus under pretence of military duty, and when Cæsar was gone upon his expedition to Gaul, finding the populace now looking to him as the leader who did every thing according to their pleasure, he attempted forthwith to repeal some of Pompey's decrees; he took Tigranes, the captive, out of prison, and kept him about him as his companion; and commenced actions against several of Pompey's friends, thus designing to try the extent of his power. At last, upon a time when Pompey was present at the hearing of a certain cause, Clodius, accompanied with a crowd of profligate and impudent ruffians, standing up in a place above the rest, put questions to the populace as follows: "Who is the dissolute general? who is the man that seeks another man? who scratches his head with one finger?" and the rabble, upon the signal of his shaking his gown, with a great shout to every question, like singers making responses in a chorus, made answer, "Pompey."

This indeed was no small annoyance to Pompey, who was quite unaccustomed to hear any thing ill of himself, and unexperienced altogether in such encounters; and he was yet more vexed, when he saw that the senate rejoiced at this foul usage, and regarded it as a just punishment upon him for his treachery to Cicero. But when it came even to blows and wounds in the forum, and that one of Clodius's bondslaves was apprehended, creeping through the crowd towards Pompey with a sword in his hand, Pompey laid hold of this pretence, though perhaps otherwise apprehensive of Clodius's insolence and bad language, and never appeared again in the forum during all the time he was tribune, but kept close at home, and passed his time in consulting with his friends, by what means he might best allay the displeasure of the senate and nobles against him. Among other expedients, Culleo advised the divorce of Julia, and to abandon Cæsar's friendship to gain that of the senate; this he would not hearken to. Others again advised him to call home Cicero from banishment, a man who was always the great adversary of Clodius, and as great a favorite of the senate; to this he was easily persuaded. And therefore he brought Cicero's brother into the forum, attended with a strong party, to petition for his return; where, after a warm dispute, in which several were wounded and some slain, he got the victory over Clodius. No sooner was Cicero returned home upon this decree, but immediately he used his efforts to reconcile the senate to Pompey; and by speaking in favor of the law upon the importations of corn, did again, in effect, make Pompey sovereign lord of all the Roman possessions by sea and land. For by that law, there were placed under his control all ports, markets, and storehouses, and in short, all the concerns both of the merchants and the husbandmen; which gave occasion to the charge brought against it by Clodius, that the law was not made because of the scarcity of corn, but the scarcity of corn was made, that they might pass a law, whereby that power of his, which was now grown feeble and consumptive, might be revived again, and Pompey reinstated in a new empire. Others look upon it as a politic device of Spinther, the consul, whose design it was to secure Pompey in a greater authority, that he himself might be sent in assistance to king Ptolemy. However, it is certain that Canidius, the tribune, preferred a law to despatch Pompey in the character of an ambassador, without an army, attended only with two lictors, as a mediator betwixt the king and his subjects of Alexandria. Neither did this proposal seem unacceptable to Pompey, though the senate cast it out upon the specious pretence, that they were unwilling to hazard his person. However, there were found several writings scattered about the forum and near the senate-house, intimating how grateful it would be to Ptolemy to have Pompey appointed for his general instead of Spinther. And Timagenes even asserts that Ptolemy went away and left Egypt, not out of necessity, but purely upon the persuasion of Theophanes, who was anxious to give Pompey the opportunity for holding a new command, and gaining further wealth. But Theophanes's want of honesty does not go so far to make this story credible as does Pompey's own nature, which was averse, with all its ambition, to such base and disingenuous acts, to render it improbable.

Thus Pompey being appointed chief purveyor, and having within his administration and management all the corn trade, sent abroad his factors and agents into all quarters, and he himself sailing into Sicily, Sardinia, and Africa, collected vast stores of corn. He was just ready to set sail upon his voyage home, when a great storm arose upon the sea, and the ships' commanders doubted whether it were safe. Upon which Pompey himself went first aboard, and bid the mariners weigh anchor, declaring with a loud voice, that there was a necessity to sail, but no necessity to live. So that with this spirit and courage, and having met with favorable fortune, he made a prosperous return, and filled the markets with corn, and the sea with ships. So much so that this great plenty and abundance of provisions yielded a sufficient supply, not only to the city of Rome, but even to other places too, dispersing itself, like waters from a spring, into all quarters.

Meantime Cæsar grew great and famous with his wars in Gaul, and while in appearance he seemed far distant from Rome, entangled in the affairs of the Belgians, Suevians, and Britons, in truth he was working craftily by secret practices in the midst of the people, and countermining Pompey in all political matters of most importance. He himself, with his army close about him, as if it had been his own body, not with mere views of conquest over the barbarians, but as though his contests with them where but mere sports and exercises of the chase, did his utmost with this training and discipline to make it invincible and alarming. And in the mean time his gold and silver and other spoils and treasure which he took from the enemy in his conquests, he sent to Rome in presents, tempting people with his gifts, and aiding ædiles, prætors, and consuls, as also their wives, in their expenses, and thus purchasing himself numerous friends. Insomuch, that when he passed back again over the Alps, and took up his winter-quarters in the city of Luca, there flocked to him an infinite number of men and women, striving who should get first to him, two hundred senators included, among whom were Pompey and Crassus; so that there were to be seen at once before Cæsar's door no less than sixscore rods of proconsuls and prætors. The rest of his addressers he sent all away full fraught with hopes and money; but with Crassus and Pompey, he entered into special articles of agreement, that they should stand candidates for the consulship next year; that Cæsar on his part should send a number of his soldiers to give their votes at the election; that as soon as they were elected, they should use their interest to have the command of some provinces and legions assigned to themselves, and that Cæsar should have his present charge confirmed to him for five years more. When these arrangements came to be generally known, great indignation was excited among the chief men in Rome; and Marcellinus, in an open assembly of the people, demanded of them both, whether they designed to sue for the consulship or no. And being urged by the people for their answer, Pompey spoke first, and told them, perhaps he would sue for it, perhaps he would not. Crassus was more temperate, and said, that he would do what should be judged most agreeable with the interest of the Commonwealth; and when Marcellinus persisted in his attack on Pompey, and spoke, as it was thought, with some vehemence, Pompey remarked that Marcellinus was certainly the unfairest of men, to show him no gratitude for having thus made him an orator out of a mute, and converted him from a hungry starveling into a man so full-fed that he could not contain himself.

Most of the candidates nevertheless abandoned their canvass for the consulship; Cato alone persuaded and encouraged Lucius Domitius not to desist, "since," said he, "the contest now is not for office, but for liberty against tyrants and usurpers." Therefore those of Pompey's party, fearing this inflexible constancy in Cato, by which he kept with him the whole senate, lest by this he should likewise pervert and draw after him all the well-affected part of the commonalty, resolved to withstand Domitius at once, and to prevent his entrance into the forum. To this end, therefore, they sent in a band of armed men, who slew the torchbearer of Domitius, as he was leading the way before him, and put all the rest to flight; last of all, Cato himself retired, having received a wound in his right arm while defending Domitius. Thus by these means and practices they obtained the consulship; neither did they behave themselves with more decency in their further proceedings; but in the first place, when the people were choosing Cato prætor, and just ready with their votes for the poll, Pompey broke up the assembly, upon a pretext of some inauspicious appearance, and having gained the tribes by money, they publicly proclaimed Vatinius prætor. Then, in pursuance of their covenants with Cæsar, they introduced several laws by Trebonius, the tribune, continuing Cæsar's commission to another five years' charge of his province ; to Crassus there were appointed Syria, and the Parthian war; and to Pompey himself, all Africa, together with both Spains, and four legions of soldiers, two of which he lent to Cæsar upon his request, for the wars in Gaul.

Crassus, upon the expiration of his consulship, departed forthwith into his province ; but Pompey spent some time in Rome, upon the opening or dedication of his theatre, where he treated the people with all sorts of games, shows, and exercises, in gymnastics alike and in music. There was likewise the hunting or baiting of wild beasts, and combats with them, in which five hundred lions were slain ; but above all, the battle of elephants was a spectacle full of horror and amazement.

These entertainments brought him great honor and popularity ; but on the other side he created no less envy to himself, in that he committed the government of his provinces and legions into the hands of friends as his lieutenants, whilst he himself was going about and spending his time with his wife in all the places of amusement in Italy ; whether it were he was so fond of her himself, or she so fond of him, and he unable to distress her by going away, for this also is stated. And the love displayed by this young wife for her elderly husband was a matter of general note, to be attributed, it would seem, to his constancy in married life, and to his dignity of manner, which in familiar intercourse was tempered with grace and gentleness, and was particularly attractive to women, as even Flora, the courtesan, may be thought good enough evidence to prove. It once happened in a public assembly, as they were at an election of the ædiles, that the people came to blows, and several about Pompey were slain, so that he, finding himself all bloody, ordered a change of apparel ; but the servants who brought home his clothes, making a great bustle and hurry about the house, it chanced that the young lady, who was then with child, saw his gown all stained with blood ; upon which she dropped immediately into a swoon, and was hardly brought to life again ; however, what with her fright and suffering, she fell into labor and miscarried ; even those who chiefly censured Pompey for his friendship to Cæsar, could not reprove him for his affection to so attached a wife. Afterwards she was great again, and brought to bed of a daughter, but died in childbed ; neither did the infant outlive her mother many days. Pompey had prepared all things for the interment of her corpse at his house near Alba, but the

people seized upon it by force, and performed the solemnities
in the field of Mars, rather in compassion for the young lady,
than in favor either for Pompey or Cæsar; and yet of these
two, the people seemed at that time to pay Cæsar a greater
share of honor in his absence, than to Pompey, though he
was present.

For the city now at once began to roll and swell, so to say,
with the stir of the coming storm. Things everywhere were
in a state of agitation, and everybody's discourse tended to
division, now that death had put an end to that relation which
hitherto had been a disguise rather than restraint to the am
bition of these men. Besides, not long after came messengers from Parthia with intelligence of the death of Crassus
there, by which another safeguard against civil war was removed, since both Cæsar and Pompey kept their eyes on
Crassus, and awe of him held them together more or less
within the bounds of fair-dealing all his lifetime. But when
fortune had taken away this second, whose province it might
have been to revenge the quarrel of the conquered, you might
then say with the comic poet,

> The combatants are waiting to begin,
> Smearing their hands with dust and oiling each his skin.

So inconsiderable a thing is fortune in respect of human nature, and so insufficient to give content to a covetous mind,
that an empire of that mighty extent and sway could not satisfy the ambition of two men; and though they knew and had
read, that

> The gods, when they divided out 'twixt three,
> This massive universe, heaven, hell, and sea,
> Each one sat down contented on his throne,
> And undisturbed each god enjoys his own,

yet they thought the whole Roman empire not sufficient to
contain them, though they were but two.

Pompey once in an oration to the people, told them, that
he had always come into office before he expected he should,
and that he had always left it sooner than they expected he
would, and, indeed, the disbanding of all his armies witnessed as much. Yet when he perceived that Cæsar would
not so willingly discharge his forces, he endeavored to strength-
en himself against him by offices and commands in the city;
but beyond this he showed no desire for any change, and
would not seem to distrust, but rather to disregard and contemn him. And when he saw how they bestowed the places

of government quite contrary to his wishes, because the citizens were bribed in their elections, he let things take their course, and allowed the city to be left without any government at all. Hereupon there was mention straightway made of appointing a dictator. Lucullus, a tribune of the people, was the man who first adventured to propose it, urging the people to make Pompey dictator. But the tribune was in danger of being turned out of his office, by the opposition that Cato made against it. And for Pompey, many of his friends appeared and excused him, alleging that he never was desirous of that government, neither would he accept of it. And when Cato therefore made a speech in commendation of Pompey and exhorted him to support the cause of good order in the Commonwealth, he could not for shame but yield to it, and so for the present Domitius and Messala were elected consuls. But shortly afterwards, when there was another anarchy, or vacancy in the government, and the talk of a dictator was much louder and more general than before, those of Cato's party, fearing lest they should be forced to appoint Pompey, thought it policy to keep him from that arbitrary and tyrannical power, by giving him an office of more legal authority. Bibulus himself, who was Pompey's enemy, first gave his vote in the senate, that Pompey should be created consul alone; alleging, that by these means either the Commonwealth would be freed from its present confusion, or that its bondage should be lessened by serving the worthiest. This was looked upon as a very strange opinion, considering the man that spoke it; and therefore on Cato's standing up, everybody expected that he would have opposed it; but after silence made, he said that he would never have been the author of that advice himself, but since it was propounded by another, his advice was to follow it, adding, that any form of government was better than none at all; and that in a time so full of distraction, he thought no man fitter to govern than Pompey. This counsel was unanimously approved of, and a decree passed that Pompey shou'd be made sole consul, with this clause, that if he thought it necessary to have a colleague, he might choose whom he pleased, provided it were not till after two months expired

Thus was Pompey created and declared sole consul by Sulpicius, regent in this vacancy; upon which he made very cordial acknowledgments to Cato, professing himself much his debtor, and requesting his good advice in conducting the government; to this Cato replied, that Pompey had no reason to thank him, for all that he had said was for the service of the commonwealth, not of Pompey; but that he would be always ready to give his advice privately, if he were asked for it; and if not, he should not fail to say what he thought in public. Such was Cato's conduct on all occasions.

On his return into the city Pompey married Cornelia, the daughter of Metellus Scipio, not a maiden, but lately left a widow by Publius, the son of Crassus, her first husband, who had been killed in Parthia. The young lady had other attractions besides those of youth and beauty; for she was highly educated, played well upon the lute, and understood geometry, and had been accustomed to listen with profit to lectures on philosophy; all this, too, without in any degree becoming unamiable or pretentious, as sometimes young women do when they pursue such studies. Nor could any fault be found either with her father's family or reputation. The disparity of their ages was, however, not liked by everybody; Cornelia being in this respect a fitter match for Pompey's son. And wiser judges thought it rather a slight upon the commonwealth when he, to whom alone they had committed their broken fortunes, and from whom alone, as from their physician, they expected a cure to these distractions, went about crowned with garlands and celebrating his nuptial feasts, never considering that his very consulship was a public calamity, which would never have been given him, contrary to the rules of law, had his country been in a flourishing state. Afterwards, however, he took cognizance of the cases of those that had obtained offices by gifts and bribery, and enacted laws and ordinances, setting forth the rules of judgment by which they should be arraigned; and regulating all things with gravity and justice, he restored security, order, and silence to their courts of judicature, himself giving his presence there with a band of soldiers. But when his father-in-law, Scipio, was accused, he sent for the three hundred and sixty judges to his house, and entreated them to be favorable to him; whereupon his accuser, seeing Scipio come into the court, accompanied by the judges themselves, withdrew the prosecution. Upon this Pompey was very ill spoken of, and much worse in the case of Plancus; for whereas he himself had made a law, putting a stop to the practice of making speeches in praise of persons under trial, yet notwithstanding this prohibition, he came into court and spoke openly in commendation of Plancus, insomuch that Cato, who happened to be one of the judges at that time stopping his ears with his hands, told him, he could not in conscious listen to commendations contrary to law. Cato upon this was refused, and set aside from being a judge, before sentence was given, but Plancus was condemned by the rest of the judges, to Pompey's dishonor. Shortly after Hypsæus, a man of consular dignity, who was under accusation, waited for Pompey's return from his bath to his supper, and falling down at his feet, implored his favor; but he disdainfully passed him by, saying, that he did nothing else but spoil his supper. Such partiality was looked upon as a great fault in Pompey, and highly condemned; however, he managed all things else discreetly, and having put the government in very good order, he chose his father-in-law to be his colleague in the consulship for the last five months. His provinces were continued to him for the term of four years longer, with a commission to take one thousand talents yearly out of the treasury for the payment of his army.

This gave occasion to some of Cæsar's friends to think it reasonable, that some consideration should be had of him too, who had done such signal services in war and fought so many battles for the empire, alleging, that he deserved at least a second consulship, or to have the government of his province continued, that so he might command and enjoy in peace what he had obtained in war, and no successor come in to reap the fruits of his labor, and carry off the glory of his actions. There arising some debate about this matter, Pompey took upon him, as it were out of kindness to Cæsar, to plead his cause, and allay any jealousy that was conceived against him, telling them that he had letters from Cæsar, expressing his desire for a successor, and his own discharge from the command; but it would be only right that they should give him leave to stand for the cousulship though in his absence. But those of Cato's party withstood this, saying that if he expected any favor from the citizens, he ought to leave his army, and come in a private capacity to canvass for it. And Pompey's making no rejoinder, but letting it pass as a matter in which he was overruled, increased the suspicion of his real feelings towards Cæsar. Presently, also, under pretence of a war with Parthia, he sent for his two legions which he had lent him. However, Cæsar, though he well knew why they were asked for, sent them home very liberally rewarded.

About that time Pompey recovered of a dangerous fit of sickness which seized him at Naples, where the whole city upon the suggestion of Praxagoras, made sacrifices of thanks giving to the gods for his recovery The neighboring towns likewise happening to follow their example, the thing then went its course throughout all Italy, so that there was not a city, either great or small, that did not feast and rejoice for many days together. And the company of those that came from all parts to meet him was so numerous, that no place was able to contain them, but the villages, seaport towns, and the very highways, were all full of people, feasting and sacrificing to the gods. Nay, many went to meet him with garlands on their heads, and flambeaux in their hands, casting flowers and nosegays upon him as he went along; so that this progress of his, and reception, was one of the noblest and most glorious sights imaginable. And yet it is thought that this very thing was not one of the least causes and occasions of the civil war. For Pompey, yielding to a feeling of exultation, which in the greatness of the present display of joy lost sight of more solid grounds of consideration, and abandoning that prudent temper which had guided him hitherto to a safe use of all his good fortune and his successes, gave himself up to an extravagant confidence in his own, and contempt of Cæsar's power; insomuch that he thought neither force of arms nor care necessary against him, but that he could pull him down much easier than he had set him up. Besides this, Appius, under whose command those legions which Pompey lent to Cæsar were returned, coming lately out of Gaul, spoke slightingly of Cæsar's actions there, and spread scandalous reports about him, at the same time telling Pompey, that he was unacquainted with his own strength and reputation, if he made use of any other forces against Cæsar than Cæsar's own; for such was the soldiers' hatred to Cæsar, and their love to Pompey so great, that they would all come over to him upon his first appearance. By these flatteries Pompey was so puffed up, and led on into such a careless security, that he could not choose but laugh at those who seemed to fear a war; and when some were saying, that if Cæsar should march against the city, they could not see what forces there were to resist him, he replied with a smile, bidding them be in no concern, "for," said he, "whenever I stamp with my foot in any part of Italy, there will rise up forces enough in an instant, both horse and foot."

Cæsar, on the other side, was more and more vigorous in his proceedings, himself always at hand about the frontiers of Italy, and sending his soldiers continually into the city to attend all elections with their votes. Besides, he corrupted several of the magistrates, and kept them in his pay; among others, Paulus, the consul, who was brought over by a bribe of one thousand and five hundred talents; and Curio, tribune of the people, by a discharge of the debts with which he was overwhelmed; together with Mark Antony, who, out of friendship to Curio, had become bound with him in the same obligations for them all. And it was stated as a fact, that a centurion of Cæsar's, waiting at the senate-house, and hearing that the senate refused to give him a longer term of his government, clapped his hand upon his sword, and said, "But this shall give it." And indeed all his practices and preparations seemed to bear this appearance. Curio's demands, however, and requests in favor of Cæsar, were more popular in appearance; for he desired one of these two things, either that Pompey also should be called upon to resign his army, or that Cæsar's should not be taken away from him; for if both of them became private persons, both would be satisfied with simple justice; or if both retained their present power, each being a match for the other, they would be contented with what they already had; but he that weakens one, does at the same time strengthen the other, and so doubles that very strength and power which he stood in fear of before. Marcellus, the consul, replied nothing to all this, but that Cæsar was a robber, and should be proclaimed an enemy to the state, if he did not disband his army. However, Curio, with the assistance of Antony and Piso, prevailed, that the matter in debate should be put to the question, and decided by vote in the senate. So that it being ordered upon the question for those to withdraw, who were of opinion that Cæsar only should lay down his army, and Pompey command, the majority withdrew. But when it was ordered again for those to withdraw, whose vote was, that both should lay down their arms, and neither command, there were but twenty-two for Pompey, all the rest remained on Curio's side. Whereupon he, as one proud of his conquest, leaped out in triumph among the people, who received him with as great tokens of joy, clapping their hands, and crowning him with garlands and flowers. Pompey was not then present in the senate, because it is not lawful for generals in command of an army to come into the city But Marcellus rising up, said that he would not sit there hearing speeches, when he saw ten legions already passing the Alps on their march toward the city but on his own authority would send some one to oppose them in defence of the country.

Upon this the city went into mourning, as in a public calamity, and Marcellus, accompanied by the senate, went solemnly through the forum to meet Pompey, and made him this address. "I hereby give you orders, O Pompey, to defend your country, to employ the troops you now command, and to levy more." Lentulus, consul elect for the year following, spoke to the same purpose. Antony, however, contrary to the will of the senate, having in a public assembly read a letter of Cæsar's, containing various plausible overtures such as were likely to gain the common people, proposing, namely, that both Pompey and he quitting their governments and dismissing their armies, should submit to the judgment of the people, and give an account of their actions before them, the consequence was that when Pompey began to make his levies, he found himself disappointed in his expectations. Some few, indeed, came in, but those very unwillingly; others would not answer to their names, and the generality cried out for peace. Lentulus, notwithstanding he was now entered upon his consulship, would not assemble the senate; but Cicero, who was lately returned from Cilicia, labored for a reconciliation, proposing that Cæsar should leave his province of Gaul and army, reserving two legions only, together with the government of Illyricum, and should thus be put in nomination for a second consulship. Pompey disliking this motion, Cæsar's friends were contented that he should surrender one of the two; but Lentulus still opposing, and Cato crying out that Pompey did ill to be deceived again, the reconciliation did not take effect.

In the mean time, news was brought that Cæsar had occupied Ariminum, a great city in Italy, and was marching directly towards Rome with all his forces. But this latter was altogether false, for he had no more with him at that time than three hundred horse and five thousand foot; and he did not mean to tarry for the body of his army, which lay beyond the Alps, choosing rather to fall in on a sudden upon his enemies, while they were in confusion, and did not expect him, than to give them time, and fight them after they had made preparations. For when he came to the banks of the Rubicon, a river that made the bounds of his province, there he made a halt, pausing a little, and considering, we may suppose, with himself the greatness of the enterprise which he had undertaken; then, at last, like men that are throwing themselves headlong from some precipice into a vast abyss, having shut, as it were, his mind's eyes and put away from his sight the idea of danger, he merely uttered to those near him in Greek the words, "Anerriphtho kubos" (let the die be cast), and led his army through it. No sooner was the news arrived, but there was an uproar throughout all the city, and a consternation in the people even to astonishment, such as never was known in Rome before; all the senate ran immediately to Pompey, and the magistrates followed. And when Tullus made inquiry about his legions and forces, Pompey seemed to pause a little, and answered with some hesitation, that he had those two legions ready that Cæsar sent back, and that out of the men who had been previously enrolled he believed he could shortly make up a body of thirty thousand men. On which Tullus crying out aloud, "O Pompey, you have deceived us," gave his advice to send off a deputation to Cæsar. Favonius, a man of fair character, except that he used to suppose his own petulance and abusive talking a copy of Cato's straightforwardness, bade Pompey stamp upon the ground, and call forth the forces he had promised. But Pompey bore patiently with this unseasonable raillery; and on Cato putting him in mind of what he had foretold from the very beginning about Cæsar, made this answer only, that Cato indeed had spoken more like a prophet, but he had acted more like a friend. Cato then advised them to choose Pompey general with absolute power and authority, saying that the same men who do great evils, know best how to cure them. He himself went his way forthwith into Sicily, the province that was allotted him, and all the rest of the senators likewise departed every one to his respective government.

Thus all Italy in a manner being up in arms, no one could say what was best to be done. For those that were without, came from all parts flocking into the city; and they who were within, seeing the confusion and disorder so great there, all good things impotent, and disobedience and insubordination grown too strong to be controlled by the magistrates, were quitting it as fast as the others came in. Nay, it was so far from being possible to allay their fears, that they would not suffer Pompey to follow out his own judgment, but every man pressed and urged him according to his particular fancy, whether it proceeded from doubt, fear, grief, or any meaner passion; so that even in the same day quite contrary counsels were acted upon. Then, again, it was as impossible to have any good intelligence of the enemy; for what each man heard by chance upon a flying rumor, he would report for truth, and exclaim against Pompey if he did not believe it. Pompey, at length, seeing such a confusion in Rome, determined with himself to put an end to their clamors by his departure, and therefore commanding all the senate to follow him, and declaring, that whosoever tarried behind, should be judged a confederate of Cæsar's, about the dusk of the evening he went out and left the city. The consuls also followed after in a hurry, without offering the sacrifices to the gods, usual before a war. But in all this, Pompey himself had the glory, that in the midst of such calamities, he had so much of men's love and good-will. For though many found fault with the conduct of the war, yet no man hated the general; and there were more to be found of those that went out of Rome, because that they could not forsake Pompey, than of those that fled for love of liberty.

Some few days after Pompey was gone out, Cæsar came into the city, and made himself master of it, treating every one with a great deal of courtesy, and appeasing their fears, except only Metellus, one of the tribunes; on whose refusing to let him take any money out of the treasury, Cæsar threatened him with death, adding words yet harsher than the threat, that it was far easier for him to do it than say it. By this means removing Metellus, and taking what moneys were of use for his occasions, he set forwards in pursuit of Pompey, endeavoring with all speed to drive him out of Italy before his army, that was in Spain, could join him.

But Pompey arriving at Brundusium, and having plenty of ships there, bade the two consuls embark immediately, and with them shipped thirty cohorts of foot, bound before him for Dyrrhachium. He sent likewise his father-in-law, Scipio, and Cnæus, his son, into Syria, to provide and fit out a fleet there; himself in the mean time having blocked up the gates, placed his lightest soldiers as guards upon the walls; and giving express orders that the citizens should keep within doors, he dug up all the ground inside the city, cutting trenches, and fixing stakes and palisades throughout all the streets of the city, except only two that led down to the sea-side. Thus in three days space having with ease put all the rest of his army on shipboard, he suddenly gave the signal to those that guarded the walls who nimbly repairing to the ships, were received on board and carried off. Cæsar meantime perceiving their departure by seeing the walls unguarded, hastened after, and in the heat of pursuit was all but entangled himself among the stakes and trenches. But the Brundusians discovering the danger to him, and showing him the way, he wheeled about, and taking a circuit round the city, made towards the haven, where he found all the ships on their way, excepting only two vessels that had but a few soldiers aboard.

Most are of opinion, that this departure of Pompey's is to be counted among the best of his military performances, but Cæsar himself could not but wonder that he, who was thus ingarrisoned in a city well fortified, who was in expectation of his forces from Spain, and was master of the sea besides, should leave and abandon Italy. Cicero accuses him of imitating the conduct of Themistocles, rather than of Pericles, when the circumstances were more like those of Pericles than they were like those of Themistocles. However, it appeared plainly, and Cæsar showed it by his actions, that he was in great fear of delay, for when he had taken Numerius, a friend of Pompey's, prisoner, he sent him as an ambassador to Brundusium, with offers of peace and reconciliation upon equal terms; but Numerius sailed away with Pompey. And now Cæsar having become master of all Italy in sixty days, without a drop of blood shed, had a great desire forthwith to follow Pompey; but being destitute of shipping, he was forced to divert his course, and march into Spain, designing to bring over Pompey's forces there to his own.

In the mean time Pompey raised a mighty army both by sea and land. As for his navy, it was irresistible. For there were five hundred men of war, besides an infinite company of light vessels, Liburnians, and others; and for his land forces, the cavalry made up a body of seven thousand horse, the very flower of Rome and Italy, men of family, wealth, and high spirit; but the infantry was a mixture of inexperienced soldiers drawn from different quarters, and these he exercised and trained near Berœa, where he quartered his army; himself noways slothful, but performing all his exercises as if he had been in the flower of his youth, conduct which raised the spirits of his soldiers extremely. For it was no small encouragement for them to see Pompey the Great, sixty years of age wanting two, at one time handling his arms among the foot then again mounted among the horse, drawing out his sword with ease in full career, and sheathing it up as easily; and in darting the javelin, showing not only skill and dexterity in hitting the mark, but also strength and activity in throwing it so far that few of the young men went beyond him.

Several kings and princes of nations came thither to him

and there was a concourse of Roman citizens who had held
the magistracies, so numerous that they made up a complete
senate. Labienus forsook his old friend Cæsar, whom he
had served throughout all his wars in Gaul, and came over to
Pompey; and Brutus, son to that Brutus that was put to death
in Gaul, a man of a high spirit, and one that to that day had
never so much as saluted or spoke to Pompey, looking upon
him as the murderer of his father, came then and submitted
himself to him as the defender of their liberty. Cicero likewise, though he had written and advised otherwise, yet was
ashamed not to be accounted in the number of those that
would hazard their lives and fortunes for the safeguard of
their country. There came to him also into Macedonia, Tidius
Sextius, a man extremely old, and lame of one leg; so that
others indeed mocked and laughed at the spectacle, but Pompey, as soon as he saw him, rose and ran to meet him, esteeming it no small testimony in his favor, when men of such age
and infirmities should rather choose to be with him in danger, than in safety at home. Afterwards in a meeting of their
senate they passed a decree, on the motion of Cato, that no
Roman citizen should be put to death but in battle, and that
they should not sack or plunder any city that was subject to
the Roman empire, a resolution which gained Pompey's party
still greater reputation, insomuch that those who were noways at all concerned in the war, either because they dwelt
afar off, or were thought incapable of giving help, were yet
in their good wishes, upon his side, and in all their words,
so far as that went, supported the good or just cause, as they
called it; esteeming those as enemies to the gods and men,
that wished not victory to Pompey.

Neither was Pompey's clemency such, but that Cæsar
likewise showed himself as merciful a conqueror; for when
he had taken and overthrown all Pompey's forces in Spain, he
gave them easy terms, leaving the commanders at their liberty, and taking the common soldiers into his own pay. Then
repassing the Alps, and making a running march through Italy,
he came to Brundusium about the winter solstice, and crossing the sea there, landed at the port of Oricum. And having
Jubius, an intimate friend of Pompey's with him as his prisoner, he despatched him to Pompey with an invitation, that they,
meeting together in a conference, should disband both their
armies within three days, and renewing their former friendship
with solemn oaths, should return together into Italy. Pompey
looked upon this again as some new stratagem, and therefore

marching down in all haste to the sea coast, possessed himself of all forts and places of strength suitable to encamp in, and to secure his land forces, as likewise of all ports and harbors commodious to receive any that came by sea, so that what wind soever blew, it must needs, in some way or other, be favorable to him, bringing in either provision, men, or money; while Cæsar, on the contrary, was so hemmed in both by sea and land, that he was forced to desire battle, daily provoking the enemy, and assailing them in their very forts; and 'n these light skirmishes for the most part had the better. Once only he was dangerously overthrown, and was within a little of losing his whole army, Pompey having fought nobly, routing the whole force, and killing two thousand on the spot. But either he was not able, or was afraid, to go on and force his way into their camp with them; so that Cæsar made the remark, that "To-day the victory had been the enemy's had there been any one among them to gain it." Pompey's soldiers were so encouraged by this victory that they were eager now to have all put to the decision of a battle; but Pompey himself, though he wrote to distant kings, generals, and states in confederacy with him, as a conqueror, yet was afraid to hazard the success of a battle, choosing rather by delays, and distress of provisions, to tire out a body of men, who had never yet been conquered by force of arms, and had long been used to fight and conquer together; while their time of life, now an advanced one, which made them quickly weary of those other hardships of war, such as were long marches, and frequent decampings, making trenches, and building fortifications, made them eager to come to close combat and venture a battle with all speed.

Pompey had all along hitherto by his persuasions pretty well quieted his soldiers; but after this last engagement, when Cæsar, for want of provisions, was forced to raise his camp, and passed through Athamania into Thessaly, it was impossible to curb or allay the heat of their spirits any longer. For all crying out with a general voice, that Cæsar was fled, some were for pursuing and pressing upon him, others for returning into Italy; some there were that sent their friends and servants beforehand to Rome, to hire houses near the forum, that they might be in readiness to sue for offices; several of their own motion sailed off at once to Lesbos to carry to Cornelia (whom Pompey had conveyed thither to be in safety), the joyful news, that the war was ended. And a senate being called, and the matter being under debate, Afranius was of opinion, that Italy should first be regained, for that it was the grand prize and crown of all the war; and they who were masters of that, would quickly have at their devotion all the provinces of Sicily, Sardinia, Corsica, Spain, and Gaul; but what was of greatest weight and moment to Pompey, it was his own native country that lay near, reaching out her hand for his help; and certainly it could not be consistent with his honor to leave her thus exposed to all indignities, and in bondage under slaves and the flatterers of a tyrant. But Pompey himself, on the contrary, thought it neither honorable to fly a second time before Cæsar, and be pursued, when fortune had given him the advantage of a pursuit; nor indeed lawful before the gods to forsake Scipio and divers other men of consular dignity dispersed throughout Greece and Thessaly, who must necessarily fall into Cæsar's hands, together with large sums of money and numerous forces; and as to his care for the city of Rome, that would most eminently appear, by removing the scene of war to a greater distance, and leaving her, without feeling the distress or even hearing the sound of these evils, to await in peace the return of which ever should be the victor.

With this determination, Pompey marched forwards in pursuit of Cæsar, firmly resolved with himself not to give him battle, but rather to besiege and distress him, by keeping close at his heels, and cutting him short. There were other reasons that made him continue this resolution, but especially because a saying that was current among the Romans serving in the cavalry came to his ear, to the effect, that they ought to beat Cæsar as soon as possible, and then humble Pompey too. And some report, it was for this reason that Pompey never employed Cato in any matter of consequence during the whole war, but now when he pursued Cæsar, left him to guard his baggage by sea, fearing lest, if Cæsar should be taken off, he himself also by Cato's means not long after should be forced to give up his power.

Whilst he was thus slowly attending the motions of the enemy, he was exposed on all sides to outcries, and imputations of using his generalship to defeat, not Cæsar, but his country and the senate, that he might always continue in authority, and never cease to keep those for his guards and servants, who themselves claimed to govern the world. Domitius Ænobarbus, continually calling him Agamemnon, and king of kings, excited jealousy against him; and Favonius, by his unseasonble raillery, did him no less injury than those ho openly attacked him, as when he cried out, Good friends, ou must not expect to gather any figs in Tusculum this year." ut Lucius Afranius, who had lain under an imputation of eachery for the loss of the army in Spain, when he saw Pomey purposely declining an engagement, declared openly, that he could not but admire, why those who were so ready to accuse him, did not go themselves and fight this buyer and seller of their provinces.

With these and many such speeches they wrought upon Pompey who never could bear reproach, or resist the expectations of his friends; and thus they forced him to break his measures, so that he forsook his own prudent resolution to follow their vain hopes and desires: weakness that would have been blamable in the pilot of a ship, how much more in the sovereign commander of such an army, and so many nations. But he, though he had often commended those physicians who did not comply with the capricious appetites of their patients, yet himself could not but yield to the malady and disease of his companions and advisers in the war, rather than use some severity in their cure. Truly who could have said that health was not disordered and a cure not required in the case of men who went up and down the camp, suing already for the consulship and office of prætor, while Spinther, Domitius, and Scipio made friends, raised factions, and quarrelled among themselves, who should succeed Cæsar in the dignity of his high-priesthood, esteeming all as lightly, as if they were to engage only with Tigranes, king of Armenia, or some petty Nabathæan king, not with that Cæsar and his army that had stormed a thousand towns, and subdued more than three hundred several nations; that had fought innumerable battles with the Germans and Gauls, and always carried the victory; that had taken a million of men prisoners, and slain as many upon the spot in pitched battles?

But they went on soliciting and clamoring, and on reaching the plain of Pharsalia, they forced Pompey by their pressure and importunities to call a council of war, where Labienus, general of the horse, stood up first and swore that he would not return out of the battle if he did not rout the enemies; and all the rest took the same oath. That night Pompey dreamed that as he went into the theatre, the people received him with great applause, and that he himself adorned the temple of Venus the Victorious, with many spoils. This vision partly encouraged, but partly also disheartened him, fearing lest that splendor and ornament to Venus should be made with spoils furnished by himself to Cæsar, who derived his family from that goddess. Besides there were some panic fears and alarms that ran through the camp, with such a noise that it awaked him out of his sleep. And about the time of renewing the watch towards morning, there appeared a great light over Cæsar's camp, whilst they were all at rest, and from thence a ball of flaming fire was carried into Pompey's camp, which Cæsar himself says he saw, as he was walking his rounds.

Now Cæsar having designed to raise his camp with the morning and move to Scotussa, whilst the soldiers were busy in pulling down their tents, and sending on their cattle and servants before them with their baggage, there came in scouts who brought word that they saw arms carried to and fro in the enemy's camp, and heard a noise and running up and down, as of men preparing for battle; not long after there came in other scouts with further intelligence, that the first ranks were already set in battle array. Thereupon Cæsar, when he had told them that the wished for day was come at last, when they should fight with men, not with hunger and famine, instantly gave orders for the red colors to be set up before his tent, that being the ordinary signal of battle among the Romans. As soon as the soldiers saw that, they left their tents, and with great shouts of joy ran to their arms; the officers, likewise, on their parts drawing up their companies in order of battle, every man fell into his proper rank without any trouble or noise, as quietly and orderly as if they had been in a dance.

Pompey himself led the right wing of his army against Antony, and placed his father-in-law, Scipio, in the middle against Lucius Calvinus. The left wing was commanded by Lucius Domitius, and supported by the great mass of the horse. For almost the whole cavalry was posted there in the hope of crushing Cæsar, and cutting off the tenth legion, which was spoken of as the stoutest in all the army, and in which Cæsar himself usually fought in person. Cæsar observing the left wing of the enemy to be lined and fortified with such a mighty guard of horse, and alarmed at the gallantry of their appearance, sent for a detachment of six cohorts out of the reserves, and placed them in the rear of the tenth legion, commanding them not to stir, lest they should be discovered by the enemy; but when the enemy's horse should begin to charge, and press upon them, that they should make up with all speed to the front through the foremost ranks, and not throw their javelins at a distance, as is usual with brave soldiers, that they may come to a close fight with their swords the sooner, but that they should strike them upwards into the eyes and faces of the enemy; telling them that those fine young dancers would never endure the steel shining in their eyes, but would fly to save their handsome faces. This was Cæsar's employment at that time. But while he was thus instructing his soldiers, Pompey on horseback was viewing the order of both armies, and when he saw how well the enemy kept their ranks, expecting quietly the signal of battle, and, on the contrary, how impatient and unsteady his own men were, waving up and down in disorder for want of experience, he was very much afraid that their ranks would be broken upon the first onset; and therefore he gave out orders that the van should make a stand, and keeping close in their ranks should receive the enemy's charge. Cæsar much condemns this command; which, he says, not only took off from the strength of the blows, which would otherwise have been made with a spring, but also lost the men the impetus, which, more than any thing, in the moment of their coming upon the enemy, fills soldiers with impulse and inspiration, the very shouts and rapid pace adding to their fury; of which Pompey deprived his men, arresting them in their course and cooling down their heat.

Cæsar's army consisted of twenty-two thousand, and Pompey's of somewhat above twice as many. When the signal of battle was given on both sides, and the trumpets began to sound a charge, most men of course were fully occupied with their own matters; only some few of the noblest Romans, together with certain Greeks there present, standing as spectators without the battle seeing the armies now ready to join, could not but consider in themselves to what a pass private ambition and emulation had brought the empire. Common arms, and kindred ranks drawn up under the self-same standards, the whole flower and strength of the same single city here meeting in collision with itself, offered plain proof how blind and how mad a thing human nature is, when once possessed with any passion; for if they had been desirous only to rule, and enjoy in peace what they had conquered in war, the greatest and best part of the world was subject to them both by sea and land. But if there was yet a thirst in their ambition, that must still be fed with new trophies and triumphs, the Parthian and German wars would yield matter enough to satisfy the most covetous of honor. Scythia, moreover, was yet unconquered, and the Indians too, where their ambition might be colored over with the specious pretext of civilizing barbarous nations. And what Scythian horse, Parthian arrows, or Indian riches, could be able to resist seventy thousand Roman soldiers, well appointed in arms, under the command of two such generals as Pompey and Cæsar, whose names they had heard of before that of the Romans, and whose prowess, by their conquests of such wild, remote, savage, and brutish nations, was spread further than the fame of the Romans themselves? To-day they met in conflict, and could no longer be induced to spare their country, even out of regard for their own glory or the fear of losing the name which till this day both had held, of having never yet been defeated. As for their former private ties, and the charms of Julia, and the marriage that had made them near connections, these could now only be looked upon as tricks of state, the mere securities of a treaty made to serve the needs of an occasion, not the pledges of any real friendship.

Now, therefore, as soon as the plains of Pharsalia were covered with men, horse, and armor, and that the signal of battle was raised on either side, Caius Crassianus, a centurion, who commanded a company of one hundred and twenty men, was the first that advanced out of Cæsar's army, to give the charge, and acquit himself of a solemn engagement that he had made to Cæsar. He had been the first man that Cæsar had seen going out of the camp in the morning, and Cæsar, after saluting him, had asked him what he thought of the coming battle. To which he, stretching out his right hand, replied aloud, "Thine is the victory, O Cæsar, thou shalt conquer gloriously, and I myself this day will be the subject of thy praise either alive or dead." In pursuance of this promise he hastened forward, and being followed by many more, charged into the midst of the enemy. There they came at once to a close fight with their swords, and made a great slaughter; but as he was still pressing forward, and breaking the ranks of the vanguard, one of Pompey's soldiers ran him in at the mouth, so that the point of the sword came out behind at his neck; and Crassianus being thus slain, the fight became doubtful, and continued equal on that part of the battle.

Pompey had not yet brought on the right wing, but stayed and looked about, waiting to see what execution his cavalry would do on the left. They had already drawn out their squadrons in form, designing to turn Cæsar's flank, and force those few horse, which he had placed in the front, to give back upon the battalion of foot. But Cæsar, on the other side, having given the signal, his horse retreated back a little, and gave way to those six subsidiary cohorts, which had been posted in the rear, as a reserve to cover the flank, and which now came out, three thousand men in number, and met the enemy; and when they came up, standing by the horses, struck their javelins upwards, according to their instructions, and hit the horsemen full in their faces. They, unskilful in any manner of fight, and least of all expecting or understanding such a kind as this, had not courage enough to endure the blows upon their faces, but turning their backs, and covering their eyes with their hands, shamefully took to flight. Cæsar's men, however, did not follow them, but marched upon the foot, and attacked the wing, which the flight of the cavalry had left unprotected, and liable to be turned and taken in the rear, so that this wing now being attacked in the flank by these, and charged in the front by the tenth legion, was not able to abide the charge, or make any longer resistance, especially when they saw themselves surrounded and circumvented in the very way in which they had designed to invest the enemy. Thus these being likewise routed and put to flight, when Pompey, by the dust flying in the air, conjectured the fate of his horse, it were very hard to say what his thoughts or intentions were, but looking like one distracted and beside himself, and without any recollection or reflection that he was Pompey the Great, he retired slowly towards his camp, without speaking a word to any man, exactly according to the description in the verses,

> But Jove from heaven struck Ajax with a fear;
> Ajax the bold then stood astonished there,
> Flung o'er his back the mighty sevenfold shield,
> And trembling gazed and spied about the field.

In this state and condition he went into his own tent, and sat down, speechless still, until some of the enemy fell in together with his men, that were flying into the camp, and then he let fall only this one word, "What! into the very camp?" and said no more, but rose up, and putting on a dress suitable to his present fortune, made his way secretly out.

By this time the rest of the army was put to flight, and there was a great slaughter in the camp among the servants and those that guarded the tents, but of the soldiers themselves there were not above six thousand slain, as is stated by Asinius Pollio, who himself fought in this battle on Cæsar's side. When Cæsar's soldiers had taken the camp, they saw clearly the folly and vanity of the enemy; for all their tents and pavilions were richly set out with garlands of myrtle, embroidered carpets and hangings, and tables laid and covered with goblets. There were large bowls of wine ready, and every thing prepared and put in array, in the manner rather of people who had offered sacrifice and were going to celebrate a holiday, than of soldiers who had armed themselves to go out to battle, so possessed with the expectation of success and so full of empty confidence had they gone out that morning.

When Pompey had got a little way from the camp, he dismounted and forsook his horse, having but a small retinue with him; and finding that no man pursued him, walked on softly afoot, taken up altogether with thoughts, such as probably might possess a man that for the space of thirty-four years together had been accustomed to conquest and victory, and was then at last, in his old age, learning for the first time what defeat and flight were. And it was no small affliction to consider, that he had lost in one hour all that glory and power, which he had been getting in so many wars, and bloody battles; and that he who but a little before was guarded with such an army of foot, so many squadrons of horse, and such a mighty fleet, was now flying in so mean a condition, and with such a slender retinue, that his very enemies who fought him could not know him. Thus, when he had passed by the city of Larissa, and came into the pass of Tempe, being very thirsty, he kneeled down and drank out of the river; then rising up again, he passed through Tempe, until he came to the seaside, and there he betook himself to a poor fisherman's cottage, where he rested the remainder of the night. The next morning about break of day he went into one of the river boats, and taking none of those that followed him except such as were free, dismissed his servants, advising them to go boldly to Cæsar, and not be afraid. As he was rowing up and down near the shore, he chanced to spy a large merchant-ship, lying off, just ready to set sail; the master of which was a Roman citizen, named Peticius, who, though he was not familiarly acquainted with Pompey, yet knew him well by sight. Now it happened that this Peticius dreamed, the night before, that he saw Pompey, not like the man he had often seen him, but in a humble and dejected condition, and in that posture discoursing with him. He was then telling his dream to the people on board, as men do when at lei sure, and especially dreams of that consequence when of a sudden one of the mariners told him, he saw a river boat with oars putting off from shore, and that some of the men there shook their garments, and held out their hands, with signs to take them in ; thereupon Peticius, looking attentively, at once recognized Pompey, just as he appeared in his dream, and smiting his hand on his head, ordered the mariners to let down the ship's boat, he himself waving his hand, and calling to him by his name, already assured of his change and the change of his fortune by that of his garb. So that without waiting for any further entreaty or discourse, he took him into his ship, together with as many of his company as he thought fit, and hoisted sail. There were with him the two Lentuli, and Favonius ; and a little after they spied king Deiotarus, making up towards them from the shore ; so they stayed and took him in along with them. At supper time, the master of the ship having made ready such provisions as he had aboard, Pompey, for want of his servants, began to undo his shoes himself, which Favonius noticing ran to him and undid them, and helped him to anoint himself, and always after continued to wait upon, and attended him in all things, as servants do their masters, even to the washing of his feet, and preparing his supper. Insomuch that any one there present, observing the free and unaffected courtesy of these services, might have well exclaimed,

> O heavens, in those that noble are,
> Whate'er they do is fit and fair.

Pompey, sailing by the city of Amphipolis, crossed over from thence to Mitylene, with a design to take in Cornelia and his son ; and as soon as he arrived at the port in that island, he despatched a messenger into the city, with news very different from Cornelia's expectation. For she, by all the former messages and letters sent to please her, had been put in hopes that the war was ended at Dyrrhachium, and that there was nothing more remaining for Pompey, but the pursuit of Cæsar. The messenger finding her in the same hopes still, was not able to salute or speak to her, but declaring the greatness of her misfortune by his tears rather than his words, desired her to make haste if she would see Pompey, with one ship only, and that not of his own. The young lady hearing this, fell down in a swoon, and continued a long time senseless and speechless. And when with some trouble she was brought to her senses again, being conscious to her self that this was no time for lamentation and tears, she started up and ran through the city towards the seaside, where Pompey meeting and embracing her, as she sank down, supported by his arms, "This, sir," she exclaimed, "is the effect of my fortune, not of yours, that I see you thus reduced to one poor vessel, who before your marriage with Cornelia, were wont to sail in these seas with a fleet of five hundred ships. Why therefore should you come to see me, or why not rather have left to her evil genius one who has brought upon you her own ill-fortune? How happy a woman had I been, if I had breathed out my last, before the news came from Parthia of the death of Publius, the husband of my youth, and how prudent if I had followed his destiny, as I designed! But I was reserved for a greater mischief, even the ruin of Pompey the Great."

Thus, they say, Cornelia spoke to him, and this was Pompey's reply: "You have had, Cornelia, but one season of a better fortune, which, it may be, gave you unfounded hopes, by attending me a longer time than is usual. It behoves us, who are mortals born, to endure these events, and to try fortune yet again; neither is it any less possible to recover our former state, than it was to fall from that into this." Thereupon Cornelia sent for her servants and baggage out of the city. The citizens also of Mitylene came out to salute and invite Pompey into the city, but he refused, advising them to be obedient to the conqueror, and fear not, for that Cæsar was a man of great goodness and clemency. Then turning to Cratippus, the philosopher, who came among the rest out of the city to visit him, he began to find some fault, and briefly argued with him upon Providence, but Cratippus modestly declined the dispute, putting him in better hopes only, lest by opposing, he might seem too austere or unseasonable. For he might have put Pompey a question in his turn, in defence of Providence; and might have demonstrated the necessity there was that the commonwealth should be turned into a monarchy, because of their ill government in the state; and could have asked, "How, O Pompey, and by what token or assurance can we ascertain, that if the victory had been yours, you would have used your fortune better than Cæsar? We must leave the divine power to act as we find it do?"

Pompey having taken his wife and friends aboard, set sail, making no port, or touching anywhere, but when he was necessitated to take in provisions, or fresh water. The first city he entered was Attalia, in Pamphylia, and whilst he was there, there came some galleys thither to him out of Cilicia, together with a small body of soldiers, and he had almost sixty senators with him again; then hearing that his navy was safe too, and that Cato had rallied a considerable body of soldiers after their overthrow, and was crossing with them over into Africa, he began to complain and blame himself to his friends that he had allowed himself to be driven into engaging by land, without making use of his other forces, in which he was irresistibly the stronger, and had not kept near enough to his fleet, that failing by land, he might have reinforced himself from the sea, and would have been again at the head of a power quite sufficient to encounter the enemy on equal terms. And in truth, neither did Pompey during all the war commit a greater oversight, nor Cæsar use a more subtle stratagem, than in drawing the fight so far off from the naval forces.

As it now was, however, since he must come to some decision, and try some plan within his present ability, he despatched his agents to the neighboring cities, and himself sailed about in person to others, requiring their aid in money and men for his ships. But, fearing lest the rapid approach of the enemy might cut off all his preparations, he began to consider what place would yield him the safest refuge and retreat at present. A consultation was held, and it was generally agreed that no province of the Romans was secure enough. As for foreign kingdoms, he himself was of opinion, that Parthia would be the fittest to receive and defend them in their present weakness, and best able to furnish them with new means, and send them out again with large forces. Others of the council were for going into Africa, and to king Juba. But Theophanes the Lesbian, thought it madness to leave Egypt, that was but at a distance of three days' sailing, and make no use of Ptolemy, who was still a boy, and was highly indebted to Pompey for the friendship and favor he had shown to his father, only to put himself under the Parthian, and trust the most treacherous nation in the world; and rather than make any trial of the clemency of a Roman, and his own near connection, to whom if he would but yield to be second, he might be the first and chief over all the rest, to go and place himself at the mercy of Arsaces, which even Crassus had not submitted to, while alive; and, moreover, to expose his young wife, of the family of the Scipios, among a barbarous people, who govern by their lusts, and measure their greatness by their power to commit affronts and insotencies; from whom, though she suffered no dishonor, yet it might be thought she did, being in the hands of those who had the power to do it. This argument alone, they say, was persuasive enough to divert his course, that was designed towards Euphrates, if it were so indeed that any counsel of Pompey's, and not some superior power, made him take this other way.

As soon, therefore, as it was resolved upon, that he should fly into Egypt, setting sail from Cyprus in a galley of Seleucia, together with Cornelia, while the rest of his company sailed along near him, some in ships of war, and others in merchant vessels, he passed over sea without danger. But on hearing that king Ptolemy was posted with his army at the city of Pelusium, making war against his sister, he steered his course that way, and sent a messenger before to acquaint the king with his arrival, and to crave his protection. Ptolemy himself was quite young, and therefore Pothinus, who had the principal administration of all affairs, called a council of the chief men, those being the greatest whom he pleased to make so, and commanded them every man to deliver his opinion touching the reception of Pompey. It was, indeed, a miserable thing, that the fate of the great Pompey should be left to the determinations of Pothinus the eunuch, Theodotus of Chios, the paid rhetoric master, and Achillas the Egyptian. For these, among the chamberlains and menial domestics, that made up the rest of the council, were the chief and leading men. Pompey, who thought it dishonorable for him to owe his safety to Cæsar, riding at anchor at a distance from shore, was forced to wait the sentence of this tribunal. It seems they were so far different in their opinions, that some were for sending the man away, and others, again, for inviting and receiving him; but Theodotus, to show his cleverness and the cogency of his rhetoric, undertook to demonstrate, that neither the one nor the other was safe in that juncture of affairs. For if they entertained him, they would be sure to make Cæsar their enemy, and Pompey their master; or if they dismissed him, they might render themselves hereafter obnoxious to Pompey, for that inhospitable expulsion, and to Cæsar, for the escape; so that the most expedient course would be to send for him and take away his life, for by that means they would ingratiate themselves with the one, and have no reason to fear the other; adding, it is related, with a smile, that ' a dead man cannot bite."

This advice being approved of, they committed the execu

tion of it to Achillas. He, therefore, taking with him as his accomplices one Septimius, a man that had formerly held a command under Pompey, and Salvius, another centurion, with three or four attendants, made up towards Pompey's galley. In the mean time, all the chiefest of those who accompanied Pompey in this voyage, were come into his ship to learn the event of their embassy. But when they saw the manner of their reception, that in appearance it was neither princely nor honorable, nor indeed in any way answerable to the hopes of Theophanes, or their expectation (for there came but a few men in a fisherman's boat to meet them), they began to suspect the meanness of their entertainment, and gave warning to Pompey that he should row back his galley, whilst he was out of their reach, and make for the sea. By this time the Egyptian boat drew near, and Septimius standing up first, saluted Pompey in the Latin tongue, by the title of imperator. Then Achillas, saluting him in the Greek language, desired him to come aboard his vessel, telling him, that the sea was very shallow towards the shore, and that a galley of that burden could not avoid striking upon the sands. At the same time they saw several of the king's galleys getting their men on board, and all the shore covered with soldiers; so that even if they changed their minds, it seemed impossible for them to escape, and besides, their distrust would have given the assassins a pretence for their cruelty. Pompey, therefore, taking his leave of Cornelia, who was already lamenting his death before it came, bade two centurions, with Philip, one of his freedmen, and a slave called Scythes, go on board the boat before him. And as some of the crew with Achillas were reaching out their hands to help him, he turned about towards his wife and son, and repeated those iambics of Sophocles,

> He that once enters at a tyrant's door,
> Becomes a slave, though he were free before.

These were the last words he spoke to his friends, and so he went aboard. Observing presently that notwithstanding there was a considerable distance betwixt his galley and the shore, yet none of the company addressed any words of friendliness or welcome to him all the way, he looked earnestly upon Septimius, and said, "I am not mistaken, surely, in believing you to have been formerly my fellow-soldier." But he only nodded with his head, making no reply at all, nor showing any other courtesy. Since, therefore, they continued silent, Pompey took a little book in his hand, in which was written out an address in Greek, which he intended to make to king Ptolemy, and began to read it. When they drew near to the shore, Cornelia, together with the rest of his friends in the galley, was very impatient to see the event, and began to take courage at last, when she saw several of the royal escort coming to meet him, apparently to give him a more honorable reception; but in the meantime, as Pompey took Philip by the hand to rise up more easily, Septimius first stabbed him from behind with his sword, and after him likewise Salvius and Achillas drew out their swords. He, therefore, taking up his gown with both hands, drew it over his face, and neither saying nor doing any thing unworthy of himself, only groaning a little, endured the wounds they gave him, and so ended his life, in the fifty-ninth year of his age, the very next day after the day of his birth.

Cornelia, with her company from the galley, seeing him murdered, gave such a cry that it was heard to the shore, and weighing anchor with all speed, they hoisted sail, and fled. A strong breeze from the shore assisted their flight into the open sea, so that the Egyptians, though desirous to overtake them, desisted from the pursuit. But they cut off Pompey's head, and threw the rest of his body overboard, leaving it naked upon the shore, to be viewed by any that had the curiosity to see so sad a spectacle. Philip stayed by and watched till they had glutted their eyes in viewing it; and then washing it with sea-water, having nothing else, he wrapped it up in a shirt of his own for a winding-sheet. Then seeking up and down about the sands, at last he found some rotten planks of a little fisher-boat, not much, but yet enough to make up a funeral pile for a naked body, and that not quite entire. As Philip was busy in gathering and putting these old planks together, an old Roman citizen, who in his youth had served in the wars under Pompey, came up to him and demanded, who he was that was preparing the funeral of Pompey the Great. And Philip making answer, that he was his freedman, "Nay, then," said he, "you shall not have this honor alone; let even me, too, I pray you, have my share in such a pious office, that I may not altogether repent me of this pilgrimage in a strange land, but in compensation of many misfortunes, may obtain this happiness at last, even with mine own hands to touch the body of Pompey, and do the last duties to the greatest general among the Romans." And in this manner were the obsequies of Pompey performed. The next day Lucius Lentulus, not knowing what had passed came sailing from Cyprus along the shore of that coast, and seeing a funeral pile, and Philip standing by, exclaimed, before he was yet seen by any one, "Who is this that has found his end here?" adding, after a short pause, with a sigh, "Possibly even thou, Pompeius Magnus!" and so going ashore, he was presently apprehended and slain. This was the end of Pompey.

Not long after, Cæsar arrived in the country that was polluted with this foul act, and when one of the Egyptians was sent to present him with Pompey's head, he turned away from him with abhorrence as from a murderer; and on receiving his seal, on which was engraved a lion holding a sword in his paw, he burst into tears. Achillas and Pothinus he put to death; and king Ptolemy himself, being overthrown in battle upon the banks of the Nile, fled away and was never heard of afterwards. Theodotus, the rhetorician, flying out of Egypt, escaped the hands of Cæsar's justice, but lived a vagabond in banishment, wandering up and down, despised and hated of all men, till at last Marcus Brutus, after he had killed Cæsar, finding him in his province of Asia, put him to death, with every kind of ignominy. The ashes of Pompey were carried to his wife Cornelia, who deposited them at his country house near Alba.

COMPARISON OF POMPEY AND AGESILAUS.

Thus having drawn out the histroy of the lives of Agesilaus and Pompey, the next thing is to compare them; and in order to this, to take a cursory view, and bring together the points in which they chiefly disagree; which are these. In the first place, Pompey attained to all his greatness and glory by the fairest and justest means, owing his advancement to his own efforts, and to the frequent and important aid which he rendered Sylla, in delivering Italy from its tyrants. But Agesilaus appears to have obtained his kingdom, not without offence both towards gods and towards men, towards these, by procuring judgment of bastardy against Leotychides, whom his brother had declared his lawful son, and towards those, by putting a false gloss upon the oracle, and eluding its sentence against his lameness. Secondly, Pompey never ceased to display his respect for Sylla during his lifetime, and expressed it also after his death, by enforcing the honorable interment of his corpse, in despite of Lepidus, and by giving his daughter in marriage to his son Faustus. But Agesilaus, upon a slight pretence, cast off Lysander with reproach and dishonor. Yet Sylla in fact had owed to Pompey's services, as much as Pompey ever received from him, whereas Lysander made Agesilaus king of Sparta, and general of all Greece. Thirdly, Pompey's transgressions of right and justice in his political life were occasioned chiefly by his relations with other people, and most of his errors had some affinity, as well as himself, to Cæsar and Scipio, his fathers-in-law. But Agesilaus, to gratify the fondness of his son, saved the life of Sphodrias by a sort of violence, when he deserved death for the wrong he had done to the Athenians; and when Phœbidas treacherously broke the peace with Thebes, zealously abetted him for the sake, it was clear, of the unjust act itself. In short, what mischief soever Pompey might be said to have brought on Rome through compliance with the wishes of his friends or through inadvertency, Agesilaus may be said to have brought on Sparta out of obstinacy and malice, by kindling the Bœotian war. And if, moreover, we are to attribute any part of these disasters to some personal ill-fortune attaching to the men themselves, in the case of Pompey, certainly the Romans had no reason to anticipate it. Whereas Agesilaus would not suffer the Lacedæmonians to avoid what they foresaw and were forewarned must attend the "lame sovereignty." For had Leotychides been chargeable ten thousand times as foreign and spurious, yet the race of the Eurypontidæ was still in being, and could easily have furnished Sparta with a lawful king, that was sound in his limbs, had not Lysander darkened and disguised the true sense of the oracle in favor of Agesilaus.

Such a politic piece of sophistry as was devised by Agesilaus, in that great perplexity of the people as to the treatment to be given to those who had played the coward at the battle of Leuctra, when after that unhappy defeat he decreed, that the laws should sleep for that day, it would be hard to find any parallel to; neither indeed have we the fellow of it in all Pompey's story. But on the contrary, Pompey for a friend thought it no sin to break those very laws which he himself had made, as if to show at once the force of his friendship, and the greatness of his power; whereas Agesilaus, under the necessity, as it seemed of either rescinding the laws, or not saving the citizens, contrived an expedient by the help of which the laws should not touch these citizens, and yet should not, to avoid it, be overthrown. Then I must commend it as an incomparable act of civil virtue and obedience in Agesilaus, that immediately upon the receipt of the scytala, he left the wars in Asia, and returned into his country. For he did not, like Pompey, merely advance his country's interest by acts that contributed at the same time to promote his own greatness, but looking to his country's good, for its sake laid aside as great authority and honor as ever any man had before or since, except Alexander the Great.

But now to take another point of view, if we sum up Pompey's military expeditions and exploits of war, the number of his trophies, and the greatness of the powers which he subdued, and the multitude of battles in which he triumphed, I am persuaded even Xenophon himself would not put the victories of Agesilaus in balance with his though Xenophon has this privilege allowed him, as a sort of special reward for his other excellences, that he may write and speak, in favor of his hero, whatever he pleases. Methinks, too, there is a great deal of difference betwixt these men, in their clemency and moderation towards their enemies. For Agesilaus, while attempting to enslave Thebes and exterminate Messene, the latter, his country's ancient associate, and Thebes, the mother-city of his own royal house, almost lost Sparta itself, and did really lose the government of Greece; whereas Pompey gave cities to those of the pirates who were willing to change their manner of life; and when it was in his power to lead Tigranes, king of Armenia, in triumph, he chose rather to make him a confederate of the Romans, saying, that a single day was worth less than all future time. But if the pre-eminence in that which relates to the office and virtues of a general, should be determined by the greatest and most important acts and counsels of war, the Lacedæmonian would not a little exceed the Roman. For Agesilaus never deserted his city, though it was besieged by an army of seventy thousand men, when there were very few soldiers within to defend it, and those had been defeated too, but a little before, at the battle of Leuctra. But Pompey, when Cæsar, with a body only of fifty-three hundred men, had taken but one town in Italy, departed in a panic out of Rome, either through cowardice, when there were so few, or at least through a false and mistaken belief that there were more; and having conveyed away his wife and children, he left all the rest of the citizens defenceless, and fled; whereas he ought either to have conquered in fight for the defence of his country, or yielded upon terms to the conqueror, who was, moreover, his fellow-citizen, and allied to him; but now to the same man to whom he refused a prolongation of the terms of his government, and thought it intolerable to grant another consulship, to him he gave the power, by letting him take the city, to tell Metellus, together with all the rest, that they were his prisoners.

That which is chiefly the office of a general, to force the enemy into fighting when he finds himself the stronger, and to avoid being driven into it himself when he is the weaker this excellence Agesilaus always displayed and by it kept himself invincible; whereas in contending with Pompey, Cæsar, who was the weaker, successfully declined the danger, and his own strength being in his land forces, drove him into putting the conflict to issue with these, and thus made himself master of the treasure, stores, and the sea too, which were all in his enemy's hands, and by the help of which the victory could have been secured without fighting. And what is alleged as an apology in vindication of Pompey, is to a general of his age and standing the greatest of disgraces. For, granting that a young commander might by clamor and outcry be deprived of his fortitude and strength of mind, and weakly forsake his better judgment, and the thing be neither strange nor altogether unpardonable, yet for Pompey, the Great, whose camp the Romans called their country, and his tent the senate, styling the consuls, prætors, and all other magistrates who were conducting the government at Rome, by no better title than that of rebels and traitors, for him, whom they well knew never to have been under the command of any but himself, having served all his campaigns under himself as sole general, for him upon so small a provocation as the scoffs of Favonius and Domitius, and lest he should bear the nick-name of Agamemnon, to be wrought upon, and even forced to hazard the whole empire and liberty of Rome upon the cast of a die, was surely indeed intolerable. Who, if he had so much regarded a present infamy, should have guarded the city at first with his arms, and fought the battle in defence of Rome, not have left it as he did: nor while declaring his flight from Italy an artifice in the manner of Themistocles, nevertheless be ashamed in Thessaly of a prudent delay before engaging. Heaven had not appointed the Pharsalian fields to be the stage and theatre upon which they should contend for the empire of Rome, neither was he summoned thither by any herald upon challenge, with intimation that he must either undergo the combat, or surrender the prize to another. There were many other fields, thousands of cities, and even the whole earth placed at his command, by the advantage of his fleet, and his superiority at sea, if he would but have followed the examples of Maximus, Marius, Lucullus, and even Agesilaus himself, who endured no less tumults within the city of Sparta, when the Thebans provoked him to come out and fight in defence of the land, and sustained in Egypt also numerous calumnies, slanders, and suspicions on the part of the king, whom he counselled to abstain from a battle. And thus following always what he had determined in his own judgment upon mature advice, by that means he not only preserved the Egyptians, against their wills, not only kept Sparta, in those desperate convulsions, by his sole act, safe from overthrow, but even was able to set up trophies likewise in the city over the Thebans, having given his countrymen an occasion of being victorious afterwards by not at first leading them out, as they tried to force him to do, to their own destruction. The consequence was that in the end Agesilaus was commended by the very men, when they found themselves saved, upon whom he had put this compulsion, whereas Pompey, whose error had been occasioned by others, found those his accusers whose advice had misled him. Some indeed profess that he was deceived by his father-in-law Scipio, who, designing to conceal and keep to himself the greatest part of that treasure which he had brought out of Asia, pressed Pompey to battle, upon the pretence that there would be a want of money. Yet admitting he was deceived, one in his place ought not to have been so, nor should have allowed so slight an artifice to cause the hazard of such mighty interests. And thus we have taken a view of each, by comparing together their conduct, and actions in war.

As to their voyages into Egypt, one steered his course thither out of necessity in flight; the other neither honorably, nor of necessity, but as a mercenary soldier, having enlisted himself into the service of a barbarous nation for pay, that he might be able afterwards to wage war upon the Greeks. And secondly, what we charge upon the Egyptians in the name of Pompey, the Egyptians lay to the charge of Agesilaus. Pompey trusted them and was betrayed and murdered by them Agesilaus accepted their confidence and deserted them, transferring his aid to the very enemies who were now attacking those whom he had been brought over to assist.

ALEXANDER.

It being my purpose to write the lives of Alexander the king, and of Cæsar, by whom Pompey was destroyed, the multitude of their great actions affords so large a field that I were to blame if I should not by way of apology forewarn my reader that I have chosen rather to epitomize the most celebrated parts of their story, than to insist at large on every particular circumstance of it. It must be borne in mind that my design is not to write histories, but lives. And the most glorious exploits do not always furnish us with the clearest discoveries of virtue or vice in men; sometimes a matter of less moment, an expression or a jest, informs us better of their characters and inclinations, than the most famous sieges, the greatest armaments, or the bloodiest battles whatsoever. Therefore as portrait-painters are more exact in the lines and features of the face, in which the character is seen, than in the other parts of the body, so I must be allowed to give my more particular attention to the marks and indications of the souls of men, and while I endeavor by these to portray their lives, may be free to leave more weighty matters and great battles to be treated of by others.

It is agreed on by all hands, that on the father's side, Alexander descended from Hercules by Caranus, and from Æacus by Neoptolemus on the mother's side. His father Philip, being in Samothrace, when he was quite young, fell in love there with Olympias, in company with whom he was initiated in the religious ceremonies of the country, and her father and mother being both dead, soon after, with the consent of her brother, Arymbas, he married her. The night before the consummation of their marriage, she dreamed that a thunderbolt fell upon her body, which kindled a great fire, whose divided flames dispersed themselves all about, and then were extinguished. And Philip, some time after he was married, dreamt that he sealed up his wife's body with a seal, whose impression, as he fancied, was the figure of a lion. Some of the diviners interpreted this as a warning to Philip to look narrowly to his wife; but Aristander of Telmessus, considering how unusual it was to seal up anything that was empty, assured him the meaning of his dream was, that the queen was with child of a boy, who would one day prove as stout and courageous as a lion. Once, moreover, a serpent was found lying by Olmypias as she slept, which more than any thing else, it is said, abated Philip's passion for her; and whether he feared her as an enchantress, or thought she had commerce with some god, and so looked on himself as excluded, he was ever after less fond of her conversation. Others say, that the women of this country having always been extremely addicted to the enthusiastic Orphic rites, and the wild worship of Bacchus (upon which account they were called Clodones, and Mimallones), imitated in many things the practices of the Edonian and Thracian women about Mount Hæmus, from whom the word *threskeuein* seems to have been derived, as a special term for superfluous and over-curious forms of adoration; and that Olympias, zealously affecting these fanatical and enthusiastic inspirations, to perform them with more barbaric dread, was wont in the dances proper to these ceremonies to have great tame serpents about her, which sometimes creeping out of the ivy and the mystic fans, sometimes winding themselves about the sacred spears, and the women's chaplets, made a spectacle which men could not look upon without terror.

Philip, after this vision, sent Chæron of Megalopolis to consult the oracle of Apollo at Delphi, by which he was commanded to perform sacrifice, and henceforth pay particular honor, above all other gods, to Ammon; and was told he should one day lose that eye with which he presumed to peep through the chink of the door, when he saw the god, under the form of a serpent, in the company of his wife. Eratosthenes says that Olympias, when she attended Alexander on his way to the army in his first expedition, told him the secret of his birth, and bade him behave himself with courage suitable to his divine extraction. Others again affirm that she wholly disclaimed any pretensions of the kind, and was wont to say, "When will Alexander leave off slandering me to Juno?"

Alexander was born the sixth of Hecatombæon, which month the Macedonians call Lous, the same day that the temple of Diana at Ephesus was burnt; which Hegesias of Magnesia makes the occasion of a conceit, frigid enough to have stopped the conflagration. The temple, he says, took fire and was burnt while its mistress was absent, assisting at the birth of Alexander. And all the Eastern soothsayers who happened to be then at Ephesus, looking upon the ruin of this temple to be the forerunner of some other calamity, ran about the town, beating their faces, and crying that this day had brought forth something that would prove fatal and destructive to all Asia.

Just after Philip had taken Potidæa, he received these three messages at one time, that Parmenio had overthrown the Illyrians in a great battle, that his race-horse had won the course at the Olympic games, and that his wife had given birth to Alexander; with which being naturally well pleased, as an addition to his satisfaction, he was assured by the diviners that a son, whose birth was accompanied with three such successes, could not fail of being invincible.

The statues that gave the best representation of Alexander's person, were those of Lysippus (by whom alone he would suffer his image to be made), those peculiarities which many of his successors afterwards and his friends used to affect to imitate, the inclination of his head a little on one side towards his left shoulder, and his melting eye, having been expressed by this artist with great exactness. But Apelles, who drew him with thunderbolts in his hand, made his complexion browner and darker than it was naturally; for he was fair and of a light color, passing into ruddiness in his face and upon his breast. Aristoxenus in his Memoirs tells us that a most agreeable odor exhaled from his skin, and that his breath and body all over was so fragrant as to perfume the clothes which he wore next him; the cause of which might probably be the hot and adust temperament of his body. For sweet smells, Theophrastus conceives, are produced by the concoction of moist humors by heat, which is the reason that those parts of the world which are driest and most burnt up, afford spices of the best kind, and in the greatest quantity; for the heat of the sun exhausts all the superfluous moisture which lies in the surface of bodies, ready to generate putrefaction. And this hot constitution, it may be, rendered Alexander so addicted to drinking, and so choleric. His temperance, as to the pleasures of the body, was apparent in him in his very childhood, as he was with much difficulty incited to them, and always used them with great moderation; though in other things he was extremely eager and vehement, and in his love of glory, and the pursuit of it, he showed a solidity of high spirit and magnanimity far above his age. For he neither sought nor valued it upon every occasion, as his father Philip did (who affected to show his eloquence almost to a degree of pedantry, and took care to have the victories of his racing chariots at the Olympic games engraven on his coin), but when he was asked by some about him, whether he would run a race in the Olympic games, as he was very swift-footed, he answered, he would, if he might have kings to run with him. Indeed, he seems in general to have looked with indifference, if not with dislike, upon the professed athletes. He often appointed prizes, for which not only tragedians and musicians, pipers and harpers, but rhapsodists also, strove to outvie one another; and delighted in all manner of hunting and cudgel-playing, but never gave any encouragement to contests either of boxing or of the pancratium.

While he was yet very young, he entertained the ambassadors from the king of Persia, in the absence of his father, and entering much into conversation with them, gained so much upon them by his affability, and the questions he asked them, which were far from being childish or trifling (for he inquired of them the length of the ways, the nature of the road into inner Asia, the character of their king, how he carried himself to his enemies, and what forces he was able to bring into the field), that they were struck with admiration of him, and looked upon the ability so much famed of Philip, to be nothing in comparison with the forwardness and high purpose that appeared thus early in his son. Whenever he heard Philip had taken any town of importance, or won any signal victory, instead of rejoicing at it altogether, he would tell his companions that his father would anticipate every thing, and leave him and them no opportunities of performing great and illustrious actions. For being more bent upon action and glory than either upon pleasure or riches, he esteemed all that he should receive from his father as a diminution and prevention of his own future achievements; and would have chosen rather to succeed to a kingdom involved in troubles and wars, which would have afforded him frequent exercise of his courage, and a large field of honor, than to one already flourishing and settled, where his inheritance would be an inactive life, and the mere enjoyment of wealth and luxury.

The care of his education, as it might be presumed, was committed to a great many attendants, preceptors, and teachers, over the whole of whom Leonidas, a near kinsman of Olympias, a man of an austere temper, presided, who did not indeed himself decline the name of what in reality is a noble and honorable office, but in general his dignity, and his near relationship, obtained him from other people the title of Alexander's foster-father and governor. But he who took upon him the actual place and style of his pedagogue, was Lysimachus the Acarnanian, who, though he had nothing specially to recommend him, but his lucky fancy of calling himself Phœnix, Alexander Achilles, and Philip Peleus, was therefore well enough esteemed, and ranked in the next degree after Leonidas.

Philonicus the Thessalian brought the horse Bucephalas to Philip, offering to sell him for thirteen talents; but when they went into the field to try him, they found him so very vicious and unmanageable, that he reared up when they endeavored to mount him, and would not so much as endure the voice of any of Philip's attendants. Upon which, as they were leading him away as wholly useless and untractable, Alexander, who stood by, said, "What an excellent horse do they lose, for want of address and boldness to manage him!" Philip at first took no notice of what he said; but when he heard him repeat the same thing several times, and saw he was much vexed to see the horse sent away, "Do you reproach," said he to him, "those who are older than yourself, as if you knew more, and were better able to manage him than they?" "I could manage this horse," replied he, "better than others do." "And if you do not," said Philip, "what will you forfeit for your rashness?" "I will pay," answered Alexander, "the whole price of the horse." At this the whole company fell a laughing; and as soon as the wager was settled amongst them, he immediately ran to the horse, and taking hold of the bridle, turned him directly towards the sun, having, it seems, observed that he was disturbed at and afraid of the motion of his own shadow; then letting him go forward a little, still keeping the reins in his hand, and stroking him gently when he found him begin to grow eager and fiery, he let fall his upper garment softly, and with one nimble leap securely mounted him, and when he was seated, by little and little drew in the bridle, and curbed him without either striking or spurring him. Presently, when he found him free from all rebelliousness, and only impatient for the course, he let him go at full speed, inciting him now with a commanding voice, and urging him also with his heel. Philip and his friends looked on at first in silence and anxiety for the result, till seeing him turn at the end of his career, and come back rejoicing and triumphing for what he had performed, they all burst out into acclamations of applause; and his father shedding tears, it is said for joy, kissed him as he came down from his horse, and in his transport, said, "O my son, look thee out a kingdom equal to and worthy of thyself, for Macedonia is too little for thee."

After this, considering him to be of a temper easy to be led to his duty by reason, but by no means to be compelled, he always endeavored to persuade rather than to command or force him to any thing; and now looking upon the instruction and tuition of his youth to be of greater difficulty and importance, than to be wholly trusted to the ordinary masters in music and poetry, and the common school subjects, and to require, as Sophocles says,

The bridle and the rudder too,

he sent for Aristotle, the most learned and most celebrated philosopher of his time, and rewarded him with a munificence proportionable to and becoming the care he took to instruct his son. For he repeopled his native city Stagira, which he had caused to be demolished a little before, and restored all the citizens, who were in exile or slavery, to their habitations. As a place for the pursuit of their studies and exercise, he assigned the temple of the Nymphs, near Mieza, where, to this very day, they show you Aristotle's stone seats, and the shady walks which he was wont to frequent. It would appear that Alexander received from him not only his doctrines of Morals, and of Politics, but also something of those more abstruse and profound theories which these philosophers, by the very names they gave them, professed to reserve for oral communication to the initiated, and did not allow many to become acquainted with. For when he was in Asia, and heard Aristotle had published some treatises of that kind, he wrote to him, using very plain language to him in behalf of philosophy, the following letter. "Alexander to Aristotle, greeting. You have not done well to publish your books of oral doctrine; for what is there now that we excel others in, if those things which we have been particularly instructed in be laid open to all? For my part, I assure you, I had rather excel others in the knowledge of what is excellent, than in the extent of my power and dominion. Farewell." And Aristotle, soothing this passion for preëminence, speaks, in his excuse for himself, of these doctrines as in fact both published and not published: as indeed, to say the truth, his books on metaphysics are written in a style which makes them useless for ordinary teaching, and instructive only, in the way of memoranda, for those who have been already conversant in that sort of learning.

Doubtless also it was to Aristotle, that he owed the inclination he had, not to the theory only, but likewise to the practice of the art of medicine. For when any of his friends were sick, he would often prescribe them their course of diet, and medicines proper to their disease, as we may find in his epistles. He was naturally a great lover of all kinds of learning and reading ; and Onesicritus informs us, that he constantly laid Homer's Iliads, according to the copy corrected by Aristotle, called the casket copy, with his dagger under his pillow, declaring that he esteemed it a perfect portable treasure of all military virtue and knowledge. When he was in the upper Asia, being destitute of other books, he ordered Harpalus to send him some ; who furnished him with Philistus's History, a great many of the plays of Euripides, Sophocles, and Æschylus, and some dithyrambic odes, composed by Telestes and Philoxenus. For awhile he loved and cherished Aristotle no less, as he was wont to say himself, than if he had been his father, giving this reason for it, that as he had received life from the one, so the other had taught him to live well. But afterwards, upon some mistrust of him, yet not so great as to make him do him any hurt, his familiarity and friendly kindness to him abated so much of its former force and affectionateness, as to make it evident he was alienated from him. However, his violent thirst after and passion for learning, which were once implanted, still grew up with him, and never decayed ; as appears by his veneration of Anaxarchus, by the present of fifty talents which he sent to Xenocrates, and his particular care and esteem of Dandamis and Calanus.

While Philip went on his expedition against the Byzantines, he left Alexander, then sixteen years old, his lieutenant in Macedonia, committing the charge of his seal to him ; who, not to sit idle, reduced the rebellious Mædi, and having taken their chief town by storm, drove out the barbarous inhabitants, and planting a colony of several nations in their room, called the place after his own name, Alexandropolis. At the battle of Chæronea, which his father fought against the Grecians, he is said to have been the first man that charged the Thebans' sacred band. And even in my remembrance, there stood an old oak near the river Cephisus, which people called Alexander's oak, because his tent was pitched under it. And not far off are to be seen the graves of the Macedonians who fell in that battle. This early bravery made Philip so fond of him, that nothing pleased him more than to hear his subjects call himself their general and Alexander their king.

But the disorders of his family, chiefly caused by his new marriages and attachments (the troubles that began in the women's chambers spreading, so to say, to the whole kingdom) raised various complaints and differences between them, which the violence of Olympias, a woman of a jealous and implacable temper, made wider, by exasperating Alexander against his father. Among the rest, this accident contributed most to their falling out. At the wedding of Cleopatra, whom Ph. ; fell in love with and married, she being much too young for him, her uncle Attalus in his drink desired the Macedonians would implore the gods to give them a lawful successor to the kingdom by his niece. This so irritated Alexander, that throwing one of the cups at his head, "You villain," said he, "what, am I then a bastard?" Then Philip taking Attalus's part, rose up and would have run his son through; but by good fortune for them both, either his over-hasty rage, or the wine he had drunk, made his foot slip, so that he fell down on the floor. At which Alexander reproachfully insulted over him: "See there," said he, "the man who makes preparations to pass out of Europe into Asia, overturned in passing from one seat to another." After this debauch, he and his mother Olympias withdrew from Philip's company, and when he had placed her in Epirus, he himself retired into Illyria.

About this time, Demaratus the Corinthian, an old friend of the family, who had the freedom to say any thing among them without offence, coming to visit Philip, after the first compliments and embraces were over, Philip asked him, whether the Grecians were at amity with one another. "It ill becomes you," replied Demaratus, "to be so solicitous about Greece, when you have involved your own house in so many dissensions and calamities." He was so convinced by this seasonable reproach, that he immediately sent for his son home, and by Demaratus's mediation prevailed with him to return. But this reconciliation lasted not long; for when Pixodorus, viceroy of Caria, sent Aristocritus to treat for a match between his eldest daughter and Philip's son, Arrhidæus, hoping by this alliance to secure his assistance upon occasion, Alexander's mother, and some who pretended to be his friends, presently filled his head with tales and calumnies, as if Philip, by a splendid marriage and important alliance, were preparing the way for settling the kingdom upon Arrhidæus. In alarm at this, he despatched Thessalus, the tragic actor into Caria, to dispose Pixodorus to slight Arrhidæus. both as illegitimate and a fool, and rather to accept of himself for his son-in-law. This proposition was much more agreeable to Pixodorus than the former. But Philip, as soon as he was made acquainted with this transaction, went to his son's apartment, taking with him Philotas, the son of Parmenio, one of Alexander's intimate friends and companions, and there reproved him severely, and reproached him bitterly, that he should be so degenerate, and unworthy of the power he was to leave him, as to desire the alliance of a mean Carian, who was at best but the slave of a barbarous prince. Nor did this satisfy his resentment, for he wrote to the Corinthians, to send Thessalus to him in chains, and banished Harpalus, Nearchus, Erigyius, and Ptolemy, his son's friends and favorites, whom Alexander afterwards recalled, and raised to great honor and preferment.

Not long after this, Pausanias, having had an outrage done to him at the instance of Attalus and Cleopatra, when he found he could get no reparation for his disgrace at Philip's hands, watched his opportunity and murdered him. The guilt of which fact was laid for the most part upon Olympias, who was said to have encouraged and exasperated the enraged youth to revenge ; and some sort of suspicion attached even to Alexander himself, who, it was said, when Pausanias came and complained to him of the injury he had received, repeated the verse out of Euripides's Medea :—

> On husband, and on father, and on bride.

However, he took care to find out and punish the accomplices of the conspiracy severely, and was very angry with Olympias for treating Cleopatra inhumanly in his absence.

Alexander was but twenty years old when his father was murdered, and succeeded to a kingdom beset on all sides with great dangers, and rancorous enemies. For not only the barbarous nations that bordered on Macedonia were impatient of being governed by any but their own native princes, but Philip likewise, though he had been victorious over the Grecians, yet, as the time had not been sufficient for him to complete his conquest and accustom them to his sway, had simply left all things in a general disorder and confusion. It seemed to the Macedonians a very critical time ; and some would have persuaded Alexander to give up all thought of retaining the Grecians in subjection by force of arms, and rather to apply himself to win back by gentle means the allegiance of the tribes who were designing revolt, and try the effect of indulgence in arresting the first motions towards revolution.

But he rejected this counsel as weak and timorous, and looked upon it to be more prudence to secure himself by resolution and magnanimity, than, by seeming to truckle to any, to encourage all to trample on him. In pursuit of this opinion, he reduced the barbarians to tranquillity, and put an end to all fear of war from them, by a rapid expedition into their country as far as the river Danube, where he gave Syrmus, king of the Triballians, an entire overthrow. And hearing the Thebans were in revolt, and the Athenians in correspondence with them, he immediately marched through the pass of Thermopylæ, saying that to Demosthenes, who had called him a child while he was in Illyria and in the country of the Triballians, and a youth when he was in Thessaly, he would appear a man before the walls of Athens.

When he came to Thebes, to show how willing he was to accept of their repentance for what was past, he only demanded of them Phœnix and Prothytes, the authors of the rebellion, and proclaimed a general pardon to those who would come over to him. But when the Thebans merely retorted by demanding Philotas and Antipater to be delivered into their hands, and by a proclamation on their part, invited all who would assert the liberty of Greece to come over to them, he presently applied himself to make them feel the last extremities of war. The Thebans indeed defended themselves with a zeal and courage beyond their strength, being much outnumbered by their enemies. But when the Macedonian garrison sallied out upon them from the citadel, they were so hemmed in on all sides, that the greater part of them fell in the battle; the city itself being taken by storm, was sacked and razed. Alexander's hope being that so severe an example might terrify the rest of Greece into obedience, and also in order to gratify the hostility of his confederates, the Phocians and Platæans. So that, except the priests, and some few who had heretofore been the friends and connections of the Macedonians, the family of the poet Pindar, and those who were known to have opposed the public vote for the war, all the rest, to the number of thirty thousand, were publicly sold for slaves; and it is computed that upwards of six thousand were put to the sword. Among the other calamities that befell the city, it happened that some Thracian soldiers, having broken into the house of a matron of high character and repute, named Timoclea, their captain, after he had used violence with her, to satisfy his avarice as well as lust, asked her, if she knew of any money concealed; to which she readily answered she did.

and bade him follow her into a garden, where she showed him a well, into which, she told him, upon the taking of the city, she had thrown what she had of most value. The greedy Thracian presently stooping down to view the place where he thought the treasure lay, she came behind him, and pushed him into the well, and then flung great stones in upon him, till she had killed him. After which, when the soldiers led her away bound to Alexander, her very mien and gait showed her to be a woman of dignity, and of a mind no less elevated, not betraying the least sign of fear or astonishment. And when the king asked her who she was, "I am," said she, "the sister of Theagenes, who fought the battle of Chæronea with your father Philip, and fell there in command for the liberty of Greece." Alexander was so surprised, both at what she had done, and what she said, that he could not choose but give her and her children their freedom to go whither they pleased.

After this he received the Athenians into favor, although they had shown themselves so much concerned at the calamity of Thebes that out of sorrow they omitted the celebration of the Mysteries, and entertained those who escaped with all possible humanity. Whether it were, like the lion, that his passion was now satisfied, or that after an example of extreme cruelty, he had a mind to appear merciful, it happened well for the Athenians; for he not only forgave them all past offences, but bade them look to their affairs with vigilance, remembering that if he should miscarry, they were likely to be the arbiters of Greece. Certain it is, too, that in after-time he often repented of his severity to the Thebans, and his remorse had such influence on his temper as to make him ever after less rigorous to all others. He imputed also the murder of Clitus, which he committed in his wine, and the unwillingness of the Macedonians to follow him against the Indians, by which his enterprise and glory was left imperfect, to the wrath and vengeance of Bacchus, the protector of Thebes. And it was observed that whatsoever any Theban, who had the good fortune to survive this victory, asked of him, he was sure to grant without the least difficulty.

Soon after, the Grecians, being assembled at the Isthmus, declared their resolution of joining with Alexander in the war against the Persians, and proclaimed him their general. While he stayed here, many public ministers and philosophers came from all parts to visit him, and congratulated him on his election, but contrary to his expectation, Diogenes of Sinope, who then was living at Corinth, thought so little of him, that instead of coming to compliment him, he never so much as stirred out of the suburb called the Cranium, where Alexander found him lying along in the sun. When he saw so much company near him, he raised himself a little, and vouchsafed to look upon Alexander; and when he kindly asked him whether he wanted any thing, "Yes," said he, "I would have you stand from between me and the sun." Alexander was so struck at this answer, and surprised at the greatness of the man, who had taken so little notice of him, that as he went away, he told his followers who were laughing at the moroseness of the philosopher, that if he were not Alexander, he would choose to be Diogenes.

Then he went to Delphi, to consult Apollo concerning the success of the war he had undertaken, and happening to come on one of the forbidden days, when it was esteemed improper to give any answer from the oracle, he sent messengers to desire the priestess to do her office; and when she refused, on the plea of a law to the contrary, he went up himself, and began to draw her by force into the temple, until tired and overcome with his importunity, "my son," said she, "thou art invincible." Alexander taking hold of what she spoke, declared he had received such an answer as he wished for, and that it was needless to consult the god any further. Among other prodigies that attended the departure of his army, the image of Orpheus at Libethra, made of Cypress-wood, was seen to sweat in great abundance, to the discouragement of many. But Aristander told him that, far from presaging any ill to him, it signified he should perform acts so important and glorious as would make the poets and musicians of future ages labor and sweat to describe and celebrate them.

His army, by their computation who make the smallest amount, consisted of thirty thousand foot, and four thousand horse; and those who make the most of it, speak but of forty-three thousand foot, and three thousand horse. Aristobulus says, he had not a fund of above seventy talents for their pay, nor had he more than thirty days' provision, if we may believe Duris; Onesicritus tells us he was two hundred talents in debt. However narrow and disproportionable the beginnings of so vast an undertaking might seem to be, yet he would not embark his army until he had informed himself particularly what means his friends had to enable them to follow him, and supplied what they wanted, by giving good farms to some, a village to one, and the revenue of some hamlet or harbor town to another. So that at last he had portioned ou' or engaged almost all the royal property; which giving Perdiccas an occasion to ask him what he would leave himself, he replied, his hopes. "Your soldiers," replied Perdiccas, "will be your partners in those," and refused to accept of the estate he had assigned him. Some others of his friends did the like, but to those who willingly received, or desired assistance of him, he liberally granted it, as far as his patrimony in Macedonia would reach, the most part of which was spent in these donations.

With such vigorous resolutions, and his mind thus disposed, he passed the Hellespont, and at Troy sacrificed to Minerva, and honored the memory of the heroes who were buried there, with solemn libations; especially Achilles, whose gravestone he anointed, and with his friends, as the ancient custom is, ran naked about his sepulchre, and crowned it with garlands, declaring how happy he esteemed him, in having while he lived so faithful a friend, and when he was dead, so famous a poet to proclaim his actions. While he was viewing the rest of the antiquities and curiosities of the place, being told he might see Paris's harp, if he pleased, he said he thought it not worth looking on, but he should be glad to see that of Achilles, to which he used to sing the glories and great actions of brave men.

In the mean time, Darius's captains having collected large forces, were encamped on the further bank of the river Granicus, and it was necessary to fight, as it were, in the gate of Asia for an entrance into it. The depth of the river, with the unevenness and difficult ascent of the opposite bank, which was to be gained by main force, was apprehended by most, and some pronounced it an improper time to engage, because it was unusual for the kings of Macedonia to march with their forces in the month called Dæsius. But Alexander broke through these scruples, telling them they should call it a second Artemisius. And when Parmenio advised him not to attempt any thing that day, because it was late, he told him that he should disgrace the Hellespont, should he fear the Granicus. And so without more saying, he immediately took the river with thirteen troops of horse, and advanced against whole showers of darts thrown from the steep opposite side, which was covered with armed multitudes of the enemy's horse and foot, notwithstanding the disadvantage of the ground and the rapidity of the stream; so that the action seemed to have more of frenzy and desperation in it, than of prudent conduct. However, he persisted obstinately to gain the passage, and at last with much ado making his way up the banks, which were extremely muddy and slippery, he had instantly to join in a mere confused hand-to-hand combat with the enemy, before he could draw up his men, who were still passing over, into any order. For the enemy pressed upon him with loud and warlike outcries; and charging horse against horse, with their lances, after they had broken and spent these, they fell to it with their swords. And Alexander, being easily known by his buckler, and a large plume of white feathers on each side of his helmet, was attacked on all sides, yet escaped wounding, though his cuirass was pierced by a javelin in one of the joinings. And Rhœsaces and Spithridates, two Persian commanders, falling upon him at once, he avoided one of them, and struck at Rhœsaces, who had a good cuirass on, with such force, that his spear breaking in his hand, he was glad to betake himself to his dagger. While they were thus engaged, Spithridates came up on one side of him, and raising himself upon his horse, gave him such a blow with his battle-axe on the helmet, that he cut off the crest of it, with one of his plumes, and the helmet was only just so far strong enough to save him, that the edge of the weapon touched the hair of his head. But as he was about to repeat his stroke, Clitus, called the black Clitus, prevented him, by running him through the body with his spear. At the same time Alexander despatched Rhœsaces with his sword. While the horse were thus dangerously engaged, the Macedonian phalanx passed the river, and the foot on each side advanced to fight. But the enemy hardly sustaining the first onset, soon gave ground and fled, all but the mercenary Greeks, who, making a stand upon a rising ground, desired quarter, which Alexander, guided rather by passion than judgment, refused to grant, and charging them himself first, had his horse (not Bucephalus, but another) killed under him. And this obstinacy of his to cut off these experienced desperate men, cost him the lives of more of his own soldiers than all the battle before, besides those who were wounded. The Persians lost in this battle twenty thousand foot, and two thousand five hundred horse. On Alexander's side, Aristobulus says there were not wanting above four and thirty, of whom nine were foot-soldiers; and in memory of them he caused so many statues of brass, of Lysippus's making, to be erected. And that the Grecians might participate in the honor of his victory, he sent a portion of the spoils home to them, particularly to the Athenians three hundred bucklers, and upon all the rest he ordered this inscription to be set: "Alexander the son of Philip, and the Grecians, except the Lacedæmonians, won these from the barbarians who inhabit Asia." All the plate and purple garments, and other things of the same kind that he took from the Persians, except a very small quantity which he reserved for himself, he sent as a present to his mother.

This battle presently made a great change of affairs to Alexander's advantage. For Sardis itself, the chief seat of the barbarian's power in the maritime provinces, and many other considerable places, were surrendered to him; only Halicarnassus and Miletus stood out, which he took by force, together with the territory about them. After which he was a little unsettled in his opinion how to proceed. Sometimes he thought it best to find out Darius as soon as he could, and put all to the hazard of a battle; another while he looked upon it as a more prudent course to make an entire reduction of the sea-coast, and not to seek the enemy till he had first exercised his power here and made himself secure of the resources of these provinces. While he was thus deliberating what to do, it happened that a spring of water near the city of Xanthus in Lycia, of its own accord, swelled over its banks, and threw up a copper plate, upon the margin in which was engraven in ancient characters, that the time would come when the Persian empire should be destroyed by the Grecians. Encouraged by this accident, he proceeded to reduce the maritime parts of Cilicia and Phœnicia, and passed his army along the sea-coasts of Pamphylia with such expedition that many historians have described and extolled it with that height of admiration, as if it were no less than a miracle, and an extraordinary effect of divine favor, that the waves which usually come rolling in violently from the main, and hardly ever leave so much as a narrow beach under the steep, broken cliffs at any time uncovered, should on a sudden retire to afford him passage. Menander, in one of his comedies, alludes to this marvel when he says,

> Was Alexander ever favored more?
> Each man I wish for meets me at my door,
> And should I ask for passage through the sea,
> The sea I doubt not would retire for me.

But Alexander himself in his epistles mentions nothing unusual in this at all, but says he went from Phaselis, and passed through what they call the Ladders. At Phaselis he stayed some time, and finding the statue of Theodectes, who was a native of this town and was now dead, erected in the market-place, after he had supped, having drunk pretty plentifully, he went and danced about it, and crowned it with garlands, honoring not ungracefuly in his sport, the memory of a philosopher whose conversation he had formerly enjoyed, when he was Aristotle's scholar.

Then he subdued the Pisidians who made head against him, and conquered the Phrygians, at whose chief city Gordium, which is said to be the seat of the ancient Midas, he saw the famous chariot fastened with cords made of the rind of the cornel-tree, which whosoever should untie, the inhabitants had a tradition, that for him was reserved the empire of the world. Most authors tell the story that Alexander finding himself unable to untie the knot, the ends of which were secretly twisted round and folded up within it, cut it asunder with his sword. But Aristobulus tells us it was easy for him to undo it, by only pulling the pin out of the pole, to which the yoke was tied, and afterwards drawing off the yoke itself from below. From hence he advanced into Paphlagonia and Cappadocia, both which countries he soon reduced to obedience, and then hearing of the death of Memnon, the best commander Darius had upon the sea-coasts, who if he had lived, might, it was supposed, have put many impediments and difficulties in the way of the progress of his arms, he was the rather encouraged to carry the war into the upper provinces of Asia.

Darius was by this time upon his march from Susa, very confident, not only in the number of his men, which amounted to six hundred thousand, but likewise in a dream, which the Persian soothsayers interpreted rather in flattery to him, than according to the natural probability. He dreamed that he saw the Macedonian phalanx all on fire, and Alexander waiting on him, clad in the same dress which he himself had been used to wear when he was courier to the late king; after which, going into the temple of Belus, he vanished out of his sight. The dream would appear to have supernaturally signified to him the illustrious actions the Macedonians were to perform, and that as he, from a courier's place, had risen to the throne, so Alexander should come to be master of Asia, and not long surviving his conquests, conclude his life with glory. Darius's confidence increased the more, because Alexander spent so much time in Cilicia, which he imputed to his cowardice. But it was sickness that detained him there, which some say he contracted from his fatigues, others from bathing in the river Cydnus, whose waters were exceeding cold. However it happened, none of his physicians would venture to give him any remedies, they thought his case so desperate, and were so afraid of the suspicions and ill-will of the Macedonians if they should fail in the cure; till Philip, the Acarnanian, seeing how critical his case was, but relying on his own well-known friendship for him, resolved to try the last efforts of his art, and rather hazard his own credit and life, than suffer him to perish for want of physic, which he confidently administered to him, encouraging him to take it boldly, if he desired a speedy recovery, in order to prosecute the war. At this very time, Parmenio wrote to Alexander from the camp, bidding him have a care of Philip, as one who was bribed by Darius to kill him, with great sums of money, and a promise of his daughter in marriage. When he had perused the letter, he put it under his pillow, without showing it so much as to any of his most intimate friends, and when Philip came in with the potion, he took it with great cheerfulness and assurance, giving him meantime the letter to read. This was a spectacle well worth being present at, to see Alexander take the draught, and Philip read the letter at the same time, and then turn and look upon one another, but with different sentiments; for Alexander's looks were cheerful and open, to show his kindness to and confidence in his physician, while the other was full of surprise and alarm at the accusation, appealing to the gods to witness his innocence, sometimes lifting up his hands to heaven, and then throwing himself down by the bedside, and beseeching Alexander to lay aside all fear, and follow his directions without apprehension. For the medicine at first worked so strongly as to drive, so to say, the vital forces into the interior; he lost his speech, and falling into a swoon, had scarce any sense or pulse left. However, in no long time, by Philip's means, his health and strength returned, and he showed himself in public to the Macedonians, who were in continual fear and dejection until they saw him abroad again.

There was at this time in Darius's army a Macedonian refugee, named Amyntas, one who was pretty well acquainted with Alexander's character. This man, when he saw Darius intended to fall upon the enemy in the passes and defiles, advised him earnestly to keep where he was, in the open and extensive plains, it being the advantage of a numerous army to have field-room enough when it engages with a lesser force. Darius, instead of taking his counsel, told him he was afraid the enemy would endeavor to run away, and so Alexander would escape out of his hands. "That fear," replied Amyntas, "is needless, for assure yourself that far from avoiding you, he will make all the speed he can to meet you, and is now most likely on his march towards you." But Amyntas's counsel was to no purpose, for Darius immediately decamping, marched into Cilicia at the same time that Alexander advanced into Syria to meet him; and missing one another in the night they both turned back again. Alexander, greatly pleased with the event, made all the haste he could to fight in the defiles, and Darius to recover his former ground, and draw his army out of so disadvantageous a place. For now he began to perceive his error in engaging himself too far in a country in which the sea, the mountains, and the river Pinarus running through the midst of it, would necessitate him to divide his forces, render his horse almost unserviceable, and only cover and support the weakness of the enemy. Fortune was not kinder to Alexander in the choice of the ground, than he was careful to improve it to his advantage. For being much inferior in numbers, so far from allowing himself to be outflanked, he stretched his right wing much further out than the left wing of his enemies, and fighting there himself in the very foremost ranks, put the barbarians to flight. In this battle he was wounded in the thigh, Chares says, by Darius, with whom he fought hand to hand. But in the account which he gave Antipater of the battle, though indeed he owns he was wounded in the thigh with a sword, though not dangerously, yet he takes no notice who it was that wounded him.

Nothing was wanting to complete this victory, in which he overthrew above an hundred and ten thousand of his enemies, but the taking the person of Darius, who escaped very narrowly by flight. However, having taking his chariot and his bow, he returned from pursuing him, and found his own men busy in pillaging the barbarians' camp, which (though to disburden themselves, they had left most of their baggage at Damascus) was exceedingly rich. But Darius's tent, which was full of splendid furniture, and quantities of gold and silver, they reserved for Alexander himself, who, after he had put off his arms, went to bathe himself, saying, "Let us now cleanse ourselves from the toils of war in the bath of Darius." "Not so," replied one of his followers, "but in Alexander's rather; for the property of the conquered is, and should be called the conqueror's." Here, when he beheld the bathing vessels, the water-pots, the pans and the ointment boxes, all of gold, curiously wrought, and smelt the fragrant odors with which the whole place was exquisitely perfumed, and from thence passed into a pavilion of great size and height, where the couches and tables and preparations for an entertainment were perfectly magnificent, he turned to those about him and said, "This, it seems, is royalty."

But as he was going to supper, word was brought him that Darius's mother and wife and two unmarried daughters, being taken among the rest of the prisoners, upon the sight of his chariot and bow, were all in mourning and sorrow, imagining him to be dead. After a little pause, more livelily affected with their affliction than with his own success, he sent Leonnatus to them, to let them know Darius was not dead, and that they need not fear any harm from Alexander, who made war upon him only for dominion; they should themselves be provided with every thing they had been used to receive from Darius. This kind message could not but be very welcome to the captive ladies, especially being made good by actions no less humane and generous. For he gave them leave to bury whom they pleased of the Persians, and to make use for this purpose of what garments and furniture they thought fit out of the booty. He diminished nothing of their equipage, or of the attentions and respect formerly paid them, and allowed larger pensions for their maintenance than they had before. But the noblest and most royal part of their usage was, that he treated these illustrious prisoners according to their virtue and character, not suffering them to hear, or receive, or so much as to apprehend any thing that was unbecoming. So that they seemed rather lodged in some temple, or some holy virgin chambers, where they enjoyed their privacy sacred and uninterrupted, than in the camp of an enemy. Nevertheless Darius's wife was accounted the most beautiful princess then living, as her husband the tallest and handsomest man of his time, and the daughters were not unworthy of their parents. But Alexander, esteeming it more kingly to govern himself than to conquer his enemies, sought no intimacy with any one of them, nor indeed with any other woman before marriage, except Barsine, Memnon's widow, who was taken prisoner at Damascus. She had been instructed in the Grecian learning, was of a gentle temper, and by her father, Artabazus, royally descended, with good qualities, added to the solicitations and encouragement of Parmenio, as Aristobulus tells us, made him the more willing to attach himself to so agreeable and illustrious a woman. Of the rest of the female captives, though remarkably handsome and well proportioned, he took no further notice than to say jestingly that Persian women were terrible eyesores. And he himself, retaliating, as it were, by the display of the beauty of his own temperance and self-control, bade them be removed, as he would have done so many lifeless images. When Philoxenus, his lieutenant on the sea-coast, wrote to him to know if he would buy two young boys, of great beauty, whom one Theodorus, a Tarentine, had to sell, he was so offended, that he often expostulated with his friends, what baseness Philoxenus had ever observed in him that he should presume to make him such a reproachful offer. And he immediately wrote him a very sharp letter, telling him Theodorus and his merchandise might go with his good-will to destruction. Nor was he less severe to Hagnon, who sent him word he would buy a Corinthian youth named Crobylus, as a present for him. And hearing that Damon and Timotheus, two of Parmenio's Macedonian soldiers, had abused the wives of some strangers who were in his pay, he wrote to Parmenio, charging him strictly, if he found them guilty, to put them to death, as wild beasts that were only made for the mischief of mankind. In the same letter he added, that he had not so much as seen or desired to see the wife of Darius, no, nor suffered anybody to speak of her beauty before him. He was wont to say that sleep and the act of generation chiefly made him sensible that he was mortal; as much as to say, that weariness and pleasure proceed both from the same frailty and imbecility of human nature.

In his diet, also, he was most temperate, as appears, omitting many other circumstances, by what he said to Ada, whom he adopted, with the title of mother, and afterwards created queen of Caria. For when she, out of kindness, sent him every day many curious dishes and sweatmeats, and would have furnished him with some cooks and pastry-men, who were thought to have great skill, he told her he wanted none of them, his preceptor, Leonidas, having already given him the best, which were a night march to prepare for breakfast, and a moderate breakfast to create an appetite for supper. Leonidas also, he added, used to open and search the furniture of his chamber and his wardrobe, to see if his mother had left him any thing that was delicate or superfluous. He was much less addicted to wine than was generally believed; that which gave people occasion to think so of him was, that when he had nothing else to do, he loved to sit long and talk, rather than drink, and over every cup hold a long conversation. For when his affairs called upon him, he would not be detained, as other generals often were, either by wine, or sleep, nuptial solemnities, spectacles, or any other diversion whatsoever; a convincing argument of which is, that in the short time he lived, he accomplished so many and so great actions. When he was free from employment, after he was up, and had sacrificed to the gods, he used to sit down to breakfast, and then spend the rest of the day in hunting, or writing memoirs, giving decisions on some military questions, or reading. In marches that required no great haste, he would practise shooting as he went along, or to mount a chariot, and alight from it in full speed. Sometimes, for sport's sake, as his journals tell us, he would hunt foxes and go fowling. When he came in for the evening, after he had bathed and was anointed, he would call for his bakers and chief cooks, to know if they had his dinner ready. He never cared to dine till it was pretty late and beginning to be dark, and was wonderfully circumspect at meals that every one who sat with him should be served alike and with proper attention; and his love of talking, as was said before, made him delight to sit long at his wine. And then, though otherwise no prince's conversation was ever so agreeable, he would fall into a temper of ostentation and soldierly boasting, which gave his flatterers a great advantage to ride him, and made his better friends very uneasy. For though they thought it too base to strive who should flatter him most, yet they found it hazardous not to do it; so that between the shame and the danger, they were in a great strait how to behave themselves. After such an entertainment, he was wont to bathe, and then perhaps he would sleep till noon, and sometimes all day long. He was so very temperate in his eating, that when any rare fish or fruits were sent him, he would distribute them among his friends, and often reserve nothing for himself. His table, however, was always magnificent, the expense of it still increasing with his good fortune, till it amounted to ten thousand drachmas a day, to which sum he limited it, and beyond this he would suffer none to lay out in any entertainment where he himself was the guest.

After the battle of Issus, he sent to Damascus to seize upon the money and baggage, the wives and children of the Persians, of which spoil the Thessalian horsemen had the greatest share; for he had taken particular notice of their gallantry in the fight, and sent them thither on purpose to make their reward suitable to their courage. Not but that the rest of the army had so considerable a part of the booty as was sufficient to enrich them all. This first gave the Mace donians such a taste of the Persian wealth and women and barbaric splendor of living, that they were ready to pursue and follow upon it with all the eagerness of hounds upon a scent. But Alexander, before he proceeded any further, thought it necessary to assure himself of the sea-coast. Those who governed in Cyprus, put that island into his possession, and Phœnicia, Tyre only excepted, was surrendered to him During the siege of this city, which with mounds of earth cast up, and battering engines, and two hundred galleys by sea, was carried on for seven months together, he dreamt that he saw Hercules upon the walls, reaching out his hands, and calling to him. And many of the Tyrians in their sleep, fancied that Apollo told them he was displeased with their actions, and was about to leave them and go over to Alexander. Upon which, as if the god had been a deserting soldier, they seized him, so to say, in the act, tied down the statue with ropes, and nailed it to the pedestal, reproaching him, that he was a favorer of Alexander. Another time Alexander dreamed he saw a Satyr mocking him at a distance, and when he endeavored to catch him, he still escaped from him, till at last with much perseverance, and running about after him, he got him into his power. The soothsayers making two words of *Satyrus*, assured him, that Tyre should be his own. The inhabitants at this time show a spring of water, near which they say Alexander slept, when he fancied the Satyr appeared to him.

While the body of the army lay before Tyre, he made an excursion against the Arabians who inhabit the Mount Antilibanus, in which he hazarded his life extremely to bring off his master Lysimachus, who would needs go along with him, declaring he was neither older nor inferior in courage to Phœnix, Achilles's guardian. For when, quitting their horses, they began to march up the hills on foot, the rest of the soldiers outwent them a great deal, so that night drawing on, and the enemy near, Alexander was fain to stay behind so long, to encourage and help up the lagging and tired old man, that before he was aware, he was left behind, a great way from his soldiers, with a slender attendance, and forced to pass an extremely cold night in the dark, and in a very inconvenient place ; till seeing a great many scattered fires of the enemy at some distance, and trusting to his agility of body, and as he was always wont by undergoing toils and labors himself to cheer and support the Macedonians in any distress, he ran straight to one of the nearest fires, and with his dagger de patching two of the barbarians that sat by it, snatched up a lighted brand, and returned with it to his own men. They immediately made a great fire, which so alarmed the enemy that most of them fled, and those that assaulted them were soon routed, and thus they rested securely the remainder of the night. Thus Chares writes.

But to return to the siege, it had this issue. Alexander, that he might refresh his army, harassed with many former encounters, had led only a small party towards the walls, rather to keep the enemy busy, than with any prospect of much advantage. It happened at this time that Aristander, the soothsayer, after he had sacrificed, upon view of the entrails, affirmed confidently to those who stood by, that the city should be certainly taken that very month, upon which there was a laugh and some mockery among the soldiers, as this was the last day of it. The king seeing him in perplexity, and always anxious to support the credit of the predictions, gave order that they should not count it as the thirtieth, but as the twenty-third of the month, and ordering the trumpets to sound, attacked the walls more seriously than he at first intended. The sharpness of the assault so inflamed the rest of his forces who were left in the camp, that they could not hold from advancing to second it, which they performed with so much vigor, that the Tyrians retired, and the town was carried that very day. The next place he sat down before was Gaza, one of the largest cities of Syria, when this accident befell him. A large bird flying over him, let a clod of earth fall upon his shoulder, and then settling upon one of the battering engines, was suddenly entangled and caught in the nets, composed of sinews, which protected the ropes with which the machine was managed. This fell out exactly according to Aristander's prediction, which was, that Alexander should be wounded, and the city reduced.

From hence he sent great part of the spoils to Olympias, Cleopatra, and the rest of his friends, not omitting his preceptor Leonidas, on whom he bestowed five hundred talents' weight of frankincense, and an hundred of myrrh, in remembrance of the hopes he had once expressed of him when he was but a child. For Leonidas, it seems, standing by him one day while he was sacrificing, and seeing him take both his hands full of incense to throw into the fire, told him it became him to be more sparing in his offerings, and not to be so profuse till he was master of the countries which those sweet gums and spices come from. So Alexander now wrote to him, saying, "We have sent you abundance of myrrh and frankincense, that for the future you may not be stingy to the gods." Among the treasures and other booty that was taken from Darius, there was a very precious casket, which being brought to Alexander for a great rarity, he asked those about him what they thought fittest to be laid up in it; and when they had delivered their various opinions, he told them he should keep Homer's Iliad in it. This is attested by many credible authors, and if what those of Alexandria tell us, relying upon the authority of Heraclides, be true, Homer was neither an idle nor an unprofitable companion to him in his expedition. For when he was master of Egypt, designing to settle a colony of Grecians there, he resolved to build a large and populous city, and give it his own name. In order to which, after he had measured and staked out the ground with the advice of the best architects, he chanced one night in his sleep to see a wonderful vision; a grey-headed old man, of a venerable aspect appeared to stand by him, and pronounce these verses:—

> An island lies, where loud the billows roar,
> Pharos they call it, on the Egyptian shore.

Alexander upon this immediately rose up and went to Pharos, which, at that time, was an island lying a little above the Canobic mouth of the river Nile, though it has now been joined to the main land by a mole. As soon as he saw the commodious situation of the place, it being a long neck of land, stretching like an isthmus between large lagoons and shallow waters one side, and the sea on the other, the latter at the end of it making a spacious harbor, he said, Homer, besides his other excellences, was a very good architect, and ordered the plan of a city to be drawn out answerable to the place. To do which, for want of chalk, the soil being black, they laid out their lines with flour, taking in a pretty large compass of ground in a semicircular figure, and drawing into the inside of the circumference equal straight lines from each end, thus giving it something of the form of a cloak or cape. While he was pleasing himself with his design, on a sudden an infinite number of great birds of several kinds, rising like a black cloud out of the river and the lake, devoured every morsel of the flour that had been used in setting out the lines; at which omen even Alexander himself was troubled, till the augurs restored his confidence again by telling him, it was a sign the city he was about to build would not only abound in all things within itself, but a so be the nurse and feeder of many nations. He commanded the workmen to proceed, while he went to visit the temple of Ammon.

This was a long and painful, and, in two respects, a dangerous journey; first, if they should lose their provision of water, as for several days none could be obtained; and, secondly, if a violent south wind should rise upon them, while they were travelling through the wide extent of deep sands, as it is said to have done when Cambyses led his army that way, blowing the sand together in heaps, and raising, as it were, the whole desert like a sea upon them, till fifty thousand were swallowed up and destroyed by it. All these difficulties were weighed and represented to him; but Alexander was not easily to be diverted from any thing he was bent upon. For fortune having hitherto seconded him in his designs, made him resolute and firm in his opinions, and the boldness of his temper raised a sort of passion in him for surmounting difficulties; as if it were not enough to be always victorious in the field, unless places and seasons and nature herself submitted to him. In this journey, the relief and assistance the gods afforded him in his distresses, were more remarkable, and obtained greater belief than the oracles he received afterwards, which, however, were valued and credited the more on account of those occurrences. For first, plentiful rains that fell, preserved them from any fear of perishing by drought, and, allaying the extreme dryness of the sand, which now became moist and firm to travel on, cleared and purified the air. Besides this, when they were out of their way, and were wandering up and down, because the marks which were wont to direct the guides were disordered and lost, they were set right again by some ravens, which flew before them when on their march, and waited for them when they lingered and fell behind; and the greatest miracle, as Callisthenes tells us, was that if any of the company went astray in the night, they never ceased croaking and making a noise till by that means they had brought them into the right way again. Having passed through the wilderness, they came to the place where the high-priest, at the first salutation, bade Alexander welcome from his father Ammon. And being asked by him whether any of his father's murderers had escaped punishment, he charged him to speak with more respect, since his was not a mortal father. Then Alexander, changing his expression, desired to know of him if any of those who murdered Philip were yet unpunished, and further concerning dominion, whether the empire of the world was reserved for him? This, the god answered, he should obtain, and that Philip's death was fully revenged, which gave him so much satisfaction that he made splendid offerings to Jupiter, and gave the priests very rich presents. This is what most authors write concerning the oracles. But Alexander, in a letter to his mother, tells her there were some secret answers, which at his return he would communicate to her only. Others say that the priest, desirous as a piece of courtesy to address him in Greek, "O Paidion," by a slip in pronunciation ended with the *s* instead of the *n*, and said "O Paidios," which mistake Alexander was well enough pleased with, and it went for current that the oracle had called him so.

Among the sayings of one Psammon, a philosopher, whom he heard in Egypt, he most approved of this, that all men are governed by God, because in every thing, that which is chief and commands, is divine. But what he pronounced himself upon this subject, was even more like a philosopher, for he said, God was the common father of us all, but more particularly of the best of us. To the barbarians he carried himself very haughtily, as if he were fully persuaded of his divine birth and parentage; but to the Grecians more moderately, and with less affectation of divinity, except it were once in writing to the Athenians about Samos, when he tells them that he should not himself have bestowed upon them that free and glorious city; "You received it," he says, "from the bounty of him who at that time was called my lord and father," meaning Philip. However, afterwards being wounded with an arrow, and feeling much pain, he turned to those about him, and told them, "This, my friends, is real flowing blood, not Ichor,

"Such as immortal gods are wont to shed."

And another time, when it thundered so much that everybody was afraid, and Anaxarchus, the sophist, asked him if he who was Jupiter's son could do any thing like this, "Nay," said Alexander, laughing, "I have no desire to be formidable to my friends, as you would have me, who despised my table for being furnished with fish, and not with the heads of governors of provinces." For in fact it is related as true, that Anaxarchus, seeing a present of small fishes, which the king sent to Hephæstion, had used this expression, in a sort of irony, and disparagement of those who undergo vast labors and encounter great hazards in pursuit of magnificent objects which after all bring them little more pleasure or enjoyment than what others have. From what I have said upon this subject, it is apparent that Alexander in himself was not foolishly affected, or had the vanity to think himself really a god, but merely used his claims to divinity as a means of maintaining among other people the sense of his superiority.

At his return out of Egypt into Phœnicia, he sacrificed and made solemn processions, to which were added shows of lyric dances and tragedies, remarkable not merely for the splendor of the equipage and decorations, but for the competition among those who exhibited them. For the kings of Cyprus were here the exhibitors, just in the same manner as at Athens those who are chosen by lot out of the tribes. And, indeed, they showed the greatest emulation to outvie each other ; especially Nicocreon, king of Salamis, and Pasicrates of Soli, who furnished the chorus, and defrayed the expenses of the two most celebrated actors, Athenodorus and Thessalus, the former performing for Pasicrates, and the latter for Nicocreon. Thessalus was most favored by Alexander, though it did not appear till Athenodorus was declared victor by the plurality of votes. For then at his going away, he said the judges deserved to be commended for what they had done, but that he would willingly have lost part of his kingdom rather than to have seen Thessalus overcome. However, when he understood Athenodorus was fined by the Athenians for being absent at the festivals of Bacchus, though he refused his request that he would write a letter in his behalf, he gave him a sufficient sum to satisfy the penalty. Another time, when Lycon of Scarphia happened to act with great applause in the theatre, and in a verse which he introduced into the comic part which he was acting, begged for a present of ten talents, he laughed and gave him the money.

Darius wrote him a letter, and sent friends to intercede with him, requesting him to accept as a ransom of his captives the sum of a thousand talents, and offering him in exchange for his amity and alliance, all the countries on this side the river Euphrates, together with one of his daughters in marriage. These propositions he communicated to his friends, and when Parmenio told him, that for his part, if he were Alexander, he should readily embrace them, " So would I," said Alexander, " if I were Parmenio." Accordingly, his answer to Darius was, that if he would come and yield himself up into his power, he would treat him with all possible kindness ; if not, he was resolved immediately to go himself and seek him. But the death of Darius's wife in childbirth made him soon after regret one part of this answer and he showed evident marks of grief at being thus deprived of a further opportunity of exercising his clemency and good nature, which he manifested, however, as far as he could, by giving her a most sumptuous funeral.

Among the eunuchs who waited in the queen's chamber, and were taken prisoners with the women, there was one Tireus, who, getting out of the camp, fled away on horseback to Darius, to inform him of his wife's death. He, when he heard it, beating his head, and bursting into tears and lamentations, said, "Alas! how great is the calamity of the Persians! Was it not enough that their king's consort and sister was a prisoner in her lifetime, but she must, now she is dead, also be but meanly and obscurely buried?" "Oh king," replied the eunuch, "as to her funeral rites, or any respect or honor that should have been shown in them, you have not the least reason to accuse the ill-fortune of your country; for to my knowledge neither your queen Statira when alive, nor your mother, nor children, wanted any thing of their former happy condition, unless it were the light of your countenance, which I doubt not but the lord Oromasdes will yet restore to its former glory. And after her decease, I assure you, she had not only all due funeral ornaments, but was honored also with the tears of your very enemies; for Alexander is as gentle after victory, as he is terrible in the field." At the hearing of these words, such was the grief and emotion of Darius's mind, that they carried him into extravagant suspicions; and taking Tireus aside into a more private part of his tent, "Unless thou likewise," said he to him, "hast deserted me, together with the good fortune of Persia, and art become a Macedonian in thy heart; if thou yet ownest me for thy master Darius, tell me, I charge thee, by the veneration thou payest the light of Mithras, and this right hand of thy king, do I not lament the least of Statira's misfortunes in her captivity and death? Have I not suffered something more injurious and deplorable in her lifetime? And had I not been miserable with less dishonor, if I had met with a more severe and inhuman enemy? For how is it possible a young man as he is, should treat the wife of his opponent with so much distinction, were it not from some motive that does me disgrace?" Whilst he was yet speaking, Tireus threw himself at his feet, and besought him neither to wrong Alexander so much, nor his dead wife and sister, as to give utterance to any such thoughts, which deprived him of the greatest consolation left him in his adversity, the belief that he was overcome by a man whose virtues raised him above human nature; that he ought to look upon Alexander with love and admiration, who had given no less proofs of his continence towards the Persian women, than of his valor among the men. The eunuch confirmed all he said with solemn and dreadful oaths, and was further enlarging upon Alexander's moderation and magnanimity on other occasions, when Darius, breaking away from him into the other division of the tent, where his friends and courtiers were, lifted up his hands to heaven, and uttered this prayer, "Ye gods," said he, " of my family, and of my kingdom, if it be possible, I beseech you to restore the declining affairs of Persia, that I may leave them in as flourishing a condition as I found them, and have it in my power in make a grateful return to Alexander for the kindness which in my adversity he has shown to those who are dearest to me. But if, indeed, the fatal time be come, which is to give a period to the Persian monarchy, if our ruin be a debt that must be paid to the divine jealousy and the vicissitude of things, then I beseech you grant that no other man but Alexander may sit upon the throne of Cyrus." Such is the narrative given by the greater number of the historians.

But to return to Alexander. After he had reduced all Asia on this side the Euphrates, he advanced towards Darius, who was coming down against him with a million of men. In his march a very ridiculous passage happened. The servants who followed the camp, for sport's sake divided themselves into two parties, and named the commander of one of them Alexander, and the other Darius. At first they only pelted one another with clods of earth, but presently took to their fists, and at last, heated with contention, they fought in good earnest with stones and clubs, so that they had much ado to part them; till Alexander, upon hearing of it, ordered the two captains to decide the quarrel by single combat, and armed him who bore his name himself, while Philotas did the same to him who represented Darius. The whole army were spectators of this encounter, willing from the event of it to derive an omen of their own future success. After they had fought stoutly a pretty long while, at last he who was called Alexander had the better, and for a reward of his prowess, had twelve villages given him, with leave to wear the Persian dress. So we are told by Eratosthenes.

But the great battle of all that was fought with Darius,

was not, as most wri.ers tell us, at Arbela, but at **Gaugamela**, which, in their language, signifies the camel's house, forasmuch as one of their ancient kings having escaped the pursuit of his enemies on a swift camel, in gratitude to his beast, settled him at this place, with an allowance of certain villages and rents for his maintenance. It came to pass that in the month Boëdromion, about the beginning of the feast of Mysteries at Athens, there was an eclipse of the moon, the eleventh night after which, the two armies being now in view of one another, Darius kept his men in arms, and by torchlight took a general review of them. But Alexander, while his soldiers slept, spent the night before his tent with his diviner, Aristander, performing certain mysterious ceremonies, and sacrificing to the god Fear. In the mean while the oldest of his commanders, and chiefly Parmenio, when they beheld all the plain between Niphates and the Gordyæan mountains shining with the lights and fires which were made by the barbarians, and heard the uncertain and confused sound of voices out of their camp, like the distant roaring of a vast ocean, were so amazed at the thoughts of such a multitude, that after some conference among themselves, they concluded it an enterprise too difficult and hazardous for them to engage so numerous an enemy in the day, and therefore meeting the king as he came from sacrificing, besought him to attack Darius by night, that the darkness might conceal the danger of the ensuing battle. To this he gave them the celebrated answer, "I will not steal a victory," which though some at the time thought a boyish and inconsiderate speech, as if he played with danger, others, however, regarded as an evidence that he confided in his present condition, and acted on a true judgment of the future, not wishing to leave Darius, in case he were worsted, the pretext of trying his fortune again, which he might suppose himself to have, if he could impute his overthrow to the disadvantage of the night, as he did before to the mountains, the narrow passages, and the sea. For while he had such numerous forces and large dominions still remaining, it was not any want of men or arms that could induce him to give up the war, but only the loss of all courage and hope upon the conviction of an undeniable and manifest defeat.

After they were gone from him with this answer, he laid himself down in his tent and slept the rest of the night more soundly than was usual with him, to the astonishment of the commanders, who came to him early in the morning, and were tain themselves to give order that the soldiers should break-fast. But at last, time not giving them leave to wait any longer, Parmenio went to his bedside, and called him twice or thrice by his name, till he waked him, and then asked him how it was possible, when he was to fight the most important battle of all, he could sleep as soundly as if he were already victorious. "And are we not so, indeed," replied Alexander, smiling, "since we are at last relieved from the trouble of wandering in pursuit of Darius through a wide and wasted country, hoping in vain that he would fight us?" And not only before the battle, but in the height of the danger, he showed himself great, and manifested the self-possession of a just foresight and confidence. For the battle for some time fluctuated and was dubious. The left wing, where Parmenic commanded, was so impetuously charged by the Bractrian horse that it was disordered and forced to give ground, at the same time that Mazæus had sent a detachment round about to fall upon those who guarded the baggage, which so disturbed Parmenio, that he sent mesengers to acquaint Alexander that the camp and baggage would be all lost unless he immediately relieved the rear by a considerable reinforcement drawn out of the front. This message being brought him just as he was giving the signal to those about him for the onset, he bade them tell Parmenio that he must have surely lost the use of his reason, and had forgotten, in his alarm, that soldiers, if victorious, become masters of their enemies' baggage; and if defeated, instead of taking care of their wealth or their slaves, have nothing more to do but to fight gallantly and die with honor. When he had said this, he put on his helmet, having the rest of his arms on before he came out of his tent, which were a coat of the Sicilian make, girt close about him, and over that a breastpiece of thickly quilted linen, which was taken among other booty at the battle of Issus. The helmet, which was made by Theophilus, though of iron, was so well wrought and polished, that it was as bright as the most refined silver. To this was fitted a gorget of the same metal, set with precious stones. His sword, which was the weapon he most used in fight, was given him by the king of the Citieans, and was of an admirable temper and lightness. The belt which he also wore in all engagements, was of much richer workmanship than the rest of his armor. It was a work of the ancient Helicon, and had been presented to him by the Rhodians, as a mark of their respect to him. So long as he was engaged in drawing up his men, or riding about to give orders or directions, or to view them, he spared Bucephalus, who was now growing old, and made use of another horse; but when he was actually to fight, he sent for him again, and as soon as he was mounted, commenced the attack.

He made the longest address that day to the Thessalians and other Greeks, who answered him with loud shouts, desiring him to lead them on against the barbarians, upon which he shifted his javelin into his left hand, and with his right lifted up towards heaven, besought the gods, as Callisthenes tells us, that if he was of a truth the son of Jupiter, they would be pleased to assist and strengthen the Grecians. At the same time the augur Aristander, who had a white mantle about him, and a crown of gold on his head, rode by and showed them an eagle that soared just over Alexander, and directed his flight towards the enemy; which so animated the beholders, that after mutual encouragements and exhortations, the horse charged at full speed, and were followed in a mass by the whole phalanx of the foot. But before they could well come to blows with the first ranks, the barbarians shrunk back, and were hotly pursued by Alexander, who drove those that fled before him into the middle of the battle, where Darius himself was in person, whom he saw from a distance over the foremost ranks, conspicuous in the midst of his life-guard, a tall and fine-looking man, drawn in a lofty chariot, defended by an abundance of the best horse, who stood close in order about it ready to receive the enemy. But Alexander's approach was so terrible, forcing those who gave back upon those who yet maintained their ground, that he beat down and dispersed them almost all. Only a few of the bravest and valiantest opposed the pursuit, who were slain in their king's presence, falling in heaps upon one another, and in the very pangs of death striving to catch hold of the horses. Darius now seeing all was lost, that those who were placed in front to defend him were broken and beat back upon him, that he could not turn or disengage his chariot without great difficulty, the wheels being clogged and entangled among the dead bodies, which lay in such heaps as not only stopped, but almost covered the horses, and made them rear and grow so unruly, that the frighted charioteer could govern them no longer, in this extremity was glad to quit his chariot and his arms, and mounting, it is said, upon a mare that had been taken from her foal, betook himself to flight. But he had not escaped so either, if Parmenio had not sent fresh messengers to Alexander, to desire him to return and assist him against a considerable body of the enemy which yet stood together, and would not give ground. For, indeed, Parmenio is on all hands accused of having been sluggish and unserviceable in this battle, whether age had impaired his courage, or that, as Callisthenes says, he secretly disliked and envied Alexander's growing greatness. Alexander, though he was not a little vexed to be so recalled and hindered from pursuing his victory, yet concealed the true reason from his men, and causing a retreat to be sounded, as if it were too late to continue the execution any longer, marched back towards the place of danger, and by the way met with the news of the enemy's total overthrow and flight.

This battle being thus over, seemed to put a period to the Persian empire; and Alexander, who was now proclaimed king of Asia, returned thanks to the gods in magnificent sacrifices, and rewarded his friends and followers with great sums of money, and places, and governments of provinces. And eager to gain honor with the Grecians, he wrote to them that he would have all tyrannies abolished, that they might live free according to their own laws, and specially to the Platæans, that their city should be rebuilt, because their ancestors had permitted their countrymen of old to make their territory the seat of the war, when they fought with the barbarians for their common liberty. He sent also part of the spoils into Italy, to the Crotoniats, to honor the zeal and courage of their citizen Phayllus, the wrestler, who, in the Median war when the other Grecian colonies in Italy disowned Greece, that he might have a share in the danger, joined the fleet at Salamis, with a vessel set forth at his own charge. So affectionate was Alexander to all kind of virtue, and so desirous to preserve the memory of laudable actions.

From hence he marched through the province of Babylon, which immediately submitted to him, and in Ecbatana was much surprised at the sight of the place where fire issues in a continuous stream, like a spring of water, out of a cleft in the earth, and the stream of naphtha, which, not far from this spot, flows out so abundantly as to form a sort of lake. This naphtha, in other respects resembling bitumen, is so subject to take fire, that before it touches the flame, it will kindle at the very light that surrounds it, and often inflame the intermediate air also. The barbarians, to show the power and nature of it, sprinkled the street that led to the king's lodgings with little drops of it, and when it was almost night, stood at the further end with torches, which being applied to the moist ened places, the first at once taking fire, instantly, as quick as a man could think of it, it caught from one end to another, in such a manner that the whole street was one continued flame. Among those who used to wait on the king and find occasion to amuse him when he anointed and washed himself, there was one Athenophanes, an Athenian, who desired him to make an experiment of the naphtha upon Stephanus, who stood by in the bathing place, a youth with a ridiculously ugly face, whose talent was singing well, "For," said he, "if it take hold of him and is not put out, it must undeniably be allowed to be of the most invincible strength." The youth, as it happened, readily consented to undergo the trial, and as soon as he was anointed and rubbed with it, his whole body broke out into such a flame, and was so seized by the fire, that Alexander was in the greatest perplexity and alarm for him, and not without reason; for nothing could have pervented his being consumed by it, if by good chance there had not been people at hand with a great many vessels of water for the service of the bath, with all which they had much ado to extinguish the fire; and his body was so burned all over, that he was not cured of it a good while after. And thus it is not without some plausibility that they endeavor to reconcile the fable to truth, who say this was the drug in the tragedies with which Medea anointed the crown and veil which she gave to Creon's daughter. For neither the things themselves, nor the fire, could kindle of its own accord, but being prepared for it by the naphtha, they imperceptibly attracted and caught a flame which happened to be brought near them. For the rays and emanations of fire at a distance have no other effect upon some bodies than bare light and heat, but in others, where they meet with airy dryness, and also sufficient rich moisture, they collect themselves and soon kindle and create a transformation. The manner, however, of the production of naphtha admits of a diversity of opinion. . . . . . . or whether this liquid substance that feeds the flame does not rather proceed from a soil that is unctuous and productive of fire, as that of the province of Babylon is, where the ground is so very hot, that oftentimes the grains of barley leap up and are thrown out, as if the violent inflammation had made the earth throb; and in the extreme heats the inhabitants are wont to sleep upon skins filled with water. Harpalus, who was left governor of this country, and was desirous to adorn the palace gardens and walks with Grecian plants, succeeded in raising all but ivy, which the earth would not bear, but constantly killed. For being a plant that loves a cold soil, the temper of this hot and fiery earth was improper for it. But such digressions as these the impatient reader will be more willing to pardon, if they are kept within a moderate compass.

At the taking of Susa, Alexander found in the palace forty thousand talents in money ready coined, besides an unspeakable quantity of other furniture and treasure; amongst which was five thousand talents' worth of Hermionian purple, that had been laid up there an hundred and ninety years, and yet kept its color as fresh and lively as at first. The reason of which, they say, is that in dyeing the purple they made use of honey, and of white oil in the white tincture, both which after the like space of time preserve the clearness and brightness of their lustre. Dinon also relates that the Persian kings had water fetched from the Nile and the Danube, which they laid up in their treasuries as a sort of testimony of the greatness of their power and universal empire.

The entrance into Persia was through a most difficult country, and was guarded by the noblest of the Persians, Darius himself having escaped further. Alexander, however, chanced to find a guide in exact correspondence with what the Pythia had foretold when he was a child, that a lycus should conduct him into Persia. For by such an one, whose father was a Lycian, and his mother a Persian, and who spoke both languages, he was now led into the country, by a way something about, yet without fetching any considerable compass. Here a great many of the prisoners were put to the sword, of which himself gives this account, that he commanded them to be killed in the belief that it would be for his advantage. Nor was the money found here less, he says, than at Susa, besides other movables and treasure, as much as ten thousand pair of mules and five thousand camels could well carry away. Amongst other things he happened to observe a large statue of Xerxes thrown carelessly down to the ground in the confusion made by the multitude of soldiers pressing into the palace. He stood still, and accosting it as if it had been alive, " Shall we," said he, " neglectfully pass thee by, now thou art prostrate on the ground, because thou once invadest Greece, or shall we erect thee again in consideration of the greatness of thy mind and thy other virtues ? " But at last, after he had paused some time, and silently considered with himself, he went on without taking any further notice of it. In this place he took up his winter-quarters, and stayed four months to refresh his soldiers. It is related that the first time he sat on the royal throne of Persia under the canopy of gold, Demaratus, the Corinthian, who was much attached to him and had been one of his father's friends, wept, in an old man's manner, and deplored the misfortune of those Greeks whom death had deprived of the satisfaction of seeing Alexander seated on the throne of Darius.

From hence designing to march against Darius, before he set out, he diverted himself with his officers at an entertainment of drinking and other pastimes, and indulged so far as to let every one's mistress sit by and drink with them. The most celebrated of them was Thais, an Athenian, mistress of Ptolemy, who was afterwards king of Egypt. She, partly as a sort of well-turned compliment to Alexander, partly out of sport, as the drinking went on, at last was carried so far as to utter a saying, not misbecoming her native country's character, though somewhat too lofty for her own condition. She said it was indeed some recompense for the toils she had undergone in following the camp all over Asia, that she was that day treated in, and could insult over, the stately palace of the Persian monarchs. But, she added, it would please her much better if, while the king looked on, she might in sport, with her own hands, set fire to the court of that Xerxes who reduced the city of Athens to ashes, that it might be recorded to posterity, that the women who followed Alexander had taken a severer revenge on the Persians for the sufferings and affronts of Greece, than all the famed commanders had been able to do by sea or land. What she said was received with such universal liking and murmurs of applause, and so seconded by the encouragement and eagerness of the company, that the king himself, persuaded to be of the party, started from his seat, and with a chaplet of flowers on his head, and a lighted torch in his hand, led them the way, while they went after him in a riotous manner, dancing and making loud cries about the place; which when the rest of the Macedonians perceived, they also in great delight ran thither with torches; for they hoped the burning and destruction of the royal palace was an argument that he looked homeward, and had no design to reside among the barbarians. Thus some writers give their account of this action, while others say it was done deliberately; however all agree that he soon repented of it, and gave order to put out the fire.

Alexander was naturally most munificent, and grew more so as his fortune increased, accompanying what he gave with that courtesy and freedom, which, to speak truth, is necessary to make a benefit really obliging. I will give a few instances of this kind. Ariston, the captain of the Pæonians, having killed an enemy, brought his head to show him, and told him that in his country, such a present was recompensed with a cup of gold. "With an empty one," said Alexander, smiling, "but I drink to you in this, which I give you full of wine." Another time, as one of the common soldiers was driving a mule laden with some of the king's treasure, the beast grew tired, and the soldier took it upon his own back, and began to march with it, till Alexander seeing the man so overcharged asked what was the matter; and when he was informed, just as he was ready to lay down his burden for weariness, "Do not faint now," said he to him, "but finish the journey, and carry what you have there to your own tent for yourself." He was always more displeased with those who would not accept of what he gave than with those who begged of him. And therefore he wrote to Phocion, that he would not own him for his friend any longer, if he refused his presents. He had never given any thing to Serapion, one of the youths that played at ball with him, because he did not ask of him, till one day, it coming to Serapion's turn to play, he still threw the ball to others, and when the king asked him why he did not direct it to him, "Because you do not ask for it," said he; which answer pleased him so, that he was very liberal to him afterwards. One Proteas, a pleasant, jesting, drinking fellow, having incurred his displeasure, got his friends to intercede for him, and begged his pardon himself with tears, which at last prevailed, and Alexander declared he was friends with him. "I cannot believe it," said Proteas, "unless you first give me some pledge of it." The king understood his meaning, and presently ordered five talents to be given him. How magnificent he was in enriching his friends, and those who attended on his person, appears by a letter which Olympias wrote to him, where she tells him he should reward and honor those about him in a more moderate way. "For now," said she, "you make them all equal to kings, you give them power and opportunity of making many friends of their own, and in the mean time you leave yourself destitute." She often wrote to him to this purpose, and he never communicated her letters to anybody, unless it were one which he opened when Hephæstion was by, whom he permitted, as his custom was, to read it along with him; but then as soon as he had done, he took off his ring, and set the seal upon Hephæstion's lips. Mazæus, who was the most considerable man in Darius's court, had a son who was already governor of a prov· Alexander bestowed another upon him that was better; he, however, modestly refused, and told him, instead of one Darius, he went the way to make many Alexanders. To Parmenio he gave Bagoas's house, in which he found a wardrobe of apparel worth more than a thousand talents. He wrote to Antipater, commanding him to keep a life-guard about him for the security of his person against conspiracies. To his mother he sent many presents, but would never suffer her to meddle with matters of state or war, not indulging her busy temper, and when she fell out with him on this account, he bore her ill-humor very patiently. Nay more, when he read a long letter from Antipater, full of accusations against her, "Antipater," he said, "does not know that one tear of a mother effaces a thousand such letters as these."

But when he perceived his favorites grow so luxurious and extravagant in their way of living and expenses, that Hagnon, the Teian, wore silver nails in his shoes, that Leonnatus enployed several camels, only to bring him powder out of Egypt to use when he wrestled, and that Philotas had hunting nets a hundred furlongs in length, that more used precious ointment than plain oil when they went to bathe, and that they carried about servants everywhere with them to rub them and wait upon them in their chambers, he reproved them in gentle and reasonable terms, telling them he wondered that they who had been engaged in so many single battles did not know by experience, that those who labor sleep more sweetly and soundly than those who are labored for, and could fail to see by comparing the Persians' manner of living with their own, that it was the most abject and slavish condition to be voluptuous, but the most noble and royal to undergo pain and labor. He argued with them further, how it was possible for any one who pretended to be a soldier, either to look well after his horse, or to keep his armor bright and in good order, who thought it much to let his hands be serviceable to what was nearest to him his own body. "Are you still to learn," said he, "that the end and perfection of our victories is to avoid the vices and infirmities of those whom we subdue?" And to strengthen his precepts by example, he applied himself now more vigorously than ever to hunting and warlike expeditions, embracing all opportunities of hardship and danger, insomuch that a Lacedæmonian, who was there on an embassy to him, and chanced to be by when he encountered with and mastered a huge lion, told him he had fought gallantly with the beast, which of the two should be king Craterus caused a representation to be made of this adventure, consisting of the lion and the dogs, of the king engaged with the lion, and himself coming in to his assistance, all expressed n figures of brass, some of which were by Lysippus, and the rest by Leochares; and had it dedicated in the temple of Apollo at Delphi. Alexander exposed his person to danger in this manner, with the object both of inuring himself, and inciting others to the performance of brave and virtuous actions.

But his followers, who were grown rich, and consequently proud, longed to indulge themselves in pleasure and idleness, and were weary of marches and expeditions, and at last went on so far as to censure and speak ill of him. All which at first he bore very patiently, saying it became a king well to do good to others, and be evil spoken of. Meantime, on the smallest occasions that called for a show of kindness to his friends, there was every indication on his part of tenderness and respect. Hearing Peucestes was bitten by a bear, he wrote to him that he took it unkindly he should send others notice of it, and not make him acquainted with it; " But now," said he, "since it is so, let me know how you do, and whether any of your companions forsook you when you were in danger, that I may punish them." He sent Hephæstion, who was absent about some business, word how while they were fighting for their diversion with an ichneumon, Craterus was by chance run through both thighs with Perdiccas's javelin. And upon Peucestes's recovery from a fit of sickness, he sent a letter of thanks to his physician Alexippus. When Craterus was ill, he saw a vision in his sleep, after which he offered sacrifices for his health, and bade him do so likewise. He wrote also to Pausanias, the physician, who was about to purge Craterus with hellebore, partly out of an anxious concern for him, and partly to give him a caution how he used that medicine. He was so tender of his friends' reputation that he imprisoned Ephialtes and Cissus, who brought him the first news of Harpalus's flight and withdrawal from his service, as if they had falsely accused him. When he sent the old and infirm soldiers home, Eurylochus, a citizen of Ægæ, got his name enrolled among the sick, though he ailed nothing, which being discovered, he confessed he was in love with a young woman named Telesippa, and wanted to go along with her to the seaside. Alexander inquired to whom the woman belonged, and being told she was a free courtesan, " I will assist you," said he to Eurylochus, "in your amour if your mistress be to be gained either by presents or persuasions; but we must use no other means, because she is free-born."

It is surprising to consider upon what slight occasions he would write letters to serve his friends. As when he wrote one in which he gave order to search for a youth that belonged to Seleucus, who was run away into Cilicia; and in another thanked and commended Peucestes for apprehending Nicon a servant of Craterus; and in one to Megabyzus, concerning a slave that had taken sanctuary in a temple, gave direction that he should not meddle with him while he was there, but if he could entice him out by fair means, then he gave him leave to seize him. It is reported of him that when he first sat in judgment upon capital causes, he would lay his hand upon one of his ears while the accuser spoke, to keep it free and unprejudiced in behalf of the party accused. But afterwards such a multitude of accusations were brought before him, and so many proved true, that he lost his tenderness of heart, and gave credit to those also that were false; and especially when anybody spoke ill of him, he would be transported out of his reason, and show himself cruel and inexorable, valuing his glory and reputation beyond his life or kingdom.

He now, as we said, set forth to seek Darius, expecting he should be put to the hazard of another battle, but heard he was taken and secured by Bessus, upon which news he sent home the Thessalians, and gave them a largess of two thousand talents over and above the pay that was due to them. This long and painful pursuit of Darius, for in eleven days he marched thirty-three hundred furlongs, harassed his soldiers so that most of them were ready to give it up, chiefly for want of water. While they were in this distress, it happened that some Macedonians who had fetched water in skins upon their mules from a river they had found out, came about noon to the place where Alexander was, and seeing him almost choked with thirst, presently filled an helmet and offered it him. He asked them to whom they were carrying the water, they told him to their children, adding, that if his life were but saved, it was no matter for them, they should be able well enough to repair that loss, though they all perished. Then he took the helmet into his hands, and looking round about, when he saw all those who were near him stretching their heads out and looking earnestly after the drink, he returned it again with thanks without tasting a drop of it. "For,' said he, "if I alone should drink, the rest will be out of heart.'

The soldiers no sooner took notice of his temperance and magnanimity upon this occasion, but they one and all cried out to him to lead them forward boldly, and began whipping on their horses. For whilst they had such a king they said they defied both weariness and thirst, and looked upon themselves to be little less than immortal. But though they were all equally cheerful and willing, yet not above threescore horse were able, it is said, to keep up, and to fall in with Alexander upon the enemy's camp, where they rode over abundance of gold and silver that lay scattered about, and passing by a great many chariots full of women that wandered here and there for want of drivers, they endeavored to overtake the first of those that fled, in hopes to meet with Darius among them. And at last, after much trouble, they found him lying in a chariot, wounded all over with darts, just at the point of death. However, he desired they would give him some drink, and when he had drunk a little cold water, he told Polystratus, who gave it him, that it had become the last extremity of his ill fortune, to receive benefits and not be able to return them. "But Alexander," said he, "whose kindness to my mother, my wife, and my children I hope the gods will recompense, will doubtless thank you for your humanity to me. Tell him, therefore, in token of my acknowledgment, I give him this right hand," with which words he took hold of Polystratus's hand and died. When Alexander came up to them, he showed manifest tokens of sorrow, and taking off his own cloak, threw it upon the body to cover it. And sometime afterwards, when Bessus was taken, he ordered him to be torn in pieces in this manner. They fastened him to a couple of trees which were bound down so as to meet, and then being let loose, with a great force returned to their places, each of them carrying that part of the body along with it that was tied to it. Darius's body was laid in state, and sent to his mother with pomp suitable to his quality. His brother Exathres, Alexander received into the number of his intimate friends.

And now with the flower of his army he marched into Hyrcania, where he saw a large bay of an open sea, apparently not much less than the Euxine, with water, however, sweeter than that of other seas, but could learn nothing of certainty concerning it, further than that in all probability it seemed to him to be an arm issuing from the lake of Mæotis. However the naturalists were better informed of the truth, and had given an account of it many years before Alexander's expedition;

that of four gulfs which out of the main sea enter into the continent, this, known indifferently as the Caspian and as the Hyrcanian sea, is the most northern. Here the barbarians, unexpectedly meeting with those who led Bucephalas, took them prisoners, and carried the horse away with them, at which Alexander was so much vexed, that he sent an herald to let them know he would put them all to the sword, men, women and children, without mercy, if they did not restore him But on their doing so, and at the same time surrendering their cities into his hands, he not only treated them kindly, but also paid a ransom for his horse to those who took him.

From hence he marched into Parthia, where not having much to do, he first put on the barbaric dress, perhaps with the view of making the work of civilizing them the easier, as nothing gains more upon men than a conformity to their fashions and customs. Or it may have been as a first trial, whether the Macedonians might be brought to *adore* him as the Persians did their kings, by accustoming them by little and little to bear with the alteration of his rule and course of life in other things. However, he followed not the Median fashion, which was altogether foreign and uncouth, and adopted neither the trousers nor the sleeved vest, nor the tiara for the head, but taking a middle way between the Persian mode and the Macedonian, so contrived his habit that it was not so flaunting as the one, and yet more pompous and magnificent than the other. At first he wore this habit only when he conversed with the barbarians, or within doors, among his intimate friends and companions, but afterwards he appeared in it abroad, when he rode out, and at public audiences, a sight which the Macedonians beheld with grief; but they so respected his other virtues and good qualities, that they felt it reasonable in some things to gratify his fancies and his passion of glory, in pursuit of which he hazarded himself so far, that, besides his other adventures, he had but lately been wounded in the leg by an arrow, which had so shattered the shank-bone that splinters were taken out. And on another occasion he received a violent blow with a stone upon the nape of the neck, which dimmed his sight for a good while afterwards. And yet all this could not hinder him from exposing himself freely to any dangers, insomuch that he passed the river Orexartes, which he took to be the Tanais, and putting the Scythians to flight, followed them above a hundred furlongs, though suffering all the time from a diarrhœa.

Here many affirm that the Amazon came to give him a

visit. So Clitarchus, Polyclitus, Onesicritus, Antigenes, and Ister, tell us. But Aristobulus and Chares, who held the office of reporter of requests, Ptolemy and Anticlides, Philon the Theban, Philip of Theangela, Hecatæus the Eretrian, Philip the Chalcidian, and Duris the Samian, say it is wholly a fiction. And truly Alexander himself seems to confirm the latter statement, for in a letter in which he gives Antipater an account of all that happened, he tells him that the king of Scythia offered him his daughter in marriage, but makes no mention at all of the Amazon. And many years after, when Onesicritus read this story in his fourth book to Lysimachus, who then reigned, the king laughed quietly and asked, "Where could I have been at that time?"

But it signifies little to Alexander whether this be credited or no. Certain it is, that, apprehending the Macedonians would be weary of pursuing the war, he left the greater part of them in their quarters; and having with him in Hyrcania the choice of his men only, amounting to twenty thousand foot, and three thousand horse, he spoke to them to this effect: That hitherto the barbarians had seen them no otherwise than as it were in a dream, and if they should think of returning when they had only alarmed Asia, and not conquered it, their enemies would set upon them as upon so many women. However, he told them he would keep none of them with him against their will, they might go if they pleased; he should merely enter his protest, that when on his way to make the Macedonians the masters of the world, he was left alone with a few friends and volunteers. This is almost word for word, as he wrote in a letter to Antipater, where he adds, that when he had thus spoken to them, they all cried out, they would go along with him whithersoever it was his pleasure to lead them. After succeeding with these, it was no hard matter for him to bring over the multitude, which easily followed the example of their betters. Now, also, he more and more accommodated himself in his way of living to that of the natives, and tried to bring them, also, as near as he could to the Macedonian customs, wisely considering that whilst he was engaged in an expedition which would carry him far from thence, it would be wiser to depend upon the good-will which might arise from intermixture and association as a means of maintaining tranquillity, than upon force and compulsion. In order to this, he chose out thirty thousand boys, whom he put under masters to teach them the Greek tongue, and to train them up to arms in the Macedonian discipline. As for his marriage with Roxana whose youthfulness and beauty had charmed him at a drinking entertainment, where he first happened to see her, taking part in a dance, it was, indeed, a love affair, yet it seemed at the same time to be conducive to the object he had in hand. For it gratified the conquered people to see him choose a wife from among themselves, and it made them feel the most lively affection for him, to find that in the only passion which he, the most temperate of men, was overcome by, he yet forebore till he could obtain her in a lawful and honorable way.

Noticing, also, that among his chief friends and favorites, Hephæstion most approved all that he did, and complied with and imitated him in his change of habits, while Craterus continued strict in the observation of the customs and fashions of his own country, he made it his practice to employ the first in all transactions with the Persians, and the latter when he had to do with the Greeks or Macedonians. And in general he showed more affection for Hephæstion, and more respect for Craterus; Hephæstion, as he used to say, being Alexander's, and Craterus the king's friend. And so these two friends always bore in secret a grudge to each other, and at times quarrelled openly, so much so, that once in India they drew upon one another, and were proceeding in good earnest, with their friends on each side to second them, when Alexander rode up and publicly reproved Hephæstion, calling him fool and madman, not to be sensible that without his favor he was nothing. He rebuked Craterus, also, in private, severely, and then causing them both to come into his presence, he reconciled them, at the same time swearing by Ammon and the rest of the gods, that he loved them two above all other men, but if ever he perceived them fall out again he would be sure to put both of them to death, or at least the aggressor. After which they neither ever did or said any thing, so much as in jest, to offend one another.

There was scarcely any one who had greater repute among the Macedonians than Philotas, the son of Parmenio. For besides that he was valiant and able to endure any fatigue of war, he was also next to Alexander himself the most munificent, and the greatest lover of his friends, one of whom asking him for some money, he commanded his steward to give it him; and when he told him he had not wherewith, "Have you not any plate, then," said he, "or any clothes of mine to sell?" But he carried his arrogance and his pride of wealth and his habits of display and luxury to a degree of assumption unbecoming a private man; and affecting all the loftiness without succeeding in showing any of the grace or gentleness of true greatness, by this mistaken and spurious majesty he gained so much envy and ill-will, that Parmenio would sometimes tell him, "My son, to be not quite so great would be better." For he had long before been complained of, and accused to Alexander. Particularly when Darius was defeated in Cilicia, and an immense booty was taken at Damascus, among the rest of the prisoners who were brought into the camp, there was one Antigone of Pydna, a very handsome woman, who fell to Philotas's share. The young man one day in his cups, in the vaunting, outspoken, soldier's manner, declared to his mistress, that all the great actions were performed by him and his father, the glory and benefit of which, he said, together with the title of king, the boy Alexander reaped and enjoyed by their means. She could not hold, but discovered what he had said to one of her acquaintance, and he, as is usual in such cases, to another, till at last the story came to the ears of Craterus, who brought the woman secretly to the king. When Alexander had heard what she had to say, he commanded her to continue her intrigue with Philotas, and give him an account from time to time of all that should fall from him to this purpose. He thus unwittingly caught in a snare, to gratify sometimes a fit of anger, sometimes a mere love of vainglory, let himself utter numerous foolish, indiscreet speeches against the king in Antigone's hearing, of which, though Alexander was informed and convinced by strong evidence, yet he would take no notice of it at present, whether it was that he confided in Parmenio's affection and loyalty, or that he apprehended their authority and interest in the army. But about this time, one Limnus, a Macedonian of Chalastra, conspired against Alexander's life, and communicated his design to a youth whom he was fond of, named Nicomachus, inviting him to be of the party. But he not relishing the thing, revealed it to his brother Balinus, who immediately addressed himself to Philotas, requiring him to introduce them both to Alexander, to whom they had something of great moment to impart which very nearly concerned him. But he, for what reason is uncertain, went not with them, professing that the king was engaged with affairs of more importance. And when they had urged him a second time, and were still slighted by him, they applied themselves to another, by whose means being admitted into Alexander's presence, they first told about Limnus's conspiracy, and by the way let Philotas's negligence appear who had twi disregarded their application to him. Alexander was greatly incensed, and on finding that Limnus had defended himself, and had been killed by the soldier who was sent to seize him, he was still more discomposed, thinking he had thus lost the means of detecting the plot. As soon as his displeasure against Philotas began to appear, presently all his old enemies showed themselves, and said openly, the king was too easily imposed on, to imagine that one so inconsiderable as Limnus, a Chalastrian, should of his own head undertake such an enterprise; that in all likelihood he was but subservient to the design, an instrument that was moved by some greater spring; that those ought to be more strictly examined about the matter whose interest it was so much to conceal it. When they had once gained the king's ear for insinuations of this sort, they went on to show a thousand grounds of suspicion against Philotas, till at last they prevailed to have him seized and put to the torture, which was done in the presence of the principal officers, Alexander himself being placed behind some tapestry to understand what passed. Where, when he heard in what a miserable tone, and with what abject submissions Philotas applied himself to Hephæstion, he broke out, it is said, in this manner: "Are you so mean-spirited and effeminate, Philotas, and yet can engage in so desperate a design?" After his death, he presently sent into Media, and put also Parmenio, his father, to death, who had done brave service under Philip, and was the only man, of his older friends and counsellors, who had encouraged Alexander to invade Asia. Of three sons whom he had had in the army, he had already lost two, and now was himself put to death with the third. These actions rendered Alexander an object of terror to many of his friends, and chiefly to Antipater, who, to strengthen himself, sent messengers privately to treat for an alliance with the Ætolians, who stood in fear of Alexander, because they had destroyed the town of the Œniadæ; on being informed of which, Alexander had said the children of the Œniadæ need not revenge their father's quarrel, for he would himself take care to punish the Ætolians.

Not long after this happened the deplorable end of Clitus, which to those who barely hear the matter-of-fact, may seem more inhuman than that of Philotas; but if we consider the story with its circumstance of time, and weigh the cause, we shall find it to have occurred rather through a sort of mischance of the king's, whose anger and over-drinking offered an occasion to the evil genius Clitus. The king had a present of Grecian fruit brought him from the sea coast, which was so fresh and beautiful, that he was surprised at it, and called Clitus to him to see it, and to give him a share of it. Clitus was then sacrificing, but he immediately left off and came, followed by three sheep, on whom the drink-offering had been already poured preparatory to sacrificing them Alexander, being informed of this, told his diviners, Aristander and Cleomantis the Lacedæmonian, and asked them what it meant; on whose assuring him it was an ill omen, he commanded them in all haste to offer sacrifices for Clitus's safety, for as much as three days before he himself had seen a strange vision in his sleep, of Clitus all in mourning, sitting by Parmenio's sons who were dead. Clitus, however, stayed not to finish his devotions, but came straight to supper with the king, who had sacrificed to Castor and Pollux. And when they had drunk pretty hard, some of the company fell a singing the verses of one Pranichus, or as others say of Pierion, which were made upon those captains who had been lately worsted by the barbarians, on purpose to disgrace and turn them to ridicule. This gave offence to the older men who were there, and they upbraided both the author and the singer of the verses, though Alexander and the younger men about him were much amused to hear them, and encouraged them to go on, till at last Clitus, who had drunk too much, and was besides of a froward and wilful temper, was so nettled that he could hold no longer, saying, it was not well done to expose the Macedonians so before the barbarians and their enemies, since though it was their unhappiness to be overcome, yet they were much better men than those who laughed at them. And when Alexander remarked, that Clitus was pleading his own cause, giving cowardice the name of misfortune, Clitus started up; "This cowardice, as you are pleased to term it," said he to him, "saved the life of a son of the gods, when in flight from Spithridates's sword; and it is by the expense of Macedonian blood, and by these wounds, that you are now raised to such a height as to be able to disown your father Philip, and call yourself the son of Ammon." "Thou base fellow," said Alexander, who was now thoroughly exasperated, "dost thou think to utter these things everywhere of me, and stir up the Macedonians to sedition, and not be punished for it?" "We are sufficiently punished already," answered Clitus, "if this be the recompense of our toils, and we must esteem theirs a happy lot, who have not lived to see their countrymen scourged with Median rods.

VOL. II.—

and forced to sue to the Persians to have access to their king." While he talked this at random, and those near Alexander got up from their seats and began to revile him in turn, the elder men did what they could to compose the disorder Alexander, in the mean time turning about to Xenodochus, the Cardian, and Artemius, the Colophonian, asked them if they were not of opinion that the Greeks, in comparison with the Macedonians, behaved themselves like so many demigods among wild beasts. But Clitus for all this would not give over, desiring Alexander to speak out if he had any thing more to say, or else why did he invite men who were freeborn and accustomed to speak their minds openly without restraint, to sup with him. He had better live and converse with barbarians and slaves who would not scruple to bow the knee to his Persian girdle and his white tunic. Which words so provoked Alexander, that, not able to suppress his anger any longer, he threw one of the apples that lay upon the table at him, and hit him, and then looked about for his sword. But Aristophanes, one of his life-guard, had hid that out of the way, and others came about him and besought him, but in vain. For breaking from them, he called out aloud to his guards in the Macedonian language, which was a certain sign of some great disturbance in him, and commanded a trumpeter to sound, giving him a blow with his clenched fist for not instantly obeying him; though afterwards the same man was commended for disobeying an order which would have put the whole army into tumult and confusion. Clitus still refusing to yield, was with much trouble forced by his friends out of the room. But he came in again immediately at another door, very irreverently and confidently singing the verses out of Euripides's Andromache,—

> In Greece, alas! how ill things ordered are!

Upon this, at last, Alexander, snatching a spear from one of the soldiers, met Clitus as he was coming forward and was putting by the curtain that hung before the door, and ran him through the body. He fell at once with a cry and a groan. Upon which the king's anger immediately vanishing, he came perfectly to himself, and when he saw his friends about him all in a profound silence, he pulled the spear out of the dead body, and would have thrust it into his own throat, if the guards had not held his hands, and by main force carried him away into his chamber, where all that night and the next day he wept bitterly, till being quite spent with lamenting and exclaiming, he lay as it were speechless, only fetching deep sighs. His friends apprehending some harm from his silence, broke into the room, but he took no notice of what any of them said, till Aristander putting him in mind of the vision he had seen concerning Clitus, and the prodigy that followed, as if all had come to pass by an unavoidable fatality, he then seemed to moderate his grief. They now brought Callisthenes, the philosopher, who was the near friend of Aristotle, and Anaxarchus of Abdera, to him. Callisthenes used moral language, and gentle and soothing means, hoping to find access for words of reason, and get a hold upon the passion. But Anaxarchus, who had always taken a course of his own in philosophy, and had a name for despising and slighting his contemporaries, as soon as he came in, cried out aloud, "Is this the Alexander whom the whole world looks to, lying here weeping like a slave, for fear of the censure and reproach of men, to whom he himself ought to be a law and measure of equity, if he would use the right his conquests have given him as supreme lord and governor of all, and not be the victim of a vain and idle opinion? Do not you know," said he, "that Jupiter is represented to have Justice and Law on each hand of him, to signify that all the actions of a conqueror are lawful and just?" With these and the like speeches, Anaxarchus indeed allayed the king's grief, but withal corrupted his character, rendering him more audacious and lawless than he had been. Nor did he fail by these means to insinuate himself into his favor, and to make Callisthenes's company, which at all times, because of his austerity, was not very acceptable, more uneasy and disagreeable to him.

It happened that these two philosophers meeting at an entertainment, where conversation turned on the subject of climate and the temperature of the air, Callisthenes joined with their opinion, who held that those countries were colder, and the winter sharper there than in Greece. Anaxarchus would by no means allow this, but argued against it with some heat. "Surely," said Callisthenes, "you cannot but admit this country to be colder than Greece, for there you used to have but one threadbare cloak to keep out the coldest winter, and here you have three good warm mantles one over another." This piece of raillery irritated Anaxarchus and the other pretenders to learning, and the crowd of flatterers in general could not endure to see Callisthenes so much admired and followed by the youth, and no less esteemed by the older men for his orderly life, and his gravity, and for being contented with his condition; all confirming what he had professed about the object he had in his journey to Alexander that it was only to get his countrymen recalled from banishment, and to rebuild and repeople his native town. Besides the envy which his great reputation raised, he also, by his own deportment, gave those who wished him ill, opportunity to do him mischief. For when he was invited to public entertainments, he would most times refuse to come, or if he were present at any, he put a constraint upon the company by his austerity and silence, which seemed to intimate his disproval of what he saw. So that Alexander himself said in application to him,

> That vain pretence to wisdom I detest,
> Where a man's blind to his own interest.

Being with many more invited to sup with the king, he was called upon when the cup came to him, to make an oration extempore in praise of the Macedonians; and he did it with such a flow of eloquence, that all who heard it rose from their seats to clap and applaud him, and threw their garland upon him; only Alexander told him out of Euripides,

> I wonder not that you have spoke so well,
> 'Tis easy on good subjects to excel.

"Therefore," said he, "if you will show the force of your eloquence, tell my Macedonians their faults, and dispraise them, that by hearing their errors they may learn to be better for the future. Callisthenes presently obeyed him, retracting all he had said before, and, inveighing against the Macedonians with great freedom, added, that Philip thrived and grew powerful, chiefly by the discord of the Grecians, applying this verse to him:—

> In civil strife e'en villains rise to fame;

which so offended the Macedonians, that he was odious to them ever after. And Alexander said, that instead of his eloquence, he had only made his ill-will appear in what he had spoken. Hermippus assures us, that one Stroebus, a servant whom Callisthenes kept to read to him, gave this account of these passages afterwards to Aristotle; and that when he perceived the king grow more and more averse to him, two or three times, as he was going away, he repeated the verses,—

> Death seiz'd at last on great Patroclus too,
> Though he in virtue far exceeded you.

Not without reason, therefore, did Aristotle give this character of Callisthenes, that he was, indeed, a powerful speaker, but had no judgment. He acted certainly a true philosopher's part in positively refusing, as he did, to pay adoration; and by speaking out openly against that which the best and gravest of the Macedonians only repined at in secret, he delivered the Grecians and Alexander himself from a great disgrace, when the practice was given up. But he ruined himself by it, because he went too roughly to work, as if he would have forced the king to that which he should have effected by reason and persuasion. Chares of Mitylene writes, that at a banquet, Alexander, after he had drunk, reached the cup to one of his friends, who, on receiving it, rose up towards the domestic altar, and when he had drunk, first adored, and then kissed Alexander, and afterwards laid himself down at the table with the rest. Which they all did one after another, till it came to Callisthenes's turn, who took the cup and drank, while the king, who was engaged in conversation with Hephæstion, was not observing, and then came and offered to kiss him. But Demetrius, surnamed Phidon, interposed, saying, "Sir, by no means let him kiss you, for he only of us all has refused to adore you;" upon which the king declined it, and all the concern Callisthenes showed was, that he said aloud, "Then I go away with a kiss less than the rest." The displeasure he incurred by this action procured credit for Hephæstion's declaration that he had broken his word to him in not paying the king the same veneration that others did, as he had faithfully promised to do. And to finish his disgrace, a number of such men as Lysimachus and Hagnon now came in with their asseverations that the sophist went about everywhere boasting of his resistance to arbitrary power, and that the young men all ran after him, and honored him as the only man among so many thousands who had the courage to preserve his liberty. Therefore when Hermolaus's conspiracy came to be discovered, the charges which his enemies brought agains him were the more easily believed, particularly that when the young man asked him what he should do to be the most illustrious person on earth, he told him the readiest way was to kill him who was already so, and that to incite him to commit the deed, he bade him not be awed by the golden couch, but remember Alexander was a man equally infirm and vulnerable as another. However, none of Hermolaus's accomplices, in the utmost extremity, made any mention of Callisthenes's being engaged in the design. Nay, Alexander himself, in the letters which he wrote soon after to Craterus, Attalus, and Alcetas, tells them that the young men who were put to the torture, declared they had entered into the conspiracy of themselves, without any others being privy to, or guilty of it. But yet afterwards, in a letter to Antipater, he accuses Callisthenes. "The young men," he says, "were stoned to death by the Macedonians, but for the sophist" (meaning Callisthenes), "I will take care to punish him with them too who sent him to me, and who harbor those in their cities who conspire against my life," an unequivocal declaration against Aristotle, in whose house Callisthenes, for his relationship's sake, being his niece Hero's son, had been educated. His death is variously related. Some say he was hanged by Alexander's orders; others, that he died of sickness in prison; but Chares writes he was kept in chains seven months after he was apprehended, on purpose that he might be proceeded against in full council, when Aristotle should be present; and that growing very fat, and contracting a disease of vermin, he there died, about the time that Alexander was wounded in India, in the country of the Malli Oxydracæ, all which came to pass afterwards.

For to go on in order, Demaratus of Corinth, now quite an old man, had made a great effort, about this time, to pay Alexander a visit; and when he had seen him, said he pitied the misfortune of those Grecians, who were so unhappy as to die before they had beheld Alexander seated on the throne of Darius. But he did not long enjoy the benefit of the king's kindness for him, any otherwise than that soon after falling sick and dying, he had a magnificent funeral, and the army raised him a monument of earth fourscore cubits high, and of a vast circumference. His ashes were conveyed in a very rich chariot drawn by four horses, to the sea-side.

Alexander now intent upon his expedition into India, took notice that his soldiers were so charged with booty that it hindered their marching. Therefore, at break of day, as soon as the baggage wagons were laden, first he set fire to his own, and to those of his friends, and then commanded those to be burnt which belonged to the rest of the army. An act which in the deliberation of it had seemed more dangerous and difficult than it proved in the execution, with which few were dissatisfied; for most of the soldiers, as if they had been inspired, uttering loud outcries and warlike shoutings, supplied one another with what was absolutely necessary, and burnt and destroyed all that was superfluous the sight of which redoubled Alexander's zeal and eagerness for his design. And, indeed, he was now grown very severe and inexorable in punishing those who committed any fault. For he put Menander, one of his friends, to death, for deserting a fortress where he had placed him in garrison, and shot Orsodates, one of the barbarians who revolted from him, with his own hand.

At this time a sheep happened to yean a lamb, with the perfect shape and color of a tiara upon the head, and testicles on each side; which portent Alexander regarded with such dislike, that he immediately caused his Babylonian priests, whom he usually carried about with him for such purposes, to purify him, and told his friends he was not so much concerned for his own sake as for theirs, out of an apprehension that after his death the divine power might suffer his empire to fall into the hands of some degenerate, impotent person. But this fear was soon removed by a wonderful thing that happened not long after, and was thought to presage better. For Proxenus, a Macedonian, who was the chief of those who looked to the king's furniture, as he was breaking up the ground near the river Oxus, to set up the royal pavilion, discovered a spring of a fat, oily liquor, which after the top was taken off, ran pure, clear oil, without any difference either of taste or smell, having exactly the same smoothness and brightness, and that, too, in a country where no olives grew. The water, indeed, of the river Oxus, is said to be the smoothest to the feeling of all waters, and to leave a gloss on the skins of those who bathe themselves in it. Whatever might be the cause, certain it is that Alexander was wonderfully pleased with it, as appears by his letters to Antipater, where he speaks of it as one of the most remarkable presages that God had ever favored him with. The diviners told him it signified his expedition would be glorious in the event, but very painful, and attended with many difficulties; for oil, they said, was bestowed on mankind by God as a refreshment of their labors.

Nor did they judge amiss, for he exposed himself to many hazards in the battles which he fought, and received very severe wounds, but the greatest loss in his army was occasioned through the unwholesomeness of the air, and the want of necessary provisions. But he still applied himself to overcome fortune and whatever opposed him, by resolution and virtue, and thought nothing impossible to true intrepidity, and on the other hand nothing secure or strong for cowardice. It is told of him that when he besieged Sisimithres, who held an inaccessible, impregnable rock against him, and his soldiers began to despair of taking it, he asked Oxyartes whether Sisimithres was a man of courage, who assuring him he was the greatest coward alive, "Then you tell me," said he, "that the place may easily be taken, since what is in command of it is weak." And in a little time he so terrified Sisimithres, that he took it without any difficulty. At an attack which he made upon such another precipitous place with some of his Macedonian soldiers, he called to one whose name was Alexander, and told him, he at any rate must fight bravely if it were but for his name's sake. The youth fought gallantly and was killed in the action, at which he was sensibly afflicted. Another time, seeing his men march slowly and unwillingly to the siege of the place called Nysa, because of a deep river between them an the town, he advanced before them, and standing upon the bank, "What a miserable man," said he, "am I, that I have not learned to swim!" and then was hardly dissuaded from endeavoring to pass it upon his shield. Here, after the assault was over, the ambassadors who from several towns which he had blocked up, came to submit to him and make their peace, were surprised to find him still in his armor, without any one in waiting or attendance upon him, and when at last some one brought him a cushion, he made the eldest of them, named Acuphis, take it and sit down upon it. The old man, marvelling at his magnanimity and courtesy, asked him what his countrymen should do to merit his friendship. "I would have them," said Alexander, "choose you to govern them, and send one hundred of the most worthy men among them to remain with me as hostages." Acuphis laughed and answered, "I shall govern them with more ease, Sir, if I send you so many of the worst, rather than the best of my subjects."

The extent of king Taxiles's dominions in India was thought to be as large as Egypt, abounding in good pastures, and producing beautiful fruits. The king himself had the reputation of a wise man, and at his first interview with Alexander, he spoke to him in these terms: "To what purpose," said he, "should we make war upon one another, if the design of your coming into these parts be not to rob us of our water or our necessary food, which are the only things that wise men are indispensably obliged to fight for? As for other riches and possessions, as they are accounted in the eye of the world, if I am better provided of them than you, I am ready to let you share with me: but if fortune has been more liberal to you than me, I have no objection to be obliged to you." This discourse pleased Alexander so much, that embracing him, "Do you think," said he to him, "your kind words and courteous behavior will bring you off in this interview without a contest? No, you shall not escape so. I shall contend and do battle with you so far, that how obliging soever you are, you shall not have the better of me." Then receiving some presents from him, he returned him others of greater value, and to complete his bounty, gave him in money ready coined one thousand talents; at which his old friends were much displeased, but it gained him the hearts of many of the barbarians. But the best soldiers of the Indians now entering into the pay of several of the cities, undertook to defend them, and did it so bravely, that they put Alexander to a great deal of trouble, till at last, after a capitulation, upon the surrender of the place, he fell upon them as they were marching away, and put them all to the sword. This one breach of his word remains as a blemish upon his achievements in war, which he otherwise had performed throughout with that justice and honor that became a king. Nor was he less incommoded by the Indian philosophers, who inveighed against those princes who joined his party, and solicited the free nations to oppose him. He took several of these also and caused them to be hanged.

Alexander, in his own letters, has given us an account of his war with Porus. He says the two armies were separated by the river Hydaspes, on whose opposite bank Porus continually kept his elephants in order of battle, with their heads towards their enemies, to guard the passage; that he, on the other hand, made every day a great noise and clamor in his camp, to dissipate the apprehensions of the barbarians; that one stormy dark night he passed the river, at a distance from the place where the enemy lay, into a little island, with part of his foot, and the best of his horse. Here there fell a most violent storm of rain, accompanied with lightning and whirlwinds, and seeing some of his men burnt and dying with the lightning, he nevertheless quitted the island and made over to the other side. The Hydaspes, he says, now after the storm, was so swollen and grown so rapid, as to have made a breach in the bank, and a part of the river was now pouring in here, so that when he came across, it was with difficulty he got a footing on the land, which was slippery and unsteady, and exposed to the force of the currents on both sides. This is the occasion when he is related to have said, "O ye Athenians, will ye believe what dangers I incur to merit your praise?' This, however, is Cnesicritus's story. Alexander says, here the men left their boats, and passed the breach in their armor, up to the breast in water, and that then he advanced with his horse about twenty furlongs before his foot, concluding that if the enemy charged him with their cavalry, he should be too strong for them; if with their foot, his own would come up time enough to his assistance. Nor did he judge amiss; for being charged by a thousand horse, and sixty armed chariots, which advanced before their main body, he took all the chariots, and kil'ed four hundred horse upon the place. Porus, by this time, guessing that Alexander himself had crossed over, came on with his whole army, except a party which he left behind, to hold the rest of the Macedonians in play, if they should attempt to pass the river. But he, apprehending the multitude of the enemy, and to avoid the shock of their elephants, dividing his forces, attacked their left wing himself, and commanded Cœnus to fall upon the right, which was performed with good success. For by this means both wings being broken, the enemies fell back in their retreat upon the centre, and crowded in upon their elephants. There rallying, they fought a hand to hand battle, and it was the eighth hour of the day before they were entirely defeated. This description the conqueror himself has left us in his own epistles.

Almost all the historians agree in relating that Porus was four cubits and a span high, and that when he was upon his elephant, which was of the largest size, his stature and bulk were so answerable, that he appeared to be proportionably mounted, as a horseman on his horse. This elephant, during the whole battle, gave many singular proofs of sagacity and of particular care of the king, whom as long as he was strong and in a condition to fight, he defended with great courage, repelling those who set upon him; and as soon as he perceived him overpowered with his numerous wounds and the multitude of darts that were thrown at him, to prevent his falling off, he softly knelt down and began to draw out the darts with his proboscis. When Porus was taken prisoner, and Alexander asked him how he expected to be used, he answered, "As a king." For that expression, he said, when the same question was put to him a second time, comprehended every thing. And Alexander, accordingly, not only suffered him to govern his own kingdom as satrap under himself, but gave him also the additional territory of various independent tribes whom he subdued, a district which, it is said, contained fifteen several nations, and five thousand considerable towns, besides abundance of villages. To another government, three times as large as this, he appointed Philip, one of his friends.

Some little time after the battle with Porus, Bucephalus died, as most of the authorities state, under cure of his wounds, or as Onesicritus says, of fatigue and age, being thirty years old. Alexander was no less concerned at his death, than if he had lost an old companion or an intimate friend, and built a city, which he named Bucephalia, in memory of him, on the bank of the river Hydaspes. He also, we are told, built another city, and called it after the name of a favorite dog, Peritas, which he had brought up himself. So Sotion assures us he was informed by Potamon of Lesbos.

But this last combat with Porus took off the edge of the Macedonians' courage, and stayed their further progress into India. For having found it hard enough to defeat an enemy who brought but twenty thousand foot and two thousand horse into the field, they thought they had reason to oppose Alexander's design of leading them on to pass the Ganges, too, which they were told was thirty-two furlongs broad and a hundred fathoms deep, and the banks on the further side covered with multitudes of enemies. For they were told the kings of the Gandaritans and Præsians expected them there with eighty thousand horse, two hundred thousand foot, eight thousand armed chariots, and six thousand fighting elephants. Nor was this a mere vain report, spread to discourage them. For Androcottus, who not long after reigned in those parts, made a present of five hundred elephants at once to Seleucus, and with an army of six hundred thousand men subdued all India. Alexander at first was so grieved and enraged at his men's reluctancy, that he shut himself up in his tent, and threw himself upon the ground, declaring, if they would not pass the Ganges, he owed them no thanks for any thing they had hitherto done, and that to retreat now, was plainly to confess himself vanquished. But at last the reasonable persuasions of his friends and the cries and lamentations of his soldiers, who in a suppliant manner crowded about the entrance of his tent, prevailed with him to think of returning. Yet he could not refrain from leaving behind him various deceptive memorials of his expedition, to impose upon after-times, and to exaggerate his glory with posterity, such as arms larger than were really worn, and mangers for horses, with bits of bridles above the usual size, which he set up, and distributed in several places. He erected altars, also, to the gods, which the kings of the

Præsians even in our time do honor to when they pass the river, and offer sacrifice upon them after the Grecian manner. Androcottus, then a boy, saw Alexander here, and is said often afterwards to have been heard to say, that he missed but little of making himself master of those countries; their king, who then reigned, was so hated and despised for the viciousness of his life, and the meanness of his extraction.

Alexander was now eager to see the ocean. To which purpose he caused a great many tow-boats and rafts to be built, in which he fell gently down the rivers at his leisure, yet so that his navigation was neither unprofitable nor inactive. For by several descents upon the bank, he made himself master of the fortified towns, and consequently of the country on both sides. But at a siege of a town of the Mallians, who have the repute of being the bravest people of India, he ran in great danger of his life. For having beaten off the defendants with showers of arrows, he was the first man that mounted the wall by a scaling-ladder, which, as soon as he was up, broke and left him almost alone, exposed to the darts which the barbarians threw at him in great numbers from below. In this distress, turning himself as well as he could, he leaped down in the midst of his enemies, and had the good fortune to light upon his feet. The brightness and clattering of his armor when he came to the ground, made the barbarians think they saw rays of light, or some bright phantom playing before his body, which frightened them so at first, that they ran away and dispersed. Till seeing him seconded but by two of his guards, they fell upon him hand to hand, and some, while he bravely defended himself, tried to wound him through his armor with their swords and spears. And one who stood further off drew a bow with such just strength, that the arrow, finding its way through his cuirass, stuck in his ribs under the breast. This stroke was so violent, that it made him give back, and set one knee to the ground, upon which the man ran up with his drawn scimitar, thinking to despatch him, and had done it, if Peucestes and Limnæus had not interposed, who were both wounded, Limnæus mortally, but Peucestes stood his ground, while Alexander killed the barbarians. But this did not free him from danger; for besides many other wounds, at last he received so weighty a stroke of a club upon his neck, that he was forced to lean his body against the wall, still, however, facing the enemy. At this extremity, the Macedonians made their way in and gathered round him. They took him up, just as he was fainting away having lost all sense of what was done near him, and conveyed him to his tent, upon which it was presently reported all over the camp that he was dead. But when they had with great difficulty and pains sawed off the shaft of the arrow, which was of wood, and so with much trouble got off his cuirass, they came to cut the head of it, which was three fingers broad and four long, and stuck fast in the bone. During the operation, he was taken with almost mortal swoonings, but when it was out he came to himself again. Yet though all danger was past, he continued very weak, and confined himself a great while to a regular diet and the method of his cure, till one day hearing the Macedonians clamoring outside in their eagerness to see him, he took his cloak and went out. And having sacrificed to the gods, without more delay he went on board again, and as he coasted along, subdued a great deal of the country on both sides, and several considerable cities.

In this voyage, he took ten of the Indian philosophers prisoners, who had been most active in persuading Sabbas to revolt, and had caused the Macedonians a great deal of trouble. These men, called Gymnosophists, were reputed to be extremely ready and succinct in their answers, which he made trial of, by putting difficult questions to them, letting them know that those whose answers were not pertinent, should be put to death, of which he made the eldest of them judge. The first being asked which he thought the most numerous, the dead or the living, answered, " The living, because those who are dead are not at all." Of the second, he desired to know whether the earth or the sea produced the largest beasts ; who told him, " the earth, for the sea is but a part of it." His question to the third was, Which is the cunningest of beasts ? " That," said he, " which men have not yet found out." He bade the fourth tell him what argument he used to Sabbas to persuade him to revolt. " No other," said he, " than that he should either live or die nobly." Of the fifth he asked, Which was eldest, night or day? The philosopher replied, " Day was eldest, by one day at least." But perceiving Alexander not well satisfied with that account, he added, that he ought not to wonder if strange questions had as strange answers made to them. Then he went on and inquired of the next, what a man should do to be exceeding y beloved. " He must be very powerful," said he, " without making himself too much feared." The answer of the seventh to his question, how a man might become a god, was, " By doing that which was impossible for men to do." The eighth told him, " Life is strong er than death, because it supports so many miseries." And the last being asked, how long he thought it decent for a man to live, said, " Till death appeared more desirable than life." Then Alexander turned to him whom he had made judge, and commanded him to give sentence. " All that I can determine," said he, " is, that they have every one answered worse than another." "Nay," said the king, "then you shall die first, for giving such a sentence." "Not so, O king," replied the gymnosophist, "unless you said falsely that he should die first who made the worst answer." In conclusion he gave them presents and dismissed them.

But to those who were in greatest reputation among them, and lived a private quiet life, he sent Onesicritus, one of Diogenes the Cynic's disciples, desiring them to come to him. Calanus, it is said, very arrogantly and roughly commanded him to strip himself and hear what he said naked, otherwise he would not speak a word to him, though he came from Jupiter himself. But Dandamis received him with more civility, and hearing him discourse of Socrates, Pythagoras, and Diogenes told him he thought them men of great parts, and to have erred in nothing so much, as in having too great respect for the laws and customs of their country. Others say, Dandamis only asked him the reason why Alexander undertook so long a journey to come into those parts. Taxiles, however, persuaded Calanus to wait upon Alexander. His proper name was Sphines, but because he was wont to say *Cale*, which in the Indian tongue is a form of salutation, to those he met with anywhere, the Greeks called him Calanus. He is said to have shown Alexander an instructive emblem of government, which was this. He threw a dry shrivelled hide upon the ground, and trod upon the edges of it. The skin when it was pressed in one place, still rose up in another, wheresoever he trod round about it, till he set his foot in the middle, which made all the parts lie even and quiet. The meaning of this similitude being that he ought to reside most in the middle of his empire, and not spend too much time on the borders of it.

His voyage down the rivers took up seven months' time, and when he came to the sea, he sailed to an island which he himself called Scillustis, others Psiltucis, where going ashore, he sacrificed, and made what observations he could as to the nature of the sea and the sea-coast. Then having besought the gods that no other man might ever go beyond the bounds of this expedition, he ordered his fleet, of which he made Nearchus admiral, and Onesicritus pilot, to sail round about, keeping the Indian shore on the right hand, and returned himself by land through the country of the Orites, where he was reduced to great straits for want of provisions, and lost a vast number of his men, so that of an army of one hundred and twenty thousand foot and fifteen thousand horse, he scarcely brought back above a fourth part out of India, they were so diminished by disease, ill diet, and the scorching heats, but most by famine. For their march was through an uncultivated country whose inhabitants fared hardly, possessing only a few sheep, and those of a wretched kind, whose flesh was rank and unsavory, by their continual feeding upon sea-fish.

After sixty days' march he came into Gedrosia, where he found great plenty of all things, which the neighboring kings and governors of provinces, hearing of his approach, had taken care to provide. When he had here refreshed his army, he continued his march through Carmania, feasting all the way for seven days together. He with his most intimate friends banqueted and revelled night and day upon a platform erected on a lofty, conspicuous scaffold, which was slowly drawn by eight horses. This was followed by a great many chariots, some covered with purple and embroidered canopies, and some with green boughs, which were continually supplied afresh, and in them the rest of his friends and commanders drinking, and crowned with garlands of flowers. Here was now no target or helmet or spear to be seen; instead of armor, the soldiers handled nothing but cups and goblets and Thericlean drinking vessels, which, along the whole way, they dipped into large bowls and jars, and drank healths to one another, some seating themselves to it, others as they went along. All places resounded with music of pipes and flutes, with harping and singing, and women dancing as in the rites of Bacchus. For this disorderly, wandering march, besides the drinking part of it, was accompanied with all the sportiveness and insolence of bacchanals, as much as if the god himself had been there to countenance and lead the procession. As soon as he came to the royal palace of Gedrosia, he again refreshed and feasted his army; and one day after he had drunk pretty hard, it is said, he went to see a prize of dancing contended for, in which his favorite Bagoas, having gained the victory, crossed the theatre in his dancing habit, and sat down close by him, which so pleased the Macedonians, that they made loud acclamations for him to kiss Bagoas, and never stopped clapping their hands and shouting till Alexander put his arms round him and kissed him.

Here his admiral, Nearchus, came to him, and delighted him so with the narrative of his voyage, that he resolved himself to sail out of the mouth of the Euphrates with a great fleet, with which he designed to go round by Arabia and Africa, and so by Hercules's Pillars into the Mediterranean; in order for which, he directed all sorts of vessels to be built at Thapsacus, and made great provisions everywhere of seamen and pilots. But the tidings of the difficulties he had gone through in his Indian expedition, the danger of his person among the Mallians, the reported loss of a considerable part of his forces, and a general doubt as to his own safety, had begun to give occasion for revolt among many of the conquered nations, and for acts of great injustice, avarice, and insolence on the part of the satraps and commanders in the provinces, so that there seemed to be an universal fluctuation and disposition to change. Even at home, Olympias and Cleopatra had raised a faction against Antipater, and divided his government between them, Olympias seizing upon Epirus, and Cleopatra upon Macedonia. When Alexander was told of it, he said his mother had made the best choice, for the Macedonians would never endure to be ruled by a woman. Upon this he despatched Nearchus again to his fleet, to carry the war into the maritime provinces, and as he marched that way himself, he punished those commanders who had behaved ill, particularly Oxyartes, one of the sons of Abuletes, whom he killed with his own hand, thrusting him through the body with his spear. And when Abuletes, instead of the necessary provisions which he ought to have furnished, brought him three thousand talents in coined money, he ordered it to be thrown to his horses, and when they would not touch it, "What good," he said, "will this provision do us?" and sent him away to prison.

When he came into Persia, he distributed money among the women, as their own kings had been wont to do, who as often as they came thither, gave every one of them a piece of gold; on account of which custom, some of them, it is said, had come but seldom, and Ochus was so sordidly covetous, that to avoid this expense, he never visited his native country once in all his reign. Then finding Cyrus's sepulchre opened and rifled, he put Polymachus, who did it, to death, though he was a man of some distinction, a born Macedonian of Pella. And after he had read the inscription, he caused it to be cut again below the old one in Greek characters; the words being these: "O man, whosoever thou art, and from whencesoever thou comest (for I know thou wilt come), I am Cyrus, the founder of the Persian empire; do not grudge me this little earth which covers my body." The reading of this sensibly touched Alexander, filling him with the thought of the uncertainty and mutability of human affairs. At the same time, Calanus having been a little while troubled with a disease in the bowels, requested that he might have a funeral pile erected, to which he came on horseback, and, after he had said some prayers and sprinkled himself and cut off some of his hair to throw into the fire, before he ascended it, he embraced and took leave of the Macedonians who stood by, desiring them to pass that day in mirth and good-fellowship with their king, whom in a little time, he said, he doubted not but to see again at Babylon. Having thus said, he lay down, and covering up his face, he stirred not when the fire came near him, but continued still in the same posture as at first, and so sacrificed himself, as it was the ancient custom of the philosophers in those countries to do. The same thing was done long after by another Indian who came with Cæsar to Athens, where they still show you "the Indian's monument." At his return from the funeral pile, Alexander invited a great many of his friends and principal officers to supper, and proposed a drinking match, in which the victor should receive a crown. Promachus drank twelve quarts of wine, and won the prize, which was a talent, from them all; but he survived his victory but three days, and was followed, as Chares says, by forty-one more, who died of the same debauch, some extremely cold weather having set in shortly after.

At Susa, he married Darius's daughter Statira, and celebrated also the nuptials of his friends, bestowing the noblest of the Persian ladies upon the worthiest of them, at the same time making it an entertainment in honor of the other Macedonians whose marriages had already taken place. At this magnificent festival, it is reported, there were no less than nine thousand guests, to each of whom he gave a golden cup for the libations. Not to mention other instances of his wonderful magnificence, he paid the debts of his army, which amounted to nine thousand eight hundred and seventy talents. But Antigenes, who had lost one of his eyes, though he owed nothing, got his name set down in the list of those who were in debt, and bringing one who pretended to be his creditor, and to have supplied him from the bank, received the money. But when the cheat was found out, the king was so incensed at it, that he banished him from court, and took away his command, though he was an excellent soldier, and a man of great courage. For when he was but a youth, and served under Philip at the siege of Perinthus, where he was wounded in the eye by an arrow shot out of an engine, he would neither let the arrow be taken out, nor be persuaded to quit the field, till he had bravely repulsed the enemy and forced them to retire into the town. Accordingly he was not able to support such a disgrace with any patience, and it was plain that grief and despair would have made him kill himself, but the king fearing it, not only pardoned him, but let him also enjoy the benefit of his deceit.

The thirty thousand boys whom he left behind him to be taught and disciplined, were so improved at his return, both in strength and beauty, and performed their exercises with such dexterity and wonderful agility, that he was extremely pleased with them, which grieved the Macedonians, and made them fear he would have the less value for them. And when he proceeded to send down the infirm and maimed soldiers to the sea, they said they were unjustly and infamously dealt with, after they were worn out in his service upon all occasions, now to be turned away with disgrace and sent home into their country among their friends and relations, in a worse condition than when they came out; therefore they desired him to dismiss them one and all, and to account his Macedonians useless, now he was so well furnished with a set of dancing boys, with whom, if he pleased, he might go on and conquer the world. These speeches so incensed Alexander, that after he had given them a great deal of reproachful language in his passion, he drove them away, and committed the watch to Persians, out of whom he chose his guards and attendants. When the Macedonians saw him escorted by these men, and themselves excluded and shamefully disgraced, their high spirits fell, and conferring with one another, they found that jealousy and rage had almost distracted them. But at last coming to themselves again, they went without their arms, with only their under garments on, crying and weeping to offer themselves at his tent, and desired him to deal with them as their baseness and ingratitude deserved. However, this would not prevail; for though his anger was already something mollified, yet he would not admit them into his presence, nor would they stir from thence, but continued two days and nights before his tent, bewailing themselves, and imploring him as their lord to have compassion on them. But the third day he came out to them, and seeing them very humble and penitent, he wept himself a great while, after a gentle reproof spoke kindly to them, and dismissed those who were unserviceable with magnificent rewards, and with this recommendation to Antipater, that when they came home, at all public shows and in the theatres, they should sit on the best and foremost seats, crowned with chaplets of flowers. He ordered, also, that the children of those who had lost their lives in his service, should have their fathers' pay continued to them.

When he came to Ecbatana in Media, and had despatched his most urgent affairs, he began to divert himself again with spectacles and public entertainments, to carry on which he had a supply of three thousand actors and artists, newly arrived out of Greece. But they were soon interrupted by Hephæstion's falling sick of a fever, in which, being a young man and a soldier, too, he could not confine himself to so exact a diet as was necessary; for whilst his physician, Glaucus, was gone to the theatre, he ate a fowl for his dinner, and drank a large draught of wine, upon which he became very ill, and shortly after died. At this misfortune, Alexander was so beyond all reason transported, that to express his sorrow, he immediately ordered the manes and tails of all his horses and mules to be cut, and threw down the battlements of the neighboring cities. The poor physician he crucified, and forbade playing on the flute, or any other musical instrument in the camp a great while, till directions came from the oracle of Ammon, and enjoined him to honor Hephæstion, and sacrifice to him as to a hero. Then seeking to alleviate his grief in war, he set out, as it were, to a hunt and chase of men, for he fell upon the Cossæans, and put the whole nation to the sword. This was called a sacrifice to Hephæstion's ghost. In his sepulchre and monument and the adorning of them, he intended to bestow ten thousand talents; and designing that the excellence of the workmanship and the singularity of the design might outdo the expense, his wishes turned, above all other artists, to Stasicrates, because he always promised something very bold, unusual, and magnificent in his projects. Once when they had met before, he had told him, that of all the mountains he knew, that of Athos in Thrace was the most capable of being adapted to represent the shape and lineaments of a man; that if he pleased to command him, he would make it the noblest and most durable statue in the world, which in its left hand should hold a city of ten thousand inhabitants, and out of its right should pour a copious river into the sea. Though Alexander declined this proposal, yet now he spent a great deal of time with workmen to invent and contrive others even more extravagant and sumptuous.

As he was upon his way to Babylon, Nearchus, who had sailed back out of the ocean up the mouth of the river Euphrates, came to tell him he had met with some Chaldæan diviners who had warned him against Alexander's going thither. Alexander, however, took no thought of it, and went on, and when he came near the walls of the place, he saw a great many crows fighting with one another, some of whom fell down just by him. After this, being privately informed that Apollodorus, the governor of Babylon, had sacrificed, to know what would become of him, he sent for Pythagoras, the soothsayer, and on his admitting the thing, asked him, in what condition he found the victim; and when he told him the liver was defective in its lobe, "A great presage indeed!" said Alexander. However, he offered Pythagoras no injury, but was sorry that he had neglected Nearchus's advice, and stayed for the most part outside the town, removing his tent from place to place, and sailing up and down the Euphrates. Besides this, he was disturbed by many other prodigies. A tame ass fell upon the biggest and handsomest lion that he kept, and killed him by a kick. And one day after he had undressed himself to be anointed, and was playing at ball, just as they were going to bring his clothes again, the young men who played with him perceived a man clad in the king's robes with a diadem upon his head, sitting silently upon his throne. They asked him who he was, to which he gave no answer a good while, till at last coming to himself, he told them his name was Dionysius, that he was of Messenia, that for some crime of which he was accused, he was brought thither from the sea-side, and had been kept long in prison, that Serapis appeared to him, had freed him from his chains, conducted him to that place, and commanded him to put on the king's robe and diadem, and to sit where they found him, and to say nothing. Alexander, when he heard this, by the direction of his soothsayers, put the fellow to death, but he lost his spirits, and grew diffident of the protection and assistance of the gods, and suspicious of his friends. His greatest apprehension was of Antipater and his sons, one of whom, Iolaus, was his chief cupbearer; and Cassander, who had lately arrived, and had been bred up in Greek manners, the first time he saw some of the barbarians adore the king, could not forbear laughing at it aloud, which so incensed Alexander, that he took him by the hair with both hands, and dashed his head against the wall. Another time, Cassander would have said something in defence of Antipater to those who accused him, but Alexander interrupting him, said, "What is it you say? Do you think people, if they had received no injury, would come such a journey only to calumniate your father?" To which when Cassander replied, that their coming so far from the evidence was a great proof of the falseness of their charges, Alexander smiled, and said those were some of Aristotle's sophisms, which would serve equally on both sides and added, that both he and his father should be severely punished, if they were found guilty of the least injustice towards those who complained. All which made such a deep impression of terror in Cassander's mind, that long after, when he was king of Macedonia, and master of Greece, as he was walking up and down at Delphi, and looking at the statues, at the sight of that of Alexander he was suddenly struck with alarm, and shook all over, his eyes rolled, his head grew dizzy, and it was long before he recovered himself.

When once Alexander had given way to fears of supernatural influence, his mind grew so disturbed and so easily alarmed, that if the least unusual or extraordinary thing happened, he thought it a prodigy or a presage, and his court was thronged with diviners and priests whose business was to sacrifice and purify and foretell the future. So miserable a thing is incredulity and contempt of divine power on the one hand, and so miserable, also, superstition on the other, which like water, where the level has been lowered, flowing in and never stopping, fills the mind with slavish fears and follies, as now in Alexander's case. But upon some answers which were brought him from the oracle concerning Hephæstion, he laid aside his sorrow, and fell again to sacrificing and drinking; and having given Nearchus a splendid entertainment, after he had bathed, as was his custom, just as he was going to bed, at Medius's request he went to supper with him. Here he drank all the next day, and was attacked with a fever, which seized him, not as some write, after he had drunk of the bowl of Hercules, nor was he taken with any sudden pain in his back, as if he had been struck with a lance, for these are the inventions of some authors who thought it their duty to make the last scene of so great an action as tragical and moving as they could. Aristobulus tells us, that in the rage of his fever and a violent thirst, he took a draught of wine, upon which he fell into delirium, and died on the thirtieth day of the month Dæsius.

But the journals give the following record. On the eighteenth day of the month, he slept in the bathing-room on account of his fever The next day he bathed and removed into his chamber, and spent his time in playing at dice with Medius. In the evening he bathed and sacrificed, and ate freely, and had the fever on him through the night. On the twentieth, after the usual sacrifices and bathing, he lay in the bathing-room and heard Nearchus's narrative of his voyage, and the observations he had made in the great sea. The twenty first he passed in the same manner, his fever still increasing, and suffered much during the night. The next day the fever was very violent, and he had himself removed and his bed set by the great bath, and discoursed with his principal officers about finding fit men to fill up the vacant places in the army. On the twenty-fourth he was much worse, and was carried out of his bed to assist at the sacrifices, and gave order that the general officers should wait within the court, whilst the inferior officers kept watch without doors. On the twenty-fifth he was removed to his palace on the other side the river, where he slept a little, but his fever did not abate, and when the generals came into his chamber, he was speechless and continued so the following day. The Macedonians, therefore, supposing he was dead, came with great clamors to the gates, and menaced his friends so that they were forced to admit them, and let them all pass through unarmed along by his bedside. The same day Python and Seleucus were despatched to the temple of Serapis to inquire if they should bring Alexander thither, and were answered by the god, that they should not remove him. On the twenty-eight, in the evening, he died. This account is most of it word for word as it is written in the diary.

At the time, nobody had any suspicion of his being poisoned, but upon some information given six years after, they say Olympias put many to death, and scattered the ashes of Iolaus, then dead, as if he had given it him. But those who affirm that Aristotle counselled Antipater to do it, and that by his means the poison was brought, adduce one Hagnothemis as their authority, who, they say, heard king Antigonus speak of it, and tell us that the poison was water, deadly cold as ice, distilled from a rock in the district of Nonacris, which they gathered like a thin dew, and kept in an ass's hoof; for it was so very cold and penetrating that no other vessel would hold it. However, most are of opinion that all this is a mere made up story, no slight evidence of which is, that during the dissensions among the commanders, which lasted several days, the body continued clear and fresh, hout any sign of such taint or corruption, though it lay d in a close sultry place.

Roxana, who was now with child, and upon that account much honored by the Macedonians, being jealous of Statira, sent for her by a counterfeit letter, as if Alexander had been still alive; and when she had her in her power, killed her and her sister, and threw their bodies into a well, which they filled up with earth, not without the privity and assistance of Perdiccas, who in the time immediately following the king's death, under cover of the name of Arrhidæus, whom he carried about him as a sort of guard to his person, exercised the chief authority. Arrhidæus, who was Philip's son by an obscure woman of the name of Philinna, was himself of weak intellect, not that he had been originally deficient either in body or mind, on the contrary, in his childhood, he had showed a happy and promising character enough. But a diseased habit of body, used by drugs which Olympias gave him, had ruined not only his health, but his understanding.

CÆSAR.

After Sylla became master of Rome, he wished to make Cæsar put away his wife Cornelia, daughter of Cinna, the late sole ruler of the commonwealth, but was unable to effect it either by promises or intimidation, and so contented himself with confiscating her dowry. The ground of Sylla's hostility to Cæsar, was the relationship between him and Marius; for Marius, the elder, married Julia, the sister of Cæsar's father, and had by her the younger Marius, who consequently was Cæsar's first cousin. And though at the beginning, while so many were to be put to death, and there was so much to do, Cæsar was overlooked by Sylla, yet he would not keep quiet, but presented himself to the people as a candidate for the priesthood, though he was yet a mere boy. Sylla, without any open opposition, took measures to have him rejected, and in consultation whether he should be put to death, when it was urged by some that it was not worth his while to contrive the death of a boy, he answered, that they knew little who did not see more than one Marius in that boy. Cæsar, on being informed of this saying, concealed himself, and for a considerable time kept out of the way in the country of the Sabines, often changing his quarters, till one night, as he was removing from one house to another on account of his health, he fell into the hands of Sylla's soldiers, who were searching those parts in order to apprehend any who had absconded. Cæsar, by a bribe of two talents, prevailed with Cornelius, their captain, to let him go, and was no sooner dismissed but he put to sea, and made for Bithynia. After a short stay there with Nicomedes, the king, in his passage back he was taken near the island Pharmacusa by some of the pirates, who, at that time, with large fleets of ships and innumerable smaller vessels, infested the seas everywhere.

When these men at first demanded of him twenty talents for his ransom, he laughed at them for not understanding the value of their prisoner, and voluntarily engaged to give them fifty. He presently despatched those about him to several places to raise the money, till at last he was left among a set of the most bloodthirsty people in the world, the Cilicians, only with one friend and two attendants. Yet he made so little of them, that when he had a mind to sleep, he would send to them, and order them to make no noise. For thirty-eight days, with all the freedom in the world, he amused himself with joining in their exercises and games, as if they had not been his keepers, but his guards. He wrote verses and speeches, and made them his auditors, and those who did not admire them, he called to their faces illiterate and barbarous, and would often, in raillery, threaten to hang them. They were greatly taken with this, and attributed his free talking to a kind of simplicity and boyish playfulness. As soon as his ransom was come from Miletus, he paid it, and was discharged, and proceeded at once to man some ships at the port of Miletus, and went in pursuit of the pirates, whom he surprised with their ships still stationed at the island, and took most of them. Their money he made his prize, and the men he secured in prison at Pergamus, and he made application to Junius, who was then governor of Asia, to whose office it belonged as prætor, to determine their punishment. Junius, having his eye upon the money, for the sum was considerable, said he would think at his leisure what to do with the prisoners, upon which Cæsar took his leave of him, and went off to Pergamus, where he ordered the pirates to be brought forth and crucified; the punishment he had often threatened them with whilst he was in their hands, and they little dreamt he was in earnest.

In the mean time Sylla's power being now on the decline, Cæsar's friends advised him to return to Rome, but he went to Rhodes, and entered himself in the school of Apollonius

Molon's son, a famous rhetorician, one who had the reputation of a worthy man, and had Cicero for one of his scholars. Cæsar is said to have been admirably fitted by nature to make a great statesman and orator, and to have taken such pains to improve his genius this way, that without dispute he might challenge the second place. More he did not aim at, as choosing to be first rather amongst men of arms and power, and, therefore, never rose to that height of eloquence to which nature would have carried him, his attention being diverted to those expeditions and designs, which at length gained him the empire. And he himself, in his answer to Cicero's panegyric on Cato, desires his reader not to compare the plain discourse of a soldier with the harangues of an orator who had not only fine parts, but had employed his life in this study.

When he was returned to Rome, he accused Dolabella of maladministration, and many cities of Greece came in to attest it. Dolabella was acquitted, and Cæsar, in return for the support he had received from the Greeks, assisted them in their prosecution of Publius Antonius for corrupt practices, before Marcus Lucullus, prætor of Macedonia. In this course he so far succeeded, that Antonius was forced to appeal to the tribunes at Rome, alleging that in Greece he could not have fair play against Grecians. In his pleadings at Rome, his eloquence soon obtained him great credit and favor, and he won no less upon the affections of the people by the affability of his manners and address, in which he showed a tact and consideration beyond what could have been expected at his age; and the open house he kept, the entertainments he gave, and the general splendor of his manner of life, contributed little by little to create and increase his political influence. His enemies slighted the growth of it at first, presuming it would soon fail when his money was gone; whilst in the mean time it was growing up and flourishing among the common people. When his power at last was established and not to be overthrown, and now openly tended to the altering of the whole constitution, they were aware too late, that there is no beginning so mean, which continued application will not make considerable, and that despising a danger at first, will make it at last irresistible. Cicero was the first who had any suspicions of his designs upon the government, and, as a good pilot is apprehensive of a storm when the sea is most smiling, saw the designing temper of the man through this disguise of good humor and affability, and said, that in general, in all he did and undertook, he detected the ambition for absolute power, "but when I see his hair so carefully arranged, and observe him adjusting it with one finger, I cannot imagine it shou'd enter into such a man's thoughts to subvert the Roman state." But of this more hereafter.

The first proof he had of the people's good-will to h m was when he received by their suffrages a tribuneship in the army, and came out on the list with a higher place than Caius Popilius. A second and clearer instance of their favor appeared upon his making a magnificent oration in praise of of his aunt Julia, wife to Marius, publicly in the forum, at whose funeral he was so bold as to bring forth the images of Marius, which nobody had dared to produce since the government came into Sylla's hands, Marius's party having from that time been declared enemies of the State. When some who were present had begun to raise a cry against Cæsar, the people answered with loud shouts and clapping in his favor, expressing their joyful surprise and satisfaction at his having, as it were, brought up again from the grave those honors of Marius, which for so long a time had been lost to the city. It had always been the custom at Rome to make funeral orations in praise of elderly matrons, but there was no precedent of any upon young women till Cæsar first made one upon the death of his own wife. This also procured him favor, and by this show of affection he won upon the feelings of the people, who looked upon him as a man of great tenderness and kindness of heart. After he had buried his wife, he went as quæstor into Spain under one of the prætors, named Vetus, whom he honored ever after, and made his son his own quæstor, when he himself came to be prætor. After this employment was ended, he married Pompeia, his third wife, having then a daughter by Cornelia, his first wife, whom he afterwards married to Pompey the Great. He was so profuse in his expenses, that before he had any public employment, he was in debt thirteen hundred talents, and many thought that by incurring such expense to be popular, he changed a solid good for what would prove but a short and uncertain return, but in truth he was purchasing what was of the greatest value at an inconsiderable rate. When he was made surveyor of the Appian way, he disbursed, besides the public money, a great sum out of his private purse; and when he was ædile, he provided such a number of gladiators, that he entertained the people with three hundred and twenty single combats, and by his great liberality and magnificence in theatrical shows in processions, and public feastings, he threw into the shade all the attempts that had been made before him, and gained so much upon the people, that every one was eager to find out new offices and new honors for him in return for his munificence.

There being two factions in the city, one that of Sylla, which was very powerful, the other that of Marius, which was then broken and in a very low condition, he undertook to revive this and to make it his own. And to this end, whilst he was in the height of his repute with the people for the magnificent shows he gave as ædile, he ordered images of Marius and figures of Victory, with trophies in their hands, to be carried privately in the night and placed in the capitol. Next morning, when some saw them bright with gold and beautifully made, with inscriptions upon them, referring them to Marius's exploits over the Cimbrians, they were surprised at the boldness of him who had set them up, nor was it difficult to guess who it was. The fame of this soon spread and brought together a great concourse of people. Some cried out that it was an open attempt against the established government thus to revive those honors which had been buried by the laws and decrees of the senate; that Cæsar had done it to sound the temper of the people whom he had prepared before, and to try whether they were tame enough to bear his humor, and would quietly give way to his innovations. On the other hand, Marius's party took courage, and it was incredible how numerous they were suddenly seen to be, and what a multitude of them appeared and came shouting into the capitol. Many, when they saw Marius's likeness, cried for joy, and Cæsar was highly extolled as the one man, in the place of all others, who was a relation worthy of Marius. Upon this the senate met, and Catulus Lutatius, one of the most eminent Romans of that time, stood up and inveighed against Cæsar, closing his speech with the remarkable saying, that Cæsar was now not working mines, but planting batteries to overthrow the state. But when Cæsar had made an apology for himself, and satisfied the senate, his admirers were very much animated, and advised him not to depart from his own thoughts for any one, since with the people's good favor he would ere long get the better of them all, and be the first man in the commonwealth.

At this time, Metellus, the High-Priest, died, and Catulus and Isauricus, persons of the highest reputation, and who had great influence in the senate, were competitors for the office yet Cæsar would not give way to them, but presented himself to the people as a candidate against them. The several parties seeming very equal, Catulus, who, because he had the most honor to lose, was the most apprehensive of the event, sent to Cæsar to buy him off, with offers of a great sum of money. But his answer was, that he was ready to borrow a larger sum than that, to carry on the contest. Upon the day of election, as his mother conducted him out of doors with tears, after embracing her, " My mother " he said, " to-day you will see me either High-Priest, or an exile." When the votes were taken, after a great struggle, he carried it, and excited among the senate and nobility great alarm lest he might now urge on the people to every kind of insolence. And Piso and Catulus found fault with Cicero for having let Cæsar escape, when in the conspiracy of Catiline he had given the government such advantage against him. For Catiline, who had designed not only to change the present state of affairs, but to subvert the whole empire and confound all, had himself taken to flight, while the evidence was yet incomplete against him, before his ultimate purposes had been properly discovered. But he had left Lentulus and Cethegus in the city to supply his place in the conspiracy, and whether they received any secret encouragement and assistance from Cæsar is uncertain; all that is certain, is, that they were fully convicted in the senate, and when Cicero, the consul, asked the several opinions of the senators, how they would have them punished, all who spoke before Cæsar sentenced them to death; but Cæsar stood up and made a set speech, in which he told them that he thought it without precedent and not just to take away the lives of persons of their birth and distinction before they were fairly tried, unless there was an absolute necessity for it; but that if they were kept confined in any towns of Italy Cicero himself should choose till Catiline was defeated, then the senate might in peace and at their leisure determine what was best to be done.

This sentence of his carried so much appearance of humanity, and he gave it such advantage by the eloquence with which he urged it, that not only those who spoke after him closed with it, but even they who had before given a contrary opinion, now come over to his, till it came about to Catulus's and Cato's turn to speak. They warmly opposed it, and Cato intimated in his speech the suspicion of Cæsar himself, and pressed the matter so strongly, that the criminals were given up to suffer execution. As Cæsar was going out of the sen ate, many of the young men who at that time acted as guards to Cicero, ran in with their naked swords to assault him. But Curio, it is said, threw his gown over him, and conveyed him away, and Cicero himself, when the young men looked up to see his wishes, gave a sign not to kill him, either for fear of the people or because he thought the murder unjust and illegal. If this be true, I wonder how Cicero came to omit all mention of it in his book about his consulship. He was blamed, however, afterwards, for not having made use of so fortunate an opportunity against Cæsar, as if he had let it escape him out of fear of the populace, who, indeed, showed remarkable solicitude about Cæsar, and some time after, when he went into the senate to clear himself of the suspicions he lay under, and found great clamors raised against him, upon the senate in consequence sitting longer than ordinary, they went up to the house in a tumult, and beset it, demanding Cæsar, and requiring them to dismiss him. Upon this, Cato, much fearing some movement among the poor citizens, who were always the first to kindle the flame among the people, and placed all their hopes in Cæsar, persuaded the senate to give them a monthly allowance of corn, an expedient which put the commonwealth to the extraordinary charge of seven million five hundred thousand drachmas in the year, but quite succeeded in removing the great cause of terror for the present, and very much weakened Cæsar's power, who at that time was just going to be made prætor, and consequently would have been more formidable by his office.

But there was no disturbance during his prætorship, only what misfortune he met with in his own domestic affairs. Publius Clodius was a patrician by descent, eminent both for his riches and eloquence, but in licentiousness of life and audacity exceeded the most noted profligates of the day. He was in love with Pompeia, Cæsar's wife, and she had no aversion to him. But there was strict watch kept on her apartment, and Cæsar's mother, Aurelia, who was a discreet woman, being continually about her, made any interview very dangerous and difficult. The Romans have a goddess whom they call Bona, the same whom the Greeks call Gynæcea. The Phrygians, who claim a peculiar title to her, say she was mother to Midas. The Romans profess she was one of the Dryads, and married to Faunus. The Grecians affirm that she is that mother of Bacchus whose name is not to be uttered, and, for this reason, the women who celebrate her festival, cover the tents with vine-branches, and, in accord ance with the fable, a consecrated serpent is placed by the goddess. It is not lawful for a man to be by, nor so much as in the house, whilst the rites are celebrated, but the women by themselves perform the sacred offices, which are said to be much the same with those used in the solemnities of Orpheus. When the festival comes, the husband, who is either consul or prætor, and with him every male creature, quits the house. The wife then taking it under her care sets it in order and the principal ceremonies are performed during the night, the women playing together amongst themselves as they keep watch, and music of various kinds going on.

As Pompeia was at that time celebrating this feast, Clodius, who as yet had no beard, and so thought to pass undiscovered, took upon him the dress and ornaments of a singing woman, and so came thither, having the air of a young girl. Finding the doors open, he was without any stop introduced by the maid, who was in the intrigue. She presently ran to tell Pompeia, but as she was away a long time, he grew uneasy in waiting for her, and left his post and traversed the house from one room to another, still taking care to avoid the lights, till at last Aurelia's woman met him, and invited him to play with her, as the women did among themselves. He refused to comply, and she presently pulled him forward, and asked him who he was, and whence he come. Clodius told her he was waiting for Pompeia's own maid, Abra, being in fact her own name also, and as he said so, betrayed himself by his voice. Upon which the woman shrieking, ran into the company where there were lights, and cried out, she had discovered a man. The women were all in a fright. Aurelia covered up the sacred things and stopped the proceedings, and having ordered the doors to be shut, went about with lights to find Clodius, who was got into the maid's room that he had come in with, and was seized there. The women knew him, and drove him out of doors, and at once, that same night, went home and told their husbands the story. In the morning, it was all about the town, what an impious attempt Clodius had made, and how he ought to be punished as an offender, not only against those whom he had offended, but also against the public and the gods. Upon which one of the tribunes impeached him for profaning the holy rites, and some of the principa senators combined together and gave evidence against him, that besides many other horrible crimes, he had been guilty of incest with his own sister, who was married to Lucullus. Bu the people set themselves against this combination of the nobility, and defended Clodius, which was of great service to him with the judges, who took alarm and were afraid to provoke the multitude. Cæsar at once dismissed Pompeia, but being summoned as a witness against Clodius, said he had nothing to charge him with. This looking like a paradox, the accuser asked him why he parted with his wife Cæsar replied, "I wished my wife to be not so much as suspected." Some say that Cæsar spoke this as his real thought, others, that he did it to gratify the people, who were very earnest to save Clodius. Clodius, at any rate, escaped; most of the judges giving their opinions so written as to be illegible that they might not be in danger from the people by condemning him, nor in disgrace with the nobility by acquitting him.

Cæsar, in the mean time, being out of his prætorship, had got the province of Spain, but was in great embarrassment with his creditors, who, as he was going off, came upon him, and were very pressing and importunate. This led him to apply himself to Crassus, who was the richest man in Rome, but wanted Cæsar's youthful vigor and heat to sustain the opposition against Pompey. Crassus took upon him to satisfy those creditors who were most uneasy to him, and would not be put off any longer, and engaged himself to the amount of eight hundred and thirty talents, upon which Cæsar was now at liberty to go to his province. In his journey, as he was crossing the Alps, and passing by a small village of the barbarians with but few inhabitants, and those wretchedly poor, his companions asked the question among themselves by way of mockery, if there were any canvassing for offices there; any contention which should be uppermost, or feuds of great men one against another. To which Cæsar made answer seriously, "For my part, I had rather be the first man among these fellows, than the second man in Rome." It is said that another time, when free from business in Spain, after reading some part of the history of Alexander, he sat a great while very thoughtful, and at last burst out into tears. His friends were surprised, and asked him the reason of it. "Do you think," said he, "I have not just cause to weep, when I consider that Alexander at my age had conquered so many nations, and I have all this time done nothing that is memorable." As soon as he came into Spain he was very active, and in a few days had got together ten new cohorts of foot in addition to the twenty which were there before. With these he marched against the Calaici and Lusitani and conquered them, and advancing as far as the ocean, subdued the tribes which never before had been subject to the Romans. Having managed his military affairs with good success, he was equally happy in the course of his civil government. He took pains to establish a good understanding amongst the several states, and no less care to heal the differences between debtors and creditors. He ordered that the creditor should receive two parts of the debtor's yearly income, and that the other part should be managed by the debtor himself, till by this method the whole debt was at last discharged. This conduct made him leave his province with a fair reputation; being rich himself, and having enriched his soldiers, and having received from them the honorable name of Imperator.

There is a law among the Romans, that whoever desires the honor of a triumph must stay without the city and expect his answer. And another, that those who stand for the consulship shall appear personally upon the place. Cæsar was come home at the very time of choosing consuls, and being in a difficulty between these two opposite laws, sent to the senate to desire that since he was obliged to be absent, he might sue for the consulship by his friends. Cato, being backed by the law, at first opposed his request; afterwards perceiving that Cæsar had prevailed with a great part of the senate to comply with it, he made it his business to gain time, and went on wasting the whole day in speaking. Upon which Cæsar thought fit to let the triumph fall, and pursued the consulship. Entering the town and coming forward immediately, he had recourse to a piece of state-policy by which everybody was deceived but Cato. This was the reconciling of Crassus and Pompey, the two men who then were most powerful in Rome. There had been a quarrel between them, which he now succeeded in making up, and by this means strengthened himself by the united power of both, and so under the cover of an action which carried all the appearance of a piece of kindness and good-nature, caused what was in effect a revolution in the government. For it was not the quarrel between Pompey and Cæsar, as most men imagine, which was the origin of the civil wars, but their union, their conspiring together at first to subvert the aristocracy, and so quarrelling afterwards between themselves. Cato, who often foretold what the consequence of this alliance would be, had then the character of a sullen, interfering man, but in the end the reputation of a wise but unsuccessful counsellor.

Thus Cæsar being doubly supported by the interests of

Crassus and Pompey, was promoted to the consulship, and triumphantly proclaimed with Calpurnius Bibulus. When he entered on his office, he brought in bills which would have been preferred with better grace by the most audacious of the tribunes than by a consul, in which he proposed the plantation of colonies and the division of lands, simply to please the commonalty. The best and most honorable of the senators opposed it, upon which, as he had long wished for nothing more than for such a colorable pretext, he loudly protested how much it was against his will to be driven to seek support from the people, and how the senate's insulting and harsh conduct left no other course possible for him, than to devote himself henceforth to the popular cause and interest. And so he hurried out of the senate, and presenting himself to the people, and there placing Crassus and Pompey, one on each side of him, he asked them whether they consented to the bills he had proposed. They owned their assent, upon which he desired them to assist him against those who had threatened to oppose him with their swords. They engaged they would, and Pompey added further, that he would meet their swords with a sword and buckler too. These words the nobles much resented, as neither suitable to his own dignity, nor becoming the reverence due to the senate, but resembling rather the vehemence of a boy, or the fury of a madman. But the people were pleased with it. In order to get a yet firmer hold upon Pompey, Cæsar having a daughter, Julia, who had been before contracted to Servilius Cæpio, now betrothed her to Pompey, and told Servilius he should have Pompey's daughter, who was not unengaged either, but promised to Sylla's son, Faustus. A little time after, Cæsar married Calpurnia, the daughter of Piso, and got Piso made consul for the year following. Cato exclaimed loudly against this, and protested with a great deal of warmth, that it was intolerable the government should be prostituted by marriages, and that they should advance one another to the commands of armies, provinces, and other great posts, by means of women. Bibulus, Cæsar's colleague, finding it was to no purpose to oppose his bills, but that he was in danger of being murdered in the forum, as also was Cato, confined himself to his house, and there let the remaining part of his consulship expire. Pompey, when he was married, at once filled the forum with soldiers, and gave the people his help in passing the new laws, and secured Cæsar the government of all Gaul, both on this and the other side of the Alps, together with Illyricum, and the command of four legions for five years. Cato made some attempts against these proceedings, but was seized and led off on the way to prison by Cæsar who expected that he would appeal to the tribunes. But when he saw that Cato went along without speaking a word, and not only the nobility were indignant, but the people, also, out of respect for Cato's virtue, were following in silence, and with dejected looks, he himself privately desired one of the tribunes to rescue Cato. As for the other senators, some few of them attended the house, the rest, being disgusted, absented themselves. Hence Considius, a very old man, took occasion one day to tell Cæsar, that the senators did not meet because they were afraid of his soldiers. Cæsar asked, "Why don't you, then, out of the same fear, keep at home?" To which Considius replied, that age was his guard against fear, and that the small remains of his life were not worth much caution. But the most disgraceful thing that was done in Cæsar's consulship, was his assisting to gain the tribuneship, for the same Clodius who had made the attempt on his wife's chastity, and intruded upon the secret vigils. He was elected on purpose to effect Cicero's downfall; nor did Cæsar leave the city to join his army, till they two had overpowered Cicero, and driven him out of Italy.

Thus far have we followed Cæsar's actions before the wars of Gaul. After this, he seems to begin his course afresh, and to enter upon a new life and scene of action. And the period of those wars which he now fought, and those many expeditions in which he subdued Gaul, showed him to be a soldier and general not in the least inferior to any of the greatest and most admired commanders who had ever appeared at the head of armies. For if we compare him with the Fabii, the Metelli, the Scipios, and with those who were his contemporaries, or not long before him, Sylla, Marius, the two Luculli, or even Pompey himself, whose glory, it may be said went up at that time to heaven for every excellence in war, we shall find Cæsar's actions to have surpassed them all. One he may be held to have outdone in consideration of the difficulty of the country in which he fought, another in the extent of territory which he conquered; some, in the number and strength of the enemy whom he defeated; one man, because of the wildness and perfidiousness of the tribes whose good-will he conciliated, another in his humanity and clemency to those he overpowered; others, again, in his gifts and kindnesses to his soldiers; all alike in the number of the battles which he fought and the enemies whom he killed. For he had not pursued the wars in Gaul full ten years, when he had taken by storm above eight hundred towns, subdued three hundred states, and of the three millions of men, who made up the gross sum of those with whom at several times he engaged, he had killed one million, and taken captive a second.

He was so much master of the good-will and hearty service of his soldiers, that those who in other expeditions were but ordinary men, displayed a courage past defeating or withstanding when they went upon any danger where Cæsar's glory was concerned. Such a one was Acilius, who, in the sea-fight before Marseilles, had his right hand struck off with a sword, yet did not quit his buckler out of his left, but struck the enemies in the face with it, till he drove them off, and made himself master of the vessel. Such another was Cassius Scæva, who, in a battle near Dyrrhachium, had one of his eyes shot out with an arrow, his shoulder pierced with one javelin, and his thigh with another; and having received one hundred and thirty darts upon his target, called to the enemy, as though he would surrender himself. But when two of them came up to him, he cut off the shoulder of one with a sword, and by a blow over the face forced the other to retire, and so with the assistance of his friends, who now came up, made his escape. Again, in Britain, when some of the foremost officers had accidentally got into a morass full of water, and there were assaulted by the enemy, a common soldier, whilst Cæsar stood and looked on, threw himself into the midst of them, and after many signal demonstrations of his valor, rescued the officers, and beat off the barbarians. He himself, in the end, took to the water, and with much difficulty, partly by swimming, partly by wading, passed it, but in the passage lost his shield. Cæsar and his officers saw it and admired, and went to meet him with joy and acclamation. But the soldier, much dejected and in tears, threw himself down at Cæsar's feet, and begged his pardon for having let go his buckler. Another time in Africa, Scipio having taken a ship of Cæsar's in which Granius Petro, lately appointed quæstor, was sailing, gave the other passengers as free prize to his soldiers, but thought fit to offer the quæstor his life. But he said it was not usual for Cæsar's soldiers to take, but give mercy, and having said so, fell upon his sword and killed himself.

This love of honor and passion for distinction were inspired into them and cherished in them by Cæsar himself.

who, by his unsparing distribution of money and honors, showed them that he did not heap up wealth from the wars for his own luxury, or the gratifying his private pleasures, but that all he received was but a public fund laid by for the reward and encouragement of valor, and that he looked upon all he gave to deserving soldiers as so much increase to his own riches. Added to this also, there was no danger to which he did not willingly expose himself, no labor from which he pleaded an exemption. His contempt of danger was not so much wondered at by his soldiers because they knew how much he coveted honor. But his enduring so much hardship which he did to all appearance beyond his natural strength, very much astonished them. For he was a spare man, had a soft and white skin, was distempered in the head and subject to an epilepsy, which, it is said, first seized him at Corduba, But he did not make the weakness of his constitution a pretext for his ease, but rather used war as the best physic against his indispositions; whilst, by indefatigable journeys, coarse diet, frequent lodging in the field, and continual laborious exercise, he struggled with his diseases, and fortified his body against all attacks. He slept generally in his chariots or litters, employing even his rest in pursuit of action. In the day he was thus carried to the forts, garrisons, and camps, one servant sitting with him, who used to write down what he dictated as he went, and a soldier attending behind him with his sword drawn. He drove so rapidly, that when he first left Rome, he arrived at the river Rhone within eight days. He had been an expert rider from his childhood; for it was usual with him to sit with his hands joined together behind his back, and so to put his horse to its full speed. And in his war he disciplined himself so far as to be able to dictate letters from on horseback, and to give directions to two who took notes at the same time, or, as Oppius says, to more. And it is thought that he was the first who contrived means for communicating with friends by cipher, when either press of business, or the large extent of the city, left him no time for a personal conference about matters that required despatch. How little nice he was in his diet, may be seen in the following instance. When at the table of Valerius Leo, who entertained him at supper at Milan, a dish of asparagus was put before him on which his host instead of oil had poured sweet ointment. Cæsar partook of it without any disgust, and reprimanded his friends for finding fault with it. "For it was enough,' said he, " not to eat what you did not like; but he who reflects on another man's want of breeding, shows he wants it as much himself." Another time upon the road he was driven by a storm into a poor man's cottage, where he found but one room, and that such as would afford but a mean reception to a single person, and therefore told his companions, places of honor should be given up to the greater men, and necessary accommodations to the weaker, and accordingly ordered that Oppius, who was in bad health, should lodge within, whilst he and the rest slept under a shed at the door.

His first war in Gaul was against the Helvetians and Tigurini, who having burnt their own towns, twelve in number, and four hundred villages, would have marched forward through that part of Gaul which was included in the Roman province, as the Cimbrians and Teutons formerly had done. Nor were they inferior to these in courage; and in numbers they were equal being in all three hundred thousand, of which one hundred and ninety thousand were fighting men. Cæsar did not engage the Tigurini in person, but Labienus, under his directions, routed them near the river Arar. The Helvetians surprised Cæsar, and unexpectedly set upon him as he was conducting his army to a confederate town. He succeeded, however, in making his retreat into a strong position, where, when he had mustered and marshalled his men, his horse was brought to him; upon which he said, "When I have won the battle, I will use my horse for the chase, but at present let us go against the enemy," and accordingly charged them on foot. After a long and severe combat, he drove the main army out of the field, but found the hardest work at their carriages and ramparts, where not only the men stood and fought, but the women also and children defended themselves till they were cut to pieces; insomuch that the fight was scarcely ended till midnight. This action, glorious in itself, Cæsar crowned with another yet more noble, by gathering in a body all the barbarians that had escaped out of the battle, above one hundred thousand in number, and obliging them to re-occupy the country which they had deserted and the cities which they had burnt. This he did for fear the Germans should pass it and possess themselves of the land whilst it lay uninhabited.

His second war was in defence of the Gauls against the Germans, though some time before he had made Ariovistus, their king, recognized at Rome as an ally. But they were very insufferable neighbors to those under his government; and it was probable, when occasion offered, they would re nounce the present arrangements, and march on to occupy Gaul. But finding his officers timorous, and especially those of the young nobility who came along with him in hopes of turning their campaigns with him into a means for their own pleasure or profit, he called them together, and advised them to march off, and not run the hazard of a battle against their inclinations, since they had such weak and unmanly feelings; telling them that he would take only the tenth legion, and march against the barbarians, whom he did not expect to find an enemy more formidable than the Cimbri, nor, he added, should they find him a general inferior to Marius. Upon this, the tenth legion deputed some of their body to pay him their acknowledgments and thanks, and the other legions blamed their officers, and all, with great vigor and zeal, followed him many day's journey, till they encamped within two hundred furlongs of the enemy. Ariovistus's courage to some extent was cooled upon their very approach; for never expecting the Romans would attack the Germans, whom he had thought it more likely they would not venture to withstand even in defence of their own subjects, he was the more surprised at Cæsar's conduct, and saw his army to be in consternation. They were still more discouraged by the prophecies of their holy women, who foretell the future by observing the eddies of rivers, and taking signs from the windings and noise of streams, and who now warned them not to engage before the next new moon appeared. Cæsar having had intimation of this, and seeing the Germans lie still, thought it expedient to attack them whilst they were under these apprehensions, rather than sit still and wait their time. Accordingly he made his approaches to the strongholds and hills on which they lay encamped, and so galled and fretted them, that at last they came down with great fury to engage. But he gained a signal victory, and pursued them for four hundred furlongs, as far as the Rhine; all which space was covered with spoils and bodies of the slain. Ariovistus made shift to pass the Rhine with the small remains of an army, for it is said the number of the slain amounted to eighty thousand.

After this action, Cæsar left his army at their winter-quarters in the country of the Sequani, and in order to attend to affairs at Rome, went into that part of Gaul which lies on the Po, and was part of his province; for the river Rubicon divides Gaul, which is on this side the Alps, from the rest of Italy. There he sat down and employed himself in courting people's favor great numbers coming to him continually, and always finding their requests answered ; for he never failed to dismiss all with present pledges of his kindness in hand, and further hopes for the future. And during all this time of the war in Gaul, Pompey never observed how Cæsar was on the one hand using the arms of Rome to effect his conquests, and on the other was gaining over and securing to himself the favor of the Romans, with the wealth which those conquests obtained him. But when he heard that the Belgæ, who were the most powerful of all the Gauls, and inhabited a third part of the country, were revolted, and had got together a great many thousand men in arms, he immediately set out and took his way hither with great expedition, and falling upon the enemy as they were ravaging the Gauls, his allies, he soon defeated and put to flight the largest and least scattered division of them. For though their numbers were great, yet they made but a slender defence, and the marshes and deep rivers were made passable to the Roman foot by the vast quantity of dead bodies. Of those who revolted, all the tribes that lived near the ocean came over without fighting, and he, therefore, led his army against the Nervii, the fiercest and most warlike people of all in those parts. These live in a country covered with continuous woods, and having lodged their children and property out of the way in the depth of the forest, fell upon Cæsar with a body of sixty thousand men, before he was prepared for them, while he was making his encampment. They soon routed his cavalry, and having surrounded the twelfth and seventh legions, killed all the officers, and had not Cæsar himself snatched up a buckler and forced his way through his own men to come up to the barbarians, or had not the tenth legion, when they saw him in danger, run in from the tops of the hills, where they lay, and broken through the enemy's ranks to rescue him, in all probability not a Roman would have been saved. But now, under the influence of Cæsar's bold example, they fought a battle, as the phrase is, of more than human courage, and yet with their utmost efforts they were not able to drive the enemy out of the field, but cut them down fighting in their defence. For out of sixty thousand men, it is stated that not above five hundred survived the battle, and of four hundred of their senators not above three.

When the Roman senate had received news of this, they voted sacrifices and festivals to the gods, to be strictly observed for the space of fifteen days, a longer space than ever was observed for any victory before. The danger to which they had been exposed by the joint outbreak of such a number of nations was felt to have been great; and the people's fondness for Cæsar gave additional lustre to successes achieved by him. He now, after settling every thing in Gaul, came back again, and spent the winter by the Po, in order to carry on the designs he had in hand at Rome. All who were candidates for offices used his assistance, and were supplied with money from him to corrupt the people and buy their votes, in return of which, when they were chosen, they did all things to advance his power. But what was more considerable, the most eminent and powerful men in Rome in great numbers came to visit him at Lucca, Pompey, and Crassus, and Appius, the governor of Sardinia, and Nepos, the proconsul of Spain, so that there were in the place at one time one hundred and twenty lictors, and more than two hundred senators. In deliberation here held, it was determined that Pompey and Crassus should be consuls again for the following year; that Cæsar should have a fresh supply of money, and that his command should be renewed to him for five years more. It seemed very extravagant to all thinking men, that those very persons who had received so much money from Cæsar should persuade the senate to grant him more, as if he were in want. Though in truth it was not so much upon persuasion as compulsion, that, with sorrow and groans for their own acts, they passed the measure. Cato was not present, for they had sent him seasonably out of the way into Cyprus; but Favonius, who was a zealous imitator of Cato, when he found he could do no good by opposing it, broke out of the house, and loudly declaimed against these proceedings to the people, but none gave him any hearing; some slighting him out of respect to Crassus and Pompey, and the greater part to gratify Cæsar, on whom depended their hopes.

After this, Cæsar returned again to his forces in Gaul, when he found that country involved in a dangerous war, two strong nations of the Germans having lately passed the Rhine, to conquer it; one of them called the Usipes, the other the Tenteritæ. Of the war with the people, Cæsar himself has given this account in his commentaries, that the barbarians, having sent ambassadors to treat with him, did, during the treaty, set upon him in his march, by which means with eight hundred men they routed five thousand of his horse, who did not suspect their coming; that afterwards they sent other ambassadors to renew the same fraudulent practices, whom he kept in custody, and led on his army against the barba rians, as judging it mere simplicity to keep faith with those who had so faithlessly broken the terms they had agreed to. But Tanusius states, that when the senate decreed festivals and sacrifices for this victory, Cato declared it to be his opinion that Cæsar ought to be given into the hands of the barbarians, that so the guilt which this breach of faith might otherwise bring upon the state, might be expiated by transferring the curse on him, who was the occasion of it. Of those who passed the Rhine, there were four hundred thousand cut off; those few who escaped were sheltered by the Sugambri, a people of Germany. Cæsar took hold of this pretence to invade the Germans, being at the same time ambitious of the honor of being the first man that should pass the Rhine with an army. He carried a bridge across it, though it was very wide, and the current at that particular point very full, strong, and violent, bringing down with its waters trunks of trees, and other lumber, which much shook and weakened the foundations of his bridge. But he drove great piles of wood into the bottom of the river above the passage, to catch and stop these as they floated down, and thus fixing his bridle upon the stream, successfully finished his bridge, which no one who saw could believe to be the work but of ten days.

In the passage of his army over it, he met with no opposition; the Suevi themselves, who are the most warlike people of all Germany, flying with their effects into the deepest and most densely wooded valleys. When he had burnt all the enemy's country, and encouraged those who embraced the Roman interest, he went back into Gaul, after eighteen days' stay in Germany. But his expedition into Britain was the most famous testimony of his courage. For he was the first who brought a navy into the western ocean, or who sailed into the Atlantic with an army to make war; and by invading an island, the reported extent of which had made its existence a matter of controversy among historians, many of whom questioned whether it were not a mere name and fiction, not a real place, he might be said to have carried the Roman empire beyond the limits of the known world. He passed thither twice from that part of Gaul which lies over against it, and in several battles which he fought, did more hurt to the enemy than service to himself, for the islanders were so miserably poor, that they had nothing worth being plundered of. When he found himself unable to put such an end to the war as he wished, he was content to take hostages from the king, and to impose a tribute, and then quitted the island. At his arrival in Gaul, he found letters which lay ready to be conveyed over the water to him from his friends at Rome, announcing his daughter's death, who died in labor of a child by Pompey. Cæsar and Pompey both were much afflicted with her death, nor were their friends less disturbed, believing that the alliance was now broken, which had hitherto kept the sickly commonwealth in peace, for the child also died within a few days after the mother. The people took the body of Julia, in spite of the opposition of the tribunes, and carried it into the field of Mars, and there her funeral rites were performed, and her remains are laid.

Cæsar's army was now grown very numerous, so that he was forced to disperse them into various camps for their winter-quarters, and he having gone himself to Italy as he used to do, in his absence a general outbreak throughout the whole of Gaul commenced, and large armies marched about the country, and attacked the Roman quarters, and attempted to make themselves masters of the forts where they lay. The greatest and strongest party of the rebels, under the command of Abriorix, cut off Cotta and Titurius with all their men, while a force sixty thousand strong besieged the legion under the command of Cicero, and had almost taken it by storm, the Roman soldiers being all wounded, and having quite spent themselves by a defence beyond their natural strength. But Cæsar, who was at a great distance, having received the news, quickly got together seven thousand men, and hastened to relieve Cicero. The besiegers were aware of it, and went to meet him, with great confidence that they should easily overpower such an handful of men. Cæsar, to increase their presumption, seemed to avoid fighting, and still marched off, till he found a place conveniently situated for a few to engage against many, where he encamped. He kept his soldiers from making any attack upon the enemy, and commanded them to raise the ramparts higher, and barricade the gates, that by show of fear, they might heighten the enemy's contempt of them. Till at last they came without any order in great security to make an assault, when he issued forth, and put them to flight with the loss of many men.

This quieted the greater part of the commotions in these parts of Gaul, and Cæsar, in the course of the winter, visited every part of the country, and with great vigilance took precautions against all innovations. For there were three legions now come to him to supply the place of the men he had lost, of which Pompey furnished him with two, out of those under his command; the other was newly raised in the part of Gaul by the Po. But in a while the seeds of war, which had long since been secretly sown and scattered by the most powerful men in those warlike nations, broke forth into the greatest and most dangerous war that was in those parts, both as regards the number of men in the vigor of their youth who were gathered and armed from all quarters, the vast funds of money collected to maintain it, the strength of the towns, and the difficulty of the country where it was carried on. It being winter, the rivers were frozen, the woods covered with snow, and the level country flooded, so that in some places the ways were lost through the depth of the snow; in others, the overflowing of marshes and streams made every kind of passage uncertain. All which difficulties made it seem impracticable for Cæsar to make any attempt upon the insurgents. Many tribes had revolted together, the chief of them being the Arverni and Carnutini; the general who had the supreme command in war was Vergentorix, whose father the Gauls had put to death on suspicion of his aiming at absolute government.

He having disposed his army in several bodies, and set officers over them, drew over to him all the country round about as far as those that lie upon the Arar, and having intelligence of the opposition which Cæsar now experienced at Rome, thought to engage all Gaul in the war. Which if he had done a little later, when Cæsar was taken up with the civil wars, Italy had been put into as great a terror as before it was by the Cimbri. But Cæsar, who above all men was gifted with the faculty of making the right use of every thing in war, and most especially of seizing the right moment, as soon as he heard of the revolt, returned immediately the same way he went, and showed the barbarians, by the quickness of his march in such a severe season, that an army was advancing against them which was invincible. For in the time that one would have thought it scarce credible that a courier or express should have come with a message from him, he himself appeared with all his army, ravaging the country, reducing their posts, subduing their towns, receiving into his protection those who declared for him. Till at last the Edui, who hitherto had styled themselves brethren to the Romans, and had been much honored by them, declared against him, and joined the rebels, to the great discouragement of his army. Accordingly he removed thence, and passed the country of the Ligones desiring to reach the territories of the

Sequani, who were his friends, and who lay like a bulwark in front of Italy against the other tribes of Gaul. There the enemy came upon him, and surrounded him with many myriads, whom he also was eager to engage; and at last, after some time and with much slaughter, gained on the whole a complete victory; though at first he appears to have met with some reverse, and the Aruveni show you a small sword hanging up in a temple, which they say was taken from Cæsar. Cæsar saw this afterwards himself, and smiled, and when his friends advised it should be taken down, would not permit it, because he looked upon it as consecrated.

After the defeat, a great part of those who had escaped fled with their king into a town called Alesia, which Cæsar besieged, though the height of the walls, and number of those who defended them, made it appear impregnable; and meantime, from without the walls, he was assailed by a greater danger than can be expressed. For the choice men of Gaul, picked out of each nation, and well armed, came to relieve Alesia, to the number of three hundred thousand; nor were there in the town less than one hundred and seventy thousand. So that Cæsar being shut up betwixt two such forces, was compelled to protect himself by two walls, one towards the town, the other against the relieving army, as knowing if these forces should join, his affairs would be entirely ruined. The danger that he underwent before Alesia, justly gained him great honor on many accounts, and gave him an opportunity of showing greater instances of his valor and conduct than any other contest had done. One wonders much how he should be able to engage and defeat so many thousands of men without the town, and not be perceived by those within, but yet more, that the Romans themselves, who guarded their wall which was next to the town, should be strangers to it. For even they knew nothing of the victory, till they heard the cries of the men and lamentations of the women who were in the town, and had from thence seen the Romans at a distance carrying into their camp a great quantity of bucklers, adorned with gold and silver, many breast-plates stained with blood, besides cups and tents made in the Gallic fashion. So soon did so vast an army dissolve and vanish like a ghost or dream, the greatest part of them being killed upon the spot. Those who were in Alesia, having given themselves and Cæsar much trouble, surrendered at last; and Vergentorix, who was the chief spring of all the war, putting his best armor on, and adorning his horse, rode out of the gates, and made a turn about Cæsar as he was sitting, then quitting his horse, threw off his armor, and remained quietly sitting at Cæsar's feet until he was led away to be reserved for the triumph.

Cæsar had long ago resolved upon the overthrow of Pompey, as had Pompey for that matter, upon his. For Crassus, the fear of whom had hitherto kept them in peace, having now been killed in Parthia, if the one of them wished to make himself the greatest man in Rome, he had only to overthrow the other ; and if he again wished to prevent his own fall, he had nothing for it but to be beforehand with him whom he feared. Pompey had not been long under any such apprehensions, having till lately despised Cæsar, as thinking it no difficult matter to put down him whom he himself had advanced. But Cæsar had entertained this design from the beginning against his rivals, and had retired, like an expert wrestler, to prepare himself apart for the combat. Making the Gallic wars his exercise-ground, he had at once improved the strength of his soldiery, and had heightened his own glory by his great actions, so that he was looked on as one who might challenge comparison with Pompey. Nor did he let go any of those ad vantages which were now given him both by Pompey himself and the times, and the ill government of Rome, where all who were candidates for offices publicly gave money, and without any shame bribed the people, who having received their pay, did not contend for their benefactors with their bare suffrages, but with bows, swords, and slings. So that after having many times stained the place of election with blood of men killed upon the spot, they left the city at last without a government at all, to be carried about like a ship without a pilot to steer her ; while all who had any wisdom could only be thankful if a course of such wild and stormy disorder and madness might end no worse than in a monarchy. Some were so bold as to declare openly, that the government was incurable but by a monarchy, and that they ought to take that remedy from the hands of the gentlest physician, meaning Pompey, who, though in words he pretended to decline it, yet in reality made his utmost efforts to be declared dictator. Cato perceiving his design, prevailed with the senate to make him sole consul, that with the offer of a more legal sort of monarchy he might be withheld from demanding the dictatorship. They over and above voted him the continuance of his provinces, for he had two, Spain and all Africa, which he governed by his lieutenants, and maintained armies under him, at the yearly charge of a thousand talents out of the public treasury.

Upon this Cæsar also sent and petitioned for the consul ship, and the continuance of his provinces. Pompey at first did not stir in it, but Marcellus and Lentulus opposed it, who had always hated Cæsar, and now did everything, whether fit or unfit, which might disgrace and affront him. For they took away the privilege of Roman citizens from the people of New Comum, who were a colony that Cæsar had lately planted in Gaul, and Marcellus, who was then consul, ordered one of the senators of that town, then at Rome, to be whipped, and told him he laid that mark upon him to signify he was no citizen of Rome, bidding him, when he went back again, to show it to Cæsar. After Marcellus's consulship, Cæsar began to lavish gifts upon all the public men out of the riches he had taken from the Gauls; discharged Curio, the tribune, from his great debts; gave Paulus, then consul, fifteen hundred talents, with which he built the noble court of justice adjoining the forum, to supply the place of that called the Fulvian. Pompey, alarmed at these preparations, now openly took steps, both by himself and his friends, to have a successor appointed in Cæsar's room, and sent to demand back the soldiers whom he had lent him to carry on the wars in Gaul. Cæsar returned them, and made each soldier a present of two hundred and fifty drachmas. The officer who brought them home to Pompey, spread amongst the people no very fair or favorable report of Cæsar, and flattered Pompey himself with false suggestions that he was wished for by Cæsar's army; and though his affairs here were in some embarrassment through the envy of some, and the ill state of the government, yet there the army was at his command, and if they once crossed into Italy, would presently declare for him; so weary were they of Cæsar's endless expeditions, and so suspicious of his designs for a monarchy. Upon this Pompey grew presumptuous, and neglected all warlike preparations, as fearing no danger, and used no other means against him than mere speeches and votes, for which Cæsar cared nothing. And one of his captains, it is said, who was sent by him to Rome, standing before the senate house one day, and being told that the senate would not give Cæsar a longer time in his government, clapped his hand on the hilt of his sword, and said "But this shall."

Yet the demands which Cæsar made had the fairest colors of equity imaginable. For he proposed to lay down his arms, and that Pompey should do the same, and both together should become private men, and each expect a reward of his services from the public. For that those who proposed to disarm him, and at the same time to confirm Pompey in all the power he held, were simply establishing the one in the tyranny which they accused the other of aiming at. When Curio made these proposals to the people in Cæsar's name, he was loudly applauded, and some threw garlands towards him, and dismissed him as they do successful wrestlers, crowned with flowers. Antony, being tribune, produced a letter sent from Cæsar on this occasion, and read it, though the consuls did what they could to oppose it. But Scipio, Pompey's father-in law, proposed in the senate, that if Cæsar did not lay down his arms within such a time, he should be voted an enemy; and the consuls putting it to the question, whether Pompey should dismiss his soldiers, and again, whether Cæsar should disband his, very few assented to the first, but almost all to the latter. But Antony proposing again, that both should lay down their commissions, all but a very few agreed to it. Scipio was upon this very violent, and Lentulus, the consul, cried aloud, that they had need of arms, and not of suffrages, against a robber; so that the senators for the present adjourned, and appeared in mourning as a mark of their grief for the dissension.

Afterwards there came other letters from Cæsar, which seemed yet more moderate, for he proposed to quit every thing else, and only to retain Gaul within the Alps, Illyricum, and two legions, till he should stand a second time for consul. Cicero, the orator, who was lately returned from Cilicia, endeavored to reconcile differences, and softened Pompey, who was willing to comply in other things, but not to allow him the soldiers. At last Cicero used his persuasion with Cæsar's friends to accept of the provinces and six thousand soldiers only, and so to make up the quarrel. And Pompey was inclined to give way to this, but Lentulus, the consul, would not hearken to it but drove Antony and Curio out of the senate-house with insults, by which he afforded Cæsar the most plausible pretence that could be, and one which he could readily use to inflame the soldiers, by showing them two persons of such repute and authority, who were forced to escape in a hired carriage in the dress of slaves. For so they were glad to disguise themselves, when they fled out of Rome.

There were not about him at that time above three hundred horse, and five thousand foot; for the rest of his army, which was left behind the Alps, was to be brought after him by officers who had received orders for that purpose But he thought the first motion towards the design which he had on foot did not require large forces at present, and that what was wanted was to make this first step suddenly, and so as to astound his enemies with the boldness of it; as it would be easier, he thought, to throw them into consternation by doing what they never anticipated, than fairly to conquer them, if he had alarmed them by his preparations. And therefore, he commanded his captains and other officers to go only with their swords in their hands, without any other arms, and make themselves masters of Ariminum, a large city of Gaul, with as little disturbance and bloodshed as possible. He committed the care of these forces to Hortensius, and himself spent the day in public as a stander-by and spectator of the gladiators, who exercised before him. A little before night he attended to his person, and then went into the hall, and conversed for some time with those he had invited to supper, till it began to grow dusk, when he rose from table, and made his excuses to the company, begging them to stay till he came back, having already given private directions to a few immediate friends, that they should follow him, not all the same way, but some one way, some another. He himself got into one of the hired carriages, and drove at first another way, but presently turned towards Ariminum. When he came to the river Rubicon, which parts Gaul within the Alps from the rest of Italy, his thoughts began to work, now he was just entering upon the danger, and he wavered much in his mind, when he considered the greatness of the enterprise into which he was throwing himself. He checked his course, and ordered a halt, while he revolved with himself, and often changed his opinion one way and the other, without speaking a word. This was when his purposes fluctuated most; presently he also discussed the matter with his friends who were about him (of which number Asinius Pollio was one), computing how many calamities his passing that river would bring upon mankind, and what a relation of it would be transmitted to posterity. At last, in a sort of passion, casting aside calculation, and abandoning himself to what might come, and using the proverb frequently in their mouths who enter upon dangerous and bold attempts, "The die is cast," with these words he took the river. Once over, he used all expedition possible, and before it was day reached Ariminum, and took it. It is said that the night before he passed the river, he had an impious dream, that he was unnaturally familiar with his own mother.

As soon as Ariminum was taken, wide gates, so to say

were thrown open, to let in war upon every land alike and sea, and with the limits of the province, the boundaries of the laws were transgressed. Nor would one have thought that, as at other times, the mere men and women fled from one town of Italy to another in their consternation, but that the very towns themselves left their sites, and fled for succor to each other. The city of Rome was overrun, as it were, with a deluge, by the conflux of people flying in from all the neighboring places. Magistrates could no longer govern, nor the eloquence of any orator quiet it ; it was all but suffering shipwreck by the violence of its own tempestuous agitation. The most vehement contrary passions and impulses were at work everywhere. Nor did those who rejoiced at the prospect of the change altogether conceal their feelings, but when they met, as in so great a city they frequently must, with the alarmed and dejected of the other party, they provoked quarrels by their bold expressions of confidence in the event. Pompey, sufficiently disturbed of himself, was yet more perplexed by the clamors of others ; some telling him that he justly suffered for having armed Cæsar against himself and the government ; others blaming him for permitting Cæsar to be insolently used by Lentulus, when he made such ample concessions, and offered such reasonable proposals towards an accommodation. Favonius bade him now stamp upon the ground ; for once talking big in the senate, he desired them not to trouble themselves about making any preparations for the war, for that he himself, with one stamp of his foot, would fill all Italy with soldiers. Yet still Pompey at that time had more forces than Cæsar ; but he was not permitted to pursue his own thoughts, but being continually disturbed with false reports and alarms, as if the enemy was close upon him and carrying all before him, he gave way, and let himself be borne down by the general cry. He put forth an edict declaring the city to be in a state of anarchy, and left it with orders that the senate should follow him, and that no one should stay behind who did not prefer tyranny to their country and liberty.

The consuls at once fled, without making even the usual sacrifices ; so did most of the senators, carrying off their own goods in as much haste as if they had been robbing their neighbors. Some, who had formerly much favored Cæsar's cause, in the prevailing alarm, quitted their own sentiments, and without any prospect of good to themselves, were carried along by the common stream. It was a melancholy thing to see the city tossed in these tumults like a ship given up by

VOL. II.—34

her pilots, and left to run as chance guides her, upon any rock in her way. Yet, in spite of their sad condition, people still esteemed the place of their exile to be their country for Pompey's sake, and fled from Rome, as if it had been Cæsar's camp. Labienus even, who had been one of Cæsar's nearest friends, and his lieutenant, and who had fought by him zealously in the Gallic wars, now deserted him, and went over to Pompey. Cæsar sent all his money and equipage after him, and then sat down before Corfinium, which was garrisoned with thirty cohorts under the command of Domitius. He, in despair of maintaining the defence, requested a physician, whom he had among his attendants, to give him poison; and taking the dose, drank it, in hopes of being dispatched by it. But soon after, when he was told that Cæsar showed the utmost clemency towards those he took prisoners, he lamented his misfortnne, and blamed the hastiness of his resolution. His physician consoled him, by informing him that he had taken a sleeping draught, not a poison; upon which, much rejoiced, and rising from his bed, he went presently to Cæsar, and gave him the pledge of his hand, yet afterwards again went over to Pompey. The report of these actions at Rome, quieted those who were there, and some who had fled thence returned.

Cæsar took into his army Domitius's soldiers, as he did all those whom he found in any town enlisted for Pompey's service. Being now strong and formidable enough, he advanced against Pompey himself, who did not stay to receive him, but fled to Brundisium, having sent the consuls before with a body of troops to Dyrrhachium. Soon after, upon Cæsar's approach, he set to sea, as shall be more particularly related in his Life. Cæsar would have immediately pursued him, but wanted shipping, and therefore went back to Rome, having made himself master of all Italy without bloodshed in the space of sixty days. When he came thither, he found the city more quiet than he expected, and many senators present, to whom he addressed himself with courtesy and deference, desiring them to send to Pompey about any reasonable accommodations towards a peace. But nobody complied with this proposal; whether out of fear of Pompey, whom they had deserted, or that they thought Cæsar did not mean what he said, but thought it his interest to talk plausibly. Afterwards, when Metellus, the tribune, would have hindered him from taking money out of the public reasure, and adduced some laws against it, Cæsar replied, that arms and laws had each their own time; "If what I do displeases you, leave the place; war allows no free talking. When I have laid down my arms, and made peace, come back and make what speeches you please. And this," he added, "I tell you in diminution of my own just right, as indeed you and all others who have appeared against me and are now in my power, may be treated as I please." Having said this to Metellus, he went to the doors of the treasury, and the keys being not to be found, sent for smiths to force them open. Metellus again making resistance and some encouraging him in it, Cæsar, in a louder tone, told him he would put him to death, if he gave him any further disturbance. "And this," said he, "you know, young man, is more disagreeable for me to say, than to do." These words made Metellus withdraw for fear, and obtained speedy execution henceforth for all orders that Cæsar gave for procuring necessaries for the war.

He was now proceeding to Spain, with the determination of first crushing Afranius and Varro, Pompey's lieutenants, and making himself master of the armies and provinces under them, that he might then more securely advance against Pompey, when he had no enemy left behind him. In this expedition his person was often in danger from ambuscades, and his army by want of provisions, yet he did not desist from pursuing the enemy, provoking them to fight, and hemming them with his fortifications, till by main force he made himself master of their camps and their forces. Only the generals got off, and fled to Pompey.

When Cæsar came back to Rome, Piso, his father-in-law, advised him to send men to Pompey, to treat of a peace; but Isauricus, to ingratiate himself with Cæsar, spoke against it. After this, being created dictator by the senate, he called home the exiles, and gave back their rights as citizens to the children of those who had suffered under Sylla; he relieved the debtors by an act remitting some part of the interest on their debts, and passed some other measures of the same sort, but not many. For within eleven days he resigned his dictatorship, and having declared himself consul, with Servilius Isauricus, hastened again to the war. He marched so fast, that he left all his army behind him, except six hundred chosen horse, and five legions, with which he put to sea in the very middle of winter, about the beginning of the month January (which corresponds pretty nearly with the Athenian month Posideon), and having past the Ionian Sea, took Oricum and Apollonia, and then sent back the ships to Brundisium, to bring over the soldiers who were left behind in the march. They, while yet on the march, their bodies now no longer in the full vigor of youth, and they themselves weary with such a multitude of wars, could not but exclaim against Cæsar, "When at last, and where, will this Cæsar let us be quiet? He carries us from place to place, and uses us as if we were not to be worn out, and had no sense of labor. Even our iron itself is spent by blows, and we ought to have some pity on our bucklers and breast-plates, which have been used so long. Our wounds, if nothing else, should make him see that we are mortal men, whom he commands, subject to the same pains and sufferings as other human beings. The very gods themselves cannot force the winter season, or hinder the storms in their time; yet he pushes forward, as if he were not pursuing, but flying from an enemy." So they talked as they marched leisurely towards Brundisium. But when they came thither, and found Cæsar gone off before them, their feelings changed, and they blamed themselves as traitors to their general. They now railed at their officers for marching so slowly, and placing themselves on the heights overlooking the sea towards Epirus, they kept watch to see if they could espy the vessels which were to transport them to Cæsar.

He in the mean time was posted in Apollonia, but had not an army with him able to fight the enemy, the forces from Brundisium being so long in coming, which put him to great suspense and embarrassment what to do. At last he resolved upon a most hazardous experiment, and embarked, without any one's knowledge, in a boat of twelve oars, to cross over to Brundisium, though the sea was at that time covered with a vast fleet of the enemies. He got on board in the night time, in the dress of a slave, and throwing himself down like a person of no consequence, lay along at the bottom of the vessel. The river Anius was to carry them down to sea, and there used to blow a gentle gale every morning from the land, which made it calm at the mouth of the river, by driving the waves forward; but this night there had blown a strong wind from the sea, which overpowered that from the land, so that where the river met the influx of the sea-water and the opposition of the waves, it was extremely rough and angry; and the current was beaten back with such a violent swell, that the master of the boat could not make good his passage, but ordered his sailors to tack about and return Cæsar, upon this, discovers himself, and taking the man by the hand, who was surprised to see him there, said, "Go on my friend, and fear nothing ; you carry Cæsar and his fortune in your boat." The mariners, when they heard that, forgot the storm, and laying all their strength to their oars, did what they could to force their way down the river. But when it was to no purpose, and the vessel now took in much water, Cæsar finding himself in such danger in the very mouth of the river, much against his will permitted the master to turn back. When he was come to land, his soldiers ran to him in a multitude, reproaching him for what he had done, and indignant that he should think himself not strong enough to get a victory by their sole assistance, but must disturb himself, and expose his life for those who were absent, as if he could not trust those who were with him.

After this, Antony came over with the forces from Brundisium, which encouraged Cæsar to give Pompey battle, though he was encamped very advantageously, and furnished with plenty of provisions both by sea and land, whilst he himself was at the beginning but ill-supplied, and before the end was extremely pinched for want of necessaries, so that his soldiers were forced to dig up a kind of root which grew there, and tempering it with milk, to feed on it. Sometimes they made a kind of bread of it, and advancing up to the enemy's outposts, would throw in these loaves, telling them, that as long as the earth produced such roots they would not give up blockading Pompey. But Pompey took what care he could, that neither the loaves nor the words should reach his men, who were out of heart and despondent, through terror at the fierceness and hardihood of their enemies, whom they looked upon as a sort of wild beasts. There were continual skirmishes about Pompey's outworks, in all which Cæsar had the better, except one, when his men were forced to fly in such a manner that he had like to have lost his camp. For Pompey made such a vigorous sally on them that not a man stood his ground ; the trenches were filled with the slaughter, many fell upon their own ramparts and bulwarks, whither they were driven in flight by the enemy. Cæsar met them, and would have turned them back, but could not. When he went to lay hold of the ensigns, those who carried them threw them down, so that the enemy took thirty-two of them. He himself narrowly escaped ; for taking hold of one of his soldiers, a big and strong man, that was flying by him, he bade him stand and face about ; but the fellow, full of apprehensions from the danger he was in, laid hold of his sword, as if he would strike Cæsar, but Cæsar's armor-bearer cut off his arm. Cæsar's affairs were so desperate at that time, that when Pompey, either through over-cautiousness, or his ill-fortune, did not give the finishing stroke to that great success but retreated after he had driven the routed enemy within their camp, Cæsar, upon seeing his withdrawal, said to his friends, "The victory to-day had been on the enemies' side, if they had had a general who knew how to gain it." When he was retired into his tent, he laid himself down to sleep but spent that night as miserable as ever he did any, in perplexity and consideration with himself, coming to the conclusion that he had conducted the war amiss. For when he had a fertile country before him, and all the wealthy cities of Macedonia and Thessaly, he had neglected to carry the war thither, and had sat down by the seaside, where his enemies had such a powerful fleet, so that he was in fact rather besieged by the want of necessaries, than besieging others with his arms. Being thus distracted in his thoughts with the view of the difficulty and distress he was in, he raised his camp, with the intention of advancing towards Scipio, who lay in Macedonia; hoping either to entice Pompey into a country where he should fight without the advantage he now had of supplies from the sea, or to overpower Scipio, if not assisted.

This set all Pompey's army and officers on fire to hasten and pursue Cæsar, whom they concluded to be beaten and flying. But Pompey was afraid to hazard a battle on which so much depended, and being himself provided with all necessaries for any length of time, thought to tire out and waste the vigor of Cæsar's army, which could not last long. For the best part of his men, though they had great experience and showed an irresistible courage in all engagements, yet by their frequent marches, changing their camps, attacking fortifications, and keeping long night-watches, were getting worn out and broken; they being now old, their bodies less fit for labor, and their courage, also, beginning to give way with the failure of their strength. Besides, it was said that an infectious disease, occasioned by their irregular diet, was prevailing in Cæsar's army, and what was of greatest moment, he was neither furnished with money nor provisions so that in a little time he must needs fall of himself.

For these reasons Pompey had no mind to fight him, but was thanked for it by none but Cato, who rejoiced at the prospect of sparing his fellow-citizens. For he, when he saw the dead bodies of those who had fallen in the last battle on

Cæsar's side, to the number of a thousand, turned away, covered his face, and shed tears. But every one else upbraided Pompey for being reluctant to fight, and tried to goad him on by such nicknames as Agamemnon, and king of kings, as if he were in no hurry to lay down his sovereign authority, but was pleased to see so many commanders attending on him, and paying their attendance at his tent. Favonius, who affected Cato's free way of speaking his mind, complained bitterly that they should eat no figs even this year at Tusculum, because of Pompey's love of command. Afranius, who was lately returned out of Spain, and on account of his ill success there, labored under the suspicion of having been bribed to betray the army, asked why they did not fight this purchaser of provinces. Pompey was driven, against his own will, by this kind of language, into offering battle, and proceeded to follow Cæsar. Cæsar had found great difficulties in his march, for no country would supply him with provisions, his reputation being very much fallen since his late defeat. But after he took Gomphi, a town of Thessaly, he not only found provisions for his army, but physic too. For there they met with plenty of wine, which they took very freely, and heated with this, sporting and revelling on their march in bacchanalian fashion, they shook off the disease, and their whole constitution was relieved and changed into another habit.

When the two armies were come into Pharsalia, and both encamped there, Pompey's thoughts ran the same way as they had done before, against fighting, and the more because of some unlucky presages, and a vision he had in a dream. But those who were about him were so confident of success, that Domitius, and Spinther, and Scipio, as if they had already conquered, quarrelled which should succeed Cæsar in the pontificate. And many sent to Rome to take houses fit to accommodate consuls and prætors, as being sure of entering upon those offices, as soon as the battle was over. The cavalry especially were obstinate for fighting, being splendidly armed and bravely mounted, and valuing themselves upon the fine horses they kept, and upon their own handsome persons; as also upon the advantage of their numbers, for they were five thousand against one thousand of Cæsar's. Nor were the numbers of the infantry less disproportionate, there being forty-five thousand of Pompey's against twenty two thousand of the enemy.

Cæsar, collecting his soldiers together, told them that

Corfinius was coming up to them with two legions, and that fifteen cohorts more under Calenus were posted at Megara and Athens; he then asked them whether they would stay till these joined them, or would hazard the battle by themselves. They all cried out to him not to wait, but on the contrary to do whatever he could to bring about an engagement as soon as possible. When he sacrificed to the gods for the lustration of his army, upon the death of the first victim, the augur told him, within three days he should come to a decisive action. Cæsar asked him whether he saw any thing in the entrails which promised a happy event. "That," said the priest, "you can best answer yourself; for the gods signify a great alteration from the present posture of affairs. If, therefore, you think yourself well off now, expect worse fortune; if unhappy, hope for better." The night before the battle, as he walked the rounds about midnight, there was a light seen in the heavens, very bright and flaming, which seemed to pass over Cæsar's camp, and fall into Pompey's. And when Cæsar's soldiers came to relieve the watch in the morning, they perceived a panic disorder among the enemies. However, he did not expect to fight that day, but set about raising his camp with the intention of marching towards Scotussa.

But when the tents were now taken down, his scouts rode up to him, and told him the enemy would give him battle. With this news was he was extremely pleased, and having performed his devotions to the gods, set his army in battle array, dividing them into three bodies. Over the middlemost he placed Domitius Calvinus; Antony commanded the left wing, and he himself the right, being resolved to fight at the head of the tenth legion. But when he saw the enemies' cavalry taking position against him, being struck with their fine appearance and their number, he gave private orders that six cohorts from the rear of the army should come round and join him, whom he posted behind the right wing, and instructed them what they should do, when the enemy's horse came to charge. On the other side, Pompey commanded the right wing, Domitius the left, and Scipio, Pompey's father-in-law, the centre. The whole weight of the cavalry was collected on the left wing, with the intent that they should outflank the right wing of the enemy, and rout that part where the general himself commanded. For they thought no phalanx of infantry could be solid enough to sustain such a shock, but that they must necessarily be broken and shattered all to pieces upon the onset of so immense a force of cavalry When they were ready on both sides to give the signal for battle, Pompey commanded his foot, who were in the front, to stand their ground, and without breaking their order, receive, quietly, the enemy's first attack, till they came within javelin's cast. Cæsar, in this respect, also, blames Pompey's generalship, as if he had not been aware how the first encounter, when made with an impetus and upon the run, gives weight and force to the strokes, and fires the men's spirits into a flame, which the general concurrence fans to full heat. He himself was just putting the troops into motion and advancing to the action, when he found one of his captains, a trusty and experienced soldier, encouraging his men to exert their utmost. Cæsar called him by his name, and said, "What hopes, Caius Crassinius, and what grounds for encouragement?" Crassinius stretched out his hand, and cried in a loud voice, "We shall conquer nobly, Cæsar; and I this day will deserve your praises, either alive or dead." So he said, and was the first man to run in upon the enemy, followed by the hundred and twenty soldiers about him, and breaking through the first rank, still pressed on forwards with much slaughter of the enemy, till at last he was struck back by the wound of a sword, which went in at his mouth with such force that it came out at his neck behind.

Whilst the foot was thus sharply engaged in the main battle, on the flank Pompey's horse rode up confidently, and opened their ranks very wide, that they might surround the right wing of Cæsar. But before they engaged, Cæsar's cohorts rushed out and attacked them, and did not dart their javelins at a distance, nor strike at the thighs and legs, as they usually did in close battle, but aimed at their faces. For thus Cæsar had instructed them, in hopes that young gentlemen, who had not known much of battles and wounds, but came wearing their hair long, in the flower of their age and height of their beauty, would be more apprehensive of such blows, and not care for hazarding both a danger at present and a blemish for the future. And so it proved, for they were so far from bearing the stroke of the javelins, that they could not stand the sight of them, but turned about, and covered their faces to secure them. Once in disorder, presently they turned about to fly; and so most shamefully ruined all. For those who had beat them back, at once outflanked the infantry, and falling on their rear, cut them to pieces. Pompey, who commanded the other wing of the army, when he saw his cavalry thus broken and flying, was no longer himself, nor did he now remember that he was Pompey the Great, but like one whom some god had deprived of his senses, retired to his tent without speaking a word, and there sat to expect the event, till the whole army was routed, and the enemy appeared upon the works which were thrown up before the camp, where they closely engaged with his men, who were posted there to defend it. Then first he seemed to have recovered his senses, and uttering, it is said, only these words, "What, into the camp too?" he laid aside his general's habit, and putting on such clothes as might best favor his flight, stole off. What fortune he met with afterwards, how he took shelter in Egypt, and was murdered there, we tell you in his Life.

Cæsar, when he came to view Pompey's camp, and saw some of his opponents dead upon the ground, others dying, said, with a groan, "This they would have; they brought me to this necessity. I, Caius Cæsar, after succeeding in so many wars, had been condemned, had I dismissed my army.' These words, Pollio says, Cæsar spoke in Latin at that time, and that he himself wrote them in Greek; adding, that those who were killed at the taking of the camp, were most of them servants; and that not above six thousand soldiers fell. Cæsar incorporated most of the foot whom he took prisoners, with his own legions, and gave a free pardon to many of the distinguished persons, and amongst the rest, to Brutus, who afterwards killed him. He did not immediately appear after the battle was over, which put Cæsar, it is said, into great anxiety for him; nor was his pleasure less when he saw him present himself alive.

There were many prodigies that foreshowed this victory, but the most remarkable that we are told of, was that at Tralles. In the temple of Victory stood Cæsar's statue. The ground on which it stood was naturally hard and solid, and the stone with which it was paved still harder; yet it is said that a palm-tree shot itself up near the pedestal of this statue In the city of Padua, one Caius Cornelius, who had the character of a good augur, the fellow-citizen and acquaintance of Livy, the historian, happened to be making some augural observations that very day when the battle was fought. And first, as Livy tells us, he pointed out the time of the fight, and said to those who were by him, that just then the battle was begun, and the men engaged. When he looked a second time, and observed the omens, he leaped up as if he had been inspired, and cried out, "Cæsar, you are victorious." This much surprised the standers by, but he took the garland which he had on from his head, and swore he would never wear it again till the event should give authority to his art. This Livy positively states for a truth.

Cæsar, as a memorial of his victory, gave the Thessalians their freedom, and then went in pursuit of Pompey. When he was come into Asia, to gratify Theopompus, the author of the collection of fables, he enfranchised the Cnidians, and remitted one-third of their tribute to all the people of the province of Asia. When he came to Alexandria, where Pompey was already murdered, he would not look upon Theodotus, who presented him with his head, but taking only his signet, shed tears. Those of Pompey's friends who had been arrested by the king of Egypt, as they were wandering in those parts, he relieved, and offered them his own friendship. In his letter to his friends at Rome, he told them that the greatest and most signal pleasure his victory had given him, was to be able continually to save the lives of fellow-citizens who had fought against him. As to the war in Egypt, some say it was at once dangerous and dishonorable, and noways necessary, but occasioned only by his passion for Cleopatra. Others blame the ministers of the king, and especially the eunuch Pothinus, who was the chief favorite, and had lately killed Pompey, who had banished Cleopatra, and was now secretly plotting Cæsar's destruction (to prevent which, Cæsar from that time began to sit up whole nights, under pretence of drinking, for the security of his person), while openly he was intolerable in his affronts to Cæsar, both by his words and actions. For when Cæsar's soldiers had musty and unwholesome corn measured out to them, Pothinus told them they must be content with it, since they were fed at another's cost. He ordered that his table should be served with wooden and earthen dishes, and said Cæsar had carried off all the gold and silver plate, under pretence of arrears of debt. For the present king's father owed Cæsar one thousand seven hundred and fifty myriads of money. Cæsar had formerly remitted to his children the rest, but thought fit to demand the thousand myriads at that time, to maintain his army. Pothinus told him that he had better go now and attend to his other affairs of greater consequence, and that he should receive his money at another time with thanks. Cæsar replied that he did not want Egyptians to be his counsellors, and soon after privately sent for Cleopatra from her retirement.

She took a small boat, and one only of her confidants, Apollodorus, the Sicilian, along with her, and in the dusk of the evening landed near the palace. She was at a loss how to get in undiscovered, till she thought of putting herself into the coverlet of a bed and lying at length, whilst Apollodorus tied up the bedding and carried it on his back through the gates to Cæsar's apartment. Cæsar was first captivated by this proof of Cleopatra's bold wit, and was afterwards so overcome by the charm of her society, that he made a reconciliation between her and her brother, on condition that she should rule as his colleague in the kingdom. A festival was kept to celebrate this reconciliation, where Cæsar's barber, a busy listening fellow, whose excessive timidity made him inquisitive into every thing, discovered that there was a plot carrying on against Cæsar by Achillas, general of the king's forces, and Pothinus, the eunuch. Cæsar, upon the first intelligence of it, set a guard upon the hall where the feast was kept, and killed Pothinus. Achillas escaped to the army, and raised a troublesome and embarrassing war against Cæsar, which it was not easy for him to manage with his few soldiers against so powerful a city and so large an army. The first difficulty he met with was want of water, for the enemies had turned the canals. Another was, when the enemy endeavored to cut off his communication by sea, he was forced to divert that danger by setting fire to his own ships, which after burning the docks, thence spread on and destroyed the great library. A third was, when in an engagement near Pharos, he leaped from the mole into a small boat, to assist his soldiers who were in danger, and when the Egyptians pressed him on every side, he threw himself into the sea, and with much difficulty swam off. This was the time when, according to the story, he had a number of manuscripts in his hand, which, though he was continually darted at, and forced to keep his head often under water, yet he did not let go, but held them up safe from wetting in one hand, whilst he swam with the other. His boat, in the mean time, was quickly sunk. At last, the king having gone off to Achillas and his party, Cæsar engaged and conquered them. Many fell in that battle, and the king himself was never seen after. Upon this, he left Cleopatra queen of Egypt, who soon after had a son by him, whom the Alexandrians called Cæsarion, and then departed for Syria.

Thence he passed to Asia, where he heard that Domitius was beaten by Pharnaces, son of Mithridates, and had fled out of Pontus with a handful of men ; and that Pharnaces pursued the victory so eagerly, that though he was already master of Bithynia and Cappadocia, he had a further design of attempting the Lesser Armenia, and was inviting all the kings and tetrarchs there to rise. Cæsar immediately marched against him with three legions, fought him near Zela, drove him out of Pontus, and totally defeated his army. When he gave Amantius, a friend of his at Rome, an account of this action, to express the promptness and rapidity of it, he used three words, I came, saw, and conquered, which in Latin, having all the same cadence, carry with them a very suitable air of brevity.

Hence he crossed into Italy, and came to Rome at the end of that year, for which he had been a second time chosen dictator, though that office had never before lasted a whole year, and was elected consul for the next. He was ill spoken of, because upon a mutiny of some soldiers, who killed Cosconius and Galba, who had been prætors, he gave them only the slight reprimand of calling them *Citizens* instead of *Fellow-Soldiers*, and afterwards assigned to each man a thousand drachmas, besides a share of lands in Italy. He was also reflected on for Dolabella's extravagance, Amantius's covetousness, Antony's debauchery, and Corfinius's profuseness, who pulled down Pompey's house, and rebuilt it, as not magnificent enough ; for the Romans were much displeased with all these. But Cæsar, for the prosecution of his own scheme of government, though he knew their characters and disapproved them, was forced to make use of those who would serve him.

After the battle of Pharsalia, Cato and Scipio fled into Africa, and there, with the assistance of king Juba, got together a considerable force, which Cæsar resolved to engage He, accordingly, passed into Sicily about the winter solstice, and to remove from his officers' minds all hopes of delay there, encamped by the sea-shore, and as soon as ever he had a fair wind, put to sea with three thousand foot and a few horse. When he had landed them, he went back secretly, under some apprehensions for the larger part of his army, but met them upon the sea, and brought them all to the same camp. There he was informed that the enemies relied much upon an ancient oracle, that the family of the Scipios should be always victorious in Africa. There was in his army a man, otherwise mean and contemptible, but of the house of the Africani, and his name Scipio Sallutio. This man Cæsar (whether in rallery to ridicule Scipio, who commanded the enemy, or seriously to bring over the omen to his side, it were hard to say), put at the head of his troops, as if he were general, in all the frequent battles which he was compelled to fight. For he was in such want both of victualling for his men, and forage for his horses, that he was forced to feed the horses with sea-weed, which he washed thoroughly to take off its saltness, and mixed with a little grass, to give it a more agreeable taste. The Numidians, in great numbers, and well horsed, whenever he went, came up and commanded the country. Cæsar's cavalry being one day unemployed, diverted themselves with seeing an African, who entertained them with dancing and at the same time played upon the pipe to admiration. They were so taken with this, that they alighted, and gave their horses to some boys, when on a sudden the enemy surrounded them, killed some, pursued the rest, and fell in with them into their camp; and had not Cæsar himself and Asinius Pollio come to their assistance, and put a stop to their flight, the war had been then at an end. In another engagement, also, the enemy had again the better, when Cæsar, it is said, seized a standard-bearer, who was running away, by the neck, and forcing him to face about, said, "Look, that is the way to the enemy."

Scipio, flushed with this success at first, had a mind to come to one decisive action. He therefore left Afranius and Juba in two distinct bodies not far distant, and marched himself towards Thapsus, where he proceeded to build a fortified camp above a lake, to serve as a centre-point for their operations, and also as a place of refuge. Whilst Scipio was thus employed, Cæsar with incredible despatch made his way through thick woods, and a country supposed to be impassable, cut off one part of the enemy, and attacked another in the front. Having routed these, he followed up his opportunity and the current of his good fortune, and on the first onset carried Afranius's camp, and ravaged that of the Numidians, Juba, their king, being glad to save himself by flight; so that in a small part of a single day he made himself master of three camps, and killed fifty thousand of the enemy, with the loss only of fifty of his own men. This is the account some give of that fight. Others say, he was not in the action, but that he was taken with his usual distemper just as he was setting his army in order. He perceived the approaches of it, and before it had too far disordered his senses, when he was already beginning to shake under its influence, withdrew into a neighboring fort where he reposed himself. Of the men of consular and prætorian dignity that were taken after the fight several Cæsar put to death, others anticipated him by killing themselves.

Cato had undertaken to defend Utica, and for that reason was not in the battle. The desire which Cæsar had to take him alive, made him hasten thither ; and upon the intelligence that he had despatched himself, he was much discomposed, for what reason is not so well agreed. He certainly said, " Cato, I must grudge you your death, as you grudged me the honor of saving your life." Yet the discourse he wrote against Cato after his death, is no great sign of his kindness, or that he was inclined to be reconciled to him. For how is it probable that he would have been tender of his life, when he was so bitter against his memory? But from his clemency to Cicero, Brutus, and many others who fought against him, it may be divined that Cæsar's book was not written so much out of animosity to Cato, as in his own vindication. Cicero had written an encomium upon Cato, and called it by his name. A composition by so great a master upon so excellent a subject, was sure to be in every one's hands. This touched Cæsar, who looked upon a panegyric on his enemies, as no better than an invective against himself ; and therefore he made in his Anti-Cato, a collection of whatever could be said in his derogation. The two compositions, like Cato and Cæsar themselves, have each of them their several admirers.

Cæsar, upon his return to Rome, did not omit to pronounce before the people a magnificent account of his victory, telling them that he had subdued a country which would supply the public every year with two hundred thousand attic bushels of corn, and three million pounds weight of oil. He then led three triumphs for Egypt, Pontus, and Africa, the last for the victory over, not Scipio, but king Juba, as it was professed, whose little son was then carried in the triumph, the happiest captive that ever was, who of a barbarian Numidian, came by this means to obtain a place among the most learned historians of Greece. After the triumphs, he distributed rewards to his soldiers, and treated the people with feasting and shows. He entertained the whole people together at one feast, where twenty-two thousand dining couches were laid out ; and he made a display of gladiators, and of battles by sea, in nonor, as he said, of his daughter Julia, though she had been long since dead. When these shows were over, an account was taken of the people, who, from three hundred and twenty thousand, were now reduced to one hundred and fifty thousand. So great a waste had the civil war made in Rome alone, not to mention what the other parts of Italy and the provinces suffered.

He was now chosen a fourth time consul, and went into Spain against Pompey's sons. They were but young, yet had gathered together a very numerous army and showed they had courage and conduct to command it, so that Cæsar was in extreme danger. The great battle was near the town of Munda, in which Cæsar, seeing his men hard pressed, and making but a weak resistance, ran through the ranks among the soldiers, and crying out, asked them whether they were not ashamed to deliver him into the hands of boys? At last, with great difficulty, and the best efforts he could make, he forced back the enemy, killing thirty thousand of them, though with the loss of one thousand of his best men. When he came back from the fight, he told his friends that he had often fought for victory, but this was the first time he had ever fought for life. This battle was won on the feast of Bacchus, the very day in which Pompey, four years before, had set out for the war. The younger of Pompey's sons escaped; but Didius, some days after the fight, brought the head of the elder to Cæsar. This was the last war he was engaged in. The triumph which he celebrated for this victory displeased the Romans beyond any thing. For he had not defeated foreign generals, or barbarian kings, but had destroyed the children and family of one of the greatest men of Rome, though unfortunate; and it did not look well to lead a procession in celebration of the calamities of his country, and to rejoice in those things for which no other apology could be made either to gods or men, than their being absolutely necessary. Besides that, hitherto he had never sent letters or messengers to announce any victory over his fellow-citizens, but had seemed rather to be ashamed of the action, than to expect honor from it.

Nevertheless his countrymen, conceding all to his fortune, and accepting the bit, in the hope that the government of a single person would give them time to breathe after so many civil wars and calamities, made him dictator for life. This was indeed a tyranny avowed, since his power now was not only absolute but perpetual too Cicero made the first proposals to the senate for conferring honors upon him, which might in some sort be said not to exceed the limits of ordinary human moderation. But others, striving which should deserve most, carried them so excessively high, that they made Cæsar odious to the most indifferent and moderate sort of men, by the pretensions and extravagance of the titles which they decreed him. His enemies, too, are thought to have had some share in this, as well as his flatterers. It gave them advantage against him, and would be their justification for any attempt they should make upon him; for since the civil wars were ended, he had nothing else that he could be charged with. And they had good reason to decree a temple to Clemency, in token of their thanks for the mild use he made of his victory. For he not only pardoned many of those who fought against him, but, further, to some gave honors and offices; as particularly to Brutus and Cassius, who both of them were prætors. Pompey's images that were thrown down, he set up again, upon which Cicero also said that by raising Pompey's statues he had fixed his own. When his friends advised him to have a guard, and several offered their services, he would not hear of it; but said it was better to suffer death once, than always to live in fear of it. He looked upon the affections of the people to be the best and surest guard, and entertained them again with public feasting, and general distributions of corn; and to gratify his army, he sent out colonies to several places, of which the most remarkable were Carthage and Corinth; which as before they had been ruined at the same time, so now were restored and repeopled together.

As for the men of high rank, he promised to some of them future consulships and prætorships, some he consoled with other offices and honors, and to all held out hopes of favor by the solicitude he showed to rule with the general good-will, insomuch that upon the death of Maximus one day before his consulship was ended, he made Caninius Revilius consul for that day. And when many went to pay the usual compliments and attentions to the new consul, "Let us make haste," said Cicero, "lest the man be gone out of his office before we come."

Cæsar was born to do great things, and had a passion after honor, and the many noble exploits he had done did not now serve as an inducement to him to sit still and reap the fruit of his past labors, but were incentives and encouragements to go on, and raised in him ideas of still greater actions, and a desire of new glory, as if the present were all spent. It was in fact a sort of emulous struggle with himself, as it had been with another, how he might outdo his past actions by his future. In pursuit of these thoughts, he resolved to make war upon the Parthians, and when he had subdued them, to pass through Hyrcania; thence to march along by the Caspian Sea to Mount Caucasus, and so on about Pontus, till he came into Scythia; then to overrun all the countries bordering upon Germany, and Germany itself; and so to return through Gaul into Italy, after completing the whole circle of his intended empire, and bounding it on every side by the ocean. While preparations were making for this expedition, he proposed to dig through the isthmus on which Corinth stands; and appointed Anienus to superintend the work. He had also a design of diverting the Tiber, and carrying it by a deep channel directly from Rome to Circeii, and so into the sea near Tarracina, that there might be a safe and easy passage for all merchants who traded to Rome. Besides this, he intended to drain all the marshes by Pomentium and Setia, and gain ground enough from the water to employ many thousands of men in tillage. He proposed further to make great mounds on the shore nearest Rome, to hinder the sea from breaking in upon the land, to clear the coast at Ostia of all the hidden rocks and shoals that made it unsafe for shipping, and to form ports and harbors fit to receive the large number of vessels that would frequent them.

These things were designed without being carried into effect; but his reformation of the calendar in order to rectify the irregularity of time, was not only projected with great scientific ingenuity, but was brought to its completion, and proved of very great use. For it was not only in ancient times that the Romans had wanted a certain rule to make the revolutions of their months fall in with the course of the year, so that their festivals and solemn days for sacrifice were removed by little and little, till at last they came to be kept at seasons quite the contrary to what was at first intended, but even at this time the people had no way of computing the solar year; only the priests could say the time, and they, at their pleasure, without giving any notice, slipped in the intercalary month, which they called Mercedonius. Numa was the first who put in this month, but his expedient was but a poor one and quite inadequate to correct all the errors that arose in the returns of the annual cycles, as we have shown in his life. Cæsar called in the best philosophers and mathematicians of his time to settle the point, and out of the systems he had before him, formed a new and more exact method of correcting the calendar, which the Romans use to this day, and seem to succeed better than any nation in avoiding the errors occasioned by the inequality of the cycles. Yet even this gave offence to those who looked with an evil eye on his position, and felt oppressed by his power. Cicero the orator, when some one in his company chanced to say, the next morning Lyra would rise, replied, "Yes, in accordance with the edict," as if even this were a matter of compulsion

But that which brought upon him the most apparent and mortal hatred, was his desire of being king; which gave the common people the first occasion to quarrel with him, and proved the most specious pretence to those who had been his secret enemies all along. Those who would have procured him that title gave it out, that it was foretold in the Sybils' books that the Romans should conquer the Parthians when they fought against them under the conduct of a king, but not before. And one day, as Cæsar was coming down from Alba to Rome, some were so bold as to salute him by the name of king; but he, finding the people disrelish it, seemed to resent it himself, and said his name was Cæsar, not king. Upon this, there was a general silence, and he passed on looking not very well pleased or contented. Another time, when the senate had conferred on him some extravagant honors, he chanced to receive the message as he was sitting on the rostra, where, though the consuls and prætors themselves waited on him, attended by the whole body of the senate, he did not rise, but behaved himself to them as if they had been private men, and told them his honors wanted rather to be retrenched than increased. This treatment offended not only the senate, but the commonalty too, as if they thought the affront upon the senate equally reflected upon the whole republic; so that all who could decently leave him went off, looking much discomposed. Cæsar, perceiving the false step he had made, immediately retired home; and laying his throat bare, told his friends that he was ready to offer this to any one who would give the stroke. But afterwards he made the malady from which he suffered, the excuse for his sitting, saying that those who are attacked by it, lose their presence of mind, if they talk much standing; that they presently grow giddy, fall into convulsions, and quite lose their reason. But this was not the reality, for he would willingly have stood up to the senate, had not Cornelius Balbus, one of his friends, or rather flatterers, hindered him. "Will you not remember," said he, "you are Cæsar, and claim the honor which is due to your merit?"

He gave a fresh occasion of resentment by his affront to the tribunes. The Lupercalia were then celebrated, a feast at the first institution belonging, as some writers say, to the shepherds, and having some connection with the Arcadian Lycæa. Many young noblemen and magistrates run up and down the city with their upper garments off, striking all they meet with thongs of hide, by way of sport; and many women, even of the highest rank, place themselves in the way, and hold out their hands to the lash, as boys in a school do to the master, out of a belief that it procures an easy labor to those who are with child, and makes those conceive who are barren. Cæsar, dressed in a triumphal robe, seated himself in a gold en chair at the rostra, to view this ceremony. Antony, as consul, was one of those who ran this course, and when he came into the forum, and the people made way for him, he went up and reached to Cæsar a diadem wreathed with laurel. Upon this, there was a shout, but only a slight one, made by the few who were planted there for that purpose; but when Cæsar refused it, there was universal applause. Upon the second offer, very few, and upon the second refusal, all again applauded. Cæsar finding it would not take, rose up, and ordered the crown to be carried into the capitol. Cæsar's statues were afterwards found with royal diadems on their heads. Flavius and Marullus, two tribunes of the people, went presently and pulled them off, and having apprehended those who first saluted Cæsar as king committed them to prison. The people followed them with acclamations, and called them by the name of Brutus, because Brutus was the first who ended the succession of kings, and transferred the power which before was lodged in one man into the hands of the senate and people. Cæsar so far resented this, that he displaced Marullus and Flavius; and in urging his charges against them, at the same time ridiculed the people, by himself giving the men more than once the names of Bruti and Cumæi.

This made the multitude turn their thoughts to Marcus Brutus, who by his father's side, was thought to be descended from that first Brutus, and by his mother's side from the Servilii, another noble family, being besides nephew and son-in-law to Cato. But the honors and favors he had received from Cæsar took off the edge from the desires he might himself have felt for overthrowing the new monarchy. For he had not only been pardoned himself after Pompey's defeat at Pharsalia, and had procured the same grace for many of his friends, but was one in whom Cæsar had a particular confidence. He had at that time the most honorable prætorship for the year, and was named for the consulship four years after, being preferred before Cassius, his competitor. Upon the question as to the choice, Cæsar, it is related, said that Cassius had the fairer pretensions, but that he could not pass by Brutus. Nor would he afterwards listen to some who spoke against Brutus, when the conspiracy against him was already afoot, but laying his hand on his body, said to the informers, "Brutus will wait for this skin of mine," intimating that he was worthy to bear rule on account of his virtue, but would not be base and ungrateful to gain it. Those who desired a change, and looked on him as the only, or at least the most proper, person to effect it, did not venture to speak with him; but in the night-time laid papers about his chair of state, where he used to sit and determine causes, with such sentences in them as, "You are asleep, Brutus," "You are no longer Brutus." Cassius, when he perceived his ambition a little raised upon this, was more instant than before to work him yet further, having himself a private grudge against Cæsar for some reasons that we have mentioned in the Life of Brutus. Nor was Cæsar without suspicions of him, and said once to his friends, "What do you think Cassius is aiming at? I don't like him, he looks so pale." And when it was told him that Antony and Dolabella were in a plot against him, he said he did not fear such fat, luxurious men, but rather the pale, lean fellows, meaning Cassius and Brutus.

Fate, however, is to all appearance more unavoidable than unexpected. For many strange prodigies and apparitions are said to have been observed shortly before this event. As to the lights in the heavens, the noises heard in the night, and the wild birds which perched in the forum, these are not perhaps worth taking notice of in so great a case as this. Strabo, the philosopher, tells us that a number of men were seen, looking as if they were heated through with fire, contending with each other; that a quantity of flame issued from the hand of a soldier's servant, so that they who saw it thought he must be burnt, but that after all he had no hurt. As Cæsar was sacrificing, the victim's heart was missing, a very bad omen, because no living creature can subsist without a heart. One finds it also related by many, that a soothsayer bade him prepare for some great danger on the ides of March. When this day was come, Cæsar, as he went to the senate, met this soothsayer, and said to him by way of raillery, "The ides of

March are come," who answered him calmly, "Yes, they are come, but they are not past." The day before his assassination he supped with Marcus Lepidus ; and as he was signing some letters according to his custom, as he reclined at table, there arose a question what sort of death was the best. At which he immediately, before any one could speak, said, 'A sudden one."

After this, as he was in bed with his wife, all the doors and windows of the house flew open together ; he was startled at the noise, and the light which broke into the room, and sat up in his bed, where by the moonshine he perceived Calpurnia fast asleep, but heard her utter in her dream some indistinct words and inarticulate groans. She fancied at that time she was weeping over Cæsar, and holding him butchered in her arms. Others say this was not her dream, but that she dreamed that a pinnacle, which the senate, as Livy relates, had ordered to be raised on Cæsar's house by way of ornament and grandeur, was tumbling down, which was the occasion of her tears and ejaculations. When it was day, she begged of Cæsar, if it were possible, not to stir out, but to adjourn the senate to another time ; and if he slighted her dreams, that she would be pleased to consult his fate by sacrifices, and other kinds of divination. Nor was he himself without some suspicion and fears ; for he never before discovered any womanish superstition in Calpurnia, whom he now saw in such great alarm. Upon the report which the priests made to him, that they had killed several sacrifices, and still found them inauspicious, he resolved to send Antony to dismiss the senate.

In this juncture, Decimus Brutus, surnamed Albinus, one whom Cæsar had such confidence in that he made him his second heir, who nevertheless was engaged in the conspiracy with the other Brutus and Cassius, fearing lest if Cæsar should put off the senate to another day, the business might get wind, spoke scoffingly and in mockery of the diviners, and blamed Cæsar for giving the senate so fair an occasion of saying he had put a slight upon them, for that they were met upon his summons, and were ready to vote unanimously that he should be declared king of all the provinces out of Italy, and might wear a diadem in any other place but Italy, by sea or land. If any one should be sent to tell them they might break up for the present, and meet again when Calpurnia should chance to have better dreams, what would his enemies say ? Or who would with any patience hear his friends, if they should presume to defend his government as not arbitrary and tyrannical?

But if he was possessed so far as to think this day unfortunate, yet it were more decent to go himself to the senate, and to adjourn it in his own person. Brutus, as he spoke these words, took Cæsar by the hand, and conducted him forth. He was not gone far from the door, when a servant of some other person's made towards him, but not being able to come up to him, on account of the crowd of those who pressed about him, he made his way into the house, and committed himself to Calpurnia, begging of her to secure him till Cæsar returned, because he had matters of great importance to communicate to him.

Artemidorus, a Cnidian, a teacher of Greek logic, and by that means so far acquainted with Brutus and his friends as to have got into the secret, brought Cæsar in a small written memorial, the heads of what he had to depose. He had observed that Cæsar, as he received any papers, presently gave them to the servants who attended on him; and therefore came as near to him as he could, and said, "Read this, Cæsar, alone, and quickly, for it contains matter of great importance which nearly concerns you." Cæsar received it, and tried several times to read it, but was still hindered by the crowd of those who came to speak to him. However, he kept it in his hand by itself till he came into the senate. Some say it was another who gave Cæsar this note, and that Artemidorus could not get to him, being all along kept off by the crowd.

All these things might happen by chance. But the place which was destined for the scene of this murder, in which the senate met that day, was the same in which Pompey's statue stood, and was one of the edifices which Pompey had raised and dedicated with his theatre to the use of the public, plainly showing that there was something of a supernatural influence which guided the action and ordered it to that particular place. Cassius, just before the act, is said to have looked towards Pompey's statue, and silently implored his assistance, though he had been inclined to the doctrines of Epicurus. But this occasion, and the instant danger, carried him away out of all his reasonings, and filled him for the time with a sort of inspiration. As for Antony, who was firm to Cæsar, and a strong man, Brutus Albinus kept him outside the house, and delayed him with a long conversation contrived on purpose. When Cæsar entered, the senate stood up to show their respect to him, and of Brutus's confederates, some came about his chair and stood behind it, others met him, pretending to add their petitions to those of Tillius Cimber, in behalf of his brother, who was in exile; and they followed him with their joint applications till he came to his seat. When he was sat down, he refused to comply with their requests, and upon their urging him further began to reproach them severally for their importunities, when Tillius, laying hold of his robe with both his hands, pulled it down from his neck, which was the signal for the assault. Casca gave him the first cut in the neck, which was not mortal nor dangerous, as coming from one who at the beginning of such a bold action was probably very much disturbed; Cæsar immediately turned about, and laid his hand upon the dagger and kept hold of it. And both of them at the same time cried out, he that received the blow, in Latin, "Vile Casca, what does this mean?" and he that gave it, in Greek, to his brother, "Brother, help!" Upon this first onset, those who were not privy to the design were astonished, and their horror and amazement at what they saw were so great, that they durst not fly nor assist Cæsar, nor so much as speak a word. But those who came prepared for the business inclosed him on every side, with their naked daggers in their hands. Which way soever he turned, he met with blows, and saw their swords levelled at his face and eyes, and was encompassed, like a wild beast in the toils, on every side. For it had been agreed they should each of them make a thrust at him, and flesh themselves with his blood; for which reason Brutus also gave him one stab in the groin. Some say that he fought and resisted all the rest, shifting his body to avoid the blows, and calling out for help, but that when he saw Brutus's sword drawn, he covered his face with his robe and submitted, letting himself fall, whether it were by chance, or that he was pushed in that direction by his murderers, at the foot of the pedestal on which Pompey's statue stood, and which was thus wetted with his blood. So that Pompey himself seemed to have presided, as it were, over the revenge done upon his adversary, who lay here at his feet, and breathed out his soul through his multitude of wounds, for they say he received three and twenty. And the conspirators themselves were many of them wounded by each other, whilst they all levelled their blows at the same person.

When Cæsar was dispatched, Brutus stood forth to give a reason for what they had done, but the senate would not hear him, but flew out of doors in all haste, and filled the people with so much alarm and distraction, that some shut up their houses, others left their counters and shops. All ran one way or the other, some to the place to see the sad spectacle others back again after they had seen it. Antony and Lepidus, Cæsar's most faithful friends, got off privately, and hid themselves in some friends' houses. Brutus and his followers, being yet hot from the deed, marched in a body from the senate-house to the capitol with their drawn swords, not like persons who thought of escaping, but with an a.r of confidence and assurance, and as they went along, called to the people to resume their liberty, and invited the company of any more distinguished people whom they met. And some of these joined the procession and went up along with them, as if they also had been of the conspiracy, and could claim a share in the honor of what had been done. As, for example, Caius Octavius and Lentulus Spinther, who suffered afterwards for their vanity, being taken off by Antony and the young Cæsar, and lost the honor they desired, as well as their lives, which it cost them, since no one believed they had any share in the action. For neither did those who punished them profess to revenge the fact, but the ill-will. The day after, Brutus with the rest came down from the capitol, and made a speech to the people, who listened without expressing either any pleasure or resentment, but showed by their silence that they pitied Cæsar, and respected Brutus. The senate passed acts of oblivion for what was past, and took measures to reconcile all parties. They ordered that Cæsar should be worshipped as a divinity, and nothing, even of the slightest consequence, should be revoked, which he had enacted during his government. At the same time they gave Brutus and his followers the command of provinces, and other considerable posts. So that all people now thought things were well settled, and brought to the happiest adjustment.

But when Cæsar's will was opened, and it was found that he had left a considerable legacy to each one of the Roman citizens, and when his body was seen carried through the market-place all mangled with wounds, the multitude could no longer contain themselves within the bounds or tranquillity and order, but heaped together a pile of benches, bars and tables, which they placed the corpse on, and setting fire to it, burnt it on them. Then they took brands from the pile and ran some to fire the houses of the conspirators, others up and down the city, to find out the men and tear them to pieces, but met, however, with none of them, they having taken effectual care to secure themselves.

One Cinna, a friend of Cæsar's, chanced the night before to have an odd dream. He fancied that Cæsar invited him to supper, and that upon his refusal to go with him, Cæsar took him by the hand and forced him, though he hung back. Upon hearing the report that Cæsar's body was burning in the market-place, he got up and went thither, out of respect to his memory, though his dream gave him some ill apprehensions, and though he was suffering from a fever. One of the crowd who saw him there asked another who that was, and having learned his name, told it to his next neighbor. It presently passed for a certainty that he was one of Cæsar's murderers, as, indeed, there was another Cinna, a conspirator, and they, taking this to be the man, immediately seized him, and tore him limb from limb upon the spot.

Brutus and Cassius, frightened at this, within a few days retired out of the city. What they afterwards did and suffered, and how they died, is written in the Life of Brutus. Cæsar died in his fifty-sixth year, not having survived Pompey above four years. That empire and power which he had pursued through the whole course of his life with so much hazard, he did at last with much difficulty compass, but reaped no other fruits from it than the empty name and invidious glory. But the great genius which attended him through his lifetime, even after his death remained as the avenger of his murder, pursuing through every sea and land all those who were concerned in it, and suffering none to escape, but reaching all who in any sort or kind were either actually engaged in the fact, or by their counsels any way promoted it.

The most remarkable of mere human coincidences was that which befell Cassius, who, when he was defeated at Philippi, killed himself with the same dagger which he had made use of against Cæsar. The most signal preternatural appearances were the great comet, which shone very bright for seven nights after Cæsar's death, and then disappeared, and the dimness of the sun, whose orb continued pale and dull for the whole of that year, never showing its ordinary radiance at its rising, and giving but a weak and feeble heat. The air consequently was damp and gross, for want of stronger rays to open and rarify it. The fruits, for that reason, never properly ripened, and began to wither and fall off for want of heat before they were fully formed. But above all, the phantom which appeared to Brutus showed the murder was not pleasing to the gods. The story of it is this.

Brutus, being to pass his army from Abydos to the continent on the other side, aid himself down one night, as he used to do, in his tent, and was not asleep, but thinking of his affairs, and what events he might expect. For he is related to have been the least inclined to sleep of all men who have commanded armies, and to have had the greatest natural capacity for continuing awake, and employing himself without need of rest. He thought he heard a noise at the door of his tent, and looking that way, by the light of his lamp, which was almost out, saw a terrible figure, like that of a man, but of unusual stature and severe countenance. He was somewhat frightened at first, but seeing it neither did nor spoke any thing to him, only stood silently by his bed-side, he asked who it was. The spectre answered him, "Thy evil genius, Brutus, thou shalt see me at Philippi." Brutus answered courageously, "Well, I shall see you," and immediately the appearance vanished. When the time was come, he drew up his army near Philippi against Antony and Cæsar, and in the first battle won the day, routed the enemy, and plundered Cæsar's camp. The night before the second battle, the same phantom appeared to him again, but spoke not a word. He presently understood his destiny was at hand, and exposed himself to all the danger of the battle. Yet he did not die in the fight, but seeing his men defeated, got up to the top of a rock, and there presenting his sword to his naked breast, and assisted, as they say, by a friend, who helped him to give the thrust, met his death.

PHOCION.

Demades, the orator, when in the height of the power which he obtained at Athens by advising the state in the interest of Antipater and the Macedonians, being necessitated to write and speak many things below the dignity, and contrary to the character, of the city, was wont to excuse himself by saying he steered only the shipwrecks of the commonwealth. This hardy saying of his might have some appearance of truth, if applied to Phocion's government. For Demades, indeed, was himself the mere wreck of his country, living and ruling so dissolutely, that Antipater took occasion to say of him, when he was now grown old, that he was like a sacrificed beast, all consumed except the tongue and the belly. But Phocion's was a real virtue, only overmatched in the unequal contest with an adverse time and rendered, by the ill fortunes of Greece, inglorious and obscure. We must not indeed, allow ourselves to concur with Sophocles in so far diminishing the force of virtue as to say that

> When fortune fails, the sense we had before
> Deserts us also, and is our's no more.

Yet thus much indeed, must be allowed to happen in the conflicts between good men and ill fortune, that instead of due returns of honor and gratitude, obloquy and unjust surmises may often prevail, to weaken, in a considerable degree, the credit of their virtue.

It is commonly said that public bodies are most insulting and contumelious to a good man, when they are puffed up with prosperity and success. But the contrary often happens; afflictions and public calamities naturally imbittering and souring the minds and tempers of men, and disposing them to such peevishness and irritability that hardly any word or sentiment of common vigor can be addressed to them, but they will be apt to take offence. He that remonstrates with them on their errors, is presumed to be insulting over their misfortunes, and any free spoken expostulation is construed into contempt. Honey itself is searching in sore and ulcerated parts; and the wisest and most judicious counsels prove provoking to distempered minds, unless offered with those soothing and compliant approaches which made the poet, for instance, characterize agreeable things in general, by a word expressive of a grateful and easy touch, exciting nothing of offence or resistance. Inflamed eyes require a retreat into dusky places, amongst colors of the deepest shades, and are unable to endure the brilliancy of light. So fares it in the body politic, in times of distress and humiliation; a certain sensitiveness and soreness of humor prevail, with a weak incapacity of enduring any free and open advice, even when the necessity of affairs most requires such plain dealing, and when the consequences of any single error may be beyond retrieving. At such times the conduct of public affairs is on all hands most hazardous. Those who humor the people are swallowed up in the common ruin; those who endeavor to lead them aright, perish the first in their attempt.

Astronomers tell us, the sun's motion is neither exactly parallel with that of the heavens in general, nor yet directly and diametrically opposite, but describing an oblique line, with insensible declination he steers his course in such a gentle, easy curve, as to dispense his light and influence, in his annual revolution, at several seasons, in just proportions to the whole creation. So it happens in political affairs; it the motions of rulers be constantly opposite and cross to the tempers and inclinations of the people, they will be resented as arbitrary and harsh; as, on the other side, too much deference, or encouragement, as too often it has been, to popular faults and errors, is full of danger and ruinous consequences. But where concession is the response to willing obedience, and a statesman gratifies his people, that he may the more imperatively recall them to a sense of the common interest, then, indeed, human beings, who are ready enough to serve well and submit to much, if they are not always ordered about and roughly handled, like slaves, may be said to be guided and governed upon the method that leads to safety. Though it must be confessed it is a nice point, and extremely difficult, so to temper this lenity as to preserve the authority of the government. But if such a blessed mixture and temperament may be obtained, it seems to be of all concords and harmonies the most concordant and most harmonious. For thus we are taught even God governs the world, not by irresistible force, but persuasive argument and reason, controlling it into compliance with his eternal purposes.

Cato the younger is a similar instance. His manners were little agreeable or acceptable to the people, and he received very slender marks of their favor; witness his repulse when he sued for the consulship, which he lost, as Cicero says, for acting rather like a citizen in Plato's commonwealth, than among the dregs of Romulus's posterity, the same thing happening to him, in my opinion, as we observe in fruits ripe before their season, which we rather take pleasure in looking at and admiring, than actually use; so much was his old-fashioned virtue out of the present mode, among the depraved customs which time and luxury had introduced, that it appeared, indeed, remarkable and wonderful, but was too great and too good to suit the present exigencies, being so out of all proportion to the times. Yet his circumstances were not altogether like Phocion's, who came to the helm when the ship of the state was just upon sinking. Cato's time was, indeed, stormy and tempestuous, yet so as he was able to assist in managing the sails, and lend his helping hand to those who, which he was not allowed to do, commanded at the helm. Others were to blame for the result; yet his courage and virtue made it in spite of all a hard task for fortune to ruin the commonwealth, and it was only with long time and effort and by slow degrees, when he himself had all but succeeded in averting it, that the catastrophe was at last effected.

Phocion and he may be well compared together, not for any mere general resemblances, as though we should say both were good men and great statesmen. For assuredly, there is difference enough among virtues of the same denomination, as between the bravery of Alcibiades and that of Epaminondas, the prudence of Themistocles and that of Aristides, the justice of Numa and that of Agesilaus. But these men's virtue, even looking to the most minute points of difference, bear the same color, stamp and character impressed upon them, so as not to be distinguishable. The mixture is still made in the same exact proportions whether we look at the combination to be found in them, both of lenity on the one hand, with austerity on the other; their boldness upon some occasions, and caution on others; their extreme solicitude for the public, and perfect neglect of themselves; their fixed and immovable bent to all virtuous and honest actions, accompanied with an extreme tenderness and scrupulosity as to doing any thing which might appear mean or unworthy; so that we should need a very nice and subtle logic of discrimination to detect and establish the distinctions between them.

As to Cato's extraction, it is confessed by all to have been illustrious, as will be said hereafter, nor was Phocion's, I feel assured, obscure or ignoble. For had he been the son of a turner, as Idomeneus reports, it had certainly not been forgotten to his disparagement by Glaucippus, the son of Hyperides, when heaping up a thousand spiteful things to say against him. Nor, indeed, had it been possible for him, in such circumstances, to have had such a liberal breeding and education in his youth, as to be first Plato's and afterwards Xenocrates's scholar in the Academy, and to have devoted himself from the first to the pursuit of the noblest studies and practices. His countenance was so composed, that scarcely was he ever seen by any Athenian either laughing, or in tears. He was rarely known, so Duris has recorded, to appear in the public baths, or was observed with his hand exposed outside his cloak, when he wore one. Abroad, and in the camp, he was so hardy in going always thin clad and barefoot, except in a time of excessive and intolerable cold, that the soldiers used to say in merriment, that it was like to be a hard winter when Phocion wore his coat.

Although he was most gentle and humane in his disposition, his aspect was stern and forbidding, so that he was seldom accosted alone by any who were not intimate with him. When Chares once made some remark on his frowning looks, and the Athenians laughed at the jest, "My sullenness," said Phocion, "never yet made any of you sad, but these men's jollities have given you sorrow enough." In like manner Phocion's language, also, was full of instruction, abounding in happy maxims and wise thoughts, but admitted no embellishment to its austere and commanding brevity. Zeno said a philosopher should never speak till his words had been steeped in meaning; and such, it may be said, were Phocion's, crowding the greatest amount of significance into the smallest allowance of space. And to this, probably, Polyeuctus, the Sphettian, referred, when he said that Demosthenes was, indeed, the best orator of his time, but Phocion the most powerful speaker. His oratory, like small coin of great value, was to be estimated, not by its bulk, but its intrinsic worth. He was once observed, it is said, when the theatre was filling with the audience, to walk musing alone behind the scenes, which one of his friends taking notice of said, "Phocion, you seem to be thoughtful." "Yes," replied he, "I am considering how I may shorten what I am going to say to the Athenians." Even Demosthenes himself, who used to despise the rest of the haranguers, when Phocion stood up, was wont to say quietly to those about him, "Here is the pruning-knife of my periods." This, however, might refer, perhaps, not so much to his eloquence, as to the influence of his character, since not only a word, but even a nod from a person who is esteemed, is of more force than a thousand arguments or studied sentences from others.

In his youth he followed Chabrias, the general, from whom he gained many lessons in military knowledge, and in return did something to correct his unequal and capricious humor. For whereas at other times Chabrias was heavy and phlegmatic, in the heat of battle he used to be so fired and transported, that he threw himself headlong into danger beyond the forwardest, which indeed, in the end, cost him his life in the island of Chios, he having pressed his own ship foremost to force a landing. But Phocion, being a man of temper as well as courage, had the dexterity at some times to rouse the general, when in his procrastinating mood, to action, and at others to moderate and cool the impetuousness of his unseasonable fury. Upon which account Chabrias, who was a good-natured, kindly-tempered man, loved him much, and procured him commands and opportunities for action, giving himself means to make himself known in Greece, and using his assistance in all his affairs o moment. Particularly the sea-fight of Naxos added not a little to Phocion's reputation, when he had the left squadron committed to him by Chabrias, as in this quarter the battle was sharply contested, and was decided by a speedy victory And this being the first prosperous sea-battle the city had engaged in with its own force since 'ts captivity Chabrias won great popularity by it, and Phocion, also, got the reputation of a good commander. The victory was gained at the time of the Great Mysteries, and Chabrias used to keep the commemoration of it by distributing wine among the Athenians, yearly, on the sixteenth day of Boëdromion.

After this, Chabrias sent Phocion to demand their quota of the charges of the war from the islanders, and offered him a guard of twenty ships. Phocion told him, if he intended him to go against them as enemies, that force was insignificant; if as to friends and allies, one vessel was sufficient. So he took his own single galley, and having visited the cities, and treated with the magistrates in an equitable and open manner, he brought back a number of ships, sent by the confederates to Athens, to convey the supplies. Neither did his friendship and attention close with Chabrias's life, but after his decease he carefully maintained it to all that were related to him, and chiefly to his son, Ctesippus, whom he labored to bring to some good, and although he was a stupid and intractable young fellow, always endeavored, so far as in him lay, to correct and cover his faults and follies. Once, however, when the youngster was very impertinent and troublesome to him in the camp, interrupting him with idle questions, and putting forward his opinions and suggestions of how the war should be conducted, he could not forbear exclaiming, "O Chabrias, Chabrias, how grateful I show myself for your friendship, in submitting to endure your son."

Upon looking into public matters, and the way in which they were now conducted, he observed that the administration of affairs was cut and parcelled out, like so much land by allotment, between the military men and the public speakers, so that neither these nor those should interfere with the claims of the others. As the one were to address the assemblies, to draw up votes and prepare motions, men, for example, like Eubulus, Aristophon, Demosthenes, Lycurgus, and Hyperides, and were to push their interests here; so, in the meantime, Diopithes, Menestheus, Leosthenes, and Chares, were to make their profit by war and in military commands

Phocion, on the other hand, was desirous to restore and carry out the old system, more complete in itself, and more harmonious and uniform, which prevailed in the times of Pericles, Aristides, and Solon; when statesmen showed themselves, to use Archilochus's words,—

> Mars' and the Muses' friends alike designed,
> To arts and arms indifferently inclined,

and the presiding goddess of his country was, he did not fail to see, the patroness and protectress of both civil and military wisdom. With these views, while his advice at home was always for peace and quietness, he nevertheless held the office of general more frequently than any of the statesmen, not only of his own times, but of those preceding, never, indeed, promoting or encouraging military expeditions, yet never, on the other hand, shunning or declining, when he was called upon by the public voice. Thus much is well known, that he was no less than forty-five several times chosen general, he being never on any one of those occasions present at the election, but having the command, in his absence, by common suffrage, conferred on him, and he sent for on purpose to undertake it. Insomuch that it amazed those who did not well consider, to see the people always prefer Phocion, who was so far from humoring them or courting their favor, that he always thwarted and opposed them. But so it was, as great men and princes are said to call in their flatterers when dinner has been served, so the Athenians, upon slight occasions, entertained and diverted themselves with their spruce speakers and trim orators, but when it came to action, they were sober and considerate enough to single out the austerest and wisest for public employment, however much he might be opposed to their wishes and sentiments. This, indeed, he made no scruple to admit, when the oracle from Delphi was read, which informed them that the Athenians were all of one mind, a single dissentient only excepted, frankly coming forward and declaring that they need look no further; he was the man; there was no one but he who was dissatisfied with everything they did. And when once he gave his opinion to the people, and was met with the general approbation and applause of the assembly, turning to some of his friends, he asked them, "Have I inadvertently said something foolish?"

Upon occasion of a public festivity, being solicited for his contribution by the example of others, and the people pressing him much he bade them apply themselves to the wealthy for his part he should blush to make a present here, rather than a repayment *there*, turning and pointing to Callicles, the money-lender. Being still clamored upon and importuned, he told them this tale. A certain cowardly fellow setting out for the wars, hearing the ravens croak in his passage, threw down his arms, resolving to wait. Presently he took them and ventured out again, but hearing the same music, once more made a stop. "For," said he, "you may croak till you are tired, but you shall make no dinner upon me."

The Athenians urging him at an unseasonable time to lead them out against the enemy, he peremptorily refused, and being upbraided by them with cowardice and pusillanimity, he told them, "Just now, do what you will, I shall not be brave; and do what I will, you will not be cowards. Nevertheless, we know well enough what we are." And when again, in a time of great danger, the people were very harsh upon him, demanding a strict account how the public money had been employed, and the like, he bade them, "First, good friends, make sure you are safe." After a war, during which they had been very tractable and timorous, when, upon peace being made, they began again to be confident and overbearing, and to cry out upon Phocion, as having lost them the honor of victory, to all their clamor he made only this answer, "My friends, you are fortunate in having a leader who knows you; otherwise, you had long since been undone."

Having a controversy with the Bœotians about boundaries, which he counselled them to decide by negotiation, they inclined to blows. "You had better," said he, "carry on the contest with the weapons in which you excel (your tongues), and not by war, in which you are inferior." Once, when he was addressing them, and they would not hear him or let him go on, said he, "You may compel me to act against my wishes, but you shall never force me to speak against my judgment." Among the many public speakers who opposed him, Demosthenes, for example, once told him, "The Athenians, Phocion, will kill you some day when they once are in a rage." "And you," said he, "if they once are in their senses." Polyeuctus, the Sphettian, once on a hot day was urging war with Philip, and being a corpulent man, and out of breath and in a great heat with speaking, took numerous draughts of water as he went on. "Here, indeed," said Phocion, "is a fit man to lead us into a war! What think you he will do when he is carrying his corslet and his shield to meet the enemy, if even here, delivering a prepared speech to you has almost killed him with exhaustion?" When Lycurgus in the assembly made many reflections on his past conduct, upbraiding him above all for having advised them to deliver up the ten citizens whom Alexander had demanded, he replied that he had been the author of much safe and wholesome counsel, which had not been followed.

There was a man called Archibiades, nick-named the Lacedæmonian, who used to go about with a huge, overgrown beard, wearing an old threadbare cloak, and affecting a very stern countenance. Phocion once, when attacked in council by the rest, appealed to this man for his support and testimony. And when he got up and began to speak on the popular side, putting his hand to his beard, "O Archibiades," said he, "it is time you should shave." Aristogiton, a common accuser, was a terrible man of war within the assembly, always inflaming the people to battle, but when the muster-roll came to be produced, he appeared limping on a crutch, with a bandage on his leg; Phocion descried him afar off, coming in, and cried out to the clerk, "Put down Aristogiton, too, as lame and worthless."

So that it is a little wonderful, how a man so severe and harsh upon all occasions should, notwithstanding, obtain the name of the Good. Yet, though difficult, it is not, I suppose, impossible for men's tempers, any more than for wines, to be at the same time harsh and agreeable to the taste; just as on the other hand many that are sweet at the first taste, are found, on further use, extremely disagreeable and unwholesome. Hyperides, we are told, once said to the people, "Do not ask yourselves, men of Athens, whether or not I am bitter, but whether or not I am paid for being so," as though a covetous purpose were the only thing that should make a harsh temper insupportable, and as if men might not even more justly render themselves obnoxious to popular dislike and censure, by using their power and influence in the indulgence of their own private passions of pride and jealousy, anger and animosity. Phocion never allowed himself from any feeling of personal hostility to do hurt to any fellow-citizen, nor, indeed, reputed any man his enemy, except so far as he could not but contend sharply with such as opposed the measures he urged for the public good; in which argument he was, indeed, a rude, obstinate, and uncompromising adversary. For his general conversation, it was easy, courteous, and obliging to all, to that point that he would befriend his very opponents in their distress, and espouse the cause of those who differed most from him, when they needed his patronage. His friends reproaching him for pleading in behalf of a man of indifferent character, he told them the innocent had no need of an advocate. Aristogiton, the sycophant, whom we mentioned before, having, after sentence passed upon him, sent earnestly to Phocion to speak with him in the prison, his friends dissuaded him from going; "Nay, by your favor," said he, "where should I rather choose to pay Aristogiton a visit?"

As for the allies of the Athenians, and the islanders, whenever any admiral besides Phocion was sent, they treated him as an enemy suspect, barricaded their gates, blocked up their havens, brought in from the country their cattle, slaves, wives, and children, and put them in garrison; but upon Phocion's arrival, they went out to welcome him in their private boats and barges, with streamers and garlands, and received him at landing with every demonstration of joy and pleasure.

When king Philip was effecting his entry into Eubœa, and was bringing over troops from Macedonia, and making himself master of the cities, by means of the tyrants who ruled in them, Plutarch of Eretria sent to request aid of the Athenians for the relief of the island, which was in imminent danger of falling wholly into the hands of the Macedonians. Phocion was sent thither with a handful of men in comparison, in expectation that the Eubœans themselves would flock in and join him. But when he came, he found all things in confusion, the country all betrayed, the whole ground, as it were, undermined under his feet, by the secret pensioners of king Philip, so that he was in the greatest risk imaginable. To secure himself as far as he could, he seized a small rising ground, which was divided from the level plains about Tamynæ by a deep watercourse, and here he inclosed and fortified the choicest of his army. As for the idle talkers and disorderly bad citizens who ran off from his camp and made their way back, he bade his officers not regard them, since here they would have been not only useless and ungovernable themselves, but an actual hindrance to the rest; and further, being conscious to themselves of the neglect of their duty, they would be less ready to misrepresent the action, or raise a cry against them at their return home. When the enemy drew nigh, he bade his men stand to their arms, until he had finished the sacrifice, in which he spent a considerable time, either by some difficulty of the thing itself, or on purpose to invite the enemy nearer. Plutarch, interpreting this tardiness as a failure in his courage, fell on alone with the mercenaries, which the cavalry perceiving, could not be contained, but issuing also out of the camp, confusedly and in disorder, spurred up to the enemy. The first who came up were defeated, the rest were put to the rout. Plutarch himself took to flight, and a body of the enemy advanced in the hope of carrying the camp, supposing themselves to have secured the victory. But by this time, the sacrifice being over, the Athenians within the camp came forward and falling upon them put them to flight, and killed the greater number as they fled among the intrenchments, while Phocion, ordering his infantry to keep on the watch and rally those who came in from the previous flight, himself, with a body of his best men, engaged the enemy in a sharp and bloody fight, in which all of them behaved with signal courage and gallantry. Thallus, the son of Cineas, and Glaucus, of Polymedes, who fought near the general, gained the honors of the day. Cleophanes, also, did good service in the battle. Recovering the calvary from its defeat, and with his shouts and encouragement bringing them up to succor the general, who was in danger, he confirmed the victory obtained by the infantry. Phocion now expelled Plutarch from Eretria, and possessed himself of the very important fort of Zaretra, situated where the island is pinched in, as it were, by the seas on each side, and its breadth most reduced to a narrow girth. He released all the Greeks whom he took, out of fear of the public speakers at Athens, thinking they might very likely persuade the people in their anger into committing some act of cruelty.

This affair thus despatched and settled, Phocion set sail homewards, and the allies had soon as good reason to regret the loss of his just and humane dealing, as the Athenians that of his experience and courage. Molossus, the commander who took his place, had no better success than to fall alive into the enemy's hands.

Philip, full of great thoughts and designs, now advanced with all his forces into the Hellespont, to seize the Chersonesus and Perinthus, and after them, Byzantium. The Athenians raised a force to relieve them, but the popular leaders made it their business to prefer Chares to be general, who sailing thither, effected nothing worthy of the means placed in his hands. The cities were afraid, and would not receive his ships into their harbors, so that he did nothing but wander about, raising money from their friends, and despised by their enemies. And when the people, chafed by the orators, were extremely indignant, and repented having ever sent any help to the Byzantines, Phocion rose and told them they ought not to be angry with the allies for distrusting, but with their generals for being distrusted. "They make you suspected," he said, "even by those who cannot possibly subsist without your succor." The assembly being moved with this speech of his. changed their minds on the sudden, and commanded him immediately to raise another force, and go himself to assist their confederates in the Hellespont; an appointment which, in effect, contributed more than anything to the relief of Byzantium.

For Phocion's name was already honorably known; and an old acquaintance of his, who had been his fellow-student in the Academy, Leon, a man of high renown for virtue among the Byzantines, having vouched for Phocion to the city, they opened their gates to receive him, not permitting him, though he desired it, to encamp without the walls, but entertained him and all the Athenians with perfect reliance, while they, to requite their confidence, behaved among their new hosts soberly and inoffensively, and exerted themselves on all occasions with the greatest zeal and resolution for their defence. Thus king Philip was driven out of the Hellespont, and was despised to boot, whom, till now, it had been thought impossible to match, or even to oppose. Phocion also took some of his ships, and recaptured some of the places he had garrisoned, making besides several inroads into the country, which he plundered and overran, until he received a wound from some of the enemy who came to the defence, and, thereupon, sailed away home.

The Megarians at this time privately praying aid of the Athenians, Phocion, fearing lest the Bœotians should hear of it, and anticipate them, called an assembly at sunrise, and brought forward the petition of the Megarians, and immediately after the vote had been put, and carried in their favor, he sounded the trumpet, and led the Athenians straight from the assembly, to arm and put themselves in posture. The Megarians received them joyfully, and he proceeded to fortify Nisæa, and built two new long walls from the city to the arsenal, and so joined it to the sea, so that having now little reason to regard the enemies on the land side. it placed its dependence entirely on the Athenians.

When final hostilities with Philip were now certain, and in Phocion's absence other generals had been nominated, he, on his arrival from the islands. dealt earnestly with the Athenians, that since Philip showed peaceable inclinations towards them, and greatly apprehended the danger, they would consent to a treaty. Being contradicted in this by one of the ordinary frequenters of the courts of justice, a common accuser, who asked him if he durst presume to persuade the Athenians to peace, now their arms were in their hands, "Yes," said he, "though I know that if there be war, I shall be in office over you, and if peace, you over me." But when he could not prevail, and Demosthenes's opinion carried it, advising them to make war as far off from home as possible, and fight the battle out of Attica, "Good friends," said Phocion, "let us not ask where we shall fight, but how we may conquer in the war. That will be the way to keep it at a distance. If we are beaten, it will be quickly at our doors." After the defeat, when the clamorers and incendiaries in the town would have brought up Charidemus to the hustings, to be nominated to the command, the best of the citizens were in a panic, and supporting themselves with the aid of the council of the Areopagus, with entreaties and tears, hardly prevailed upon the people to have Phocion intrusted with the care of the city. He was of opinion, in general, that the fair terms to be expected from Philip should be accepted, yet after Demades had made a motion that the city should receive the common conditions of peace in concurrence with the rest of the states of Greece, he opposed it, till it were known what the particulars were which Philip demanded. He was overborne in this advice, under the pressure of the time, but almost immediately after the Athenians repented it, when they understood that by these articles they were obliged to furnish Philip both with horse and shipping. "It was the fear of this," said Phocion, "that occasioned my opposition. But since the thing is done, let us make the best of it, and not be discouraged. Our forefathers were sometimes in command, and sometimes under it; and by doing their duty, whether as rulers or as subjects, saved their own country and the rest of Greece."

Upon the news of Philip's death, he opposed himself to any public demonstrations of joy and jubilee, saying it would be ignoble to show malice upon such an occasion, and that the army that had fought them at Chæronea was only diminished by a single man.

When Demosthenes made his invectives against Alexander, now on his way to attack Thebes he repeated those verses of Homer —

"Unwise one, wherefore to a second stoke
His anger be foolhardy to provoke?'

and asked, "Why stimulate his already eager passion for glory? Why take pains to expose the city to the terrible conflagration now so near? We, who accepted office to save our fellow-citizens, will not, however they desire it, be consenting to their destruction."

After Thebes was lost, and Alexander had demanded Demosthenes, Lycurgus, Hyperides, and Charidemus to be delivered up, the whole assembly turning their eyes to him, and calling on him by name to deliver his opinion, at last he rose up, and showing them one of his most intimate friends, whom he loved and confided in above all others, told them, "You have brought things amongst you to that pass, that for my part, should he demand this my friend Nicocles, I would not refuse to give him up. For as for myself, to have it in my power to sacrifice my own life and fortune for the common safety, I should think the greatest of good fortune. Truly," he added, "it pierces my heart to see those who are fled hither for succor from the desolation of Thebes. Yet it is enough for Greece to have Thebes to deplore. It will be more for the interest of all that we should deprecate the conqueror's anger, and intercede for both, than run the hazard of another battle."

When this was decreed by the people, Alexander is said to have rejected their first address when it was presented, throwing it from him scornfully, and turning his back upon the deputation, who left him in affright. But the second, which was presented by Phocion, he received, understanding from the older Macedonians how much Philip had admired and esteemed him. And he not only gave him audience and listened to his memorial and petition, but also permitted him to advise him, which he did to this effect, that if his designs were for quietness, he should make peace at once; if glory were his aim, he should make war, not upon Greece, but on the barbarians. And with various counsels and suggestions happily designed to meet the genius and feelings of Alexander, he so won upon him, and softened his temper, that he bade the Athenians not forget their position, as if any thing went wrong with him, the supremacy belonged to them. And to Phocion himself, whom he adopted as his friend and guest, he showed a respect, and admitted him to distinctions, which few of those who were continually near his person ever received. Duris, at any rate, tells us, that when he became great, and had conquered Darius, in the heading of all his letters he left off the word *Greeting*, except in those he wrote to Phocion. To him, and to Antipater alone, he condescended to use it. This, also, is stated by Chares.

As for his munificence to him, it is well known he sent him a present at one time of one hundred talents; and this being brought to Athens, Phocion asked of the bearers, how it came to pass, that among all the Athenians, he alone should be the object of this bounty. And being told that Alexander esteemed him alone a person of honor and worth, "Let him, then," said he, "permit me to continue so and be still so reputed." Following him to his house, and observing his simple and plain way of living, his wife employed in kneading bread with her own hands, himself drawing water to wash his feet, they pressed him to accept it, with some indignation, being ashamed, as they said, that Alexander's friend should live so poorly and pitifully. So Phocion, pointing out to them a poor old fellow, in a dirty worn-out coat, passing by, asked them if they thought him in worse condition than this man. They bade him not mention such a comparison. "Yet," said Phocion, "he, with less to live upon than I, finds it sufficient, and in brief," he continued, "if I do not use this money, what good is there in my having it; and if I do use it, I shall procure an ill name, both for myself and for Alexander, among my countrymen." So the treasure went back again from Athens, to prove to Greece, by a signal example, that he who could afford to give so magnificent a present, was yet not so rich as he who could afford to refuse it. And when Alexander was displeased, and wrote back to him to say that he could not esteem those his friends, who would not be obliged by him, not even would this induce Phocion to accept the money, but he begged leave to intercede with him in behalf of Echecratides, the sophist, and Athenodorus, the Imbrian, as also for Demaratus and Sparton, two Rhodians, who had been arrested upon some charges, and were in custody at Sardis. This was instantly granted by Alexander, and they were set at liberty. Afterwards, when sending Craterus into Macedonia, he commanded him to make him an offer of four cities in Asia, Cius, Gergithus, Mylasa, and Elæa, any one of which, at his choice, should be delivered to him; insisting yet more positively with him, and declaring he should resent it, should he continue obstinate in his refusal. But Phocion was not to be prevailed with at all and, shortly after, Alexander died.

Phocion's house is shown to this day in Melita, ornamented with small plates of copper, but otherwise plain and homely. Concerning his wives, of the first of them there is little said, except that she was sister of Cephisodotus, the statuary. The other was a matron of no less reputation for her virtues and simple living among the Athenians, than Phocion was for his probity. It happened once when the people were entertained with a new tragedy, that the actor just as he was to enter the stage to perform the part of a queen, demanded to have a number of attendants sumptuously dressed, to follow in his train, and on their not being provided, was sullen and refused to act, keeping the audience waiting, till at last Melanthius, who had to furnish the chorus, pushed him on the stage, crying out, "What, don't you know that Phocion's wife is never attended by more than a single waiting woman, but you must needs be grand, and fill our women's head with vanity?" This speech of his, spoken loud enough to be heard, was received with great applause, and clapped all round the theatre. She herself, when once entertaining a visitor out of Ionia, who showed her all her rich ornaments, made of gold and set with jewels, her wreaths, necklaces, and the like, "For my part," said she, "all my ornament is my husband, Phocion, now for the twentieth year in office as general at Athens."

He had a son named Phocus, who wished to take part in the games at the great feast of Minerva. He permitted him so to do, in the contest of leaping, not with any view to the victory, but in the hope that the training and discipline for it would make him a better man, the youth being in a general way a lover of drinking, and ill-regulated in his habits. On his having succeeded in the sports, many were eager for the honor of his company at banquets in celebration of the victory. Phocion declined all these invitations but one, and when he came to this entertainment and saw the costly preparations, even the water brought to wash the guests' feet being mingled with wine and spices, he reprimanded his son, asking him why he would so far permit his friend to sully the honor of his victory. And in the hope of wholly weaning the young man from such habits and company, he sent him to Lacedæmon, and placed him among the youth, then under the course of the Spartan discipline. This the Athenians took offence at, as though he slighted and contemned the education at home; and Demades twitted him with it publicly "Suppose, Phocion, you and I advise the Athenians to adopt the Spartan constitution. If you like, I am ready to introduce a bill to that effect, and to speak in its favor.' "Indeed," said Phocion, "you, with that strong scent of perfumes about you, and with that mantle on your shoulders, are just the very man to speak in honor of Lycurgus, and recommend the Spartan table."

When Alexander wrote to demand a supply of galleys, and the public speakers objected to sending them, Phocion, on the council requesting his opinion, told them freely, 'Sirs, I would either have you victorious yourselves, or friends of those who are so." He took up Pytheas, who about this time first began to address the assembly, and already showed himself a confident, talking fellow, by saying that a young slave whom the people had but bought yesterday, ought to have the manners to hold his tongue. And when Harpalus, who had fled from Alexander out of Asia, carrying off a large sum of money, came to Attica, and there was a perfect race among the ordinary public men of the assembly who should be the first to take his pay, he distributed amongst these some trifling sums by way of a bait and provocative, but to Phocion he made an offer of no less than seven hundred talents and all manner of other advantages he pleased to demand; with the compliment that he would entirely commit himself and all his affairs to his disposal. Phocion answered sharply, Harpalus should repent of it, if he did not quickly leave off corrupting and debauching the city, which for the time silenced him, and checked his proceedings. But afterwards, when the Athenians were deliberating in council about him, he found those that had received money from him to be his greatest enemies, urging and aggravating matters against him, to prevent themselves being discovered, whereas Phocion, who had never touched his pay, now, so far as the public interest would admit of it, showed some regard to his particular security. This encouraged him once more to try his inclinations, and upon further survey finding that he himself was a fortress, inaccessible on every quarter to the approaches of corruption, he professed a particular friendship to Phocion's son-in-law, Charicles. And admitting him into his confidence in all his affairs, and continually requesting his assistance, he brought him under some suspicion. Upon the occasion, for example, of the death of Pythonice, who was Harpalus's mistress, for whom he had a great fondness, and had a child by her, he resolved to build her a sumptuous monument, and committed the care of it to his friend Charicles. This commission, disreputable enough in itself, was yet further disparaged by the figure the piece of workmanship made after it was finished. It is yet to be seen in the Hermeum, as you go from Athens to Eleusis, with nothing in its appearance answerable to the sum of thirty talents, with which Charicles is said to have charged Harpalus for its erection. After Harpalus's own decease, his daughter was educated by Phocion and Charicles with great care. But when Charicles was called to account for his dealings with Harpalus, and entreated his father-in-law's protection, begging that he would appear for him in the court, Phocion refused, telling him, "I did not choose you for my son-in-law for any but honorable purposes."

Asclepiades, the son of Hipparchus, brought the first tidings of Alexander's death to Athens, which Demades told them was not to be credited; for were it true, the whole world would ere this have stunk with the dead body. But Phocion, seeing the people eager for an instant revolution, did his best to quiet and repress them. And when numbers of them rushed up to the hustings to speak, and cried out that the news was true, and Alexander was dead, "If he is dead today," said he, "he will be so to-morrow and the day after to-morrow equally. So that there is no need to take counsel hastily or before it is safe."

When Leosthenes now had embarked the city in the Lamian war, greatly against Phocion's wishes, to raise a laugh against Phocion, he asked him scoffingly, what the State had been benefited by his having now so many years been general. "It is not a little," said Phocion, "that the citizens have been buried in their own sepulchres." And when Leosthenes continued to speak boldly and boastfully in the assembly, "Young man," he said, "your speeches are like cypress-trees, stately and tall, and no fruit to come of them." And when he was then attacked by Hyperides, who asked him when the time would come, that he would advise the Athenians to make war, "As soon," said he, "as I find the young men keep their ranks, the rich men contribute their money, and the orators leave off robbing the treasury." Afterwards, when many admired the forces raised, and the preparations for war that were made by Leosthenes, they asked Phocion how he approved of the new levies. "Very well," said he, "for the short course; but what I fear, is the long race. Since, however late the war may last, the city has neither money, ships, nor soldiers, but these." And the event justified his prognostics. At first all things appeared fair and promising Leos thenes gained great reputation by worsting the Bœotians in battle, and driving Antipater within the walls of Lamia, and the citizens were so transported with the first successes, that they kept solemn festivities for them, and offered public sacrifices to the gods. So that some, thinking Phocion must now be convinced of his error, asked him whether he would not willingly have been author of these successful actions. "Yes," said he, "most gladly, but also of the former counsel." And when one express after another came from the camp, confirming and magnifying the victories, "When," said he, "will the end of them come?"

Leosthenes, soon after, was killed, and now those who feared lest if Phocion obtained the command, he would put an end to the war, arranged with an obscure person in the assembly, who should stand up and profess himself to be a friend and old confidant of Phocion's, and persuade the people to spare him at this time, and reserve him (with whom none could compare) for a more pressing occasion, and now to give Antiphilus the command of the army. This pleased the generality, but Phocion made it appear he was so far from having any friendship with him of old standing, that he had not so much as the least familiarity with him; "Yet now, sir," says he, "give me leave to put you down among the number of my friends and well-wishers, as you have given a piece of advice so much to my advantage."

And when the people were eager to make an expedition against the Bœotians, he at first opposed it; and on his friends telling him the people would kill him for always running counter to them, "That will be unjust of them," he said, "if I give them honest advice, if not, it will be just of them." But when he found them persisting and shouting to him to lead them out, he commanded the crier to make proclamation, that all the Athenians under sixty should instantly provide themselves with five days' provision, and follow him from the assembly. This caused a great tumult. Those in years were startled, and clamored against the order; he demanded wherein he injured them, "For I," says he, "am now fourscore, and am ready to lead you." This succeeded in pacifying them for the present.

But when Micion, with a large force of Macedonians and mercenaries, began to pillage the sea-coast, having made a descent upon Rhamnus, and overrun the neighboring country, Phocion led out the Athenians to attack him. And when sundry private persons came, intermeddling with his dispositions, and telling him that he ought to occupy such or such a hill, detach the cavalry in this or that direction, engage the enemy on this point or that, "O Hercules," said he, "how many generals have we here, and how few soldiers!" Afterwards, having formed the battle, one who wished to show his bravery, advanced out of his post before the rest, but on the enemy's approaching, lost heart, and retired back into his rank. "Young man," said Phocion, "are you not ashamed twice in one day to desert your station, first that on which I had placed you, and secondly, that on which you had placed yourself?" However, he entirely routed the enemy, killing Micion and many more on the spot. The Grecian army, also, in Thessaly, after Leonnatus and the Macedonians who came with him out of Asia, had arrived and joined Antipater, fought and beat them in a battle. Leonnatus was killed in the fight, Antiphilus commanding the foot, and Menon, the Thessalian, the horse.

But not long after, Craterus crossed from Asia with numerous forces; a pitched battle was fought at Cranon; the Greeks were beaten; though not, indeed, in a signal defeat, nor with any great loss of men. But what with their want of obedience to their commanders, who were young and over-indulgent with them, and what with Antipater's tampering and treating with their separate cities, one by one, the end of it was that the army was dissolved, and the Greeks shamefully surrendered the liberty of their country.

Upon the news of Antipater's now advancing at once against Athens with all his force, Demosthenes and Hyperides deserted the city, and Demades, who was altogether insolvent for any part of the fines that had been laid upon him by the city, for he had been condemned no less than seven times for introducing bills contrary to the laws, and who had been disfranchised, and was no longer competent to vote in the assembly, laid hold of this season of impunity, to bring in a bill for sending ambassadors with plenipotentiary power to Antipater, to treat about a peace. But the people distrusted him and called upon Phocion to give his opinion, as the person they only and entirely confided in. He told them, "If my former counsels had been prevalent with you, we had not been reduced to deliberate on the question at all." However, the vote passed; and a decree was made, and he with others deputed to go to Antipater, who lay now encamped in the Theban territories, but intended to dislodge immediately, and pass into Attica. Phocion's first request was, that he would make the treaty without moving his camp. And when Craterus declared that it was not fair to ask them to be burdensome to the country of their friends and allies by their stay, when they might rather use that of their enemies for provisions and the support of their army, Antipater taking him by the hand, said, "We must grant this favor to Phocion." For the rest he bade them return to their principals, and acquaint them that he could only offer them the same terms, namely, to surrender at discretion, which Leosthenes had offered to him when he was shut up in Lamia.

When Phocion had returned to the city, and acquainted them with this answer, they made a virtue of necessity, and complied, since it would be no better. So Phocion returned to Thebes with the other ambassadors, and among the rest, Xenocrates, the philosopher, the reputation of whose virtue and wisdom was so great and famous everywhere, that they conceived there could not be any pride, cruelty, or anger arising in the heart of man, which would not at the mere sight of him be subdued into something of reverence and admiration. But the result, as it happened, was the very opposite, Antipater showed such a want of feeling, and such a dislike of goodness. He saluted every one else, but would not so much as notice Xenocrates. Xenocrates, they tell us, observed upon it, that Antipater, when meditating such cruelty to Athens, did well to be ashamed of seeing him. When he began to speak, he would not hear him, but broke in and rudely interrupted him, until at last he was obliged to be silent. But when Phocion had declared the purport of their embassy, he replied shortly, that he would make peace with the Athenians on these conditions, and no others; that Demosthenes and Hyperides should be delivered up to him; that they should retain their ancient form of government, the franchise being determined by a property qualification; that they should receive a garrison into Munychia, and pay a certain sum for the cost of the war. As things stood, these terms were judged tolerable by the rest of the ambassadors; Xenocrates only said, that if Antipater considered the Athenians slaves, he was treating them fairly; but if free, severely. Phocion pressed him only to spare them the garrison, and used many arguments and entreaties. Antipater replied, "Phocion, we are ready to do you any favor, which will not bring ruin both on ourselves and on you." Others report it differently; that Antipater asked Phocion, supposing he remitted the garrison to the Athenians, would he, Phocion, stand surety for the city's observing the terms and attempting no revolution? And when he hesitated, and did not at once reply Callimedon, the Carabus, a hot partisan and professed enemy of free states, cried out, "And if he should talk so idly, Antipater, will you be so much abused as to believe him and not carry out your own purpose?" So the Athenians received the garrison, and Menyllus for the governor, a fair-dealing man, and one of Phocion's acquaintance.

But the proceeding seemed sufficiently imperious and arbitrary, indeed rather a spiteful and insulting ostentation of power, than that the possession of the fortress would be of any great importance. The resentment felt upon it was heightened by the time it happened in, for the garrison was brought in on the twentieth of the month of Bœdromion, just at the time of the great festival, when they carry forth Iacchus with solemn pomp from the city to Eleusis; so that the solemnity being disturbed, many began to call to mind instances, both ancient and modern, of divine interventions and intimations. For in old time, upon the occasions of their happiest successes, the presence of the shapes and voices of the mystic ceremonies had been vouchsafed to them, striking terror and amazement into their enemies; but now, at the very season of their celebration, the gods themselves stood witnesses of the saddest oppressions of Greece, the most holy time being profaned, and their greatest jubilee made the unlucky date of their most extreme calamity. Not many years before, they had a warning from the oracle at Dodona, that they should carefully guard the summits of Diana, lest haply strangers should seize them. And about this very time, when they dyed the ribbons and garlands with which they adorn the couches and cars of the procession, instead of a purple, they received only a faint yellow color; and to make the omen yet greater, all the things that were dyed for common use, took the natural color. While a candidate for initiation was washing a young pig in the haven of Cantharus, a shark seized him, bit off all his lower parts up to the belly, and devoured them, by which the god gave them manifestly to understand, that having lost the lower town and sea-coast, they should keep only the upper city.

Menyllus was sufficient security that the garrison should behave itself inoffensively. But those who were now excluded from the franchise by poverty, amounted to more than twelve thousand; so that both those that remained in the city thought themselves oppressed and shamefully used, and those who on this account left their homes and went away into Thrace, where Antipater offered them a town and some territory to inhabit, regarded themselves only as a colony of slaves and exiles. And when to this was added the deaths of Demosthenes at Calauria, and of Hyperides at Cleonae, as we have elsewhere related, the citizens began to think with regret of Philip and Alexander, and almost to wish the return of those times. And as, after Antigonus was slain, when those that had taken him off were afflicting and oppressing the people, a countryman in Phrygia, digging in the fields, was asked what he was doing, "I am," said he, fetching a deep sigh, "searching for Antigonus;" so said many that remembered those days, and the contests they had with those kings, whose anger, however great, was yet generous and placable; whereas Antipater, with the counterfeit humility of appearing like a private man, in the meanness of his dress and his homely fare, merely belied his real love of that arbitrary power, which he exercised, as a cruel master and despot, to distress those under his command. Yet Phocion had interest with him to recall many from banishment by his intercession, and prevailed also for those who were driven out, that they might not, like others, be hurried beyond Tænarus, and the mountains of Ceraunia, but remain in Greece, and plant themselves in Peloponnesus, of which number was Agnonides, the sycophant. He was no less studious to manage the affairs within the city with equity and moderation, preferring constantly those that were men of worth and good education to the magistracies, and recommending the busy and turbulent talkers, to whom it was a mortal blow to be excluded from office and public debating, to learn to stay at home, and be content to till their land. And observing that Xenocrates paid his alien-tax as a foreigner, he offered him the freedom of the city, which he refused, saying he could not accept a franchise which he had been sent, as an ambassador, to deprecate.

Menyllus wished to give Phocion a considerable present of money, who, thanking him, said, neither was Menyllus greater than Alexander, nor his own occasions more urgent to receive it now, than when he refused it from him. And on his pressing him to permit his son Phocus to receive it, he replied, "If my son returns to a right mind, his patrimony is sufficient; if not, all supplies will be insufficient." But to Antipater he answered more sharply, who would have him engaged in something dishonorable. "Antipater," said he, "cannot have me both as his friend and his flatterer." And, indeed, Antipater was wont to say he had two friends at Athens, Phocion and Demades; the one would never suffer him to gratify him at all, the other would never be satisfied. Phocion might well think that poverty a virtue, in which, after having so often been general of the Athenians, and admitted to the friendship of potentates and princes, he had now grown old. Demades, meantime, delighted in lavishing his wealth even in positive transgressions of the law. For there having been an order that no foreigner should be hired to dance in any chorus on the penalty of a fine of one thousand drachmas on the exhibitor, he had the vanity to exhibit an entire chorus of a hundred foreigners, and paid down the penalty of a thousand drachmas a head upon the stage itself. Marrying his son Demeas, he told him with the like vanity, "My son, when I married your mother, it was done so privately it was not known to the next neighbors, but kings and princes give presents at your nuptials."

The garrison in Munychia continued to be felt as a great grievance, and the Athenians did not cease to be importunate upon Phocion, to prevail with Antipater for its removal; but whether he despaired of effecting it, or perhaps observed the people to be more orderly, and public matters more reasonably conducted by the awe that was thus created, he constantly declined the office, and contented himself with obtaining from Antipater the postponement for the present of the payment of the sum of money in which the city was fined. So the people, leaving him off, applied themselves to Demades, who readily undertook the employment, and took along with him his son also into Macedonia; and some superior power, as it seems, so ordering it, he came just at that nick of time when Antipater was already seized with his sickness, and Cassander, taking upon himself the command, had found a letter of Demades's, formerly written by him to Antigonus in Asia, recommending him to come and possess himself of the empire of Greece and Macedon, now hanging, he said (a scoff at Antipater), "by an old and rotten thread." So when Cassander saw him come, he seized him: and first brought out the son, and killed him so close before his face, that the blood ran all over his clothes and person, and then, after bitterly taunting and upbraiding him with his ingratitude and treachery, despatched him himself.

Antipater being dead, after nominating Polysperchon general-in-chief and Cassander commander of the cavalry, Cassander at once set up for nimself, and immediately despatched Nicanor to Menyllus, to succeed him in the command of the garrison, commanding him to possess himself of Munychia before the news of Antipater's death should be heard; which being done, and some days after the Athenians hearing the report of it, Phocion was taxed as privy to it before, and censured heavily for dissembling it, out of friendship for Nicanor. But he slighted their talk, and making it his duty to visit and confer continually with Nicanor, he succeeded in procuring his good-will and kindness for the Athenians, and induced him even to put himself to trouble and expense to seek popularity with them, by undertaking the office of presiding at the games.

In the mean time Polysperchon, who was intrusted with the charge of the king, to countermine Cassander, sent a letter to the city, declaring in the name of the king, that he restored them their democracy, and that the whole Athenian people were at liberty to conduct their commonwealth according to their ancient customs and constitutions. The object of these pretences was merely the overthrow of Phocion's influence, as the event manifested. For Polysperchon's design being to possess himself of the city, he despaired altogether of bringing it to pass, whilst Phocion retained his credit; and the most certain way to ruin him, would be again to fill the city with a crowd of disfranchised citizens, and let loose the tongues of the demagogues and common accusers.

With this prospect, the Athenians were all in excitement and Nicanor, wishing to confer with them on the subject, at a meeting of the Council in Piræus, came himself, trusting for the safety of his person to Phocion. And when Dercyllus, who commanded the guard there, made an attempt to seize him, upon notice of it beforehand, he made his escape, and there was little doubt he would now lose no time in righting himself upon the city for the affront; and when Phocion was found fault with for letting him get off and not securing him, he defended himself by saying that he had no mistrust of Nicanor, nor the least reason to expect any mischief from him, but should it prove otherwise, for his part he would have them all know, he would rather receive than do the wrong. And so far as he spoke for himself alone, the answer was honorable and high-minded enough, but he who hazards his country's safety, and that, too, when he is her magistrate and chief commander, can scarcely be acquitted, I fear, of transgressing a higher and more sacred obligation of justice, which he owed to his fellow-citizens. For it will not even do to say, that he dreaded the involving the city in war, by seizing Nicanor, and hoped by professions of confidence and just-dealing, to retain him in the observance of the like; but it was, indeed, his credulity and confidence in him, and an over-weening opinion of his sincerity, that imposed upon him. So that notwithstanding the sundry intimations he had of his making preparations to attack Piræus, sending soldiers over into Salamis, and tampering with, and endeavoring to corrupt various residents in Piræus, he would, notwithstanding all this evidence, never be persuaded to believe it. And even when Philomedes of Lampra had got a decree passed, that all the Athenians should stand to their arms, and be ready to follow Phocion their general, he yet sat still and did nothing, until Nicanor actually led his troops out from Munychia, and drew trenches about Piræus; upon which, when Phocion at last would have let out the Athenians, they cried out against him, and slighted his orders.

Alexander, the son of Polysperchon, was at hand with a considerable force, and professed to come to give them succor against Nicanor, but intended nothing less, if possible, than to surprise the city, whilst they were in tumult and divided among themselves. For all that had previously been expelled from the city, now coming back with him, made their way into it, and were joined by a mixed multitude of foreigners and disfranchised persons, and of these a motley and irregular public assembly came together, in which they presently divested Phocion of all power, and chose other generals; and if by chance Alexander had not been spied from the walls, alone in close conference with Nicanor, and had not this, which was often repeated, given the Athenians cause of suspicion, the city had not escaped the snare. The orator Agnonides, however, at once fell foul upon Phocion, and impeached him of treason; Callimedon and Charicles, fearing the worst, consulted their own security by flying from the city; Phocion, with a few of his friends that stayed with him, went over to Polysperchon, and out of respect for him, Solon of Platæa, and Dinarchus of Corinth, who were reputed friends and confidants of Polysperchon, accompanied him. But on account of Dinarchus falling ill, they remained several days in Elatea, during which time, upon the persuasion of Agnonides and on the motion of Archestratus, a decree passed that the people should send delegates thither to accuse Phocion. So both parties reached Polysperchon at the same time, who was going through the country with the king, and was then at a small village of Phocis, Pharygæ under the mountain now called Galate, but then Acrurium.

There Polysperchon, having set up the golden canopy, and seated the king and his company under it, ordered Dinarchus at once to be taken, and tortured, and put to death; and that done, gave audience to the Athenians, who filled the place with noise and tumult, accusing and recriminating on one another, till at last Agnonides came forward, and requested they might all be shut up together in one cage, and conveyed to Athens, there to decide the controversy. At that the king could not forbear smiling, but the company that attended, for their own amusement, Macedonians and strangers, were eager to hear the altercation, and made signs to the delegates to go on with their case at once. But it was no sort of fair hearing, Polysperchon frequently interrupted Phocion, till at last Phocion struck his staff on the ground, and declined to speak further. And when Hegemon said, Polysperchon himself could bear witness to his affection for the people, Polysperchon called out fiercely, "Give over slandering me to the king," and the king starting up was about to have run him through with his javelin, but Polysperchon interposed and hindered him; so that the assembly dissolved.

Phocion, then, and those about him, were seized; those of his friends that were not immediately by him, on seeing this, hid their faces, and saved themselves by flight. The rest Clitus took and brought to Athens, to be submitted to trial; but, in truth, as men already sentenced to die. The manner of conveying them was indeed extremely moving; they were carried in chariots through the Ceramicus, straight to the place of judicature, where Clitus secured them till they had convoked an assembly of the people, which was open to all comers, neither foreigners, nor slaves, nor those who had been punished with disfranchisement, being refused admittance, but all alike, both men and women, being allowed to come into the court, and even upon the place of speaking. So having read the king's letters, in which he declared he was satisfied himself that these men were traitors, however, they being a free city, he willingly accorded them the grace of trying and judging them according to their own laws, Clitus brought in his prisoners. Every respectable citizen, at the sight of Phocion, covered up his face, and stooped down to conceal his tears. And one of them had the courage to say, that since the king had committed so important a cause to the judgment of the people, it would be well that the strangers, and those of servile condition, should withdraw. But the populace would not endure it, crying out they were oligarchs, and enemies to the liberty of the people, and deserved to be stoned; after which no man durst offer any thing further in Phocion's behalf. He was himself with difficulty heard at all, when he put the question, "Do you wish to put us to death lawfully or unlawfully?" Some answered, "According to law." He replied, "How can you, except we have a fair hearing?" But when they were deaf to all he said, approaching nearer, "As to myself," said he, "I admit my guilt, and pronounce my public conduct to have deserved sentence of death. But why, O men of Athens, kill others who have offended in nothing?" The rabble cried out, they were his friends, that was enough. Phocion therefore drew back, and said no more.

Then Agnonides read the bill, in accordance with which the people should decide by show of hands whether they judged them guilty, and if so it should be found, the penalty should be death. When this had been read out, some desired it might be added to the sentence, that Phocion should be tortured also, and the rack should be produced with the executioners. But Agnonides perceiving even Clitus to dislike this, and himself thinking it horrid and barbarous, said, "When we catch that slave, Callimedon, men of Athens, we will put him to the rack, but I shall make no motion of the kind in Phocion's case." Upon which one of the better citizens remarked, he was quite right; "If he should torture Phocion, what could we do to you?" So the form of the bill was approved of, and the show of hands called for; upon which, not one man retaining his seat, but all rising up, and some with garlands on their heads, they condemned them all to death.

There were present with Phocion, Nicocles, Thudippus, Hegemon, and Pythocles. Demetrius the Phalerian, Callimedon, Charicles, and some others, were included in the condemnation, being absent.

After the assembly was dismissed, they were carried to the prison; the rest with cries and lamentations, their friends and relatives following and clinging about them, but Phocion looking (as men observed with astonishment at his calmness and magnanimity), just the same as when he had been used to return to his home attended, as general, from the assembly

His enemies ran along by his side, reviling and abusing him. And one of them coming up to him, spat in his face; at which Phocion, turning to the officers, only said, "You should stop this indecency." Thudippus, on their reaching the prison, when he observed the executioner tempering the poison and preparing it for them, gave away to his passion, and began to bemoan his condition and the hard measure he received, thus unjustly to suffer with Phocion. "You cannot be contented," said he, "to die with Phocion?" One of his friends that stood by, asked him if he wished to have any thing said to his son. "Yes, by all means," said he, "bid him bear no grudge against the Athenians." Then Nicocles, the dearest and most faithful of his friends, begged to be allowed to drink the poison first. "My friend," said he, "you ask what I am loath and sorrowful to give, but as I never yet in all my life was so thankless as to refuse you, I must gratify you in this also." After they had all drunk of it, the poison ran short; and the executioner refused to prepare more, except they would pay him twelve drachmas, to defray the cost of the quantity required. Some delay was made, and time spent, when Phocion called one of his friends, and observing that a man could not even die at Athens without paying for it, requested him to give the sum.

It was the nineteenth day of the month Munychion, on which it was the usage to have a solemn procession in the city, in honor of Jupiter. The horsemen, as they passed by, some of them threw away their garlands, others stopped, weeping, and casting sorrowful looks towards the prison doors, and all the citizens whose minds were not absolutely debauched by spite and passion, or who had any humanity left, acknowledged it to have been most impiously done, not, at least, to let that day pass, and the city so be kept pure from death and a public execution at the solemn festival. But as if this triumph had been insufficient, the .nance of Phocion's enemies went yet further; his dead body was excluded from burial within the boundaries of the country, and none of the Athenians could light a funeral pile to burn the corpse; neither durst any of his friends venture to concern themselves about it. A certain Conopion, a man who used to do these offices for hire, took the body and carried it beyond Eleusis, and procuring fire from over the frontier of Megara, burned it. Phocion's wife, with her servant-maids, being present and assisting at the solemnity, raised there an empty tomb, and performed the customary libations, and gathering up the bones in her lap, and bringing them home by night, aug a place for them by the fireside in her house, saying, "Blessed hearth, to your custody I commit the remains of a good and brave man, and, I beseech you, protect and restore them to the sepulchre of his fathers, when the Athenians return to their right minds.

And, indeed, a very little time and their own sad experience soon informed them what an excellent governor, and how great an example and guardians of justice and of temperance they had bereft themselves of. And now they decreed him a statue of brass, and his bones to be buried honorably at the public charge; and for his accusers, Agnonides they took themselves, and caused him to be put to death. Epicurus and Demophilus, who fled from the city for fear, his son met with, and took his revenge upon them. This son of his, we are told, was in general of an indifferent character, and once when enamored of a slave girl kept by a common harlot merchant, happened to hear Theodorus, the atheist, arguing in the Lyceum, that if it were a good and honorable thing to buy the freedom of a friend in the masculine, why not also of a friend in the feminine, if, for example, a master, why not also a mistress? So putting the good argument and his passion together, he went off and purchased the girl's freedom. The death which was thus suffered by Phocion, revived among the Greeks the memory of that of Socrates, the two cases being so similar, and both equally the sad fault and misfortune of the city.